Information Technology for Management

On-Demand Strategies for Performance, Growth and Sustainability

Eleventh Edition

Information Technology for Management

On-Demand Strategies for Performance, Growth and Sustainability

Eleventh Edition

EFRAIM TURBAN

CAROL POLLARD
Appalachian State University

GREGORY WOOD
Canisius College

WILEY

VP AND EDITORIAL DIRECTOR	Mike McDonald
EXECUTIVE EDITOR	Lise Johnson
EDITORIAL ASSISTANT	Ethan Lipson
EDITORIAL MANAGER	Judy Howarth
CONTENT MANAGEMENT DIRECTOR	Lisa Wojcik
CONTENT MANAGER	Nichole Urban
SENIOR CONTENT SPECIALIST	Nicole Repasky
PRODUCTION EDITOR	Loganathan Kandan
PHOTO RESEARCHER	Billy Ray
COVER PHOTO CREDIT	© Ditty_about_summer/Shutterstock

This book was set in 9.5/12.5 pt Source Sans Pro by SPi Global and printed and bound by Quad/Graphics.

Founded in 1807, John Wiley & Sons, Inc. has been a valued source of knowledge and understanding for more than 200 years, helping people around the world meet their needs and fulfill their aspirations. Our company is built on a foundation of principles that include responsibility to the communities we serve and where we live and work. In 2008, we launched a Corporate Citizenship Initiative, a global effort to address the environmental, social, economic, and ethical challenges we face in our business. Among the issues we are addressing are carbon impact, paper specifications and procurement, ethical conduct within our business and among our vendors, and community and charitable support. For more information, please visit our website: www.wiley.com/go/citizenship.

ISBN: 978-1-118-89079-0 (PBK)
ISBN: 978-1-119-39783-0 (EVALC)

Library of Congress Cataloging in Publication Data:

Names: Turban, Efraim, author. | Pollard, Carol (Carol E.), author. | Wood, Gregory R., author.
Title: Information technology for management : on-demand strategies for performance, growth and sustainability / Efraim Turban, Carol Pollard, Gregory R. Wood.
Description: 11th edition. | Hoboken, NJ : John Wiley & Sons, 2018. | Includes bibliographical references and index. |
Identifiers: LCCN 2017037711 (print) | LCCN 2017046158 (ebook) | ISBN 9781118890868 (epub) | ISBN 9781119172390 (pdf) | ISBN 9781118890790 (pbk.)
Subjects: LCSH: Management information systems.
Classification: LCC T58.6 (ebook) | LCC T58.6 .T765 2017 (print) | DDC 658.4/038011—dc23
LC record available at https://lccn.loc.gov/2017037711

The inside back cover will contain printing identification and country of origin if omitted from this page. In addition, if the ISBN on the back cover differs from the ISBN on this page, the one on the back cover is correct.

V10007160_122818

Brief Contents

PREFACE xiii

ACKNOWLEDGMENTS xviii

PART 1 Reshaping Enterprises and Consumers in the On-Demand Economy

1 Disruptive IT Impacts Companies, Competition, and Careers 1

2 Information Systems, IT Architecture, Data Governance, and Cloud Computing 25

3 Data Management, Data Analytics, and Business Intelligence 65

4 Networks, Collaborative Technology, and the Internet of Things 101

5 Cybersecurity and Risk Management Technology 127

PART 2 Winning, Engaging, and Retaining Consumers for Growth

6 Search, Semantic, and Recommendation Technology 165

7 Web 2.0 and Social Technology 199

8 Retail, E-commerce, and Mobile Commerce Technology 240

PART 3 Optimizing Performance, Processes, and Productivity

9 Functional Business Systems 269

10 Enterprise Systems 300

11 Data Visualization and Geographic Information Systems 331

PART 4 Managing Business Relationships, Projects, and Ethical Responsibilities

12 IT Strategy, Sourcing, and Strategic Technology Trends 354

13 Systems Development and Project Management 385

14 IT Ethics, Privacy, and Sustainability 417

GLOSSARY 443

ORGANIZATION INDEX 448

NAME INDEX 450

SUBJECT INDEX 451

Contents

PREFACE   xiii

ACKNOWLEDGMENTS   xviii

PART 1   Reshaping Enterprises and Consumers in the On-Demand Economy

1   Disruptive IT Impacts Companies, Competition, and Careers   1

Case 1.1   **Opening Case: Uber and Airbnb Revolutionize Business Models in the On-Demand Economy**   3

1.1   **Doing Business in the On-Demand Economy**   4
Growth of the On-Demand Economy   5
Digital Business Models   6
IT's Role in the On-Demand Economy   7
IT Business Objectives   8

1.2   **Business Process Improvement and Competitive Advantage**   8
What Is a Business Process?   9
Improving Business Processes   9
Don't Automate, Obliterate!   10
Gaining a Competitive Advantage   11
Software Support for BPM   13

1.3   **IT Innovation and Disruption**   13
Social–Mobile–Analytics–Cloud (SMAC) Model   13
Technology Mega Trends   14
Lessons Learned from Companies Using Disruptive Technologies   16

1.4   **IT and You**   17
On-Demand Workers   17
IT Adds Value to Your Performance and Career   19
Becoming an Informed IT User   21

Case 1.2   **Business Case: The Internet of Things Comes to the NFL**   23

Case 1.3   **Video Case: Knowing More and Doing More**   24

2   Information Systems, IT Architecture, Data Governance, and Cloud Computing   25

Case 2.1   **Opening Case: Detoxing Location-Based Advertising Data at MEDIATA**   27

2.1   **IS Concepts and Classification**   28

Components of an IS   29
Data, Information, Knowledge, and Wisdom   30
Types of ISs   31
Transaction Processing System (TPS)   32
Management Information System (MIS)   33
Decision Support System (DSS)   34
Executive Information System (EIS)   35
ISs Exist within Corporate Culture   36

2.2   **IT Infrastructure, IT Architecture, and Enterprise Architecture**   37
EA Helps to Maintain Sustainability   38
Developing an Enterprise Architecture (EA)   41

2.3   **Information Management and Data Governance**   42
Information Management Harnesses Scattered Data   43
Reasons for Information Deficiencies   43
Factors Driving the Shift from Silos to Sharing and Collaboration   45
Business Benefits of Information Management   45
Data Governance: Maintaining Data Quality and Cost Control   46

2.4   **Data Centers and Cloud Computing**   48
Data Centers   48
Integrating Data to Combat Data Chaos   50
Cloud Computing   52
Selecting a Cloud Vendor   52
Cloud Infrastructure   54
Issues in Moving Workloads from the Enterprise to the Cloud   54

2.5   **Cloud Services and Virtualization**   55
Anything as a Service (XAAS) Models   55
Going Cloud   58
Virtualization and Virtual Machines   58

Case 2.2   **Business Case: Data Chaos Creates Risk**   62

Case 2.3   **Video Case: Cloud Computing at Coca-Cola Is Changing Everything**   63

3   Data Management, Data Analytics, and Business Intelligence   65

Case 3.1   **Opening Case: Coca-Cola Strategically Manages Data to Retain Customers and Reduce Costs**   66

3.1   **Data Management and Database Technologies**   69
Database Management Systems and SQL   69
DBMS and Data Warehousing Vendors Respond to Latest Data Demands   72

3.2   **Centralized and Distributed Database Architectures**   **73**
Garbage In, Garbage Out   75
Data Ownership and Organizational Politics   76
Data Life Cycle and Data Principles   77
Master Data and Master Data Management   78

3.3   **Data Warehouses**   **79**
Procedures to Prepare EDW Data for Analytics   80
Building a Data Warehouse   80
Real-Time Support from an Active Data Warehouse   81

3.4   **Big Data Analytics and Data Discovery**   **83**
Human Expertise and Judgment are Needed   85
Data and Text Mining   88
Creating Business Value   88
Text Analytics Procedure   90
Analytics Vendor Rankings   90

3.5   **Business Intelligence and Electronic Records Management**   **91**
Business Benefits of BI   92
Common Challenges: Data Selection and Quality   92
Aligning BI Strategy with Business Strategy   92
BI Architecture and Analytics   93
Electronic Records Management   94
Legal Duty to Retain Business Records   94
ERM Best Practices   94
ERM Benefits   95
ERM for Disaster Recovery, Business Continuity, and Compliance   95

Case 3.2   **Business Case: Big Data Analytics is the "Secret Sauce" for Revitalizing McDonald's**   **98**

Case 3.3   **Video Case: Verizon Improves Its Customer Experience with Data Driven Decision-Making**   **99**

4   **Networks, Collaborative Technology, and the Internet of Things**   **101**

Case 4.1   **Opening Case: Sony Builds an IPv6 Network to Fortify Competitive Edge**   **102**

4.1   **Network Fundamentals**   **104**
Network Types   104
Intranets, Extranets, and Virtual Private Networks   105
Network Terminology   105
Functions Supported by Business Networks   106
Quality of Service   107

4.2   **Internet Protocols (IP), APIs, and Network Capabilities**   **109**

Comparing 3G, 4G, 4G LTE, and 5G Network Standards   110
Circuit versus Packet Switching   111
Application Program Interfaces and Operating Systems   111

4.3   **Mobile Networks and Near-Field Communication**   **113**
Increase in Mobile Network Traffic and Users   114
Higher Demand for High-Capacity Mobile Networks   115
Mobile Infrastructure   115
Two Components of Wireless Infrastructure   116
Business Use of Near-Field Communication   117
Choosing Mobile Network Solutions   118

4.4   **Collaborative Technologies and the Internet of Things**   **119**
Virtual Collaboration   120
Group Work and Decision Processes   120
The Internet of Things (IoT)   121
IoT Sensors, Smart Meters, and the Smart Grid   121

Case 4.2   **Business Case: Google Maps API for Business**   **125**

Case 4.3   **Video Case: Small Island Telecom Company Goes Global**   **126**

5   **Cybersecurity and Risk Management Technology**   **127**

Case 5.1   **Opening Case: Yahoo Wins the Gold and Silver Medal for the Worst Hacks in History!**   **129**

5.1   **The Face and Future of Cyberthreats**   **130**
Intentional Threats   132
Unintentional Threats   132
Hacking   133
Cyber Social Engineering and Other Related Web-Based Threats   134
Denial-of-Service   137
Insider and Privilege Misuse   137
Physical Theft or Loss   138
Miscellaneous Errors   138
New Attack Vectors   138

5.2   **Cyberattack Targets and Consequences**   **139**
"High-Profile" and "Under-the-Radar" Attacks   139
Critical Infrastructure Attacks   140
Theft of Intellectual Property   141
Identity Theft   142
Bring Your Own Device   142
Social Media Attacks   144

5.3   **Cyber Risk Management**   **146**
IT Defenses   146
Business Continuity Planning   149
Government Regulations   149

5.4   Defending Against Fraud   150
Occupational Fraud Prevention
and Detection   151
General Controls   152
Internal Controls   153
Cyber Defense Strategies   153
Auditing Information Systems   155

5.5   Frameworks, Standards, and Models   155
Risk Management and IT Governance
Frameworks   155
Industry Standards   157
IT Security Defense-In-Depth Model   157

Case 5.2   **Business Case: Lax Security at LinkedIn
Exposed   161**

Case 5.3   **Video Case: Botnets, Malware Security, and
Capturing Cybercriminals   163**

PART 2   Winning, Engaging, and Retaining Consumers for Growth

6   Search, Semantic, and Recommendation Technology   165

Case 6.1   **Opening Case: Mint.com Uses Search
Technology to Rank Above Established
Competitors   166**

**6.1   Using Search Technology for Business
Success   168**
How Search Engines Work   168
Web Directories   168
How Crawler Search Engines Work   169
Why Search Is Important for Business   172

**6.2   Organic Search and Search Engine
Optimization   178**
Strategies for Search Engine Optimization   178
Content and Inbound Marketing   180
Black Hat versus White Hat SEO: Ethical Issues
in Search Engine Optimization   181

6.3   Pay-Per-Click and Paid Search Strategies   182
Creating a PPC Advertising Campaign   182
Metrics for Paid Search Advertising   184

6.4   A Search for Meaning—Semantic Technology   184
What Is the Semantic Web?   185
The Language(s) of Web 3.0   185
Semantic Web and Semantic Search   186
Semantic Web for Business   187

6.5   Recommendation Engines   188
Recommendation Filters   189

Case 6.2   **Business Case: Deciding What to Watch—Video
Recommendations at Netflix   195**

Case 6.3   **Video Case: Power Searching with
Google   196**

7   Web 2.0 and Social Technology   199

Case 7.1   **Opening Case: Social Customer Service Takes
Off at KLM   200**

7.1   Web 2.0—The Social Web   201
The Constantly Changing Web   201
Invention of the World Wide Web   202
A Platform for Services and Social Interaction   202
Emergence of Social Applications, Networks,
and Services   203
Why Managers Should Understand Web
Technology   205
Communicating on the Web   206
Social Media Applications and Services   207
Social Media Is More than Facebook, YouTube, and
Twitter   207
With Web 2.0, Markets are Conversations   209

7.2   Social Networking Services and Communities   210
The Power of the Crowd   212
Crowdfunding   212
Social Networking Services   213
Facebook Dominates Social Networking   214
Google Takes on Facebook with G+   216
Be in the Now with Snapchat   217
And Now for Something Different: Second Life   218
Private Social Networks   219
Future of Social Networking Systems   220

**7.3   Engaging Consumers with Blogs and
Microblogs   220**
What Is the Purpose of a Blog?   220
Blogging and Public Relations   222
Reading and Subscribing to Blogs   222
Blogging Platforms   222
Microblogs   223
Twitter   223
Tumblr Blogs   225

**7.4   Mashups, Social Metrics, and
Monitoring Tools   226**
What Makes a Mashup Social   226
RSS Technology   227
Social Monitoring Services   227

**7.5   Enterprise 2.0: Workplace Collaboration and
Knowledge Sharing   229**
Tools for Meetings and Discussions   230
Social Tools for Information Retrieval and
Knowledge Sharing   230
Social Bookmarking Tools   231
Content Creation and Sharing   232

Case 7.2   **Business Case: Facebook Helps Songkick Rock
the Ticket Sales Industry   236**

Case 7.3   **Business Case: AT&T's "It Can Wait" Campaign
against Distracted Driving   237**

8 Retail, E-commerce, and Mobile Commerce Technology 240

Case 8.1 **Opening Case: Macy's Races Ahead with Mobile Retail Strategies 241**

8.1 Retailing Technology 243
Keeping Up with Consumer Demands and Behavior 243
The Omni-Channel Retailing Concept 244

8.2 Business-to-Consumer (B2C) E-commerce 246
Online Banking 246
International and Multiple-Currency Banking 246
Online Recruiting 246
Issues in Online Retailing 250
Online Business and Marketing Planning 250

8.3 Business-to-Business (B2B) E-commerce and E-procurement 251
Sell-Side Marketplaces 251
E-Sourcing 252
E-Procurement 252
Electronic Data Interchange (EDI) Systems 253
Public and Private Exchanges 253

8.4 Mobile Commerce 253
Information: Competitive Advantage in Mobile Commerce 255
Mobile Entertainment 258
Hotel Services and Travel Go Wireless 259
Mobile Social Networking 259

8.5 Mobile Transactions and Financial Services 260
Mobile Payment Systems 260
Mobile Banking and Financial Services 262
Short Codes 263
Security Issues 263

Case 8.2 **Business Case: Chegg's Mobile Strategy 266**

Case 8.3 **Video Case: Searching with Pictures Using MVS 267**

PART 3 Optimizing Performance, Processes, and Productivity

9 Functional Business Systems 269

Case 9.1 **Opening Case: Ducati Redesigns Its Operations 271**

9.1 Business Management Systems and Functional Business Systems 272
Business Management Systems (BMSs) 273
Management Levels 273
Business Functions vs. Cross-Functional Business Processes 274
Transaction Processing Systems 275

9.2 Production and Operations Management Systems 277
Transportation Management Systems 278
Logistics Management 278
Inventory Control Systems 279
Computer-Integrated Manufacturing and Manufacturing Execution Systems 281

9.3 Sales and Marketing Systems 282
Data-Driven Marketing 284
Sales and Distribution Channels 284
Social Media Customer Service 284
Marketing Management 285

9.4 Accounting, Finance, and Regulatory Systems 286
Financial Disclosure: Reporting and Compliance 286
Fraud Prevention and Detection 289
Auditing Information Systems 291
Financial Planning and Budgeting 291

9.5 Human Resource Systems, Compliance, and Ethics 293
HR Information Systems 293
Management and Employee Development 295
HR Planning, Control, and Management 295

Case 9.2 **Business Case: HSBC Combats Fraud in Split-second Decisions 297**

Case 9.3 **Video Case: United Rentals Optimizes Its Workforce with Human Capital Management 298**

10 Enterprise Systems 300

Case 10.1 **Opening Case: 3D Printing Drives the "Always-On" Supply Chain 301**

10.1 Enterprise Systems 303
Implementation Challenges of Enterprise Systems 305
Investing in Enterprise Systems 305
Implementation of Best Practices 306
Enterprise Systems Insights 307

10.2 Enterprise Resource Planning (ERP) 307
Brief History of ERP 308
Technology Perspective 308
Achieving ERP Success 311

10.3 Supply Chain Management Systems 313
Managing the Flow of Materials, Data, and Money 315
Order Fulfillment and Logistics 315
Steps in the Order Fulfillment Process 315
Innovations Driving Supply Chain Strategic Priorities 316

10.4 Customer Relationship Management Systems 319
How are CRM Apps Different from ERP? Why are they Different? 319
CRM Technology Perspective 320

Customer Acquisition and Retention **320**
CRM for a Competitive Edge **320**
Common CRM Mistakes: How to Avoid
Them **321**
Justifying CRM **322**
10.5 Enterprise Social Platforms 323
Growth of Enterprise Social Investments
and Markets **323**
Sharepoint **324**
Oracle's Social Network **326**
Jive **326**
Chatter **326**
Case 10.2 **Business Case: Lowe's Fresh Approach to
Supply Chain Management 328**
Case 10.3 **Video Case: Procter & Gamble: Creating
Conversations in the Cloud with 4.8 Billion
Consumers 329**

11 Data Visualization and Geographic Information Systems 331

Case 11.1 **Opening Case: Safeway and PepsiCo
Collaborate to Reduce Stock Outages using Data
Visualization 332**
11.1 Data Visualization and Learning 334
Learning, Exploration, and Discovery with
Visualization **336**
Data Discovery Market Separates from the
BI Market **336**
How Is Data Visualization Used in Business? **340**
Data Visualization Tools **341**
11.2 Enterprise Data Mashups 342
Mashup Architecture **343**
Why Do Business Users Need Data Mashup
Technology? **344**
Enterprise Mashup Technology **344**
11.3 Digital Dashboards 345
Dashboards are Real Time **347**
How Operational and Strategic
Dashboards Work **348**
Benefits of Digital Dashboards **348**
**11.4 Geographic Information Systems and
Geospatial Data 349**
Geocoding **350**
GIS Is Not Your Grandfather's Map **350**
Infrastructure and Location-Aware Collection
of Geospatial Data **350**
Applying GIS in Business **351**
Case 11.2 **Visualization Case: Are You Ready for
Football? 353**
Case 11.3 **Video Case: The Beauty of Data
Visualization—Data Detective 353**

PART 4 Managing Business Relationships, Projects, and Ethical Responsibilities

12 IT Strategy, Sourcing, and Strategic Technology Trends 354

Case 12.1 **Opening Case: Intel Reaps Rewards from
Sustainable IT Strategy 355**
12.1 IT Strategic Planning 357
Value Drivers **358**
IT Strategic Plan Objectives **358**
IT and Business Disconnects **359**
Corporate and IT Governance **359**
Reactive Approach to IT Investments Will Fail **359**
IT Strategic Planning Process **359**
12.2 Aligning IT with Business Objectives 362
Achieving and Sustaining a Competitive
Advantage **364**
12.3 IT Sourcing Strategies 367
Sourcing and Cloud Services **368**
Factors Driving Outsourcing **369**
Outsourcing Risks and Hidden Costs **370**
Offshoring **370**
Outsourcing Life Cycle **371**
Managing IT Vendor Relationships **373**
Contracts: Get Everything in Writing **373**
12.4 Balanced Scorecard 374
The Balanced Scorecard **374**
Using the Balance Scorecard **375**
Applying the BSC **377**
12.5 Strategic Technology Trends 378
Strategic Technology Scanning **380**
Finding Strategic Technologies **380**
Case 12.2 **Business Case: Cisco IT Improves Strategic
Vendor Management 382**
Case 12.3 **Data Analysis: Third-Party versus Company-
Owned Offshoring 383**

13 Systems Development and Project Management 385

Case 13.1 **Opening Case: Denver International Airport
Learns from Mistakes Made in Failed Baggage-
Handling System Project 386**
13.1 System Development Life Cycle 388
Stages of the SDLC **388**
13.2 Systems Development Methodologies 391
Waterfall Model **391**
Object-Oriented Analysis and Design **392**
Agile Methodology **392**

The DevOps Approach to Systems
Development **394**

13.3 **Project Management Fundamentals   395**
What Is a Project?   **396**
Choosing Projects   **396**
The Triple Constraint   **397**
The Project Management Framework   **397**

13.4 **Initiating, Planning, and Executing Projects   399**
Project Initiation   **400**
Project Planning   **400**
Project Execution   **403**

13.5 **Monitoring/Controlling and Closing
Projects   404**
Project Monitoring and Controlling   **404**
Project Closing or Post Mortem   **407**
Why Projects Fail   **408**
IT Project Management Mistakes   **410**

Case 13.2 **Business Case: Steve Jobs' Shared Vision
Project Management Style   412**

Case 13.3 **Demo Case: Mavenlink Project Management
and Planning Software   413**

14 IT Ethics, Privacy, and Sustainability   417

Case 14.1 **Opening Case: Lessons Learned: How Google
Glass Raised Risk and Privacy Challenges   418**

14.1 **IT Ethics   420**
Ethical versus Unethical Behavior   **420**
Competing Responsibilities   **423**

14.2 **Privacy and Civil Rights   424**
Privacy and the New Privacy
Paradox   **424**
Social Media Recruiting   **425**
Legal Note: Civil Rights   **426**
Competing Legal Concerns   **427**
Financial Organizations Must Comply with Social
Media Guidelines   **428**

14.3 **Technology Addictions and Focus
Management   430**
Digital Distractions and Loss of Focus   **430**
Focus Management   **430**

14.4 **ICT and Sustainable Development   432**
Global Temperature Rising Too Much
Too Fast   **432**
IT and Global Warming   **433**
Technology to Transform Business and
Society   **436**
Next Wave of Disruption Will Be More
Disruptive   **438**

Case 14.2 **Business Case: Android Auto and
CarPlay Keep Drivers Safe, Legal, and
Productive   439**

Case 14.3 **Video Case: IT Ethics in the
Workplace   440**

GLOSSARY   **443**
ORGANIZATION INDEX   **448**
NAME INDEX   **450**
SUBJECT INDEX   **451**

Information Technology for Management discusses a variety of business strategies and explains how they rely on data, digital technology, and mobile devices to support them in the on-demand economy. Our goal is to provide students from any business discipline with a strong foundation for understanding the critical role that digital technology plays in enhancing business sustainability, profitability, and growth and excel in their careers. Enabling technologies discussed in this textbook include the following:

- **Performance**   Combining the latest capabilities in big data analytics, reporting, collaboration, search, and digital communication helps enterprises be more agile and cuts costs to optimize business performance and profitability.
- **Growth**   Strategic technologies enable business to create new core competencies, expand their markets, and move into new markets to experience exponential growth in the on-demand economy.
- **Sustainability**   Cloud services are fundamental to sustaining business profitability and growth in today's on-demand economy. They play a critical role in managing projects and sourcing agreements, respecting personal privacy, encouraging social responsibility, and attracting and engaging customers across multimedia channels to promote sustainable business performance and growth.

In this 11th edition, students learn, explore, and understand the importance of IT's role in supporting the three essential components of business performance improvement: *technology, business processes,* and *people.*

What's New in the 11th Edition?

In the 11th edition of IT *for Management,* we present and discuss concepts in a comprehensive yet easy-to-understand format by actively engaging students through a wide selection of case studies, interactive figures, video animations, tech notes, concept check questions, online and interactive exercises, and critical thinking questions. We have enhanced the 11th edition in the following ways:

New Author   Dr. Carol Pollard, Professor of Computer Information Systems at the Walker College of Business and former Executive Director of the Center for Applied Research in Emerging Technologies (CARET) at Appalachian State University in North Carolina, has taken the helm for the 11th edition. Carol

has applied her innovative teaching and learning techniques to create a stronger pedagogical focus and more engaging format for the text.

Diverse Audience   *IT for Management* is directed toward undergraduate, introductory MBA courses, and Executive Education courses in Management Information Systems and General Business programs. Concepts are explained in a straightforward way, and interactive elements, tools, and techniques provide tangible resources that appeal to all levels of students.

Strong Pedagogical Approach   To encourage improved learning outcomes, we employed a blended learning approach, in which different types of delivery and learning methods, enabled and supported by technology, are blended with traditional learning methods. For example, case study and theoretical content are presented visually, textually, and/or interactively to enable different groups of students to use different learning strategies in different combinations to fit their individual learning style and enhance their learning. Throughout the book, content has been reorganized to improve development of the topics and improve understanding and readability. A large number of images that did not enhance understanding have been removed and replaced with informative and interactive figures and tables that better convey critical concepts.

Leading-Edge Content   Prior to and during the writing process, we consulted with a number of vendors, IT professionals, and managers who are hands-on users of leading technologies, to learn about their IT/business successes, challenges, experiences, and recommendations. To integrate the feedback of these business and IT professionals, new or updated chapter opening and closing cases have been added to many of the chapters along with the addition of relevant, leading-edge content in the body of the chapters.

New Technologies and Expanded Topics   New to this edition are the IT framework, business process reengineering, geocoding, systems developments methodologies, including Waterfall, object-oriented analysis, Agile and DevOps, advances in Search Technology, the growth of Mobile Commerce and Mobile Payment Systems, the Always-On Supply Chain, and the Project Management framework. In addition, with more purchases and transactions starting online and attention being a scarce resource, students learn how search, semantic, and recommendation technologies function to improve revenue. Table P-1 provides a detailed list of new and expanded topics.

Useful Tools and Techniques   New to this edition is a feature we call the "IT Toolbox." This involves the provision of a set of useful tools or techniques relevant to chapter content. Collectively, these tools and techniques equip readers with a suite of IT tools that will be useful in their university classes, workplace, and personal life.

Engaging Students to Assure Learning

The 11th edition of *Information Technology for Management* engages students with up-to-date coverage of the most important IT trends today. Over the years, this IT textbook has distinguished itself with an emphasis on illustrating the use of cutting-edge business technologies for supporting and achieving managerial goals and objectives. The 11th edition continues this tradition with more interactive activities and analyses.

Real-World Case Studies Each chapter contains numerous real-world examples illustrating how businesses use IT to increase productivity, improve efficiency, enhance communication and collaboration, and gain a competitive edge. Faculty will appreciate a variety of options for reinforcing student learning that include three different types of **Case Studies** (opening case, video case, and business case), along with interactive figures and whiteboard animations that provide a multimedia overview of each chapter.

Interactive Figures and Whiteboard Animations The unique presentation of interactive figures and whiteboard animations facilitates reflection on the textual content of the book and provides a clear path to understanding key concepts. The whiteboard animations fit particularly well with the "flipping the classroom" model and complement additional functionality and assets offered throughout the 11th edition. The interactive figures actively engage the students in their own learning to effectively reinforce concepts.

Learning Aids Each chapter contains various learning aids, which include the following:

- **Learning Objectives** are listed at the beginning of each chapter to help students focus their efforts and alert them to the important concepts that will be discussed.

- **IT at Work** boxes spotlight real-world cases and innovative uses of IT.
- Definitions of **Key Terms** appear in the margins throughout the book.
- **Tech Note** boxes explore topics such as "Key Performance Indicators" and "Six Basic Systems Development Guidelines."
- **Career Insight** boxes highlight different jobs in the IT for management field.

End-of-Chapter Activities At the end of each chapter, features designed to assure student learning include the following:

- **Critical Thinking Questions** are designed to facilitate student discussion.
- **Online and Interactive Exercises** encourage students to explore additional topics.
- **Analyze and Decide** questions help students apply IT concepts to business decisions.
- **Concept Questions** test students' comprehension of each learning objective at the end of each chapter to ensure that the students are clear on the concepts. Students are provided with immediate feedback on their performance.

Details of New and Enhanced Features of the 11th Edition

The textbook consists of 14 chapters organized into four modules. All chapters have new or updated sections, as shown in Table P-1.

TABLE P-1 Overview of New and Expanded Topics and Innovative Enterprises Discussed in the Chapters

Chapter	New and Expanded IT and Business Topics	Innovative Enterprises
1. Disruptive IT Impacts Companies, Competition, and Careers	• IT's role in the on-demand economy • Business process improvement • Business process re-engineering • SMAC model • Nature of on-demand work • Becoming an informed IT user • Technology mega trends	• Uber • Airbnb • FitBit • NFL • Teradata
2. Information Systems, IT Architecture, Data Governance, and Cloud Computing	• IS concepts and framework • Information, knowledge, wisdom model • Software-defined data center	• Mediata • National Climatic Data center • U.S. National Security Agency • Apple • Uber • WhatsApp • Slack • Vanderbilt University Medical Center • Coca-Cola

TABLE P-1   Overview of New and Expanded Topics and Innovative Enterprises Discussed in the Chapters *(continued)*

Chapter	New and Expanded IT and Business Topics	Innovative Enterprises
3. Data Management, Data Analytics, and Business Intelligence	• Dirty data costs and consequences • Data life cycle • Genomics and big data • Aligning business intelligence with business strategy	• Coca-Cola • Capitol One • Travelocity • First Wind • Argo Corporation • Walmart • Infinity Insurance • DoD and Homeland Security • CarMax • McDonald's • Verizon
4. Networks, Collaborative Technology, and the Internet of Things	• IPv6 protocol • Types of networks • Network terminology • Quality of service • Net neutrality • Mobile networks and near-field communication • Internet of Things	• Sony • AT & T • Time-Warner • Amazon • Warner Music • Proctor & Gamble • Walmart • Ford • Asda • Unilever • Caterpillar • Santander • Google • Isle of Man
5. Cybersecurity and Risk Management Technology	• Data breaches • Major sources of cyberthreats • Classes of hackers • Spear phishing • Crimeware categories • Denial of service • KPMG data loss barometer • Enterprise risk management framework	• Yahoo • Global Payments, Inc. • Government of China • Google • U.S. Chamber of Commerce • Brookings Institution • LinkedIn • Damballa
6. Search, Semantic, and Recommendation Technology	• Social search technologies • Personal assistant and voice search • Mobile search and mobile SEO • On-page and off-page SEO factors • Updates to Google's ranking algorithm • Semantic search technologies	• Mint.com • Google • Microsoft • Yahoo • Netflix • Apple • Amazon • Diigo • World Wide Web Consortium (W3C)

(continued)

TABLE P-1 Overview of New and Expanded Topics and Innovative Enterprises Discussed in the Chapters *(continued)*

Chapter	New and Expanded IT and Business Topics	Innovative Enterprises
7. Web 2.0 and Social Technology	• Snapchat, the #2 social platform • Social bookmarking • Social customer service moves from optional to essential • Role of APIs in development of new Web applications and functionality • The dominance of Facebook and the demise of Google+ • Emerging virtual-world technology	• KLM Royal Dutch Airlines • Facebook, Inc. • Myntra • Snap, Inc. • Kickstarter.com • GoFundMe.com • Oculus VR • High Fidelity • Twitter • Social Mention • Diigo • Clipix • Dropbox
8. Retail, E-commerce, and Mobile Commerce Technology	• Direct and marketplace B2B ecommerce • In-store retail technology • Omni-channel retailing • Growth of mobile commerce • Growth of the mobile gaming market • Mobile payment methods • Mobile visual search	• Macys Department Stores • Amazon.com • Ally Bank • LinkedIn.com • Alibaba.com • Dell, Inc. • The Walt Disney Company • PayPal, Inc. • Chegg.com
9. Functional Business Systems	• Business management systems • Cross-functional coordination and integration of systems • Systems that support supply-chain management • Social customer service • eXtensible Business Reporting Language (XBRL)	• Ducati Motor Holding S.p.A. • Office Depot • Schurman Fine Papers • BAE Systems • Adweek • Salesforce.com • LinkedIn • HSBC Bank • United Rentals
10. Enterprise Systems	• 3D printing impact on supply chain • Selecting an ERP vendor • Factors for ERP success • Order fulfillment • Always-on supply chain • Enterprise social platforms	• Organovo • Ferrari • GE • Siemens • Organic Valley Family of Farms • Boers & Co. • Peters Ice Cream • ScanSource • Avanade • Dillards • FoxMeyer Drugs • Joint Munitions Command • Flower.com • Red Robin • Lowe's • Procter & Gamble

TABLE P-1 Overview of New and Expanded Topics and Innovative Enterprises Discussed in the Chapters *(continued)*

Chapter	New and Expanded IT and Business Topics	Innovative Enterprises
11. Data Visualization and Geographic Information Systems	• Increasing reliance on data discovery • Data visualization tools • Enterprise data mashups • Geocoding	• Safeway • PepsiCo • IBM • ADP Corp. • Department of Veterans Affairs • General Motors
12. IT Strategy, Sourcing, and Strategic Technology Trends	• Business–IT alignment • IT strategic planning • Porter's competitive forces model • Porter's value chain model • Five-phase outsourcing life cycle • IT sourcing strategies • Strategic technology trends • Technology scanning	• Intel • Nestle Nespresso • LinkedIn • ESSA Academy • Cisco • Citigroup
13. Systems Development and Project Management	• SDLC stages • Systems development methodologies • DevOps • Project management framework • PM core and support knowledge areas • Responsibility matrix	• Denver International Airport • U.S. Census Bureau • Apple • Mavenlink
14. IT Ethics, Privacy, and Sustainability	• Ethical vs. unethical behavior • Privacy paradox • Climate change • Technology addiction • "People-first" approach to technology • Disruptive technologies	• Google • Target • Facebook • SnapChat • NASA • Apple

Supplemental Materials

An extensive package of instructional materials is available to support this 11th edition. These materials are accessible from the book companion website at **www.wiley.com/college/turban**.

• **Instructor's Manual** The Instructor's Manual presents objectives from the text with additional information to make them more appropriate and useful for the instructor. The manual also includes practical applications of concepts, case-study elaboration, answers to end-of-chapter questions, questions for review, questions for discussion, and Internet exercises.

• **Test Bank** The test bank contains over 1,000 questions and problems (about 75 per chapter) consisting of multiple-choice, short answer, fill-ins, and critical thinking/essay questions.

• **PowerPoint Presentation** A series of slides designed around the content of the text incorporates key points from the text and illustrations where appropriate.

• **Chapter Summary Whiteboard Animations** A series of video animations that summarize the content of each chapter in an entertaining way to engage the students in grasping the subject matter.

Acknowledgments

No book is produced through the sole efforts of its authors, and this book is no exception. Many people contributed to its creation, both directly and indirectly, and we wish to acknowledge their contributions.

Special thanks go to the team at John Wiley, particularly Darren Lalonde, Emma Townsend-Merino, Ethan Lipson, and Loganathan Kandan for their ongoing and encouraging editorial expertise and leadership. Their guidance, patience, humor, and support during the development and production of this most recent version of the textbook made the process much easier. We couldn't have done it without you!

Our sincere thanks also go to the following reviewers of the 11th edition. Their feedback, insights, and suggestions were invaluable in ensuring the accuracy and readability of the book:

Joni Adkins, Northwest Missouri State University

Ahmad Al-Omari, Dakota State University

Rigoberto Chinchilla, Eastern Illinois University

Michael Donahue, Towson University

Samuel Elko, Seton Hill University

Robert Goble, Dallas Baptist University

Eileen Griffin, Canisius College

Binshan Lin, Louisiana State University in Shreveport

Thomas MacMullen, Eastern Illinois University

James Moore, Canisius College

Beverly S. Motich, Messiah College

Barin Nag, Towson University

Luis A. Otero, Inter-American University of Puerto Rico, Metropolitan Campus

John Pearson, Southern Illinois University

Daniel Riding, Florida Institute of Technology

Josie Schneider, Columbia Southern University

Derek Sedlack, South University

Eric Weinstein, The University of La Verne

Patricia White, Columbia Southern University

Gene A. Wright, University of Wisconsin–Milwaukee

Many thanks also go to our dedicated graphic designers, Kevin Hawley and Nathan Sherrill, without whose help we would not have been able to create the innovative Whiteboard Animations, and to Senior Photo Editor, Billy Ray, whose extensive and expert research into the images used in the textbook greatly enhanced the overall "look" of this 11th edition.

Extra special thanks go to our families, friends, and colleagues for the enormous encouragement, support, and understanding they provided as we dedicated time and effort to creating this new edition.

Finally, we dedicate the 11th edition of *Information Technology for Management* to the Memory of Dr. Linda Volonino, the driving force behind editions 7 through 10 of *IT for Management*. Thank you Linda, for all your hard work in providing the foundation for this latest edition of the textbook.

CAROL POLLARD
GREGORY WOOD

CHAPTER 1

Disruptive IT Impacts Companies, Competition, and Careers

CHAPTER OUTLINE

Case 1.1 Opening Case: Uber, Airbnb, and the On-Demand Economy

1.1 Doing Business in the On-Demand Economy

1.2 Business Process Improvement and Competitive Advantage

1.3 IT Innovation and Disruption

1.4 IT and You

Case 1.2 Business Case: The Internet of Things Comes to the NFL

Case 1.3 Video Case: What Is the Value of Knowing More and Doing More?

LEARNING OBJECTIVES

1.1 Describe how the on-demand economy is changing the way that business is conducted.

1.2 Explain the role of IT in business process improvement. Understand the concepts of business process reengineering and competitive advantage.

1.3 Describe innovating technologies and explain how they are disrupting enterprises.

1.4 Understand the value of being an "informed user" of IT and the ways in which IT can add value to your career path and performance in the on-demand economy.

Introduction

The more digital technology advances, the more it is almost instantly integrated into our daily lives. Many managers and entrepreneurs recognize the need to integrate digital technology into their products and services. For example, it has been estimated that 78% of business leaders expect their organizations to be a digital business by 2020. Outdated and complex application architectures with a mix of interfaces can delay or prevent the release of new products and services, and maintaining these obsolete systems absorbs large portions of the information technology (IT) budget.

Companies such as Uber, Airbnb, Shyp, TaskRabbit, and other participants in the on-demand economy are leveraging IT to create exciting new business models and revolutionize the way workers, businesses, and customers interact and compete. Peter Hinssen, a well-known business author, university lecturer, and digital consultant, described the change in digital technology as follows:

> *Technology used to be nice. It used to be about making things a little bit better, a little bit more efficient. But, technology stopped being nice: it's disruptive. It's changing our business models, our consumer markets, our organizations. (MacIver, 2015)*

As businesses continue to join the on-demand economy, IT professionals must constantly scan for innovative new technologies to provide business value and help shape the future of the business. For example, smart devices, mobile apps, sensors, and technology platforms—along with increased customer demand for digital interactions and on-demand services—have moved commerce in fresh new directions. We've all heard the phrase "there's an app for that" and that kind of consumer thinking is what drives the on-demand economy.

Business leaders today need to know what steps to take to get the most out of mobile, social, cloud, big data, analytics, visualization technologies, and the Internet of Things (IoT) to move their business forward and enable new on-demand business models. Faced with opportunities and challenges, managers need to know how to leverage IT earlier and more efficiently than their competitors.

A goal of this book is to empower you to improve your use and management of IT at work by raising your understanding of IT terminology, practices, and tools and developing your IT skills to transform you into an informed IT user. Throughout this book, you will learn how digital technology is transforming business and society in the on-demand economy as the IT function takes on key strategic and operational roles that determine an enterprise's success or failure. You will also be provided with an in-depth look at IT trends that have immediate and future capacity to influence products, services competition, and business relationships. Along the way, we'll describe many different ways in which IT is being used and can be used in business and provide you with the some of the terminology, techniques and tools that enable organizations to leverage IT to improve growth, performance, and sustainability.

In this opening chapter, you will learn about the powerful impacts of digital technology on people, business, government, entertainment, and society that are occurring in today's on-demand economy. You will also discover how leading companies are deploying digital technology and changing their business models, business processes, customer experiences, and ways of working. We will present examples of innovative products, services, and distribution channels to help you understand the digital revolution that is currently shaping the future of business, the economy and society and changing management careers. And, we'll explain why IT is important to you and how becoming an "informed user" of IT will add significant value to your career and overall quality of life.

Case 1.1 Opening Case

THE ON-DEMAND BUSINESS FRAMEWORK

NICOLAS MAETERLINCK / Stringer / Getty Images

Uber and Airbnb Revolutionize Business Models in the On-Demand Economy

If you've used Uber or Airbnb, then you have participated in the on-demand economy where speed, convenience, and simplicity are key factors in consumer behavior and purchasing decisions. Michael Boland, author of *What's Driving the Local On-Demand Economy*, explains that as consumers, "We're being conditioned to expect everything on-demand as the mobile device increasingly becomes the *remote control for the physical world*" (Boland, 2015). For example, the majority of consumers who tap an Uber app to get a ride would not consider dialing an 800 number for a taxi. With all transactions performed by apps and automated processes, the entire process from hailing to paying for a ride is slick, quick, and easy, without cash or credit cards.

Tech Platforms Enabled On-Demand Services to Take Off

Decades of technological innovation have given us smartphone apps, mobile payment platforms, GPS and map technology, and social authentication. These technologies are being used to build the infrastructure needed for **on-demand services**. This infrastructure—also referred to as a **technology platform** or **technology stack**—supports the exchange and coordination of staggering amounts of data. The term technology stack reflects the fact that the platform is made up of multiple layers (stacks) of hardware, software, network connectivity, and **data analytics** capabilities.

In many consumer markets today, companies that do not have iPhone or Android apps or technology platforms that support the exchange of goods and services—no matter how useful their website—may find themselves losing their competitive edge.

On-Demand Economy Requires a New Business Model

Uber and Airbnb are popular examples of companies that developed on-demand business models to transform slow-to-innovate industries. A simple definition of **business model** is the way a company generates revenue and makes a profit. On-demand business models provide real-time fulfillment of goods and services, which have attracted millions of users worldwide. This model fits best when speed and convenience matter the most. The ground transportation, grocery, and restaurant industries are examples of hyper-growth

categories in the on-demand world. Forward-thinking companies are reshaping these industries.

Uber Business Model

Uber disrupted the taxi industry with a workforce that is essentially any person with a smartphone and a car. Location-aware smartphone apps bring drivers and passengers together, while in-app accounts make the cashless payment process effortless. By simply opening the Uber app and pressing the middle button for several seconds (a long press), customers can order a ride to their current location, selecting the kind of car they want. Payment is automatically charged to the credit card on file with receipts via email.

The Uber concept developed in response to taxi scarcities. It started on a snowy Paris night in 2008 when the two founders could not get a cab. They wanted a dead-simple app that could get them a car with a tap. On June 1, 2015, the entrepreneurs celebrated Uber fifth anniversary and announced that the company had grown into a transportation network covering 311 cities in 58 countries in North and South Americas, Europe, Africa, Asia Pacific, and the Middle East.

Uber has invested in new and developing technologies and partnerships. The company partnered with Carnegie Mellon University to build robotic cars and new mapping software. In March 2015, Uber purchased deCarta, a 40-person mapping start-up to reduce its dependence on Google maps.

Airbnb Business Model

Another disruption to a traditional industry occurred when Airbnb blindsided the hotel industry. Airbnb allows anyone with a spare apartment or room—even if only for a day—to run their own bed and breakfast by giving them a technology platform to market themselves to a global market. By 2016, the Airbnb site had over 1.5 million listings in 190 countries and 34,000 cities. Over 40 million guests have used Airbnb worldwide. For comparison, Hilton, InterContinental, and Marriott, the largest hotel chains in the world, have less than 1 million rooms each.

Uber and Airbnb do not own inventory. Instead, they scale up (expand) by improving their ability to acquire and match customers and service providers.

Business Success in Terms of Company Growth and Valuation

The ride-hailing app Uber and the housing rental app Airbnb are two of the most valuable start-ups, as displayed in **Figure 1.1**. **Valuation** of a company at its early stages is based heavily on its growth potential and future value. In contrast, the valuation of an established company is based on its present value, which is calculated using traditional financial ratios and techniques related to revenues or other assets.

Uber's massive market value—estimated at $60 billion—is greater than 80% of all Standard & Poor (S&P) 500 companies, many of which have been around for 25, 50, or 100 years. Investors valued Airbnb at $24 billion—higher than the value of the hotel giant Marriott International. These companies would never have been able to grow in the old way as a traditional organization, with their own inventory of products, services, and workforce and traditional forms of technology.

Questions

1. In what ways are the Uber and Airbnb business similar or different?
2. How did Uber achieve its new business model?
3. To what extent do you think changing their business models contributed to the success of Uber and Airbnb?

Sources: Compiled from Primack (2015), Storbaek (2015), Winkler and MacMillan (2015,) Jaconi (2014), *Uber.com* (2017), *Airbnb.com* (2017).

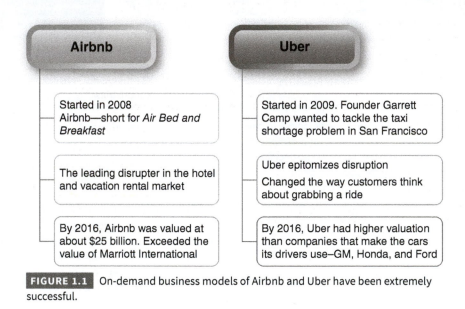

FIGURE 1.1   On-demand business models of Airbnb and Uber have been extremely successful.

1.1 | Doing Business in the On-Demand Economy

The on-demand economy is revolutionizing commercial activities in businesses around the world. The businesses in this new economy are fueled by years of technology innovation and a radical change in consumer behavior. As companies become more highly digitized, it becomes more and more apparent that what companies can do depends on what their IT and data management systems can do. For over a decade, powerful new digital approaches to doing business have emerged. And there is sufficient proof to expect even more rapid and dramatic changes due to IT breakthroughs and advances.

In market segment after market segment, mobile communications and technology stacks make it financially feasible for companies to bring together consumers and providers of products and services. These capabilities have created the **on-demand economy**. As Ev Williams, cofounder of Twitter says,

On-demand economy is the economic activity created by technology companies that fulfill consumer demand through the immediate provisioning of products and services.

> *The internet makes human desires more easily attainable. In other words, it offers convenience. Convenience on the internet is basically achieved by two things: speed, and cognitive ease. If you study what the really big things on the internet are, you realize they are masters at making things fast and not making people think.*

The proliferation of smartphone-connected consumers, simple and secure purchase flows, and location-based services are a few of the market conditions and technological innovations that are propelling the explosion of on-demand services.

Just as the rapid growth of online-only Amazon and eBay transformed retail, the even faster growth of app-driven companies, like Uber, Airbnb, and Grubhub, has disrupted the taxi, hotel, and restaurant markets. As you read in the opening case, in six short years, Uber changed the taxi industry as it rose from start-up to the world's most valuable private technology company, and Airbnb tackled the fiercely competitive hotel market and attracted more than 60 million customers to become the third most valuable venture-capital-backed company in the world. Another example is Grubhub who became No. 1 in online food ordering, controlling over 20% of that $9 billion market. What today's successful technology businesses have in common are platform-based business models. Platforms consist of hardware, software, and networks that provide the connectivity for diverse transactions, such as ordering, tracking, user authentication, and payments. These business models are designed to serve today's on-demand economy, which is all about time (on-demand), convenience (tap an app), and personalized service (my way). For example, millennials want the ease of online payment over cash and insist on efficiency for all aspects of their lives, including shopping, delivery, and travel.

Key strategic and tactical questions that determine an organization's profitability and management performance are shown in **Figure 1.2**. Answers to each question require an understanding of the capabilities of mundane to complex IT, which ones to implement and how to manage them.

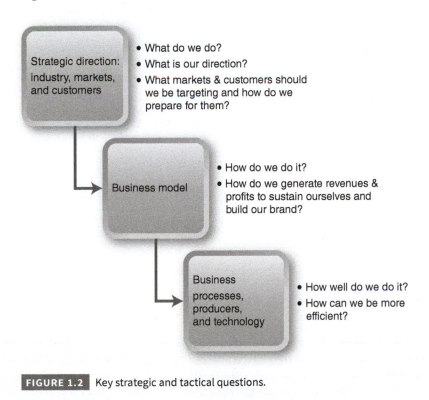

FIGURE 1.2   Key strategic and tactical questions.

Growth of the On-Demand Economy

Whether it is ease of scheduled deliveries or the corresponding time savings, the growth of the on-demand economy is a product of its alignment with consumers' growing appetite for greater convenience, speed, and simplicity. A recent survey reported that 86.5 million Americans have used the services of at least one on-demand start-up company (Chriss, 2016).

The growth of the on-demand economy demonstrates the high level of interest consumers have in on-demand services from dog walking to laundry services, short-term home rentals, massages, and truck hauling. Although just applying a mobile app to an existing service will not ensure a company's success, IT is a vital and integral part of the all businesses that are part of the on-demand economy.

Low Cost of Entry One of the reasons that the on-demand economy has taken off is that it is easier than ever to become an on-demand business. Companies like Dispatch, a software as-a-service company, allow entrepreneurs to move into the on-demand world quickly and inexpensively. For example, Aatlantic Fitness, a fitness equipment repair service company, moved into the on-demand economy using Dispatch, and Handyman Connection, a 20-year-old home repair service company, is using Dispatch's platform to compete with Handy, an on-demand service for house cleaning that has raised $60 million in venture capital.

Digital Business Models

The on-demand economy is driving the transformation of traditional business models to digital business models to serve customers what they want and where they want it.

Business models are the ways enterprises generate revenue or sustain themselves. Digital business models define how businesses make money via digital technology. Companies that adopt digital business models are better positioned to take advantage of business opportunities and survive, according to the Accenture *Technology Vision* 2013 report (Accenture, 2013). **Figure 1.3** contains examples of new technologies that destroyed old business models and created new ones.

Twitter dominates the reporting of news and events as they are still happening

Facebook became the most powerful sharing network in the world

Location-aware technologies track items through production and delivery to reduce wasted time and inefficiency in supply chains and other business-to-business (B2B) transactions

Smartphones, tablets, other touch devices, and their apps reshaped how organizations interact with customers—and how customers want businesses to interact with them

FIGURE 1.3 Digital business models refer to how companies engage their customers digitally to create value via websites, social channels, and mobile devices.

The ways in which market leaders are transitioning to digital business models include the following:

- **NBA talent scouts rely on sports analytics and advanced scouting systems** NBA talent scouts used to crunch players' stats, watch live player performances, and review hours of tapes to create player profiles. Now software that tracks players' performance has changed how basketball and soccer players are evaluated. For example, STATS' SportVU technology is revolutionizing the way sports contests are viewed, understood, played, and enjoyed. SportVU uses six palm-sized digital cameras that track the movement of every player on the court, record ball movement 25 times per second, and convert movements into statistics. SportVU produces real-time and highly complex statistics to complement the traditional play-by-play. Predictive sport analytics can provide a 360-degree view of a player's performance and help teams make trading decisions. Sports analytics bring about small competitive advantages that can shift games and even playoff series.

- **Dashboards keep casino floor staff informed of player demand** Competition in the gaming industry is fierce, particularly during bad economic conditions. The use of manual spreadsheets and gut-feeling decisions did not lead to optimal results. Casino operators facing pressure to increase their bottom line have invested in analytic tools, such as

Tangam's Yield Management solution (TYM). TYM is used to increase the yield (profitability) of blackjack, craps, and other table games. The analysis and insights from real-time apps are used to improve the gaming experience and comfort of players.

Today, a top concern of well-established corporations, global financial institutions, born-on-the-Web retailers, and government agencies is how to design their **digital business models** in order to

- Deliver an incredible customer experience
- Turn a profit
- Increase market share
- Engage their employees

In the digital (online) space, the **customer experience** must measure up to the very best the Web has to offer. Stakes are high for those who get it right—or get it wrong. Forrester research repeatedly confirms there is a strong relationship between the quality of a firm's customer experience and loyalty, which, in turn, increases revenue (Schmidt-Subramanian et al., 2013).

IT's Role in the On-Demand Economy

According to the 2016 survey conducted by the Society of Information Management (SIM), 1,213 IT leaders (including 490 chief information officers (CIOs)) from 801 companies reported companies that are more highly digitized and tightly connected are putting a greater emphasis on the strategic use of IT to enhance growth and improve performance. As a result, IT priorities and spending are changing (Kappelman et al., 2017).

A review of the top 10 IT management priorities reported in the survey results is shown in **Table 1.1**. Along with business-IT alignment and security, Table 1.1 clearly demonstrates a need for companies to focus on strategic and organizational priorities such as innovation, IT and business agility, speed of IT delivery, and business **productivity** and efficiency.

TABLE 1.1   10 Top IT Management Priorities

	IT Management Issues
1	Technology Alignment with the Business
2	Security, Cybersecurity & Privacy
3	Innovation
4	IT Agility & Flexibility
5	Business Agility & Flexibility
6	Business Cost Reduction & Controls
7	IT Cost Reduction & Controls
8	Speed of IT Delivery & IT Time to Market
9	Business Strategic Planning
10	Business Productivity & Efficiency

Adapted from Kappelman et al. (2017).

To address these issues, IT leaders said they need to focus on relationships, meet more frequently with top management, and spend significant amounts of time with functional leaders, customers, and suppliers. Companies also need to emphasize finding, keeping, and developing IT talent and on improving IT to improve business performance. These findings point to one clear message—IT in the on-demand economy is about meeting customer needs.

IT Business Objectives

Now, more than ever, IT must be responsive to the needs of consumers who are demanding a radical overhaul of business processes in companies across diverse industry sectors. Intuitive interfaces, around-the-clock availability, real-time fulfillment, personalized treatment, global consistency, and zero errors—this is the world to which customers have become increasingly accustomed. And, it's not just about providing a superior user or customer experience—when companies get it right, they can also offer more competitive prices because of lower costs, better operational controls, and open themselves up to less risk.

According to Chirantan Basu of Chron (Basu, 2017), to stay abreast of the ever-changing business landscape and customer needs, IT today must concentrate on the following six business objectives:

1. **Product development** From innovations in microprocessors to efficient drug-delivery systems, IT helps businesses respond quickly to changing customer demands.

2. **Stakeholder integration** Companies use their investor relations websites to communicate with shareholders, research analysts, and others in the market.

3. **Process improvement** An ERP system replaces dozens of legacy systems for finance, human resources, and other functional areas, to increase efficiency and cost-effectiveness of internal business processes.

4. **Cost efficiencies** IT allows companies to reduce transaction and implementation costs, such as costs of duplication and postage of email versus snail mail.

5. **Competitive advantage** Companies can use agile development, prototyping, and other systems methodologies to being a product to market cost-effectively and quickly.

6. **Globalization** Companies can outsource most of their noncore functions, such as HR and finance, to offshore companies and use ICT to stay in contact with its global employees, customers, and suppliers 24/7.

Every technology innovation triggers opportunities and threats to business models and strategies. With rare exceptions, every business model depends on a mix of IT, knowledge of its potential, the requirements for success, and, equally important, its limitations.

Questions

1. What precipitated the on-demand economy?
2. How is IT contributing to the success of the on-demand economy?
3. List the six IT business objectives.
4. What are the key strategic and tactical questions that determine an organization's profitability and management performance?
5. What is a business model?
6. What is a digital business model?
7. Give two examples of how companies are transitioning to digital business models.
8. What factors are driving the move to digital business models?

1.2 Business Process Improvement and Competitive Advantage

Given that a company's success depends on the efficiency of its business processes, even small improvements in key processes can have significant payoff. All functions and departments in the enterprise have tasks they need to complete to produce outputs, or deliverables, in order to meet their **objectives**.

Before you can begin to improve something, you have to understand what it is you are improving. We'll start by defining a business process, looking at its characteristics, and then exploring ways in which a business process can be improved either incrementally or radically through Business Process Reengineering.

What Is a Business Process?

Business processes are series of steps by which organizations coordinate and organize tasks to get work done. In the simplest terms, a **process** consists of activities that convert inputs into outputs by doing work.

Examples of common business processes are as follows:

- **Accounting**   Invoicing; reconciling accounts; auditing
- **Finance**   Credit card or loan approval; estimating credit risk and financing terms
- **Human resources (HR)**   Recruiting and hiring; assessing compliance with regulations; evaluating job performance
- **IT or information systems**   Generating and distributing reports and data visualizations; data analytics; data archiving
- **Marketing**   Sales; product promotion; design and implementation of sales campaigns; qualifying a lead
- **Production and operations**   Shipping; receiving; quality control; inventory management
- **Cross-functional business processes**   Involving two or more functions, for example, order fulfillment and product development

Three Components of a Business Process   Business processes have the three basic components shown in **Figure 1.4**. They involve inputs, activities, and deliverables.

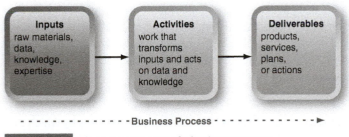

FIGURE 1.4   Three components of a business process.

Processes can be formal or informal. **Formal processes** are documented and have well-established steps. Order taking and credit approval processes are examples. Routine formal processes are referred to as **standard operating procedures (SOPs)**. An SOP is a well-defined and documented way of doing something. An effective SOP documents who will perform the tasks; what materials to use; and where, how, and when the tasks are to be performed. SOPs are needed for the handling of food, hazardous materials, or situations involving safety, security, or compliance. In contrast, **informal processes** are typically undocumented, have inputs that may not yet been identified, and are knowledge-intensive. Although enterprises would prefer to formalize their informal processes in order to better understand, share, and optimize them, in many situations process knowledge remains in people's heads.

Processes range from slow, rigid to fast-moving, adaptive. Rigid processes can be structured to be resistant to change, such as those that enforce security or compliance regulations. Adaptive processes are designed to respond to change or emerging conditions, particularly in marketing and IT.

Improving Business Processes

Designing an effective process can be complex because you need a deep understanding of the inputs and outputs (also known as **deliverables**), how things can go wrong, and how to prevent

Deliverables   are the outputs or tangible things that are produced by a business process. Common deliverables are products, services, actions, plans, or decisions, such as to approve or deny a credit application. Deliverables are produced in order to achieve specific objectives.

things from going wrong. For example, Dell had implemented a new process to reduce the time that tech support spent handling customer service calls. In an effort to minimize the length of the call, tech support's quality dropped so much that customers had to call multiple times to solve their problems. The new process had backfired—increasing the time to resolve computer problems and aggravating Dell customers.

The importance of efficient business processes and continuous process improvement cannot be overemphasized. Why? Because 100% of an enterprise's performance is the result of its processes. Maximizing the use of inputs in order to carry out similar activities better than one's competitors is a **critical success factor (CSF)**. Poorly designed, flawed, or outdated business processes waste resources, increase costs, cause delays, and aggravate customers. For example, when customers' orders are not filled on time or correctly, customer loyalty suffers, returns increase, and reshipping increases costs. The blame may not be employee incompetence, but a flawed order fulfillment process.

Don't Automate, Obliterate!

In today's on-demand economy, incrementally improving a business process isn't always sufficient to create the type of change required. Instead, radical changes need to occur to meet higher customer expectations. To do this, companies have to go beyond simply automating an existing process. They must reinvent the entire business process, including reducing the number of steps required, eliminating documents, developing automated decision-making, and dealing with regulatory and fraud issues. Operating models, skills, organizational structures, and roles need to be redesigned to match the reinvented processes. Data models should be adjusted and rebuilt to enable better decision-making, performance tracking, and customer insights.

Leading organizations have come to recognize that it can take a long time to see the benefits of traditional large-scale projects that migrate all current processes to digital and sometimes they don't work. Instead, successful companies are reinventing processes, challenging everything related to an existing process and rebuilding it using cutting-edge digital technology. For example, rather than creating technology tools to help back-office employees type customer complaints into their systems, leading organizations create self-serve options for customers to type in their own complaints.

Business Process Reengineering (BPR)   The process by which these types of radical process change can be achieved is referred to as **business process reengineering (BPR)**, its slogan is "Don't automate, obliterate!" (Hammer and Champy, 2006). Consisting of eight stages, shown in **Figure 1.5**, BPR proposes that simply applying IT to a manual or outdated process does not always optimize it. Instead, processes need to be examined to determine whether they are still necessary. After unnecessary processes are identified and eliminated, the remaining ones are redesigned (or reengineered) in order to automate or streamline them. Next, the new process is implemented and put into operation and its performance is evaluated. Finally, the process is reassessed over time to continually improve it.

The goal of BPR is to eliminate unnecessary, non-value-added processes, and simplify and automate the remaining processes to significantly reduce cycle time, labor, and costs. For example, reengineering the credit approval process cuts time from several days or hours to minutes or less. Simplifying processes naturally reduces the time needed to complete the process, which also cuts down on errors.

After eliminating waste, technology can enhance processes by (1) automating existing manual processes; (2) expanding the data flows to reach more functions in order to make it possible for sequential activities to occur in parallel; and (3) creating innovative business processes that, in turn, create new business models. For instance, consumers can scan an image of a product and land on an e-commerce site, such as Amazon.com, selling that product. This process flips the traditional selling process by making it customer-centric.

You will read more about optimizing business processes and role of business process management (BPM) role in the alignment of IT and business strategy in Chapter 13.

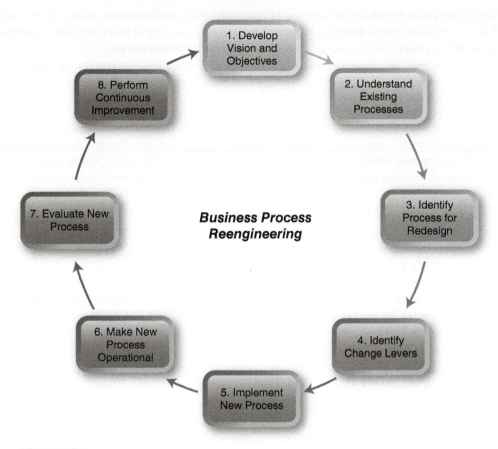

FIGURE 1.5 Eight phases of business process reengineering.

Gaining a Competitive Advantage

Understanding trends that affect the new ways business is being done and getting in front of those trends by changing adding, deleting, and changing existing business processes gives organizations an important **competitive advantage** over their competitors. Helping a company gain, maintain, and sustain a competitive advantage in the market is a very important function of IT. In business, as in sports or politics, companies want to win—customers, market share, and position in the industry. Basically, this requires gaining an edge over competitors by being first to take advantage of market opportunities, providing better customer experiences, offering unique products or services, or convincing customers why your business is a more attractive alternative than your competitors.

Influential industry leaders cite "new competition" as their largest business challenge. Once an enterprise has developed a competitive edge, it can only be sustained by continually pursuing new and better ways to compete. Maintaining a competitive advantage requires forecasting trends and industry changes and figuring out what the company needs to do to stay ahead of the game. It demands continuously tracking competitors and their future plans and promptly taking corrective actions. Competitiveness depends heavily on IT **agility** and **responsiveness**. The benefit of IT agility is that it enables organizations to take advantage of opportunities faster or more effectively.

Closely related to IT agility is **flexibility**. For example, mobile networks are flexible—able to be set up, moved, or removed easily, without dealing with cables and other physical requirements of wired networks. Mass migration to mobile devices from PCs has expanded the scope of IT beyond traditional organizational boundaries—making location practically irrelevant.

IT agility, flexibility, and mobility are tightly interrelated and fully dependent on an organization's IT infrastructure and architecture, which are discussed in Chapter 2.

With mobile devices, applications, platforms, and social media becoming inseparable parts of work life and corporate collaboration and with more employees working from home, the result is the rapid consumerization of IT. **IT consumerization** is the migration of consumer

Competitive advantage is an edge that enables a company to outperform its average competitor.

Agility means being able to respond quickly.

Responsiveness means that IT capacity can be easily scaled up or down as needed, which essentially requires cloud computing.

Flexibility means having the ability to quickly integrate new business functions or to easily reconfigure software or applications.

technology into enterprise IT environments. This shift has occurred because personally owned IT is as capable and cost–effective as its enterprise equivalents. **IT at Work 1.1** demonstrates how FitBit has maintained a competitive advantage with its fitness tracker.

As evidenced by the mergers of Grubhub/Seamless in food delivery and Handybook/Exec in home services, consolidation will accelerate as competition grows. This trend is underscored in the following examples:

- Collaboration of complementary, noncompetitive businesses will become commonplace as a means to collectively educate consumers about the benefits of on-demand services, increase awareness, and provide added value to core users. These range from cross-promotions similar to that of Instacart/Washio to close partnerships such as that of WunWun/Gett.

- Legacy providers in hospitality, transportation, and other Fortune 500s will "partner with" or "acquire" more innovative on-demand companies. Ken Chenault, Chairman and CEO of American Express, conceded in their annual report, "Our industry is being redefined by many forces, including the continued revolution in online and mobile technologies, which is transforming commerce and society." Given the emerging influence of on-demand services, Amex launched a partnership with Uber earlier this year. American Express was able to get a foot in the door by allowing customers to earn 2× points for its spend on Uber with an American Express credit card.

- As on-demand businesses solve for the current technological and logistical challenges, design will increasingly become one of the most meaningful forms of competitive advantage. Creating a memorable, frictionless user interface is the next battleground for addressing consumers' insatiable appetite for greater simplicity and convenience. Scott Belsky points out, "A new cohort of design-driven companies are adding a layer of convenience between us and the underlying services and utilities that improve our lives. This could change everything."

IT at Work 1.1

FitBit: Smart, Connected Device Transforms Competition and Promotes Sustainability

In the first year of its existence, FitBit sold 100,000 devices. At the time, there were countless weight loss and exercise programs, plans, and gimmicks. But smart, connected wearable activity trackers were virtually nonexistent. Five years later, FitBit managed to take the title *biggest selling manufacturer of wearable tech* when it sold a whopping 21 million devices in 1 year. It still holds that title today.

Vision: Simple Approach Plus Smart Device

FitBit was launched in San Francisco, California, by Eric Friedman and James Park. These entrepreneurs took a basic approach to personal health and fitness—eating right and keeping active. Their vision was to develop a smart device that would motivate users to be more active, eat a well-rounded diet, and ultimately become healthier.

Throughout the day, FitBit logs data about the wearer's activities, including the number of steps taken, distance travelled, calories burned, and what needs to be done to reach a personal daily goal, for example, walking 2 miles. FitBit's internal memory can store at least a week of activity data.

One of FitBit's competitive strengths is the app that is accessible from a smartphone. Users can sync FitBit devices and view their online profile, activity levels, and sleep patterns on **dashboards** that display on more than 150 mobile devices, including iOS, Android, and Windows Phone products. This compatibility maximizes the number of friends and family in each user's network to share performance stats. It also motivates and increases user retention.

First Class Fitness

A smart wearable product that fits effortlessly into users' life styles launched an industry and made FitBit a market leader. In the second quarter of 2015 (2Q15), FitBit shipped 4.4 million units, up 159% from the same quarter a year ago (2Q14) and held 24.3% global market share. Second in line was Apple with 3.6 million units shipped in 2Q15 and 19.9% global market share. Thanks to the technology that enabled FitBit and the company's growing reputation, Friedman and Park are likely to be in business for a long time.

IT at Work Questions

1. How did FitBit manage to take the title of biggest selling manufacturer of **wearable technology** tech and sustain it?

2. What could other companies who produce fitness trackers challenge FitBit in the marketplace?

3. What other features do you think consumers would like FitBit to incorporate into its fitness tracker to further improve it? How would consumers and FitBit benefit from these improvements?

Sources: Compiled from Ashcroft (2015), Nusca (2015), Grand View Research (2016), and Fitbit.com (2016).

Software Support for BPM

The purpose of **business process management (BPM)** is to help enterprises become more agile and effective by enabling them to better understand, manage, and adapt their business processes. Vendors, consulting and tech firms offer BPM expertise, services, software suites, and tools.

BPM software is used to map processes performed either by computers or manually—and to design new ones. The software includes built-in templates showing workflows and rules for various functions, such as rules for credit approval. These templates and rules provide consistency and high-quality outcomes. For example, Oracle's WebLogic Server Process Edition includes server software and process integration tools for automating complex business processes, such as handling an insurance claim.

But, BPM initiatives can be extremely challenging, and in order to be successful, BPM requires buy-in from a broad cross section of the business, the right technology selection, and highly effective change management processes.

> **Business process management** consists of methods, tools, and technology to support and continuously improve business processes.

Questions

1. What is a business process? Give three examples.
2. What is the difference between business deliverables and objectives?
3. List and give examples of the three components of a business process.
4. Explain the differences between formal and informal processes.
5. What is an SOP?
6. What is the purpose of BPM?

1.3 | IT Innovation and Disruption

Digital technology creates new markets, businesses, products, and careers. As digital changes the way consumers and retailers buy and sell products, companies must adapt and innovate to ensure their product offerings, platforms, technologies, and search options cater to these changing needs.

Social–Mobile–Analytics–Cloud (SMAC) Model

We are in the era of **social–mobile–analytics–cloud (SMAC)** computing that is reshaping business strategies and day-to-day operations (**Figure 1.6**).

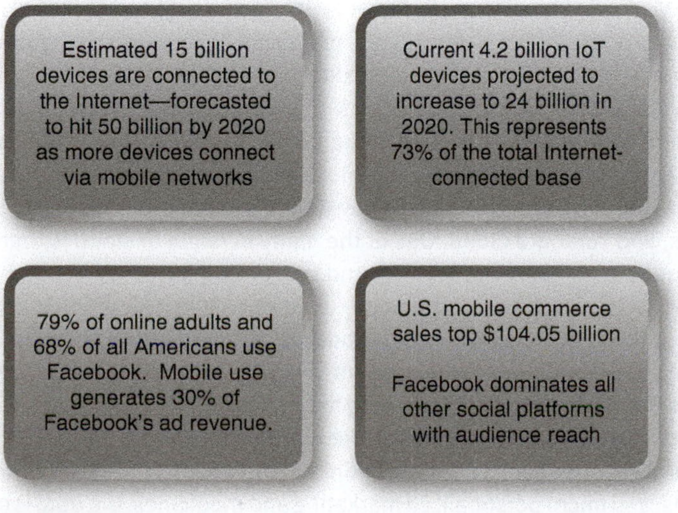

Estimated 15 billion devices are connected to the Internet—forecasted to hit 50 billion by 2020 as more devices connect via mobile networks

Current 4.2 billion IoT devices projected to increase to 24 billion in 2020. This represents 73% of the total Internet-connected base

79% of online adults and 68% of all Americans use Facebook. Mobile use generates 30% of Facebook's ad revenue.

U.S. mobile commerce sales top $104.05 billion

Facebook dominates all other social platforms with audience reach

FIGURE 1.6   SMAC reshapes business strategies and day-to-day operations.

The cloud consists of huge data centers accessible via the Internet and forms the core by providing 24/7 access to storage, applications, and services. Handhelds and wearables, such as FitBit, Pebble, and the Apple Watch, and their users form the edge. Social channels connect the core and edge. The SMAC integration creates the technical and services infrastructure needed for digital business. This infrastructure makes it possible to meet the expectations of employees, customers, and business partners given that almost everyone is connected (social), everywhere they go (mobile), gets the information they need (analytics), and has 24/7 access to products and services (cloud).

Here are three examples of SMAC's influence:

1. **Powerful social influences impact advertising and marketing**   Connections and feedback via social networks have changed the balance of influence. Consumers are more likely to trust tweets from ordinary people than recommendations made by celebrity endorsements. And, negative sentiments posted or tweeted can damage brands.

2. **Consumer devices go digital and offer new services**   The Nike+ FuelBand wristband helps customers track their exercise activities and calories burned. The device links to a mobile app that lets users post their progress on Facebook.

3. **eBay's move to cloud technology improves sellers' and buyers' experiences**   The world's largest online marketplace, eBay, moved its IT infrastructure to the cloud. With cloud computing, eBay is able to introduce new types of landing pages and customer experiences without the delay associated with having to buy additional computing resources.

The balance of power has shifted as business is increasingly driven by individuals for whom mobiles are an extension of their body and mind. They expect to use location-aware services, apps, alerts, social networks, and the latest digital capabilities at work and outside work. To a growing extent, customer loyalty and revenue growth depend on a business's ability to offer unique customer experiences that wow customers more than competitors can.

Technology Mega Trends

Mega trends are forces that shape or create the future of business, the economy, and society.

For 21st-century enterprises, connectivity, big data and analytics, and digitization are technology **mega trends** that cannot be ignored. Business breakthroughs and innovation would be impossible without them. They also mark the difference between outdated 20th-century business models and practices and those of today's on-demand economy.

The most influential IT mega trends driving digital transformation of companies in the on-demand economy are discussed next.

Connectivity   Companies need to connect with consumers and business partners across multiple channels and devices using digital platforms that consist of hardware, software (mobile apps), networks (social media), (embedded sensors), and **cloud computing**.

For example, rather than run applications or programs from software stored on a computer or server owned by the company, cloud computing allows companies to access the same kinds of applications through the Internet. Major business cloud computing providers include Amazon Web Services (AWS), Cisco Powered, Dell Cloud Solutions, Google Cloud, IBM Cloud Solutions, and Teradata Cloud. One of the many benefits of cloud is that it provides the flexibility to acquire or expand connectivity and computing power as needed for operations, business transactions, and communication.

Expanded connectivity supports smart products, which have the ability to sense, process, report, and take corrective action, such as smart clothing, watches, phones, to smart buildings and smart cities. This IoT is becoming a driving force in the on-demand economy.

Connectivity pushes other sub trends, like big data, to create market opportunities for new products and services, such as social sentiment analysis, open innovation, new insurance business models, and micro personalized marketing and medicines. Big data is one of the many disruptive technologies that are impacting people, processes, and profits.

Big Data and Data Analytics   There is no question that the increasing volume of data can be valuable, but only if they are processed and available when and where they are needed. The problem is that the amount, variety, structure, and speed of data being generated or collected by enterprises differ significantly from traditional data. **Big data** are what high-volume, mostly text data are called. Big data stream in from multiple channels and sources, including the following:

- Mobile devices and machine-to-machine sensors embedded in everything from airport runways to casino chips (Later in this chapter, you will read more about the IoT.)
- Social content from texts, tweets, posts, blogs
- Clickstream data from the Web and Internet searches
- Video data and photos from retail and user-generated content
- Financial, medical, research, customer, and **business-to-business** transactions.

Big data are 80% to 90% unstructured. **Unstructured data** do not have a predictable format like a credit card application form. Huge volumes of unstructured data flooding into an enterprise are too much for traditional technology to process and analyze quickly. Big data tend to be more time-sensitive than traditional (or small) data. Data collected from social, mobile, and other channels are analyzed to gain insights and make smart decisions that drive up the bottom line. Machine-generated data from sensors and social media texts are main sources of big data.

Big data has been one of the most disruptive forces businesses have seen in a long time. But when an enterprise harnesses its data and is able to act on analytic insights, it can turn the challenges into opportunities.

Digitization   Across industries, companies are attempting to transform their disconnected or disjointed approaches to customers, products, services, and operating models to an always-on, real-time, and information-rich marketplace. Some leaders are redesigning their capabilities and operating models to take full advantage of digital technologies to keep step with the "connected" consumer and attract talent. Others are creating qualitatively new business models—and tremendous value—around disruptive digital opportunities. In doing so, these companies secure not only continued relevance but also superior returns.

Digitization often requires that old wisdom be combined with new skills, for example, by training a merchandising manager to program a pricing algorithm and creating new roles, such as user-experience designer. The benefits of digitizing processes, through business process reengineering, are huge. By digitizing information-intensive processes, costs can be cut by up to 90% and turnaround times improved by several orders of magnitude.

Examples span multiple industries. For example, one bank digitized its mortgage application and decision process, cutting the cost per new mortgage by 70% and slashing time to preliminary approval from several days to just one minute. A telecommunications company created a self-serve, prepaid service where customers could order and activate phones without back-office involvement. A shoe retailer built a system to manage its in-store inventory that enabled it to know immediately whether a shoe and size was in stock—saving time for customers and sales staff. An insurance company built a digital process to automatically adjudicate a large share of its simple claims.

In addition, replacing paper and manual processes with software allows businesses to automatically collect data that can be mined to better understand process performance, cost drivers, and causes of risk. Real-time reports and dashboards on digital-process performance enable managers to address problems before they get out of control. For example, quality issues in a company's supply chain can be identified and remedied more rapidly by monitoring customer buying behavior and feedback in digital channels.

Digitization   is the process of transforming any kind of activity or information into a digital format that can be collected, stored, searched, and analyzed electronically—and efficiently.

Machine-to-Machine Technology   Sensors can be embedded in most products. Objects that connect themselves to the Internet include cars, heart monitors, stoplights, and appliances. Sensors are designed to detect and react, such as Ford's rain-sensing front wipers that use an advanced optical sensor to detect the intensity of rain or snowfall and adjust wiper speed

Internet of Things (IoT) refers to a set of capabilities enabled when physical things are connected to the Internet via sensors.

accordingly. **Machine-to-machine (M2M) technology** enables sensor-embedded products to share reliable real-time data via radio signals. M2M and the **Internet of Things (IoT)** are widely used to automate business processes in industries ranging from transportation to health care. By adding sensors to trucks, turbines, roadways, utility meters, heart monitors, vending machines, and other equipment they sell, companies can track and manage their products remotely.

When devices or products are embedded with sensors, companies can track their movements or monitor interactions with them. Business models can be adjusted to take advantage of what is learned from this behavioral data. For example, an insurance company offers to install location sensors in customers' cars. By doing so, the company develops the ability to price the drivers' policies on how a car is driven and where it travels. Pricing is customized to match the actual risks of operating a vehicle rather than based on general proxies—driver's age, gender, or location of residence. **Table 1.2** lists a number of opportunities for improvement through the application of embedded physical things.

TABLE 1.2 **Improvement Opportunities from Embedded Sensors**

Industry Sector	Application	Payoff
Oil and gas	Exploration and development rely on extensive sensor networks placed in the earth's crust. Sensors can produce accurate readings of the location, structure, and dimensions of potential fields	Lower development costs and improved oil flows
Health care	Sensors and data links can monitor patients' behavior and symptoms in real time and at low cost allowing physicians to more precisely diagnose disease and prescribe treatment regimens	Reduce hospitalization and treatment costs by $1 billion per year in the United States
Retail	Sensors can capture shoppers' profile data stored in their membership cards to help close purchases	Additional information and discounts at point of sale
Farming	Ground sensors can take into account crop and field conditions and adjust the amount of fertilizer that is spread on areas that need more nutrients	Reduction in time and cost
Advertising	Billboards can scan people passing by, assessing how they fit consumer profiles, and instantly change displayed messages based on those assessments	Better targeted marketing campaigns; flexibility; increased revenues
Automotive	Systems can detect imminent collisions and take evasive action, such as automatic braking systems	Potential accident reduction savings of more than $100 billion annually

Lessons Learned from Companies Using Disruptive Technologies

Those companies who have adapted to change by exploiting digital technology and software are outperforming their peers. According to a survey conducted by CA Associates, companies who have turned the way they use technology from being a cost center and operational function to being a genuine competitive differentiator are reaping the benefits. Many reported doubling their revenue growth, experiencing a higher profit by a factor of 2.5 and increasing new business-based revenue by a factor of 1.5 (Vaughn-Brown, 2014). The five factors to which companies attribute these benefits can be summed up in the following Lessons Learned:

1. **Exploit the power of software** Become "app-centric" and extend core business functions to include software development.
2. **Develop, deliver, disrupt—quickly!** Embrace agile development techniques and broadly implement DevOps.
3. **Boost speed and efficiency with automated programming interfaces (APIs)** Take a managed approach to use APIs for building full-function Web applications (particularly mobile apps) and for integrating back-office systems.

4. **Leverage third-party innovation**   Take a more managed approach to use APIs for integrating third-party services into applications and enable external develop access to systems and data.

5. **Maximize returns with smarter IT investments**   Get smarter at assessing and prioritizing IT investments to maximize return on investment and put portfolio management in place to prioritize and track IT programs.

Business opportunities and challenges presented by today's technology innovations are on an unprecedented scale. **Cloud services**, big data, mobility, digitization, and the IoT are likely to disrupt many industries and shake up competitive positions.

Innovation is necessary for any company that wants to remain relevant, retain customers, and increase profits. Increased competition, expanded global markets, and empowered customers define today's on-demand business environment.

Cloud service   is any computing resource that is provided over the Internet on demand.

Questions

1. What are the benefits of cloud computing?
2. What is M2M technology? Give an example of a business process that could be automated with M2M.
3. Describe the relationships in the SMAC model.
4. What impacts is the SMAC model having on business?
5. Why have mobile devices given consumers more power in the marketplace?
6. Explain why connectivity is important in today's on-demand economy.
7. In what ways is IT disrupting business?

1.4   IT and You

Today, IT and information systems touch nearly all aspects of our lives. IT is a part of our social life, our work, and every business process, and it is no longer the sole responsibility of the IT department. Just think about much of your day you spend interacting with technology—your iPad, PC, and smartphone. It has been reported that the average American checks his/her phone 46 times every day! That's an increase of 35% over the 33 looks per day reported in a similar study just one year earlier. Aggregated across the 185 million American smartphone users, that's 8 billion "looks" per day (Eadicicco, 2015).

IT impacts the way you work, the way you learn, the way you communicate and socialize and the way you entertain yourself. Today, success in any field, be it health care, marketing, finance, accounting, law, education, sports, entertainment, etc. requires much more than a cursory knowledge of IT. IT is and will remain the foundation of the global economy and is especially important in the on-demand economy.

On-Demand Workers

A recent survey of on-demand economy (Chriss, 2016) in the United States and online talent recruiters reported an increase in people working in the on-demand economy who are enjoying a new way of working. Other facts and stats from the survey reveal the U.S. On-Demand workforce as a community of 45 million workers, the majority of whom are younger, optimistic, and urban-based (**Table 1.3**).

The survey also revealed that fewer and fewer people are looking for traditional employment. For example, 91% like the control over where, when, and how they work that the on-demand jobs offer them. The motivation for most is not to replace a traditional job, but to earn supplemental income (**Table 1.4**).

TABLE 1.3 Profile of U.S. On-Demand Workers

Characteristic	Number
Financial situation had improved over the past year	23 million
Expected their financial situation to improve over the coming year	28.8 million
Under 35 years of age	23 million
Live in urban areas	18.45 million

TABLE 1.4 Motivation to Work in the On-Demand Economy

Motivation	Percent
Earn supplemental income	63
Create and control their own schedule	46
Turned to on-demand work because they couldn't find another traditional job	11

The data also shows a strong entrepreneurial drive behind people choosing on-demand work. Just over one-third of respondents owned full- or part-time business and approximately one quarter reporting they are working in the on-demand economy to build a business. This entrepreneurial spirit is reflected in the ways that on-demand worker are compensated. While the 40-hour workweek is still alive and well, sources of income have changed. Instead of one paycheck, on-demand workers typically receive their income from three different sources:

1. On-demand work
2. Contracting and consulting
3. Running a business

Changes in Work Status While the on-demand economy provides positive opportunities, it can also offer limited benefits and inferior infrastructure. Take, for example, the "contractor" model that companies like Uber use. Initially, Uber set the standard for on-demand business by labeling its drivers "independent contractors" and essentially claiming that all of its 160,000 drivers were self-employed. This pushed many of the costs of doing business onto the independent contractors' shoulders and deprived them of baseline labor protections such as worker's compensation, social security contributions, minimum wage, and discrimination protections.

This business model also allowed companies using the Uber model to sidestep federal, state, and county taxes and insurance premiums and undercuts competitors that used a traditional W-2 hiring model. However, not all on-demand businesses use the Uber model.

Some companies treat their workers as employees from the start, while others have switched to the W-2 model and both approaches are reaping benefits. Shyp CEO Kevin Gibbon posted on LinkedIn that the move to employee status was "an investment in a longer-time relationship with our couriers, which we believe will ultimately create the best experience for our customers." After moving to the W-2 model, Shyp had only 1 out of 245 employees quit and customer complaints decreased at the package delivery company. And Instacart, a food shopping and delivery service, offered its shoppers the option to convert to part-time employees so they could offer training to ensure a consistent customer experience and greater customer satisfaction (National Employment Law Project, 2016).

Regardless of their work status, it would appear that overall on-demand workers are highly satisfied with their work environment, perhaps because it fits a unique need. Intuit's on-demand economy survey reported the following:

- 70% of on-demand workers are satisfied with their work.
- 81% plan to continue working with the same provider over the next year.
- 63% are happier to be working in the on-demand economy.

Overall, on-demand workers are forward-looking, eager to embrace new opportunities, and want to take charge of their careers.

IT Adds Value to Your Performance and Career

Whether you join the ranks of the on-demand workers, or choose to stay in a traditional job, IT can greatly enhance your performance at work and the ways you move through your career path.

Staying current in emerging technologies affecting markets is essential to the careers of knowledge workers, entrepreneurs, managers, and business leaders—not just IT and CIO.

In the current marketplace, organizations are finding it particularly difficult to find qualified IT Talent, as illustrated in **IT at Work 1.2**.

IT at Work 1.2

Scott Zulpo Is Facing Stiff Competition

He's adding a senior project manager, a network analyst, and a help desk worker to his 55-member IT staff at BCU, a Vernon Hills, Illinois-based credit union where he is vice president of IT. And, Zulpo will need to add even more people to keep up with an increasing demand for tech-driven innovations.

"The challenge is twofold—first finding talent, and then determining if that talent has the skills, experience and personality to thrive in the position," says Zulpo, who's mindful that "the cost and impact of not hiring an 'A' player is huge."

Zulpo has his work cut out for him. He's hiring at time when very few IT professionals are out of work. Consequently, competition for tech talent is fierce. The unemployment rate for tech workers is about 2%, according to reports on recent data from the U.S. Bureau of Labor Statistics (Bureau of Labor Statistics, 2016).

And, Zulpo isn't the only one who's having a difficult time finding good IT talent. Many of his fellow IT leaders are seeking the same skills. Computerworld's Forecast 2017 survey of 196 IT professionals found that both project management and technical support were among the top 10 most sought-after skills among companies that plan to recruit in the new year.

"The IT labor market is still very hot. The candidate is very much in the driver's seat," says Jason Hayman, market research manager for IT staffing firm TEKsystems.

Hayman cites a government report that estimates that 500,000 to 1 million IT jobs go unfilled every year, but notes that some analysts say the figure is closer to 2 million. He says there's a classic supply-and-demand scenario working here, with demand for talent far exceeding supply.

The takeaway is that there are not enough IT workers!

Compiled from: Bureau of Labor Statistics (2016), Pratt (2016), and Computerworld (2017).

IT at Work Questions

1. What are two reasons why Zulpo had trouble finding qualified IT talent?
2. What of position was Zulpo trying to fill?
3. What methods would you recommend to Zulpo help him in his efforts to recruit new IT personnel?

IT as a Career Fueled by corporate growth, systems expansion, need for competitive or unique services to increase business and security initiatives, companies are increasing their IT hires. Companies need new tech hires who have a background in both technology and business and who can articulate IT's value in meeting business goals. In particular, companies are seeking IT employees with skills in programming, application development, technical support, security, cloud, business intelligence, Web development, database administration, and project management.

According to the **U.S. Department of Labor (2016)**, IT job growth is estimated at 12% from 2014 to 2024, faster than the average for all other occupations. This means about 488,500 new jobs. The median annual wage for computer and IT occupations was $81,430 in May 2015, which was considerably higher than the median annual wage of $36,200 for all other occupations. Here are some common IT jobs and their activities:

IT managers Play a vital role in the implementation and administration of digital technology. They plan, coordinate, and direct research on the computer-related activities of firms. In consultation with other managers, they help determine the goals of an organization and then implement technology to meet those goals.

Chief technology officers (CTOs) Evaluate the newest and most innovative technologies and determine how they can be applied for competitive advantage. CTOs develop technical standards, deploy technology, and supervise workers who deal with the daily IT issues of the firm. When innovative and useful new ITs are launched, the CTO determines implementation strategies, performs cost–benefit or **SWOT analysis**, and reports those strategies to top management, including the CIO.

IT project managers   Develop requirements, budgets, and schedules for their firm's IT projects. They coordinate such projects from development through implementation, working with their organization's IT workers, as well as clients, vendors, and consultants. These managers are increasingly involved in projects that upgrade the information security of an organization.

Data scientists   Manage and analyze massive sets of data for purposes such as target marketing, trend analysis, and the creation of individually tailored products and services. Enterprises that want to take advantage of big data use real-time data from tweets, sensors, and their big data sources to gain insights into their customers' interests and preference, to create new products and services, and to respond to changes in usage patterns as they occur. Big data analytics has increased the demand for data scientists, as described in **Career Insight 1.1**.

Career Insight 1.1

Data Scientists Analyze Business Data for Actionable Business Intelligence

Online searches for data scientist are outpacing the number of job postings by more than 20% and the large business consulting firm, Price-Waterhouse-Cooper, recently announced they would be adding more than 1,000 data scientists during the next 2 years.

Big data, analytics tools, powerful networks, and greater processing power have contributed to growth of the field of **data science**. According to Glassdoor data (glassdoor.com, 2017), the median annual salary for data scientists in the United States is $113,436 and experienced data scientists who manage teams of 5 to 10 people are earning more than $250,000 per annum.

But, it's not just about the money—data scientists enjoy what they do. The job is interesting, spanning many different aspects of the organization and in some cases involves analyzing community outreach programs supported by organizations.

What Does a Data Scientist Do?

Enterprises need people who are capable of analyzing and finding insights in data captured from a range of sources, including customer transactions, click streams, sensors, social media, log files, and GPS plots. Their mission is to unlock valuable and predictive insights that will influence business decisions and spur a competitive advantage. According to Gregg Gordon, VP of the Big Data practice group at Kronos, provider of workforce management solutions in the cloud,

> It's not sitting in a room all day – we take our work and apply it to customer problems. We're working and interacting with customers on a daily basis talking about real problems, then attempting to replicate, model and solve them.

An interesting example of what a data scientist can achieve can be found by studying Jonathan Goldman, the person who transformed LinkedIn. At the time Goldman joined, LinkedIn had less than 8 million members. Goldman noticed that existing members were inviting their friends and colleagues to join, but they were not making connections with other members at the rate executives had expected. A LinkedIn manager said, "It was like arriving at a conference reception and realizing you don't know anyone. So you just stand in the corner sipping your drink—and you probably leave

early." Goldman began analyzing the data from user profiles and looked for patterns to predict whose networks a given profile would land in. While most LinkedIn managers saw no value in Goldman's work, Reid Hoffman, LinkedIn's cofounder and CEO at the time, understood the power of analytics because of his experiences at PayPal. With Hoffman's approval, Goldman applied data analytics to test what would happen if a member were presented with names of other members they had not yet connected with, but seemed likely to know. He displayed the three best new matches for each member based on his or her LinkedIn profile. Within days, the click-through rate on those matches skyrocketed and things really took off. Thanks to this one feature, LinkedIn's growth increased dramatically.

Artist or Scientist?

The most successful—and sought-after—data scientists possess a combination of analytical skills, technical prowess and business acumen needed to effectively analyze massive data sets while thinking critically and shifting assumptions on the fly, ultimately transforming raw intelligence into concise and actionable insights.

The LinkedIn example shows that good data scientists do much more than simply try to solve obvious business problems. Creative and critical thinking are part of their job—that is, part analyst and part artist. They dig through incoming data with the goal of discovering previously hidden insights that could lead to a competitive advantage or detect a business crisis in enough time to prevent it. Data scientists often need to evaluate and select those opportunities and threats that would be of greatest value to the enterprise or brand.

Questions

1. What types of IT career have the most potential in the current hiring market?

2. What factors does Zulpo take into consideration when he's evaluating job applicants?

3. Why is IT a major enabler of business performance and success?

4. Explain why it is beneficial to be an informed user of IT.

5. Do you think IT job prospects are strong? Explain.

Sources: Darrow (2015), Marr (2016), U.S. Department of Labor (2016), and Bureau of Labor Statistics (2016).

IT Job Prospects   In 2017, only 2% of all IT workers are unemployed. Workers with specialized technical knowledge and strong communications and business skills, as well as those with an MBA with a concentration in an IT area, will have the best prospects. Job openings will be the result of employment growth and the need to replace workers who transfer to other occupations or leave the labor force (Bureau of Labor Statistics, 2016)

Dow Chemical set up its own social network to help managers identify the talent they need to carry out projects across its diverse business units and functions. To expand its talent pool, Dow extended the network to include former employees and retirees.

Other companies are using networks to tap external talent pools. These networks include online labor markets such as Amazon Mechanical Turk and contest services such as InnoCentive that help solve business problems.

- Amazon Mechanical Turk is a marketplace for work that requires human intelligence. Its Web service enables companies to access a diverse, on-demand workforce.

- InnoCentive is an "open innovation" company that takes R&D problems in a broad range of areas such as engineering, computer science, and business and frames them as "challenge problems" for anyone to solve. It gives cash awards for the best solutions to solvers who meet the challenge criteria.

Becoming an Informed IT User

Knowing how best to you use IT and how and when to interact with IT personnel, and they with you, will help you perform better at home and at work and enable you to become an **informed user** of technology.

Informed user   is a person knowledgeable about information systems and IT.

The department or functional area that handles the collection, processing, storing, analysis and distribution of information using a computer-based tool can be referred to by many names—some companies refer to it as information technology (IT), while others refer to it as information systems (IS), management information systems (MIS), IT support, IT services or computer information systems (CIS). Whatever the name, its purpose is the same—to support a company's information needs by developing, operating, securing, and maintaining one or more information systems.

To become an informed IT user, you will learn how the six components of an information system—hardware, software, procedures, people, networks, and data—interact to provide you with the information that you need, when you need it, and in the format you need. These components will be discussed in detail in Chapter 2.

By reading this book, you will become an informed user and you gain more value from IT to improve your performance and widen your career opportunities. For example, you will learn to

- Understand how using IT can improve organizational performance
- Understand how and why IT can benefit organizational growth
- Understand how business can use IT to enhance the customer experience
- Use how companies use IT to analyze business data and offer important insights
- Be able to offer input into the development and use of IT
- Be able to recommend and select IT applications at work
- Know how to find emerging technologies to make radical improvement in business processes
- Understand how IT can facilitate teamwork and improve individual productivity
- Appreciate the importance of ethical behavior when using IT and explain the associated risks and responsibilities
- Foster your entrepreneurial tendencies to start your own on-demand business.

Key Terms

agility 11
barriers to entry 23
big data 15
business model 3
business process 9
business process management (BPM) 13
business process reengineering (BPR) 10
business-to-business 15
chief technology officers (CTOs) 19
cloud computing 14
cloud services 17
competitive advantage 11
critical success factor (CSF) 10

cross-functional business process 9
customer experience 7
cycle time 22
dashboards 12
data analytics 3
data science 20
deliverables 9
digital business model 7
digitization 15
flexibility 11
informed user 21
Internet of Things (IoT) 16
IT consumerization 11

IT project managers 20
machine-to-machine (M2M) technology 16
mega trends 14
objectives 8
on-demand economy 4
productivity 7
responsiveness 11
social, mobile, analytics and cloud (SMAC) 13
standard operating procedures (SOPs) 9
SWOT analysis 19
unstructured data 15
wearable technology 12

Assuring Your Learning

Discuss: Critical Thinking Questions

1. Why are businesses experiencing a digital transformation?

2. More data are collected in a day now than existed in the world 10 years ago. What factors have contributed to this volume of data?

3. Assume you had no smartphone, other mobile device, or mobile apps to use for 24 hours. How would that mobile blackout disrupt your ability to function?

4. Name three highly disruptive digital technologies. Give an example of one disruption for each technology.

5. Why are enterprises adopting cloud computing?

6. What is the value of M2M technology? Give two examples.

7. Starbucks monitors tweets and other sources of big data. How might the company increase revenue from big data analytics?

8. Select three companies in different industries, such as banking, retail store, supermarket, airlines, or package delivery, that you do business with. What digital technologies does each company use to engage you, keep you informed, or create a unique customer experience? How effective is each use of digital technology to keeping you a loyal customer?

9. Describe two examples of the influence of SMAC on the financial industry.

10. What is the potential impact of the IoT on the health-care industry?

11. Why does reducing the **cycle time** of a business process also help to reduce errors?

12. Research firm Gartner defines competitive advantage as a difference between a company and its competitors *that matters to customers*. Describe one use of M2M technology that could provide a manufacturer with a competitive advantage.

13. What IT careers are forecasted to be in high demand? Explain why.

14. Why or how would understanding the latest IT trends influence your career?

Explore: Online and Interactive Exercises

1. Research the growing importance of the IoT. Find two forecasts of its growth. What do they forecast?

2. Go to "9 Successful Digital Disruption Examples" on the IT Business Edge website. Close the pop-up to view the slideshow and read the descriptions of each of the ways in which technology is disrupting our lives. Answer the following questions:

a. Which of the following disruptions resonated best with you and your lifestyle? Explain.

b. Which of the disruptions was most surprising to you? Why?

c. Rank order the disruptions in their order of importance to you? Write a short report explaining your rankings.

Analyze & Decide: Apply IT Concepts to Business Decisions

1. A transportation company is considering investing in a truck tire with embedded sensors. Outline the benefits of this investment. Would this investment create a long-term competitive advantage for the transportation company?

2. Visit the website of UPS (ups.com), Federal Express (fedex.com), and one other logistics and delivery company.

   a. At each site, describe what information is available to customers before and after they send a package?

   b. Compare the three customer experiences. Which one do you prefer? Why?

3. Visit Dell.com and Apple.com to simulate buying a laptop computer. Compare and contrast the selection process, degree of customization, and other buying features. What are the **barriers to entry** into this market, based on what you learned from this exercise?

Case 1.2

Business Case: The Internet of Things Comes to the NFL

People love sports statistics and the more the better. Responding to this customer demand, the NFL increased the quality and quantity of statistics available to coaches and fans with radio frequency identification (RFID) chips.

Player RFID Project

When the 2015 National Football League played its first game in New England, each player was equipped with a set of RFID sensors. Each sensor, about the size of a quarter, is embedded in players' shoulder pads and emits a unique radio frequency. Every stadium used by the NFL is equipped with 20 receivers to pick up the RFID signals and pinpoint every player on the field. It also records speed, distance traveled, acceleration in real time, and the direction the player is facing.

The NFL plans to use the data it collects to power an Xbox One and Windows NFL apps to allow fans to call up stats for each player tied into the highlight clips posted on the app. The data will also be fed to broadcasters, leveraged for in-stadium displays, and provided to coaching staff and players.

"We've always had these traditional NFL stats," says Matt Swensson, senior director of Emerging Products and Technology at the NFL. "The league has been very interested in trying to broaden that and bring new statistics to the fans. Along the way, there's been more realization about how the data can be leveraged to make workflow more efficient around the game."

Zebra Technologies Software Vendor

The NFL's technology partner in its IoT push was Zebra Technologies of Lincolnshire, Illinois.

Zebra was well known for its manufacturing and selling marking, tracking and printing technologies such as thermal barcode label and receipt printers, RFID smart label printer/encoders, and card and kiosk printers. As it moved into IoT and M2M applications, Zebra launched its MotionWorks Sports Solution, which powers the NFL IoT initiative. Zebra was able to develop RFID tags that blink up to 85 times per second to track motion of athletes in subseconds. Then it had to find a customer for the product—so it turned to the biggest fish in the pond—the NFL. Zebra trialed the tags by equipping more than 2,000 players, 18 NFL stadiums and officials, markers, and pylons. Over the course of the season, more than 1.7 billion sets of XY player coordinates were measured, transmitted, and stored during the games. Every stadium was connected to a command station in San Jose, California, that controls when the data are collected, where they are sent, and stores them in the cloud.

The Need for the Right People

An important lesson that Zebra learned is that generic data scientists weren't sufficient to gain insight into the data. Zebra needed football experts. "When you look at analytics in football, you really need people. We had to go out and hire football people. The analytics from manufacturing weren't the same as the analytics from football. We could see correlations in the data that seemed important and then found out they weren't. We had to bring in people that had the football expertise who could say 'Look, this is why it matters'," said Jill Stelfox, Zebra Technologies Vice President and General Manager, Location Solutions.

The latest development in this IoT initiative is its integration with NFL's fantasy football offerings.

Questions

1. Why did NFL equip its players with RFID tags?
2. What factors contributed to the success of the IoT initiative at the NFL?
3. What other types of IoT applications can you think of that could be used in sports stadiums?

Case 1.3

Video Case: Knowing More and Doing More

Teradata is a leading provider of big data and data analytics solutions. In a video, Teradata explains that when you know the right thing to do, you can do more of what truly matters for your business and your customers. Visit **Teradata's website**, search for and view the video entitled "Manufacturing: What Would You Do If You Knew?"™ (the video runs for 1:26 minutes).

Questions

1. What did you learn from the video?
2. What is the value of knowing more?

References

Accenture. *Accenture Technology Vision* 2013.

Ashcroft, S. "Fitbit sold 4.5 million trackers last quarter and smashed financial estimates." *Wareable.com*, August 6, 2015.

Barry Libert, B., Y. Wind, and M.B. Fenley. "What Airbnb, Uber, and Alibaba Have in Common." *Harvard Business Review*, November 20, 2014.

Basu, C. "The Six Important Business Objectives of Information Technology." *Chron*, 2017. Accessible from http://smallbusiness.chron.com/six-important-business-objectives-information-technology-25220.html

Boland, M. "What's Driving the Local on Demand Economy?" *BIA/Kelsey blog*, May 5, 2015.

Bureau of Labor Statistics. *Occupational Outlook Handbook*. U.S. Department of Labor, 2016–2017.

Chandler, N. "How FitBit Works." *HowStuffWorks.com*, May 2, 2012.

Chriss, A. "How the On-Demand Economy Is Reshaping the 40 Hour Work Week." 2016.

Computerworld. "2017 Tech Forecast: IT Sharpens Its Focus." *Computerworld*, 2017.

Darrow, B. "Data Science Is Still White Hot, but Nothing Lasts Forever." *Fortune*, 2015.

Eadicicco, L. "American Check Their Phones 8 Billion Times a Day." *Time*, December 15, 2015.

glassdoor.com. "Data Scientist Salaries." April 7, 2017.

Grand View Research. "Wearable Technology Market Analysis By Product (Wrist-Wear, Eye-Wear, Foot-Wear, Neck-Wear, Body-Wear), by Application (Fitness & Wellness, Healthcare, Infotainment, Defense, Enterprise and Industrial) and Segment Forecasts to 2022." Grand View Research, 2016.

Hammer, M. and J. Champy. "Re-engineering the Corporation: A Manifesto for Business Revolution." Updated and revised edition. Harper Business Essentials, 2006.

Jaconi, M. "The 'On-Demand Economy' Is Revolutionizing Consumer Behavior—Here's How." *Business Insider*, July 13, 2014.

Kappelman, L., E. McLean, V. Johnson, R. Torres, Q. Nguyen, C. Maurer, and M. Snyder. "The 2016 SIM IT Key Issues and Trends Study." *MIS Quarterly Executive*, March 2017.

MacIver, K. "Digital Business in an Era of Disruptive Innovation." *I-CIO.com*, November 2015.

Marr, B. "Is Being a Data Scientist Really the Best Job in America?" *Forbes*, February 25, 2016.

National Employment Law Project. "Employers in the On-Demand Economy: Why Treating Workers as Employees is Good for Business." http://www.nelp.org/content/uploads/Fact-Sheet-Employers-in-the-On-Demand-Economy.pdf, 2016.

Nusca, A. "The Numbers Are in: Apple Is No. 2 in Wearables." *Fortune*, August 27, 2015.

Pratt, M. "10 Hottest Tech Skills for 2017." *Computerworld*, December 7, 2016.

Primack, D. "GrubHub Makes Major Move in Restaurant Delivery Wars." *Fortune*, February 5, 2015.

Schmidt-Subramanian, M., H. Manning, J. Knott, and Murphy. "The Business Impact of Customer Experience, 2013." *Forrester Research*, June 10, 2013.

Storbaek, D. "The 5-Step Uber Playbook That Will Disrupt the On-Demand Economy." *TechCrunch.com*, October 15, 2015.

U.S. Department of Labor (2016). "Computer and Information Technology Occupations". https://www.bls.gov/ooh/computer-and-information-technology/home.htm

Vaughn-Brown, J. "The Digital Transformation Journey: Key Technology Considerations." *CA Technologies*, 2014.

Winkler, R. and D. Macmillan. "The Secret Math of Airbnb's $24 Billion Valuation." *The Wall Street Journal*, June 17, 2015.

CHAPTER 2

Information Systems, IT Architecture, Data Governance, and Cloud Computing

CHAPTER OUTLINE	LEARNING OBJECTIVES
Case 2.1 Opening Case: Detoxing Location-Based Advertising Data at MEDIATA	
2.1 IS Concepts and Classifications	**2.1 Name** the six components of an **information** system and match the various types of information systems to the type of support needed by business operations and decision-makers.
2.2 IT Infrastructure, IT Architecture, and Enterprise Architecture	**2.2 Describe** an IT infrastructure, an IT architecture, and an enterprisewide architecture (EA) and compare and contrast their roles in guiding IT growth and sustaining long-term performance.
2.3 Information Management and Data Governance	**2.3 Explain** the business benefits of information management and understand the importance of data governance and master data management in providing trusted data that is available when and where needed to support sustainability.
2.4 Data Centers and Cloud Computing	**2.4 Understand** the concepts of data centers and cloud computing and understand how they add value in an organization.
2.5 Cloud Services and Virtualization	**2.5 Describe** the different types of cloud services and the various forms of virtualization and understand how they add value in an organization.
Case 2.2 Business Case: Data Chaos Creates Risk	
Case 2.3 Video Case: Cloud Computing at Coca-Cola Is Changing Everything	

Introduction

One of the most popular business strategies for achieving success is the development of a competitive advantage. Competitive advantage exists when a company has superior resources and capabilities than its competitors that allow it to achieve either a lower cost structure or a differentiated product. For long-term business success, companies strive to develop *sustainable competitive advantages*, or competitive advantages that cannot be easily copied by the competition (Porter, 1998). To stay ahead, corporate leaders must constantly seek new ways to grow their business in the face of rapid technology changes, increasingly empowered consumers and employees, and ongoing changes in government regulation. Effective ways to thrive over the long term are to launch new business **models** and strategies or devise new ways to outperform competitors. Because these new business models, strategies, and performance capabilities will frequently be the result of advances in technology, the company's ability to leverage technological innovation over time will depend on its approach to enterprise IT architecture, information management, and data governance. The *enterprisewide IT architecture,* or simply the **enterprise architecture (EA)**, guides the evolution, expansion, and integration of information systems (ISs), digital technology, and business processes. This guidance enables companies to more effectively leverage their IT capability to achieve maximum competitive advantage and growth over the long term. **Information management** guides the acquisition, custodianship, and distribution of corporate data and involves the management of data systems, technology, processes, and corporate strategy. Data governance, or *information governance,* controls enterprise data through formal policies and procedures. One goal of data governance is to provide employees and business partners with high-quality data they can trust and access on demand.

Dirty data are data of such poor quality that they cannot be trusted or relied upon for decisions.

Bad decisions can result from the analysis of inaccurate data, which is widely referred to as **dirty data,** and lead to increased costs, decreased revenue, and legal, reputational, and performance-related consequences. For example, if data is collected and analyzed based on inaccurate information because advertising was conducted in the wrong location for the wrong audience, marketing campaigns can become highly skewed and ineffective. Companies must then begin costly repairs to their datasets to correct the problems caused by dirty data. This creates a drop in customer satisfaction and a misuse of resources in a firm. One example of an organization taking strides to clean the dirty data collected through inaccurate marketing is the data management platform, MEDIATA, which runs bidding systems and ad location services for firms looking to run ads on websites (see **Table 2.1**). Let's see how they did this.

Case 2.1   Opening Case

Courtesy of Billy Ray

Detoxing Location-Based Advertising Data at MEDIATA

TABLE 2.1	Opening Case Overview
Company	MEDIATA was launched as Valued Interactive Media (VIM) in 2009. Rebranded in 2013 as MEDIATA
Industry	Communications; Advertising
Product Lines	Wide range of programmatic solutions and products to provide practical solutions for digital marketing campaigns to deliver successful online advertising campaigns to organizations across Australia, Hong Kong, and New Zealand
Digital Technology	Information management and data governance to increase trust and accessibility of data to facilitate a company's vision
Business Vision	Shake up the online advertising industry. Improve transparency and foster greater cooperation between partners
Website	www.mediataplatform.com

Company Overview

MEDIATA uses its audience and media delivery platform to deliver thousands of successful online advertising campaigns across Australia, Hong Kong, and New Zealand. Known as a "programmatic solution specialist," the MEDIATA platform is truly cutting-edge. It runs bidding systems and ad location services for companies that are looking to run ads on websites and provides its clients with high-impact, fully managed, 100% transparent advertising campaigns that produce results. MEDIATA is committed to shaking up the online advertising industry and is evolving into a fast-growing international business. MEDIATA clients include Qantas, LG, Virgin Money, Konica Minolta, Optus, Carlsberg, Honda, ACCOR Hotels, Air New Zealand, Heinz, Woolworths, Citibank, and JP Morgan.

The Problem

MEDIATA uses IP address data to locate customers and ad effectiveness. Unfortunately, *as much as **80% of ad inventories come with an incorrect location*** and MEDIATA realized that this "dirty data" was adversely affecting their business. Location-based advertising provides organizations and companies alike with massive benefits. Target customers can be reached easily and effectively through marketing campaigns tailored specifically for them. For example, utility companies and internet service providers usually have certain areas or regions that they service. Using location-based targeting (see **Figure 2.1**), these companies can target television, newspaper, and online display ads to attract new customers. Another benefit includes the reduced waste of running marketing campaigns in unprofitable areas. Firms can choose precisely where their advertisements are displayed without wasting resources on customer segments that will not respond because of location or preference discrepancies.

Advanced data analytics in location-based advertising also allows companies like MEDIATA to reach customers where and when they are in decision-making mode using programmatic bidding algorithms and ad inventories. Browser-based ads use these algorithms to predict which customer segments will click on certain ads at certain times of the day. Automated bidding then ensues, with the ad spot on the page going to the highest bidder (Cailean, 2016). However, the data must be accurate to be useful and MEDIATA realized that their data could be much better than it was. Given the importance of this technology to advertisers and digital advertising agencies, there are overwhelming issues to overcome.

The issues stem from outdated methods of locating Internet users through IP addresses. These old systems do not pinpoint where exactly traffic is coming from, rather they give advertising agencies broad geographic regions to work with, and the ads go to random coordinates within the regions. Since the value of these activities comes from having accurate targeting, the inaccuracies of the antiquated systems severely impact profitability. As targeting regions shrink, information becomes more valuable and accurate, but even small inaccuracies dilute the value of demographic information applied to an audience.

The Solution

In 2016, MEDIATA established a data governance program in which it partnered with Skyhook, a U.S. global location software company to

FIGURE 2.1 Location-based advertising.

improve the effectiveness of MEDIATA's user profile data by more precisely locating IP addresses resolving MEDIATA's challenges related to dirty data. Skyhook's Context Accelerator Hyperlocal IP uses big data analytics to provide over 1 billion IP addresses to advertising platforms and cleaned MEDIATA's dirty data to pinpoint customers within 100 meters, thus increasing ad effectiveness for its clients. Hyperlocal IP achieves this by using big data analytics to provide over 1 billion IP addresses to advertising platforms.

Now, every time a device like a cell phone or laptop requests a location, the on-device software scans for Wi-Fi, GPS, or cell tower data. Combining all of these data points allows Skyhook to provide extremely accurate coordinates and pass this information along to MEDIATA to use.

While this approach still is not perfect, it allows MEDIATA's advertisements to become closer than ever to their target customers. A nine-month study conducted after implementing Skyhook showed that MEDIATA saw a 20% increase in marketing campaign effectiveness.

Creating and employing this data governance system allowed MEDIATA to clean its datasets and create new, effective methods to reach target audiences.

Questions

1. What business challenges did MEDIATA face because of its dirty data?
2. What is the function of location-based advertising?
3. Why is it important to maintain accurate location data?
4. How did Skyhook and data governance enable MEDIATA to achieve its vision?
5. What benefits did MEDIATA achieve as a result of implementing data governance?

Sources: Compiled from Cailean (2016), Schneider (2014), and Schneider (2015).

2.1 IS Concepts and Classification

Information systems (ISs) is a combination of information technology and people's activities using the technology to support business processes, operations, management, and decision-making at different levels of the organization.

IPOS is the cycle of inputting, processing, outputting, and storing information in an information system.

Before we being to explore the value of **information systems (ISs)** to an organization, it's useful to understand what an IS is, what it does, and what types of ISs are typically found at different levels of an organization.

In addition to supporting decision-making, coordination, and control in an organization, ISs also help managers and workers analyze problems, visualize complex sets of data, and create new products. ISs collect (**input**) and manipulate data (**process**), and generate and distribute reports (**output**) and based on the data-specific IT services, such as processing customer orders and generating payroll, are delivered to the organization. Finally, the ISs save (**store**) the data for future use. In addition to the four functions of **IPOS**, an information needs **feedback** from its users and other stakeholders to help improve future systems as demonstrated in **Figure 2.2**.

The following example demonstrates how the components of the IPOS work together: To access a website, Amanda opens an Internet browser using the keyboard and enters a Web address into the browser (input). The system then uses that information to find the correct website (processing) and the content of the desired site is displayed in the Web browser (output). Next, Amanda bookmarks the desired website in the Web browser for future use (storage). The system then records the time that it took to produce the output to compare actual versus expected performance (feedback).

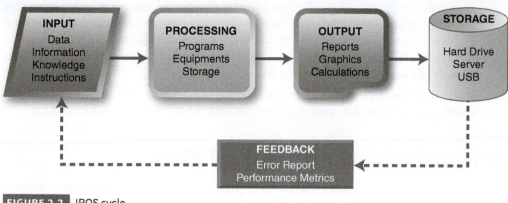

FIGURE 2.2   IPOS cycle.

Components of an IS

A computerized IS consists of six interacting components. Regardless of type and where and by whom they are used within an organization, the components of an IS must be carefully managed to provide maximum benefit to an organization (see **Figure 2.3**).

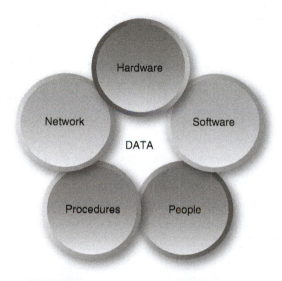

FIGURE 2.3   Components of an IS.

1. **Hardware**   Any physical device used in a computerized IS. Examples include central processing unit (CPU), sound card, video card, network card, hard drive, display, keyboard, motherboard, processor, power supply, modem, mouse, and printer.

2. **Software**   A set of machine-readable instructions (code) that makes up a computer application that directs a computer's processor to perform specific operations. Computer software is nontangible, contrasted with system hardware, which is the physical component of an IS. Examples include Internet browser, operating system (OS), Microsoft Office, Skype, and so on.

3. **People**   Any person involved in using an IS. Examples include programmers, operators help desk, and end-users.

4. **Procedures**   Documentation containing directions on how to use the other components of an IS. Examples include operational manual and user manual.

5. **Network**   A combination of lines, wires, and physical devices connected to each other to create a telecommunications network. In computer networks, networked computing

devices exchange data with each other using a data link. The connections between nodes are established using either cable media or wireless media. Networks can be internal or external. If they are available only internally within an organization, they are called "intranets." If they are available externally, they are called "internets." The best-known example of a computer network is the World Wide Web.

6. **Data**   Raw or unorganized facts and figures (such as invoices, orders, payments, customer details, product numbers, product prices) that describe conditions, ideas, or objects.

Data, Information, Knowledge, and Wisdom

Data   describe products, customers, events, activities, and transactions that are recorded, classified, and stored.

Information   is data that have been processed, organized, or put into context so that they have meaning and value to the person receiving them.

Knowledge   adds understanding, experience, accumulated learning, and expertise as they apply to a current problem or activity, to information.

As you can see in Figure 2.3, **data** is the central component of any **information** system. Without data, an IS would have no purpose and companies would unable to conduct business. Generally speaking, ISs process **data** into meaningful *information* that produces corporate **knowledge** and ultimately creates *wisdom* that fuels corporate strategy.

Data are the raw material from which information is produced; the quality, reliability, and integrity of the data must be maintained for the information to be useful. Data are the raw facts and figures that are not organized in any way. Examples are the number of hours an employee worked in a certain week or the number of new Ford vehicles sold from the first quarter (Q1) of 2015 through the second quarter (Q2) of 2017 (**Figure 2.4**).

Information is an organization's most important asset, second only to people. Information provides the "who," "what," "where," and "when" of data in a given context. For example,

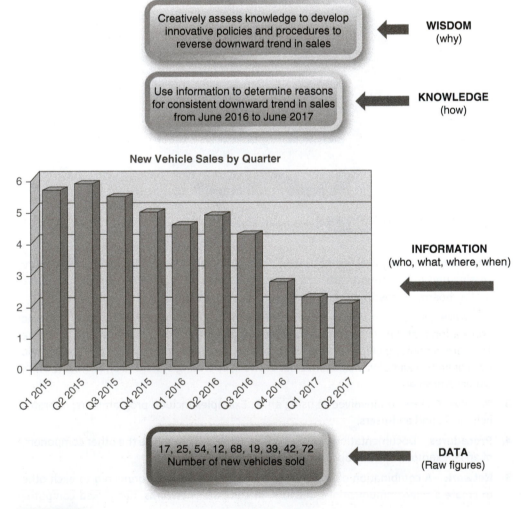

FIGURE 2.4   Examples of data, information, knowledge, and wisdom.

summarizing the quarterly sales of new Ford vehicles from Q1 2015 through Q2 2017 provides information that shows sales have steadily decreased from Q2 2016.

Knowledge is used to answer the question "how." In our example, it would involve determining how the trend can be reversed, for example, customer satisfaction can be improved, new features can be added, and pricing can be adjusted.

Wisdom is more abstract than data and information (that can be harnessed) and knowledge (that can be shared). Wisdom adds value and increases effectiveness. It answers the "why" in a given situation. In the Ford example, wisdom would be corporate strategists evaluating the various reasons for the sales drop, creatively analyzing the situation as a whole, and developing innovative policies and procedures to reverse the recent downward trend in new vehicle sales.

ISs collect or input and process data to create and distribute reports or other outputs based on information gleaned from the raw data to support decision-making and business processes that, in turn, produce corporate knowledge that can be stored for future use. **Figure 2.5** shows the input-processing-output-storage (IPOS) cycle.

Wisdom is a collection of values, ethics, moral codes, and prior experiences that form an evaluated understanding or common-sense judgment.

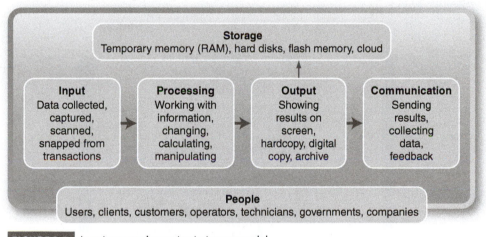

FIGURE 2.5   Input-processing-output-storage model.

Types of ISs

An IS may be as simple as a single computer and a printer used by one person, or as complex as several thousand computers of various types (tablets, desktops, laptops, mainframes) with hundreds of printers, scanners, and other devices connected through an elaborate network used by thousands of geographically dispersed employees. Functional ISs that support business analysts and other departmental employees range from simple to complex, depending on the type of employees supported. The following examples show the support that IT provides to major functional areas.

1. **Marketing**   Utilizing IBM software, Bolsa de Comercio de Santiago, a large stock exchange in Chile, is able to process its ever-increasing, high-volume trading in microseconds. The Chilean stock exchange system can do the detective work of analyzing current and past transactions and market information, learning, and adapting to market trends and connecting its traders to business information in real time. Immediate throughput in combination with analytics allows traders to make more accurate decisions.

2. **Sales**   According to the *New England Journal of Medicine*, one in five patients suffers from preventable readmissions, which cost taxpayers over $17 billion a year. In the past, hospitals have been penalized for high readmission rates with cuts to the payments they receive from the government (Zuckerman et al., 2016). Using effective management information systems (MISs), the health-care industry can leverage unstructured information in ways not possible before, according to Matt McClelland, manager of information

governance for Blue Cross Blue Shield of North Carolina. "With proper support, information governance can bridge the gaps among the need to address regulation and litigation risk, the need to generate increased sales and revenue, and the need to cut costs and become more efficient. When done right, information governance positively impacts every facet of the business," McClelland said in the Information Governance Initiative (Jarousse, 2016).

Figure 2.6 illustrates the classification of the different types of ISs used in organizations, the typical level of workers who use them and the types of input/output (I/O) produced by each of the ISs. At the operational level of the organization, line workers use **transaction processing systems (TPSs)** to capture raw *data* and pass it along (output) to middle managers. The raw data is then input into office automation (OA) and MISs by middle managers to produce *information* for use by senior managers. Next, information is input into **decision support systems (DSSs)** for processing into explicit *knowledge* that will be used by senior managers to direct current corporate strategy. Finally, corporate executives input the explicit knowledge provided by the DSSs into **executive information systems (EISs)** and apply their experience, expertise, and skills to create *wisdom* that will lead to new corporate strategies.

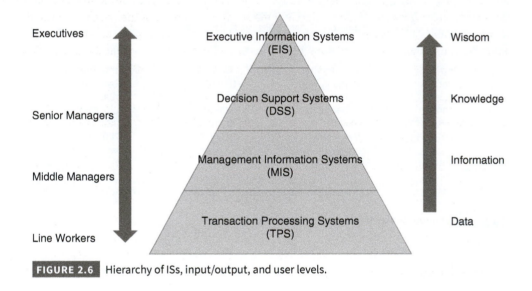

FIGURE 2.6 Hierarchy of ISs, input/output, and user levels.

Transaction Processing System (TPS)

A TPS is designed to process specific types of data input from ongoing transactions. TPSs can be manual, as when data are typed into a form on a screen, or automated by using scanners or sensors to capture barcodes or other data (**Figure 2.7**). TPSs are usually operated directly by frontline workers and provide the key data required to support the management of operations.

Organizational data are processed by a TPS, for example, sales orders, reservations, stock control, and payments by payroll, accounting, financial, marketing, purchasing, inventory control, and other functional departments. The data are usually obtained through the automated or semiautomated tracking of low-level activities and basic transactions. Transactions are either:

- **internal transactions** that originate within the organization or that occur within the organization, for example, payroll, purchases, budget transfers, and payments (in accounting terms, they are referred to as *accounts payable*); or
- **external transactions** that originate from outside the organization, for example, from customers, suppliers, regulators, distributors, and financing institutions.

TPSs are essential systems. Transactions that are not captured can result in lost sales, dissatisfied customers, unrecorded payments, and many other types of data errors with financial

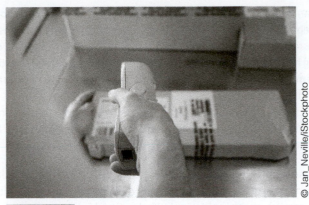

FIGURE 2.7 Scanners automate the input of data into a transaction processing system (TPS).

impacts. For example, if the accounting department issued a check to pay an invoice (bill) and it was cashed by the recipient, but information about that transaction was not captured, then two things happen. First, the amount of cash listed on the company's financial statements is incorrect because no deduction was made for the amount of the check. Second, the accounts payable (A/P) system will continue to show the invoice as unpaid, so the accounting department might pay it a second time. Likewise, if services are provided, but the transactions are not recorded, the company will not bill for them and thus lose service revenue.

Batch versus Online Real-Time Processing   Data captured by a TPS are processed and stored in a **database**; they then become available for use by other systems. Processing of transactions is done in one of two modes:

1. **Batch processing**   A TPS in **batch processing** mode collects all transaction for a day, shift, or other time period, and then processes the data and updates the data stores. Payroll processing done weekly or bi-weekly is an example of batch mode.

2. **Online transaction processing (OLTP) or real-time processing**   The TPS processes each transaction as it occurs, which is what is meant by the term *real-time processing*. In order for OLTP to occur, the input device or website must be directly linked via a network to the TPS. Airlines need to process flight reservations in real time to verify that seats are available.

Batch processing costs less than real-time processing. A disadvantage is that data are inaccurate because they are not updated immediately, in real time.

Processing Impacts Data Quality   As data are collected or captured, they are validated to detect and correct obvious errors and omissions. For example, when a customer sets up an account with a financial services firm or retailer, the TPS validates that the address, city, and postal code provided are consistent with one another and also that they match the credit card holder's address, city, and postal code. If the form is not complete or errors are detected, the customer is required to make the corrections before the data are processed any further.

Data errors detected later may be time-consuming to correct or cause other problems. You can better understand the difficulty of detecting and correcting errors by considering identity theft. Victims of identity theft face enormous challenges and frustration trying to correct data about them.

Management Information System (MIS)

An MIS is built on the data provided by TPS. MISs are management-level systems that are used by middle managers to help ensure the smooth running of an organization in the short to medium term. The highly structured information provided by these systems allows managers to evaluate an organization's performance by comparing current with previous outputs. Functional areas or departments—accounting, finance, production/operations, marketing and sales, human resources, and engineering and design—are supported by ISs designed for their particular reporting needs. General-purpose reporting systems are referred to as **management information systems (MISs)**. Their objective is to provide reports to managers for tracking operations, monitoring, and control.

Typically, a functional system provides reports about such topics as operational efficiency, effectiveness, and productivity by extracting information from databases and processing it according to the needs of the user. Types of reports include the following:

- **Periodic**   These reports are created or run according to a pre-set schedule. Examples are daily, weekly, and quarterly. Reports are easily distributed via e-mail, blogs, internal websites (called *intranets*), or other electronic media. Periodic reports are also easily ignored if workers do not find them worth the time to review.

- **Exception**   **Exception reports** are generated only when something is outside the norm, either higher or lower than expected. Sales in hardware stores prior to a hurricane may be much higher than the norm. Or sales of fresh produce may drop during a food contamination crisis. Exception reports are more likely to be read because workers know that some unusual event or deviation has occurred.

- **Ad hoc, or on demand**   **Ad hoc reports** are unplanned reports. They are generated to a mobile device or computer on demand *as needed*. They are generated on request to learn more about a situation, problem, or opportunity.

Reports typically include interactive data visualizations, such as column and pie charts, as shown in **Figure 2.8**.

FIGURE 2.8   Sample report produced by an MIS.

Decision Support System (DSS)

A DSS is a knowledge-based system used by senior managers to facilitate the creation of knowledge and allow its integration into the organization. More specifically, a DSS is an interactive application that supports decision-making by manipulating and building upon the information from an MIS and/or a TPS to generate insights and new information.

Configurations of a DSS range from relatively simple applications that support a single user to complex enterprisewide systems. A DSS can support the analysis and solution of a specific problem, evaluate a strategic opportunity, or support ongoing operations. These systems support unstructured and semistructured decisions, such as make-or-buy-or-outsource decisions, or what products to develop and introduce into existing markets.

Degree of Structure of Decisions   Decisions range from structured to unstructured. Structured decisions are those that have a well-defined method for solving and the data necessary to reach a sound decision. An example of a structured decision is determining whether an applicant qualifies for an auto loan, or whether to extend credit to a new customer— and the terms of those financing options. **Structured decisions** are relatively straightforward and made on a regular basis, and an IS can ensure that they are done consistently.

At the other end of the continuum are **unstructured decisions** that depend on human intelligence, knowledge, and/or experience—as well as data and models to solve. Examples include deciding which new products to develop or which new markets to enter. Semistructured decisions fall in the middle of the continuum. DSSs are best suited to support these types of decisions, but they are also used to support unstructured ones. To provide such support, DSSs have certain characteristics to support the decision-maker and the overall decision-making process.

The main characteristic that distinguishes a DSS from an MIS is the inclusion of models. Decision-makers can manipulate models to conduct experiments and sensitivity analyses, for example, *what-if* and *goal seeking*. **What-if analysis** refers to changing assumptions or data in the model to observe the impacts of those changes on the outcome. For example, if sales forecasts are based on a 5% increase in customer demand, a what-if analysis would replace the 5% with higher and/or lower estimates to determine *what* would happen to sales *if* demand changed. With **goal seeking**, the decision-maker has a specific outcome in mind and needs to determine how that outcome could be achieved and whether it is feasible to achieve that desired outcome. A DSS can also estimate the risk of alternative strategies or actions.

California Pizza Kitchen (CPK) uses a DSS to support inventory decisions. CPK has over 200 locations in 32 U.S. states and 13 other countries, including 17 California Pizza Kitchen non-traditional, franchise concepts designed for airports, universities, and stadiums. Maintaining optimal inventory levels at all its restaurants was challenging and time-consuming. The original MIS was replaced by a DSS to make it easy for the chain's managers to maintain updated records, generate reports as and when needed, and make corporate- and restaurant-level decisions. Many CPK restaurants reported a 5% increase in sales after the DSS was implemented.

Executive Information System (EIS)

EISs are strategic-level information systems that help executives and senior managers analyze the environment in which the organization exists. They typically are used to identify long-term trends and to plan appropriate courses of action. The information in such systems is often weakly structured and comes from both internal and external sources. EISs are designed to be operated directly by executives without the need for intermediaries and easily tailored to the preferences of the individual using them. An EIS organizes and presents data and information from both external data sources and internal MIS or TPS in an easy-to-use dashboard format to support and extend the inherent capabilities of senior executives.

Initially, EISs were custom-made for an individual executive. However, a number of off-the-shelf EIS packages now exist and some enterprise-level systems offer a customizable EIS module.

The ways in which the different characteristics of the various types of ISs are classified is shown in **Table 2.2**.

Here's an example of how these ISs are used together to add value in an organization. Day-to-day transaction data collected by the TPS are converted into prescheduled summarized reports by middle managers using an MIS. The findings in these reports are then analyzed by senior managers who use a DSS to support their semistructured or unstructured decision-making. DSSs contain models that consist of a set of formulas and functions, such as statistical, financial, optimization, and/or simulation models. Corporations, government agencies, the military, health care, medical research, major league sports, and nonprofits depend on their DSSs to answer what-if questions to help reduce waste in production operations, improve inventory management, support investment decisions, and predict demand and help sustain a competitive edge.

Customer data, sales, and other critical data produced by the DSS are then selected for further analysis, such as trend analysis or forecasting demand and are input into an EIS for

TABLE 2.2   Characteristics of Types of Information Systems

Type	Characteristics
TPS	Used by operations personnel
	Produce information for other ISs
	Use internal and external data
	Efficiency oriented
MIS	Used by lower and middle managers
	Based on internal information
	Support structured decisions
	Inflexible
	Lack analytical capabilities
	Focus on past and present data
DSS	Used by senior managers
	Support semistructured or unstructured decisions
	Contain models or formulas that enable sensitivity analysis, what-if analysis, goal seeking, and risk analysis
	Use internal and external data plus data added by the decision-maker who may have insights relevant to the decision situation
	Predict the future
EIS	Used by C-level managers
	Easy-to-use, customizable interface
	Support unstructured decisions
	Use internal and external data sources
	Focus on effectiveness of the organization
	Very flexible
	Focus on the future

use by top level management, who add their experience and expertise to make unstructured decisions that will affect the future of the business.

Figure 2.9 shows how the major types of ISs relate to one another and how data flow among them. In this example,

1. Data from online purchases are captured and processed by the TPS and then stored in the transactional database.

2. Data needed for reporting purposes are extracted from the database and used by the MIS to create periodic, ad hoc, or other types of reports.

3. Data are output to a DSS where they are analyzed using formulas, financial ratios, or models.

ISs Exist within Corporate Culture

It is important to remember that ISs do not exist in isolation. They have a purpose and a social (organizational) context. A common *purpose* is to provide a solution to a business problem. The *social context* of the system consists of the values and beliefs that determine what is admissible and possible within the culture of the organization and among the people involved. For example, a company may believe that superb customer service and on-time delivery are critical success factors. This belief system influences IT investments, among other factors.

The business value of IT is determined by the people who use them, the business processes they support, and the culture of the organization. That is, IS value is determined by the

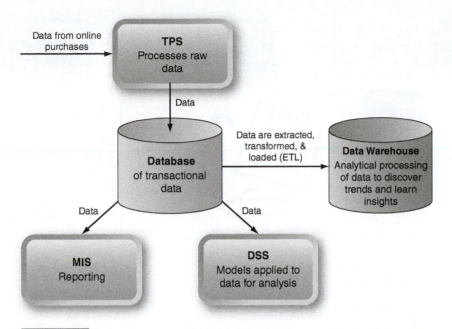

FIGURE 2.9   Flow of data from point of sale (POS) through processing, storage, reporting, decision support, and analysis. Also shows the relationships among different types of ISs.

relationships among ISs, people, and business processes—all of which are influenced strongly by organizational culture.

In an organization, there may be a culture of distrust between the technology and business employees. No enterprise IT architecture methodology or data governance can bridge this divide unless there is a genuine commitment to change. That commitment must come from the highest level of the organization—senior management. Methodologies cannot solve people problems; they can only provide a framework in which those problems can be solved.

Questions

1. Name the six components of an IS.
2. Describe the differences between data, information, knowledge, and wisdom.
3. Define TPS and give an example.
4. Explain why TPSs need to process incoming data before they are stored.
5. Define MIS and DSS and give an example of each.
6. What characteristic distinguishes a DSS from an MIS?
7. What level of personnel typically uses an EIS?
8. What factors determine IS value?

2.2 | IT Infrastructure, IT Architecture, and Enterprise Architecture

Every enterprise has a core set of ISs and business processes that execute the transactions that keep it in business. Transactions include processing orders, order fulfillment and delivery, purchasing inventory and supplies, hiring and paying employees, and paying bills. To most effectively utilize its IT assets, an organization must create an IT infrastructure, IT architecture, and an enterprise architecture (EA) as shown in **Figure 2.10**.

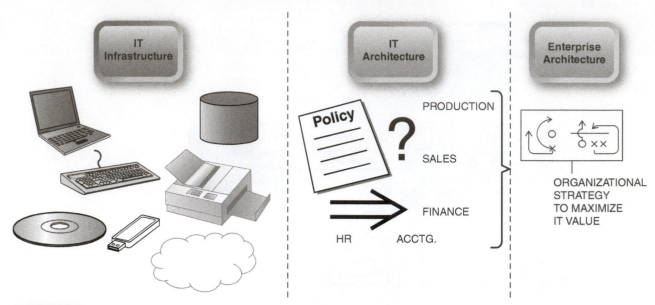

FIGURE 2.10 Comparing IT infrastructure, IT architecture, and enterprise architecture.

IT infrastructure *is an inventory of the physical IT devices that an organization owns and operates.* The IT infrastructure *describes an organization's entire collection* of hardware, software, networks, **data centers**, facilities, and other related equipment used to develop, test, operate, manage, and support IT services. It does **NOT** include the people or process components of an information system.

IT architecture guides the *process of planning, acquiring, building, modifying, interfacing, and deploying IT resources in a single department* within an organization. The IT architecture should offer a way to systematically identify technologies that work together to satisfy the needs of the departments' users. The IT architecture is a blueprint for how future technology acquisitions and deployment will take place. It consists of standards, investment decisions, and product selections for hardware, software, and communications. The IT architecture is developed first and foremost based on department direction and business requirements.

Enterprise architecture (EA) *reviews all the information systems across all departments in an organization to develop a strategy to organize and integrate the organization's IT infrastructures to help it meet the current and future goals of the enterprise and maximize the value of technology to the organization.* In this way, EA provides a holistic view of an organization with graphic and text descriptions of strategies, policies, information, ISs, and business processes and the relationships between them.

The EA adds value in an organization in that it can provide the basis for organizational change just as architectural plans guide a construction project. Since a poorly crafted **enterprise architecture (EA)** can also hinder day-to-day operations and efforts to execute business strategy, it is more important than ever before to carefully consider the EA within your organization when deciding on an approach to business, technology, and corporate strategy. Simply put, EA helps solve two critical challenges: *where an organization is going*, and *how it will get there*.

The success of EA is measured not only in financial terms, such as profitability and return on investment (ROI), but also in nonfinancial terms, for example, improved customer satisfaction, faster speed to market, and lower employee turnover as diagrammed in **Figure 2.11** and demonstrated in **IT at Work 2.1**.

EA Helps to Maintain Sustainability

As you read in Chapter 1, the volume, variety, and speed of data being collected or generated have increased dramatically over the past decade. As enterprise ISs become more complex,

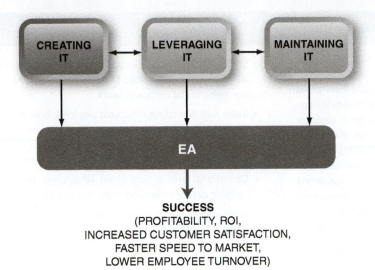

FIGURE 2.11   Enterprise architecture success.

IT at Work 2.1

A New Enterprise Architecture Improves Data Quality and EIS Use

Executives at a large chemical corporation were supported by an IS specifically designed for their needs—called an executive information system (EIS). The EIS was designed to provide senior managers with internal and external data and key performance indicators (KPIs) that were relevant to their specific needs. **Tech Note 2.1** describes KPIs. As with any system, the value of the EIS depends on the data quality.

Too Much Irrelevant Data

Unfortunately, the EIS was a failure. Executives soon discovered that only half of the data available through the EIS related to their level of analysis and decision-making at the corporate level. A worse problem was that the data they needed were not available when and how they wanted them. For example, executives needed to analyze current detailed sales revenue and cost data for every strategic business unit (SBU), product line, and operating business to compare performance. But, data were not in standardized format as needed, making analysis difficult or impossible. A large part of the problem was that SBUs reported sales revenues in different time frames (e.g., daily, weekly, monthly, or quarterly), and many of those reports were not available when needed. As a result, senior management could not get a *trusted* view of the company's current overall performance and did not know which products were profitable.

There were two reasons for the failure of the EIS:

1. **IT architecture was not designed for customized reporting**
   The design of the IT architecture had been based on financial accounting rules. That is, the data were organized to make it easy to collect and consolidate the data needed to prepare financial statements and reports that had to be submitted to the SEC (Securities and Exchange Commission) and other regulatory agencies. These statements and reports have well-defined or standardized formats and only need to be prepared at specific times during the year, typically annually or quarterly. The organization of the data (for financial reporting)

did not have the flexibility needed for the customized ad hoc (unplanned) data needs of the executives. For example, it was nearly impossible to generate customized sales performance (nonfinancial) reports or do ad hoc analyses, such as comparing inventory turnover rates by product for each region for each sales quarter. Because of lags in reports from various SBUs, executives could not trust the underlying data.

2. **Complicated user interface**   Executives could not easily review the KPIs. Instead, they had to sort through screens packed with too much data—some of interest and some irrelevant. To compensate for poor interface design, several IT analysts themselves had to do the data and KPI analyses for the executives—delaying response time and driving up the cost of reporting.

Solution: New Enterprise Architecture with Standardized Data Formats

The CIO worked with a task force to design and implement an entirely new EA. Data governance policies and procedures were implemented to standardize data formats companywide. Data governance eliminated data inconsistencies to provide reliable KPI reports on inventory turns, cycle times, and profit margins of all SBUs.

The new architecture was business-driven instead of financial reporting-driven. It was easy to modify reports—eliminating the costly and time-consuming ad hoc analyses. Fewer IT resources are needed to maintain the system. Because the underlying data are now relatively reliable, EIS use by executives increased significantly.

IT at Work Questions

1. Why was an EIS designed and implemented at the large chemical corporation?
2. What problems did the executives have with the EIS?
3. What were the two reasons for those EIS problems?
4. How did the CIO improve the EIS?
5. What are the benefits of the new IT enterprise architecture?
6. What are the benefits of data governance?

Tech Note 2.1

Key Performance Indicators (KPIs)

KPIs are a set of quantifiable measures used to evaluate factors that are crucial to the success of an organization. KPIs present data in easy-to-comprehend and comparison-ready formats to gauge or compare performance in terms of meeting an organization's operational and strategic goals. KPIs are used in four main areas: increasing revenue; reducing costs; improving process cycle-time; and improving customer satisfaction. Examples of key comparisons include actual versus budget, actual versus forecasted, and the ROI for this year versus prior years. KPIs help reduce the complex nature of organizational performance to a small number of understandable measures, including:

- Financial KPIs: accounts payable turnover; inventory turnover; net profit margin; sum of difference between planned and actual project budgets

- Social media KPIs: social traffic and conversions (number of visitors who are converted to customers); likes; new followers per week; social visits and leads

- Sales and marketing KPIs: cost per lead; how much revenue a marketing campaign generates; number of customer complaints; cycle time from customer request to delivery, percentage of correspondence replied to on time

- Operational and supply chain KPIs: units per transaction; carrying cost of inventory; order status; back order rate

- Environmental and carbon-footprint KPIs: energy, water, or other resource use; spend by utility; weight of landfill waste.

---

long-range IT planning is critical. Companies cannot simply add storage, new apps, or data analytics on an as-needed basis and expect those additional IT assets to work with existing systems.

The relationship between complexity and planning for the future is easier to see in physical things such as buildings and transportation systems. For example, if you are constructing a simple holiday cabin in a remote area, there is no need to create a detailed plan for future expansion. On the other hand, if you are building a large commercial development in a highly populated area, you're not likely to succeed without a detailed project plan. Relating this to the case of enterprise ISs, if you are building a simple, single-user, nondistributed system, you would not need to develop a well-thought-out growth plan. However, this approach would not be feasible to enable you to successfully manage big data, copious content from mobiles and social networks, and data in the cloud. Instead, you would need a well-designed set of plans, or blueprints, provided by an EA to align IT with business objectives by guiding and controlling hardware acquisition, software add-ons and upgrades, system changes, network upgrades, choice of cloud services, and other digital technology investments that you will need to make your business sustainable.

There are two specific strategic issues that the EA is designed to address:

1. **IT systems' complexity**   IT systems have become unmanageably complex and expensive to maintain.
2. **Poor business alignment**   Organizations find it difficult to keep their increasingly expensive IT systems aligned with business needs.

Business and IT Benefits of EA
Having the right EA in place is important for the following reasons:

- EA cuts IT costs and increases productivity by giving decision-makers access to information, insights, and ideas where and when they need them.
- EA determines an organization's competitiveness, flexibility, and IT economics for the next decade and beyond. That is, it provides a long-term view of a company's processes, systems, and technologies so that IT investments do not simply fulfill immediate needs.
- EA helps align IT capabilities with business strategy—to grow, innovate, and respond to market demands, supported by an IT practice that is 100% in accord with business objectives.
- EA can reduce the risk of buying or building systems and enterprise applications that are incompatible or unnecessarily expensive to maintain and integrate.

Developing an Enterprise Architecture (EA)

Developing an EA starts with the organization's goals, for example, *where does it want to be in three years?* and identifies the strategic direction in which it is heading and the business drivers to which it is responding. The goal is to make sure that everyone understands and shares a single vision. As soon as managers have defined this single shared vision of the future, they then consider the impact this vision will have on the business, technical, information, and solutions architectures of the enterprise. This shared vision of the future will dictate changes in all these architectures, assign priorities to those changes, and keep those changes grounded in business value.

According to Microsoft, the EA should include the four different perspectives shown in **Table 2.3**.

TABLE 2.3	Components of an Enterprise Architecture
Business architecture	How the business works. Includes broad business strategies and plans for moving the organization from where it is now to where it wants to be. Processes the business uses to meet its goals.
Application architecture	Portfolio of organization's applications. Includes descriptions of automated services that support business processes; descriptions of interactions and interdependencies between the organization's ISs.
Information architecture	What the organization needs to know to perform its business processes and operations. Includes standard data models; data management policies and descriptions of patterns of information production and use in an organization.
Technology architecture	Hardware and software that supports the organization. Examples include desktop and server software; OSs; network connectivity components; printers, modems.

It is important to recognize that the EA must be dynamic, not static. To sustain its effectiveness, it should be an ongoing process of aligning the creation, operation, and maintenance of IT across the organization with the ever-changing business objectives. As business needs change, so must the EA, as demonstrated in **IT at Work 2.2**.

IT at Work 2.2

EA Must Be Dynamic and Evolving

In order to keep IT aligned with the business, the EA must be a dynamic plan. As shown in the model in **Figure 2.12**, the EA evolves toward the target architecture, which represents the company's future IT needs. According to this model, EA defines the following:

1. The organization's mission, business functions, and future direction
2. Information and information flows needed to perform the mission
3. The current baseline architecture
4. The desired target architecture
5. The sequencing plan or strategy to progress from the baseline to the target architecture.

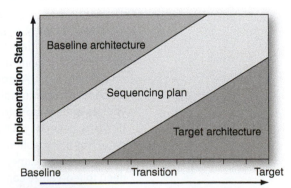

FIGURE 2.12   **The importance of viewing EA as a dynamic and evolving plan**   The purpose of the EA is to maintain IT–business alignment. Changes in priorities and business are reflected in the target architecture to help keep IT aligned with them (Bloomberg, 2016).

Career Insight 2.1

Essential Skills of an Enterprise Architect (EA)

Enterprise architects need much more than technology skills. On a daily basis, an enterprise architect's activities can change quickly and significantly. Ideally, enterprise architects should come from a highly technical background. Even though enterprise architects deal with many other factors besides technology, it is still important to keep technical skills current. The job performance and success of such an architect—or anyone responsible for large-scale IT projects—depend on a broad range of skills.

- **Interpersonal or people skills**   The job requires interacting with people and getting their cooperation.
- **Ability to influence and motivate**   A large part of the job is motivating users to comply with new processes and practices.
- **Negotiating skills**   The project needs resources—time, money, and personnel—that must be negotiated to get things accomplished.

- **Critical-thinking and problem-solving skills**   Architects face complex and unique problems. Being able to expedite solutions prevents bottlenecks.
- **Business and industry expertise**   Knowing the business and industry improves the outcomes and the architect's credibility.
- **Process orientation**   Thinking in terms of process is essential for an enterprise architect. Building repeatable and reusable processes as artifacts from the work they do and how they work themselves.

The most common function an enterprise architect will perform is that of overseeing a large-scale program. Programs are a group of related projects and as such, managing EA implementations requires someone who is able to handle multiple aspects of a project at one time. Project management is covered in Chapter 13.

Questions

1. What is the purpose of the IT infrastructure?
2. How is the IT infrastructure different from the IT architecture?
3. What is the purpose of an EA?
4. What are the business benefits of EA?
5. Explain why it is necessary to ensure that an EA maintains alignment between IT and business strategy?
6. Explain KPIs and give an example.

2.3 Information Management and Data Governance

As shown in Figure 2.3, data is the heart of the business and the central component of an IS. Most business initiatives succeed or fail based on the quality of their data. Effective planning and decision-making depend on systems being able to make data available in usable formats on a timely basis. Almost everyone manages information. You manage your social and cloud accounts across multiple mobile devices and computers. You update or synchronize ("synch") your calendars, appointments, contact lists, media files, documents, and reports. Your productivity depends on the compatibility of devices and applications and their ability to share data. Not being able to transfer and synch whenever you add a device or app is bothersome and wastes your time. For example, when you switch to the latest mobile device, you might need to reorganize content to make dealing with data and devices easier. To simplify add-ons, upgrades, sharing, and access, you might leverage cloud services such as iTunes, Instagram, Diigo, and Box.

Information management is the use of IT tools and methods to collect, process, consolidate, store, and secure data from sources that are often fragmented and inconsistent.

This is just a glimpse at some of the **information management** situations that organizations face today and shows why a continuous plan is needed to guide, control, and govern IT growth. As with building construction (**Figure 2.13**), blueprints and models help guide and govern future IT and digital technology investments.

© Martin Barraud/Alamy

FIGURE 2.13   Blueprints and models, like those used for building construction, are needed to guide and govern an enterprise's IT assets.

Information Management Harnesses Scattered Data

Business information is generally scattered throughout an enterprise, stored in separate systems dedicated to specific purposes, such as operations, supply chain management, or customer relationship management. Major organizations have over 100 data repositories (storage areas). In many companies, the integration of these disparate systems is limited—as is users' ability to access all the information they need. As a result, despite all the information flowing through companies, executives, managers, and workers often struggle to find the information they need to make sound decisions or do their jobs. The overall goal of information management is to eliminate that struggle through the design and implementation of a sound data governance program and a well-planned EA.

Providing easy access to large volumes of information is just one of the challenges facing organizations. The days of simply managing structured data are over. Now, organizations must manage semistructured and unstructured content from social and mobile sources even though that data may be of questionable quality.

Information management is critical to data security and compliance with continually evolving regulatory requirements, such as the Sarbanes-Oxley Act, Basel III, the Computer Fraud and Abuse Act (CFAA), the USA PATRIOT Act, and the Health Insurance Portability and Accountability Act (HIPAA).

Issues of information access, management, and security must also deal with information degradation and disorder—where people do not understand what data mean or how the data can be useful.

Reasons for Information Deficiencies

Organizational information and decision support technologies have developed over many decades. During that time management teams' priorities have changed along with their understanding of the role of IT within the organization; technology has advanced in unforeseeable ways, and IT investments have been increased or decreased based on competing demands on the budget. Other common reasons why information deficiencies are still a problem include:

1. **Data silos**   Information can be *trapped* in departmental **data silos** (also called *information silos*), such as marketing or production databases. Data silos are illustrated in **Figure 2.14**. Since silos are unable to share or exchange data, they cannot consistently be updated. When data are inconsistent across multiple enterprise applications, data quality cannot (and should not) be trusted without extensive verification. Data silos exist when there is no overall IT architecture to guide IT investments, data coordination, and communication. Data silos support a single function and, as a result, do not support an organization's cross-functional needs.

Data silo   are stand-alone data stores. Their data are not accessible by other ISs that need it or outside that department.

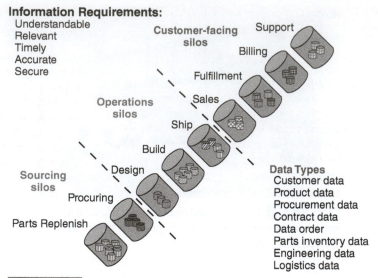

Information Requirements:
Understandable
Relevant
Timely
Accurate
Secure

Customer-facing silos

Support
Billing
Fulfillment
Sales

Operations silos

Ship
Build
Design

Sourcing silos

Procuring
Parts Replenish

Data Types
Customer data
Product data
Procurement data
Contract data
Data order
Parts inventory data
Engineering data
Logistics data

FIGURE 2.14 Data (or information) silos are ISs that do not have the capability to exchange data with other systems, making timely coordination and communication across functions or departments difficult.

For example, most health-care organizations are drowning in data, yet they cannot get reliable, actionable insights from these data. Physician notes, registration forms, discharge summaries, documents, and more are doubling every five years. Unlike structured machine-ready data, these are messy data that take too much time and effort for health-care providers to include in their business analysis. So, valuable messy data are routinely left out. Millions of insightful patient notes and records sit inaccessible or unavailable in separate clinical data silos because historically there has been no easy way to analyze the information they contain.

2. **Lost or bypassed data**   Data can get lost in transit from one system to another. Or, data might never get captured because of inadequately tuned data collection systems, such as those that rely on sensors or scanners. Or, the data may not get captured in sufficient detail, as described in **Tech Note 2.2**.

3. **Poorly designed interfaces**   Despite all the talk about user-friendly interfaces, some ISs are horrible to deal with. Poorly designed interfaces or formats that require extra time and effort to figure out increase the risk of errors from misunderstanding the data or ignoring them.

4. **Nonstandardized data formats**   When users are presented with data in inconsistent or nonstandardized formats, errors increase. Attempts to compare or analyze data are more difficult and take more time. For example, if the Northeast division reports weekly gross sales revenues per product line and the Southwest division reports monthly net sales per product, you cannot compare their performance without converting the data to a common format. Consider the extra effort needed to compare temperature-related sales, such as air conditioners, when some temperatures are expressed in degrees Fahrenheit and others in Centigrade.

5. **Difficult to hit moving targets**   The information that decision-makers want keeps changing—and changes faster than ISs can respond to because of the first four reasons in this list. Tracking tweets, YouTube hits, and other unstructured content requires expensive investments—which managers find risky in an economic downturn.

These are the data challenges managers have to face when there is little or no information management. Companies undergoing fast growth or merger activity or those with decentralized systems (each division or business unit manages its own IT) will end up with a patchwork of reporting processes. As you would expect, patchwork systems are more complicated to modify, too rigid to support an agile business, and more expensive to maintain.

Tech Note 2.2

Need to Measure in Order to Manage

A residential home construction company had two divisions: standard homes and luxury homes. The company was not capturing material, labor, and other costs associated with each type of construction. Instead, these costs were pooled, making it impossible to allocate costs to each type of construction and then to calculate the profit margins of each division. They had no way of calculating profit margins on each type of home within the divisions. Without the ability to measure costs, they did not have any cost control.

After upgrading their ISs, they began to capture detailed data at the division level. They discovered a wide profit margin on standard homes, which was hiding the losses occurring in the luxury home division. Without cost control data, the profitable standard homes division had been subsidizing the luxury home division for many years. Based on the cost control data, the company decided to focus more on standard homes and adjust their pricing on luxury homes. This new cost control strategy increased the company's long-term performance.

Factors Driving the Shift from Silos to Sharing and Collaboration

Senior executives and managers are aware of the problems associated with their data silos and information management problems, but they also know about the huge cost and disruption associated with converting to newer IT architectures. The "silo effect" occurs when different departments of an organization do not share data and/or communicate effectively enough to maintain productivity. Surprisingly, 75% of employers believe team work and collaboration are essential, but only 18% of employees receive communication evaluations during performance critiques (Marchese, 2016). In the new age of efficiency of service, many companies like Formaspace, an industrial manufacturing and service corporation, must work toward complete cloud integration of old silos to increase customer service and generate more revenue. Enabling applications to interact with one another in an automated fashion to gain better access to data increases meaningful productivity and decreases time and effort spent in manual collaboration efforts. In an illustration of how silo integration is essential for a modern corporation, IT technician at Formaspace, Loddie Alspach, claims that in 2015, the company managed to increase revenues by 20% using Amazon-based cloud technology (Shore, 2015). However, companies are struggling to integrate thousands of siloed global applications, while aligning them to business operations. To remain competitive, they must be able to analyze and adapt their business processes quickly, efficiently, and without disruption.

Greater investments in collaboration technologies have been reported by the research firm Forrester (Keitt, 2014). A recent study identified four main factors that have influenced the increased use of cloud technologies, as shown in **Table 2.4** (Rai et al., 2015).

TABLE 2.4	Key Factors Leading to Increased Migration to the Cloud
Cost Savings	
Efficient Use of Resources	
Unlimited Scalability of Resources	
Lower Maintenance	

Business Benefits of Information Management

Based on the examples you have read, the obvious benefits of information management are:

1. **Improves decision quality**   Decision quality depends on accurate and complete data.
2. **Improves the accuracy and reliability of management predictions**   It is essential for managers to be able to predict sales, product demand, opportunities, and competitive

threats. Management predictions focus on "what is going to happen" as opposed to financial reporting on "what has happened."

3. **Reduces the risk of noncompliance** Government regulations and compliance requirements have increased significantly in the past decade. Companies that fail to comply with laws on privacy, fraud, anti-money laundering, cybersecurity, occupational safety, and so on face harsh penalties.

4. **Reduces the time and cost** of locating and integrating relevant information.

Data Governance: Maintaining Data Quality and Cost Control

The success of every data-driven strategy or marketing effort depends on data governance. **Data governance** policies must address structured, semistructured, and unstructured data (discussed in Section 2.3) to ensure that insights can be trusted.

Data governance is the control of enterprise data through formal policies and procedures to help ensure data can be trusted and are accessible.

Enterprisewide Data Governance With an effective data governance program, managers can determine where their data are coming from, who owns them, and who is responsible for what—in order to know they can trust the available data when needed. Data governance is an enterprisewide project because data cross boundaries and are used by people throughout the enterprise. New regulations and pressure to reduce costs have increased the importance of effective data governance. Governance eliminates the cost of maintaining and archiving bad, unneeded, or inaccurate data. These costs grow as the volume of data grows. Governance also reduces the legal risks associated with unmanaged or inconsistently managed information.

Three industries that depend on data governance to comply with regulations or reporting requirements are the following:

- **Food industry** In the food industry, data governance is required to comply with food safety regulations. Food manufacturers and retailers have sophisticated control systems in place so that if a contaminated food product, such as spinach or peanut butter, is detected, they are able to trace the problem back to a particular processing plant or even the farm at the start of the food chain.

- **Financial services industry** In the financial services sector, strict reporting requirements of the Dodd–Frank Wall Street Reform and Consumer Protection Act of 2010 are leading to greater use of data governance. The Dodd–Frank Act regulates Wall Street practices by enforcing transparency and accountability in an effort to prevent another significant financial crisis like the one that occurred in 2008.

- **Health-care industry** Data are health care's most valuable asset. Hospitals have mountains of electronic patient information. New health-care accountability and reporting obligations require data governance models for transparency to defend against fraud and to protect patients' information.

Master Data and Master Data Management (MDM) **Master data** is the term used to describe business-critical information on customers, products and services, vendors, locations, employees, and other things needed for operations and business transactions. Master data are fundamentally different from the high volume, velocity, and variety of big data and traditional data. For example, when a customer applies for automobile insurance, data provided on the application become the master data for that customer. In contrast, if the customer's vehicle has a device that sends data about his or her driving behavior to the insurer, those machine-generated data are transactional or operational, but not master data.

Data are used in two ways—both depend on high-quality trustworthy data:

1. **For running the business**   Transactional or operational use
2. **For improving the business**   Analytic use

Master data are typically quite stable and typically stored in a number of different systems spread across the enterprise. **Master data management (MDM)** links and synchronizes all critical data from those disparate systems into one file called a **master file**, to provide a common point of reference. MDM solutions can be complex and expensive. Given their complexity and cost, most MDM solutions are out of reach for small and medium companies. Vendors have addressed this challenge by offering cloud-managed MDM services. For example, in 2013, Dell Software launched its next-generation Dell Boomi MDM. Dell Boomi provides MDM, data management, and data quality services (DQS)—and they are 100% cloud-based with near real-time synchronization.

Data governance and MDM manage the availability, usability, integrity, and security of data used throughout the enterprise. Strong data governance and MDM are needed ensure data are of sufficient quality to meet business needs. The characteristics and consequences of weak or nonexistent data governance are listed in **Table 2.5**.

Data governance and MDM are a powerful combination. As data sources and volumes continue to increase, so does the need to manage data as a strategic asset in order to extract its full value. Making business data consistent, trusted, and accessible across the enterprise is a critical first step in **customer-centric** business models. With data governance, companies are able to extract maximum value from their data, specifically by making better use of opportunities that are buried within behavioral data.

TABLE 2.5	**Characteristics and Consequences of Weak or Nonexistent Data Governance and MDM**

- Data duplication causes isolated data silos.
- Inconsistency exists in the meaning and level of detail of data elements.
- Users do not trust the data and waste time verifying the data rather than analyzing them for appropriate decision-making.
- Leads to inaccurate data analysis.
- Bad decisions are made on perception rather than reality, which can negatively affect the company and its customers.
- Results in increased workloads and processing time.

Questions

1. What is information management?
2. What is the "silo effect" and how does it affect business performance?
3. What three factors are driving collaboration and information sharing?
4. What are the business benefits of information management?
5. Explain why it is important to develop an effective data governance program?
6. Explain the purposes of master data management.
7. Why has interest in data governance and MDM increased?

2.4 Data Centers and Cloud Computing

Data centers and cloud computing are types of **IT infrastructures** or computing systems. Data center also refers to the building or facility that houses the servers and equipment. In the past, there were few IT infrastructure options. Companies owned their servers, storage, and network components to support their business applications and these computing resources were on their premises. Now, there are several choices for an IT infrastructure strategy—including cloud computing. As is common to IT investments, each infrastructure configuration has strengths, weaknesses, and cost considerations.

Data Centers

Traditionally, data and database technologies were kept in data centers that were typically run by an in-house IT department (**Figure 2.15**) and consisted of on-premises hardware and equipment that store data within an organization's local area network.

Today, companies may own and manage their own on-premises data centers or pay for the use of their vendors' data centers, such as in cloud computing, virtualization, and software-as-a-service arrangements (**Figure 2.16**).

© Oleksiy Mark/Shutterstock

FIGURE 2.15 A row of network servers in a data center.

© Michael D Brown/Shutterstock

FIGURE 2.16 Data centers are the infrastructure underlying cloud computing, virtualization, networking, security, delivery systems, and software-as-a-service.

In an on-premises data center connected to a local area network, it is easier to restrict access to applications and information to authorized, company-approved people and equipment. In the cloud, the management of updates, security, and ongoing maintenance are outsourced to a third-party cloud provider where data is accessible to anyone with the proper credentials and Internet connection. This arrangement can make a company more vulnerable since it increases exposure of company data at many more entry and exit points. Here are some examples of data centers.

- **National Climatic Data Center**   The National Climatic Data Center is an example of a public data center that stores and manages the world's largest archive of weather data.

- **U.S. National Security Agency**   The National Security Agency's (NSA) data center, shown in **Figure 2.17** is located in Bluffdale, UT. It is the largest spy data center for the NSA. People who think their correspondence and postings through sites like Google, Facebook, and Apple are safe from prying eyes should rethink that belief. You will read more about reports exposing government data collection programs in Chapter 5.

- **Apple**   Apple has a 500,000-square-foot data center in Maiden, NC, that houses servers for various iCloud and iTunes services. The center plays a vital role in the company's back-end IT infrastructure. In 2014 Apple expanded this center with a new, smaller 14,250-square-foot tactical data center that also includes office space, meeting areas, and breakrooms.

Since only the company owns the infrastructure, a data center is more suitable for organizations that run many different types of applications and have complex workloads. A data center, like a factory, has limited capacity. Once it is built, the amount of storage and the workload the center can handle does not change without purchasing and installing more equipment.

© epa european pressphoto agency b.v./Alamy

FIGURE 2.17   The NSA data center in Bluffdale, UT.

When a Data Center Goes Down, so Does Business

Data center failures disrupt all operations regardless of who owns the data center. Here are two examples.

- **Uber**   The startup company Uber experienced an hour-long outage in February 2014 that brought its car-hailing service to a halt across the country. The problem was caused by an outage at its vendor's West Coast data center. Uber users flooded social media sites with complaints about problems kicking off Uber's app to summon a driver-for-hire.

- **WhatsApp**   WhatsApp also experienced a server outage in early 2014 that took the service offline for 2.5 hours. WhatsApp is a smartphone text-messaging service that had been bought by Facebook for $19 billion. "Sorry we currently experiencing server issues. We hope to be back up and recovered shortly," WhatsApp said in a message on Twitter that was retweeted more than 25,000 times in just a few hours. The company has grown rapidly to 450 million active users within five years, nearly twice as many as Twitter. More than two-thirds of these global users use the app daily. WhatsApp's server failure drove millions of users to a competitor. Line, a messaging app developed in Japan, added 2 million new registered users within 24 hours of WhatsApp's outage—the biggest increase in Line's user base within a 24-hour period.

These outages point to the risks of maintaining the complex and sophisticated technology needed to power digital services used by millions or hundreds of millions of people.

Integrating Data to Combat Data Chaos

An enterprise's data are stored in many different or remote locations—creating data chaos at times. And some data may be duplicated so that they are available in multiple locations that need a quick response. Therefore, the data needed for planning, decision-making, operations, queries, and reporting are scattered or duplicated across numerous servers, data centers, devices, and cloud services. Disparate data must be unified or integrated in order for the organization to function.

Data Virtualization

As organizations have transitioned to a cloud-based infrastructure, data centers have become virtualized. For example, Cisco offers data virtualization, which gives greater IT flexibility. The process of data virtualization involves abstracting, transforming, merging, and delivering data from disparate sources. The main goal of data virtualization is to provide a single point of access to the data. By aggregating data from a wide range of sources users can access applications without knowing their exact location. Using data virtualization methods, enterprises can respond to change more quickly and make better decisions in real time without physically moving their data, which significantly cuts costs. Cisco Data Virtualization makes it possible to:

- Have instant access to data at any time and in any format.
- Respond faster to changing data analytics needs.
- Cut complexity and costs.

Compared to traditional (nonvirtual) data integration and replication methods, data virtualization accelerates time to value with:

- **Greater agility** Speeds 5–10 times faster than traditional data integration methods
- **Streamlined approach** 50–75% time savings over data replication and consolidation methods
- **Better insight** Instant access to data

Software-Defined Data Center

Data virtualization has led to the latest development in data centers—the **software-defined data center (SDDC)**. An SDDC facilitates the integration of the various infrastructures of the SDDC silos within organizations and optimizes the use of resources, balances workloads, and maximizes operational efficiency by dynamically distributing workloads and provisioning networks. The goal of the SDDC is to decrease costs and increase agility, policy compliance, and security by deploying, operating, managing, and maintaining applications. In addition, by providing organizations with their own private cloud, SDDCs provide greater flexibility by allowing organizations to have on-demand access to their data instead of having to request permission from their cloud provider (see **Figure 2.18**).

The base resources for the SDDC are *computation, storage, networking, and security*. Typically, the SDDC includes limited functionality of service portals, applications, OSs, VM hardware, hypervisors, physical hardware, software-defined networking, software-defined storage, a security layer, automation and management layers, catalogs, a gateway interface module, and third-party plug-ins (**Figure 2.19**).

It is estimated that the market share for SDDCs will grow from the current level of $22 billion to more than $77 billion in the next five years. As the use of SDDCs grows at this extraordinary rate, data center managers will be called upon to scale their data centers exponentially at a moment's notice. Unfortunately, this is impossible to achieve using the traditional data center infrastructure. In the SDDC, software placement and optimization decisions are based on business logic, not technical provisioning directives. This requires changes in culture,

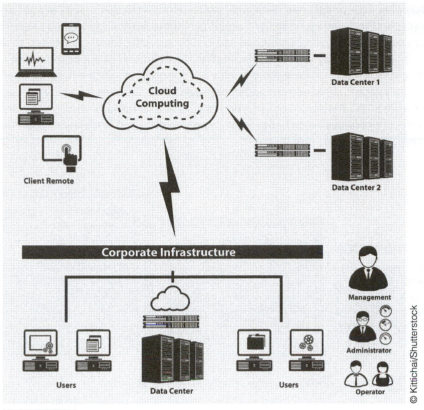

© Kittichai/Shutterstock

FIGURE 2.18 Corporate IT infrastructures can consist of an on-premises data center and off-premises cloud computing.

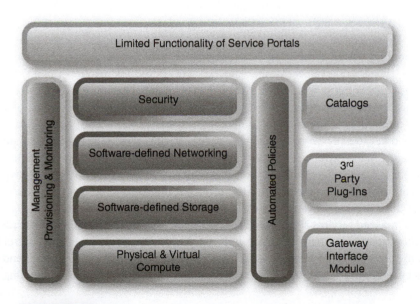

FIGURE 2.19 SDDC infrastructure (adapted from Sturm et al., 2017).

processes, structure, and technology. The SDDC isolates the application layer from the physical infrastructure layer to facilitate faster and more effective deployment, management, and monitoring of diverse applications. This is achieved by finding each enterprise application an optimal home in a public or private cloud environment or draw from a diverse collection of resources.

From a business perspective moving to a SDDC is motivated by the need to improve security, increase alignment of the IT infrastructure with business objectives and provision of applications more quickly.

Traditional data centers had dedicated, isolated hardware that results in poor utilization of resources and very limited flexibility. Second-generation virtualization data cases improved resource use by consolidating virtualized servers. By reducing the steps needed to decrease the time it takes to deploy workloads, facilitating the definition of applications and resource needs, the SDDC creates an even more flexible environment in which enterprise applications can be quickly reconfigured and supported to provide infrastructure-as a service (IaaS). Transitioning to an SDDC enables an organization to optimize its resource usage, provide capacity on demand, improve business-IT alignment, improve agility and flexibility of operations, and save money (**Figure 2.20**).

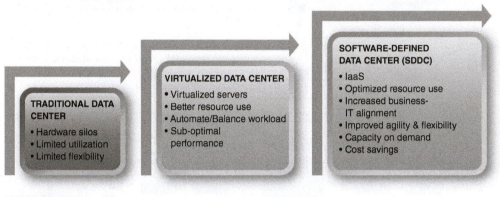

FIGURE 2.20 Evolution of data centers (adapted from Sturm et al., 2017).

Cloud Computing

In a business world where first movers gain the advantage, IT responsiveness and agility provide a competitive edge and lead to sustainable business practices. Yet, many IT infrastructures are extremely expensive to manage and too complex to easily adapt. A common solution is cloud computing. **Cloud computing** is the general term for infrastructures that use the Internet and private networks to access, share, and deliver computing resources. More specifically, IBM defines cloud computing as "the delivery of on-demand computing resources—everything from applications to data centers—over the Internet on a pay-for-use basis" (IBM, 2016).

Cloud computing is the delivery of computing and storage resources as a service to end-users over a network. Cloud systems are *scalable.* That is, they can be adjusted to meet changes in business needs. At the extreme, the cloud's capacity is unlimited depending on the vendor's offerings and service plans. A drawback of the cloud is control because a third party manages it. Unless the company uses a **private cloud** within its network, it shares computing and storage resources with other cloud users in the vendor's **public cloud**. Public clouds allow multiple clients to access the same virtualized services and utilize the same pool of servers across a public network. In contrast, private clouds are single-tenant environments with stronger security and control for regulated industries and critical data. In effect, private clouds retain all the IT security and control provided by traditional IT infrastructures with the added advantages of cloud computing.

Selecting a Cloud Vendor

Because cloud is still a relatively new and evolving business model, the decision to select a cloud service provider should be approached with even greater diligence than other IT decisions. As cloud computing becomes an increasingly important part of the IT delivery model, assessing and selecting the right cloud provider also become the most strategic decisions that business leaders undertake. Providers are not created equally, so it is important to investigate each provider's offerings prior to subscribing. When selecting and investing in cloud services, there are several service factors a vendor needs to address. These evaluation factors are listed in **Table 2.6**.

TABLE 2.6	Service Factors to Consider when Evaluating Cloud Vendors or Service Providers	
Factors	**Examples of Questions to Be Addressed**	
Delays	What are the estimated server delays and network delays?	
Workloads	What is the volume of data and processing that can be handled during a specific amount of time?	
Costs	What are the costs associated with workloads across multiple cloud computing platforms?	
Security	How are data and networks secured against attacks? Are data encrypted and how strong is the encryption? What are network security practices?	
Disaster recovery and business continuity	How is service outage defined? What level of redundancy is in place to minimize outages, including backup services in different geographical regions? If a natural disaster or outage occurs, how will cloud services be continued?	
Technical expertise and understanding	Does the vendor have expertise in your industry or business processes? Does the vendor understand what you need to do and have the technical expertise to fulfill those obligations?	
Insurance in case of failure	Does the vendor provide cloud insurance to mitigate user losses in case of service failure or damage? This is a new and important concept.	
Third-party audit or an unbiased assessment of the ability to rely on the service provided by the vendor	Can the vendor show objective proof with an audit that it can live up to the promises it is making?	

Vendor Management and Cloud Service Agreements (CSAs) The move to the cloud is also a move to vendor-managed services and **cloud service agreements (CSAs).** Also referred to as cloud service level agreements (SLAs), the CSA or SLA is a negotiated agreement between a company and service provider that can be a legally binding contract or an informal contract. You can review a sample CSA used by IBM by visiting **http://www-05. ibm.com/support/operations/files/pdf/csa_us.pdf**.

Staff experienced in managing outsourcing projects may have the necessary expertise for managing work in the cloud and policing SLAs with vendors. The goal is not building the best CSA terms, but negotiating the terms that align most closely with the business needs. For example, if a server becomes nonoperational and it does not support a critical business operation, it would not make sense to pay a high premium for reestablishing the server within one hour. On the other hand, if the data on the server support a business process that would effectively close down the business for the period of time that it was not accessible, it would be prudent to negotiate the fastest possible service in the CSA and pay a premium for that high level of service.

In April 2015, the Cloud Standards Customer Council (CSCC) published the *Practical Guide to Cloud Service Agreements, Version 2.0,* to reflect changes that have occurred since 2012 when it first published the *Practical Guide to Cloud Service Level Agreements*. The new guide provides a practical reference to help enterprise IT and business decision-makers analyze CSAs from different cloud service providers. The main purpose of a CSA is to set clear expectations for service between the cloud customer (buyer) and the cloud provider (seller), but CSAs should also exist between a customer and other cloud entities, such as the cloud carrier, the cloud broker, and even the cloud auditor. Although the various service delivery models, that is, IaaS, PaaS, SaaS, and so on, may have different requirements, the guide focuses on the requirements that are common across the various service models (Cloud Standards Customer Council, 2015, p. 4).

Implementing an effective management process is an important step in ensuring internal and external user satisfaction with cloud services. **Table 2.7** lists the 10 steps that should be taken by cloud customers to evaluate cloud providers' CSAs in order to compare CSAs across multiple providers or to negotiate terms with a selected provider.

TABLE 2.7	Ten Steps to Evaluate a CSA
1.	Understand roles and responsibilities of the CSA customer and provider
2.	Evaluate business-level policies and compliance requirements relevant to the CSA customer
3.	Understand service and deployment model differences
4.	Identify critical performance objectives such as availability, response time, and processing speed. Ensure they are measurable and auditable
5.	Evaluate security and privacy requirements for customer information that has moved into the provider's cloud and applications, functions, and services being operated in the cloud to provide required service to the customer
6.	Identify service management requirements such as auditing, monitoring and reporting, measurement, provisioning, change management, and upgrading/patching
7.	Prepare for service failure management by explicitly documenting cloud service capabilities and performance expectations with remedies and limitations for each
8.	Understand the disaster recovery plan
9.	Develop a strong and detailed governance plan of the cloud services on the customer side
10.	Understand the process to terminate the CSA

Cloud Infrastructure

The cloud has greatly expanded the options for enterprise IT infrastructures because any device that accesses the Internet can access, share, and deliver data. Cloud computing is a valuable infrastructure because:

1. It is dynamic, not static and provides a way to make applications and computing power available on demand. Applications and power are available on demand because they are provided *as a service*. For example, any software that is provided on demand is referred to as **software as a service (SaaS)**. Typical SaaS products are Google Apps and **www. Salesforce.com**. Section 2.5 discusses SaaS and other cloud services.

2. Helps companies become more agile and responsive while significantly reducing IT costs and complexity through improved workload optimization and service delivery.

Move to Enterprise Clouds   A majority of large organizations have hundreds or thousands of software licenses that support business processes, such as licenses for Microsoft Office, Oracle database management, IBM CRM (customer relationship management), and various network security software. Managing software and their licenses involves deploying, provisioning, and updating them—all of which are time-consuming and expensive. Cloud computing overcomes these problems.

Issues in Moving Workloads from the Enterprise to the Cloud

Building a cloud strategy is a challenge, and moving existing applications to the cloud is stressful. Despite the business and technical benefits, the risk exists of disrupting operations or customers in the process. With the cloud, the network and WAN (wide area network) become an even more critical part of the IT infrastructure. Greater network bandwidth is needed to support the increase in network traffic. And, putting part of the IT architecture or workload into the cloud requires different management approaches, different IT skills, and knowing how to manage vendor relationships and contracts.

Infrastructure Issues   There is a big difference because cloud computing runs on a shared infrastructure, so the arrangement is less customized to a specific company's requirements. A comparison to help understand the challenges is that outsourcing is like renting an apartment, while the cloud is like getting a room at a hotel.

With cloud computing, it may be more difficult to get to the root of performance problems, like the unplanned outages that occurred with Google's Gmail and Workday's human resources apps. The trade-off is cost versus control.

Increasing demand for faster and more powerful computers, and increases in the number and variety of applications are driving the need for more capable IT architectures.

Questions

1. What is a data center?
2. What is the difference between on-premises data centers and cloud computing?
3. What is an SDDC?
4. What are the advantages of using an SDDC?
5. How can cloud computing solve the problems of managing software licenses?
6. What factors should be considered when selecting a cloud vendor or provider?
7. When are private clouds used instead of public clouds?
8. Explain three issues that need to be addressed when moving to cloud computing or services.

2.5 | Cloud Services and Virtualization

Managers want streamlined, real-time, data-driven enterprises, yet they may face budget cuts. Sustaining performance requires the development of new business applications and analytics capabilities, which comprise the *front end* and the data stores and digital infrastructure, or back end, to support them. The back end is where the data reside. The problem is that data may have to navigate through a congested IT infrastructure that was first designed decades ago. These network or database bottlenecks can quickly wipe out the competitive advantages from big data, mobility, and so on. Traditional approaches to increasing database performance—manually tuning databases, adding more disk space, and upgrading processors—are not enough when you are you are dealing with streaming data and real-time big data analytics. Cloud services help to overcome these limitations. Cloud services are outsourced to a third-party cloud provider who manages the updates, security, and ongoing maintenance.

At first glance, virtualization and cloud computing may appear to be quite similar. However, cloud computing and virtualization are inherently different. Unlike cloud computing that involves multiple computers or hardware devices sending data through vendor-provided networks, virtualization is the replacement of a tangible physical component with a virtual one. Each of these concepts are described and discussed in the following sections.

Anything as a Service (XAAS) Models

The cloud computing model for on-demand delivery of and access to various types of computing resources also extends to the development of business apps. **Figure 2.21** shows four "as a service" (XaaS) solutions based on the concept that the resource—software, platform, infrastructure, or data—can be provided on demand regardless of geolocation. As these as service solutions develop, the focus is changing from massive technology implementation costs to business-reengineering programs that enable XaaS platforms (Fresht, 2014).

Cloud services are services made available to users on demand via the Internet from a cloud computing provider's servers instead of being accessed through an organization's

FIGURE 2.21 Four as a service solutions: software, platform, infrastructure, and data as a service.

on-premises servers. Cloud services are designed to provide easy, scalable access to applications, resources, and services, and are fully managed by a cloud services provider.

Cloud computing is often referred to as a **"stack"** or broad range of services built on top of each other under the name *cloud*. These cloud services can be defined as follows:

- **Software as a service (SaaS)** is a widely used model in which software is available to users from a service provider as needed. A provider licenses a SaaS application to customers as an on-demand service, through a subscription, a pay-as-you-go model, or free of charge (where revenue can be generated by other means, such as through sale of advertisements).

- **Platform as a service (PaaS)** is a computing platform that enables the quick and easy creation, testing, and deployment of web applications without the necessity of buying and maintaining the software and infrastructure underneath it. It is a set of tools and services that make coding and deploying these applications faster and more efficient.

- **Infrastructure as a service (IaaS)** is a way of delivering servers, storage, networks, work-load balancers, and OSs as an on-demand service.

- **Data as a service (DaaS)** is an information provision and distribution model in which data files (including text, images, sounds, and videos) are made available to customers over a network by a service provider.

Software as a Service (SaaS) SaaS is a rapidly growing method of delivering software and is particularly useful in applications in which there are considerable interactions between the organization and external entities that do not confer a competitive advantage, for example, e-mail and newsletters. It is also useful when an organization is going to be needing a particular type of software for a short period of time or for a specific project, and for software that is used periodically, for example, tax, payroll, or billing software. SaaS is not appropriate for accessing applications that require fast processing of real-time data or applications where regulation does not permit data being hosted externally.

Other terms for SaaS are *on-demand computing* and *hosted services*. The idea is basically the same: Instead of buying and installing expensive packaged enterprise applications, users can access software applications over a network, using an Internet browser. To use SaaS, a service provider hosts the application at its data center and customers access it via a standard Web browser.

The SaaS model was developed to overcome the common challenge to an enterprise of being able to meet fluctuating demands on IT resources efficiently. It is used in many business functions, primarily customer relationship management (CRM), accounting, human resources (HR), service desk management, communication, and collaboration.

There are thousands of SaaS vendors. **www.Salesforce.com** is one of the most widely known SaaS providers. Other examples are Google Docs and collaborative presentation software Prezi. For instance, instead of installing Microsoft Word on your own computer, and then loading Word to create a document, you use a browser to log into Google Docs. Only the browser uses your computer's resources.

Platform as a Service (PaaS)

PaaS provides a standard unified platform for developing, testing, and deploying software over the Web. This computing platform allows the creation of Web applications quickly and easily without the complexity of buying and maintaining the underlying infrastructure. Without PaaS, the cost of developing some applications would be prohibitive. Examples of PaaS include databases, Web servers, development tools, and execution runtime. PaaS is particularly useful when multiple software developers are working on a software development project of when other external parties need to interact with the development process and for when developers want to automate testing and deployment services. It is less useful in those instances where application performance needs to be customized to the underlying hardware and software or an application needs to be highly portable in terms of where it is hosted. Some examples of PaaS include Microsoft Azure Service, **www.Force.com**, and Google App Engine.

Infrastructure as a Service (IaaS)

Rather than purchasing all the components of its IT infrastructure, organizations buy their computing resources as a fully outsourced Infrastructure as a Service (IaaS) on demand. Generally, IaaS can be acquired as a Public or Private infrastructure or a combination of the two (Hybrid). A public IaaS is one that consists of shared resources deployed on a self-service basis over the Internet. On the other hand, a private IaaS is provided on a private network. And, a hybrid IaaS is a combination of both public and private. IaaS is useful where organizations experience significant highs and lows in terms of demand on the infrastructure, for new or existing organizations who have budgetary constraints on hardware investment and in situations where an organization has temporary infrastructure needs. Some IaaS providers you may be familiar with include Amazon Web Services (AWS) and Rackspace.

Data as a Service (DaaS)—The New Kid on the Block

DaaS is the newest entrant into the XaaS arena. DaaS enables data to be shared among clouds, systems, apps, and so on regardless of the data source or where they are stored. Data files, including text, images, sound, and video, are made available to customers over a network, typically the Internet. DaaS makes it easier for data architects to select data from different pools, filter out sensitive data, and make the remaining data available on demand.

A key benefit of DaaS is that it transfers the risks and responsibilities associated with data management to a third-party cloud provider. Traditionally, organizations stored and managed their data within a self-contained storage system, however, as data become more complex, it is increasingly difficult and expensive to maintain using the traditional data model. Using DaaS, organizational data are readily accessible through a cloud-based platform and can be delivered to users despite organizational or geographical constraints. This model is growing in popularity as data become more complex, difficult, and expensive to maintain. Some of the most common business applications currently using DaaS are CRM and enterprise resource planning (ERP). For an example of Daas, see **IT at Work 2.3**.

IT at Work 2.3

Slack

Slack, the successful social chat app for companies and their executives and/or employees, has announced a "deep product partnership" with Salesforce (Lunden, 2016). The partnership includes a new data sharing platform for businesses to easily share information about conversations they are having within the app. More specifically, businesses will be able to share details about client accounts in real time with automatic updates for new leads about the accounts. The new partnership will allow Slack and its users to be even more effective in collaboration and data sharing across many platforms and departments (Lunden, 2016).

As a Service Models Are Enterprisewide and Can Trigger Lawsuits The various As a Service models are used in various aspects of business. You will read how these specific services, such as CRM and HR management, are being used for operational and strategic purposes in later chapters. Companies are frequently adopting software, platform, infrastructure, data management, and starting to embrace *mobility as a service* and *big data as a service* because they typically no longer have to worry about the costs of buying, maintaining, or updating their own data servers. Both hardware and human resources expenses can be cut significantly. Service arrangements all require that managers understand the benefits and trade-offs—and how to negotiate effective SLAs and CSAs. Regulations mandate that confidential data be protected regardless of whether the data are on-premises or in the cloud. Therefore, a company's legal department needs to get involved in these IT decisions. Put simply, moving to cloud services is not simply an IT decision because the stakes around legal and compliance issues are very high.

Going Cloud

Cloud services can advance the core business of delivering superior services to optimize business performance. Cloud can cut costs and add flexibility to the performance of critical business apps. And, it can improve responsiveness to end-consumers, application developers, and business organizations. But to achieve these benefits, there must be IT, legal, and senior management oversight because a company still must meet its legal obligations and responsibilities to employees, customers, investors, business partners, and society.

Virtualization and Virtual Machines

There are many types of virtualization, such as virtual storage devices, virtual desktops, virtual OSs, and virtual servers for network virtualization. You can think of virtualization as a model for a physical component that is built into computer code, to create a software program that acts in the same way as the physical component it is modeling. For example, a virtual machine is a software representation of a computer, rather than an actual computer and a virtual server sends and receives signals just like a physical one, even though it doesn't have its own circuitry and other physical components.

You might ask why organizations want to virtualize their physical computing and networking devices. The answer is a gross underutilization of inefficient use of resources. Computer hardware had been designed to run a single OS and a single app, which leaves most computers vastly underutilized. Virtualization is a technique that creates a virtual (i.e., nonphysical) layer and multiple virtual machines (VMs) to run on a single physical machine. The virtual (or virtualization) layer makes it possible for each VM to share the resources of the hardware. **Figure 2.22** shows the relationship among the VMs and physical hardware.

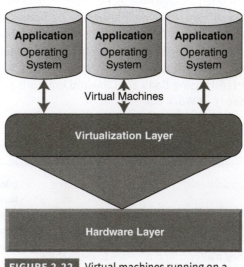

FIGURE 2.22 Virtual machines running on a simple computer hardware layer.

What Is a Virtual Machine?   Just as *virtual reality* is not real, but a software-created world, a virtual machine is a software-created computer. Technically, a **virtual machine (VM)** is created by a software layer, called the *virtualization layer,* as shown in Figure 2.22. That layer has its own Windows or other OS and apps, such as Microsoft Office, as if it were an actual physical computer. A VM behaves exactly like a physical computer and contains its own virtual—that is, *software-based*—CPU, RAM (random access memory), hard drive, and network interface card (NIC). An OS cannot tell the difference between a VM and a physical machine, nor can applications or other computers on a network tell the difference. Even the VM thinks it is a "real" computer. Users can set up multiple real computers to function as a single PC through virtualization to pool resources to create a more powerful VM.

Virtualization is a concept that has several meanings in IT and therefore several definitions. The major type of virtualization is hardware virtualization, which remains popular and widely used. Virtualization is often a key part of an enterprise's disaster recovery plan. In general, virtualization separates business applications and data from hardware resources. This separation allows companies to pool hardware resources—rather than dedicate servers to applications—and assign those resources to applications as needed.

Different types of virtualization include:

- *Storage virtualization* is the pooling of physical storage from multiple network storage devices into what appears to be a single storage device managed from a central console.
- *Server virtualization* consolidates multiple physical servers into virtual servers that run on a single physical server.
- *Desktop virtualization* is software technology that separates the desktop environment and associated application software from the physical machine that is used to access it.
- *Application virtualization* is the practice of running software from a remote server rather than on the user's computer.
- *Network virtualization* combines the available resources in a network by splitting the network load into manageable parts, each of which can be assigned (or reassigned) to a particular server on the network.
- *Hardware virtualization* is the use of software to emulate hardware or a total computer environment other than the one the software is actually running in. It allows a piece of hardware to run multiple OS images at once. This kind of software is sometimes known as a virtual machine.

Virtualization Characteristics and Benefits   Virtualization increases the flexibility of IT assets, allowing companies to consolidate IT infrastructure, reduce maintenance and administration costs, and prepare for strategic IT initiatives. Virtualization is not primarily about cost-cutting, which is a tactical reason. More importantly, for strategic reasons, virtualization is used because it enables flexible sourcing and cloud computing.

The characteristics and benefits of virtualization are as follows:

1. **Memory-intensive**   VMs need a huge amount of RAM (random access memory, or primary memory) because of their massive processing requirements.
2. **Energy-efficient**   VMs minimize energy consumed running and cooling servers in the data center—representing up to a 95% reduction in energy use per server.
3. **Scalability and load balancing**   When a big event happens, such as the Super Bowl, millions of people go to a website at the same time. Virtualization provides load balancing to handle the demand for requests to the site. The VMware infrastructure automatically distributes the load across a cluster of physical servers to ensure the maximum performance of all running VMs. Load balancing is key to solving many of today's IT challenges.

Virtualization consolidates servers, which reduces the cost of servers, makes more efficient use of data center space, and reduces energy consumption. All of these factors reduce the total cost of ownership (TCO). Over a three-year life cycle, a VM costs approximately 75% less to operate than a physical server. **IT at Work 2.4** describes one example of how virtualization can help organizations provide higher levels of customer service and improve productivity.

IT at Work 2.4

Business Continuity with Virtualization

Liberty Wines supplies to restaurants, supermarkets, and independent retailers from its headquarters in central London. Recipient of multiple international wine awards—including the International Wine Challenge on Trade Supplier of the Year for two years running—Liberty Wines is one of the United Kingdom's foremost wine importers and distributors.

IT Problems and Business Needs

As the business expanded, the existing servers did not have the capacity to handle increased data volumes, and maintenance of the system put a strain on the IT team of two employees. Existing systems were slow and could not provide the responsiveness that employees expected.

Liberty Wines had to speed up business processes to meet the needs of customers in the fast-paced world of fine dining. To provide the service their customers expect, employees at Liberty Wines needed quick and easy access to customer, order, and stock information. In the past, the company relied on 10 physical servers for applications and services, such as order processing, reporting, and e-mail.

Virtualized Solution

Liberty Wines deployed a virtualized server solution incorporating Windows Server 2008 R2. The 10 servers were replaced with 3 physical servers, running 10 virtual servers. An additional server was used as part of a backup system, further improving resilience and stability.

By reducing the number of physical servers from 10 to 4, power use and air conditioning costs were cut by 60%. Not only was the bottom line improved, but the carbon footprint was also reduced, which was good for the environment.

The new IT infrastructure cut hardware replacement costs by £45,000 (U.S. $69,500) while enhancing stability with the backup system. Applications now run faster, too, so employees can provide better customer service with improved productivity. When needed, virtual servers can be added quickly and easily to support business growth.

Questions

1. What is SaaS?
2. What is PaaS?
3. What is IaaS?
4. How might companies risk violating regulation or compliance requirements with cloud services?
5. In what ways is a virtualized information system different from a traditional information system?
6. Describe the different types of virtualization.
7. What is load balancing and why is it important?

Key Terms

ad hoc report   34
batch processing   33
cloud computing   52
cloud service agreements (CSAs)   53
customer-centric   47
data   30
data as a service (DaaS)   56
data center   38
data governance   46

data silo   43
database   33
decision support systems (DSS)   32
dirty data   26
enterprise architecture (EA)   26
exception report   34
executive information systems (EISs)   32
goal seeking   35
information   30

information management   42
information systems (ISs)   28
infrastructure as a service (IaaS)   56
IT infrastructure   38
IPOS   28
knowledge   30
management information systems (MIS)   34
master data   46
master data management (MDM)   47

master file   47
model   26
online transaction processing (OLTP)   33
platform as a service (PaaS)   56
private cloud   52
public cloud   52

real-time processing   33
service level agreement (SLA)   61
software as a service (SaaS)   54
software-defined data center (SDDC)   50
stack   56
structured decisions   35

transaction processing systems (TPS)   32
unstructured decisions   35
virtualization   59
virtual machine (VM)   59
what-if analysis   35
wisdom   31

Assuring Your Learning

Discuss: Critical Thinking Questions

1. Why is a strong market position or good profit performance only temporary?

2. Assume you had:

    a. A tall ladder with a sticker that lists a weight allowance only five pounds more than you weigh. You know the manufacturer and model number.

    b. Perishable food with an expiration date two days into the future.

    c. A checking account balance that indicates you have sufficient funds to cover the balance due on an account.

    In all three cases, trusting the data to be exactly correct could have negative consequences. Explain the consequences of trusting the data in each instance. How might you determine the correct data for each instance? Which data might not be possible to verify? How does dirty data impact your decision-making?

3. If business data are scattered throughout the enterprise and not synched until the end of the month, how does that impact day-to-day decision-making and planning?

4. Assume a bank's data are stored in silos based on financial product—checking accounts, saving accounts, mortgages, auto loans, and so on. What problems do these data silos create for the bank's managers?

5. Why do managers and workers still struggle to find information that they need to make decisions or take action despite advances in digital technology? That is, what causes data deficiencies?

6. According to a Tech CEO Council Report, Fortune 500 companies waste $480 billion every year on inefficient business processes. What factors cause such huge waste? How can this waste be reduced?

7. Explain why organizations need to implement EA and data governance.

8. What two problems can EA solve?

9. Name two industries that depend on data governance to comply with regulations or reporting requirements. Given an example of each.

10. Why is it important for data to be standardized? Give an example of unstandardized data.

11. Why are TPSs critical systems?

12. Discuss why the cloud acts as the *great IT delivery frontier*.

13. What are the functions of data centers?

14. What factors need to be considered when selecting a cloud vendor?

15. What protection does an effective SLA or CSA provide?

16. Why is an SLA or a CSA a legal document?

17. How can virtualization reduce IT costs while improving performance?

Explore: Online and Interactive Exercises

1. When selecting a cloud vendor to host your enterprise data and apps, you need to evaluate the **service level agreement (SLA)**.

    a. Research the SLAs of two cloud vendors, such as Rackspace, Amazon, or Google.

    b. For the vendors you selected, what are the SLAs' uptime percentages? Expect them to be 99.9% or less.

    c. Does each vendor count both scheduled downtime and planned downtime toward the SLA uptime percentage?

    d. Compare the SLAs in terms of two other criteria.

    e. Decide which SLA is better based on your comparisons.

    f. Report your results and explain your decision.

2. Many organizations initiate data governance programs because of pressing compliance issues that impact data usage. Organizations may need data governance to be in compliance with one or more regulations, such as the Gramm–Leach Bliley Act (GLB), HIPAA, Foreign Corrupt Practices Act (FCPA), Sarbanes–Oxley Act, and several state and federal privacy laws.

    a. Research and select two U.S. regulations or privacy laws.

    b. Describe how data governance would help an enterprise comply with these regulations or laws.

3. Visit **www.eWeek.com** Cloud Computing Solutions Center for news and reviews at **www.eweek.com/c/s/Cloud-Computing**. Select one of the articles listed under Latest Cloud Computing News. Prepare an executive summary of the article.

4. Visit Rackspace.com and review the company's three types of cloud products. Describe each of those cloud solutions.

5. Visit Oracle.com. Describe the types of virtualization services offered by Oracle.

6. Visit YouTube.com and search for two videos on virtualization. For each video, report what you learned. Specify the complete URL, video title, who uploaded the video and the date, video length, and number of views.

Analyze & Decide: Apply IT Concepts to Business Decisions

1. Financial services firms experience large fluctuations in business volumes because of the cyclical nature of financial markets. These fluctuations are often caused by crises—such as the subprime mortgage problems, the discovery of major fraud, or a slowdown in the economy. These fluctuations require that executives and IT leaders have the ability to cut spending levels in market downturns and quickly scale up when business volumes rise again. Research SaaS solutions and vendors for the financial services sector. Would investment in SaaS help such firms align their IT capacity with their business needs and also cut IT costs? Explain your answer.

2. Despite multimillion-dollar investments, many IT organizations cannot respond quickly to evolving business needs. Also, they cannot adapt to large-scale shifts like mergers, sudden drops in sales, or new product introductions. Can cloud computing help organizations improve their responsiveness and get better control of their IT costs? Explain your answer.

3. Describe the relationship between enterprise architecture and organizational performance.

4. Identify four **KPIs** for a major airline (e.g., American, United, Delta) or an automobile manufacturer (e.g., GM, Ford, BMW). Which KPI would be the easiest to present to managers on an online dashboard? Explain why.

Case 2.2

Business Case: Data Chaos Creates Risk

Data chaos often runs rampant in service organizations, such as health care and the government. For example, in many hospitals, each line of business, division, and department has implemented its own IT applications, often without a thorough analysis of its relationship with other departmental or divisional systems. This arrangement leads to the hospital having IT groups that specifically manage a particular type of application suite or data silo for a particular department or division.

Data Management

When applications are not well managed, they can generate terabytes of irrelevant data, causing hospitals to drown in such data. This data chaos could lead to medical errors. In the effort to manage excessive and massive amounts of data, there is increased risk of relevant information being lost (missing) or inaccurate—that is, faulty or dirty data. Another risk is data breaches.

- **Faulty data**   By 2015, 96% of health-care organizations had adopted electronic health records, or EHRs (Office of the National Coordinator for HIT, 2016). It is well known that an unintended consequence of EHR is faulty data. According to a study published in the *Journal of the American Medical Association*, data in EHR systems may not be as accurate and complete as expected (Conn, 2016). Incorrect lab values, imaging results, or physician documentation lead to medical errors, harm patients, and damage the organization's accreditation and reputation.

- **Data breaches**   More than 25 million people have been affected by health-care system data breaches since the Office for Civil Rights, a division of the U.S. Department of Health and Human Services, began reporting breaches in 2009. Most breaches involved lost or stolen data on laptops, removable drives, or other portable media. Breaches are extremely expensive and destroy trust.

Accountability in health-care demands compliance with strong data governance efforts. Data governance programs verify that data input into EHR, clinical, financial, and operational systems are accurate and complete—and that only authorized edits can be made and logged.

Vanderbilt University Medical Center Adopts EHR and Data Governance

Vanderbilt University Medical Center (VUMC) in Nashville, TN, was an early adopter of EHR and implemented data governance in 2009. VUMC's experience provides valuable lessons.

VUMC consists of three hospitals and the Vanderbilt Clinic, which have 918 beds, discharge 53,000 patients each year, and count 1.6 million clinic visits each year. On average, VUMC has an 83% occupancy rate and has achieved HIMSS Stage 6 hospital EHR adoption. HIMSS (Healthcare Information and Management Systems Society, himss.org) is a global, nonprofit organization dedicated to better health-care outcomes through IT. There are seven stages of EHR adoption, with Stage 7 being a fully paperless environment. That means all clinical data are part of an electronic medical record and, as a result, can be shared across and outside the enterprise. At Stage 7, the health-care organization is getting full advantage of the *health information exchange* (*HIE*). HIE provides interoperability so that information can flow back and forth among physicians, patients, and health networks (NextGen Healthcare, 2016).

VUMC began collecting data as part of its EHR efforts in 1997. By 2009, the center needed stronger, more disciplined data management. At that time, hospital leaders initiated a project to build a data governance infrastructure.

Data Governance Implementation

VUMC's leadership team had several concerns.

1. IT investments and tools were evolving rapidly, but they were not governed by HIM (Healthcare Information and Management) policies.

2. As medical records became electronic so they might be transmitted and shared easily, they became more vulnerable to hacking.

3. As new uses of electronic information were emerging, the medical center struggled to keep up.

Health Record Executive Committee

Initially, VUMC's leaders assigned data governance to their traditional medical records committee, but that approach failed. Next, they hired consultants to help develop a data governance structure and organized a *health record executive committee* to oversee the project. The committee reports to the medical board and an executive committee to ensure executive involvement and sponsorship. The committee is responsible for developing the strategy for standardizing health record practices, minimizing risk, and maintaining compliance. Members include the chief medical information officer (CMIO), CIO, legal counsel, medical staff, nursing informatics, HIM, administration, risk management, compliance, and accreditation. In addition, a legal medical records team was formed to support additions, corrections, and deletions to the EHR. This team defines procedures for removal of duplicate medical record numbers and policies for data management and compliance.

Costs of Data Failure

Data failures incur the following costs:

- Rework
- Loss of business
- Patient safety errors
- Malpractice lawsuits
- Delays in receiving payments because billing or medical codes data are not available.

Benefits Achieved from Data Governance

As in other industries, in health care, data are the most valuable asset. The handling of data is the real risk. EHRs are effective only if the data are accurate and useful to support patient care. Effective ongoing data governance has achieved that goal at VUMC.

Questions

1. What might happen when each line of business, division, and department develops its own IT apps?
2. What are the consequences of poorly managed apps?
3. What two risks are posed by data chaos? Explain why.
4. What are the functions of data governance in the health-care sector?
5. Why is it important to have executives involved in data governance projects?
6. List and explain the costs of data failure.
7. Why are data the most valuable asset in health care?

Sources: Compiled from NextGen Healthcare (2016), Office of the National Coordinator for HIT (2016), and Conn (2016).

Case 2.3

Video Case: Cloud Computing at Coca-Cola Is Changing Everything

When organizations say they are "using the cloud," they can mean a number of very different things. Using an IaaS service such as Amazon EC2 or Terremark is different from using Google Apps to outsource e-mail, which is different again from exposing an API in Facebook.

In this video Alan Boehme, CIO of the Coca-Cola Company discusses how Coca-Cola uses cloud computing to more effectively interact with its customers and describes the challenges Coca-Cola is facing in establishing SaaS partnerships with new start-ups.

Complete these three steps:

1. Visit **https://www.youtube.com/watch?v=hCxmsSED2DY**
2. View the 13-minute video.
3. Answer each of the three parts of the following question.

Question

1. Explain the value of Coca-Cola's cloud partnerships with start-up companies to:
   a. Coca-Cola
   b. The start-up companies
   c. Coca-Cola's customers

IT Toolbox

Accurately Measuring the Value of Data Governance

When developing a data governance program, it's important to present a strong business case to get buy-in from top executives and stakeholders. A crucial part of the business case is an estimate of the data governance program's return on investment (ROI) to show how it will add value to the company. You will need to justify the ROI based on both business and IT strategy to ensure that available funds are used to best meet the business objectives.

To do this you will need to carefully analyze the IT infrastructure with regard to how different components of the IT infrastructure work together to support business processes, how data needed by one system can be received and used by another, how easily data can be communicated and/or repurposed. You will also need to factor in risks and adverse events such as costs associated with rework in data collection, costs associated with unreliable or unfit data, and delays associated with untimely or unavailable data. Now, all of these costs must be quantified and your level of confidence in the corporate data has to be calculated to ensure your business case accurately reflects the value of a data governance program.

One metric used to make this calculation is the *confidence in data-dependent assumptions* metric, or CIDDA (Reeves & Bowen, 2013). The CIDDA identifies specific areas of deficiency.

So, to sum up, when building a data governance model, it is necessary to:

1. Establish a leadership team
2. Define the program's scope
3. Calculate the ROI using the CIDDA.

CIDDA is computed by multiplying three confidence estimates using the following formula:

$$CIDDA = G \times M \times TS$$

where

G = Confidence that data are *good* enough for their intended purpose

M = Confidence that data *mean* what you think they do

TS = Confidence that you know where the data come from and *trust the source.*

CIDDA is a subjective metric for which there are no industry benchmarks, yet it can be evaluated over time to gauge improvements in data quality confidence.

To ensure your understanding of this IT Toolbox item, calculate the CIDDA of Company A over time, using the stated levels of confidence in the different aspects of its corporate data over Q1–Q4 2017:

Q1_2017: G = 40%, M = 50%, TS = 20%
Q2_2017: G = 50%, M = 55%, TS = 30%
Q3_2017: G = 60%, M = 60%, TS = 40%
Q4_2017: G = 60%, M = 70%, TS = 45%

References

Bloomberg, J. "Change as Core Competency: Transforming the Role of the Enterprise Architect." *Forbes*, June 16, 2016.

Cailean, I. "What Role Do Algorithms Play in Programmatic Advertising?" *Trade Mod*, January 6, 2016. http://www.trademob.com/what-role-do-algorithms-play-in-programmatic-advertising

Cloud Standards Customer Council. *Practical Guide to Cloud Service Agreements, Version 2.0.* April 2015. http://www.cloud-council.org/deliverables/CSCC-Practical-Guide-to-Cloud-Service-Agreements.pdf

Conn, J. "EHRs vs. Paper: A Split-decision on Accuracy." *Modern Healthcare*, July 8, 2016.

Fresht, P. "The Ten Tenets Driving the As-a-service Economy." *Horses for Sources*, October 6, 2014. http://www.horsesforsources.com/as a service-economy_100614

IBM. "What is Cloud Computing?" *IBM*, June 6, 2016. https://www.ibm.com/cloud-computing/learn-more/what-is-cloud-computing

Jarousse, L. A. "Information Governance for Hospitals." *Hospitals & Health Networks*, February 18, 2016.

Keitt, T. J. "Collaboration Technology Should Be Part of Your Customer Experience Tool Kit." *Forrester.com*, June 30, 2014.

Lunden, I. "Enterprise Chat App Slack Ties up with Salesforce in a Deep Product Partnership." *Tech Crunch*, September 27, 2016. https://techcrunch.com/2016/09/27/enterprise-chat-app-slack-ties-up-with-salesforce-in-a-deep-platform-partnership

Marchese, L. "How the 'Silo Effect' Is Hurting Cross Team Collaboration." *Trello*, May 10, 2016.

NextGen Healthcare. "Health Information Exchange (HIE)." *NextGen Healthcare*, March 31, 2016.

Office of the National Coordinator for Health Information Technology. "Percent of Hospitals, By Type, that Possess Certified Health IT." *Office of the National Coordinator for Health Information Technology*, May 31, 2016.

Porter, M. *Competitive Advantage: Creating and Sustaining Superior Performance*. Free Press, 1998.

Rai, R., G. Sahoo, and S. Mehfuz. "Exploring the Factors Influencing the Cloud Computing Adoption: A Systematic Study on Cloud Migration." *Springerplus*, April 25, 2015, *4*, 197.

Reeves, M. G. and R. Bowen. "Developing a Data Governance Model in Health Care." *Healthcare Financial Management*, February 2013, *67*(2): 82–86.

Schneider, M. "Case Study: How MEDIATA Increased Campaign Performance with Hyperlocal Targeting." *Skyhook Wireless*, July 22, 2014.

Schneider, M. "Solving the Dirty Data Problem in Location-Based Advertising." *Street Fight*, January 7, 2015.

Shore, J. "Cloud-Based Integration Seeks to Tear Down Data Silos." *Tech Target*, August 19, 2015.

Sturm, R., C. Pollard, and J. Craig. *Application Performance Management in the Digital Enterprise*. Elsevier, March 2017.

Zuckerman, M.P.H., Sheingold, Ph.D., Orav, Ph.D., Ruhter, M.P.P., M.H.S.A., and Epstein, M.D. "Readmissions, Observation, and the Hospital Readmissions Reduction Program." *The New England Journal of Medicine*, April 21, 2016.

CHAPTER 3

Data Management, Data Analytics, and Business Intelligence

CHAPTER OUTLINE

Case 3.1 Opening Case: Coca-Cola Strategically Manages Data to Retain Customers and Reduce Costs

3.1 Data Management and Database Technologies

3.2 Centralized and Distributed Database Architectures

3.3 Data Warehouses

3.4 Data Analytics and Data Discovery

3.5 Business Intelligence and Electronic Records Management

Case 3.2 Business Case: Big Data Analytics is the "Secret Sauce" for Revitalizing McDonald's

Case 3.3 Video Case: Verizon Improves its Customer Experience with Data-Driven Decision-Making

LEARNING OBJECTIVES

3.1 Describe the purpose and benefits of data management and how database technologies help support business processes.

3.2 Describe the differences between centralized and distributed database architectures and the importance of creating and maintaining data that can be trusted.

3.3 Understand the concepts of data analytics and data warehousing and evaluate their tactical and strategic benefits.

3.4 Explain benefits of data and text mining and business intelligence and how they benefit an organization.

3.5 Describe electronic records management and how it helps companies to meet their compliance, regulatory, and legal obligations.

Introduction

As discussed in Chapter 2, collecting and maintaining trusted data is a critical aspect of any business. Knowing how and where to find data, store it efficiently, analyze it in new ways to increase the organization's competitive advantage, and enable the right people to access it at the right time are all fundamental components of managing the ever-increasing amounts of corporate data. Indeed, data analytics is the primary differentiator when doing business in the 21st century. Transactional, social, mobile, cloud, Web, and sensor data offer enormous potential. But without tools to analyze these data types and volumes, there would not be much difference between business in the 20th century and business today—except for mobile access. High-quality data and human expertise are essential to the value of analytics.

Human expertise is necessary because analytics alone cannot explain the reasons for trends or relationships; know what action to take; or provide sufficient context to determine what the numbers represent and how to interpret them.

Database, data warehouse, data analytics, and business intelligence (BI) technologies interact to create a new biz-tech ecosystem. Data analytics and BI discover insights or relationships of interest that otherwise might not have been recognized. They make it possible for managers to make decisions and act with clarity, speed, and confidence. Data analytics is not just about managing more or varied data. Rather, it is about asking new questions, formulating new hypotheses, exploration and discovery, and making data-driven decisions. Ultimately, a big part of data analysis efforts is the use of new analytics techniques.

Mining data or text taken from day-to-day business operations reveals valuable information, such as customers' desires, products that are most important, or processes that can be made more efficient. These insights expand the ability to take advantage of opportunities, minimize risks, and control costs.

While you might think that physical pieces of paper are a relic of the past, in most offices the opposite is true. Aberdeen Group's survey of 176 organizations worldwide found that the volume of physical documents is growing by up to 30% per year. Document management technology archives digital and physical data to meet business needs, as well as regulatory and legal requirements (Eisenhauer, 2015).

Case 3.1 Opening Case

Coca-Cola Strategically Manages Data to Retain Customers and Reduce Costs

Coca-Cola's Data Management Challenges

The Coca-Cola Company is a Fortune 100 company with over $43.7 billion in sales revenue and $7.35 billion in profit (Figure 3.1). The market leader manages and analyzes several **petabytes** (Pb) of data generated or collected from more than 500 brands and consumers in 206 countries. To understand the size of one petabyte of data, it would take 223,000 DVDs (4.7 Gb each) to hold 1 Pb of data!

Coca-Cola's bottling partners provide sales and shipment data, while retail customers transmit transaction and merchandising data. Other data sources are listed in Table 3.1. Before the introduction of its newest BI system, Coca-Cola knew there were BI opportunities in the mountains of data its bottlers were storing, but finding and accessing all of that data for analytics proved to be nearly impossible. The disparate data sources caused long delays in getting analytics reports from IT to sales teams. The company decided to replace the legacy software at each bottling facility and standardize them on a new BI system—a combination of MicroStrategy and Microsoft BI products.

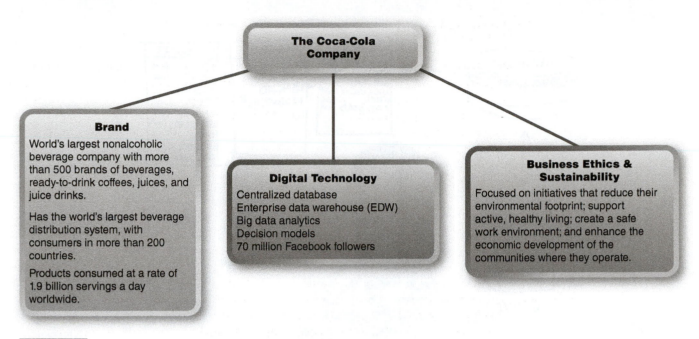

FIGURE 3.1   The Coca-Cola Company overview.

TABLE 3.1   **Opening Case Overview**

Company	• The Coca-Cola Company, **www.coca-cola.com** • Sustainability: **www.coca-colacompany.com/sustainability** • $43.7 billion in sales revenue and profits of $7.35 billion, 2016
Industry	• The global company manufactures, sells, and distributes nonalcoholic beverages
Product lines	• More than 500 brands of still and sparkling beverages, ready-to-drink coffees, juices, and juice drinks
Digital technology	• Enterprise data warehouse (EDW) • Big data and analytics • Business intelligence • In 2014, moved from a decentralized approach to a centralized approach, where the data are combined centrally and available via the shared platforms across the organization
Business challenges	• Coca-Cola had 74 unique databases, many of them used different software to store and analyze data. Dealing with incompatible databases and reporting systems was a major problem. Coca-Cola had to take a strategic approach instead of a tactical approach with big data
Global data sources	• Transaction and merchandising data • Data from nationwide network of more than 900 bottlers and manufacturing facilities • Multichannel retail data • Customer profile data from loyalty programs • Social media data • Supply chain data • Competitor data • Sales and shipment data from bottling partners
Taglines	"Taste the feeling!"
Website	**www.coca-cola.com**

Enterprise Data Management

Like most global companies, Coca-Cola relies on sophisticated enterprise data management, BI, and analytic technologies to sustain its performance in fiercely competitive markets. Data are managed in a **centralized database**. They use **data warehousing**, data analytics, data modeling, and social media to respond to competitors' activity, market changes, and consumer preferences.

To support its business strategy and operations, Coca-Cola changed from a decentralized database approach to a centralized database approach (**Figure 3.2**). Now its data are combined centrally

FIGURE 3.2 Data from online and offline transactions are stored in databases. Data about entities such as customers, products, orders, and employees are stored in an organized way.

and accessible via shared platforms across the organization to help its major retail customers such as Walmart sell more Coca-Cola products and to improve the consumer experience and implemented a data governance program to ensure that cultural data sensitivities are respected.

Sustaining Business Performance

All data are standardized through a series of master data management (MDM) processes. An enterprise data warehouse (EDW) generates a single view of all multichannel retail data and creates a trusted view of customers, sales, and transactions. This enables Coca-Cola to respond quickly and accurately to changes in market conditions.

Throughout Coca-Cola huge volumes of data are analyzed to make more and better time-sensitive, critical decisions about products, shopper marketing, the supply chain, and production. Point-of-sale (POS) data are captured from retail channels and communicated via a centralized iPad reporting system to created customer profiles. POS data are analyzed to support collaborative planning, forecasting, and replenishment processes within its supply chain.

Coca-Cola's Approach to Big Data and Decision Models Coca-Cola takes a strategic approach instead of a tactical approach to big data. The company is far advanced in the use of big data to manage its products, sales revenue, and customer experiences in near real time and reduce costs. For example, it cut overtime costs almost in half by analyzing service center data. Big data help Coca-Cola relate to its millions of Facebook followers—many of whom bolster the Coke brand.

Big data play a key role in ensuring that its orange juice tastes the same year-round and is readily available anywhere in the world. Oranges used by Coca-Cola have a peak growing season of only three months. Producing orange juice with a consistent taste year-round despite the

inconsistent quality of the orange supply is complex. To deal with this complexity, an orange juice decision model was developed, the *Black Book model.* A **decision model** quantifies the relationship between variables to reduce uncertainty. Black Book combines detailed data on the 6001 flavors that make up an orange, weather, customer preferences, expected crop yields, cost pressures, regional consumer preferences, and acidity or sweetness rate. The model specifies how to blend the orange juice to create a consistent taste. Coke's Black Book juice model is considered one of the most complex **business analytics** apps. It requires analyzing up to 1 quintillion (10E18) decision variables to consistently deliver the optimal blend.

With the power of big data and decision models, Coca-Cola is prepared for disruptions in supply far in advance. According to Doug Bippert, Coca-Cola's vice president of business acceleration, "If we have a hurricane or a freeze, we can quickly re-plan the business in 5 or 10 minutes just because we've mathematically modeled it" (**www.Business Intelligence.com**, 2013b).

Questions

1. Why does the Coca-Cola Company have petabytes of data?
2. Why is it important for Coca-Cola to be able to process POS data in near real time?
3. How does Coca-Cola attempt to create favorable customer experiences?
4. What is the importance of having a trusted view of the data?
5. What is the benefit of a decision model?
6. What is the Black Book model?
7. Explain the strategic benefit of the Black Book model.

Sources: Compiled from Burns (2013), BusinessIntelligence.com (2013), CNNMoney (2014), HBS (2015), Liyakas (2015), and Ransbothom (2015).

3.1 | Data Management and Database Technologies

Due to the incredible volume of data that the typical organization creates, effective data management is vital to prevent storage costs from spiraling out of control and controlling data growth while supporting greater performance. **Data management** oversees the end-to-end lifecycle of data from creation and initial storage to the time when it becomes obsolete and is deleted.

The objectives of data management include the following:

1. Mitigating the risks and costs of complying with regulations.
2. Ensuring legal requirements are met.
3. Safeguarding data security.
4. Maintaining accuracy of data and availability.
5. Certifying consistency in data that come from or go to multiple locations.
6. Ensuring that data conform to organizational best practices for access, storage, backup, and disposal.

Typically, newer data, and data that is accessed more frequently, is stored on faster, but more expensive storage media while less critical data is stored on cheaper, slower media.

The main benefits of data management include greater compliance, higher security, less legal liability, improved sales and marketing strategies, better product classification, and improved data governance to reduce risk. The following data management technologies keep users informed and support the various business demands:

- **Databases** store data generated by business apps, sensors, operations, and transaction-processing systems (TPS). Data in some databases can be extremely **volatile**. Medium and large enterprises typically have many databases of various types—centralized and distributed.
- **Data warehouses** integrate data from multiple databases and data silos across the organization, and organize them for complex analysis, knowledge discovery, and to support decision-making. For example, data are extracted from a database, processed to standardize their format, and then loaded into data warehouses at specific times, such as weekly. As such, data in data warehouses are nonvolatile—and are ready for analysis.
- **Data marts** are small-scale data warehouses that support a single function or one department. Enterprises that cannot afford to invest in data warehousing may start with one or more data marts.
- **Business intelligence (BI)**—tools and techniques process data and do statistical analysis for insight and discovery—that is, to discover meaningful relationships in the data, keep informed in real time, detect trends, and identify opportunities and risks.

Each of these database management technologies will be discussed in greater detail later in this chapter.

Database Management Systems and SQL

Data-processing techniques, processing power, and enterprise performance management capabilities have undergone revolutionary advances in recent years for reasons you are already familiar with—big data, mobility, and cloud computing. The last decade, however, has seen the emergence of new approaches, first in data warehousing and, more recently, for transaction processing. Given the huge number of transactions that occur daily in an organization, the data in databases are constantly in use or being updated. The volatility of databases makes it impossible to use them for complex decision-making and problem-solving tasks. For this reason, data are extracted from the database, transformed (processed to standardize the data), and then loaded into a data warehouse.

Data management is the management of the flow of data from creation and initial storage to the time when the data become obsolete and are deleted.

Databases are collections of data sets or records stored in a systematic way.

Database management systems (DBMSs) are software used to manage the additions, updates, and deletions of data as transactions occur, and to support data queries and reporting. They are online transaction-processing (OLTP) systems.

Database management systems (DBMSs) integrate with data collection systems such as TPS and business applications; store the data in an organized way; and provide facilities for accessing and managing that data. Factors to consider when evaluating the performance of a database management system are listed in **Tech Note 3.1**. Over the past 25 years, the **relational database** has been the standard database model adopted by most enterprises. Relational databases store data in tables consisting of columns and rows, similar to the format of a spreadsheet, as shown in **Figure 3.3**.

Tech Note 3.1

Factors That Determine the Performance of a DBMS

Factors to consider when evaluating the performance of a database management system include:

- **Data latency** **Latency** is the elapsed time (or delay) between when data are created and when they are available for a **query** or report. Applications have different tolerances for latency. Database systems tend to have shorter latency than data warehouses. Short latency imposes more restrictions on a system.

- **Ability to handle the volatility of the data** The database has the processing power to handle the volatility of the data. The rates at which data are added, updated, or deleted determine the workload that the database must be able to control to prevent problems with the response rate to queries.

- **Query response time** The volume of data impacts response times to queries and data explorations. Many databases

pre-stage data—that is, summarize or precalculate results—so queries have faster response rates.

- **Data consistency** **Immediate consistency** means that as soon as data are updated, responses to any new query will return the updated value. With **eventual consistency**, not all query responses will reflect data changes uniformly. Inconsistent query results could cause serious problems for analyses that depend on accurate data.

- **Query predictability** The greater the number of ad hoc or unpredictable queries, the more flexible the database needs to be. Database or query performance management is more difficult when the workloads are so unpredictable that they cannot be prepared for in advance. The ability to handle the workload is the most important criterion when choosing a database.

- **Query processing capabilities** Database queries are processed in real time and results are transmitted via wired or wireless networks to computer screen or handheld devices.

Query are ad hoc (unplanned) user requests for specific data.

© Alexander Fediachov/Alamy

FIGURE 3.3 Illustration of structured data format. Numeric and alphanumeric data are arranged into rows and predefined columns similar to those in an Excel spreadsheet.

Structured query language (SQL) is a standardized query language for accessing databases.

Relational management systems (RDBMSs) provide access to data using a declarative language—**structured query language (SQL)**. **Declarative languages** simplify data access by requiring that users only specify what data they want to access without defining how access will be achieved. The format of a basic SQL statement is

```
SELECT column_name(s)
FROM table_name
WHERE condition
```

An instance of SQL is shown in **Figure 3.4**.

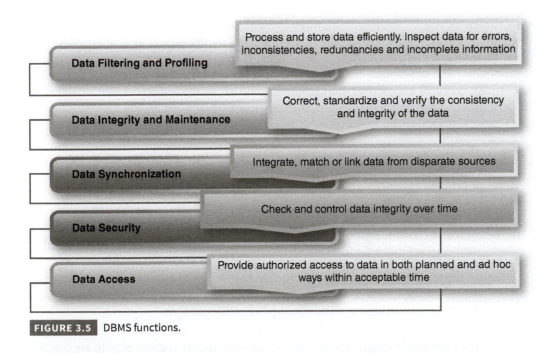

```
SELECT        EmployeeID, FirstName, LastName, HireDate, Ci
FROM          Employees
WHERE         HireDate BETWEEN '1-june-2012' AND '15-decemb


SELECT EmployeeID, FirstName, LastName, HireDate, City
WHERE City IN ('Seattle', 'Tacoma', 'Redmond')


SELECT        EmployeeID, FirstName, LastName, HireDate, Ci
FROM          Employees
WHERE         HireDate NOT BETWEEN '1-june-2012' AND '15-de
```

© Piotr Adamowicz/Shutterstock

FIGURE 3.4   An instance of SQL to access employee information based on date of hire.

DBMS Functions   An accurate and consistent view of data throughout the enterprise is needed so one can make informed, actionable decisions that support the business strategy. Functions performed by a DBMS to help create such a view are shown in **Figure 3.5**.

Data Filtering and Profiling — Process and store data efficiently. Inspect data for errors, inconsistencies, redundancies and incomplete information

Data Integrity and Maintenance — Correct, standardize and verify the consistency and integrity of the data

Data Synchronization — Integrate, match or link data from disparate sources

Data Security — Check and control data integrity over time

Data Access — Provide authorized access to data in both planned and ad hoc ways within acceptable time

FIGURE 3.5   DBMS functions.

Online Transaction Processing and Online Analytics Processing   When

most business transactions occur—for instance, an item is sold or returned, an order is sent or cancelled, a payment or deposit is made—changes are made immediately to the database. These online changes are additions, updates, or deletions. DBMSs record and process transactions in the database, and support queries and reporting. Given their functions, DBMSs are referred to as **online transaction processing (OLTP) systems**. OLTP is a database design that

Online transaction processing (OLTP) systems are designed to manage transaction data, which are volatile.

breaks down complex information into simpler data tables to strike a balance between transaction-processing efficiency and query efficiency. OLTP databases process millions of transactions per second. However, databases cannot be optimized for data mining, complex **online analytics processing (OLAP) systems**, and decision support. These limitations led to the introduction of data warehouse technology. Data warehouses and data marts are optimized for OLAP, data mining, BI, and decision support. OLAP is a term used to describe the analysis of complex data from the data warehouse. In summary, databases are optimized for extremely fast transaction processing and query processing. Data warehouses are optimized for analysis.

DBMS and Data Warehousing Vendors Respond to Latest Data Demands

One of the major drivers of change in the data management market is the increased amount of data to be managed. Enterprises need powerful DBMSs and data warehousing solutions, analytics, and reporting. The four vendors that dominate this market—Oracle, IBM, Microsoft, and Teradata—continue to respond to evolving data management needs with more intelligent and advanced software and hardware. Advanced hardware technology enables scaling to much higher data volumes and workloads than previously possible, or it can handle specific workloads. Older general-purpose relational databases DBMSs lack the scalability or flexibility for specialized or very large workloads, but are very good at what they do.

Trend Toward NoSQL Systems RDBMSs are still the dominant database engines, but the trend toward **NoSQL** (short for "not only SQL") systems is clear. NoSQL systems increased in popularity by 96% from 2014 to 2016. Although NoSQL have existed for as long as relational DBMS, the term itself was not introduced until 2009. That was when many new systems were developed in order to cope with the unfolding requirements for DBMS—namely, handling big data, scalability, and fault tolerance for large Web applications. **Scalability** means the system can increase in size to handle data growth or the load of an increasing number of concurrent users. To put it differently, scalable systems efficiently meet the demands of high-performance computing. **Fault tolerance** means that no single failure results in any loss of service.

NoSQL systems are such a heterogeneous group of database systems that attempts to classify them are not very helpful. However, their general advantages are the following:

- higher performance
- easy distribution of data on different nodes, which enables scalability and fault tolerance
- greater flexibility
- simpler administration

Starting in 2010 and continuing through 2016, Microsoft has been working on the first rewrite of SQL Server's query execution since Version 7 was released in 1998. The goal is to offer NoSQL-like speeds without sacrificing the capabilities of a relational database.

With most NoSQL offerings, the bulk of the cost does not lie in acquiring the database, but rather in implementing it. Data need to be selected and migrated (moved) to the new database. Microsoft hopes to reduce these costs by offering migration solutions.

DBMS Vendor Rankings The top five enterprise database systems of 2016 are Oracle's 12c Database, Microsoft SQL Server, IBM DB2, SAP Sybase ASE, and PostgreSQL:

1. **Oracle 12c Database** consolidates and manages databases as cloud services via Oracle's multitenant architecture and in-memory data processing capabilities and can be rapidly provisioned.

2. **Microsoft SQL Server** ease of use, availability, and Windows operating system integration make it an easy choice for firms that choose Microsoft products for their enterprises.

3. **IBM DB2** is widely used in large data centers and runs on Linux, UNIX, Windows, IBM iSeries, and mainframes.

4. **SAP Sybase ASE** is a major force after 25 years of success and improvements. Supports partition locking, relaxed query limits, query plan optimization, and dynamic thread assignment.

5. **PostgreSQL** is the most advanced open source database, often used by online gaming applications and Skype, Yahoo!, and MySpace. This database runs on a wide variety of operating systems including Linux, Windows, FreeBSD, and Solaris.

Questions

1. Describe a database and a database management system (DBMS).
2. Explain what an online transaction-processing (OLAP) system does.
3. Why are data in databases volatile?
4. Describe the functions of a DBMS.
5. Describe the purpose and benefits of data management.
6. What is a relational database management system?

3.2 | Centralized and Distributed Database Architectures

Databases can be **centralized** or **distributed**, as shown in **Figure 3.6**. Both types of databases need one or more backups and should be archived on- and offsite in case of a crash or security incident.

For decades the main database platform consisted of centralized database files on massive mainframe computers. Benefits of centralized database configurations include the following:

1. **Better control of data quality**   Data consistency is easier when data are kept in one physical location because data additions, updates, and deletions can be made in a supervised and orderly fashion.

2. **Better IT security**   Data are accessed via the centralized host computer, where they can be protected more easily from unauthorized access or modification.

A major disadvantage of centralized databases, like all centralized systems, is transmission delay when users are geographically dispersed. More powerful hardware and networks compensate for this disadvantage.

In contrast, distributed databases use client/server architecture to process information requests. The databases are stored on servers that reside in the company's data centers, a private cloud, or a public cloud (**Figure 3.7**). Advantages of a distributed database include reliability—if one site crashes, the system will keep running—and speed—it's faster to search a part of a database than the whole. However, if there's a problem with the network that the distributed database is using, it can cause availability issues and the appropriate hardware and software can be expensive to purchase.

Centralized database   stores all data in a single central compute such as a mainframe or server.

Distributed database   stores portions of the database on multiple computers within a network.

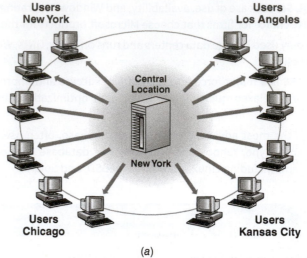

(a)

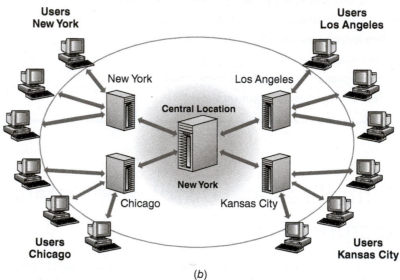

(b)

FIGURE 3.6 Comparison of (a) centralized and (b) distributed databases.

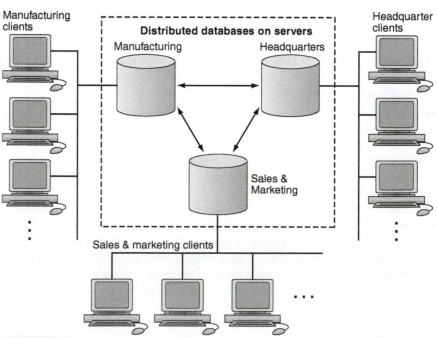

FIGURE 3.7 Distributed database architecture for headquarters, manufacturing, and sales and marketing.

Garbage In, Garbage Out

Data collection is a highly complex process that can create problems concerning the quality of the data being collected. Therefore, regardless of how the data are collected, they need to be validated so users know they can trust them. Classic expressions that sum up the situation are "garbage in, garbage out" (GIGO) and the potentially riskier "garbage in, gospel out." In the latter case, poor-quality data are trusted and used as the basis for planning. For example, you have probably encountered data safeguards, such as integrity checks, to help improve data quality when you fill in an online form, such as when the form will not accept an e-mail address or a credit card number that is not formatted correctly.

Table 3.2 lists the characteristics typically associated with dirty or poor-quality data.

TABLE 3.2   Characteristics of Poor-Quality or Dirty Data

Characteristic of Dirty Data	Description
Incomplete	Missing data
Outdated or invalid	Too old to be valid or useful
Incorrect	Too many errors
Duplicated or in conflict	Too many copies or versions of the same data—and the versions are inconsistent or in conflict with each other
Nonstandardized	Data are stored in incompatible formats—and cannot be compared or summarized
Unusable	Data are not in context to be understood or interpreted correctly at the time of access

Dirty Data Costs and Consequences   As discussed in Chapter 2, too often managers and information workers are actually constrained by data that cannot be trusted because they are incomplete, out of context, outdated, inaccurate, inaccessible, or so overwhelming that they require weeks to analyze. In such situations, the decision-maker is facing too much uncertainty to make intelligent business decisions.

On average, an organization experiences 40% data growth annually, and 20% of that data is found to be dirty. Each **dirty data** point, or record, costs $100 if not resolved (Ring-Lead, 2015). The costs of poor-quality data spread throughout a company, affecting systems from shipping and receiving to accounting and customer service. Data errors typically arise from the functions or departments that generate or create the data—and not within the IT department. When all costs are considered, the value of finding and fixing the causes of data errors becomes clear. In a time of decreased budgets, some organizations may not have the resources for such projects and may not even be aware of the problem. Others may be spending most of their time fixing problems, thus leaving them with no time to work on preventing them. However, the benefits of acting preventatively against dirty data are astronomical. It costs $1 to prevent and $10 to correct dirty data. While the short-run cost of cleaning and preventing dirty data is unrealistic for some companies, the long-term conclusion is far more expensive (Kramer, 2015).

Bad data are costing U.S. businesses hundreds of billions of dollars a year and affecting their ability to ride out the tough economic climate. Incorrect and outdated values, missing data, and inconsistent data formats can cause lost customers, sales, and revenue; misallocation of resources; and flawed pricing strategies.

Consider a corporation that follows the cost structure associated with clean/dirty data explained above with 100,000 data points. Over a three-year span, by cleaning the 20% of dirty data during the first year and using prevention methods for the following years, the corporation will save $8,495,000. Purely based on the quality of its data, a corporation with a large amount of data can hypothetically increase its revenue by 70% (RingLead, 2015).

Dirty data is poor-quality data that lacks integrity and cannot be trusted.

The cost of poor-quality data may be expressed as a formula:

Cost of Poor-Quality Data = Lost Business + Cost to Prevent Errors + Cost to Correct Errors

Examples of these costs include the following:

- **Lost business**   Business is lost when sales opportunities are missed, orders are returned because wrong items were delivered, or errors frustrate and drive away customers.
- **Time spent preventing errors**   If data cannot be trusted, then employees need to spend more time and effort trying to verify information in order to avoid mistakes.
- **Time spent correcting errors**   Database staff need to process corrections to the database. For example, the costs of correcting errors at U-rent Corporation are estimated as follows:
  a. Two database staff members spend 25% of their workday processing and verifying data corrections each day:

  2 people * 25% of 8 hours / day = 4 hours / day correcting errors

  b. Hourly salaries are $50 per hour based on pay rate and benefits:

  $50 / hour * 4 hours / day = $200 / day correcting errors

  c. 250 workdays per year:

  $200 / day * 250 days = $50,000 / year to correct errors

For a particular company, it is difficult to calculate the full cost of poor-quality data and its long-term effects. Part of the difficulty is the time delay between the mistake and when it is detected. Errors can be very difficult to correct, especially when systems extend across the enterprise. Another concern is that the impacts of errors can be unpredictable, far-reaching, and serious.

Data Ownership and Organizational Politics

Compliance with numerous federal and state regulations relies on rock-solid data and trusted metrics used for regulatory reporting. Data ownership, data quality, and formally managed data are high priorities on the agenda of CFOs and CEOs who are held personally accountable if their company is found to be in violation of regulations.

Despite the need for high-quality data, organizational politics and technical issues make that difficult to achieve. The source of the problem is data ownership—that is, who owns or is responsible for the data. Data ownership problems exist when there are no policies defining responsibility and accountability for managing data. Inconsistent data formats of various departments create an additional set of problems as organizations try to combine individual applications into integrated enterprise systems.

The tendency to delegate data-quality responsibilities to the technical teams who have no control over data quality, as opposed to business users who do have such control, is another common pitfall that stands in the way of accumulating high-quality data.

Those who manage a business or part of a business are tasked with trying to improve business performance and retain customers. Compensation is tied to improving profitability, driving revenue growth, and improving the quality of customer service. These key performance indicators (KPIs) are monitored closely by senior managers who want to find and eliminate defects that harm performance. It is strange then that so few managers take the time to understand how performance is impacted by poor-quality data. Two examples make a strong case for investment in high-quality data.

Retail banking: For retail bank executives, risk management is the number one issue. Disregard for risk contributed to the 2008 financial services meltdown. Despite risk management strategies, many banks still incur huge losses. Part of the problem in many banks is that their ISs enable them to monitor risk only at the product level—mortgages, loans, or credit cards. Product-level risk management ISs monitor a customer's risk exposure for mortgages, or for loans, or for credit cards, and so forth—but not for a customer for all products. With product-level ISs, a bank cannot see the full risk exposure of a customer. The limitations of these siloed product-level risks have serious implications for business performance because bad-risk customers cannot be identified easily, and customer data in the various ISs may differ. However, banks are beginning to use big data to analyze risk more effectively. Although they are still very limited to credit card, loan, and mortgage risk data, cheaper and faster computing power allows them to keep better and more inclusive records of customer data. Portfolio monitoring offers earlier detection and predictive analytics for potential customers, and more advanced risk models show intricate patterns unseen by the naked eye in large data sets. Also, more fact-based inputs and standardized organizational methods are being implemented to reduce loan and credit officer bias to take risks on undesirable customers.

Marketing: Consider what happens when each product-level risk management IS feeds data to marketing ISs. Marketing may offer bad-risk customers incentives to take out another credit card or loan that they cannot repay. And since the bank cannot identify its best customers either, they may be ignored and enticed away by better deals offered by competitors. This scenario illustrates how data ownership and data-quality management are critical to risk management. Data defects and incomplete data can quickly trigger inaccurate marketing and mounting losses. Banks' increasing dependence on business modeling requires that risk managers understand and manage model risk better. Although losses often go unreported, the consequences of errors in the model can be extreme. For instance, a large Asia–Pacific bank lost $4 billion when it applied interest-rate models that contained incorrect assumptions and data-entry errors. Risk mitigation will entail rigorous guidelines and processes for developing and validating models, as well as the constant monitoring and improvement of them (Harle et al., 2016).

Manufacturing: Many manufacturers are at the mercy of a powerful customer base—large retailers. Manufacturers want to align their processes with those of large retail customers to keep them happy. This alignment makes it possible for a retailer to order centrally for all stores or to order locally from a specific manufacturer. Supporting both central and local ordering makes it difficult to plan production runs. For example, each manufacturing site has to collect order data from central ordering and local ordering systems to get a complete picture of what to manufacture at each site. Without accurate, up-to-date data, orders may go unfilled, or manufacturers may have excess inventory. One manufacturer who tried to keep its key retailer happy by implementing central and local ordering could not process orders correctly at each manufacturing site. No data ownership and lack of control over how order data flowed throughout business operations had negative impacts. Conflicting and duplicate business processes at each manufacturing site caused data errors, leading to mistakes in manufacturing, packing, and shipments. Customers were very dissatisfied.

These examples demonstrate the consequences of a lack of data ownership and data quality. Understanding the impact mismanaged data can have on business performance highlights the need to make data ownership and data accuracy a high priority.

Data Life Cycle and Data Principles

The data life cycle is a model that illustrates the way data travel through an organization as shown in **Figure 3.8**. The data life cycle begins with storage in a database, to being loaded into a data warehouse for analysis, then reported to knowledge workers or used in business

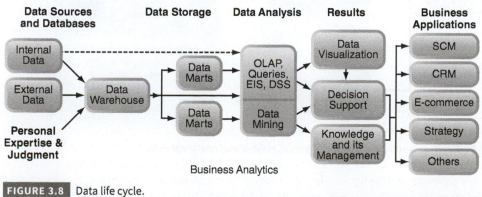

FIGURE 3.8 Data life cycle.

apps. Supply chain management (SCM), customer relationship management (CRM), and e-commerce are enterprise applications that require up-to-date, readily accessible data to function properly.

Three general data principles relate to the data life cycle perspective and help to guide IT investment decisions:

1. **Principle of diminishing data value**   The value of data diminishes as they age. This is a simple, yet powerful principle. Most organizations cannot operate at peak performance with blind spots (lack of data availability) of 30 days or longer. Global financial services institutions rely on near real-time data for peak performance.

2. **Principle of 90/90 data use**   According to the 90/90 data-use principle, a majority of stored data, as high as 90%, is seldom accessed after 90 days (except for auditing purposes). That is, roughly 90% of data lose most of their value after three months.

3. **Principle of data in context**   The capability to capture, process, format, and distribute data in near real time or faster requires a huge investment in data architecture (Chapter 2) and infrastructure to link remote POS systems to data storage, data analysis systems, and reporting apps. The investment can be justified on the principle that data must be integrated, processed, analyzed, and formatted into "actionable information."

Master Data and Master Data Management

As data become more complex and their volumes explode, database performance degrades. One solution is the use of master data and **master data management (MDM)** as introduced in Chapter 2. MDM processes integrate data from various sources or enterprise applications to create a more complete (unified) view of a customer, product, or other entity. **Figure 3.9** shows how master data serve as a layer between transactional data in a database and analytical data in a data warehouse. Although vendors may claim that their MDM solution creates "a single version of the truth," this claim is probably not true. In reality, MDM cannot create a single unified version of the data because constructing a completely unified view of all master data is simply not possible.

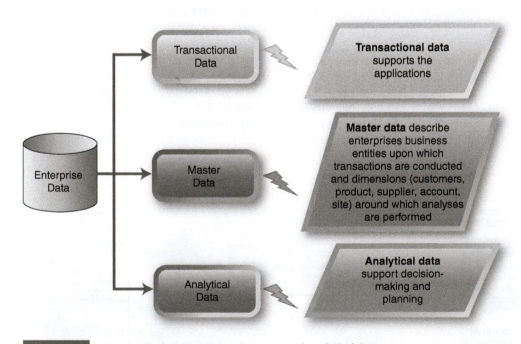

FIGURE 3.9   An enterprise has transactional, master, and analytical data.

Master Reference File and Data Entities Realistically, MDM consolidates data from various data sources into a master reference file, which then feeds data back to the applications, thereby creating accurate and consistent data across the enterprise. In **IT at Work 3.1**, participants in the health-care supply chain essentially developed a master reference file of its key data entities. A **data entity** is anything real or abstract about which a company wants to collect and store data. Master data entities are the main entities of a company, such as customers, products, suppliers, employees, and assets.

IT at Work 3.1

Data Errors Increase Costs Downstream

At an insurance company, the cost of processing each claim is $1, but the average downstream cost due to errors in a claim is $300. The $300 average downstream costs included manual handling of exceptions, customer support calls initiated due to errors in claims, and reissuing corrected documents for any claims processed incorrectly the first time. In addition, the company faced significant soft costs from regulatory risk, lost revenues due to customer dissatisfaction, and overpayment on claims due to claims-processing errors. These soft costs are not included in the hard cost of $300.

Every day health-care administrators and others throughout the health-care supply chain waste 24–30% of their time correcting data errors. Each transaction error costs $60 to $80 to correct.

In addition, about 60% of all invoices among supply chain partners contain errors, and each invoice error costs $40 to $400 to reconcile. Altogether, errors and conflicting data increase supply costs by 3–5%. In other words, each year billions of dollars are wasted in the health-care supply chain because of supply chain data disconnects, which refer to one organization's IS not understanding data from another's IS.

IT at Work Questions

1. Why are the downstream costs of data errors so high?
2. What are soft costs?
3. Explain how soft costs might exceed hard costs. Give an example.

Each department has distinct master data needs. Marketing, for example, is concerned with product pricing, brand, and product packaging, whereas production is concerned with product costs and schedules. A customer master reference file can feed data to all enterprise systems that have a customer relationship component, thereby providing a more unified picture of customers. Similarly, a product master reference file can feed data to all the production systems within the enterprise.

An MDM includes tools for cleaning and auditing the master data elements as well as tools for integrating and synchronizing data to make them more accessible. MDM offers a solution for managers who are frustrated with how fragmented and dispersed their data sources are.

Questions

1. Describe the data life cycle.
2. What is the function of master data management (MDM)?
3. What are the consequences of not cleaning "dirty data"?
4. Describe the differences between centralized and distributed databases.
5. Discuss how data ownership and organizational politics affect the quality of an organization's data.

3.3 | Data Warehouses

Data warehouses are the primary source of cleansed data for analysis, reporting, and business intelligence (BI). Often the data are summarized in ways that enable quick responses to queries. For instance, query results can reveal changes in customer behavior and drive the decision to redevelop the advertising strategy.

Enterprise data warehouses (EDWs) is a data warehouse that integrates data from databases across an entire enterprise.

Data warehouses that pull together data from disparate sources and databases across an entire enterprise are called **enterprise data warehouses (EDWs)**.

Data warehouses store data from various source systems and databases across an enterprise in order to run analytical queries against huge datasets collected over long time periods.

The high cost of data warehouses can make them too expensive for a company to implement. **Data marts** are lower-cost, scaled-down versions of a data warehouse that can be implemented in a much shorter time, for example, in less than 90 days. Data marts serve a specific department or function, such as finance, marketing, or operations. Since they store smaller amounts of data, they are faster and easier to use, and navigate.

Procedures to Prepare EDW Data for Analytics

Consider a bank's database. Every deposit, withdrawal, loan payment, or other transaction adds or changes data. The volatility caused by constant transaction processing makes data analysis difficult—and the demands to process millions of transactions per second consume the database's processing power. In contrast, data in warehouses are relatively stable, as needed for analysis. Therefore, select data are moved from databases to a warehouse. Specifically, data are as follows:

1. *Extracted* from designated databases.
2. *Transformed* by standardizing formats, cleaning the data, integrating them.
3. *Loaded* into a data warehouse.

These three procedures—**extract, transform, and load**—are referred to by their initials **ETL** (**Figure 3.10**). In a warehouse, data are *read-only*; that is, they do not change until the next ETL.

FIGURE 3.10 Data enter databases from transaction systems. Data of interest are extracted from databases, transformed to clean and standardize them, and then loaded into a data warehouse. These three processes are called ETL.

Three technologies involved in preparing raw data for analytics include ETL, **change data capture (CDC),** and data deduplication ("deduping the data"). CDC processes capture the changes made at data sources and then apply those changes throughout enterprise data stores to keep data synchronized. CDC minimizes the resources required for ETL processes by only dealing with data changes. Deduping processes remove duplicates and standardize data formats, which helps to minimize storage and data synch.

Building a Data Warehouse

Figure 3.11 diagrams the process of building and using a data warehouse. The organization's data from operational transaction processes systems are stored in operational databases

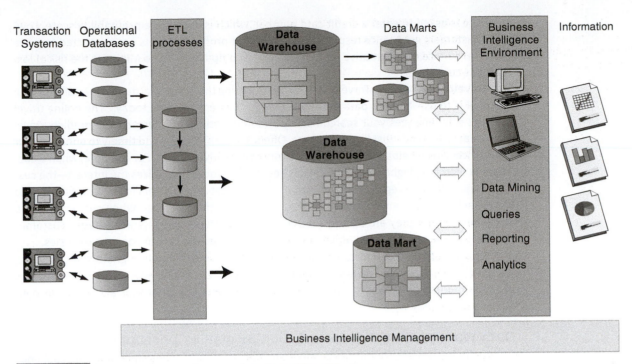

FIGURE 3.11 Database, data warehouse and marts, and BI architecture.

(left side of the figure). Not all data are transferred to the data warehouse. Frequently, only summary data are transferred. The warehouse organizes the data in multiple ways—by subject, functional area, vendor, and product. As shown, the data warehouse architecture defines the flow of data that starts when data are captured by transaction systems; the source data are stored in transactional (operational) databases; ETL processes move data from databases into data warehouses or data marts, where the data are available for access, reports, and analysis.

Real-Time Support from an Active Data Warehouse

Early data warehouse technology primarily supported strategic applications that did not require instant response time, direct customer interaction, or integration with operational systems. ETL might have been done once per week or once per month. But, demand for information to support real time customer interaction and operations leads to real-time data warehousing and analytics—known as an **active data warehouse (ADW).** Massive increases in computing power, processing speeds, and memory made ADW possible. ADW are not designed to support executives' strategic decision-making, but rather to support operations. For example, shipping companies like DHL use huge fleets of trucks to move millions of packages. Every day and all day, operational managers make thousands of decisions that affect the bottom line, such as: "Do we need four trucks for this run?" "With two drivers delayed by bad weather, do we need to bring in extra help?" Traditional data warehousing is not suited for immediate operational support, but active data warehousing is. For example, companies with an ADW are able to:

- Interact with a customer to provide superior customer service.
- Respond to business events in near real time.
- Share up-to-date status data among merchants, vendors, customers, and associates.

Here are some examples of how two companies use ADW.

Capital One. Capital One uses its ADW to track each customer's "profitability score" to determine the level of customer service to provide for that person. Higher-cost personalized service is only given to those with high scores. For instance, when a customer calls Capital One, he or she is asked to enter a credit card number, which is linked to a profitability score. Low-profit customers get a voice response unit only; high-profit customers are connected to a live customer service representative (CSR) because the company wants to minimize the risk of losing those customers.

Travelocity. If you use Travelocity, an ADW is finding the best travel deals especially for you. The goal is to use "today's data today" instead of "yesterday's data today." The online travel agency's ADW analyzes your search history and destinations of interest; then predicts travel offers that you would most likely purchase. Offers are both relevant and timely to enhance your experience, which helps close the sale in a very competitive market. For example, when a customer is searching flights and hotels in Las Vegas, Travelocity recognizes the interest—the customer wants to go to Vegas. The ADW searches for the best-priced flights from all carriers, builds a few package deals, and presents them in real time to the customer. When customers see a personalized offer they are already interested in, the ADW helps generate a better customer experience. The real-time data-driven experience increases the conversion rate and sales.

Data warehouse content can be delivered to decision-makers throughout the enterprise via the cloud or company-owned intranets. Users can view, query, and analyze the data and produce reports using Web browsers. These are extremely economical and effective data delivery methods.

Data Warehousing Supports Action as well as Decisions   Many organizations built data warehouses because they were frustrated with inconsistent data that could not support decisions or actions. Viewed from this perspective, data warehouses are infrastructure investments that companies make to support ongoing and future operations, including the following:

- **Marketing**   Keeps people informed of the status of products, marketing program effectiveness, and product line profitability; and allows them to take intelligent action to maximize per-customer profitability.

- **Pricing and contracts**   Calculates costs accurately in order to optimize pricing of a contract. Without accurate cost data, prices may be below or too near to cost; or prices may be uncompetitive because they are too high.

- **Forecasting**   Estimates customer demand for products and services.

- **Sales**   Calculates sales profitability and productivity for all territories and regions; analyzes results by geography, product, sales group, or individual.

- **Financial**   Provides real-time data for optimal credit terms, portfolio analysis, and actions that reduce risk or bad debt expense.

Table 3.3 summarizes several successful applications of data warehouses.

TABLE 3.3   Data Warehouse Applications by Industry

Industry	Applications
Airline	Crew assignment, aircraft deployment, analysis of route profitability, and customer loyalty promotions
Banking and financial	Customer service, trend analysis, product and service services promotions, and reduction of IS expenses
Credit card	Customer service, new information service for a fee, fraud detection
Defense contracts	Technology transfer, production of military applications
E-business	Data warehouses with personalization capabilities, marketing/shopping preferences allowing for up-selling and cross-selling
Government	Reporting on crime areas, homeland security
Health care	Reduction of operational expenses
Investment and insurance	Risk management, market movements analysis, customer tendencies analysis, and portfolio management
Retail chain	Trend analysis, buying pattern analysis, pricing policy, inventory control, sales promotions, and optimal distribution channel decision

Questions

1. What are the differences between databases and data warehouses?
2. What are the differences between data warehouses and data marts?
3. Explain ETL.
4. Explain CDC.
5. What is an advantage of an enterprise data warehouse (EDW)?
6. Why might a company invest in a data mart instead of a data warehouse?
7. What types of decisions can benefit from a data warehouse?

3.4 Big Data Analytics and Data Discovery

Like mobile and cloud, **big data** and advanced **data analytics** are reshaping organizations and business processes to increase efficiency and improve performance. Research firm IDC forecasts that big data and analytics spending will reach $187 billion in 2019 (Ovalsrud, 2016).

Data analytics is an important tool across organizations, which helps users discover meaningful real-time insights to meet customer expectations, achieve better results and stay competitive. These deeper insights combined with human expertise enable people to recognize meaningful relationships more quickly or easily; and furthermore, realize the strategic implications of these situations. Imagine trying to make sense of the fast and vast data generated by social media campaigns on Facebook or by sensors attached to machines or objects. Low-cost sensors make it possible to monitor all types of physical things—while analytics makes it possible to understand those data in order to take action in real time. For example, sensors data can be analyzed in real time:

- To monitor and regulate the temperature and climate conditions of perishable foods as they are transported from farm to supermarket.
- To sniff for signs of spoilage of fruits and raw vegetables and detect the risk of *E. coli* contamination.
- To track the condition of operating machinery and predict the probability of failure.
- To track the wear of engines and determine when preventive maintenance is needed.

In this section, you will learn about the value, challenges, and technologies involved in putting data and analytics to use to support decisions and action, together with examples of skill sets currently in high demand by organizations expanding their efforts to train, hire and retain competent data professionals (**Career Insight 3.1**).

> **Big data** is an extremely large data set that is too large or complex to be analyzed using traditional data processing techniques.
>
> **Data analytics** is a technique of qualitatively or quantitatively analyzing a data set to reveal patterns, trends, and associations that often relate to human behavior and interactions, to enhance productivity and business gain.

Career Insight 3.1

Managing and Interpreting Big Data are High Demand Skills

Concerns about the analytics skills gap have existed for years. It is increasingly clear that the shortage isn't just in data scientists, but also data engineers, data analysts, and even the executives required to manage data initiatives. As a result, organizations and institutions are expanding their efforts to train, hire, and retain data professionals. Here are two of those skill sets that are in high demand.

Big data specialists manage and package big data collections, analyze, and interpret trends and present their findings in easy to understand ways to "C"-level executives. Those who can present the data through user-friendly data visualizations will be particularly sought after. Skills required of these big data professionals include big data visualization, statistical analysis, Big Data reporting and presentation, Apache Hadoop, NoSQL Database Skills, and machine learning.

Business intelligence (BI) analysts use tools and techniques to go beyond the numbers of big data and take action based on the findings of the big data analyses. Successful BI professionals use self-service BI platforms, like Tableau, SAP, Oracle BI, Microsoft BI, and IBM Cognos, to create BI reports and visualizations to streamline the process and reduce reliance on additional staff. Additional skills of critical thinking, creative problem solving, effective communication, and presentations further enhance their attractiveness to employers (Hammond, 2015).

Big data analytics   process of examining large and varied data sets to identify hidden patterns and correlations, market trends, customer preferences and other useful information to enable better business decisions.

When the data set is too large or complex to be analyzed using traditional data processing applications, **big data analytics** tools are used. One of the biggest sectors of customer relations relative to big data is customer value analytics (CVA). CVA studies the recent phenomenon that customers are more willing to use and purchase innovative products, services, and customer service channels while demanding an increasing amount of high-quality, personalized products. Companies and producers use big data analytics to capture this combination to transform the information into usable data to track and predict trends. If companies know what customers like, what makes them spend more, and when they are happy, they can leverage the information to keep them happy and provide better products and services.

Companies can also use big data analytics to store and use their data across the supply chain. To maximize the effectiveness of data analytics, companies usually complete these objectives throughout their input transformation process:

- Invest heavily in IT to collect, integrate, and analyze data from each store and sales unit.
- Link these data to suppliers' databases, making it possible to adjust prices in real time, to reorder hot-selling items automatically, and to shift items from store to store easily.
- Constantly test, integrate, and report information instantly available across the organization—from the store floor to the CFO's office.

These big data programs enable them to pinpoint improvement opportunities across the supply chain—from purchasing to in-store availability management. Specifically, the companies are able to predict how customers *will behave* and use that knowledge to be prepared to respond quickly. According to Louis Columbus at Forbes, the market demand for big data analytics is about to hit its largest increase in history. Software for business analytics will increase by more than 50% by 2019. Prescriptive analytics software will be worth $1.1B in 2019, compared to its value of $415M in 2014. Since increasing the focus on customer demand trends, effectively entering new markets and producing better business models, and enhancing organizational performance are the most important goals for 21st-century companies, business analytics will be needed in almost every instance. Taking advantage of the benefits of business intelligence is allowing sectors like health care to compete in areas they would have not been able to enter before (Columbus, 2016).

To be effective in using data analysis, organization must pay attention to the four Vs of analytics—variety, volume, velocity, and veracity—shown in **Figure 3.12**.

Big data can have a dramatic impact on the success of any enterprise, or they can be a low-contributing major expense. However, success is not achieved with technology alone. Many companies are collecting and capturing huge amounts of data, but spending very little effort to ensure the veracity and value of data captured at the transactional stage or point of origin. Emphasis in this direction will not only increase confidence in the datasets, but also significantly reduce the efforts for analytics and enhance the quality of decision-making. Success depends also on ensuring that you avoid invalid assumptions, which can be done by testing the assumptions during analysis.

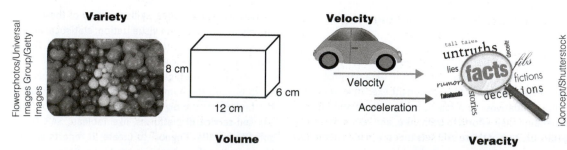

The analytic environment has expanded from pulling data from enterprise systems to include big data unstructured sources

Speed of access reports that are drawn from data defines the difference between effective and ineffective analytics

Variety

Velocity

8 cm

6 cm

12 cm

Velocity

Acceleration

Volume

Large volumes of structured and unstructured data are analyzed

Veracity

Validating data and extracting insights that managers and workers can trust are key factors of successful analytics. Trust in analytics has grown more difficult with the explosion of data sources

FIGURE 3.12   The four Vs of data analytics.

Human Expertise and Judgment are Needed

Human expertise and judgment are needed to interpret the output of analytics (refer to **Figure 3.13**). Data are worthless if you cannot analyze, interpret, understand, and apply the results in context. This brings up several challenges:

- **Data need to be prepared for analysis**   For example, data that are incomplete or duplicated need to be fixed.

- **Dirty data degrade the value of analytics**   The "cleanliness" of data is very important to data mining and analysis projects. Analysts have complained that data analytics is like janitorial work because they spend so much time on manual, error-prone processes to clean the data. Large data volumes and variety mean more data that are dirty and harder to handle.

- **Data must be put into meaningful context**   If the wrong analysis or datasets are used, the output would be nonsense, as in the example of the Super Bowl winners and stock market performance. Stated in reverse, managers need context in order to understand how to interpret traditional and big data.

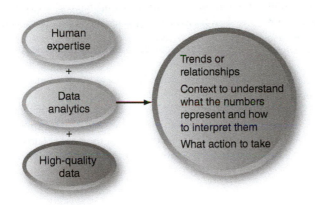

FIGURE 3.13   Data analytics, human expertise, and high-quality data are needed to obtain actionable information.

IT at Work 3.2 describes how big data analytics, collaboration, and human expertise have transformed the new drug development process.

Machine-generated sensor data are becoming a larger proportion of big data (**Figure 3.14**), according to a research report by IDC (2015). It is predicted that these data will increase to two-thirds of all data by 2020, representing a significant increase from the 11% level of 2005. In addition to its growth as a portion of analyzed data, the market for sensor data will increase to $1.7 trillion in 2020.

On the consumer side, a significant factor in this market is the boom in wearable technology—products like FitBit and the Apple Watch. Users no longer even have to input data to these devices as it is automatically gathered and tracked in real time. On the public sector and enterprise side, sensor data and the Internet of Things (IoT) are being used in the advancement of IT-enabled business processes like automated factories and distribution centers and IT-enabled products like the wearable tech (IDC, 2015). Federal health reform efforts have pushed health-care organizations toward big data and analytics. These organizations are planning to use big data analytics to support revenue cycle management, resource utilization, fraud prevention, health management, and quality improvement.

Hadoop and MapReduce   Big data volumes exceed the processing capacity of conventional database infrastructures. A widely used processing platform is **Apache Hadoop**.

IT at Work 3.2

Researchers Use Genomics and Big Data in Drug Discovery

Drug development is a high-risk business. Almost 90% of new drugs ultimately fail to reach the market. One of the challenges has been the amount, variety, and complexity of the data that need to be systematically analyzed. Big data technologies and private–public partnerships have made biomedical analytics feasible.

New Drug Development Had Been Slow and Expensive

Biotechnology advances have produced massive data on the biological causes of disease. However, analyzing these data and converting discoveries into treatments are much more difficult. Not all biomedical insights lead to effective drug targets, and choosing the wrong target leads to failures late in the drug development process, costing time, money, and lives. Developing a new drug—from early discovery through Food and Drug Administration (FDA) approval—takes over a decade. As a consequence, each success ends up costing more than $1 billion. Sometimes much more! For example, by the time Pfizer Inc., Johnson & Johnson, and Eli Lilly & Co. announced their new drugs had only limited benefit for Alzheimer's patients in late-stage testing, the industry had spent more than $30 billion researching amyloid plaque in the brain.

Reducing Risk of Failure

Drug makers, governments, and academic researchers have partnered to improve the odds of drug success and after years of decline, the pharmaceutical industry is beginning to experience a greater rate of success with its clinical trials. Partnerships bring together the expertise of scientists from biology, chemistry, bioinformatics, genomics, and big data. They are using big data to identify biological targets for drugs and eliminate failures before they reach the human testing stage and many anticipate that big data and the analytics that go with it could be a key element in further increasing the success rates in pharmaceutical R&D (Cattell et al., 2016).

GlaxoSmithKline, the European Bioinformatics Institute (EBI), and the Wellcome Trust Sanger Institute established the Centre for Therapeutic Target Validation (CTTV) near Cambridge, England. CTTV partners combine cutting-edge genomics with the ability to collect and analyze massive amounts of biological data. By not developing drugs that target the wrong biological pathways, they avoid wasting billions of research dollars.

With biology now a data-driven discipline, collaborations such as CTTV are needed to improve efficiencies, cut costs, and provide the best opportunities for success. Other private–public partnerships that had formed to harness drug research and big data include the following:

- **Accelerating Medicines Partnership and U.S. National Institutes of Health (NIH)**   In February 2014 the NIH announced that the agency, 10 pharmaceutical companies, and nonprofit organizations were investing $230 million in the Accelerating Medicines Partnership.

- **Target Discovery Institute and Oxford University**   Oxford University opened the Target Discovery Institute in 2013. Target Discovery helps to identify drug targets and molecular interactions at a critical point in a disease-causing pathway—that is, when those diseases will respond to drug therapy. Researchers try to understand complex biological processes by analyzing image data that have been acquired at the microscopic scale.

"The big data opportunity is especially compelling in complex business environments experiencing an explosion in the types and volumes of available data. In the health-care and pharmaceutical industries, data growth is generated from several sources, including the R&D process itself, retailers, patients and caregivers. Effectively utilizing these data will help pharmaceutical companies better identify new potential drug candidates and develop them into effective, approved and reimbursed medicines more quickly" (Cattell et al., 2016).

IT at Work Questions

1. What are the consequences of new drug development failures?

2. What factors have made biomedical analytics feasible? Why?

3. Large-scale big data analytics are expensive. How can the drug makers justify investments in big data?

4. Why would drug makers such as Glaxo and Pfizer be willing to share data given the fierce competition in their industry?

Sources: Compiled from Cattell et al. (2016), *HealthCanal* (2014), Kitamura (2014), and NIH (2014).

It places no conditions on the structure of the data it can process. Hadoop distributes computing problems across a number of servers. Hadoop implements **MapReduce** in two stages:

1. **Map stage**   MapReduce breaks up the huge dataset into smaller subsets; then distributes the subsets among multiple servers where they are partially processed.

2. **Reduce stage**   The partial results from the map stage are then recombined and made available for analytic tools.

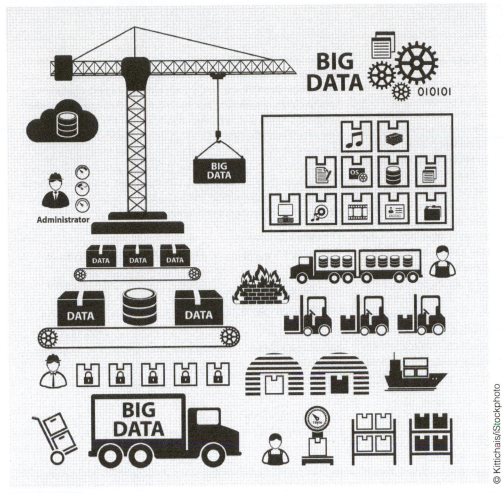

FIGURE 3.14 Machine-generated data from physical objects are becoming a much larger portion of big data and analytics.

To store data, Hadoop has its own distributed file system, *Hadoop File System* (HDFS), which functions in three stages:

- Loads data into HDFS.
- Performs the MapReduce operations.
- Retrieves results from HDFS.

Figure 3.15 diagrams how Facebook uses database technology and Hadoop. **IT at Work 3.3** describes how First Wind has applied big data analytics to improve the operations of its wind farms and to support sustainability of the planet by reducing environmentally damaging carbon emissions.

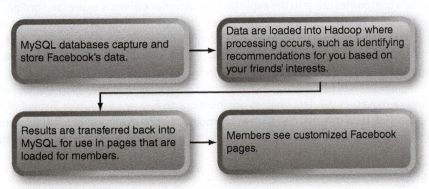

FIGURE 3.15 Facebook's MySQL database and Hadoop technology provide customized pages for its members.

IT at Work 3.3

Industrial Project Relies on Big Data Analytics

Wind power can play a major role in meeting America's rising demand for electricity—as much as 20% by 2030. Using more domestic wind power would reduce the nation's dependence on foreign sources of natural gas and also decrease carbon dioxide (CO_2) emissions that contribute to adverse climate change.

First Wind is an independent North American renewable energy company focused on the development, financing, construction, ownership, and operation of utility-scale power projects in the United States. Based in Boston, First Wind has developed and operates 980 megawatts (MW) of generating capacity at 16 wind energy projects in Maine, New York, Vermont, Utah, Washington, and Hawaii. First Wind has a large network of sensors embedded in the wind turbines, which generate huge volumes of data continuously. The data are transmitted in real time and analyzed on a 24/7 real time basis to understand the performance of each wind turbine.

Sensors collect massive amounts of data on the temperature, wind speeds, location, and pitch of the blades. The data are analyzed to study the operation of each turbine in order to adjust them to maximum efficiency. By analyzing sensor data, highly refined measurements of wind speeds are possible. In wintry conditions, turbines can detect when they are icing up, and speed up or change pitch to knock off the ice. In the past, when it was extremely windy, turbines in the entire farm had been turned off to prevent damage from rotating too fast. Now First Wind can identify the specific portion of turbines that need to be shut down. Based on certain alerts, decisions often need to be taken within a few seconds.

Upgrades on 123 turbines on two wind farms have improved energy output by 3%, or about 120 megawatt hours per turbine per year. That improvement translates to $1.2 million in additional revenue a year from these two farms.

IT at Work Questions

1. What are the benefits of big data analytics to First Wind?
2. What are the benefits of big data analytics to the environment and the nation?
3. How do big data analytics impact the performance of wind farms?

Sources: Compiled from **www.FirstWind.com** (2014) and U.S. Department of Energy (2015).

Data and Text Mining

Data and text mining are different from DBMS and data analytics. As you have read earlier in this chapter, a DBMS supports queries to extract data or get answers from huge databases. But, in order to perform queries in a DBMS you must first know the question you want to be answered. You also have read that Data Analytics describes the entire function of applying technologies, algorithms, human expertise, and judgment. **Data and text mining** are specific analytic techniques that allow users to discover knowledge that they didn't know existed in the databases.

Data mining software enables users to analyze data from various dimensions or angles, categorize them, and find correlations or patterns among fields in the data warehouse. Up to 75% of an organization's data are nonstructured word-processing documents, social media, text messages, audio, video, images and diagrams, faxes and memos, call center or claims notes, and so on.

IT at Work 3.4 describes one example of how the U.S. government is using data mining software to continuously improve its detection and deterrence systems.

Text mining is a broad category that involves interpreting words and concepts in context. Any customer becomes a brand advocate or adversary by freely expressing opinions and attitudes that reach millions of other current or prospective customers on social media. Text mining helps companies tap into the explosion of customer opinions expressed online. Social commentary and social media are being mined for **sentiment analysis** or to understand consumer intent. Innovative companies know they could be more successful in meeting their customers' needs, if they just understood them better. Tools and techniques for analyzing text, documents, and other nonstructured content are available from several vendors.

Combining data and text mining can create even greater value. Burns (2016) pointed out that mining text or nonstructural data enables organizations to forecast the future instead of merely reporting the past. He also noted that forecasting methods using existing structured data and nonstructured text from both internal and external sources provide the best view of what lies ahead.

Creating Business Value

Enterprises invest in data mining tools to add business value. Business value falls into three categories, as shown in **Figure 3.16**.

IT at Work 3.4

DoD and Homeland Security Use Data Mining Spy Machine for Threat Intelligence

Digital Reasoning, a large player in the field of big data analytics has upgraded its software that is currently contracted by the Department of Defense and Homeland Security. Synthesys 4, the name for the brand new software, allows the agencies to monitor threats in the homeland and gather data about potential attacks. Ironically, one of the main tactics employed with this software is to track and deter potential employees or contractors who have access to it. Vice President of Federal Programs Eric Hansen says that the software excels at monitoring behavioral patterns, language, and data to act and respond like a human detective would to a potential threat.

While Digital Reasoning also contracts out to other organizations like Goldman Sachs, the US government is probably its most interesting and important client. Using automatic computer software

to analyze data is much more effective at hindering attacks and quicker for analyzing large amounts of data about potential threats domestically and abroad. For instance, the software knows exactly what to look for without being bogged down and distracted by superfluous data. As available data and analytical capabilities increase, the US government is continuously aiming to improve its detection and deterrence systems using software like **Synthesys 4** (Bing, 2016).

IT at Work Questions

1. What is Synthesys 4?
2. How does data mining help the DoD achieve its mission?
3. What are the main threats to the government's data sources?
4. Why does the government see Synthesys 4 as essential to its threat deterrence measures?

Sources: Compiled from Bing (2016) and syntheses.net (2017).

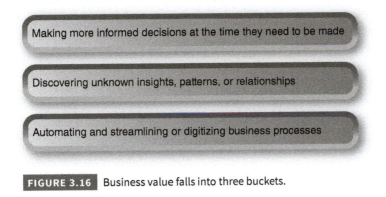

FIGURE 3.16   Business value falls into three buckets.

Here are some brief cases illustrating the types of business value created by data and text mining.

1. Using pattern analysis, **Argo Corporation,** an agricultural equipment manufacturer based in Georgia, was able to optimize product configuration options for farm machinery and real-time customer demand to determine the optimal base configurations for its machines. As a result, Argo reduced product variety by 61% and cut days of inventory by 81% while still maintaining its service levels.

2. The mega-retailer **Walmart** wanted its online shoppers to find what they were looking for faster. Walmart analyzed clickstream data from its 45 million monthly online shoppers; then combined that data with product- and category-related popularity scores. The popularity scores had been generated by text mining the retailer's social media streams. Lessons learned from the analysis were integrated into the Polaris search engine used by customers on the company's website. Polaris has yielded a 10% to 15% increase in online shoppers completing a purchase, which equals roughly $1 billion in incremental online sales.

3. **McDonald's** bakery operation replaced manual equipment with high-speed photo analyses to inspect thousands of buns per minute for color, size, and sesame seed distribution. Automatically, ovens and baking processes adjust instantly to create uniform buns and reduce thousands of pounds of waste each year. Another food products company also uses photo analyses to sort every french fry produced in order to optimize quality.

4. **Infinity Insurance** discovered new insights that it applied to improve the performance of its fraud operation. The insurance company text mined years of adjuster reports to look for key drivers of fraudulent claims. As a result, the company reduced fraud by 75%, and eliminated marketing to customers with a high likelihood of fraudulent claims.

Text Analytics Procedure

With text analytics, information is extracted from large quantities of various types of textual information. The basic steps involved in text analytics include the following:

1. **Exploring** First, documents are explored. This might occur in the form of simple word counts in a document collection, or by manually creating topic areas to categorize documents after reading a sample of them. For example, what are the major types of issues (brake or engine failure) that have been identified in recent automobile warranty claims? A challenge of the exploration effort is misspelled or abbreviated words, acronyms, or slang.

2. **Preprocessing** Before analysis or the automated categorization of content, the text may need to be preprocessed to standardize it to the extent possible. As in traditional analysis, up to 80% of preprocessing time can be spent preparing and standardizing the data. Misspelled words, abbreviations, and slang may need to be transformed into consistent terms. For instance, BTW would be standardized to "by the way" and "left voice message" could be tagged as "lvm."

3. **Categorizing and modeling** Content is then ready to be categorized. Categorizing messages or documents from information contained within them can be achieved using statistical models and business rules. As with traditional model development, sample documents are examined to train the models. Additional documents are then processed to validate the accuracy and precision of the model, and finally new documents are evaluated using the final model (scored). Models can then be put into production for the automated processing of new documents as they arrive.

Analytics Vendor Rankings

Analytics applications cover business intelligence functions sold as a standalone application for decision support or embedded in an integrated solution. The introduction of intuitive decision support tools, dashboards, and data visualization (discussed in detail in Chapter 11) have

TABLE 3.4 Top Analytics Vendors

Rank	Vendor	Focus	Products
1	SAP	Market lines of analytics products that cove BI and reporting, predictive analysis, performance management and governance, risk and compliance applications	SAP Business Objects Predictive Analytics SAP Business Objects BI SAP Business Objects Planning and Consolidation
2	SAS	Offer simple desktop solutions to high performance distributed processing solutions	SAS Analytics Pro SAS Enterprise Minder SAS Visual Analytics SAS Customer Intelligence 360
3	IBM	Allow users to quickly discover patterns and meanings in data with guided data discovery, automated predictive analytics, one-click analysis, self-service dashboards, and a natural language dialogue	Watson Analytics
4	Oracle	Offer a complete solution for connecting and collaborating with analytics in the cloud. Products allow users to aggregate, experiment, manage, and analyze/act	Oracle Data Integrator Oracle Big Data Cloud Service Oracle R Advanced Analytics for Hadoop BI Cloud Service Oracle Stream Explore
5	Microsoft	Provide a broad range of products from standalone solutions to integrated tools that provide data preparation, data discovery, and interactive dashboard capabilities in a single tool	Excel HDInsight Machine Learning Stream Analytics Power BI Embedded

added some interesting interactive components to big data analytics to bring the data to life and enable nonexperts to use it.

Organizations invest in analytics, BI, and data/text mining applications based on new features and capabilities beyond those offered by their legacy systems. Analytics vendors offer everything from simple-to-use reporting tools to highly sophisticated software for tackling the most complex data analysis problems. A list of the top five analytics and BI application vendors are shown in **Table 3.4.**

Questions

1. Why are human expertise and judgment important to data analytics? Give an example.
2. What is the relationship between data quality and the value of analytics?
3. Why do data need to be put into a meaningful context?
4. How can manufacturers and health care benefit from data analytics?
5. How does data mining provide value? Give an example.
6. What is text mining?
7. What are the basic steps involved in text analytics?

3.5 | Business Intelligence and Electronic Records Management

Continuing developments in data analytics and **business intelligence (BI)** make it increasingly necessary for organizations to be aware of the differences between these terms and the different ways in which they add value in an organization. The field of BI started in the late 1980s and has been a key to competitive advantage across industries and in enterprises of all sizes. Unlike data analytics that has predictive capabilities, BI is a comprehensive term that refers to analytics and reporting tools that were traditionally used to determine trends in historical data.

> **Business intelligence (BI)** is a set of tools and techniques for acquiring and transforming raw data into meaningful and useful information for business analysis purposes in the forms of reports, dashboards, or interactive visualizations.

The key distinction between data analytics and BI is that analytics uses algorithms to statistically determine the relationships between data whereas BI presents data insights established by data analytics in reports, easy-to-use dashboards, and interactive visualizations. BI can also make it easier for users to ask data-related questions and obtain results that are presented in a way that they can easily understand.

What started as a tool to support sales, marketing, and customer service departments has widely evolved into an enterprise wide strategic platform. While BI software is used in the operational management of divisions and business processes, they are also used to support strategic corporate decision-making. The dramatic change that has taken effect over the last few years is the growth in demand for operational intelligence across multiple systems and businesses—increasing the number of people who need access to increasing amounts of data. Complex and competitive business conditions do not leave much slack for mistakes.

Unfortunately, some companies are not able to use their data efficiently, creating a higher cost to gather information than the benefits it provides. Luckily, BI software brings decision-making information to businesses in as little as two clicks. Small businesses have a shared interest with large corporations to enlist BI to help with decision-making, but they are usually unequipped to build data centers and use funds to hire analysts and IT consultants. However, small business BI software is rapidly growing in the analytics field, and it is increasingly cheaper to implement it as a decision-making tool. Small businesses do not always have workers specialized in certain areas, but BI software makes it easy for all employees to analyze the data and make decisions (King, 2016).

Business Benefits of BI

BI provides data at the *moment of value* to a decision-maker—enabling it to extract crucial facts from enterprise data in real time or near real time. A BI solution with a well-designed dashboard, for example, provides retailers with better visibility into inventory to make better decisions about what to order, how much, and when in order to prevent stock-outs or minimize inventory that sits on warehouse shelves.

Companies use BI solutions to determine what questions to ask and find answers to them. BI tools integrate and consolidate data from various internal and external sources and then process them into information to make smart decisions. BI answers questions such as these: Which products have the highest repeat sales rate in the last six months? Do customer likes on Facebook relate to product purchase? How does the sales trend break down by product group over the last five years? What do daily sales look like in each of my sales regions?

According to The Data Warehousing Institute, BI "unites data, technology, analytics, and human knowledge to optimize business decisions and ultimately drive an enterprise's success. BI programs usually combine an enterprise data warehouse and a BI platform or tool set to transform data into usable, actionable business information" (The Data Warehousing Institute, 2014). For many years, managers have relied on business analytics to make better-informed decisions. Multiple surveys and studies agree on BI's growing importance in analyzing past performance and identifying opportunities to improve future performance.

Common Challenges: Data Selection and Quality

Companies cannot analyze all of their data—and much of them would not add value. Therefore, an unending challenge is how to determine which data to use for BI from what seems like unlimited options (Oliphant, 2016). One purpose of a BI strategy is to provide a framework for selecting the most relevant data without limiting options to integrate new data sources. **Information overload** is a major problem for executives and for employees. Another common challenge is data quality, particularly with regard to online information, because the source and accuracy might not be verifiable.

Aligning BI Strategy with Business Strategy

Reports and dashboards are delivery tools, but they may not be delivering business intelligence. To get the greatest value out of BI, the CIO needs to work with the CFO and other business leaders to create a BI governance program whose mission is to achieve the following (Ladley, 2016):

1. Clearly articulate business strategies.
2. Deconstruct the business strategies into a set of specific goals and objectives—the *targets*.
3. Identify the key performance indicators (KPIs) that will be used to measure progress toward each target.
4. Prioritize the list of KPIs.
5. Create a plan to achieve goals and objectives based on the priorities.
6. Estimate the costs needed to implement the BI plan.
7. Assess and update the priorities based on business results and changes in business strategy.

After completing these activities, BI analysts can identify the data to use in BI and the source systems. This is a **business-driven development approach** that starts with a business strategy and work backward to identify data sources and the data that need to be acquired and analyzed.

Businesses want KPIs that can be utilized by both departmental users and management. In addition, users want real-time access to these data so that they can monitor processes with the smallest possible latency and take corrective action whenever KPIs deviate from their target values. To link strategic and operational perspectives, users must be able to drill down from highly consolidated or summarized figures into the detailed numbers from which they were derived to perform in-depth analyses.

BI Architecture and Analytics

BI architecture is undergoing technological advances in response to big data and the performance demands of end-users (Wise, 2016). BI vendors are facing the challenges of social, sensor, and other newer data types that must be managed and analyzed. One technology advance that can help handle big data is BI in the cloud. **Figure 3.17** lists the key factors contributing to the increased use of BI. It can be hosted on a public or private cloud. Although cloud services come with more upkeep, optimizing the service and customizing it for one's company brings undeniable benefits in data security. With a public cloud, a service provider hosts the data and/or software that are accessed via an Internet connection. For private clouds, the company hosts its own data and software, but uses cloud-based technologies.

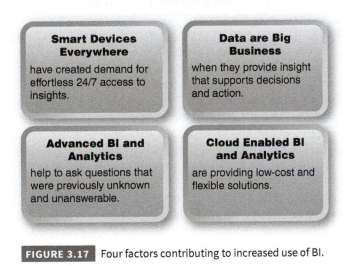

Smart Devices Everywhere have created demand for effortless 24/7 access to insights.

Data are Big Business when they provide insight that supports decisions and action.

Advanced BI and Analytics help to ask questions that were previously unknown and unanswerable.

Cloud Enabled BI and Analytics are providing low-cost and flexible solutions.

FIGURE 3.17   Four factors contributing to increased use of BI.

For cloud-based BI, a popular option offered by a growing number of BI tool vendors is software as a service (SaaS). MicroStrategy offers MicroStrategy Cloud, which provides fast deployment with reduced project risks and costs. This cloud approach appeals to small and midsized companies that have limited IT staff and want to carefully control costs. The potential downsides include slower response times, security risks, and backup risks.

Competitive Analytics in Practice: CarMax   CarMax, Inc. is the nation's largest retailer of used cars and for a decade has remained one of *FORTUNE* Magazine's "100 Best Companies to Work For." CarMax was the fastest retailer in U.S. history to reach $1 billion in revenues. In 2016 the company had over $15 billion in net sales and operating revenues, representing a 6.2% increase over the prior year's results. The company grew rapidly because of its compelling customer offer—no-haggle prices and quality guarantees backed by a 125-point inspection that became an industry benchmark—and auto financing. As of November 30, 2016, CarMax operated in 169 locations across 39 U.S. states and had more than 22,000 full- and part-time employees.

CarMax continues to enhance and refine its information systems, which it believes to be a core competitive advantage. CarMax's IT includes the following:

- A proprietary IS that captures, analyzes, interprets, and distributes data about the cars CarMax sells and buys.
- Data analytics applications that track every purchase; number of test drives and credit applications per car; color preferences in every demographic and region.

- Proprietary store technology that provides management with real-time data about every aspect of store operations, such as inventory management, pricing, vehicle transfers, wholesale auctions, and sales consultant productivity.
- An advanced inventory management system that helps management anticipate future inventory needs and manage pricing.

Throughout CarMax, analytics are used as a strategic asset and insights gained from analytics are available to everyone who needs them.

Electronic Records Management

All organizations create and retain **business records.** A record is documentation of a business event, action, decision, or transaction. Examples are contracts, research and development, accounting source documents, memos, customer/client communications, hiring and promotion decisions, meeting minutes, social posts, texts, e-mails, website content, database records, and paper and electronic files. Business documents such as spreadsheets, e-mail messages, and word-processing documents are a type of record. Most records are kept in electronic format and maintained throughout their life cycle—from creation to final archiving or destruction by an **electronic records management system (ERMS).**

One application of an ERMS would be in a company that is required by law to retain financial documents for at least seven years, product designs for many decades, and e-mail messages about marketing promotions for a year. The major ERM tools are workflow software, authoring tools, scanners, and databases. ERM systems have query and search capabilities so documents can be identified and accessed like data in a database. These systems range from those designed to support a small workgroup to full-featured, Web-enabled enterprise-wide systems.

Electronic records management system (ERMS) consists of hardware and software that manage and archive electronic documents and image paper documents; then index and store them according to company policy.

Legal Duty to Retain Business Records

Companies need to be prepared to respond to an audit, federal investigation, lawsuit, or any other legal action against them. Types of lawsuits against companies include patent violations, product safety negligence, theft of intellectual property, breach of contract, wrongful termination, harassment, discrimination, and many more.

Because senior management must ensure that their companies comply with legal and regulatory duties, managing electronic records (e-records) is a strategic issue for organizations in both the public and private sectors. The success of ERM depends greatly on a partnership of many key players, namely, senior management, users, records managers, archivists, administrators, and most importantly, IT personnel. Properly managed, records are strategic assets. Improperly managed or destroyed, they become liabilities.

ERM Best Practices

Effective ERM systems capture all business data and documents at their first touchpoint—data centers, laptops, the mailroom, at customer sites, or remote offices. Records enter the enterprise in multiple ways—from online forms, bar codes, sensors, websites, social sites, copiers, e-mails, and more. In addition to capturing the entire document as a whole, important data from within a document can be captured and stored in a central, searchable repository. In this way, the data are accessible to support informed and timely business decisions.

In recent years, organizations such as the Association for Information and Image Management (**AIIM**), National Archives and Records Administration (NARA), and **ARMA International** (formerly the Association of Records Managers and Administrators) have created and published industry standards for document and records management. Numerous best practices articles, and links to valuable sources of information about document and records management, are available on their websites. The IT Toolbox describes ARMA's eight generally accepted recordkeeping principles framework.

ERM Benefits

Departments or companies whose employees spend most of their day filing or retrieving documents or warehousing paper records can reduce costs significantly with ERM. These systems minimize the inefficiencies and frustration associated with managing paper documents and workflows. However, they do not create a paperless office as had been predicted.

An ERM can help a business to become more efficient and productive by the following:

- Enabling the company to access and use the content contained in documents.
- Cutting labor costs by automating business processes.
- Reducing the time and effort required to locate information the business needs to support decision-making.
- Improving the security of content, thereby reducing the risk of intellectual property theft.
- Minimizing the costs associated with printing, storing, and searching for content.

When workflows are digital, productivity increases, costs decrease, compliance obligations are easier to verify, and green computing becomes possible. Green computing is an initiative to conserve our valuable natural resources by reducing the effects of our computer usage on the environment. You can read about green computing and the related topics of reducing an organization's carbon footprint, sustainability, and ethical and social responsibilities in Chapter 14.

ERM for Disaster Recovery, Business Continuity, and Compliance

Businesses also rely on their ERM system for disaster recovery and business continuity, security, knowledge sharing and collaboration, and remote and controlled access to documents. Because ERM systems have multilayered access capabilities, employees can access and change only the documents they are authorized to handle.

When companies select an ERM to meet compliance requirements, they should ask the following questions:

1. Does the software meet the organization's needs? For example, can the DMS be installed on the existing network? Can it be purchased as a service?
2. Is the software easy to use and accessible from Web browsers, office applications, and e-mail applications? If not, people will not use it.
3. Does the software have lightweight, modern Web and graphical user interfaces that effectively support remote users?
4. Before selecting a vendor, it is important to examine workflows and how data, documents, and communications flow throughout the company. For example, know which information on documents is used in business decisions. Once those needs and requirements are identified, they guide the selection of technology that can support the input types—that is, capture and index them so they can be archived consistently and retrieved on-demand.

IT at Work 3.5 describes how several companies currently use ERM. Simply creating backups of records is not sufficient because the content would not be organized and indexed to retrieve them accurately and easily. The requirement to manage records—regardless of whether they are physical or digital—is not new.

IT at Work 3.5

ERM Applications

Here some examples of how companies use ERM in the health-care, finance, and education sectors:

- The Surgery Center of Baltimore stores all medical records electronically, providing instant patient information to doctors and nurses anywhere and at any time. The system also routes charts to the billing department, which can then scan and e-mail any relevant information to insurance providers and patients. The ERM system helps maintain the required audit trail, including the provision of records when they are needed for legal purposes. How valuable has ERM been to the center? Since it was implemented, business processes have been expedited by more than 50%, the costs of these processes have been significantly reduced, and the morale of office employees in the center has improved noticeably.

- American Express (AMEX) uses TELEform, developed by Alchemy and Cardiff Software, to collect and process more than 1 million customer satisfaction surveys every year. The data are collected in templates that consist of more than 600 different survey forms in 12 languages and 11 countries. AMEX integrated TELEform with AMEX's legacy system, which enables it to distribute processed results to many managers. Because the survey forms are now readily accessible, AMEX has reduced the number of staff who process these forms from 17 to 1, thereby saving the company more than $500,000 a year.

- The University of Cincinnati provides authorized access to the personnel files of 12,000 active employees and tens of thousands of retirees. The university receives more than 75,000 queries about personnel records every year and then must search more than 3 million records to answer these queries. Using a microfilm system to find answers took days. The solution was an ERM that digitized all paper and microfilm documents, without help from the IT department, making them available via the Internet and the university's intranet. Authorized employees access files using a browser.

IT at Work Questions

1. What are the business benefits of BI?
2. What are two-related challenges that must be resolved for BI to produce meaningful insights?
3. What are the steps in a BI governance program?
4. What does it mean to drill down into data, and why is it important?
5. What four factors are contributing to increased use of BI?
6. Why is ERM a strategic issue rather than simply an IT issue?
7. Why might a company have a legal duty to retain records? Give an example.
8. Why is creating backups an insufficient way to manage an organization's documents?

Key Terms

active data warehouse (ADW)   81
big data   83
big data analytics   84
business analytics   68
business intelligence (BI)   91
business record   94
business-driven development approach   92
centralized database   73
change data capture (CDC)   80
data analytics   83
data entity   79
data management   69
data marts   80
data mining   88
data warehouse   67
database   69

database management system (DBMS)   70
decision model   68
declarative language   70
dirty data   75
distributed database   73
electronic records management system (ERMS)   94
extract, transform and load (ETL)   80
enterprise data warehouses (EDWs)   80
eventual consistency   70
fault tolerance   72
Hadoop   85
information overload   92
immediate consistency   70
latency   70
MapReduce   86

master data management (MDM)   78
NoSQL   72
online transaction processing (OLTP) systems   71
online analytical processing (OLAP) systems   72
petabyte   66
query   70
relational database   70
relational management systems (RDBMSs)   70
sentiment analysis   88
scalability   72
structured query language (SQL)   70
text mining   88

Assuring Your Learning

Discuss: Critical Thinking Questions

1. What are the functions of databases and data warehouses?

2. How does data quality impact business performance?

3. List three types of waste or damages that data errors can cause.

4. What is the role of a master reference file?

5. Give three examples of business processes or operations that would benefit significantly from having detailed real-time or near real-time data and identify the benefits.

6. What are the tactical and strategic benefits of big data analytics?

7. Explain the four Vs of data analytics.

8. Select an industry. Explain how an organization in that industry could improve consumer satisfaction through the use of data warehousing.

9. Explain the principle of 90/90 data use.

10. Why is master data management (MDM) important in companies with multiple data sources?

11. Why would a company invest in a data mart instead of a data warehouse?

12. Why is data mining important?

13. What are the operational benefits and competitive advantages of business intelligence?

14. How can ERM decrease operating costs?

Explore: Online and Interactive Exercises

1. Visit www.YouTube.com and search for SAS Enterprise Miner Software Demo in order to assess the features and benefits of SAS Enterprise Miner. The URL is https://www.youtube.com/watch?v=Nj4L5RFvkMg.

   a. View the SAS Enterprise Miner Software demo, which is about seven minutes long.

   b. Based on what you learn in the demo, what skills or expertise are needed to build a predictive model?

   c. At the end of the demo, you hear the presenter say that "SAS Enterprise Miner allows end-users to easily develop predictive models and to generate scoring to make better decisions about future business events." Do you agree that SAS Enterprise Miner makes it easy to develop such models? Explain.

   d. Do you agree that if an expert develops predictive models, it will help managers make better decisions about future business events? Explain.

   e. Based on your answers to (c), (d), and (e), under what conditions would you recommend SAS Enterprise Miner?

2. Research two electronic records management vendors, such as Iron Mountain.

   a. What are the retention recommendations made by the vendors? Why?

   b. What services or solutions does each vendor offer?

3. View the "Edgenet Gain Real time Access to Retail Product Data with In-Memory Technology" video on YouTube. Explain the benefit of in-memory technology.

Analyze & Decide: Apply IT Concepts to Business Decisions

1. Visit www.Oracle.com. Click the Solutions tab to open the menu; then click Data Warehousing under Technology Solutions.

   a. Scroll down to view "Procter & Gamble Drives 30X Performance Gains with Oracle Exadata."

   b. Describe the Procter & Gamble's challenges, why it selected Oracle Exadata, and how that solution met their challenge.

2. Visit www.Teradata.com. Click Resources and open "Videos." Select one of the videos related to data analytics. Explain the benefits of the solution chosen.

3. Spring Street Company (SSC) wanted to reduce the "hidden costs" associated with its paper-intensive processes. Employees jokingly predicted that if the windows were open on a very windy day, total chaos

would ensue as thousands of papers started to fly. If a flood, fire, or windy day occurred, the business would literally grind to a halt. The company's accountant, Sam Spring, decided to calculate the costs of its paper-driven processes to identify their impact on the bottom line. He recognized that several employees spent most of their day filing or retrieving documents. In addition, there were the monthly costs to warehouse old paper records. Sam measured the activities related to the handling of printed reports and paper files. His average estimates were as follows:

a. **Dealing with a file:** It takes an employee 12 minutes to walk to the records room, locate a file, act on it, refile it, and return to his or her desk. Employees do this 4 times per day (five days per week).

b. **Number of employees:** 10 full-time employees perform the functions.

c. **Lost document replacement:** Once per day, a document gets "lost" (destroyed, misplaced, or covered with massive coffee stains) and must be recreated. The total cost of replacing each lost document is $200.

d. **Warehousing costs:** Currently, document storage costs are $75 per month.

Sam would prefer a system that lets employees find and work with business documents without leaving their desks. He's most concerned about the human resources and accounting departments. These personnel are traditional heavy users of paper files and would greatly benefit from a modern document management system. At the same time, however, Sam is also risk averse. He would rather invest in solutions that would reduce the risk of higher costs in the future. He recognizes that the U.S. PATRIOT Act's requirements that organizations provide immediate government access to records apply to SSC. He has read that manufacturing and government organizations rely on efficient document management to meet these broader regulatory imperatives. Finally, Sam wants to implement a disaster recovery system.

Prepare a report that provides Sam with the data he needs to evaluate the company's costly paper-intensive approach to managing documents. You will need to conduct research to provide data to prepare this report. Your report should include the following information:

1. How should SSC prepare for an ERM if it decides to implement one?

2. Using the data collected by Sam, create a spreadsheet that calculates the costs of handling paper at SSC based on average hourly rates per employee of $28. Add the cost of lost documents to this. Then, add the costs of warehousing the paper, which increases by 10% every month due to increases in volume. Present the results showing both monthly totals and a yearly total. Prepare graphs so that Sam can easily identify the projected growth in warehousing costs over the next three years.

3. How can ERM also serve as a disaster recovery system in case of fire, flood, or break-in?

4. Submit your recommendation for an ERM solution. Identify two vendors in your recommendation.

Case 3.2

Business Case: Big Data Analytics is the "Secret Sauce" for Revitalizing McDonald's

With 62 million daily customers and an annual revenue of $27 billion, McDonald's has a virtually unrivaled amount of data at its disposal to analyze. In order to dominate the market, retain its loyal customers, and attract new customers who are skeptical of McDonald's practices and quality, it lends itself to its data, becoming an "information centric organization." What does it mean to be information centric? Instead of using a fixed process of production, service, etc. as a business plan that is product driven, McDonald's uses customer data to dictate its next move as a customer-driven corporation. During the inception of McDonald's in 1940, the McDonald brothers derived a product-driven business centered around fast service and tasty food. While that method was successful before other restaurants entered the fast food market, growth was stunted due to a lack of innovation and change. So, the organization began to collect customer data as a means to monitor successful products, customer demands, and the results of marketing campaigns.

This venture led to McDonald's becoming the premier fast food chain across the United States in the 1980s. Soon after becoming a customer-driven corporation, McDonald's introduced the Happy Meal so families with small children could reduce costs and waste at dinner time, released the Egg McMuffin as the most successful breakfast item of all time, equipped professionals and teenagers with free Wi-Fi to expand its customer segmentation, and provided nutrition details to become the most transparent fast food chain at the time. All of these improvements derived from McDonald's using its immense amount of data to set its chain apart from the rest.

In 2008, to further improve its ability to leverage big data, McDonald's made the transition from average-based metrics to trend analytics. The issue with average-based metrics is that it is hard to compare regions and stores. A store could be growing in its sales and productivity but have the same average metrics as a store that is declining. Using trend analytics allowed McDonald's to combine multiple datasets from multiple data sources to visualize and understand cause-and-effect relationships in individual stores and regions. The correlations it found enabled its analysts to prescribe solutions to problems in sales, production, turnover, and supply chain management to reduce costs and save time. The variables it studies allows McDonald's to create a standardized experience across the world. However, analyzing local data in each store produces minor changes around the organization. For example, most McDonald's locations look the same, but each restaurant is slightly different and optimized for the local market.

A great example of McDonald's big data analysis in action is its updated drive-thru system. All fast food chains have bottlenecks in their drive-thru lanes, but McDonald's average customer wait time is about 3 minutes, which is close to the industry's longest wait time of 214 seconds. One of the most prominent issues in its drive-thru was that customers going through the line for dinner, ordering large meals and searching over the menu for an extended period of time, created a negative experience for each car in line behind them. In response, McDonald's optimized the drive-thru across three components: design, information, and people. Design focused on the improvements to the drive-thru, including better speaker quality and higher resolution, digital menu boards. Information centered around what was on the menu board. In order to decrease order times, McDonald's removed about 40% of the drive-thru menu board. In its third aspect, people, the fast food chain attempted to reduce the negative experiences for those in line by creating a second drive-thru line with a designated order taker for each line, a third drive-thru window, and two production lines.

Another example showing McDonald's commitment to being a customer-driven corporation is its introduction of all day breakfast, which was the highest priority for customers across the United States. Being the corporation with by far the largest share of the fast food market, McDonald's will continue to use its growing data sets to provide the best experience and food to its customers (van Rijmenam, 2016).

Questions

1. Explain McDonald's mission and responsibilities.
2. What limitation did McDonald's face in gaining data that was meaningful to decision-making?
3. Describe trend analytics.
4. Is McDonald's product oriented or customer oriented?
5. Why is the ability to identify patterns and relationships critical to McDonald's operations?

Sources: Compiled from Van Rijmenam (2016) and McDonald's (2017).

Case 3.3

Video Case: Verizon Improves Its Customer Experience with Data Driven Decision-Making

Verizon leverages Teradata's data analytics platform to shift its operations from qualitative decision-making to evidence-based and data-driven decision-making to improve the customer experience. Visit **www.Teradata.com** and search for the video "Verizon: Using Advanced Analytics to Deliver on Their Digital Promise to Help Customers Innovate Their Lifestyle."

1. How does Verizon use Teradata to make decisions?
2. How do the three sectors of Verizon work together to create value for the customer?
3. How does Verizon use data analytics to "penetrate the market"?
4. What impact does customer behavior data have on Verizon's marketing strategy?

"IT Matters" Discussion Board

Research the concept of Big Data. Find at least one company that maintains a "Big Data" database.

1. What is Big Data? Give at least three examples of organizations that have Big Data sets. What are the applications?
2. Discuss one of the organizations that you identified that uses Big Data and briefly describe the use of Big Data in the organization.
3. Discuss as much as you can find about the amount of data they have and how they process it.
4. What did you learn or what lessons did you take away from this research?

Provide at least two hyperlinked references to back up your findings (one for the organization you chose to discuss and one for the concept of big data in general). Post your findings and respond to at least two comments posted by your fellow students.

IT Toolbox

Framework for Generally Accepted Recordkeeping Principles

The Framework for generally accepted recordkeeping principles is a useful tool for managing business records to ensure that they support an enterprise's current and future regulatory, legal, risk mitigation, environmental, and operational requirements.

The framework consists of eight principles or best practices, which also support data governance. These principles were created by ARMA International and legal and IT professionals.

1. **Principle of accountability** Assign a senior executive to oversee a recordkeeping program; adopt policies and procedures to guide personnel; and ensure program audit ability.
2. **Principle of transparency** Document processes and activities of an organization's recordkeeping program in an understandable manner and available to all personnel and appropriate parties.
3. **Principle of integrity** Ensure recordkeeping program is able to reasonably guarantee the authenticity and reliability of records and data.
4. **Principle of protection** Construct the recordkeeping program to ensure a reasonable level of protection to records and information that are private, confidential, privileged, secret, or essential to business continuity.
5. **Principle of compliance** Ensure recordkeeping program complies with applicable laws, authorities, and the organization's policies.
6. **Principle of availability** Maintain records in a manner that ensures timely, efficient, and accurate retrieval of needed information.
7. **Principle of retention** Maintain records and data for an appropriate time based on legal, regulatory, fiscal, operational, and historical requirements.
8. **Principle of disposition** Securely disposed of records when they are no longer required to be maintained by laws or organizational policies.

References

Bing, C. "Data Mining Software Used by Spy Agencies just got more Powerful." *FedScoop*, June 21, 2016.

Burns, E. "Coca-Cola Overcomes Challenges to Seize BI Opportunities." *TechTarget.com*. August 2013.

Burns, E. "Text Analysis Tool Helps Lenovo Zero in on the Customer." *Business Analytics*, April 8, 2016.

BusinessIntelligence.com. "Coca-Cola's Juicy Approach to Big Data." July 29, 2013b. http://businessintelligence.com/bi-insights/coca-colas-juicy-approach-to-big-data

Cattell, J., S. Chilukuri, and M. Levy. "How Big Data Can Revolutionize Pharmaceutical R&D." 2016. http://www.mckinsey.com/industries/pharmaceuticals-and-medical-products/our-insights/how-big-data-can-revolutionize-pharmaceutical-r-and-d

CNNMoney, The Coca-Cola Co (NYSE:KO) 2014.

Columbus, L. "Ten Ways Big Data Is Revolutionizing Marketing and Sales." *Forbes*, May 9, 2016.

Eisenhauer, T. "The Undeniable Benefits of Having a Well-Designed Document Management System." *Axero Solutions*, August 5, 2015.

FirstWind website www.firstwind.com, 2017.

Forbes. "Betting on Big Data." 2015.

Hammond, T. "Top IT Job Skills for 2014: Big Data, Mobile, Cloud, Security." *TechRepublic.com*, January 31, 2014.

Harle, P., A. Havas, and H. Samandari. "The Future of Bank Risk Management." McKinsey & Company, July 2016.

Harvard Business School. "How Coca-Cola Controls Nature's Oranges." November 22, 2015.

HealthCanal. "Where Do You Start When Developing a New Medicine?" March 27, 2014.

IDC. "Explosive Internet of Things Spending to Reach $1.7 Trillion in 2020, According to IDC." June 02, 2015.

King, L. "How Business Intelligence Helps Small Businesses Make Better Decisions." *Huffington Post*, July 28, 2016.

Kitamura, M. "Big Data Partnerships Tackle Drug Development Failures." *Bloomberg News*, March 26, 2014.

Kramer, S. "The High Costs of Dirty Data." *Digitalist*, May 1, 2015.

Ladley, J. "Business Alignment Techniques for Successful and Sustainable Analytics." *CIO*, May 13, 2016.

Liyakasa, K. "Coke Opens Data-Driven Happiness, Builds Out Marketing Decision Engine." *Ad Exchanger*, October 14, 2015.

McDonald's website 2017. https://www.mcdonalds.com/us/en-us/about-us/our-history.html

NIH (National Institute of Health). "Accelerating Medicines Partnership." February 2014. http://www.nih.gov/science/amp/index.htm

Oliphant, T. "How to Make Big Data Insights Work for You." *Business Intelligence*, February 24, 2016.

Ovalsrud, T. "Big Data and Analytics Spending to Hit $1.87 billion" *CIO*, May 24, 2016.

Ransbothom, S. "Coca-Cola's Unique Challenge: Turning 250 Datasets into One." *MIT Sloan Management Review*, May 27, 2015.

RingLead, Inc. "The True Cost of Bad (And Clean) Data." July 17, 2015.

syntheses.net 2017.

The Data Warehousing Institute (TDWI). tdwi.org/portals/business-intelligence.asp. 2014

U.S. Department of Energy. "Wind Vision: A New Era for Wind Power in the United States." http://energy.gov/eere/wind/maps/wind-vision, March 12, 2015.

Van Rijmenam, M. "From Big Data to Big Mac; how McDonalds leverages Big Data." *DataFloq.com*, August 15, 2016.

Van Rijmenam, M. "How Coca-Cola Takes a Refreshing Approach on Big Data." *DataFloq*, July 18, 2016.

Wise, L. "Evaluating Business Intelligence in the Cloud." *CIO*, March 9, 2016.

CHAPTER 4

Networks, Collaborative Technology, and the Internet of Things

CHAPTER OUTLINE	LEARNING OBJECTIVES
Case 4.1 Opening Case: Sony Builds an IPv6 Network to Fortify Competitive Edge	
4.1 Network Fundamentals	**4.1 Describe** the different types of networks and the basic functions of business networks.
4.2 Internet Protocols (IP), APIs, and Network Capabilities	**4.2 Understand** the purpose of IPs and APIs and compare wireless 3G, 4G, and 5G networks and how they support businesses.
4.3 Mobile Networks	**4.3 Describe** the growth in mobile data traffic and understand the components of the mobile infrastructure including near-field communication. List the business functions that near-field communication supports.
4.4 Collaborative Technologies and the Internet of Things (IoT)	**4.4 Evaluate** performance improvements gained from collaborative technology and understand concept of the Internet of Things (IoT)
Case 4.2 Business Case: Google Maps API for Business	
Case 4.3 Video Case: Small Island Telecom Company Goes Global	

Introduction

Across all types and sizes of organizations, the Internet and networks have changed the way that business is conducted. Twenty years ago, computers were glorified typewriters that could not communicate with one another. If we wanted to communicate we used the telephone. Today computers constantly exchange data with each other over distance and time to provide companies with a number of significant advantages. The convergence of access technologies, cloud, 5G networks, multitasking mobile operating systems, and collaboration platforms continues to change the nature of work, the way we do business, how machines interact, and other things not yet imagined. In this chapter you will learn about the different types of networks, how they affect the way that businesses communicate with customers, vendors, and other businesses, and how the largest network, the Internet, is enabling massive automatic data collection efforts from "things" rather than from people.

Case 4.1 Opening Case

Grasko/Shutterstock

Rob Arnold/Alamy Stock Photo

JamesBrey/Getty Images

Sony Builds an IPv6 Network to Fortify Competitive Edge

Sony's Rapid Business Growth

In the early 2000s, Sony Corporation had been engaged in strategic mergers and acquisitions to strengthen itself against intensifying competition (**Figure 4.1**). By 2007 Sony's enterprise network (internal network) had become too complex and was incapable of supporting communication, operations, and further business growth (**Table 4.1**). The enterprise network was based on IPv4. A serious limitation was that the IPv4 network could not provide real-time collaboration among business units and group companies.

Expansion efforts were taking too long because of the complicated structure of the network, and total cost of ownership (TCO) was increasing. Also, a number of technical limitations were blocking internal communications. To eliminate these limitations, Sony decided to invest in IPv6-based networks.

Network Limitations

Many of the Sony Group companies had developed independently—and had independent networks. Devices connected to the independent networks were using the same IP addresses. That situation is comparable to users having duplicate telephone numbers—making it impossible to know which phone was being called. Also, phones with the same number could not call each other.

Once these networks were integrated, the duplicate IP address caused traffic-routing conflicts. Routing conflicts, in turn, led to the following problems:

1. Sony's employee communication options were severely limited, which harmed productivity.

2. File sharing and real-time communication were not possible.

3. Introducing cloud services was difficult and time-consuming.

Migration to IPv6 Networks: An Investment in the Future

With its virtually unlimited number of IP addresses, **IPv6** would support Sony's long-term, next-generation **information and communications technology (ICT)** infrastructure strategy and improve collaboration and productivity.

Migrating from IPv4 to IPv6 involved 700 sites, hundreds of thousands of networking devices, and hundreds of thousands of network users spread around the globe. During the transition, Sony realized that it was necessary to support both IP protocols. That is, while Sony wanted to eventually completely migrate to IPv6, the IPv6 would supplement and coexist with the existing enterprise IPv4 network, rather than replace it. Running both protocols on the same network at the same time was necessary because Sony's legacy devices and apps only worked on IPv4.

Sony selected Cisco as a key partner in the migration and integration of IPv4 and IPv6 traffic because of the maturity of its IPv6

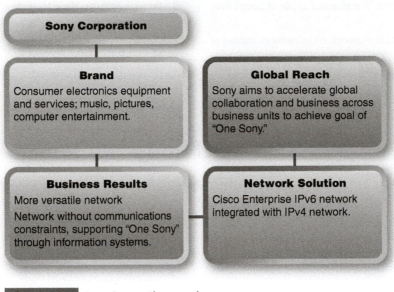

FIGURE 4.1 Sony Corporation overview.

TABLE 4.1	**Opening Case Overview**
Company	Sony Corporation, Sony.com
Location	Headquartered in Tokyo, Japan. Over 700 total network sites worldwide.
Industries	One of the largest consumer electronics and entertainment companies in the world, including audio/video equipment, semiconductors, computers, and video games. Also engaged in production and distribution of recorded music, motion picture, and video.
Business challenges	• Network expansion required too much time due to complexity of enterprise network. • Networking TCO (total cost of ownership) was continually increasing. • Numerous constraints on networks obstructing communication between companies in Sony Group.
Network technology	• Integrated its IPv4 networks with new IPv6 solutions from Cisco. The integrated IPv4/IPv6 network has been used by Sony as infrastructure for the development of new products and enterprise-wide collaboration. • Sony also upgraded its Cisco switches at the corporate data center, campuses, and remote offices to handle concurrent IPv4 and IPv6 traffic.

technology. The integrated network has been used by Sony as infrastructure for product development. Sony also upgraded its Cisco network switches at the corporate data center, campuses, and remote offices to handle concurrent IPv4 and IPv6 traffic.

Business Results

The use of IPv6 eliminated the issue of conflicting IP addresses, enabling Sony employees in all divisions to take advantage of the productivity benefits of real-time collaboration applications. Other business improvements are as follows:

- Flexibility to launch new businesses quickly.
- Reduced TCO of enterprise network.
- Network without communications constraints, supporting "One Sony" through information systems:

  ○ Decreased lead time of connecting a new group to the enterprise network.
  ○ Automated network processes by ridding of manually configured NAT devices.

However, Sony's networks are far from perfect, especially when it comes to its PlayStation Network Service. Unfortunately for gamers, the PSN consistently crashes without warning and for relatively long periods of time. The first crash of 2016 on January 4th caused the service to be down for about 8 hours for all users. During that time, many users could not play their games, use streaming services, or access the online store.

Questions

1. Explain how Sony's IPv4 enterprise network was restricting the productivity of its workers.

2. What problems did duplicate IP addresses cause at Sony? Give an analogy.

3. Why did Sony need to run both protocols on its network instead of replacing IPv4 with IPv6?

4. Describe the strategic benefit of Sony's IPv6 implementation.

5. Do research to determine the accuracy of this prediction: "Today, almost everything on the Internet is reachable over IPv4. In a few years, both IPv4 and IPv6 will be required for universal access."

Sources: Cisco (2016) and Neal (2016).

4.1 Network Fundamentals

Computer networks are a set of computers connected together for the purpose sharing resources.

Today's managers need to understand the technical side of **computer networks** to make intelligent investment decisions that impact operations and competitive position. Enterprises run on networks—wired and mobile—and depend upon their ability to interface with other networks and applications. Computer networks are changing significantly in their capacity and capabilities.

Network Types

Computers on a network are called nodes. The connection between computers can be done via cabling, most commonly through Ethernet, or wirelessly through radio waves. Connected computers share resources, such as the Internet, printers, file servers, and other devices. The multipurpose connections enabled by a network allow a single computer to do more than if it were not connected to other devices. The most well-known network is the Internet.

Computer networks are typically categorized by their scope. Common types of networks are shown in **Table 4.2**. Of these, LAN and WAN are the two primary and best-known categories of networks.

TABLE 4.2   Types of Networks

Acronym	Type	Characteristics	Example
LAN	Local Area Network	Connects network devices over a relatively short distance Owned, controlled, and managed by one individual or organization	Office building School Home
WAN	Wide Area Network	Spans a large physical distance Geographically dispersed collection of LANs Owned and managed by multiple entities	Internet Large company
WLAN	Wireless Local Area Network	LAN based on Wi-Fi wireless network technology	Internet Large company
MAN	Metropolitan Area Network	Spans a physical area larger than a LAN but smaller than a WAN Owned and operated by a single entity, e.g., government agency, large company	City Network of suburban fire stations
SAN	Storage Area Network Server Area Network	Connects servers to data storage devices	High-performance database
CAN	Campus Area Network Cluster Area Network	Spans multiple LANs but smaller than a MAN	University Local business campus
PAN	Personal Area Network	Spans a small physical space, typically 35 feet or less Connects personal IT devices of a single individual	Laptop, smartphone, and portable printer connected together

Intranets, Extranets, and Virtual Private Networks

Intranets are used within a company for data access, sharing, and collaboration. They are portals or gateways that provide easy and inexpensive browsing and search capabilities. Colleges and universities rely on intranets to provide services to students and faculty. Using screen sharing and other groupware tools, intranets can support team work.

An **extranet** is a private, company-owned network that can be logged into remotely via the Internet. Typical users are suppliers, vendors, partners, or customers. Basically, an extranet is a network that connects two or more companies so they can securely share information. Since authorized users remotely access content from a central server, extranets can drastically reduce storage space on individual hard drives.

A major concern is the security of the transmissions that could be intercepted or compromised. One solution is to use **virtual private networks (VPNs)**, which encrypt the packets before they are transferred over the network. VPNs consist of encryption software and hardware that encrypt, send, and decrypt transmissions, as shown in **Figure 4.2**. In effect, instead of using a leased line to create a dedicated, physical connection, a company can invest in VPN technology to create virtual connections routed through the Internet from the company's private network to the remote site or employee. Extranets can be expensive to implement and maintain because of hardware, software, and employee training costs if hosted internally rather than by an application service provider (ASP).

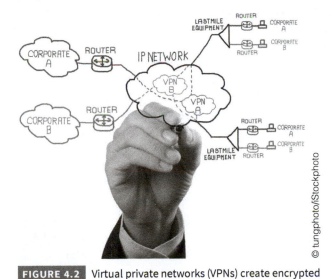

FIGURE 4.2 Virtual private networks (VPNs) create encrypted connections to company networks.

Network Terminology

To be able to evaluate the different types of networks and the factors that determine their functionality, you need to be familiar with the following network terminology:

- **Modem**   It is a device designed to adapt/modify the information signals in a way that can be transported by the media. The word modem is composed of two terms: *Modu*lator and *Dem*odulator, the modulator adapts the information signal in order to be transported by the media and the demodulator does the inverse process at reception. Digital modems are called "CSU/DSU" (Channel Service Unit/Data Service Units).

- **Modulation and coding**   These are the specific techniques used by the modem to adapt the signal to the media. There are several ways to do this process like Amplitude Modulation, Phase modulation, Frequency Modulation. In a few words modulation/coding is to decide how the "1s" and "0s" are represented in terms of voltages and/or frequencies.

- **Signal**   It is the information we want to send, every signal is composed of a combination of 1s and 0s. Every signal has a frequency spectrum.

- **Signal frequency spectrum**   These are all the frequency components of a signal. The more 1s and 0s are transmitted per unit of time (i.e., per second) the highest will be the frequency components of a signal. The bandwidth of the signal is measured in hertz or number of variations per second. The more 1s and 0s are transmitted within one second the higher will be the frequency spectrum or signal bandwidth.

- **Media bandwidth**   Every media (i.e., Copper, Coaxial, and Fiber Optics) has a limitation in the range of frequency signals that can move through it without significant attenuation. The bandwidth of the media varies by type, is limited, and typically can't accept the entire signals frequency spectrum (**Figure 4.3**). The range of frequencies that can move through the media without significant attenuation is called bandwidth and it is also measured in hertz.

  The mission of a modem/DSU-CSU is to adapt the information signal so that it can move through the media without significant attenuation. Typically "significant attenuation" means that the signal has not lost more than half of its original power.

  Generally speaking, the media bandwidth (in hertz) can be defined as the range of frequencies (i.e., fmax – fmin) at which the signal has not lost more than 50% of its power. Upon coding-modulation techniques, it is possible to pack many binary symbols in one hertz (many binary symbols per second), for example, it is possible to pack 5 bits in each hertz of the signal. So if the bandwidth is 200,000 hertz then up to 1,000,000 bits/s (2000,000 hertz *5 bits/hertz) can be transmitted.

  A different modulation/coding technique (i.e., for the same signal and the same media) might pack 10 bits per every hertz of bandwidth and up to 2 Mbits/s (200,000 hertz *10 bits/hertz = 2 Mbits/s). The media bandwidth provided should be capable of transporting this coded-modulated signal without significant attenuation.

- **Capacity or digital bandwidth**   It is the maximum amount of bits/second that can be transmitted over the media. Upon ideal conditions, it is possible to reach the maximum capacity in a connection although this seldom happens (see **Figure 4.4**).

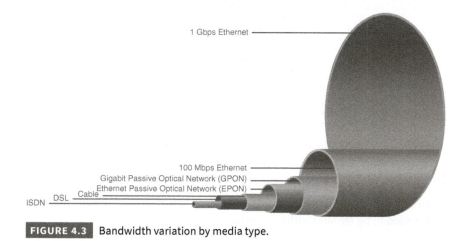

1 Gbps Ethernet

100 Mbps Ethernet
Gigabit Passive Optical Network (GPON)
Ethernet Passive Optical Network (EPON)
ISDN   DSL   Cable

FIGURE 4.3   Bandwidth variation by media type.

Functions Supported by Business Networks

Figure 4.5 describes the basic business functions supported business networks: communication, mobility, collaboration, relationships, and search. These functions depend on network **switches** and **routers**—devices that transmit data packets from their source to their destination based on IP addresses. A switch acts as a controller, enabling networked devices to talk to each other efficiently. For example, switches connect computers, printers, and servers within an office building. Switches create a network. Routers connect networks. A router links computers

Bandwidth Monitor
910
819
728
637
546
455
364
273
182
91
0
MBytes
Enterprise
Current Policy Threshold
Current Policy Threshold(06:51:55): 300
06:51:55
06:52:23
06:52:51
06:53:19
06:53:47
06:54:15
06:54:43
06:55:11
06:55:39
06:56:07
06:56:35
Current Bandwidth Usage - Last 5 Minutes

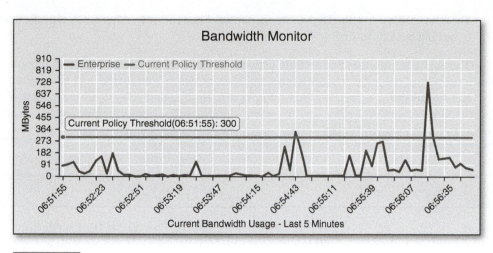

FIGURE 4.4 Bandwidth capacity monitor.

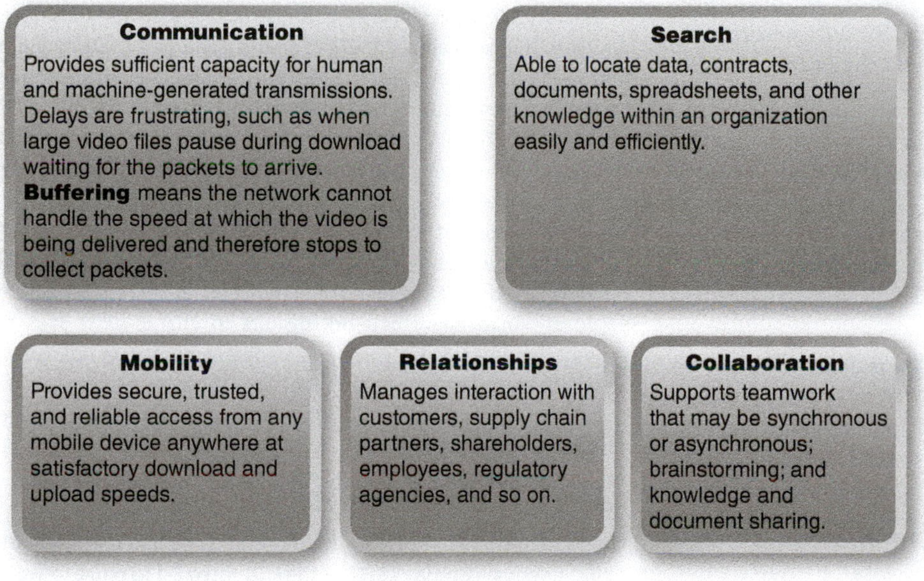

Communication
Provides sufficient capacity for human and machine-generated transmissions. Delays are frustrating, such as when large video files pause during download waiting for the packets to arrive. Buffering means the network cannot handle the speed at which the video is being delivered and therefore stops to collect packets.
Search
Able to locate data, contracts, documents, spreadsheets, and other knowledge within an organization easily and efficiently.
Mobility
Provides secure, trusted, and reliable access from any mobile device anywhere at satisfactory download and upload speeds.
Relationships
Manages interaction with customers, supply chain partners, shareholders, employees, regulatory agencies, and so on.
Collaboration
Supports teamwork that may be synchronous or asynchronous; brainstorming; and knowledge and document sharing.

FIGURE 4.5 Basic functions of business networks.

to the Internet, so users can share the connection. Routers act like a dispatcher, choosing the best paths for packets to travel.

Investments in network infrastructure, including data networks, IP addresses, routers, and switches are business decisions because of their impact on productivity, security, user experiences, and customer service.

Quality of Service

An important management decision is the network's **quality of service (QoS)**, especially for delay-sensitive data such as real-time voice and high-quality video. The higher the required QoS, the more expensive the technologies needed to manage organizational networks. Bandwidth-intensive apps are important to business processes, but they also strain network capabilities and resources. Regardless of the type of traffic, networks must provide secure, predictable, measurable, and sometimes guaranteed services for certain types of traffic. For example, QoS technologies can be applied to create two tiers of traffic:

- **Prioritize traffic** Data and apps that are time-delay-sensitive or **latency-sensitive apps**, such as voice and video, are given priority on the network.

- **Throttle traffic**   In order to give latency-sensitive apps priority, other types of traffic need to be held back (throttled).

The ability to prioritize and throttle network traffic is referred to as **traffic shaping** and forms the core of the hotly debated Net neutrality issue, which is discussed in **IT at Work 4.1**.

Net neutrality is a principle that Internet service providers (ISPs) and their regulators treat all Internet traffic the same way. It's essentially equal opportunity for Internet speeds and access to website—no unfair fast or slow lanes and no blocking of anything that's legal on your phone, computer, or table.

IT at Work 4.1

Net Neutrality Debate Intensifies

In 2016, the battle over the complicated issue of net neutrality heated up due to AT&T's purchase of Time-Warner. However, with AT&T's takeover of Time-Warner, which owns HBO and DC Comics, it is almost certain that AT&T will give priority to customers who try to access its newfound property (Pachal, 2016). On the opposing side of that issue is traffic shaping. Traffic shaping creates a two-tier system for specific purposes such as:

1. Time-sensitive data are given priority over traffic that can be delayed briefly with little-to-no adverse effect. Companies like Comcast and AT&T argue that Net neutrality rules hurt consumers. Certain applications are more sensitive to delays than others, such as streaming video and Internet phone services. Managing data transfer makes it possible to assure a certain level of performance or QoS.

2. In a corporate environment, business-related traffic may be given priority over other traffic, in effect, by paying a premium price for that service. Proponents of traffic shaping argue that ISPs should be able to charge more to customers who want to pay a premium for priority service.

Specifically, traffic is shaped by delaying the flow of less important network traffic, such as bulk data transfers, P2P file-sharing programs, and BitTorrent traffic.

Traffic shaping is hotly debated by those in favor of Net neutrality. They want a one-tier system in which all Internet data packets are treated the same, regardless of their content, destination, or source. In contrast, those who favor the two-tiered system argue that there have always been different levels of Internet service and that a two-tiered system would enable more freedom of choice and promote Internet-based commerce.

Federal Communications Commission's 2010 Decision

On December 21, 2010, the Federal Communications Commission (FCC) approved a compromise that created two classes of Internet access: one for fixed-line providers and the other for the wireless Net. In effect, the new rules are **Net semi-neutrality**. The FCC banned any outright blocking of and "unreasonable discrimination" against websites or applications by **fixed-line broadband** providers. But the rules do not explicitly forbid "paid prioritization," which would allow a company to pay an ISP for faster data transmission. Net neutrality supporters include major internet companies who provide the content you read and watch online, including AOL, Facebook, Netflix, Twitter, and Vimeo who don't want to be discriminated against by network owners. Those

against it include AT&T, Comcast Time Warner Cable, Verizon, and other internet service providers who own the networks and fear price controls.

Net Neutrality Overturned in 2014

In January 2014, an appeals court struck down the FCC's 2010 decision. The court allowed ISPs to create a two-tiered Internet, but promised close supervision to avoid anticompetitive practices, and banned "unreasonable" discrimination against providers.

On April 24, 2014 FCC Chairman Tom Wheeler reported that his agency would propose new rules to comply with the court's decision. These new rules were approved by the FCC in 2015. Wheeler stated that these rules "would establish that behavior harmful to consumers or competition by limiting the openness of the Internet will not be permitted" (Wheeler, 2014). But Wheeler's proposal would allow network owners to charge extra fees to content providers. This decision has angered consumer advocates and Net neutrality advocates who view Wheeler with suspicion because of his past work as a lobbyist for the cable industry and wireless phone companies.

Rolling Back Net Neutrality Protections in 2017

The process to overhaul how the Internet is regulated is now officially underway. On May 18, 2017 the FCC voted 2-1 to move forward with a proposal to roll back net neutrality protections. The controversial vote is the first step in a lengthy process to overturn the rules put into place during the Obama administration. Longtime net neutrality advocates predict there will be negative consequences for businesses and consumers if net neutrality is overturned. Michael Cheah, general counsel at Vimeo, summed it up by saying that net neutrality is about "allowing consumers to pick the winners and losers and not [having] the cable companies make those decisions for them" (Fiegerman, 2017).

IT at Work Questions

1. What is Net neutrality?
2. What tiers are created by traffic shaping?
3. Why did the battle over Net neutrality intensify in 2014?
4. Did the FCC's 2015 net neutrality rules favor either side of the debate? Explain.
5. What consequences may occur when the 2015 net neutrality rules are overturned?

Sources: Compiled from Federal Communications Commission (fcc.gov, 2017), Fiegerman (2017), Pachal (2016), Wheeler (2014), and various blog posts.

Questions

1. Name the different types of networks.
2. What is meant by "bandwidth"?
3. What is the difference between an intranet and an extranet?
4. How does a virtual private network (VPN) provide security?
5. What is the purpose of a modem?
6. Describe the basic functions of business networks.
7. How do investments in network infrastructure impact an organization?
8. Name the two tiers of traffic to which quality of service is applied.

4.2 | Internet Protocols (IP), APIs, and Network Capabilities

The basic technology that makes global communication possible is a network **protocol** commonly known as an **Internet Protocol (IP)**. Each device attached to a network has a unique **IP address** that enables it to send and receive files. Files are broken down into blocks known as **packets** in order to be transmitted over a network to their destination's IP address. Initially, networks used **IP Version 4 (IPv4)**. In April 2014 ARIN, the group that oversees Internet addresses, reported that IPv4 addresses were running out—making it urgent that enterprises move to the newer **IP Version 6 (IPv6)** (**Figure 4.6**).

The IPv6 Internet protocol has features that are not present in IPv4. For example, IPv6 simplifies aspects of how addresses are assigned, how networks are renumbered and places responsibility for packet fragmentation when packets are processed in routers. The IPv6 protocol does not offer direct interoperability with IPv4, instead it creates a parallel, independent network. Fortunately, several transition mechanisms, such as NAT64 and 6rd, have been developed to allow IPv6 hosts to communicate with IPv4 servers.

Network protocols serve the following three basic functions:

1. Send data to the correct recipient(s).
2. Physically transmit data from source to destination, with security protected as needed.
3. Receive messages and send responses to the correct recipient(s).

The capacity and capabilities of data networks provide opportunities for more automated operations and new business strategies. M2M communications over wireless and wired

Internet Protocol (IP) is the method by which data are sent from one device to another over a network.

IP address is a unique identifier for each device that communicates with a network that identifies and locates each device. An IP address is comparable to a telephone number or home address.

Packet is a piece of a message that is collected and re-assembled with the other pieces of the same message at their destination. To improve communication performance and reliability, each larger message sent between two network devices is often subdivided into packets.

IP Version 4 (IPv4) has been Internet protocol for over three decades, but has reached the limits of its 32-bit address design. It is difficult to configure, it is running out of addressing space, and it provides no features for site renumbering to allow for an easy change of Internet Service Provider (ISP), among other limitations.

IP Version 6 (IPv6) is the most recent version of the Internet Protocol. IPv6 is replacing IPv4 because of IPv4's limitations in number of IP addresses it can generate. IPv6 has a 128-bit address and allows 7.9×10^{28} times as many addresses as IPv4, which provides about 4.3 billion addresses.

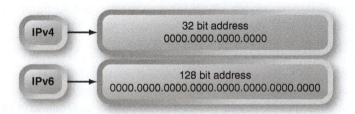

FIGURE 4.6 IPv4 addresses have 4 groups of four alphanumeric characters, which allow for 2^{32} or roughly 4.3 billion unique IP addresses. IPv6 addresses have 8 groups of alphanumeric characters, which allows for 2^{128}, or 340 trillion, trillion, trillion addresses. IPv6 also offers enhanced quality of service that is needed by the latest in video, interactive games, and e-commerce.

networks automate operations, for instance, by triggering action such as sending a message or closing a valve. The speed at which data can be sent depends on several factors, including capacity, server usage, computer usage, noise, and the amount of network traffic. Transfer rate or speed is an instantaneous measurement.

Comparing 3G, 4G, 4G LTE, and 5G Network Standards

Over the past 20 years, networks have evolved from 3G networks designed for voice and data to 4G and 5G networks that support broadband Internet connectivity. In its 2016 report, SNS Research, a major market analysis and consulting firm, announced its forecast of 5G network contribution to the world economy. Experts predict that by 2020, "LTE and 5G infrastructure investments are expected to account for a market worth $32 billion" (*PRNewswire*, 2016).

3G networks support multimedia and broadband services over a wider distance and at faster speeds than prior generation networks. 3G networks have far greater ranges than 1G and 2G networks since they use large satellite connections to telecommunication towers.

4G networks are digital, or IP, networks that enable even faster data transfer rates. 4G delivers average *realistic* download rates of 3 Mbps or higher (as opposed to *theoretical* rates, which are much higher). In contrast, today's 3G networks typically deliver average download speeds about one-tenth of that rate.

5G networks—the coming generation of broadband technology. 5G builds on the foundation created by 4G. 5G will dramatically increase the speed at which data is transferred across the network.

Unlike its predecessors, 2G and 3G that have a circuit-switched subsystem, 4G is based purely on the packet-based IP. Users can obtain 4G wireless connectivity through one of the following standards:

1. **WiMAX** is a technology standard for long-range wireless networks. WiMax is based on the IEEE 802.16 standard. IEEE 802.16 specifications are as follows:

   - Range: 30 miles (50 km) from base station.
   - Speed: 70 megabits per second (Mbps).
   - Line-of-sight not needed between user and base station.

   WiMAX operates on the same basic principles as Wi-Fi in that it transmits data from one device to another via radio signals.

2. **Long-Term Evolution (LTE)** is a GSM-based technology that provides the fastest and most consistent download speeds and most closely follows the United Nation technical standard for 4G networks. In the United States, LTE is deployed by Verizon, AT&T, and T-Mobile. LTE capabilities include the following:

   - Speed: Downlink data rates of 100 Mbps and uplink data rates of 50 Mbps.

Improved network performance, which is measured by its *data transfer capacity,* provides fantastic opportunities for mobility, mobile commerce, collaboration, supply chain management, remote work, and other productivity gains.

5G mobile networks will offer huge gains in both speed and capacity over existing 4G networks—along with opportunities at the operations and strategic levels. In the short term, the 5G infrastructure build-out will create new jobs. In the longer term, 5G will create entirely new markets and economic opportunities driven by superior mobile capabilities in industries ranging from health care to automotive.

5G networks are designed to support the escalation in mobile data consumption, with users demanding higher data speeds and traffic volumes expected to increase by hundreds or even thousands of times over the next 10 years. It is likely that 5G networks will have to deliver baseline data speeds of 100 Mbit/s and peak speeds of up to 10 Gbit/s. 5G will make it easier to send texts, make calls, and download and upload Ultra HD and 3D videos. 5G operates with a 5-Ghz signal and is set to offer speeds of up to 1 gigabyte per second for tens of thousands of connections or tens of megabytes per second for tens of thousands of connections.

The move to 5G is being driven by the significant increase in the number of devices to be supported. Mobile networks will no longer be concerned primarily with person-to-person communications, as the Internet of Things (IoT) creates billions of new devices for remote sensing, telemetry, and control applications which will lead to huge numbers of machine-to-machine and person-to-machine interactions. Although 5G isn't expected until 2020, many organizations are already investing in the infrastructure required to run this new mobile wireless standard.

Circuit versus Packet Switching

All generations of networks are based on switching. Prior to 4G, networks included **circuit switching**, which is slower than **packet switching**. 4G was first to be fully packet switched, which significantly improved performance. The two basic types of switching are as follows:

Circuit switching   A circuit is a dedicated connection between a source and destination. In the past, when a call was placed between two landline phones, a circuit or connection was created that remained until one party hung up. Circuit switching is older technology that originated with telephone calls; it is inefficient for digital transmission.

Packet switching   Packet switching transfers data or voice in packets. Files are broken into packets, numbered sequentially, and routed individually to their destination. When received at the destination, the packets are reassembled into their proper sequence.

Wireless networks use packet switching and wireless routers whose antennae transmit and receive packets. At some point, wireless routers are connected by cables to wired networks. The first real network to run on packet-switching technology was ARPAnet described in **Tech Note 4.1**.

Tech Note 4.1

Origin of the Internet, E-mail, and TCP/IP

The Advanced Research Projects Agency network (ARPAnet) was the first real network to run on packet-switching technology. In October 1969, computers at Stanford University, UCLA, and two other U.S universities connected for the first time—making them the first hosts on what would become the Internet. ARPAnet was designed for research, education, and government agencies. ARPAnet provided a communications network linking the country in the event that a military attack or nuclear war destroyed conventional communications systems.

In 1971 e-mail was developed by Ray Tomlinson, who used the @ symbol to separate the username from the network's name, which became the domain name.

On January 1, 1983, ARPAnet computers switched over to the **transmission control protocol/Internet protocols (TCP/IPs)** developed by Vinton Cerf. A few hundred computers were affected by the switch. The original ARPAnet protocol had been limited to 1,000 hosts, but the adoption of the TCP/IP standard made larger numbers of hosts possible. The number of Internet hosts in the domain name system (DNS) topped 1.05 billion in 2016, almost double the number reported in 2010.

Application Program Interfaces and Operating Systems

When software developers create applications, they must write and compile the code for a specific operating system (OS). **Figure 4.7** lists the common OSs. Each OS communicates with hardware in its own unique way; each OS has a specific API that programmers must use. Video game consoles and other hardware devices also have **application program interfaces (APIs)** that run software programs.

Application program interface (API)   An interface is the boundary where two separate systems meet. An API provides a standard way for different things, such as software, content, or websites, to talk to each other in a way that they both understand without extensive programming.

FIGURE 4.7 Common mobile and desktop operating systems. Each computer OS provides an API for programmers. Mobile OSs are designed around touchscreen input.

What Is an API?

An API consists of a set of functions, commands, and protocols used by programmers to build software for an OS. The API allows programmers to use predefined functions or reusable codes to interact with an OS without having to write a software program from scratch. APIs simplify the programmer's job.

APIs are the common method for accessing information, websites, and databases. They were created as gateways to popular apps such as Twitter, Facebook, and Amazon and enterprise apps provided by SAP, Oracle, NetSuite, and many other vendors.

Automated API

The current trend is toward automatically created APIs that are making innovative IT developments possible. Here are two examples of the benefits of automated APIs:

- Websites such as the European Union Patent office have mappings of every one of their pages to both URLs for browser access and URLs for REST APIs. Whenever a new page is published, both access methods are supported.

- McDonald's, along with Unilever and Gatorade, are using automated API's to bring advertisements to Snapchat users. The social network app is using an auction-based system and targeting to choose which users see which advertisements (Joseph, 2016).

API Value Chain in Business

APIs deliver more than half of all the traffic to major companies like Twitter and eBay. APIs are used to access business assets, such as customer information or a product or service, as shown in **Figure 4.8**. IT developers use APIs to quickly and easily connect diverse data and services to each other. APIs from Google, Twitter, Amazon, Facebook, Accuweather, Sears, and E*Trade are used to create many thousands of applications. For example, Google Maps API is a collection of APIs used by developers to create customized Google Maps that can be accessed on a Web browser or mobile devices. **Tech Note 4.2** describes a new API that Amazon developed for its Internet assistant, Alexa.

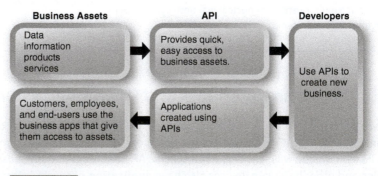

FIGURE 4.8 API value chain in business.

Tech Note 4.2

Amazon Develops New API for Alexa

Online retail giant Amazon announced in 2016 its new and improved API for its voice-automated speaker Alexa, along with other developed applications. The new API allows software developers to increase the efficiency of Alexa's list feature, which allows users to add items to their lists within Alexa. For example, a user can ask Alexa to "add buy soccer cleats" to their to-do lists (Zeman, 2016). This application extends to shopping lists, buy lists, and even music playlists.

The new API called the List Skills API means that developers will have a standardized voice interaction model instead of having to create one of their own. In other words, applications like Alexa will all have standardized instructions that users can take advantage of universally. Similarly, Apple developed Siri for iPhones, Apple compuers, and iPads. List Skills API gives customers the ability to add anything to their lists or give commands across any device or application that uses it.

The API value chain takes many forms because the organization that owns the business asset may or may not be the same as the organization that builds the APIs. Different people or organizations may build, distribute, and market the applications. At the end of the chain are end-users who benefit from the business asset. Often, many APIs are used to create a new user experience. The business benefits of APIs are listed in **Table 4.3**.

TABLE 4.3   **Business Benefits of APIs**

Characteristic	Benefit
APIs are channels to new customers and markets	APIs enable partners to use business assets to extend the reach of a company's products or services to customers and markets they might not
APIs promote innovation	Through an API, people who are committed to a challenge or problem can solve it themselves
APIs are a better way to organize IT	APIs promote innovation by allowing everyone in a company to use each other's assets without delay
APIs create a path to lots of Apps	Apps are going to be a crucial channel in the next 10 years. Apps are powered by APIs. Developers use APIs and combinations of APIs to create new user experiences

Questions

1. Why has IPv6 become increasingly important?
2. What is the difference between IPv4 and Ipv6?
3. What is the purpose of an IP address?
4. What are the benefits of using an API?
5. What is the difference between 4G and 5G?
6. What is the most current network standard?
7. What benefits will the upcoming 5G network standard offer businesses?
8. What is the difference between circuit switching and packet switching?

4.3 | Mobile Networks and Near-Field Communication

In the 21st-century global economy, advanced wireless networks are a foundation on which global economic activity takes place. Current 4G and 5G networks and technologies provide that foundation for moving entire economies. For any nation to stay competitive and prosperous, it is imperative that investment and upgrades in these technologies continue to advance to satisfy demand. Cisco forecasts that the average global mobile connection speed will more than double from the current 1.4 to 3 Mbps and 5G networks are promising speeds that will be 100 times faster than current speeds. The factors that are driving global mobile traffic are shown in **Figure 4.9**.

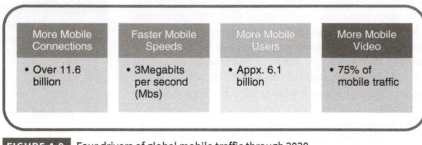

More Mobile Connections	Faster Mobile Speeds	More Mobile Users	More Mobile Video
• Over 11.6 billion	• 3Megabits per second (Mbs)	• Appx. 6.1 billion	• 75% of mobile traffic

FIGURE 4.9 Four drivers of global mobile traffic through 2020.

Increase in Mobile Network Traffic and Users

In its most recent Visual Networking Index Forecast (VNI), Cisco reported that mobile data traffic has grown 400 million times over the past 15 years. They also predict that by 2020 monthly global mobile data traffic will be 30.6 **Exabytes**; number of mobile-connected devices will exceed 11.6 billion (exceeding the world's projected population of 7.8 billion) and smartphones will account for 81% of total mobile traffic. This includes a major increase in machine-to-machine communications and the number of wearable technology devices.

Exabyte is one quintillion bytes (1,000,000,000,000,000,000 Bytes) which is the equivalent of 1,000 petabytes of data or 7 trillion online video clips. Five Exabytes is equal to all words ever spoken by human beings.

Smartphone users are expected to rise from the 2.6 billion reported in 2014 to 6.1 billion in 2020 and 80% of these new smartphone users will be located in Asia Pacific, the Middle East, and Africa. Much of that traffic will be driven by billions of devices talking to other devices wirelessly and consumers' growing demand for more and more videos.

Zettabyte is one sextillion bytes (1,000,000,000,000,000,000,000 Bytes) which is approximately equal to 1,000 Exabytes.

According to the *Cisco Visual Networking Index (VNI): Forecast and Methodology 2015–2020.* (Cisco 2016), annual global IP traffic will reach 2.3 **Zettabytes** or 194 Exabytes per month and smartphone traffic will exceed PC traffic by 2020. **Figure 4.10** lists the milestones that mobile data traffic will reach by 2020.

Busy-hour Internet Traffic	Increase by factor of 4.6 Average traffic will only increase by factor of 2
PCs	29% of network traffic
Smartphones	30% of network traffic
Wireless & Mobile	67% of total network traffic
Global Internet Traffic	Equivalent to 95 times the volume of the entire global Internet in 2005
Devices connected to IP networks	Three times the entire global population
Broadband Speeds	Increase 100%
Video	It will take an individual 5 million years to watch the amount of video that will cross global IP networks EACH month!

FIGURE 4.10 Mobile Data Traffic Milestone by 2020.

Higher Demand for High-Capacity Mobile Networks

This increase in mobile networks capacity and use is increasing the demand for high-capacity mobile networks. The four drivers of the increase in global mobile traffic demand are shown in Figure 4.10. Demand for high-capacity networks is growing at unprecedented rates. Examples of high-capacity networks are wireless mobile, satellite, wireless sensor, and VoIP (voice over Internet Protocol) such as Skype. **Voice over IP (VoIP)** networks carry voice calls by converting voice (analog signals) to digital signals that are sent as packets. With VoIP, voice and data transmissions travel in packets over telephone wires. VoIP has grown to become one of the most used and least costly ways to communicate. Improved productivity, flexibility, and advanced features make VoIP an appealing technology.

Mobile Infrastructure

Enterprises are moving away from the ad hoc adoption of mobile devices and network infrastructure to a more strategic planning build-out of their mobile capabilities. As technologies that make up the mobile infrastructure evolve, identifying strategic technologies and avoiding wasted investments require more extensive planning and forecasting. Factors to consider are the network demands of multitasking mobile devices, more robust mobile OSs, and their applications. Mobile infrastructure consists of the integration of technology, software, support, standards, security measures, and devices for the management and delivery of wireless communications, including the following.

Wi-Fi and Bluetooth   Bluetooth is a short-range—up to 100 meters or 328 feet—wireless communications technology found in billions of devices, such as smartphones, computers, medical devices, and home entertainment products. When two Bluetooth-enabled devices connect to each other, this is called pairing.

Bluetooth is a short-range wireless communications technology.

Wi-Fi is the standard way computers connect to wireless networks. Nearly all computers have built-in Wi-Fi chips that allow users to find and connect to wireless routers. The router must be connected to the Internet in order to provide Internet access to connected devices.

Wi-Fi is the standard way computers connect to wireless networks.

Wi-Fi technology allows devices to share a network or Internet connection without the need to connect to a commercial network. Wi-Fi networks beam packets over short distances using part of the radio spectrum, or they can extend over larger areas, such as municipal Wi-Fi networks. However, municipal networks are not common because of their huge costs. See **Figure 4.11** for an overview of how Wi-Fi works.

Wi-Fi Networking Standards

- **802.11ac**   This is the newest generation of Wi-Fi signaling in popular use. 802.11ac utilizes dual-band wireless technology and support simultaneous connections on both the 2.4 and 5 GHz Wi-Fi bands. 802.11ac offers backward compatibility to 802.11b/g/n and bandwidth rated up to 130 Mbps on 5 GHz, plus up to 450 Mbps on 2.4 GHz.

- **802.11b**   This standard shares spectrum with 2.4-GHz cordless phones, microwave ovens, and many Bluetooth products. Data are transferred at distances up to 100 meters or 328 feet.

- **802.11a**   This standard runs on 12 channels in the 5-GHz spectrum in North America, which reduces interference issues. Data are transferred about 5 times faster than 802.11b, improving the quality of streaming media. It has extra bandwidth for large files. Since the 802.11a and b standards are not interoperable, data sent from an 802.11b network cannot be accessed by 802.11a networks.

- **802.11g**   This standard runs on three channels in the 2.4-GHz spectrum, but at the speed of 802.11a. It is compatible with the 802.11b standard.

- **802.11n**   This standard improves upon prior 802.11 standards by adding multiple-input multiple-output (MIMO) and newer features. Frequency ranges from 2.4 to 5 GHz with a data rate of about 22 Mbps, but perhaps as high as 100 Mbps.

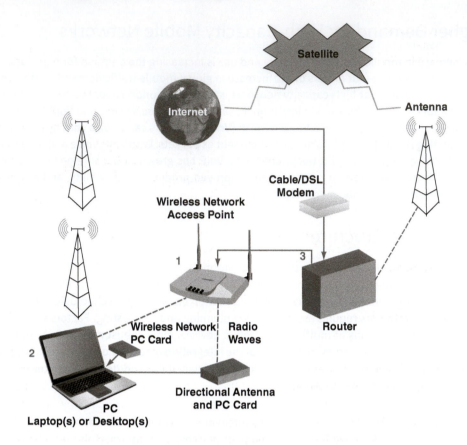

1 Radio-equipped access point connected to the Internet
  (or via a router). It generates and receives radio waves
  (up to 400 feet).
2 Several client devices, equipped with PC cards, generate
  and receive radio waves.
3 Router is connected to the Internet via a cable or
  DSL modem, or is connected via a satellite.

FIGURE 4.11   Overview of Wi-Fi.

Two Components of Wireless Infrastructure

There are three general types of mobile networks: **wide area networks (WANs), WiMAX**, and **local area networks (LANs)**. WANs for mobile computing are known as **wireless wide area networks (WWANs)**. The range of a WWAN depends on the transmission media and the wireless generation, which determines which services are available. The two components of wireless infrastructures are wireless LANs and WiMAX.

WLANs   Wireless LANs use high-frequency radio waves to communicate between computers, devices, or other nodes on the network. A wireless LAN typically extends an existing wired LAN by attaching a wireless AP to a wired network.

WiMAX   Wireless broadband WiMAX transmits voice, data, and video over high-frequency radio signals to businesses, homes, and mobile devices. It was designed to bypass traditional telephone lines and is an alternative to cable and DSL. WiMAX is based on the IEEE 802.16 set of standards and the metropolitan area network (MAN) access standard. Its range is 20–30 miles and it does not require a clear line of sight to function. **Figure 4.12** shows the components of a WiMAX/Wi-Fi network.

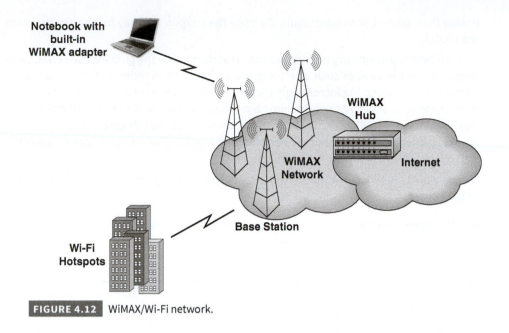

FIGURE 4.12   WiMAX/Wi-Fi network.

Mashup of GPS and Bluetooth   The **mashup** of GPS positioning and short-range wireless technologies, such as **Bluetooth** and **Wi-Fi**, can provide unprecedented intelligence. These technologies create opportunities for companies to develop solutions that make a consumer's life better. They could, for example, revolutionize traffic and road safety. Intelligent transport systems being developed by car manufacturers allow cars to communicate with each other and send alerts about sudden braking and will even allow for remote driving in the future. In the event of a collision, the car's system could automatically call emergency services. The technology can also apply the brakes automatically if it was determined that two cars were getting too close to each other or alert the driver to a car that is in their blind spot in the next lane.

Advancements in networks, devices, and RFID sensor networks are changing enterprise information infrastructures and business environments dramatically. The preceding examples and network standards illustrate the declining need for a physical computer, as other devices provide access to data, people, or services at anytime, anywhere in the world, on high-capacity networks.

Mashup is a general term referring to the integration of two or more technologies.

Business Use of Near-Field Communication

If you've used AirDrop on your smartphone you've engaged in near-field communication. NFC is a location-aware technology that is more secure than other wireless technologies like Bluetooth and Wi-Fi. And, unlike RFID, NFC is a two-way communication tool. An NFC tag contains small microchips with tiny aerials which can store a small amount of information for transfer to another **near-field communication (NFC)** device, such as a mobile phone.

Location-aware NFC technology can be used to transfer photos and files, make purchases in restaurants, resorts, hotels, theme parks and theaters, at gas stations, and on buses and trains. Here are some examples of NFC applications and their potential business value.

Near-field communication (NFC) enables two devices within close proximity to establish a communication channel and transfer data through radio waves.

- The Apple iWatch wearable device with NFC communication capabilities could be ideal for mobile payments. Instead of a wallet, users utilize their iWatch as a credit card or wave their wrists to pay for their Starbucks coffee. With GPS and location-based e-commerce services, retailers could send a coupon alert to the iWatch when a user passes their store. Consumers would then see the coupon and pay for the product with the iWatch.

- The self-healthcare industry is being radically transformed by the growing use of NFC technology. Wearable devices such as Fit-Bits, smart glucose monitors, and electrical nerve stimulators are becoming increasingly cheap and popular due to the proliferation of NFC tech. These devices can not only monitor, but they also can provide "automated or remote treatment" to users (Patrick, 2016). Remote control with health-care devices allow for smarter preventive care without the need for doctor or hospital visits and can increase the well-being of those living with chronic illnesses.

- Passengers on public transportation systems can pay fares by waving an NFC smartphone as they board.

Another interesting near-field application is described in **IT at Work 4.2** when technology was used as an incentive in a marketing campaign by Warner Music.

IT at Work 4.2

NFC-Embedded Guitar Picks

Fans attending gigs by The Wild Feathers were given guitar picks embedded with an NFC tag. Warner Music had distributed the guitar picks for fans to enter a competition, share content via social media, and vote at the gig simply by tapping with an NFC phone. NFC-embedded picks were inserted into the band's promotional flyers at six European venues. Each pick was encoded with a unique URL and also printed with a unique code for iPhone users to enable tracking and monitoring.

Marketing Campaign Success Shows an Exciting Future for NFC

The tags generated a high response rate. Over 65% of the NFC guitar picks had registered in the competition. And 35% of the fans had shared content on social media—spending an average of five minutes on the site.

   NFC is being used in marketing campaigns because the technology offers slick one-tap interaction. NFC allows brands to engage with their customers in unique ways and create exciting user experiences. With millions of NFC-equipped smartphones set to reach users over the next few years and the technology's advantages for shoppers and businesses, NFC is emerging as a major technology.

IT at Work Questions

1. Assume you attended a concert and were given a brochure similar to the one distributed to fans at The Wild Feathers concert. Would you use the guitar pick or comparable NFC-embedded item to participate in a contest? To post on Facebook or tweet about the concert? Explain why or why not.

2. How can NFC be applied to create an interesting user experience at a sporting event? At a retail store or coffee shop?

3. Refer to your answers in Question 2. What valuable information could be collected by the NFC tag in these businesses?

Bluetooth and Wi-Fi seem similar to near-field communication on the surface. All three allow wireless communication and data exchange between digital devices like smartphones. The difference is that near-field communication utilizes electromagnetic radio fields while technologies such as Bluetooth and Wi-Fi focus on radio transmissions instead.

Choosing Mobile Network Solutions

When you are choosing a mobile network solution, it's important to carefully consider the four factors shown in **Figure 4.13**.

1. **Simple**   Easy to deploy, manage, and use.
2. **Connected**   Always makes the best connection possible.
3. **Intelligent**   Works behind the scenes, easily integrating with other systems.
4. **Trusted**   Enables secure and reliable communications.

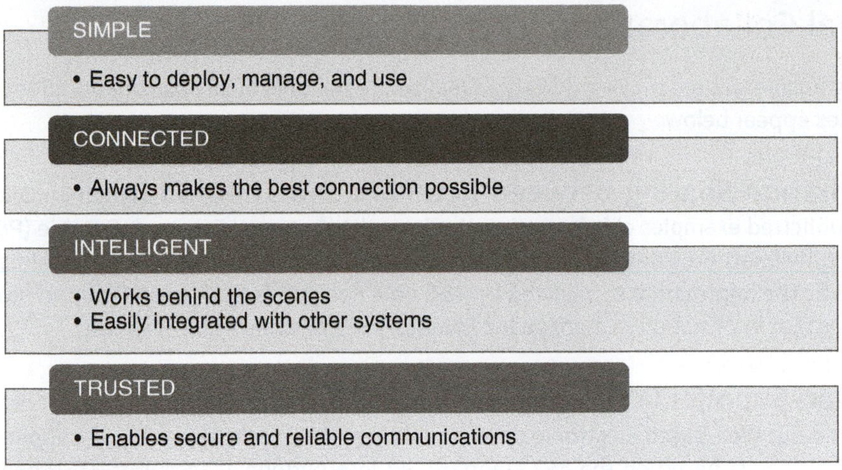

SIMPLE
- Easy to deploy, manage, and use

CONNECTED
- Always makes the best connection possible

INTELLIGENT
- Works behind the scenes
- Easily integrated with other systems

TRUSTED
- Enables secure and reliable communications

FIGURE 4.13 Four important factors to consider when choosing a mobile network solution.

Questions

1. What are the factors contribute to mobility?
2. Why is mobile global traffic increasing?
3. What accounts for the increased in mobile traffic?
4. Give some examples of VoIP networks.
5. How is NFC different from RFID?
6. What are the two components of a wireless network infrastructure?
7. What is near-field communication and how is it used in business?
8. What factors should be considered when evaluating mobile networks?

4.4 Collaborative Technologies and the Internet of Things

Now more than ever, business gets done through information sharing and collaborative planning. Business performance depends on broadband data networks for communication, mobility, and collaboration. For example, after Ford Motor Company began relying on UPS Logistics Group's data networks to track millions of cars and trucks and to analyze any potential problems before they occur, Ford realized a $1 billion reduction in vehicle inventory and $125 million reduction in inventory carrying costs annually.

More and more people need to work together and share documents over time and distance. Teams make most of the complex decisions in organizations and many teams are geographically dispersed. This makes it difficult for organizational decision-making when team members are geographically spread out and working in different time zones.

Messaging and collaboration tools include older communications media such as e-mail, videoconferencing, fax, and texts—and blogs, Skype, Web meetings, and social media. Yammer is an enterprise social network that helps employees collaborate across departments, locations, and business apps. These private social sites are used by more than 400,000 enterprises worldwide. Yammer functions as a communication and problem-solving tool and is rapidly replacing e-mail. You will read about Yammer in detail in Chapter 7.

Virtual Collaboration

Leading businesses are moving quickly to realize the benefits of virtual collaboration. Several examples appear below.

Information Sharing Between Retailers and Their Suppliers
One of the most publicized examples of information sharing exists between Procter & Gamble (P&G) and Walmart. Walmart provides P&G with access to sales information on every item Walmart buys from P&G. The information is collected by P&G on a daily basis from every Walmart store, and P&G uses that information to manage the inventory replenishment for Walmart.

Retailer–Supplier Collaboration: Asda Corporation
Supermarket chain Asda has rolled out Web-based electronic data interchange (EDI) technology to 650 suppliers. Web EDI technology is based on the AS2 standard, an internationally accepted HTTP-based protocol used to send real-time data in multiple formats securely over the Internet. It promises to improve the efficiency and speed of traditional EDI communications, which route data over third-party, value-added networks (VANs).

Lower Transportation and Inventory Costs and Reduced Stockouts: Unilever
Unilever's 30 contract carriers deliver 250,000 truckloads of shipments annually. Unilever's Web-based database, the Transportation Business Center (TBC), provides these carriers with site specification requirements when they pick up a shipment at a manufacturing or distribution center or when they deliver goods to retailers. TBC gives carriers all of the vital information they need: contact names and phone numbers, operating hours, the number of dock doors at a location, the height of the dock doors, how to make an appointment to deliver or pick up shipments, pallet configuration, and other special requirements. All mission-critical information that Unilever's carriers need to make pickups, shipments, and deliveries is now available electronically 24/7.

Reduction of Product Development Time
Caterpillar, Inc. is a multinational heavy-machinery manufacturer. In the traditional mode of operation, cycle time along the supply chain was long because the process involved paper—document transfers among managers, salespeople, and technical staff. To solve the problem, Caterpillar connected its engineering and manufacturing divisions with its active suppliers, distributors, overseas factories, and customers through an extranet-based global collaboration system. By means of the collaboration system, a request for a customized tractor component, for example, can be transmitted from a customer to a Caterpillar dealer and on to designers and suppliers, all in a very short time. Customers also can use the extranet to retrieve and modify detailed order information while the vehicle is still on the assembly line.

Group Work and Decision Processes

Managers and staff continuously make decisions as they develop and manufacture products, plan social media marketing strategies, make financial and IT investments, determine how to meet compliance mandates, design software, and so on. By design or default, group processes emerge, referred to as **group dynamics**, and those processes can be productive or dysfunctional.

Group Work and Dynamics
Group work can be quite complex depending on the following factors:

- Group members may be located in different places or work at different times.
- Group members may work for the same or different organizations.

- Needed data, information, or knowledge may be located in many sources, several of which are external to the organization.

Despite the long history and benefits of collaborative work, groups are not always successful.

Online Brainstorming in the Cloud   Brainstorming ideas is no longer limited to a room full of people offering their ideas that are written on a whiteboard or posters. Companies are choosing an alternative—online brainstorming applications, many of them cloud-based. An advantage is the avoidance of travel expenses if members are geographically dispersed, which often restricts how many sessions a company can afford to hold. The following are two examples of online brainstorming apps:

- **Evernote** is a cloud-based tool that helps users gather and share information, and brainstorm ideas. One function is Synch, which keeps Evernote notes up-to-date across a user's computers, phones, devices, and the Web. A free version of Evernote is available for download from **www.evernote.com**.
- **iMindmap Online**, from UK-based **ThinkBuzan**, relies on mind mapping and other well-known structured approaches to brainstorming. iMindmap Online helps streamline work processes, minimize information overload, generate new ideas, and boost innovation.

The Internet of Things (IoT)

The **Internet of Things** has the potential to impact how we live and how we work. The IoT is a subset of the Internet which dictates that objects we interact with everyday send and receive signals to and from each other to exchange data about almost everything. The IoT can best be described as a collection technology in that it collects data from millions of data sensors embedded in everything from cars to refrigerators to space capsules. This aggregation of data points through smart meters, sensors, etc. contribute to the "Internet of Things" (IoT).

> **Internet of Things**   is the network of physical objects or "things" embedded with electronics, software, sensors, and network connectivity, that enables these objects to collect and exchange data.

Analytics, big data, and sensor integrations are revolutionizing how we live and work. A recent study conducted by IndustryWeek (2016), reported that more than half of U.S. manufacturers report they are currently using IoT technology to collect machine data, and a significant but smaller percentage (44%) are collecting data from sensors embedded in their products.

Several things have created the "perfect storm" for the creation and growth of the IoT. These include more widely available broadband Internet, lower cost of connecting, development of more devices with Wi-Fi capabilities and embedded sensors, and the overwhelming popularity of the smartphone. In layperson's terms, the IoT is the concept of connecting any device that has an on/off switch to the Internet or each other. This includes everything from everyday items such as cellphones, coffee makers, washing machines, lamps, and headphones to airplane jet engines or an oil rig drill, smart traffic signals, smart parking, traffic congestion monitoring, air pollution sensors, potable water monitoring, and river, dam, and reservoir water level monitors. In other words, if it can be connected, it will be connected. Just think of the IoT as a giant network of connected "things" with relationships between people-to-people, people-to-things, and things-to-things.

The primary driver for IoT is the broader adoption and deployment of sensors and smart devices. Some industries have had IoT in place for quite some time, but for others it is an entirely new concept. Lately, IoT has been gaining in popularity and use. The use of the smaller sensors, as compared to the traditional IT infrastructure, enables companies to gain more computing capacity and reduce power consumption for less cost. All in all, it's a win-win situation.

IoT Sensors, Smart Meters, and the Smart Grid

It has been estimated that the number of network-connected sensors and devices could triple to 21 billion by 2020 (IndustryWeek, 2016).

Sensors   The heart of IoT resides in the source of the data, that is, the **sensors**. Sensors generate data about activities, events, and influencing factors that provide visibility into performance and support decision processes across a variety of industries and consumer channels.

Smart Grid and Smart Cities   With a combination of smart meters, wireless technology, sensors, and software, the **smart grid** allows utilities to accurately track power grids and cut back on energy use when the availability of electricity is stressed. And consumers gain insight into their power consumption to make more intelligent decisions about how to use energy.

A fully deployed smart grid has the potential of saving between $39.69 and $101.57, and up to 592 pounds of carbon dioxide emissions, per consumer per year in the United States, according to the Smart Grid Consumer Collaborative (SGCC).

On a broader scale, the IoT can be applied to things like "smart cities" that can help reduce waste and improve efficiency. **IT at Work 4.3** describes how a town in Spain is using the IoT to improve everyday life for its' citizens, or is it?

IT at Work 4.3

Smart City or Police State?

In the small city of Santander on Spain's Atlantic coast, Mayor Iñigo de la Serna raised $12 million, mostly from the European Commission, to launch *SmartSantander*. SmartSantander is a **smart city** experiment that is improving the quality of life, reducing energy consumption, and engaging its citizens in civic duties.

20,000 Sensors Embedded

The city implemented wireless sensor networks and embedded 20,000 sensors in its streets and municipal vehicles to monitor garbage collection, crime, and air quality and manage street lighting for better energy efficiency. "The internet of Things unites all the data coming from sensors, along with the data the city already has and data provided by citizens," says Joaquin Gonzalez, director of Telefonica in Cantabria (Frangoul, 2016). Sensors communicate with smartphone apps to inform drivers and commuters on parking availability, bus delays, road closures, and the current pollen count in real time. Parking apps direct drivers to available spaces via cell phone alerts. Drivers benefit from a reduction in the time and annoyance of finding parking spots. Anyone can feed his or her own data into the system by, for example, snapping a smartphone photo of a pothole or broken streetlight to notify the local government that a problem needs to be fixed. Users can even point their smartphones at landmarks in the city to learn more about them and events happening around the city.

Build-Out of Smart City Applications

This mobile technology can help cities contribute to a greener planet. Municipal landscape sprinklers can send facts to city agencies for analysis to conserve water usage. Sensors can monitor weather and pollen counts as well as water and power leaks. City officials also claim that the development has saved money through automated and data driven applications such as dimming street lights at optimal times, resulting in 25% savings on electricity bills and 20% on garbage.

Police State

The data streams and mobile apps that keep citizens informed also keep the government informed. What is the difference between a smart city and a police state? Many see the new sensor saturation as a sort of "Big Brother" experiment. Consider how data collected from sensors mounted outside a bar to track noise levels might be used.

- Scenario #1: Instances of loud noises and squealing tires are transmitted to local police. The city uses the information to enforce public nuisance laws and make arrests.
- Scenario #2: People who live in the neighborhood show civic leaders what is keeping them up at night and receive help in resolving the problem.
- Scenario #3: Landlords could use data showing less noise and cleaner air to promote their apartments or office buildings.

The Dark Side of Smart

The wireless networks and sensors need to be maintained. Thousands of batteries embedded in roadways could have expensive and disruptive maintenance requirements.

Parking space alerts might create other annoyances. If everyone becomes aware of a parking spot up the street, the rush of cars converging on a few open locations could lead to rage and defeat the purpose of such an alert.

IT at Work Questions

1. What are the benefits of a smart city?
2. What are the potential abuses of data collected in this way?
3. Consider the dark side of smart. Are you skeptical of the benefits of a smart city?
4. Would you want to live in a smart city? Explain.
5. How would you prevent Santander from becoming a police state?

Sources: Compiled from Eggers (2016), Frangoul (2016), O'Connor (2013), and Edwards (2014).

Security and Privacy in the IoT Network security and data privacy are manufacturers' top concerns about IoT technology. With billions of devices connected together there are a multitude of end-points where security breaches can occur and individuals or organizations can be hacked.

Advantages and Disadvantages of IoT Organizations are struggling with the advantages and disadvantages associated with the IoT and seeking to understand how it will impact their business.

Wireless hospitals and remote patient monitoring, for example, are growing IoT trends. Tracking medical equipment and hospital inventory, such as gurneys, is done with RFID tagging at a number of hospitals. Remote monitoring apps are making health care easier and more comfortable for patients while reaching patients in remote areas.

Organizations can expect to gain from using the IoT in a number of ways, for example, expected benefits from using IoT include the following:

1. Monitoring performance, quality, and reliability of products and services
2. Gaining insight into potential new products and service
3. Support sales
4. Better understand product use
5. Remote troubleshooting of products
6. Deliver revenue-generating post-sales service
7. More efficiently deliver post-sales services

Similarly, there are concerns around using the IoT and the ability to collect and analyze the massive amounts of data that it enables. Main *disadvantages* that organizations have about the use of IoT include the following:

1. Network security
2. Data privacy
3. Data analysis capabilities
4. Data collection capabilities
5. Realistic efficiency opportunities
6. Realistic new revenue opportunities
7. Cost

Questions

1. Why has group work becoming more challenging?
2. What might limit the use of face-to-face brainstorming?
3. How can online brainstorming tools overcome those limits?
4. List ways in which virtual collaboration can be used in business.
5. What devices do you have that take advantage of the IoT? Describe how they impact the way that you live and work.
6. What is driving the rise of the IoT?
7. What is the main concern that organizations have about the IoT?
8. Do you think the advantages outweigh the disadvantages of the IoT? Explain.

Key Terms

3G   110
4G   110
5G   110
application program interface (API)   111
Bluetooth   115
circuit switching   111
computer networks   104
Exabyte   114
extranet   105
fixed-line broadband   108
group dynamics   120
information and communications
technology (ICT)   102
Internet of Things   121
Internet Protocol (IP)   109

Intranet   105
IP address   109
IP Version 4 (IPv4)   109
IP Version 6 (IPv6)   109
latency-sensitive apps   107
local area network (LAN)   116
Long-Term Evolution (LTE)   110
mashup   117
near-field communication (NFC)   117
Net neutrality   108
Net semi-neutrality   108
packet   109
packet switching   111
protocol   109
quality of service (QoS)   107

router   106
sensors   122
smart grid   122
smart city   122
switch   106
traffic shaping   108
transmission control protocol/Internet
   protocols (TCP/IPs)   111
virtual private networks (VPNs)   105
voice over IP (VoIP)   115
wide area network (WAN)   116
Wi-Fi   115
WiMAX   116
Zettabyte   114

Assuring Your Learning

Discuss: Critical Thinking Questions

1. Explain how network capacity is measured.

2. How are devices identified to a network?

3. Explain how digital signals are transmitted.

4. Explain the functions of switches and routers.

5. QoS technologies can be applied to create two tiers of traffic. What are those tiers? Give an example of each type of traffic.

6. Typically, networks are configured so that downloading is faster than uploading. Explain why.

7. What are the differences between 3G, 4G, and 5G networks?

8. What are two 4G wireless standards?

9. How is network performance measured?

10. Discuss two applications of near-field communication (NFC).

11. What are the benefits of APIs?

12. Describe the components of a mobile communication infrastructure.

13. What is the range of WiMAX? Why does it not need a clear line of sight?

14. Why are VPNs used to secure extranets?

15. How can group dynamics improve group work? How can it disrupt what groups might accomplish?

16. What are the benefits of using software to conduct brainstorming in the cloud (remotely)?

Explore: Online and Interactive Exercises

1. Visit the Google apps website. Identify three types of collaboration support and their value in the workplace.

2. Compare the various features of broadband wireless networks (e.g., 3G, Wi-Fi, and WiMAX). Visit at least three broadband wireless network vendors.

a. Prepare a list of capabilities for each network.

b. Prepare a list of actual applications that each network can support.

c. Comment on the value of such applications to users. How can the benefits be assessed?

Analyze & Decide: Apply IT Concepts to Business Decisions

1. Visit **www.Youtube.com** and search for tutorials on the latest version of iMindMap. Watch a few of the tutorials. As an alternative, watch the video at **http://www.youtube.com/watch?v=UVt3Qu6Xcko&list =PLA42C25431E4EA4FF**. Describe the potential value of sharing maps online and synching maps with other computers or devices. What is your opinion of the ease or complexity of the iMindMap interface?

2. Visit the **AT&T website** and read the article "What you Need to Know about IoT Wide Area Networks." Write a short report discussing the benefits of each type of network that can be used in an organization's IoT and make a choice for your "business."

Case 4.2

Business Case: Google Maps API for Business

A restaurant owner has a website where customers can place orders for delivery. When a customer inputs a delivery address, a software script verifies whether the address is within the delivery range of the restaurant. If the address is not in the delivery range, the site does not let the customer check out and sends a message informing the customer that he or she is outside of the delivery range. The script requests information from Google Maps via an API to calculate whether or not the address was in the range. The free version, called *Google Maps API*, allows up to 2,500 requests per day from a single IP address and is limited to noncommercial purposes.

The owner needs to purchase a *Google Maps API for Business* license because any requests in excess of 2,500 will be ignored. The Google Maps API for Business provides better resolution, scale, and enhanced features and support to businesses that add maps to their websites, mobile apps, or asset-tracking applications.

Directions and Routing Features

The Google Maps API delivers the full power of Google's routing engine to applications. Among other features, it:

- Generates routes between up to 23 locations for driving, walking, or cycling.
- Generates routes to avoid toll roads or highways.
- Reduces travel time by calculating the optimal order to visit each location.
- Calculates travel time and distance between locations, for example, to offer users a way to filter search results by drive time.

Data Visualization

The Google Maps API lets managers visualize data using heat maps, symbols, and custom styles. For U.S. maps, companies have access to a demographics layer containing up-to-date census data provided by Nielsen and five-year projections of many data fields. The demographics layer may only be used on intranets or internal websites.

Advanced Analytics

The Google Maps API for Business offers an analytics tool that shows how visitors interact with the maps—for example, how many visitors switched to satellite view, what they zoomed, and which map features were used the most. Using this information, businesses can customize the user experience based on their preferences and better engage with customers.

Automobile Association

Google Maps is the most widely used online mapping service in the world, with more than 800,000 sites using the Google Maps API and over 250 million active users on mobile devices alone. In the United Kingdom, the Automobile Association (AA) provides roadside assistance and directions to motorists. AA invested in the Google Maps API for Business to offer interactive route planning and improve visitors' experiences. The value AA derived from the API was a 12% increase in the number of routes downloaded, hitting an average of 4 million downloads per week of its routing or trip-planning service. Approximately 20% of site visitors remained on the site for at least five minutes—up from only 6% prior to implementation. The API also cuts the time and cost of IT support for the mapping platform.

Questions

1. Describe Google Maps API.

2. Why do you think Google provides free noncommercial use of its Maps API?

3. How many times have you used a website's mapping feature for directions or to calculate distance? How did having a familiar interface improve your experience?

4. Google claims that its Maps API helps a company's customers and employees make better business and purchasing decisions by visualizing important information on a familiar map. Explain how data visualization provides these benefits. Give two examples in your explanation.

Case 4.3

Video Case: Small Island Telecom Company Goes Global

Go online to research the Isle of Man, a small island in the Irish Sea off the coast of Great Britain. Visit the **Cisco website**. Search for the video "Island Telecom Competes on a Global Level." Watch the video to learn how this small telecom company was able to evolve from a traditional local service provider to a global cloud services innovator thanks to Cisco's networking technology (video runs 2:09 minutes).

Questions

1. Describe the benefits that Island Telecom achieved through using Cisco's networking product.

2. What factors allowed Island Telecom to make the transition from local to global?

References

Cisco. "Sony Adopts Cisco Solution for Global IPv6 Project." Cisco Public Information, Customer Case Study. October 28, 2014.

Cisco. "Cisco Visual Networking Index: Forecast and Methodology, 2015–2020," 2016.

Edwards, J. "The Connected Life." *Teradata Magazine*, Q1, 2014.

Eggers, W. D. "8 Ways Digital is Transforming Governments around the World." *The Huffington Post*, July 18, 2016.

Fiegerman, S. "Trump's FCC May Try to Roll Back Net Neutrality. Here's Why it Matters." 2017. Accessed at: http://money.cnn.com/2017/01/24/technology/fcc-net-neutrality/index.html

Frangoul, A. "Thousands of Sensors are Making This Famous City Smarter." *CNBC*, May 5, 2016.

IndustryWeek. "The Internet of Things: Finding the Path to Value." *IndustryWeek*. 2016.

Joseph, S. "McDonald's, Unilever and Gatorade Among the First to Run Snapchat API Campaigns." *TheDrum*, October 6, 2016.

Neal, D. "Sony's Playstation Network Is Down in the UK, Again." *The Inquirer*, October 26, 2016.

O'Connor, M. C. "Santander: Test Bed for Smart Cities and Open Data Policies." *SmartPlanet.com*, May 8, 2013.

Pachal, P. "How the AT&T-Time Warner Deal Threatens Net Neutrality." *Mashable*, October 23, 2016.

Patrick, M. "How Will the Internet of Medical Things Change Healthcare?" *Electronic Design*, October 20, 2016.

PRNewswire. "LTE and 5G Infrastructure Investments are Expected to Account for a Market Worth $32 Billion by 2020—Research and Markets." October 20, 2016.

Wheeler, T. "Setting the Record Straight on the FCC's Open Internet Rules." *FCC blog*, April 24, 2014.

Zeman, E. "Amazon Opens Beta for Alexa List Skills API." *ProgrammableWeb*, October 13, 2016.

CHAPTER 5

Cybersecurity and Risk Management Technology

CHAPTER OUTLINE	LEARNING OBJECTIVES
Case 5.1 Opening Case: Yahoo wins the gold and silver medal for the worst hacks in history!	
5.1 The Face and Future of Cyberthreats	**5.1 Describe** the extent of incidents and data breaches in organizations and the sources of cyberthreats that are putting organizations in jeopardy.
5.2 Cyberattack Targets and Consequences	**5.2 Describe** the targets of cyberattacks and the impact these attacks have on both public and private sector organizations.
5.3 Cyber Risk Management	**5.3 Explain** why cyber risk management must be a top business priority and outline an organizational model for cybersecurity.
5.4 Internal Audits and Controls	**5.4 Describe** the internal audits and controls that are used to defend against occupational fraud at all levels of an organization.
5.5 Frameworks, Standards, and Models	**5.5 Explain** how risk management frameworks, standards, and models help ensure compliance with industry and federal regulations. Assess the risk associated with a network crash, debilitating hacker attack, or other IT disruption.
	a. Explain how compliance and security can diverge such that being compliant is not necessarily equivalent to being secure. (Home Depot, Target, and a myriad of others were all PCI compliant.)
Case 5.2 Business Case: Lax Security at LinkedIn Exposed	
Case 5.3 Video Case: Botnets, Malware Security, and Capturing Cybercriminals	

Introduction

Today, most business leaders know they are responsible for cybersecurity and privacy threats, wherever they occur. What most don't understand is how to design, implement, and manage threat-intelligent business strategies and risk management plans to prevent data breaches and protect IT and business resources.

In the digital economy, organizational data is typically available on demand 24/7 to enable companies to benefit from opportunities for productivity improvement and data sharing with customers, suppliers, and business partners. The concept of data on demand is an operational and competitive necessity for global companies, but unfortunately, it also opens them up to cyberattacks.

New vulnerabilities are continuously being found in operating systems, applications, and wired and wireless networks. Left unaddressed, vulnerabilities provide an open door for cyberattacks that can cause business disruptions and devastating financial consequences. Managers no longer question whether their networks will be breached, but when it will happen, how much damage will be done, how long the investigation will take, and how much the investigation and fines will cost.

For example, after detecting a network hack, credit card processing company Global Payments, Inc. spent 14 months investigating the resulting data breach that exposed 1.5 million U.S. debit and credit card accounts. Global's damages totaled $93 million. This loss consisted of $36 million in fraud losses and fines and $77 million for the investigation, remediation, credit monitoring, and identity theft insurance for affected consumers. And this is not an unusual occurrence, according to a global study conducted by the Ponemon Institute, the average cost of a breached record is $141 and the average cost of an overall data breach is $3.62 million (Ponemon Institute, 2017).

These reports of data breaches focus primarily on what companies are required to report publicly—theft of personally identifiable information (PII), payment data, and personal health information (PHI). Consequently, the costs commonly associated with data breaches only take into consideration these more easily understood impacts. But these are not always an attacker's objective. Rarely brought into full view are theft of intellectual property (IP), espionage, data destruction, attacks on core operations, or attempts to disable critical infrastructure. These attacks can have a much more significant impact on organizations. But the damage they cause is not widely understood and is much more difficult to quantify.

As a result, organizations need to acquire a deeper knowledge of cyberattacks and combine it with business context, valuation techniques, and financial quantification to establish the true costs of their losses. Applying this more accurate knowledge of potential business impacts, leaders can be much more effective in managing and controlling cyber risk and improve their ability to recover from a cyberattack.

In Chapter 5, you will learn about cybersecurity terminology, the rising number of data breaches, sources of cyberthreats, damage caused by cybercriminals' aggressive tactics and their impacts on organizations. You will also learn how organizations can defend against cyberattacks, correctly assess the damage they cause, and ensure the actions needed for business continuity. But, first, let's take a look at two of the biggest cyberattacks ever reported.

Case 5.1 Opening Case

G Fiume/Getty Images

Ryan Anson/Bloomberg/Getty Images

Tetiana Vitsenko/Alamy Stock Photo

Yahoo Wins the Gold and Silver Medal for the Worst Hacks in History!

It wasn't until Fall 2016 that Yahoo alerted its users and the public to the first of two of the largest known breaches of user information in history that had occurred 2–3 years earlier. On September 22, 2016, Yahoo publicly disclosed that over 1 billion Yahoo account records were stolen in mid-2013. A second news release on December 15, 2016, revealed a second attack that occurred in 2014 when the account information of over 500 million Yahoo account holders was breached. The delay in reporting is partly due to the fact that Yahoo itself did not know of the breach until shortly before releasing these statements to the public. The information leaked in the attacks included e-mail accounts, telephone numbers, street addresses, unencrypted security questions and answers, but no financial information.

To add insult to injury, at the time of the first news release, Yahoo was in negotiations with mega-corporation Verizon to acquire Yahoo for $4.83 billion. After the first news release, Verizon said that the announcement could have a negative impact on their purchasing decision. The second news release caused Verizon to further review the financial implications of the two breaches and reduce its offer by $350 million.

The 2013 breach was conducted by an unknown unauthorized third party. The information stolen in the 2014 attack was sold by a "state-sponsored actor" on the Dark Web for 3 Bitcoins (approx. $1,900). The actor, who used the name "Peace" is of Russian origin and attempted to sell data from 200 million Yahoo users online. Yahoo urged all of its users to change their passwords and security questions and to review their accounts for suspicious activity. To date, little information has been released on the 2013 breach, but more is known about the incident that occurred in 2014.

How the Second Attack was Carried Out

The data theft was similar to the way in which a typical online attack of a database is carried out. The protections used for database containing the login and personal information were insufficient to protect against the advanced methods used by the hackers. In this case, the encryption method employed in the database was broken by the hacker. Additionally, cybercrime analyst Vitali Kremez maintains that the hacker stole the information from Yahoo slowly and methodically so as to not draw attention to the breach taking place.

Since the breach was not immediately detected, the hacker had plenty of time to leverage the information in a financially, personal, or politically beneficial manner. It is not clear if the seller is the original hacker.

Impact of the Data Breach

Since the breaches were so devastating and far reaching to most of Yahoo's customer base, Verizon is having second thoughts about the acquisition. Craig Silliman, general counsel to Verizon, said Verizon has

"a reasonable basis" to believe that the data breach will have a significant impact on the deal proceedings and the likelihood that it will actually happen (Fiegerman, 2016). He furthers to explain that Yahoo will have to convince Verizon that the breach will not affect future processes in the company and that more security features have been and will be implemented. Also, the incidents could make the Yahoo deal worth about $200 million less than the $4.8 billion initially settled upon. In addition to the decreased value of Yahoo's core assets, the company's stock fell about 2% after the comments by Craig Silliman.

Justice is Served

On March 17, 2017, the U.S. Department of Justice indicted two Russian Intelligence agents and two state-sponsored hackers, Alexsey Belan and Karim Baratov, for the theft of the Yahoo user data in 2014. Belan, one of the FBI's most notorious criminal hackers, had been previously indicted in two other cases. In the indictments it was revealed that the targets of the theft included Russian journalists, U.S. and Russian government officials, military personnel, and private-sector employees of financial, transportation, and other companies (Balakrishnan, 2017).

The obvious issue surrounding the Yahoo data breaches is Internet security. Simple username, password, and security questions simply are not enough to keep hackers at bay. UC Davis professor Hemant Bhargava notes that two-factor authentication (TFA) is successful in many other companies and that Yahoo should follow suit (Matwyshyn & Bhargava, 2016). An example of TFA would be that a user is asked to enter information such as username and password, then a mobile app generates and sends a random number code for the user to enter before being granted access to his or her account. Both the Yahoo account and the mobile app are linked to a common, secure account. This method is exceptionally popular and useful since over 50% of Web users access the Web through their mobile phones.

Questions

1. Why do you think Yahoo was targeted for these data breaches?
2. Why did Yahoo keep the breaches from the public eye? How did their nondisclosure affect Yahoo's relationship with its customers and partners?
3. In addition to the data theft, what else was damaged by this incident?
4. Were these cybersecurity incidents foreseeable? Were they avoidable?
5. Assuming that the CEO and CIO were forced to resign, what message does that send to senior management at Yahoo?

Sources: Compiled from Fiegerman (2016), Hackett (2016a), Kan (2016), Lee (2016), Matwyshyn and Bhargava (2016), Murgia (2016), Sterling (2015), and Balakrishnan (2017).

5.1 | The Face and Future of Cyberthreats

Over the past several years, the number of cyberattacks in which data records have been stolen by hackers has increased at an alarming rate. In 2016, the total number of U.S. data breaches hit an all-time record high of 1,093 according to a report released on January 19, 2017, by the Identity Theft Resource Center (ITRC) (Goldman, 2017). This represents a 40% increase over the previous year. The general business sector reported the highest number of cyberattacks with 494 reported incidents, followed by the healthcare/medical industry with 377, education sector with 98, government/ military with 72, and the banking/credit/financial sector with 52 breaches (see **Figure 5.1**).

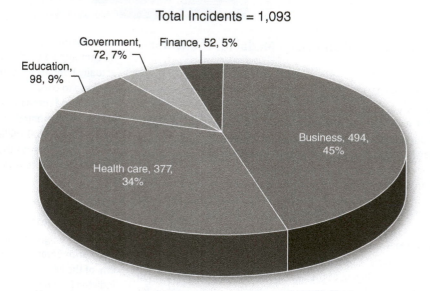

FIGURE 5.1   Number of 2016 U.S. data breaches by industry sector.

Vulnerability is a gap in IT security defenses of a network, system, or application that can be exploited by a **threat** to gain unauthorized access. Vulnerabilities can be exemplified by lack of controls around people (user training, inadequate policies), process (inadequate separation of duties, poor process controls), or tools (lack of technical controls enforcement or monitoring).

Data incidents and **breaches** in 2016 exposed everything from usernames to passwords to Social Security numbers and are caused by the successful exploitation of vulnerabilities in information systems by a threat (risk = threat × vulnerability). Vulnerabilities threaten the confidentiality, integrity, or availability (CIA) of data and information systems, as defined in **Figure 5.2**.

Data incident is an *attempted* or *successful* unauthorized access to a network, system, or application; unwanted disruption or denial of service; unauthorized use of a system for processing or storage of data; changes to system without the owners knowledge, instruction, or consent.

Data breach is the *successful retrieval* of sensitive information by an individual, group, or software system.

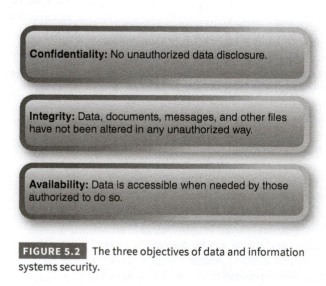

FIGURE 5.2   The three objectives of data and information systems security.

Fifty-six percent of all breaches were phishing attacks, where hackers trick an employee into clicking a specially crafted e-mail link or attachment which then provides the hackers access to the user's system and ultimately corporate network and data. These attacks were up 38% from 2015. **Table 5.1** lists the top five data breaches worldwide in 2016. Although these numbers are high, it's important to remember that a vast majority of data breaches go unreported, according to cybersecurity experts, because corporate victims fear that disclosure would damage their stock price, or because they never knew they were hacked in the first place.

The consequences of insufficient cybersecurity include damaged reputations, consumer backlash, lost market share, falling share prices, financial penalties, and federal and state government fines. As a result, companies are investing heavily in security-related technologies—worldwide spending on security-related hardware, software, and services rose to $73.7 billion in 2016 from $68.2 billion a year earlier and that number is expected to approach $90 billion in 2018.

TABLE 5.1 2016 Biggest Data Breaches Worldwide, in Terms of Number of Data Records Breached

Company	Type of Data Breach	Records Breached
Anthem Insurance	The attack against U.S.-based health insurer Anthem was an identity theft breach that resulted in the theft of 78.8 million records, making it the largest data breach of the year in terms of records compromised. Current and former members of one of Anthem's affiliated health plans, as well as some members of other independent Blue Cross and Blue Shield plans who received health-care services in any of the areas that Anthem serves, were said to be affected.	78.8 Million
Turkish General Directorate of Population and Citizenship Affairs	The Turkish government agency experienced an identity theft attack at the hands of a malicious outsider. The attack exposed 50 million records, and information pertaining to citizens was stolen.	50 Million
Korean Pharmaceutical Information Center	The South Korean organization that distributes pharmacy management software to many of the country's pharmacies was hit by an identity theft breach launched by a malicious insider. The result was the exposure of 43 million records. According to the *Korea Herald*, medical information of nearly 90% of the South Korean population was sold to a multinational firm, which processed and sold the data.	43 Million
U.S. Office of Personnel Management	The state-sponsored attack, which was described by federal officials as being among the largest breaches of government data in the history of the United States, scored a 9.6 on the risk assessment scale. The attack exposed data including PII such as Social Security numbers, names, dates and places of birth, and addresses.	22 Million
Experian	The U.S.-based credit bureau and consumer data broker experienced an identity theft breach by a malicious outsider that resulted in the theft of 15 million records. The data included some PII about consumers in the United States, including those who applied for T-Mobile services or device financing.	15 Million

Source: Breach Level Index (2016).

Hacks of high-tech companies like Yahoo, LinkedIn, Google, Amazon, eBay, and Sony, and top security agencies like the CIA and FBI are proof that no one is safe. Cyberwarriors are too well funded and motivated. Taking a global perspective, Verizon's 2016 Data Breach Investigations Report (DBIR) examined over 100,000 incidents, including 3,141 confirmed data breaches across 82 countries. Of these, 89% of the breaches were motivated by financial gain or espionage. In over 90% of the breaches, it took attackers mere minutes (or less) to compromise a system. On the other hand, it took companies weeks to months to discover that a breach had occurred and in most cases it was external sources, such as customers or law enforcement that sounded the alarm! **Cyberthreats** can be intentional or unintentional.

Table 5.2 lists eight sources of intentional and unintentional cyberthreats that account for the vast majority of data breaches and other cybersecurity incidents.

Cyberthreat is a threat posed by means of the Internet (a.k.a. cyberspace) and the potential source of malicious attempts to damage or disrupt a computer network, system, or application.

TABLE 5.2	Major Sources of Cyberthreats	
Source/Type	**Characteristics**	**Solution**
Intentional Cyberthreat		
Hacking	Unauthorized access of networks, systems or applications for economic, social, or political gain. Use of programs such as backdoor services to promote reentry or further incursion into target environment	Train your staff Change password frequently Have "strong" passwords
Phishing	Social engineering, targeting human behavior rather than computer technology	Train your staff Monitor activity
Crimeware	Use of malware and ransomware	Use antimalware/AV software Patch promptly Monitor change and watch key indicators Back-up system regularly Capture data on attacks Practice principle of least privilege
Distributed denial-of-service	Use of compromised systems to overwhelm a system with malicious traffic	Segregate key servers Choose your providers carefully Test your anti-DDoS service
Insider and privilege misuse	Employees, contractors, partners, suppliers, and other external entities with specific insider roles abusing access granted to systems for legitimate business purposes.	Monitor user behavior Track mobile media usage Know your data
Physical theft	Theft of laptops, tablets, peripherals, printed material, etc.	Encrypt your data Train your staff Reduce use of paper
Unintentional Cyberthreat		
Physical loss	Theft of laptops, tablets, and peripheral devices	Encrypt your data Train your staff
Miscellaneous errors	Any *unintentional* action that compromises security, except theft, and loss of assets	Learn from your mistakes Strengthen controls Ensure all assets go through a rigorous check by IT before they are decommissioned or disposed of

Source: Verizon (2016).

Intentional Threats

Examples of intentional threats include data theft such as inappropriate use of data (e.g., manipulating inputs); theft of computer time; theft of equipment and/or software; deliberate manipulation in handling, entering, programming, processing, or transferring data; sabotage; malicious damage to computer resources; destruction from malware and similar attacks; and miscellaneous computer abuses and Internet fraud.

Unintentional Threats

Unintentional threats fall into three major categories: human error, environmental hazards, social unrest and computer system failures.

- **Human error** can occur in the design of the hardware or information system. It can also occur during programming, testing, or data entry. Neglecting to change default passwords in applications or on systems or failing to manage patches creates security holes. Human error also includes untrained or unaware users falling prey to **social engineering** like phishing scams or ignoring security procedures. Human errors contribute to the majority of internal control and information security problems.

- **Environmental hazards**   include volcanoes, earthquakes, blizzards, floods, power failures or strong fluctuations, fires (the most common hazard), defective heating, ventilation and air-conditioning (HVAC) systems, explosions, radioactive fallout, and water-cooling-system failures. In addition to the primary damage, computer resources can be damaged by the side effects of a hazard, such as smoke and water. Such hazards may disrupt normal computer operations resulting in extended data inaccessibility and exorbitant restoration and recovery costs.

- **Computer systems failures**   can occur as the result of poor manufacturing, defective materials, or poor maintenance. Unintentional malfunctions can also occur for other reasons, ranging from administrator inexperience to inadequate testing.

In the next sections, you will learn more about the various sources of cyberthreats and their potential impact on organizations.

Hacking

Hacking is a very profitable industry. In 2016, 56% of reported data breaches were reported to be the result of hacking, which is 18% higher than those reported for 2015 (Verizon, 2016). Hacking is a big part of underworld cybercrime, and a way for **hacktivists** to protest. Both the anonymity of the Internet and lack of international treaties provide hackers with a feeling of near invincibility because they face very low risk of capture and punishment.

It is important to note that in the Hacker culture there are three classes of Hackers, shown in **Table 5.3**.

Hacking   is broadly defined as intentionally accessing a computer without authorization or exceeding authorized access. Various state and federal laws govern computer hacking.

Hacktivist   is short for hacker-activist or someone who performs hacking to promote awareness for or otherwise support a social, political, economic, or other cause. Hacking an application, system, or network without authorization, regardless of motive, is a crime.

TABLE 5.3   **Three Classes of Hackers**

Type	Characteristics	Outcome
White hat	Computer security specialist who breaks into protected systems and networks to test and assess their security.	Use their skills to improve security by exposing vulnerabilities before malicious hackers (black hats) can detect and exploit them.
Black hat	Person who attempts to find computer security vulnerabilities and exploit them for personal financial gain or other malicious reasons.	Can inflict major damage on both individual computer users and large organizations by stealing personal financial information, compromising security of major systems, or shutting down or alerting the function of websites and networks.
Gray hat	Person who may violate ethical standards or principles, but without the malicious intent ascribed to black hat hackers.	May engage in practices that are less than ethical, but are often operating for the common good, e.g., exploits a security vulnerability to spread public awareness that the vulnerability exists.

An Inside Look at How the Hacking Industry Operates   Hacking is an industry with its own way of operating, a workforce, and support services. Hackers use social networks, underground forums, and the Deep Web to rate and promote services, share exploits, and recruit others. In certain forums and in the Deep Web, hackers can purchase the use of any number of services. These include the following:

Educational services

Software platforms for building and distributing hacking tools and malware/ransomware

Sale or purchase of stolen data ranging from items as simple as e-mail accounts to credit cards, PII, and corporate data.

Contract hackers are available for hire or complete hack attacks can be bought.

Hacking help desks provide 24/7 support—making sophisticated attacks easier to manage and execute.

Organized crime groups quickly learned that cybercrime has better payoffs with substantially lower risks to life, limb, and liberty than other activities like human trafficking, smuggling, extortion, and the drug trade. They become virtually untouchable by law enforcement because often no one sees the crime and if it is identified, the lack of international treaties and cooperation make capture and trial between those non-extradition countries virtually impossible. Given this, it is not surprising that almost every survey identifies the same troubling trend—the recovery costs and frequency of cybercrimes are increasing while the costs of execution are declining. This means much stronger IT security practices and defenses are obviously needed. One of the greatest cybersecurity weaknesses is users who ignore the dangers of weak passwords—more than half of all confirmed data breaches involve weak or stolen passwords. The capture and misuse of credentials, such a user's IDs and passwords, is one of the foundations of the cybercriminal and nation-state hackers used in executing numerous other types of cyberthreats, including phishing (discussed in more detail later in the chapter). Proper credential management is essential to security.

Cyber Social Engineering and Other Related Web-Based Threats

Experts believe the greatest cybersecurity dangers over the next few years will involve persistent threats, mobile computing, and the use of social media for social engineering. From an IT security perspective, social engineering is a hacker's clever use of deception or manipulation of people's tendency to trust, be helpful, or simply follow their curiosity. Powerful IT security systems cannot defend against what appears to be authorized access.

Notorious hacker Kevin Mitnick, who served time in jail for hacking, used social engineering as his primary method to gain access to computer networks. In most cases, the criminal never comes face-to-face with the victim, but communicates via the phone or e-mail.

Humans are easily hacked, making them and their social media posts high-risk attack vectors. For instance, it is often easy to get users to infect their corporate network or mobile devices by tricking them into downloading and installing malicious applications or **backdoors**.

Phishing **Phishing** is the term used to describe a social-engineering attack that can use e-mail sent to the recipient under false pretense to steal confidential information from the target. This is done by the sender pretending to be a known person or legitimate organization, such as PayPal, a bank, credit card company, or other trusted source and asking the user to perform an action that would expose his or her computer to a cyberthreat or reveal credentials, personal, financial, or business-related private information. Phishing messages are either sent in mass campaigns or they are specifically targeted at a particular group of people or person. The former requires no front work to gain context for the target but relies on sheer volume of messages (millions to tens of millions) to achieve returns.

The latter requires more effort to gather relevant context about the message target and is therefore sent out in far smaller batches but has a higher rate of return on both the number of opened messages and the payback per message for that effort. The latter approach is discussed later in this section.

Phishing messages include a request to respond with information of some kind or a link to a fraudulent website that often looks like an authentic site the user works with. When the user clicks the link to the site, he or she falls victim to a malware download, drive-by attack, or information skimming such as being asked for a credit card number, Social Security number, account number, or password.

Criminals use the Internet and private networks to hijack large numbers of systems including PC's mobile devices, servers, and Internet of Thing (IoT) devices to spy on users, spam them, shake down businesses, and steal identities. Once captured, they are called Bots, short for robots or Internet Robots. But why are they so successful? **The Information Security Forum**, a self-help organization that includes many Fortune 100 companies, compiled a list of the top information problems and discovered that nine of the top 10 incidents were the result of three factors:

1. Mistakes or human errors leading to misconfigured systems, applications, or networks
2. Malfunctioning systems
3. Failure to patch or otherwise properly maintain software on existing systems

Unfortunately, these factors can too easily create gaps in cybersecurity controls that companies and individuals use to protect their information.

Spear Phishing
Spear phishing targets select groups of people who have something in common. They can work at the same company, bank at the same financial institution, use a specific Internet provider, or attend the same church or university. The scam e-mails appear to be sent from organizations or people the potential victims normally receive e-mails from, making them even more deceptive.

Here is how **spear phishing** works:

1. Spear phishers gather information about people's activities, social groups, companies, and/or jobs from general media announcements, social media or compromised accounts, applications that are poorly designed and leak information or they can steal it from websites, computers, or mobile devices they have compromised, and then use that information to customize messages.
2. Then they send the customized e-mails to targeted victims, creating some sort of pretext requiring the user to act or respond. These can be threats of account closure, loss of access or privilege, loss of funds or additional charges, legal actions impact to friends or family members, and so on. With the background information gained the message creates a very legitimate-sounding and compelling explanation as to why they need your personal data.
3. Finally, the victims are asked to click on a link inside the e-mail that takes them to a phony but realistic-looking website, where they are asked to provide passwords, account numbers, user IDs, access codes, PINs, and so on.

When spear phishing targets are executives or persons of significant wealth, power, influence, or control the activity is known as "whaling."

Crimeware
IT security researchers discover almost 1 million malicious programs every day. Why would so many hackers be spending so much time generating or launching these programs? The answer is simple—it pays well! Crimeware can be broken down into several categories, including **spyware**, **adware**, **malware**, and **ransomware**.

Malware Assaults are Part of Everyday Operations
There have been numerous test cases of malware overheating devices, causing them to physically distort or worse. These attacks, bundled into a cyberattack, could have devastating and lasting effects beyond what we commonly associate with an aggravating **distributed denial-of-service (DDoS) attack**.

Viruses, worms, trojans, rootkits, backdoors, and keyloggers are types of malware. Most viruses, trojans, and worms are activated when an attachment is opened or a link is clicked. But when features are automated, they may trigger malware automatically, too. For example:

- If an e-mail client, such as Microsoft Outlook or Gmail, is set to allow scripting, then virus infection occurs by simply opening a message or attachment.
- Viewing e-mail messages in HTML, instead of in plain text, can trigger virus infections.

Malware is not just about e-mail. It also includes rogue applications and malicious websites.

Spyware is tracking software that is not designed to intentionally damage or disable a system. For example, an employer may install spyware on corporate laptops to monitor employee browsing activities, or an advertiser might use cookies to track what Web pages a user visit in order to target advertising in a marketing campaign.

Adware is software that embeds advertisements in the application. It is considered a legitimate alternative offered to consumers who do not wish to pay for software.

Malware refers to hostile or intrusive software, including computer viruses, rootkits, worms, trojan horses, ransomware, and other malicious programs used to disrupt computer or mobile operations, gather sensitive information, gain access to private computer systems.

Ransomware is a type of malware that is designed to block access to a computer system until a sum of money has been paid.

Trojan horse is a program that appears harmless, but is, in fact, malicious.

Remote access trojans (RATS) are a form of **Trojan horse** that creates an unprotected backdoor into a system through which a hacker can remotely control that system. As the name implies, a backdoor provides easy access to a system, computer, or account by creating the access that may or may not require authentication.

However, hackers are very territorial and don't want someone else using systems they worked to compromise, so RATS often require some form of access control to eliminate the need to authenticate with a username and password.

A malware's **payload** is code that is dropped on the system that performs any or all of the following functions: facilitates the infection or communicates with the command and control server or downloads more code. In doing so, the payload carries out the purpose of the malware. The payload could cause damage that is visible or operate in stealth mode so as to remain undetected. A **vector** is the specific method that malware uses to *propagate,* or spread, to other machines or devices. Malware may also *replicate to* make copies of itself.

Malware creators often use social engineering to maximize the effective distribution of their creations. For example, the *ILoveYou* worm, released in May, 2000, used social engineering to entice people to open malware-infected e-mail messages. It successfully attacked tens of millions of Windows computers when it was sent as an e-mail attachment with the subject line: ILOVEYOU. Within nine days, the worm had spread worldwide, crippling networks, destroying files, and causing an estimated $5.5 billion in damages.

Malware Reinfection, Signatures, Mutations, and Variants
When a host computer is infected, attempts to remove the malware may fail—and the malware may reinfect the host for these two reasons:

1. **Malware is captured in backups or archives** Restoring the infected backup or archive also restores the malware.

2. **Malware infects removable media** Months or years after the initial infection, the removable media may be accessed, and the malware could attempt to infect the host.

Most antivirus (AV) software relies on **signatures** to identify and then block malware. According to the Worldwide Malware Signature Counter, at the start of 2013, there were an estimated 19 million malware signatures. Detecting and preventing infections are not always a possibility. **Zero-day exploits**—malware so new their signatures are not yet known—are an example. Malware authors also evade detection by AV software and firewalls by altering malware code to create *variants*, which have new signatures. But not all procedures or AV tools are capable of removing every trace of the malware. Even if the malicious parts of the infection can be cleaned from a system, the remaining pieces of code could make the system unstable or expose to future infection.

Botnets
Today's malware is often designed for long-term control of infected machines. Advanced malware sets up outbound communication channels in order to upload stolen data, download payloads, or do reconnaissance.

In contrast, a **botnet** is a group of external attacking entities and is a totally different attack method/vector from malware which is internal to the system. Infected computers, called **zombies**, can be controlled and organized into a network of zombies on the command of a remote botmaster (also called *bot herder*). Storm worm, which is spread via **spam**, is a botnet agent embedded inside over 25 million computers. Storm's combined power has been compared to the processing might of a supercomputer. Storm-organized attacks are capable of crippling any website. Zombies can be commanded to monitor and steal personal or financial data—acting as spyware. Botnets are used to send spam and phishing e-mails and launch DDoS attacks. Botnets are extremely dangerous because they scan for and compromise other computers, which then can be used for every type of crime and attack against computers, servers, and networks.

Ransomware Is Increasingly Becoming a Problem
Ransomware has been around for more than a decade. The problem began on a fairly small scale, targeting individual users, but the ransomware cyberthreat has been growing in the last couple of years and the

attacks have become large scale. Now, some company executives fear entire companies will be shut down by ransomware until they pay up, or risk losing all their data.

Ransomware works by first infiltrating a computer with malware and then encrypting all the files on the disk. The malware used to encrypt files can be difficult to defend against, and the encryption in most cases can't be broken. Then, the user is presented with a limited time offer: Lose all your data or send money with the promise the data will be unlocked. The fee typically varies from a few dollars to hundreds of dollars and often has to be transmitted in Bitcoin. One hospital in Los Angeles, whose electronic medical record system was locked out for 10 days, was forced to pay cyberattackers 40 Bitcoins to get its system unlocked when law enforcement and computer experts were unable to help in restoring the hospital's data files.

Computer security experts have theorized that this type of attack has a higher rate of success versus other cybercrime activity that has become more difficult. The best insurance against ransomware is to have offline or segregated backups of data.

Denial-of-Service

Cybersecurity experts warn that battling the increasing number of **Denial-of-Service (DoS)** threats needs to be a top priority. DoS threats come in a number of "flavors," depending on their target. The three most prominent forms are:

Distributed Denial-of-Service (DDoS)—crashes a network or website by bombarding it with traffic (i.e., *requests for service*) and effectively denying services to all those legitimately using it and leaving it vulnerable to other threats.

Telephony Denial-of-Service (TDoS)—floods a network with phone calls and keeps the calls up for long durations to overwhelm an agent or circuit and prevents legitimate callers such as customers, partners, and suppliers from using network resources.

Permanent Denial-of-Service (PDoS)—completely prevents the target's system or device from working. This attack type is unique. Instead of collecting data or providing some ongoing perverse function its objective is to completely prevent its target's device(s) from functioning. The damage PDoS causes is often so extensive that hardware must be reinstalled or reinstated. PDoS is also known as "phlashing."

A "chilling" example of the havoc that PDoS can cause was demonstrated when a PDoS attack took the building management system offline in a block of residential apartments in Finland. The system's Internet connection was blocked causing the system to repeatedly try to reconnect by rebooting itself. During this downtime, the system was unable to supply heat at a time when temperatures were below freezing! Fortunately, the energy company was able to find alternate accommodations for residents until the system was brought back online.

Insider and Privilege Misuse

Threats from employees, referred to as **internal threats**, are a major challenge largely due to the many ways an employee can carry out malicious activity. Insiders may be able to bypass physical security (e.g., locked doors) and technical security (e.g., passwords) measures that organizations have put in place to prevent unauthorized access. Why? Because defenses such as firewalls, **intrusion detection systems (IDSs)**, and locked doors mostly protect against external threats. Despite the challenges, insider incidents can be minimized with a layered defense-in-depth strategy consisting of security procedures, acceptable use policies (AUPs), and technology controls.

Data tampering is a common means of attack that is overshadowed by other types of attacks. It refers to an attack during which someone enters false or fraudulent data into a computer, or changes or deletes existing data. Data tampering is extremely serious because it may not be detected. This is the method often used by insiders.

Physical Theft or Loss

The threat of an information asset going missing, whether through negligence or malice can send companies into a panic. The "miniaturization" of computing has led to an increase in physical theft or loss. Laptops, tablets, modems, routers, and USBs are much more easily transportable than mainframes or servers! When a laptop or tablet with unencrypted sensitive documents on it goes missing it's difficult to determine if a data breach has actually occurred, but precautions must always be taken. Theft of laptops occurs primarily in victims' own work area or from their vehicles. On the positive side, lost items are much more prevalent than theft. Theft is more likely to be related to the procurement of USB drives and printer paper.

Miscellaneous Errors

The main concern related to this source of cyberthreat is a shortage of capacity, thus preventing information from being available when needed. Other threat actions that fall within this category of miscellaneous errors are shown in **Table 5.4**.

TABLE 5.4 **Threat Actions Classified as Miscellaneous Errors**

Misdelivery	Information delivered to the wrong person, when e-mails or documents are sent to the wrong people
Publishing error	Information published to an unintended audience, such as the entire Internet, enabling them to view it
Misconfiguration	A firewall rule is mistyped allowing access to a sensitive file server from all internal networks rather than a specific pool of hosts
Disposal error	A hard drive is not "wiped" on decommissioned devices
Programming error	Code is mistyped or logic is flawed
Date entry error	Data is entered incorrectly or into the incorrect file or duplicated
Omission	Data is not entered; document is not sent

New Attack Vectors

Attack vector is a path or means by which a hacker can gain access to a computer or network server in order to deliver a malicious outcome.

Vulnerabilities exist in networks, operating systems, applications, databases, mobile devices, and cloud environments. These vulnerabilities are **attack vectors** or entry points for malware, hackers, hacktivists, and organized crime. Mobile devices and apps, social media, and cloud services introduce even more attack vectors for malware, phishing, and hackers. As a result, new cyberthreats are on the horizon.

Malicious (Rogue) Mobile Applications The number of malicious Android applications is growing at an alarming rate. According to a report by AV provider and software analysis group Trend Micro, more than 850,000 Android phones worldwide have been infected by the new "Godless" malware, as of June, 2016 (Goodin, 2016). The malware is transferred to users' phones through rogue applications in the Google Play store. According to mobile security cloud service providers Marble Security and Trend Micro, over 42% of the more than 300 rogue mobile applications found in the Google Play store are published in the United States (RT.com, 2015; Duan, 2016). Almost all of these applications were found in unreliable third-party stores. Rogue mobile applications can serve up trojan attacks, other malware, or phishing attacks.

Companies offering legitimate applications for online banking, retail shopping, gaming, and other functions might not be aware of threats lurking in their app stores. And despite their best efforts, legitimate app store operators cannot reliably police their own catalogs for rogue apps.

With a single click on a malicious link, users can launch a targeted attack against their organizations.

Questions

1. Define and give an example of an intentional threat and an unintentional threat.

2. Why might management not treat cyberthreats as a top priority?

3. Describe the differences between distributed denial-of-service (DDoS), telephony denial-of-service (TDoS), and permanent denial-of-service (PDoS).

4. Why is social engineering a technique used by hackers to gain access to a network?

5. List and define three types of malware.

6. What are the risks caused by data tampering?

7. Define botnets and explain why they are dangerous.

8. Why is ransomware on the rise? How might companies guard against ransomware attacks?

5.2 | Cyberattack Targets and Consequences

Every enterprise has data that profit-motivated criminals want. Customer data, networks, websites, proprietary information systems, and patents are examples of **assets**—things of value that need to be protected. However, it would appear that management may not be doing enough to defend against cyberattacks. Even high-tech companies and market leaders appear to be detached from the value of the confidential data they store and the ways in which highly motivated hackers will try to steal them.

One of the biggest mistakes managers make is underestimating IT vulnerabilities and threats. For example, workers use their laptops and mobiles for both work and leisure, and in an era of multitasking, they often do both at the same time. Yet off-time or off-site use of devices remains risky because, despite policies, employees continue to engage in dangerous online and communication habits. Those habits make them a weak link in an organization's otherwise solid security efforts.

Some of the most prevalent and deadly targets that cyber criminals will attack in companies and governmental agencies include: critical infrastructure; theft of IP; identity theft; bring your own device (BYOD); and social media. Some of these attacks will be conducted as high-profile attacks while others will fall into the category of "under-the-radar" attacks. Before discussing the different cyberattack targets, let's take a look at the differences between these two approaches.

"High-Profile" and "Under-the-Radar" Attacks

Advanced persistent threat (APT) attackers operate "under the radar" so they can continue to steal data, as described in IT at Work 5.1 and profit from it. These APT attackers are profit-motivated cybercriminals who often operate in stealth mode. In contrast, hackers and hacktivists with personal agendas carry out high-profile attacks to gain recognition and notoriety.

Hacktivist groups, such as **Anonymous**, a loosely associated international network of activist and hacktivist entities and its spin-off hacker group, **LulzSec**, have committed daring data breaches, data compromises, data leaks, thefts, threats, and privacy invasions. Consider the following three examples:

Philippine Commission on Elections   A few months before a Philippine election, the hacker group Anonymous tapped into the commission's website and released personal information on 55 million registered voters. The demonstration was in response to the Philippines' lax security measures around its voting machines; 1.3 million overseas voters' information, which included passport numbers, were included in the breach.

Combined Systems, Inc.   Proudly displaying its hacktivist flag, Anonymous took credit for knocking Combined Systems, Inc. offline and stealing personal data from its clients. Anonymous went after Combined Systems, which sells tear gas and crowd-control devices to law enforcement and military organizations, to protest war profiteers.

CIA Twice in one year, Anonymous launched a DoS attack that forced the CIA website offline. The CIA takedown followed a busy week for the hacktivists. Within 10 days, the group also went after Chinese electronics manufacturer Foxconn, American Nazi groups, AV firm Symantec, and the office of Syria's president.

In contrast, APTs typically steal corporate and government secrets. Most APT attacks are launched through phishing. Typically, this type of attack begins with some reconnaissance on the part of attackers. This can include researching publicly available information about the company and its employees, often from social networking sites. This information is then used to create targeted phishing e-mail messages. A successful attack could give the attacker access to the enterprise's network.

APTs are designed for long-term espionage. Once installed on a network, APTs transmit copies of documents, such as Microsoft Office files and PDFs, in stealth mode. APTs collect and store files on the company's network; encrypt them; then send them in bursts to servers often in China or Russia. This type of attack has been observed in other large-scale data breaches that exposed significant numbers of identities.

Both high-profile and under-the-radar attacks can be launched against a number of different targets. We will discuss those next.

Critical Infrastructure Attacks

Critical infrastructure is defined as, "systems and assets, whether physical or virtual, so vital to the a country that the incapacity or destruction of such systems and assets would have a debilitating impact on security, national economic security, national public health or safety, or any combination of those matters" (Department of Justice, 2001).

Hackers, hacktivists, crime syndicates, militant groups, industrial spies, fraudsters, and hostile governments continue to attack networks for profit, fame, revenge, or an ideology; to wage warfare and terrorism, fight against a terrorist campaign, or disable their target. For example, the Department of Homeland Security (DHS) Industrial Control Systems Cyber Emergency Response Team (ICS-CERT) warned that attacks against **critical infrastructure** are growing. In 2015, more than 427 vulnerability incidents were reported, far surpassing the 245 total attacks reported in 2014. The most affected industry was the energy sector.

Figure 5.3 shows the 16 critical infrastructure sectors whose assets, systems, and networks, whether physical or virtual, are considered so vital to the United States that their incapacitation or destruction would have a debilitating effect on security, national economic security, national public health or safety, or any combination thereof.

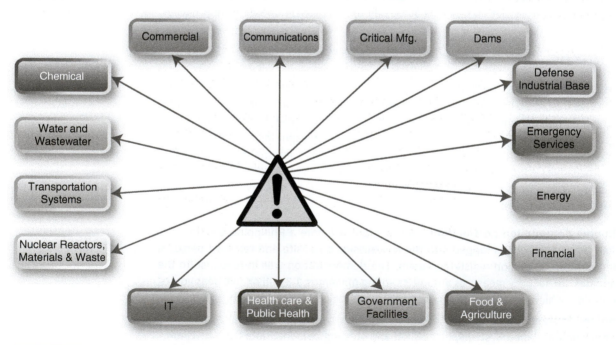

FIGURE 5.3 U.S. critical infrastructure sectors.

Attacks on critical infrastructure sectors can significantly disrupt the functioning of government and business—and trigger cascading effects far beyond the targeted sector and physical location of the incident. These cyberattacks could compromise a country's critical infrastructure and its ability to provide essential services to its citizens.

For example, the first cyberattack against a nation's power grid occurred in December, 2015, when a cyberattacker successfully seized control of the Prykarpattyaoblenergo Control Center (PCC) in the Western Ukraine leaving 230,000 citizens without power for up to six hours. The attackers carefully planned their assault over many months. They studied the networks and siphon operator credentials and finally launched their devastating synchronized assault in the middle of winter. The PCC operated a supervisory control and data acquisition (SCADA) system, which is a common form of industrial control system, that distributed electricity. The critical devices at 16 substations became unresponsive to any remote command by its operators after attackers overwrote its firmware. This type of control system is surprisingly more secure than some used in the United States since they have robust firewalls that separate them from control center business networks. Governments around the world have plans in place to deal with the consequences of natural disasters, yet none have disaster relief plans for a downed power grid. Clearly, this must change. Local and state governments must work together with their national counterparts to produce and quickly implement plans to address future attacks.

In response to the consistently growing number of cyberattacks over the past decade, the Inter-American Committee Against Terrorism (CICTE) issued a formal declaration to protect critical infrastructure from emerging threats and a Presidential executive order was signed in May 2017 to strengthen the cybersecurity of Federal networks and critical infrastructure.

Theft of Intellectual Property

Intellectual property (IP) can represent more than 80% of a company's value and as such is a critical part of all 21st-century organizations. Losing customer data to hackers can be costly and embarrassing but losing IP, commonly known as trade secrets, could threaten a company's existence. It's a business leaders' nightmare—that gut-wrenching realization that a corporate network has been breached and valuable intellectual assets have been stolen by unknown cybercriminals (Gelinne et al., 2016).

Theft of IP has always been a threat from corporate moles, disgruntled employees, and other insiders. While some IP may still be obtainable exclusively through physical means, digitization has made theft easier. Advancements in technology, increased mobility, rapid globalization, and the anonymous nature of the Internet create growing challenges in protecting IP. Hackers' preferred modus operandi is to break into employees' mobile devices and leapfrog into employers' networks—stealing trade secrets without a trace.

Cybersecurity experts and government officials are increasingly concerned about breaches from other countries into corporate and government networks either through mobile devices or other means. For example, a government agency could have blueprints for a secret new weapon system stolen by foreign agents, or an employee of a popular game developer might steal their latest game before it is released to the public.

In May of 2016, President Barack Obama signed the Defend Trade Secrets Act (DTSA), to allow "the owners of trade secrets to bring a civil action in federal court for trade secret misappropriation" (Gibson Dunn, 2016). Until the signing of the DTSA, corporations had to rely on state law regarding trade secrets. Now, every American corporation is equally protected under federal law. Moreover, it extends the power of the federal government in regulation of trade secrets through interstate and foreign commerce while maintaining existing trade secret laws.

A famous example of theft of IP is the APT attack named Operation Aurora perpetrated against Google, described in **IT at Work 5.1.**

Intellectual property is a work or invention that is the result of creativity that has commercial value, including copyrighted property such as a blueprint, manuscript, or a design, and is protected by law from unauthorized use by others.

IT at Work 5.1

Operation Aurora

Operation Aurora was a counterespionage operation being run by the Chinese government. It was a series of cyberattacks conducted by APTs with ties to the People's Liberation Army in China. Attackers successfully accessed a database that flagged Gmail accounts marked for court-ordered wiretaps to gain insights into active investigations being conducted by the FBI and other law enforcement agencies that involved undercover Chinese operatives.

To access IP, Operation Aurora exploited security flaws in e-mail attachments to sneak into the networks of major financial, defense, and technology companies and research institutions in the United States by performing six steps, as described in **Figure 5.4**. Standard IT security technologies at Google failed to prevent these six steps from occurring and neither Google nor its Gmail account holders knew they had been hacked.

Once the APTs gained access to Google's internal systems (Step 6), they were free to steal corporate secrets. Reportedly, over 30 other large companies from a wide range of industries were similarly targeted by Operation Aurora.

Most hack activities do not become headline grabbers until after the incidents are detected and reported. Even then, victimized companies are reluctant to discuss them so statistics are scarce. In the case of Operation Aurora, the attack was not discovered until almost one year after the fact!

IT at Work Questions

1. Describe the six steps of Operation Aurora.
2. What was the purpose of Operation Aurora?
3. What could Google have done to prevent Operation Aurora?

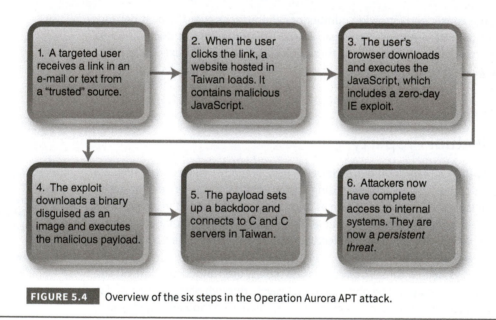

FIGURE 5.4   Overview of the six steps in the Operation Aurora APT attack.

Identity Theft

One of the worst and most prevalent cyberthreats is identity theft. Thefts where individuals' Social Security and credit card numbers are stolen and used by thieves are not new. Criminals have always obtained information about other people—by stealing wallets or dumpster diving. But widespread electronic sharing and databases have made the crime worse. Because financial institutions, data-processing firms, and retail businesses are reluctant to reveal incidents in which their customers' personal financial information may have been stolen, lost, or compromised, laws continue to be passed that force those notifications.

Bring Your Own Device

Another, more recent, vulnerability is bring your own device (BYOD). Roughly 74% of U.S. organizations are either already using or planning to use BYOD. It's an appealing concept because BYOD enables companies to cut costs by not having to purchase and maintain employees' mobile devices. Unfortunately, many companies have rushed into it without considering issues relating to security. Mobile devices rarely have strong authentication, access controls, and encryption even though they connect to mission-critical data and cloud services. For example, only 20% of androids have a security app installed.

The BYOD trend is driven by employees using their own devices for business purposes because they are more powerful than those the company has provided. Another factor is mobility. In the past, and before the BYOD push, employees worked at their desks on a land-line and on a computer plugged into the wall with a network cable. This change in exposure requires greater investment to defend against BYOD risks. As more and more people work from home and on the go, the office-bound traditional 9-to-5 workday has become a thing of the past.

Users bringing their personal mobile devices and their own mobile applications to work and connecting them to the corporate network is part of the larger **consumerization of information technology (COIT)** trend. **Bring your own device (BYOD)** and **bring your own apps (BYOA)** are practices that move enterprise data and IT assets to employees' mobile devices and the cloud, creating a new set of tough IT security challenges. **Figure 5.5** summarizes how apps, mobile devices, and cloud services put organizations at a greater risk of cyberattack. Widely used applications that are outside of the organization's firewall are Twitter, Google Analytics, Dropbox, WebEx, and Salesforce.com.

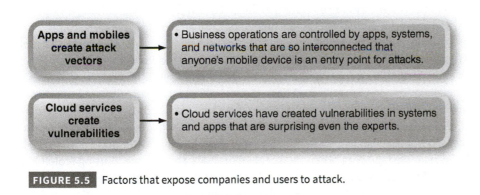

FIGURE 5.5 Factors that expose companies and users to attack.

Enterprises take risks with BYOD practices that they never would consider taking with conventional computing devices. One possible reason is that new devices, apps, and systems have been rolled out so quickly. As a result, smartphones are not being managed as secure devices, with fewer than 20% of users installing antimalware and 50% using some type of data encryption. In fact, employees expected instant approval of (or at least no disapproval of) and support for their new tablet computers within hours of the product's release.

BYOD Raises Serious and Legitimate Areas of Concern Hackers break into employees' mobile devices and leapfrog into employers' networks—stealing secrets without a trace. New vulnerabilities are created when personal and business data and communications are mixed together. All cybersecurity controls—authentication, access control, data confidentiality, and intrusion detection—implemented on corporate-owned resources can be rendered useless by an employee-owned device. The corporation's mobile infrastructure may not be able to support the increase in mobile network traffic and data processing, causing unacceptable delays or requiring additional investments.

Another serious problem arises when an employee's mobile device is lost or stolen. The company can suffer a data breach if the device is not adequately secured by a strong password and the data on the BYOD is not encrypted.

Tech Note 5.1 demonstrates why users should only download applications from trusted sources and check reviews to verify the legitimacy of the application being downloaded.

Tech Note 5.1

Android Botnet over SMS

A botnet of exploited android phones was sending massive amounts of spam via Yahoo e-mail servers using the short messaging service (SMS) as the **command and control (C&C) channel**. Infected androids, or bots, log into the owner's Yahoo Mail account to send spam. Most of the devices were located in Chile, Venezuela, Thailand, Indonesia, Lebanon, Philippines, Russia, and Saudi Arabia—in countries where users are less likely to get

their android applications from the Google Play market, which automatically ensures that the applications are safe. Users downloading free phone apps from third-party app stores to avoid paying for legitimate versions were actually downloading the android malware.

User should only download applications from trusted sources and also check the reviews to verify the applications are legitimate because there are many bogus applications.

Social Media Attacks

Companies' poor social media security practices put their brands, customers, executives, and entire organizations at serious risk. According to Cisco, Facebook scams are the most common form of malware distributed in 2015. The FBI reported that social media-related events had quadrupled over the past five years and PricewaterhouseCoopers (2015) found that more than one in eight enterprises has suffered at least one security breach due to a social media-related cyberattack.

Social networks and cloud computing increase vulnerabilities by providing a single point of failure and attack for organized criminal networks. Critical, sensitive, and private information is at risk, and like previous IT trends, such as wireless networks, the goal is connectivity, often with little concern for security. As social networks increase their offerings, the gap between services and information security also increases. For example, virus and malware attacks on a well-established service such as e-mail have decreased as e-mail security has improved over the years. Unfortunately, malware is still finding ways to successfully disrupt new services and devices, such e-readers, netbooks, Google's Chrome OS, Facebook, YouTube, Twitter, LinkedIn, and other cloud-based social media networks. For example, in Twitter and Facebook, where users build relationships with other users, cybercriminals are hacking in using stolen logins. These types of attacks that take advantage of user trust are very difficult to detect. Facebook recently reported that up to 2% of its 31 million accounts are false, Twitter estimates 5%, and LinkedIn openly admitted, that they don't have a reliable system for identifying and counting duplicate or fraudulent accounts.

To combat these cyberthreats, Web filtering, user education, and strict policies are key to preventing widespread outbreaks.

Networks and Services Increase Exposure to Risk
An overriding reason why these networks and services increase exposure to risk is the **time-to-exploitation** of today's sophisticated spyware and mobile viruses. Time-to-exploitation is the elapsed time between when vulnerability is discovered and when it is exploited. That time has shrunk from months to minutes so IT staff have ever-shorter timeframes to find and fix flaws before they are compromised by an attack. Some attacks exist for as little as two hours, which means that enterprise IT security systems must have real-time protection.

When new vulnerabilities are found in operating systems, applications, or wired and wireless networks, patches are released by the vendor or security organization. **Patches** are software programs that users download and install to fix a vulnerability. Microsoft, for example, releases patches that it calls **service packs** to update and fix vulnerabilities in its operating systems, including Vista, and applications, including Office 2010. Service packs can be downloaded from Microsoft's website.

Left undetected or unprotected, vulnerabilities provide an open door for IT attacks and business disruptions and their financial damages. Despite the best technology defenses, information security incidents will occur mostly because of the users who do not follow secure computing practices and procedures. **IT at Work 5.2** illustrates how Google's new automated cybersecurity initiative is poised to reduce Google's losses suffered due to cyberattacks in the cloud.

IT at Work 5.2

Google's Automated Game of Monkey in the Middle

Google is the world's largest Internet-based search engine, servicing 2 trillion Internet searches every year (Burgess, 2016). In addition to being the largest encyclopedia known to man, Google has also expanded its services into cloud computing and online advertising. The Internet security sector is becoming increasingly important as the amount of global cyberattacks grows every year. Encryption technologies serve the purpose of hiding information from unauthorized personnel and hackers using binary code (0 s and 1 s instead of plain text). In October, 2016, Google made the leap to becoming a security platform for Internet communication using encryption technology.

In order to do this, Google created three adversarial neural networks, that is, an information processing unit that acts very much like the brain, using interconnected processing "neurons" to gather conclusions about large data sets or other sources of information. In turn, adversarial neural networks are those that compete with each other to gain the same information more quickly or efficiently. Google named its three neural networks Eve, Alice, and Bob. Alice was tasked to send secret, encrypted messages to Bob, while Eve attempts to intercept the information before Bob receives it. The purpose of this demonstration is to test the plausibility of neural networks in Internet security applications and train them to better encrypt sensitive information.

Google's Neural Network Effectiveness

Throughout 15,000 simulations, Alice and Bob were able to send and decrypt hidden messages without Eve fully decrypting any of them. In fact, as the study progressed, Eve made more decryption errors as Bob and Alice became more effective (**Figure 5.6**). The implications of this study are significant to the future of machine learning and security. While neural networks are relatively simple in terms of cryptanalysis, because the adversarial neural networks were able to learn how to better secure information, other, more complex security technologies can also learn how to protect information and determine which information is worth protecting.

IT at Work Questions

1. Why is decryption security important in today's interconnected society?

2. What can Google's AI teach us about cybersecurity?

3. What are the future implications of this study?

Sources: Compiled from Berman (2016), Burgess (2016), and Abadi and Andersen (2016).

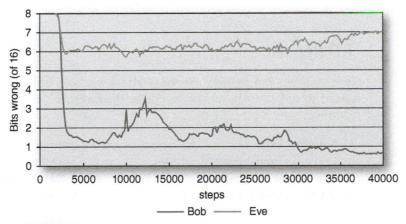

FIGURE 5.6   Effectiveness of Bob and Eve in receiving and decrypting messages over time.

Questions

1. What is a critical infrastructure?
2. List three types of critical infrastructures.
3. How do social networks and cloud computing increase vulnerability?
4. Why are patches and service packs needed?
5. Why is it important to protect IP?
6. How are the motives of hacktivists and APTs different?
7. Explain why data on laptops and computers need to be encrypted.
8. Explain how identity theft can occur.

5.3 | Cyber Risk Management

Top management needs to sponsor and promote security initiatives and fund them as a top priority. As you will read in this section, robust data security is not just the responsibility of IT and top management, but the ongoing duty of everyone in an organization.

It is becoming more important than ever that security is viewed as a high priority as the growth of mobile technologies and the IoT threaten to provide attackers with new opportunities. The five key factors contributing to the rising number of data breaches that must be addressed in a cyber **risk** management program are listed in **Table 5.5**.

Risk is the probability of a threat successfully exploiting a vulnerability and the estimated cost of the loss or damage.

TABLE 5.5   Five Key Factors Leading to an Increase in Cyberattacks

1. Interconnected, interdependent, wirelessly networked business environment
2. Smaller, faster, cheaper computers and storage devices
3. Decreasing skills necessary to be a computer hacker
4. International organized crime taking over cybercrime
5. Lack of management support

Keep in mind that security is an ongoing, unending process—something akin to painting the Golden Gate Bridge in San Francisco—and not a problem that can be solved with just hardware or software. Hardware and software security defenses cannot protect against irresponsible business practices. These are organizational and people issues.

IT Defenses

Since malware and botnets use many attack methods and strategies, multiple tools are needed to detect them and/or neutralize their effects. Three essential defenses are the following:

1. **Antivirus Software**   Antimalware tools are designed to detect malicious codes and prevent users from downloading them. They can also scan systems for the presence of worms, trojans, and other types of threats. This technology does not provide complete protection because it cannot defend against zero-day exploits. Antimalware may not be able to detect a previously unknown exploit.

2. **Intrusion Detection Systems (IDSs)**   As the name implies, an IDS scans for unusual or suspicious traffic. An IDS can identify the start of a DoS attack by the traffic pattern, alerting the network administrator to take defensive action, such as switching to another IP address and diverting critical servers from the path of the attack.

3. **Intrusion Prevention Systems (IPSs)**   An IPS is designed to take immediate action—such as blocking specific IP addresses—whenever a traffic-flow anomaly is detected. An application-specific integrated circuit (ASIC)-based IPS has the power and analysis capabilities to detect and block DDoS attacks, functioning somewhat like an automated circuit breaker.

Business policies, procedures, training, and disaster recovery plans as well as hardware and software are critical to cybersecurity. **Table 5.6** lists the characteristics of an effective cybersecurity program.

To help keep managers updated on the latest cyberthreats and prioritize defenses, KPMG publishes its *Data Loss Barometer.* The annual report describes the latest trends and statistics for data losses worldwide. Key findings and predictions are listed in **Table 5.7**.

The higher the value of the asset to the company and to cybercriminals, the greater the risk is to the company and the higher the level of security needs to be. The smart strategy is

TABLE 5.6   **Characteristics of an Effective Cybersecurity Program**

Make data and documents available and accessible 24/7 while simultaneously restricting access.
Implement and enforce procedures and AUPs for data, networks, hardware, and software that are company or employee owned, as discussed in the opening case.
Promote secure and legal sharing of information among authorized persons and partners.
Ensure compliance with government regulations and laws.
Prevent attacks by having network intrusion defenses in place.
Detect, diagnose, and respond to incidents and attacks in real time.
Maintain internal controls to prevent unauthorized alteration of data/records.
Recover from business disasters and disruptions quickly.

TABLE 5.7   **Worldwide Data Loss Key Findings and Predictions**

Key findings from *KPMG Data Loss Barometer Report* and its predictions for the next few years:

- Hacking is the number one cause of data loss.
- Internal threats have reduced significantly, while external threats are increasing significantly.
- The most hacked sectors are technology, financial services, retail, and automotive.
- Expect increased loss of data from mobile devices.
- Expect a steep rise in automated hacking and botnets.
- Expect less tolerant regulators and greater fines and negative consequences.
- Expect greater visibility and reporting of data loss as a result of less tolerant regulators.

Source: KPMG (2016).

to invest more to protect the company's most valuable assets rather than trying to protect all assets equally, as discussed in IT at Work 5.2. The IT security field—like sports and law—has its own terminology, which is summarized for quick reference in **Figure 5.7** and **Table 5.8**.

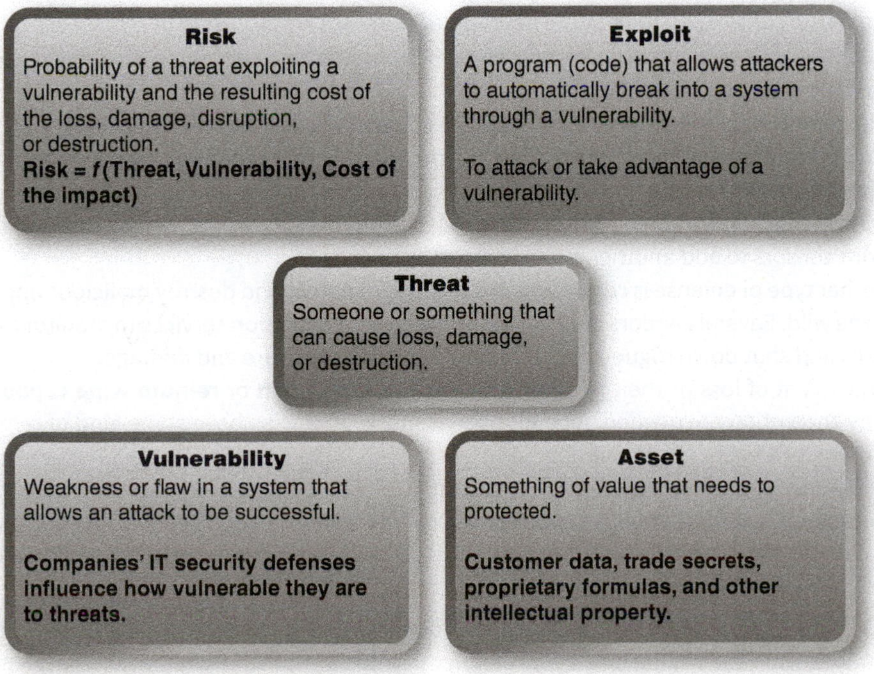

Risk
Probability of a threat exploiting a vulnerability and the resulting cost of the loss, damage, disruption, or destruction.
Risk = *f*(Threat, Vulnerability, Cost of the impact)

Exploit
A program (code) that allows attackers to automatically break into a system through a vulnerability.

To attack or take advantage of a vulnerability.

Threat
Someone or something that can cause loss, damage, or destruction.

Vulnerability
Weakness or flaw in a system that allows an attack to be successful.

Companies' IT security defenses influence how vulnerable they are to threats.

Asset
Something of value that needs to protected.

Customer data, trade secrets, proprietary formulas, and other intellectual property.

FIGURE 5.7   Basic IT security concepts.

TABLE 5.8   IT Security Terminology

Term	Definition
Exposure	Estimated cost, loss, or damage that can result if a threat exploits a vulnerability
Access control	Security feature designed to restrict who has access to a network, IS, or data
Audit	Procedure of generating, recording, and reviewing a chronological record of system events to determine their accuracy
Encryption	Transforming data into scrambled code to protect them from being understood by unauthorized users
Plaintext or clear text	Readable text
Ciphertext	Encrypted text
Authentication	Method (usually based on username and password) by which an IS validates or verifies that a user is really who he or she claims to be
Biometrics	Methods to identify a person based on a biological feature, such as a fingerprint or retina
Firewall	Software or hardware device that controls access to a private network from a public network (Internet) by analyzing data packets entering or exiting it
Intrusion detection system (IDS)	A defense tool used to monitor network traffic (packets) and provide alerts when there is suspicious traffic, or to quarantine suspicious traffic
Fault tolerance	The ability of an IS to continue to operate when a failure occurs, but usually for a limited time or at a reduced level

Minimum Security Defenses for Mobiles   Minimum security defenses for mobile devices are mobile biometrics, rogue app monitoring, remote wipe capability, and encryption. For travelers, do-not-carry rules may be a necessary defense.

A **biometric control** is an automated method of verifying the identity of a person, based on physical or behavioral characteristics. The most common biometrics are a thumbprint or fingerprint, voice print, retinal scan, and signature.

Mobile biometrics, such as voice and fingerprint biometrics, can significantly improve the security of physical devices and provide stronger authentication for remote access or cloud services. Biometric controls have been integrated into e-business hardware and software products. Biometric controls do have some limitations: They are not accurate in certain cases, and some people see them as an invasion of privacy. Most biometric systems match some personal characteristic against a stored profile.

When Apple acquired Siri, Inc., the voice-based personal assistant Siri was integrated into its Apple's operating system, Siri gave Apple the potential to move into voice biometrics.

Voice biometrics is an effective authentication solution across a wide range of consumer devices including smartphones, tablets, and TVs. Future mobile devices are expected to have fingerprint sensors to add another authentication factor.

Another type of defense is **rogue app monitoring** to detect and destroy malicious applications in the wild. Several vendors offer 24/7 monitoring and detection services to monitor major app stores and shut down rogue applications to minimize exposure and damage.

In the event of loss or theft of a device, a **mobile kill switch** or **remote wipe capability** as well as encryption are needed. All major smartphone platforms have some kind of remote-erase capability and encryption option.

In response to mobile security threats, many U.S. companies and government agencies are imposing do-not-carry rules on mobiles to prevent compromise. Travelers can bring only "clean" devices and are forbidden from connecting to the government's network while abroad.

Do-Not-Carry Rules   The U.S. Chamber of Commerce did not learn that it and its member organizations were the victims of a cybertheft for months until the FBI informed the Chamber that servers in China were stealing data from four of its Asia policy experts, individuals who frequently travel to Asia. Most likely, the experts' mobile devices had been infected with malware that was transmitting information and files back to the hackers. By the time the Chamber hardened (secured) its network, hackers had stolen at least six weeks of e-mails, most of which were communications with the largest U.S. corporations. Even later, the Chamber learned that its office printer and a thermostat in one of its corporate apartments were communicating with an Internet address in China. The Chamber did not disclose how hackers had infiltrated its systems, but its first step was to implement do-not-carry rules.

U.S. companies, government agencies, and organizations are now imposing **do-not-carry rules**, which are based on the assumption that devices will inevitably be compromised according to Mike Rogers, current chairman of the House Intelligence Committee. For example, House members can bring only "clean" devices and are forbidden from connecting to the government's network while abroad. Rogers said he travels "electronically naked" to ensure cybersecurity during and after a trip. **IT at Work 5.3** explains how one cybersecurity expert complies with do-not-carry rules while traveling.

IT at Work 5.3

Traveling Electronically Clean

When Kenneth G. Lieberthal, an expert at the Brookings Institution, travels to other countries, he follows a routine that seems straight from a secret agent movie. He leaves his smartphone and laptop at home. Instead, he brings loaner devices, which he erases before he leaves the United States and wipes clean the minute he returns. While traveling, he disables Bluetooth and Wi-Fi and never lets his phone out of his sight. While in meetings, he not only turns off his phone, but also removes the battery for fear his microphone could be turned on remotely.

Lieberthal connects to the Internet only through an encrypted, password-protected channel. He never types in a password directly, but copies and pastes his password from a USB thumb drive. By not typing his password, he eliminates the risk of having it stolen if keylogging software were to be installed on his device.

IT at Work Questions

1. Many travelers might consider Lieberthal's method too inconvenient. Clearly, his electronically clean methods are time consuming and expensive. In your opinion, is there a trade-off between cybersecurity and convenience? Explain.

2. Create a list of best cybersecurity practices for travelers based on Lieberthal's methods.

Business Continuity Planning

Risk management is not complete without a **business continuity plan** that has been tested to verify that it works. Business continuity refers to maintaining business functions or restoring them quickly when there is a major disruption. The plan covers business processes, assets, human resources, business partners, and more. Fires, earthquakes, floods, power outages, malicious attacks, and other types of disasters hit data centers. Yet, business continuity planning capabilities can be a tough sell because they do not contribute to the bottom line—that is, until it is too late. Compare them to an insurance policy: If and only if a disaster occurs, the money has been well spent. And spending on business continuity preparedness is an ongoing process because there is always more that could be done to prepare better.

The purpose of a business continuity plan is to keep the business running after a disaster occurs. Each function in the business should have a feasible backup plan. For example, if the customer service center or call center was destroyed by a storm or lost all power, would anyone know how the reps would continue to answer customer calls? The backup plan could define how to provide necessary network access to enable business to continue.

Government Regulations

Cyberattacks are now the number one type of danger facing many countries around the globe. As a result, international, federal, and state laws and industry regulations mandate that enterprises invest in cybersecurity defenses, audits, and internal controls to help secure confidential data, prevent attacks, and defend against fraud and unauthorized transactions such as money laundering (Morris 2016).

IT defenses must satisfy ever-stricter government and international regulations. All mandate the protection of PII. To protect consumers, some countries require strict compliance with these regulations. For example, in the United States the director of the Bureau of Consumer Protection at the Federal Trade Commission (FTC) warned that the agency would bring enforcement action against small businesses lacking adequate policies and procedures to protect consumer data. Some examples of major national security regulations are listed in **Figure 5.8**. Some of these regulations also apply to **occupational fraud** that is described in the next section.

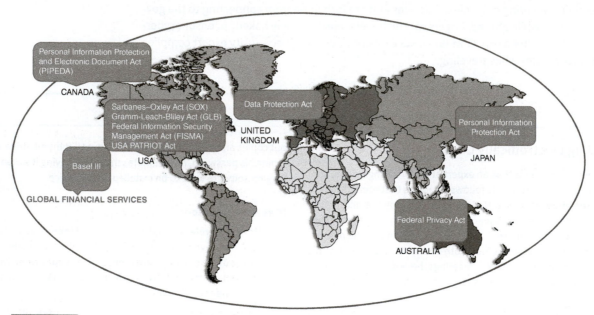

FIGURE 5.8   Global government regulations of PII.

To ensure compliance with these regulations in United Sates, the **SEC** and **FTC** impose huge fines for data breaches to deter companies from underinvesting in data protection.

Questions

1. Explain why it is becoming more important for organizations to make cyber risk management a high priority?
2. Name four U.S. government regulations that relate to cyber risk management.
3. What is the purpose of rogue application monitoring?
4. Why is a mobile kill switch or remote wipe capability an important part of managing cyber risk?
5. Why does an organization need to have a business continuity plan?
6. Name the three essential cybersecurity defenses.
7. Name three IT defenses.
8. Why do companies impose do-not-carry rules?

5.4 | Defending Against Fraud

Fraud is a nonviolent crime in which **fraudsters** use deception, confidence, and trickery for their personal gain.

Not all cybercrimes are "attacks" conducted from outside the organization. Some are conducted by employees within the organization. This is called **fraud**. Fraudsters carry out their crime by abusing the power of their position or by taking advantage of the trust, ignorance, or laziness of others. According to the latest Annual Global Fraud Survey, 81% of organizations have been victims of frauds perpetrated by insiders. Of these, 36% were carried out by senior or middle managers and 45% were attributed to junior employees. Only 23% of the reported frauds resulted from actions of an agent or nonemployee with access.

Occupational Fraud Prevention and Detection

High-profile cases of occupational fraud committed by senior executive have led to an increase in government regulations. Unfortunately, this increased legislation has not put an end to fraud.

The single most effective fraud prevention tactic is making employees aware that fraud will be detected by IT-monitoring systems and punished, with the fraudster possibly turned over to the police or FBI. The fear of being caught and prosecuted is a strong deterrent. IT must play a visible and major role in detecting fraud. A strong corporate governance program and internal audits and controls are essential to the prevention and detection of occupational fraud.

Several examples of occupational fraud, their characteristics and the extent to which they impact corporate financial statements are illustrated in **Figure 5.9.**

Type of Fraud	Impacts Financial Statements?	Typical Characteristics
Operating Management Corruption	No	Occurs *off the books*. Median loss due to corruption is 6X median loss due to misappropriation
Conflict of Interest	No	Breach of confidentiality, such as revealing competitor bids. Often occurs coincident with bribery.
Bribery	No	Uses positional power or money to influence others
Embezzlement or "misappropriation"	Yes	Employee theft. Employee access to company property creates the opportunity for embezzlement
Senior management financial reporting fraud	Yes	Involves massive breach of trust and leveraging of positional power
Accounting Cycle fraud	Yes	Also called "earnings management" or "earnings engineering." Violates generally accepted accounting principles (GAAP) and other all other accounting principles. See aicpa.org

FIGURE 5.9 Types, impact, and characteristics of occupational fraud.

Corporate Governance An enterprise-wide approach that combines risk, security, compliance, and IT specialists greatly increases the prevention and detection of fraud. Prevention is the most cost-effective approach, since detection and prosecution costs are enormous in addition to the direct cost of the loss. It starts with corporate governance culture and ethics at the top levels of the organization.

IT monitoring and control also demonstrate that the company has implemented effective **corporate governance** and fraud prevention measures. Regulators look favorably on companies that can demonstrate best practices in corporate governance and operational risk management. Management and staff would then spend less time worrying about regulations and more time adding value to their brands and business.

Internal fraud prevention measures are based on the same controls that are used to prevent external intrusions—perimeter defense technologies, such as firewalls, e-mail scanners, and biometric access. They are also based on human resource (HR) procedures, such as recruitment screening and training.

Intelligent Analysis and Anomaly Detections Most detection activity can be handled by intelligent analysis engines using advanced data warehousing and analytics techniques. These systems take in audit trails from key systems and personnel records from the HR and finance departments. The data are stored in a data warehouse where they are analyzed to detect anomalous patterns, such as excessive hours worked, deviations in patterns of behavior, copying huge amounts of data, attempts to override controls, unusual transactions, and inadequate documentation about a transaction. Information from investigations is fed back into the detection system so it learns of any anomalous patterns. Since insiders might work in collusion with organized criminals, insider profiling is important to find wider patterns of criminal networks.

General Controls

It is also important to have a set of general controls in place. The major categories of general controls are physical controls, access controls, data security controls, communication network controls, and administrative controls.

Physical Controls Physical security refers to the protection of computer facilities and resources. This includes protecting physical property such as computers, data centers, software, manuals, and networks. It provides protection against most natural hazards as well as against some human hazards. Appropriate physical security may include several **physical controls** such as the following:

- Appropriate design of the data center. For example, the data center should be noncombustible and waterproof.
- Shielding against electromagnetic fields.
- Good fire prevention, detection, and extinguishing systems, including a sprinkler system, water pumps, and adequate drainage facilities.
- Emergency power shutoff and backup batteries, which must be maintained in operational condition.
- Properly designed and maintained air-conditioning systems.
- Motion detector alarms that detect physical intrusion.

Access Controls **Access control** is the management of who is and who is not authorized to use a company's hardware and software. Access control methods, such as firewalls and access control lists, restrict access to a network, database, file, or data. It is the major line of defense against unauthorized insiders as well as outsiders. Access control involves authorization (having the right to access) and authentication, which is also called user identification (proving that the user is who he or she claims to be).

Authentication methods include:

- Something only the user knows, such as a password
- Something only the user has, for example, a smart card or a token
- Something only the user is, such as a signature, voice, fingerprint, or retinal (eye) scan; implemented via biometric controls, which can be physical or behavioral

Administrative Controls While the previously discussed general controls are technical in nature, **administrative controls** deal with issuing guidelines and monitoring compliance with the guidelines. Examples of controls are shown in **Table 5.9**.

To guard against fraud and protect clients, customers, and constituents, all public and private enterprises are subject to federal and state laws and regulations, some of which are shown in Figure 5.8. In the United States, the Sarbanes–Oxley Act requires that companies prove that their financial applications and systems are controlled (secured) to verify that financial reports can be trusted. It is intended to discourage fraud at the corporate and executive levels.

Sarbanes–Oxley Act Mandates More Accurate Business Reporting and Disclosure of Violations The **Sarbanes–Oxley Act (SOX)** mandates more accurate business reporting and disclosure of generally accepted accounting principles (GAAP) violations. Section 302 deters corporate and executive fraud by requiring that the CEO and CFO verify that they have reviewed the financial report, and, to the best of their knowledge, the report

TABLE 5.9   Representative Administrative Controls

- Appropriately selecting, training, and supervising employees, especially in accounting and information systems
- Fostering company loyalty
- Immediately revoking access privileges of dismissed, resigned, or transferred employees
- Requiring periodic modification of access controls, such as passwords
- Developing programming and documentation standards (to make auditing easier and to use the standards as guides for employees)
- Insisting on security bonds or malfeasance insurance for key employees
- Instituting separation of duties, namely, dividing sensitive computer duties among as many employees as economically feasible in order to decrease the chance of intentional or unintentional damage
- Holding periodic random audits of the system

does not contain an untrue statement or omit any material fact. To motivate honesty, executive management faces criminal penalties including long jail terms for false reports. Section 805 mandates a review of the Sentencing Guidelines to ensure that "the guidelines that apply to organizations . . . are sufficient to deter and punish organizational criminal conduct." The Guidelines also focus on the establishment of "effective compliance and ethics" programs. As indicated in the Guidelines, a precondition to an effective compliance and ethics program is "an organizational culture that encourages ethical conduct and a commitment to compliance with the law."

Among other measures, SOX requires companies to set up comprehensive internal controls. There is no question that SOX, and the complex and costly provisions it requires public companies to follow, have had a major impact on corporate financial accounting. For starters, companies have had to set up comprehensive internal controls over financial reporting to prevent fraud, catching it when it occurs. Since the collapse of Arthur Andersen, following the accounting firm's conviction on criminal charges related to the Enron case, outside accounting firms have gotten tougher with clients they are auditing, particularly with regard to their internal controls.

SOX and the SEC are making it clear that if controls can be ignored, there is no control. Therefore, fraud prevention and detection require an effective monitoring system. If a company shows its employees that it can find out everything that every employee does and use that evidence to prosecute a wrongdoer to the fullest extent possible under the law, then the likelihood of any employee adopting an "I can get away with it" attitude drops drastically.

Approximately 85% of occupational fraud could be prevented if proper IT-based internal controls had been designed, implemented, and followed.

Internal Controls

The internal control environment is the work atmosphere that a company sets for its employees. **Internal control (IC)** is a process designed to achieve:

- Reliability of financial reporting, to protect investors
- Operational efficiency
- Compliance with laws, regulations, and policies
- Safeguarding of assets

Cyber Defense Strategies

The objective of IT security management practices is to defend all of the components of an information system, specifically data, software applications, hardware, and networks, so they remain in compliance. Before they make any decisions concerning defenses, the people responsible for security must understand the requirements and operations of the business, which form the basis for a customized defense strategy.

The defense strategy and controls that should be used depend on what needs to be protected and a cost–benefit analysis. That is, companies should neither underinvest nor overinvest. The major objectives of defense strategies are listed in **Table 5.10**.

TABLE 5.10 **Major Objectives of Defense Strategies**

Action	Details
Prevention and deterrence	Properly designed controls may prevent errors from occurring, deter criminals from attacking the system, and, better yet, deny access to unauthorized people. These are the most desirable controls.
Detection	Like a fire, the earlier an attack is detected, the easier it is to combat, and the less damage is done. Detection can be performed in many cases by using special diagnostic software, at a minimal cost.
Contain the damage	This objective involves minimizing or limiting losses once a malfunction has occurred. It is also called damage control. This can be accomplished, for example, by including a *fault-tolerant system* that permits operation in a degraded mode until full recovery is made. If a fault-tolerant system does not exist, a quick and possibly expensive recovery must take place. Users want their systems back in operation as fast as possible.
Recovery	A recovery plan explains how to fix a damaged information system as quickly as possible. Replacing rather than repairing components is one route to fast recovery.
Correction	Correcting the causes of damaged systems can prevent a problem from occurring again.
Awareness and compliance	All organization members must be educated about the hazards and must comply with the security rules and regulations.

A defense strategy is also going to require several controls, as shown in **Figure 5.10**. **General controls** are established to protect the system regardless of the specific application. For example, protecting hardware and controlling access to the data center are independent of the specific application. **Application controls** are safeguards that are intended to protect specific applications. In the next two sections, we discuss the major types of these two groups of information system controls.

FIGURE 5.10 Major defense controls.

Auditing Information Systems

Some companies rely on surprise audits. But being proactive about searching for problems is more effective and can stop frauds early on, before the losses mount. An **audit** is an important part of any control system. Auditing can be viewed as an additional layer of controls or safeguards. It is considered as a deterrent to criminal actions, especially for insiders. Auditors attempt to answer questions such as these:

- Are there sufficient controls in the system? Which areas are not covered by controls?
- Which controls are not necessary?
- Are the controls implemented properly?
- Are the controls effective? That is, do they check the output of the system?
- Is there a clear separation of duties of employees?
- Are there procedures to ensure compliance with the controls?
- Are there procedures to ensure reporting and corrective actions in case of violations of controls?

Auditing a website is a good preventive measure to manage the legal risk. Legal risk is important in any IT system, but in Web systems it is even more important due to the content of the site, which may offend people or be in violation of copyright laws or other regulations (e.g., privacy protection). Auditing e-commerce is also more complex since, in addition to the website, one needs to audit order taking, order fulfillment, and all support systems.

Questions

1. What defenses help prevent occupational fraud?
2. What level of employee commits the most occupational fraud?
3. What is the purpose of internal controls?
4. What federal law requires effective internal controls?
5. Explain the concepts of intelligence analysis and anomaly detection.
6. Name the major categories of general controls.
7. Explain authentication and name two methods of authentication.
8. What are the six major objectives of a defense strategy?

5.5 Frameworks, Standards, and Models

A number of frameworks, standards, and models have been developed to guide cyber defense strategies.

Risk Management and IT Governance Frameworks

Two widely accepted frameworks that guide risk management and IT governance are **Enterprise Risk Management (ERM)** and **Control Objectives for Information and Related Technology (COBIT) 5**.

Enterprise Risk Management Framework ERM is a risk-based approach to managing an enterprise developed by the Committee of Sponsoring Organizations of the Treadway Commission (COSO). ERM integrates internal control, the Sarbanes–Oxley Act mandates, and strategic planning.

ERM consists of eight components, listed in **Table 5.11**.

TABLE 5.11 Enterprise Risk Management Components

Component	Description
Internal environment	Assess risk management philosophy and culture
Objective setting	Determine relationship of risk to organizational goals
Event identification	Differentiate between risks and opportunities; negative/positive impact
Risk assessment	Assess risk probability and impact
Risk response	Identify and evaluate risk responses
Control activities	Develop policies and procedures to ensure implementation of risk responses
Information and communication	Identify, capture, and communicate information
Monitoring	Conduct ongoing and separate evaluations of risk-related activities

These eight components can be viewed from a strategic, operations, reporting, and compliance perspective at all level of the organizations. Taking a portfolio view of risk, management must consider how individual risks are interrelated and apply a strong system of internal controls to ensure effective enterprise risk management. Those involved in ERM include management, Board of Directors, Risk officers, and internal auditors. ERM is intended to be part of routine planning processes rather than a separate initiative. The ideal place to start is with buy-in and commitment from the board and senior leadership.

COBIT 5 COBIT 5, is the internationally accepted **IT governance** and control framework created by the International Systems Audit and Control Association (ISACA) to align IT with business objectives, delivering value, and manage associated risks. It provides a framework for management, users, and IS audit, control, and security practitioners that allows them to bridge the gap between control requirements, technical issues, and business risks.

COBIT 5 is the leading framework for the governance and security of IT. COBIT 5, the most current version of the COBIT 5 framework is based on five principles, shown in **Figure 5.11**. COBIT 5 contains highly relevant guidance for IT practitioners and business leaders regarding

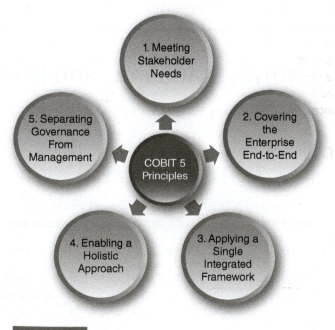

FIGURE 5.11 COBIT 5 principles.

governing and protecting data and information. COBIT 5 encourages each organization to customize COBIT to fit its priorities and circumstances and can be downloaded from isaca.org.

Three of the five COBIT 5 principles are most applicable to security:

1. A *system* needs to be in place that considers and effectively addresses enterprise information security requirements. At a minimum, this would include metrics for the number of clearly defined key security roles and the number of security-related incidents reported.

2. An established *security plan* has been accepted and communicated throughout the organization. This would include level of stakeholder satisfaction with the security plan, the number of security solutions that are different from those in the plan and the number of security solutions deviating from the enterprise security architecture that can lead to security gaps and potentially lengthen the time to resolve security or compliance issues.

3. Information security *solutions* are implemented throughout the organization. These should include the number of services and solutions that align with the security plan and security incidents caused by noncompliance with the security plan.

By following these three principles, using a specified set of IT-enabling processes, and taking additional steps to move from an application centric focus to a data centric focus, organizations that use COBIT 5 can improve the governance and protection of their data and information.

While COBIT 5 provides sound and comprehensive improvement recommendations to start the security governance journey, organizations clearly need to move beyond reactive compliance and security to proactively mandating the need for data privacy and security enterprise-wide. In this way data are always protected.

ERM and COBIT 5 can be used separately or jointly. As with most improvement methodologies, the key to success is to start using them one step at a time.

Industry Standards

Industry groups impose their own standards to protect their customers and their members' brand images and revenues. One example is the **Payment Card Industry Data Security Standard (PCI DSS)** created by Visa, MasterCard, American Express, and Discover. PCI is required for all members, merchants, or service providers that store, process, or transmit cardholder data. PCI DSS requires merchants and card payment providers to make certain their Web applications are secure. If done correctly, this could reduce the number of Web-related security breaches.

The purpose of the PCI DSS is to improve customers' trust in e-commerce, especially when it comes to online payments, and to increase the Web security of online merchants. To motivate following these standards, the penalties for noncompliance are severe. The card brands can fine the retailer, and increase transaction fees for each credit or debit card transaction. A finding of noncompliance can be the basis for lawsuits.

IT Security Defense-In-Depth Model

The Defense-in-Depth Model encourages a multilayered approach to information security. The basic principle is that when one defense layer fails, another layer provides protection. For example, if a wireless network's security was compromised, then having encrypted data would still protect the data, provided that the thieves could not decrypt it.

The success of any type of IT project depends on the commitment and involvement of executive management, also referred to as the *tone at the top*. The same is true of IT security. This information security tone makes users aware that insecure practices and mistakes will not be tolerated. Therefore, an IT security model begins with senior management commitment and support, as shown in **Figure 5.12**. The model views information security as a combination of people, policies, procedures, and technology.

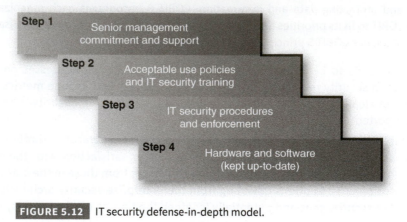

FIGURE 5.12 IT security defense-in-depth model.

To use the Defense-in-Depth Model an organization must carry out four major steps:

Step 1: Gain senior management commitment and support Senior managers' influence is needed to implement and maintain security, ethical standards, privacy practices, and internal control. IT security is best when it is top-driven. Senior managers decide how stringent infosec policies and practices should be in order to comply with laws and regulations. Financial institutions are subject to strict security and anti-money laundering (AML) rules because they face numerous national and international regulations and have high-value data. Advertising agencies and less regulated firms tend to have more lenient rules. Other factors influencing infosec policies are a corporation's culture and how valuable their data are to criminals.

For instance, management may decide to forbid employees from using company e-mail accounts for nonwork purposes, accessing social media during work hours, or visiting gambling sites. These decisions will then become rules stated in company policy, integrated into procedures, and implemented with technology defenses. Sites that are forbidden, for instance, can be blocked by firewalls.

Step 2: Develop acceptable use policies and IT security training Organizations need to put in place strong policies and processes that make responsibilities and accountabilities clear to all employees. An **acceptable use policy (AUP)** explains what management has decided are acceptable and unacceptable activities, and the consequences of noncompliance. Rules about tweets, texting, social media, e-mail, applications, and hardware should be treated as extensions of other corporate policies—such as physical safety, equal opportunity, harassment, and discrimination. No policy can address every future situation, so rules need to be evaluated, updated, or modified. For example, if a company suffers a malware infection traced to an employee using an unprotected smartphone connected to the company network, policies to restrict or prohibit those connections might be advisable.

Step 3: Create and Enforce IT security procedures and enforcement Secure procedures define how policies will be enforced, how incidents will be prevented, and how an incident will be responded. Here are the basic secure procedures to put in place:

a. **Define enforcement procedures** Rules that are defined in the AUP must be enforced and enforcement procedures must be applied consistently. Procedures for monitoring employee Internet and network usage are defined at this stage.

b. **Designate and empower an internal incident response team (IRT)** The IRT typically includes the CISO, legal counsel, senior managers, experienced communicators, and key operations staff. Minimizing the team size and bureaucracy can expedite decision making and response. Because there may be significant liability issues, legal counsel needs to be involved in incident response planning and communication.

c. **Define notification procedures** When a data breach occurs the local police department, local office of the FBI, Securities and Exchange Commission (SEC), the U.S. Secret Service, or other relevant agency need to be notified immediately. Federal and state laws or industry regulations may define how and when affected people need to be notified.

d. **Define a breach response communications plan**   Effective incident response communication plans include personnel and processes with lists, channels, and social media needed to execute all communications that might be needed.

e. **Monitor information and social media sources**   Monitor Twitter, social media, and news coverage as a standard procedure to understand how people are responding to the incident and criticizing the company. Damage control procedures may be needed.

When an incident occurs, the organization is ready to respond intelligently—having the correct information to be honest, open, and accountable, and to communicate with consumers and other important audiences as quickly as possible.

Step 4: Implement Security Tools: Hardware and software   The last step in the model is implementation of software and hardware needed to support and enforce the AUP and secure practices. The selection of hardware and software defenses is based on risk, security budget, AUP, and secure procedures. Every device that connects to an organization's network; every online activity and mobile app of employees; and each file sent or received are access points. Technology defense mechanisms need to be:

- able to provide strong authentication and access control of industrial grade
- appropriate for the types of networks and operating systems
- installed and configured correctly
- tested rigorously
- maintained regularly

How much does a cyberattack really cost an organization? Regulatory fines, public relations costs, breach notification and protection costs, and other consequences of large-scale data breaches are easy to see and quantify. However, the effects of a cyberattack can linger for years, resulting in a wide range of intangible costs tied to a damaged reputation, disruption of operations, loss of IP or other strategic assets. The latter are much more difficult to measure since they are not easily quantifiable.

No matter which frameworks, standards, and controls are used to assess, monitor, and control cyber risk, a balanced approach to measuring direct costs and intangible impacts associated with cyberattacks must be used to paint an accurate picture of the damage sustained and to guide the creation of increased security measures going forward.

Questions

1. Who created the Enterprise Risk Management Framework? What is its purpose?
2. What are the five principles of COBIT 5? Explain.
3. What is the difference between internal and external controls?
4. Why do industry groups have their own standards for cybersecurity? Name one standard.
5. Are measurements of direct costs sufficient to reflect total damage sustained by a cyberattack?
6. What four components comprise the IT security defense-in-depth model?
7. What are the four steps in the IT security defense-in-depth security model?
8. Explain why frameworks, standards, and models are important parts of a cybersecurity program.

Key Terms

acceptable use policy (AUP)   158
access control   152
administrative controls   152
advanced persistent threat (APT)   139

adware   135
Anonymous   139
application controls   154
assets   139

attack vector   138
audit   155
backdoor   134
biometric control   148

black hat   133
botnet   136
bring your own apps (BYOA)   143
bring your own device (BYOD)   143
business continuity plan   149
business impact analysis (BIA)   163
command and control (C&C) channel   144
consumerization of information technology (COIT)   143
contract hacker   134
Control Objectives for Information and Related Technology (COBIT) 5   155
corporate governance   151
critical infrastructure   140
cyberthreat   131
data breach   130
Data incident   130
data tampering   137
distributed denial-of-service (DDoS) attack   135
do-not-carry rules   149
enterprise risk management (ERM)   155
fraud   150

general controls   154
gray hat   133
hacking   133
hacktivist   133
intellectual property   141
internal control (IC)   153
internal threats   137
intrusion detection system (IDS)   137
intrusion prevention system (IPS)   146
IT governance   156
LulzSec   139
malware   135
mobile biometrics   148
occupational fraud   150
patches   144
payload   136
Payment Card Industry Data Security Standard (PCI DSS)   157
permanent denial-of-service (PDoS)   137
phishing   134
physical controls   152
ransomware   135
remote access trojan (RAT)   136

remote wipe capability   148
risk   146
rogue app monitoring   148
rootkit   135
service pack   144
signature   136
social engineering   133
spam   136
spear phishing   135
spyware   135
telephony denial-of-service (TDoS)   137
threat   130
time-to-exploitation   144
trojan   135
Trojan horse   136
vector   136
Virus   135
voice biometrics   148
vulnerability   130
white hat   133
worm   135
zero-day exploit   136
zombie   136

Assuring Your Learning

Discuss: Critical Thinking Questions

1. Why is cybercrime expanding rapidly? Discuss some possible solutions.

2. In addition to hackers, what kinds of cybercriminals do organizations need to defend against?

3. What are the major motives of cybercriminals?

4. In what ways do users make themselves vulnerable to cybercrimes?

5. Why do malware creators alter their malware?

6. Why should you set a unique password for each website, service, and device that you use?

7. How can malware be stopped from stealing or disclosing data from an organization's network?

8. What impact might huge fines have on how much a company budgets for IT security defenses?

9. Why are BYOD, BYOA, and do-not-carry rules important to IT security? Why might users resist such rules?

10. Why do users refuse to use strong passwords even though they know how dangerous weak passwords are?

11. How can the risk of occupational fraud be decreased?

12. Why should information control and security be of prime concern to management?

13. Explain what firewalls protect and what they do not protect.

14. Why are authentication and authorization important in e-commerce?

15. Some insurance companies will not insure a business unless the firm has a computer disaster recovery plan. Explain why.

16. Explain why risk management should involve the following elements: threats, exposure associated with each threat, risk of each threat occurring, cost of controls, and assessment of their effectiveness.

17. Discuss why the Sarbanes–Oxley Act focuses on internal control. How does that focus influence information security?

Explore: Online and Interactive Exercises

1. Visit http://www.informationisbeautiful.net/visualizations/worlds-biggest-data-breaches-hacks

   a. Choose two companies where data breaches have occurred.

   b. Explain the reasons for these breaches and discuss how they could have been avoided.

2. Visit https://www.identityforce.com/resources/quiz and take the Identity Theft Quiz. What was your score? Explain ways in which you could improve your score so that you are not as much at risk for identity theft.

3. Visit https://www.identityforce.com/blog/2016-data-breaches and choose one of the major data breaches listed. Read about the data breach. What lessons did you learn from the article?

4. Research vendors of biometrics. Select one vendor and discuss three of its biometric devices or technologies. Prepare a list of major capabilities. What are the advantages and disadvantages of its biometrics?

5. Visit **https://learn-umbrella.cisco.com/product-videos/what-is-a-secure-internet-gateway** to watch the video "What is a Secure Internet Gateway?", where Dan Hubbard, Cloud Security Product CTO at Cisco explains how security needs to adapt to keep up with the evolving workforce and how Cisco Umbrella can assist companies protect their employees wherever they choose to work.

a. Describe two things that you learned from watching this video.

b. Do you think Cisco Umbrella would be an effective tool for companies to use? Explain why or why not.

Analyze & Decide: Apply IT Concepts to Business Decisions

1. Many firms concentrate on the wrong questions and end up throwing a great deal of money and time at minimal security risks while ignoring major vulnerabilities. Why?

2. Assessing how much a company is legally obligated to invest in cybersecurity remains a challenge. Since there is no such thing as perfect security (i.e., there is always more that you can do), resolving these questions can significantly affect cost.

a. When are a company's security measures sufficient to comply with its obligations? For example, does installing a firewall and using virus detection software satisfy a company's legal obligations?

b. Is it necessary for an organization to encrypt all of its data?

3. Assume that the daily probability of a major earthquake in Los Angeles is .07%. The chance of your computer center being damaged during such a quake is 5%. If the center is damaged, the average estimated damage will be $1.6 million.

a. Calculate the expected loss (in dollars).

b. An insurance agent is willing to insure your facility for an annual fee of $15,000. Analyze the offer, and discuss whether to accept it.

4. Should an employer notify employees that their usage of computers is being monitored? Why or why not?

5. Twenty-five thousand messages arrive at an organization each year. Currently, there are no firewalls. On average, 1.2 successful hackings occur each year. Each successful hack attack results in a loss of about $130,000 to the company. A major firewall is proposed at a cost of $66,000. The estimated useful life is three years. The chance that an intruder will break through the firewall is 0.0002. In such a case, the damage will be $100,000 (30%), $200,000 (50%), or there will be no damage. There is an annual maintenance cost of $20,000 for the firewall.

a. Should management buy the firewall?

b. An improved firewall that is 99.9988% effective and that costs $84,000, with a life of three years and annual maintenance cost of $16,000, is available. Should this firewall be purchased instead of the first one?

Case 5.2

Business Case: Lax Security at LinkedIn Exposed

On any social network, most users mistakenly believe that their privacy is only as good as the privacy of their most careless—or temporary—friend. In fact, weak passwords and hackers can deprive users of all privacy.

When the business social networking site LinkedIn was hacked (**Figure 5.13**), hackers stole 6.5 million passwords and e-mail addresses. This data breach was discovered by IT security experts when they found millions of LinkedIn passwords posted on a Russian underground website (**Figure 5.14**). Experts also determined that a hacker named Dwdm was asking underground members for help in cracking the stolen

FIGURE 5.14 LinkedIn did not discover its own data breach and, when informed of it, delayed notifying members.

passwords. Within only 2 days, most passwords were cracked. Why were LinkedIn's passwords cracked so quickly? The simple answer is that LinkedIn was using an outdated encryption method instead of up-to-date industry-standard encryption. As a result, members' passwords were really only camouflaged—and crackable.

LinkedIn Criticized for Bad Data Security

What could hackers do to your online accounts if they had your passwords for 48 hours and you did not know? That is what LinkedIn allowed to happen by waiting 2 days before notifying members that their passwords had been stolen. The company took a lot of criticism

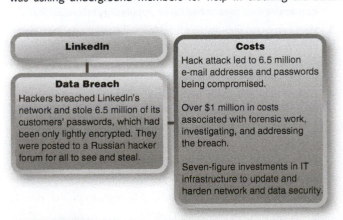

FIGURE 5.13 LinkedIn data breach overview.

for not notifying members via Twitter or Facebook immediately. According to the chief executive of the Public Relations Consultants Association, Francis Ingham, LinkedIn ignored the first rule of crisis management, which is to be first to tell your customers.

What surprised customers and IT security experts was that a company that collects and profits from vast amounts of data had taken a negligent approach to protecting it. **Figure 5.15** explains why it was surprising and alarming that LinkedIn's password protection was weak.

Its most valuable asset is data

- LinkedIn's business model: *collect and profit from data.*

It's a high-tech, public company with a brand image to protect

- LinkedIn was not some cash-poor startup company. The company had piles of cash from its successful initial public offering (IPO) in May 2011. Once it went public, LinkedIn, like all public companies, had to report hack attacks to the SEC.

It had a lot of net income to protect

- LinkedIn's net income for the first quarter of 2012 was $5 million, more than double its $2.1 million net income in the first quarter 2011. LinkedIn had a lot to protect… and lose.

FIGURE 5.15   Three reasons why LinkedIn's underinvestment in data security did not make business sense.

E-mail Addresses are Universal Usernames

At most e-commerce and social sites, usernames are e-mail addresses—making them our universal username for online accounts. If the e-mail is a work account, then everyone also knows where we work and our login name. Therefore, knowing users' usernames and passwords provides authorized access to corporate accounts with almost no risk of being detected. Hackers attacked LinkedIn to gain access to over 161 million members' credentials as a means to gain access to much more valuable business networks and databases.

Business Risks and Collateral Damage

The hack caused the following business risks and collateral damage.

- Takeover of members' other accounts by hackers, fraudsters, and other criminals. Hackers know that people reuse passwords; once their LinkedIn accounts are linked to Facebook and Twitter, far too much information may be revealed. Knowing where people worked and their e-mail accounts allowed hackers to quickly use the stolen LinkedIn passwords to log in to corporate accounts, online bank accounts, and so on to steal more data or transfer funds.

- Damage to LinkedIn's biggest revenue source—its advertising business. LinkedIn's financial success is tied to its advertising revenues, which in turn are based on the number of active members and membership growth.

- Fines for violating privacy laws and regulations. Any company exposing the confidential data of customers or employees faces steep fines. Regulators impose harsh penalties for breaking privacy laws and not taking reasonable care to defend against data breaches. Strict data privacy laws in states such as Massachusetts and California could keep LinkedIn fighting legal battles for years.

- Cleanup costs. The cleanup cost LinkedIn nearly $1 million and another $2–$3 million in upgrades. Forensic work on the password theft cost another $500,000 to $1 million.

Data Security: A Top Management Concern

Data security is a senior management concern and responsibility. It affects a company's operations, reputation, and customer trust, which ultimately impact revenue, profits, and competitive edge. Yet, defenses that could help to prevent breaches are not always implemented.

Some experts argue that senior management continues to skimp on basic protections because computer security is not regulated—that is, until a business suffers a major crisis. After the data breach, LinkedIn implemented improved password storage encryption, hired private security and forensics experts, and called in the FBI to help investigate the security breach.

Comparison with Other Cyberattacks

While 6.5 million leaked passwords represent a serious breach, it affected a relatively small percent of the more than 175 million members LinkedIn had at that time. Overall, the LinkedIn breach, while somewhat costly, did not do as much harm as those experienced by other hacked companies such as Global Payments, Sony, and Certificate Authority DigiNotar, which were literally hacked out of business.

Just the Beginning

Four years after the data breach, the number of released account details was found to be 117 million rather than 6.5 million. In May, 2016, Russian hacker "Peace," who sold the Yahoo data breach information in the Opening Case, made available for purchase LinkedIn account details on a marketplace in the Dark Web for $2,300. In response to the massive breach of additional accounts, LinkedIn required the affected accountholders to change their passwords and urged all other users to change theirs as well. In addition, LinkedIn spent about $4 million repairing and upgrading their security infrastructure to combat future leaks (Hackett, 2016b).

Questions

1. LinkedIn does not collect the credit card or other financial account information of its members. Why then would profit-motivated hackers be interested in stealing LinkedIn's stored data? What data would hackers be most interesting in accessing?

2. Companies are often slow to self-detect data breaches so a cyberattack can occur without a company even knowing it has a problem. What effect do you think LinkedIn's failure to self-detect its massive data breach had on its popularity and credibility?

3. Most corporate security incidents are uncovered by a third party, like a security firm, that picks up on evidence of malicious activity. Why do you think IT security experts and not LinkedIn discovered the data breach?

4. Explain why LinkedIn's lax approach to members' information security and weak passwords was very surprising to members and information security professionals.

5. Identify and evaluate the actual and potential business risks and damages from LinkedIn's data breach.

6. In your opinion, was LinkedIn negligent in protecting its main asset? Explain.

Sources: Compiled from Franceschi-Bicchierai (2016), Hackett (2016b), and Ponemon Institute (2017).

Case 5.3

Video Case: Botnets, Malware Security, and Capturing Cybercriminals

Gunter Ollmann, vice president of research at Damballa, Inc., explains what companies have learned from the Operation Aurora attacks against major companies. In the video, you will learn why it is difficult for law enforcement to track and prosecute cybercriminals, including botnet operators who now launch targeted botnet attacks with the help of automated tools. Also discussed is the effectiveness of Microsoft's legal action to shut down the C&C (command and control) network of the Waladec botnet. Visit **searchsecurity.techtarget.com/video/Botnets-malware-and-capturing-cybercriminals** to view the video, read its transcript and answer the following questions.

Questions

1. Why are botnets used?
2. What is needed to get started in the botnet industry? Explain why.
3. Given your answers, what should users and organizations do and/or not do to reduce the threat of botnets?

IT Toolbox

Conducting a Cost–Benefit Analysis

It is usually not economical to prepare protection against every possible threat. Therefore, an IT security program must provide a process for assessing threats and deciding which ones to prepare for, which ones to ignore and which ones to provide reduced protection against. Two commonly used cost-benefit analysis tools are risk assessment and business impact analysis. Risk assessment relies solely on quantitative measures, while the business impact analysis takes into account both qualitative and quantitative indicators.

- **Risk assessment**

Risk assessments are done using an app or spreadsheet. The basic computations are shown here:

$$\text{Expected loss} = P_1 \times P_2 \times L$$

where

P_1 = probability of attack (estimate, based on judgment)

P_2 = probability of attack being successful (estimate, based on judgment)

L = loss occurring if attack is successful

Example:

An organization estimates that the probability of a cyberattack is 2% and the attack has only a 10% chance of being successful. If the attack is successful, the company estimates that it will lose $1 million.

This would be expressed as:

$$P_1 = .02, \ P_2 = .10, \ L = \$1,000,000$$

Then expected loss from this particular attack is

$$P_1 \times P_2 \times L = 0.02 \times 0.1 \times \$1,000,000 = \$2,000$$

- **Business impact analysis**

A **business impact analysis (BIA)** estimates the consequences of disruption of a business function and collects data to develop recovery strategies.

Potential loss scenarios are first identified during the risk assessment. Operations may also be interrupted by the failure of a supplier of goods or services or delayed deliveries. There are many possible scenarios that should be considered.

The BIA identifies both operational and financial impacts resulting from a disruption. The financial impacts are easier to assess, but the operational impacts are more difficult to determine because of their qualitative nature. Several examples of operational and financial impacts to consider are shown in **Table 5.12**.

The losses assessed using these two methods should be compared with the costs for possible recovery strategies to determine net risk. The BIA report should also prioritize the order of events for restoration of the business, with processes having the greatest operational and financial impacts being restored first.

TABLE 5.12   Business Disruption Qualitative and Quantitative Impacts

Type	Metric	Description
Financial	Quantitative	Lost sales and income
		Delayed sales or income
		Increased expenses (e.g., overtime labor, outsourcing, expediting costs)
		Regulatory fines
		Contractual penalties or loss of contractual bonuses
Operational	Qualitative	Customer dissatisfaction or defection
		Delay of new business plans

References

Abadi, M., and D.G. Andersen. "Learning to Protect Communications with Adversarial Neural Cryptography." *Cornell University Library*, October 24, 2016.

Balakrishnan, A. "U.S. Accuses Russia of Hacking Yahoo." *CNBC*, March 15, 2017.

Berman, R. "Alice, Bob, and Eve Are Neural Networks. And They Have Secrets." *Big Think*, November 1, 2016.

Breach Level Index. "2015: The Year Data Breaches Got Personal." February 18, 2016.

Burgess, M. "How Google's AI taught itself to create its own encryption." *Wired*, October 31, 2016.

Department of Justice. "The USA Patriot Act: Preserving Life and Liberty". 2001. Accessed from https://www.justice.gov/archive/ll/highlights.htm

Duan, E. "DressCode and its Potential Impact for Enterprises." *Trend-Micro*, September 29, 2016.

Fiegerman, S. "Verizon says Yahoo's massive breach could impact deal." *CNN*, October 13, 2016.

Franceschi-Bicchierai, L. "Another Day, Another Hack: 117 Million LinkedIn Emails and Passwords." *Motherboard Vice*, May 18, 2016.

Gelinne, J., J. Fancher, and E. Mossburg. "The Hidden Costs of an IP Breach: Cyber Theft and the Loss of Intellectual Property." *Deloitte Review*, Issue 19, July 25, 2016.

Gibson Dunn. "President Obama Signs Federal Trade Secrets Law." May 11, 2016.

Goldman, J. "All-Time High of 1,093 Data Breaches Reported in U.S. in 2016." *E-Security Planet*, January 24, 2017. Accessed from: http://www.esecurityplanet.com/network-security/all-time-high-of-1093-data-breaches-reported-in-u.s.-in-2016.html

Goodin, D. "Godless Apps, Some Found in Google Play, Can Root 90% of Android Phones." *ArsTechnica*, June 23, 2016.

Hackett, R. "Yahoo's Titanic Data Breach Highlights Risk to M&A." *Fortune*, September 23, 2016a.

Hackett, R. "LinkedIn Lost 167 Million Account Credentials in Data Breach." *Fortune*, May 18, 2016b.

Kan, M. "Hackers Now Have a Treasure Trove of User Data with the Yahoo Breach." *International Data Group*, September 22, 2016.

KPMG. *Consumer Loss Barometer*. 2016. https://assets.kpmg.com/content/dam/kpmg/cn/pdf/en/2016/08/consumer-loss-barometer-v1.pdf

Lee, D. "'State' Hackers Stole Data from 500 Million Users." *BBC*, September 23, 2016.

Matwyshyn, A., and H. Bhargava. "Will Yahoo's Data Breach Help Overhaul Online Security?" *Knowledge@Wharton: University of Pennsylvania*, September 27, 2016. Accessed from http://knowledge.wharton.upenn.edu/article/will-yahoos-data-breach-help-overhaul-online-security/

Morris, A., D. Nathan, and A. Ayyar. "Broker-Dealers and Their Auditors Face Increased Regulatory Scrutiny." *Bloomberg Legal*, November 3, 2016.

Murgia, M. "Cyber experts look to usual suspects in Yahoo hack." *Financial Times*, September 25, 2016.

Ponemon Institute. "2017 Cost of Data Breach Study: Global Overview" June, 2017.

PricewaterhouseCoopers. "US Cybersecurity: Progress Stalled." July, 2015.

RT.com. "Buyer Beware: US Is Biggest Creator of Malicious Mobile Apps." February 4, 2015.

Sterling, G. "Bing Reaches 20 Percent Search Market Share Milestone in US." *SearchEngineLand*, April 16, 2015.

Verizon. "2016 Data Breach Investigations Report." Accessed from: http://www.verizonenterprise.com/verizon-insights-lab/dbir/2016

CHAPTER 6

Search, Semantic, and Recommendation Technology

CHAPTER OUTLINE

LEARNING OBJECTIVES

Case 6.1 Opening Case: Mint.com Uses Search Technology to Rank Above Established Competitors

6.1 Using Search Technology for Business Success

6.1 Describe how search engines work and identify ways that businesses gain competitive advantage by using search technology effectively.

6.2 Organic Search and Search Engine Optimization

6.2 Explain how to improve website ranking on search results pages by optimizing website design and creating useful content.

6.3 Pay-Per-Click and Paid Search Strategies

6.3 Describe how companies manage paid search advertising campaigns to increase awareness and drive sales volume.

6.4 A Search for Meaning—Semantic Technology

6.4 Describe how semantic Web technology enhances the accuracy of search engines results and how businesses can optimize their websites to take advantage of this emerging technology.

6.5 Recommendation Engines

6.5 Describe how recommendation engines are used to enhance user experience and increase sales on e-commerce websites.

Case 6.2 Business Case: Deciding What to Watch—Video Recommendations at Netflix

Case 6.3 Video Case: Power Searching with Google

Introduction

Every day, over 1.5 billion people around the world use what seems to be a simple tool to find information online—a search engine. We sometimes take for granted that behind a relatively simple user interface, an increasingly complex set of search engine technologies are at work, helping us find the information we need to do our jobs, conduct research, locate product reviews, or find information about the television shows we watch. Because most search engine services are free, people are not generally aware that "Search" has become a multibillion-dollar-a-year business. More importantly, the way search engines work and how they rank-order the links displayed when we conduct a search have huge implications for millions of other businesses. Because consumers typically don't look past the first few pages of search results, having your business appear at the top of a search results page can make a big difference in how much traffic your website gets. In this chapter, you will read about how search engines work and how they determine which websites are listed at the top of search results. You will also read about the strategies companies use to increase their presence on search results pages including search engine optimization (SEO) and pay-per-click (PPC) advertising.

Semantic technologies are increasingly being used by search engines to understand Web page content. In this chapter you will read about the ways that search engines are using semantic technology to improve performance, increasing relevant pages and decreasing the number of irrelevant pages that appear in search results.

Finally, you will read about recommendation engines. These tools attempt to anticipate online information you might be interested in. Netflix uses recommendation engines to suggest movies you might like to watch and news organizations use them to recommend stories you might want to read on their websites. Amazon credits its recommendation technology for increasing sales by suggesting products that customers might want to buy.

Business managers need to understand search and recommendation technologies because their influence in directing potential consumers to business websites is already significant and expected to grow substantially in the future.

Case 6.1 Opening Case

Geber86/E+/Getty Images

IanDagnall Computing/Alamy Stock Photo

filo/DigitalVision Vectors/Getty Images

Mint.com Uses Search Technology to Rank Above Established Competitors

Company Overview

Mint is a popular, Web-based personal finance service that makes it easy for users to keep track of bank, credit card, and other financial accounts using a computer or mobile device. Customers can also use the service to create budgets and monitor progress toward financial goals. Since it began in 2006, the company has grown rapidly despite competition from more established companies. In 2009, Mint was acquired by Intuit, the maker of TurboTax and Quicken financial software. Today, over 20 million people use Mint's free financial management service (**Table 6.1**).

The Business Challenge

In the months leading up to the 2006 launch of Mint.com, a personal finance service, the leadership team faced a formidable challenge: How

to establish name awareness and brand equity in a market filled with established competitors, without spending a lot of money? Mint knew it would be competing in a market space already populated by familiar brands like Quicken Online and Microsoft Money Online. Since online platforms and communication channels tend to favor existing companies with established audiences and reputations, the team knew they had to come up with a powerful strategy for overcoming the established brands.

Mint's Content Marketing Strategy

As a Web-based service, it was critical for Mint.com to rank high on **search engine results pages (SERPs)** when consumers used sites like **Google** or **Bing** to find information about personal finance services and related topics. Consumers are more likely to visit websites that appear at the top of SERPs. While the service was still in the beta (trial) stage of development, workers at Mint developed an aggressive strategy to optimize the brand's ranking on popular search engines. Their strategy involved building the company's Web presence on criteria used by

TABLE 6.1	Opening Case Overview
Company	Mint
History	Mint was launched in 2006 as a free, Web-based personal finance app by founder Aaron Patzer. In 2009, the company was acquired by the financial software company Intuit.
Growth	Within two years of launch, Mint claimed over 1.5 million users. By 2012, the company claimed 10 million users and by 2016, the number of users rose to over 20 million.
Product lines	Mint's original service allowed users to track balances and transactions on credit card, investment, and bank accounts as well as to create budgets and establish financial goals. In addition, Mint now offers users a bill pay service and credit score monitoring.
Social technology	Prior to the release of its flagship personal finance app, Mint created a large following of prospective users with **MintLife**, a blog that offered valuable advice targeted to young professionals.
Search technology	Mint utilized an aggressive SEO strategy to rank highly on search results pages. Specific actions included the following: • Creation of useful personal finance content on its blog, MintLife • Use of targeted keywords in website content • Established audiences on popular social media sites such as Facebook and Twitter • Used various strategies, including sponsorship of third-party blogs, to generate links (or "backlinks") to Mint.com from other websites
Website	**Mint.com**

search engines to determine SERP ranking. The strategy focused on the following:

- Increasing the number of other websites that linked back to Mint's website (called "backlinks")
- Creating interesting and useful content about personal finance topics that prospective customers would find helpful
- Identifying keywords and phrases used by prospective customers when searching for personal financial services, and creatively inserting these words and phrases into website content
- Regularly updating and adding to their collection of personal finance content
- Establishing a presence on popular social media sites, expanding their audience on those sites, and encouraging the audience to share links to Mint's website content

Months prior to the launch of its personal finance service, Mint rolled out a personal finance blog called **MintLife** and quickly developed a reputation for providing helpful financial advice targeted to young professionals. Blog posts on MintLife were creatively seeded with keywords and phrases the team had identified as likely to be used by prospective customers when conducting Internet searches for financial services. Mint also created landing pages on their website containing content optimized for keywords and phrases related to financial services. As search engines tracked this content, Mint began to lay a foundation for eventually being viewed by search engines as a credible authority for personal finance topics. New posts were regularly added to the blog, which further enhanced Mint's ranking since search engines favor websites with lots of content (content depth) and regular updates. To further establish its position as a useful and authoritative site, Mint sponsored several third-party blogs and cultivated relationships with authors of established finance and money management blogs. Mint's founder, Aaron Patzer, gave hundreds of interviews, resulting in print media and online articles about the start-up company. These and other actions resulted in more third-party websites posting links back to

Mint.com. These "backlinks" were tracked by search engines and resulted in additional increases to the site's ranking on SERPs. Popular search engines also track a company's presence on social media and the extent to which users share information about the company and its products. Mint's blog featured content in a variety of interesting formats: videos, podcasts, infographics, and so on. Users on social news sites like Reddit.com frequently shared and "upvoted" interesting infographics from Mint's blog. Links to other types of blog content were shared by users on Facebook, Twitter, and other social media platforms. As a result, Mint's expanding audiences on Facebook, Twitter, and other social media platforms further enhanced the new company's SERP ranking.

Results

In 2007, Mint launched its new financial services website into a market where it already enjoyed considerable name recognition and awareness. Within 2 years, the service acquired 1.5 million users and was purchased by Intuit for $170 million. The company continued its successful content marketing strategy, climbing to 10 million users in 2012 and over 20 million users today.

Questions

1. Why did Mint invest the time and effort to publish a financial services blog almost two years before the launch of its service?
2. How did Mint use social media sites to increase its ranking on the search results pages of popular search engines?
3. Why did Mint use keywords and phrases associated with personal finance when creating content for its blog?
4. Why did Mint put so much emphasis on improving the rank of its website on SERPs?
5. Why did Mint use infographics, videos, and other types of rich media in its financial services blog?

Sources: Compiled from Sukhraj (2015), Bulygo (2013a), Obi-Azubuike (2016), Prince (2016), Greene (2016).

6.1 Using Search Technology for Business Success

Search engines like Google, Bing, Yahoo, and others have traditionally been regarded as a consumer technology. But search technology has become an important business tool with many different uses and applications. In this section, you will learn how search engines work and the role they play in generating revenue and consumer awareness for organizations. You will also discover how businesses use enterprise search technology to unlock hidden content with their organizations. Finally, you will read about how search and Internet technology is evolving to provide more accurate and useful results.

How Search Engines Work

Search engine   an application for locating Web pages or other content (e.g., documents, media files) on a computer network. Popular Web-based search engines include Google, Bing, and Yahoo.

Spiders   also known as **crawlers, Web bots,** or simply "bots," spiders are small computer programs designed to perform automated, repetitive tasks over the Internet. They are used by search engines for scanning Web pages and returning information to be stored in a page repository.

People use the word **search engine** to refer to many different kinds of information retrieval (IR) services that find content on the World Wide Web. These services vary in significant ways. Understanding how these services differ can improve the quality of results obtained when conducting a search for online information. Listed below is a brief description of different IR services for finding Web content:

- **Crawler search engines** rely on sophisticated computer programs called **spiders**, **crawlers**, or **bots** that surf the Internet, locating Web pages, links, and other content that are then stored in the search engine's page repository. The most popular commercial search engines, Google and Bing, are based on crawler technology.
- **Web directories** list Web pages organized into hierarchical categories. Originally, Web directories were created and maintained by human editors who decided how a website would be categorized. Today, many Web directories use technology to automate new website listings. Web directories are typically classified as "general" directories that cover a wide-range topical categories, or "niche" directories that focus on a narrow range of topics. Examples of popular general directories include **Best of the Web**, **JoeAnt**, and **LookSmart**. **Wikipedia** maintains a list of general and niche Web directories.
- **Hybrid search engines** combine the results of a directory created by humans and results from a crawler search engine, with the goal of providing both accuracy and broad coverage of the Internet.
- **Meta-search engines** compile results from other search engines. For instance, **Dogpile** generates listings by combining results from Google and Yahoo.
- **Semantic search engines** are designed to locate information based on the nature and meaning of Web content, not simple keyword matches. The goal of these search engines is to dramatically increase the accuracy and usefulness of search results. Semantic search engines are described in more detail in Section 6.4.

Web Directories

Before crawler search engines became the dominant method for finding Web content, people relied on directories created by human editors to help them find information. Web directories are typically organized by categories (for instance, see the categories listed on **Best of the Web**). Web page content is usually reviewed by directory editors prior to its listing in a category to make sure it is appropriate. This reduces the number of irrelevant links generated in a search. The review process, however, is very slow compared to the automated process used by crawlers (described in the following section). As a result, the listings in a Web directory represent a relatively small portion of the Web. Directories are particularly useful when conducting searches on a narrow topic, such as identifying suppliers of a specific type of product or service. Companies who need to identify vendors or suppliers may consult a niche Web directory created for just this purpose. For example, see the Web directory at *business.com*.

How Crawler Search Engines Work

The two most popular commercial search engines on the Web, Google and Bing, are based on crawler technology. Behind the relatively simple interfaces of these two powerful search engines, a great deal of complex technology is at work (**Figure 6.1**). Because modern search engines use proprietary technology in the race to stay ahead of competitors, it is not possible to tell exactly how they decide what websites will appear in a SERP. While they each produce different results, it is possible to describe the basic process shared by most crawler search engines. The following description is based on publications by Grehan (2002) and Oak (2008).

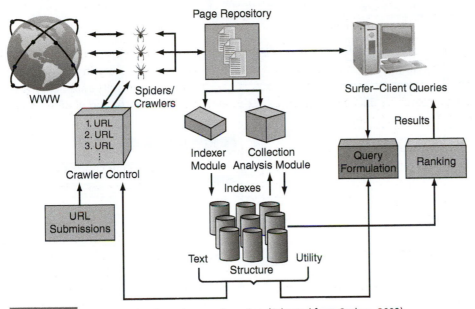

FIGURE 6.1 Components of crawler search engine (Adapted from Grehan, 2002).

1. The crawler control module assigns Web page URLs to programs called spiders or bots. The spider downloads these Web pages into a **page repository** and scans them for links. The links are transferred to the **crawler control module** and used to determine where the spiders will be sent in the future. (Most search engines also allow Web masters to submit URLs, requesting that their websites be scanned so they will appear in search results. These requests are added to the crawler control queue.)

2. The **indexer module** creates look-up tables by extracting words from the Web pages and recording the URL where they were found. The indexer module also creates an inverted index that helps search engines efficiently locate relevant pages containing **keywords** used in a search. (See **Figure 6.2** for examples of an inverted index.)

3. The **collection analysis module** creates utility indexes that aid in providing search results. The utility indexes contain information about things such as how many pages are in a website, the geographic location of the website, number of pictures on a Web page, Web page length, or other site-specific information the search engine may use to determine the relevance of a page.

4. The **retrieval/ranking module** determines the order in which pages are listed in a SERP. The methods by which search engines determine website listing order varies and the specific algorithms they use are often carefully guarded trade secrets. In some cases, a search engine may use hundreds of different criteria to determine which pages appear at the top of a SERP. Google, for instance, claims to use over 200 "clues" to determine how it ranks pages (Google.com, 2014).

Page repository a data structure that stores and manages information from a large number of Web pages, providing a fast and efficient means for accessing and analyzing the information at a later time.

Crawler control module a software program that controls a number of "spiders" responsible for scanning or crawling through information on the Web.

5. Web pages retrieved by the spiders, along with the indexes and ranking information, are stored on large servers (see **IT at Work 6.1**).

6. The **query interface** is where users enter words that describe the kind of information they are looking for. The search engine then applies various algorithms to match the query string with information stored in the indexes to determine what pages to display in the SERP.

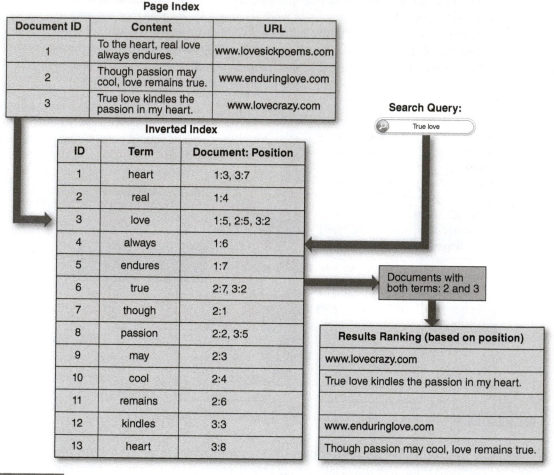

Page Index

Document ID	Content	URL
1	To the heart, real love always endures.	www.lovesickpoems.com
2	Though passion may cool, love remains true.	www.enduringlove.com
3	True love kindles the passion in my heart.	www.lovecrazy.com

Search Query:

True love

Inverted Index

ID	Term	Document: Position
1	heart	1:3, 3:7
2	real	1:4
3	love	1:5, 2:5, 3:2
4	always	1:6
5	endures	1:7
6	true	2:7, 3:2
7	though	2:1
8	passion	2:2, 3:5
9	may	2:3
10	cool	2:4
11	remains	2:6
12	kindles	3:3
13	heart	3:8

Documents with both terms: 2 and 3

Results Ranking (based on position)

www.lovecrazy.com
True love kindles the passion in my heart.
www.enduringlove.com
Though passion may cool, love remains true.

FIGURE 6.2 Search engines use inverted indexes to efficiently locate Web content based on search query terms.

Each search engine utilizes variations and refinements of the aforementioned steps in an attempt to achieve superior results. The Web search industry is highly competitive and the proprietary advances in search technology used by each company are closely guarded secrets. For instance, even the first step in the process, crawling the Web for content, can vary greatly depending on the strategic goals of the search engine. Some search engines limit the number of pages scanned at each website, seeking instead to use limited computing power and resources to cover as many websites as possible. Other search engines program their spiders to scan deep into each website, seeking more complete coverage of each site's content. Still other search engines direct their spiders to seek out websites that contain certain types of content, such as government sites or shopping (e-commerce) sites. Another decision that search engines make regarding spiders is the amount of resources directed at searching new websites versus devoting resources to exploring previously indexed pages for updates or changes.

One of the many challenges faced by large commercial search engines is storage. In the simplest sense, the crawler approach to search requires a company to store a copy of the Web in large data centers. In addition to the **petabytes** of storage required to maintain this copy of the Web, the search engine must also store the results of its indexing process and the list of links for future crawls.

Petabyte a unit of measurement for digital data storage. A petabyte is equal to one million gigabytes.

IT at Work 6.1

Google Data Centers

Not only does Google maintain a copy of the Internet for its search engine services, it is also constantly updating a map of the entire planet for users of its popular Google Earth application. In addition, the company is making a full-text, searchable copy of over 129,864,880 known books, equal to 4 billion pages or 2 trillion words. And then there are applications like Gmail, serving roughly 425 million people and YouTube, where 300 hours of video are uploaded every minute! Add all this up, and Google is facing perhaps the biggest data storage challenge ever. So where does Google store all of these data?

Challenges: Energy, Performance, and Security

Information collected by Google is housed on over 1 million servers spread across 12 different facilities worldwide. The facilities are large, factory-like installations containing row upon row of racked and stacked servers. Cooling systems, required to keep servers from overheating, are a significant component of any large data center (**Figure 6.3**). Google pioneered the software systems that connect the company's servers and make it possible for various applications to access data stored on the machines. Unlike other companies that purchase servers from outside suppliers, Google builds its own. Based on its experience creating the hardware, software, and facilities necessary to power the company on a global scale, Google is recognized as a leader in data center operations.

The company's data centers, including the servers, are built with energy efficiency, reliability, and performance in mind. As Google is a leading provider of Internet services, its data infrastructure must keep up with growing consumer demand for speedy performance and reliability. A typical Google search delivers millions of pages of results in less than half a second. Consumer expectations for performance have grown so high that waiting more than a few seconds for an e-mail to load or a search to run can cause frustration.

More recently, Google has had to contend with revelations that the U.S. National Security Agency (NSA) breached its server network security. This follows cyberattacks in 2010 and 2011 by hackers suspected of being associated with the Chinese government. Protecting company data from criminals is a significant challenge in itself, but Google is understandably frustrated by the fact that it must now fight off cyber-attacks from two world superpowers, one of which is its own government.

Environmental Impact

Industrywide, data centers used 70 billion kilowatt-hours of electricity in 2014, representing a 4% increase from the amount used in 2012. Industrywide, data center energy use and the related environmental impact have become an issue of growing concern. Google is widely recognized as operating some of the most efficient data centers in the world, but many critics are disturbed by the industry's overall level of energy consumption. According to some estimates, data centers account for about 2% of the world's energy use and the fast rate of growth is cause for concern (see **Figure 6.4**). Google has taken an active approach to reducing its environmental footprint. Beginning in 2017, Google will source 100% of its energy needs for offices and data centers from renewable sources. See Google's data center Web page **https://www.google.com/about/datacenters** for additional information.

© asharkyu/Shutterstock

FIGURE 6.4 New, large-scale data centers being constructed for companies like Google, Microsoft, and Facebook house thousands of servers and are creating concern among environmentalists over increases in energy consumption.

Google Data Center Statistics

- **Number of servers worldwide**   Over 1 million
- **Number of data centers**   Nine in North America, one in South America, two in Asia, and four in Europe
- **2016 Capital investment in data centers**   Approximately $11 billion
- **Data processing volume**   Over 100 petabytes a day
- **Average energy efficiency**   PUE* = 1.12
- **Energy use**   Continual use of about 260 megawatts of electricity, approximately 0.01% of global energy consumption
- **Energy use comparisons**   Owns about 3% of servers worldwide, but only uses about 1% of data center industry energy
- **Renewable energy**   Claims that 100% percent of its energy use comes from renewable sources

*PUE stands for Power Usage Effectiveness. A PUE of 2.0 means that for every watt of power devoted to computing, an additional watt is spent on cooling, power distribution, and overhead. The Data Center Industry average PUE falls between 1.8 and 1.89.

Sources: Jacobson (2010), Grifantini (2011), Newman (2011), Schneider (2011), Glanz (2011, 2012), Gallagher (2012), Venkatraman (2012), Anthony (2013), Miller (2013), Sverdlik (2016).

Bloomberg/Getty Images

FIGURE 6.3 Pipes pass through the chiller plant at the Google, Inc., data center in Changhua, Taiwan. Google doubled its spending plan for its new data center in Taiwan to $600 million amid surging demand from Asia for its Gmail and YouTube services.

Why Search Is Important for Business

Search engines have become a part of our everyday life. They are free, easy to use, and become more powerful and effective every day. Most of us take them for granted and are generally unaware of the complex technologies that power these tools. For the average Web user, it may not be vitally important to understand how search technology is evolving. But for business managers, understanding the potential power of search technology is crucial and becoming more important every day. It has long been recognized that access to information is a competitive advantage. Search technology impacts business in each of the following ways:

- Enterprise search—finding information within your organization
- Recommendation engines—presenting information to users without requiring them to conduct an active search
- Search engine marketing (SEM)—getting found by consumers on the Web
- Web search—finding crucial business information online

Each of these important search technology applications are described in what follows.

Enterprise Search   **Enterprise search** tools are used by employees to search for and retrieve information related to their work in a manner that complies with the organization's information-sharing and access control policies. Information can come from a variety of sources, including publicly available information, enterprise information (internal records) found in company databases and intranets, as well as information on individual employee computers (Delgado, Renaud, & Krishnamurthy, 2014). Enterprise search tools allow companies to gain competitive advantages by leveraging the value of internal information that would otherwise remain hidden or "siloed." Information can be inaccessible as a result of incompatible technologies in various units, lack of coordination or cooperation between units, security concerns, and concerns about the cost of making information accessible (Thomas, 2013; Walker, 2014).

In most organizations today, a large portion of employees are "knowledge workers" (e.g., business analysts, marketing managers, purchasing agents, IT managers, etc.). Access to information has a significant impact on their productivity. Enterprise search tools allow workers to extract internal information from databases, intranets, content management systems, files, contracts, policy manuals, and documents to make timely decisions, adding value to the company and enhancing its competitive advantage.

Structured versus unstructured data   One of the challenges encountered by developers of enterprise search tools is that information is not always in the same format. Data exist in two formats: structured or unstructured. **Structured data** can be defined as highly organized information, which is easily searchable using simple search engine algorithms or related procedures. **Unstructured data**, sometimes called messy data, refers to information that is not organized in a systematic or predefined way. Unstructured data files are also more likely to contain inaccuracies or errors. Examples of unstructured data include e-mails, articles, books, and documents. Unstructured data accounts for a majority of all the data present on computers today. Originally, enterprise search tools worked only with structured data. Many newer systems claim to work with unstructured information as well, although there is great variability in terms of how well they actually do this.

Security issues in enterprise search   Unlike a Web search, enterprise search tools must balance the goal of making information widely available throughout the organization with the need to restrict access based on an employee's job function or security clearance. Limiting access to certain documents or data is referred to as **access control**. Enterprise search tools introduce the potential for a number of security breaches or access of unauthorized information. Most of these can be addressed as long as the organization's IT workers install and maintain the search system's security features, including security integrations with other enterprise programs. An audit of requests logs should be conducted regularly to look for patterns or inconsistencies.

Enterprise search vendors   Market analysts Frost and Sullivan (Prnewswire.com, 2013) estimate that the global market for enterprise search tools was over $1.47 billion in 2012; it is predicted that the market will grow to over $5 billion by 2020. Clearly, organizations around the world recognize the value of this technology. Several different companies make and sell enterprise search systems, Autonomy, Google, Coveo, and Perceptive Software being the top contenders (Andrews & Koehler-Kruener, 2014). Vendors can be broken down into the following three categories:

- Specialized search vendors (for instance, Attivio, Endeca, Vivisimo): Software designed to target specific user information needs
- Integrated search vendors (for instance, Autonomy, IBM, and Microsoft): Software designed to combine search capabilities with information management tools
- Detached search vendors (for instance, Google, ISYS): Software designed to target flexibility and ease of use

With so many options available for enterprise search, it is important that organizations conduct a careful needs analysis prior to acquisition.

Recommendation Engines   **Recommendation engines** represent an interesting twist on IR technology. Unlike Web search engines that begin with a user query for information, recommendation engines attempt to anticipate information that a user might be interested in. Recommendation engines are used by e-commerce sites to recommend products; news organizations to recommend news articles and videos; Web advertisers to anticipate the ads people might respond to; and so on. They represent a huge potential for businesses and developers. While the use of recommendation engines is widespread, there is still much work to be done to improve the accuracy of these fascinating applications. You can read more about recommendation engines in Section 6.5.

Search Engine Marketing   Most traditional advertising methods target customers who are not actively engaged in shopping for a product. Instead, they are watching television, listening to the radio, reading a magazine, or driving down the road, paying little attention to the billboards they pass. To most people, advertising represents an unwelcome interruption. On the other hand, people using search engines are actively looking for information. As a result, they are much more likely to be interested in product and service information found in SERPs as long as it is related to the topic they are searching for. Efforts to reach this targeted audience are much more likely to produce sales. That's why **search engine marketing (SEM)** has become an important business strategy. Industry experts report that people generally engage in three basic types of searches:

1. **Informational search**   Using search engines to conduct research on a topic. This is the most common type of search.
2. **Navigational search**   Using a search engine to locate particular websites or Web pages.
3. **Transactional search**   Using a search engine to determine where to purchase a product or service.

You might think businesses would be primarily interested in transactional searches, but all three types are important and play a key role in the buying process. Say you are interested in purchasing a new tablet computer. Your first step is likely to engage in an informational search, attempting to learn about the product category of mobile tablet devices. Businesses should offer content on their websites and social media sites for consumers seeking general product information. An informational search also represents an opportunity to influence consumers early in the purchasing process.

After researching a product category, you might try finding websites of particular companies to learn more about individual tablet computer brands (navigational search). Companies need to design their websites so that they can be found easily by search engines.

Search engine marketing (SEM)   a collection of online marketing strategies and tactics that promote brands by increasing their visibility in SERPs through optimization and advertising.

Finally, you might try to determine where to buy your tablet computer by searching on terms like "lowest price," "free shipping," and so on. This is an example of a transactional search.

Search engine marketing (**Figure 6.5**) consists of designing and advertising a Web page, with the goal of increasing its visibility when consumers conduct the three types of searches just described. SEM strategies and tactics produce two different, but complementary outcomes:

1. **Organic search listings** are the result of content and website design features intended to improve a site's ranking on SERPs that result from specific keyword queries. No payments are made to the search engine service for organic search listings.

2. **Paid search listings** are a form of advertising and are purchased from search engine companies. The placement and effectiveness of paid search ads on SERPs are a function of several factors in addition to the fees paid by advertisers. You will read more about these factors in Section 6.3.

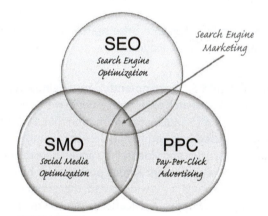

FIGURE 6.5   Search engine marketing integrates three different strategies: search engine optimization, pay-per-click advertising, and social media optimization.

Businesses utilize **search engine optimization (SEO)** to improve their website's organic listings on SERPs. SEO specialists understand how search engines work and guide companies in designing websites and creating content that will produce higher organic SERP rankings than competitive websites.

Paid search listings are often referred to as **pay-per-click (PPC)** advertising because advertisers pay search engines based on how many people click on the ads. Typically, PPC ads are listed separately from organic search results. Managing an effective PPC ad campaign involves making strategic decisions about what keyword search queries you want to trigger the display of your ad. You will read more about PPC or paid search advertising in Section 6.3.

Social media optimization refers to strategies designed to enhance a company's standing on various social media sites. Increasingly, search engines evaluate a company's presence on social media to determine its reputation, which in turn influences how the company is ranked in SERPs. You will read more about social media strategies in Chapter 7.

Growth of search engine marketing   As companies begin to realize the power of SEM, more money is being spent on this highly effective strategy. In 2016, businesses spent an estimated $65 billion on SEO services to improve the rank or listing order of their organic listings on SERPs. This figure is expected to rise to almost $80 billion in 2020 (Sullivan, 2016). In addition, the research firm eMarketer (2016) estimates that spending on PPC search advertising reached $86.25 billion in 2016, an increase of 15.4% from the year before. Both types of spending, SEO and PPC, illustrate how important search marketing is to businesses these days. Companies now spend more on SEM than they do on television or print advertising. Unlike most traditional advertising methods, return on investment (ROI) can be calculated for SEM by tracking **click-through rates (CTRs)**, changes in site traffic, and purchasing behavior.

Click-through rates (CTRs)   the percentage of people who click on a hyperlinked area of a SERP or Web page.

Mobile Search and Mobile SEO   Mobile devices have become ubiquitous. With the emergence of smartphones and tablet computers, mobile devices now account for over half of all Web traffic. In some developing countries, mobile devices account for an even larger share of Internet use since they are less expensive than computers. Since more people are using mobile devices to surf the Web, it should come as no surprise that more Internet searches are conducted using mobile devices instead of computers.

With the dramatic increase in mobile device usage, companies need to make sure their websites and content can be found via mobile search. This means optimizing mobile websites differently from desktop sites. Two issues essential to mobile SEO include:

1. Properly configuring the technical aspects of the mobile site so that it can be crawled and indexed by search engines.

2. Providing content that is useful to people using mobile devices. Webmasters should consider how people use their mobile devices differently from computers and adjust content on their mobile websites accordingly. For instance, if consumers are likely to use their mobile device to check product reviews while shopping in a store, make this information easy to find on the mobile website.

When designing a mobile site for e-commerce, Web developers should make sure that information about store location, product reviews, and promotional offers is easily available and optimized so that it will appear in a mobile SERP. Mobile shoppers also use barcode scanning apps as a kind of mobile search engine for locating product reviews and price comparisons while shopping in stores. This practice, called **showrooming**, is becoming increasingly popular with consumers and creating a great deal of frustration and worry on the part of brick-and-mortar retailers.

Social Search   Most major social media websites (i.e., Facebook, YouTube, Twitter, LinkedIn, etc.) have search engines designed to help users find content on their platforms. Of course, some search tools are better than others. It probably comes as no surprise that Facebook users have access to some advanced search features. People can search for friends by name or find information related to their friends using more complex queries such as "Movies liked by friends who liked The Godfather" or "Music liked by friends who liked Lady Gaga." Facebook search can be used to find services, events, places, and groups. You can use it to find some place to eat with a search phrase like "Seafood restaurants in New Orleans." Clearly, Facebook hopes to leverage the content and connections created by users to power a search tool that people will use instead of Google, Bing, or some other general Web search engine.

Recently, Facebook added a new image search feature powered by artificial intelligence that allows users to search for pictures using words that describe what's in the picture instead of relying on tags and captions. For instance, you might search for "Santa Claus photo" and the search engine will be able to find photos with Santa Claus even if no tags or text associate the picture with Santa Claus. Developers say that eventually the image search will be able to recognize photos based on objects, actions (e.g., walking, running, dancing), and other descriptive terms. Eventually, this technology could be used to perform similar searches for video and other immersive formats (Candela, 2017).

Facebook undoubtedly can devote more resources to innovations of this nature than other social media platforms. However, while other platforms may take longer to develop sophisticated social search tools, most have the same motivations as Facebook when it comes enhancing user experience and providing a mechanism for highlighting content from individuals and organizations with commercial interests. With over 2 billion searches conducted on Facebook each day, businesses will undoubtedly be willing to pay for ways to reach this sizable social media audience in much the same way that they currently advertise on Google, Bing, and other Internet search engines (Kraus, 2015; Constine, 2016).

Personal Assistants and Voice Search   Major Internet technology firms Apple, Amazon, Google, and Microsoft and a host of smaller firms have launched intelligent personal assistant (IPA) systems that threaten to disrupt conventional SEM paradigms. IPA software is typically designed to help people perform basic tasks like turning on/off lights and small appliances, activating household alarm systems, and searching the Internet for music, videos, weather, and other types of information. While IPAs are still in the growth stages of the product life cycle, forecasted demand for the foreseeable future seems strong.

The typical IPA system is a voice-activated program that uses commands that approximate natural language. For instance, to learn about the weather, you might ask Amazon's IPA, "Alexa, what's the weather for this weekend?" To get Apple's IPA to play a specific music genre, you might say, "Siri, play some R&B music." In the not too distant future, we can expect voice-activated IPAs will be integrated with mobile devices, televisions, automobiles, and even hotel rooms.

Business that have become skilled at using SEO and PPC campaigns to drive traffic to their websites will have to go back to the drawing board to figure out how the rise in voice search will affect some fundamental marketing strategies. Currently, IPAs act like a kind of filter, screening search results and often basing answers on a single source. Just as businesses once faced the challenge of reformatting website content for smaller screens on mobile devices, they must now determine how to serve up information in a format optimized to make it attractive to a variety of IPAs acting as proxies for their owners.

Web Search for Business
Commercial search engines and Web directories are useful tools for knowledge workers in business. To use search engines effectively, workers should familiarize themselves with all the features available on the search engine they use. Since Google is the most popular search engine, we highlight some of those features in the following list. Many of these features are also available on **Bing.com**.

- **Focused search**   You can focus your search to information in different formats—Web pages, videos, images, maps, and the like—by selecting the appropriate navigation button on the SERP page.

- **Filetype**   If you are looking specifically for information contained in a certain file format, you can use the "filetype:[file extension]" command following your keyword query. For instance, the search "private colleges filetype:xls" will produce links to MS Excel files with information related to private colleges. Use this command to find Adobe files (.pdf), MS Word files (.docx), MS PowerPoint files (.pptx), and so on.

- **Advanced search**   To narrow your search, go to the Advanced Search panel. From this page, you can set a wide range of parameters for your search, including limiting the search to certain domains (e.g., .gov, .org, .edu), languages, dates, and even reading level. You can also use this to narrow your search to a particular website.

- **Search tools button**   Allows you to narrow your results to listings from specific locations or time frames.

- **Search history**   Have you ever found a page using a search engine, but later had trouble finding it again? If you are logged into your Google account while using the search engine, it's possible to review your search history. It will show you not only your search queries but also the pages you visited following each query.

These are just a few of the many features you can use to conduct a power search. While you are in college, take the time to become proficient with using different search engine features. Not only will it help with your immediate research needs, it will help you in your career as well. At the end of this chapter, we include information for a free online Power Search course offered by Google. This is a good way to enhance your ability to find the information you need.

Finding intellectual property
Your business may have an interest in protecting certain kinds of intellectual property being used without permission on the Web. This might include confidential reports, images, copyrighted blog posts, creative writing (e.g., poetry, novels, etc.), and so on. You can use search engines to find where someone may have posted your intellectual property on the Web without permission (see Osher, 2014). You can search for text-based work by simply using queries containing strings of text from the material you're looking for. Images can be found by using **Google's reverse image search engine**. **Tin Eye** is an alternative reverse image search engine with a number of interesting features.

Real-time search   Sometimes you need information about things as they happen. For instance, you may be interested in monitoring news stories written about your company or you might need to know what people are saying about your brand or a political candidate on Twitter. For these situations, you'll need a real-time search tool.

Say your company wants to explore accepting Bitcoin payments. (Bitcoin is a digital currency that was launched in 2009.) After engaging in a traditional Web search to learn about the currency, you decide you want to learn about public interest in Bitcoin and find news stories that have recently been published about the currency. You might consider using the following tools:

- **Google Trends**   This tool will help you identify current and historical interest in the topic by reporting the volume of search activity over time. Google Trends allows you to view the information for different time periods and geographic regions.

- **Google Alerts**   Use Google Alerts to create automated searches for monitoring new Web content, news stories, videos, and blog posts about some topic. Users set up alerts by specifying a search term (e.g., a company name, product, or topic), how often they want to receive notices, and an e-mail address where the alerts are to be sent. When Google finds content that match the parameters of the search, users are notified via e-mail. Bing has a similar feature called News Alerts.

- **Twitter Search**   You can leverage the crowd of over 650 million Twitter users to find information as well as gauge sentiment on a wide range of topics and issues in real time. Twitter's search tool looks similar to other search engines and includes an advanced search mode. In addition to real-time search, the Twitter search tool is also an example of social search, which was explained earlier in the chapter.

Social bookmarking search   Social bookmarking sites like **Diigo** provide a way for users to save links to websites they want to access at a later time. When saving page links, users tag them with keywords that describe the page's content. The bookmarked links form a graph of content on the Web that can be used by others. Because the Web pages are tagged by humans, search results are often more relevant than results from commercial search engines. **Pinterest** is a variation on the social bookmarking idea, allowing users to save and share images they find online. You can find information about various topics by searching Pinterest to see what other users have collected on the subject.

Vertical search   As described previously, large commercial search engines use indicators of popularity or reputation to determine website quality. This seems to work well for a generalized Web search, but it might not be effective when users search on very specific topics such as rare disease, which, by definition, does not generate a lot of activity on the Web. Crawlers do not often index pages in the lower levels of less popular websites. **Vertical search engines** are programmed to focus on Web pages related to a particular topic and to drill down by crawling pages that other search engines are likely to ignore. Vertical search engines exist for a variety of industries. Ironically, the best way to find a vertical search engine is to search for it on a commercial search engine like Google or Bing.

Questions

1. What is the primary difference between a Web directory and a crawler-based search engine?
2. What is the purpose of an index in a search engine?
3. Why are companies increasingly interested in enterprise search tools capable of handling unstructured data?
4. What is the difference between SEO and PPC advertising?
5. Describe three different real-time search tools.

6.2 | Organic Search and Search Engine Optimization

The goal of SEO practitioners is to help organizations increase traffic to their websites. They accomplish this by optimizing websites in an effort to increase visibility and ranking on SERPs. Using Web analytics programs like *Google Analytics*, companies can determine how many people visit their site, what specific pages they visit, how long they spend on the site, and what search engines are producing the most traffic (see **Figure 6.6**). More sophisticated SEO practitioners will also attempt to determine what keywords or phrases generated traffic to their website. These are just a few of the many metrics used to measure the effectiveness of SEO strategies. In the sections that follow, we will use the most popular search engine, Google, to explain the basics of SEO. Most of what we write, however, will also apply to other popular search engines.

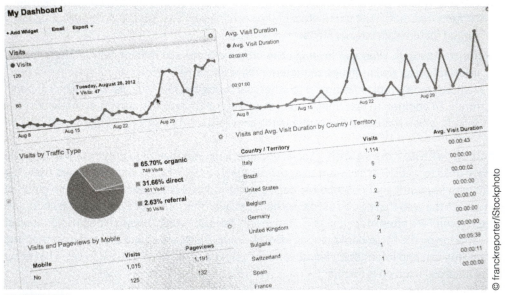

FIGURE 6.6 Tools like Google Analytics are used to monitor changes in website traffic as a result of SEO practices.

Strategies for Search Engine Optimization

As mentioned at the beginning of this chapter, all search engines use somewhat different proprietary algorithms for determining where a website will appear in search results. As a result, it is not possible to tell what specific factors will be used or how much weight they will carry in determining SERP ranking. Over time, there has been a significant increase in the number of factors that search engines like Google use to determine how a site is listed on a SERP. The general consensus among SEO experts is that Google probably uses over 200 different factors. To make things even more challenging, Google updates its algorithm hundreds of times a year. This presents somewhat of a moving target for SEO professionals hired to improve the organic SERP listings of their clients.

Why Does Google Keep Changing Its Algorithm? Google's overall goal is to constantly improve the experience of people using its search engine. Over time, Google engineers have developed ways to predict if a website will provide a positive experience for people using its search engine. Whenever a new way to improve user experience is found, they implement the change by updating the algorithm. Google also employs sophisticated technologies like artificial intelligence and semantic search algorithms to enhance the search experience.

Artificial intelligence constantly monitors how users respond to search results and modifies the listing algorithm to improve results. Semantic technology helps Google do a better job of understanding the content on a Web page and matching that content with the words and phrases people use to conduct a search.

Ranking Factors: On-Page and Off-Page SEO

To understand how Google ranks website listings in search results, we begin by dividing ranking factors into on-page factors and off-page factors.

On-page factors are elements of the Web page that can be directly controlled by the publisher or Web page creator. SEO professionals attempt to improve a website's SERP listing by optimizing on-page factors related to content, functionality, and HTML programming (Sullivan, 2015).

Content   Perhaps one of the biggest changes Google has made to its ranking algorithm over the years is an increased emphasis on high-quality content. Content marketing is a strategy that has gained popularity in recent years because of the significant weight assigned to high-quality content when determining search results and its role in attracting increased Web traffic. Some specific ways that Google determines if a website has high-quality content include the following:

- The quality of writing on the Web page
- The presence of relevant keywords and phrases associated with the topic
- How "fresh" or up-to-date the content is
- Use of multiple content formats (i.e., news, video, podcast, blog, and social content)
- Depth or quantity of topical content
- Links that point to other well-respected and trustworthy websites
- The proportion of relevant to irrelevant text about a topic
- Barriers to content have a negative impact on user satisfaction. Examples include making people register, provide names, or fill out forms to get to content.

Functionality and programming   Website functionality has an impact on SERP rankings. Pages that don't load quickly or display well on mobile devices are less likely to result in a positive user experience. Information in a page's HTML (programming language) source code also influences ranking algorithms. Functionality and programming can be assessed by factors such as the following:

- How easily search engine programs can "crawl" the Web page.
- How well the Web page works with mobile devices.
- How quickly the Web page loads.
- Availability of secure (https://) connections for visitors.
- Minimal presence of duplicate content on the website.
- Page URLs that contain keywords.
- Use of topical words and phrases in source code metadata (e.g., title tags, page descriptions, keywords).
- How frequently users click on a listing in search results. **Click-through rates (CTR)** are determined in part by how attractive a website's listing is on a SERP. The way a SERP listing looks is the result of the Web page's HTML source code.
- Hacked websites, sites that infect users with malware, and sites that fail to clean up spam or irrelevant content in comment sections are all factors that negatively impact user experience.

Off-page factors can be influenced but not directly controlled by SEO professionals. Many off-page factors are strongly related to a website's relevance and credibility. Other off-page factors are related to personalized search, a relatively new effort by Google to improve user experience (Sullivan, 2015).

Relevance and credibility   Google uses a number of different metrics to determine if a website is a trustworthy source of information on a particular topic. Many of these metrics are based on user behavior and how the site is represented on other websites and social media platforms:

- **Backlinks** to the target website on other well-respected and trustworthy websites. The use of backlinks is based on the assumption that people who create website content are more likely to place links to high-quality websites than poor-quality sites on their Web pages. Google assigns a **PageRank** score to each Web page based on the quality and quantity of backlinks associated with the page. Since the PageRank score is believed to be a heavily weighted factor, SEO professionals have developed several creative strategies for increasing legitimate backlinks to their websites while avoiding certain tactics that Google disapproves of. Google downgrades websites that use methods that artificially inflate their backlink count.

- Click-through rate (CTR) is also an indicator of relevance. Users are more likely to click on SERP listings related to the information they're searching for.

- Amount of advertising on the website—Too many ads detract from topical website content.

- **Dwell time**—This is a measure of how long a user remains on a page. Users stay on pages with useful content longer than pages that lack useful content.

- Sites listed in respected Web directories are more likely to contain quality content because they have been reviewed by human editors. Positive comments on review sites like **Yelp.com** and **Zagat.com** also have a positive impact on a website's reputation.

- High-quality or helpful websites are more likely to be discussed on social media. Examples include comments on Facebook and Google+, shares, Tweets, Likes, and so on.

- Site traffic—Sites with high-quality content tend to get more traffic over time.

Personalized search   Google uses information about the person conducting the search in an effort to enhance their experience:

- User location—the country, city or area the user is from

- Past experience—Google SERPs can be influenced by search and Web browsing history

- Social experience—the extent to which the user or people in their network engaged with or discussed the website favorably on social media including Google+, Facebook, Twitter, and so on

Content and Inbound Marketing

The ultimate goal of search engines is to help users find information. Sometimes it seems that SEO practitioners lose sight of this and spend too much time chasing down hundreds of factors they think are being used by search engine ranking algorithms. At worst, SEO can represent an attempt to "game the system" or trick search engines into ranking a site higher than its content deserves (see the discussion of black hat SEO in the next section).

Perhaps the most important action an organization can take to improve its website's ranking and satisfy website visitors is to provide helpful content that is current and updated regularly. When SEO practices are combined with valuable content, websites not only become easier to find but also contribute to building brand awareness, positive attitudes toward the brand, and brand loyalty.

Inbound marketing represents an alternative approach to traditional outbound marketing strategies (e.g., mass media advertising). Inbound marketers attract customers to their websites with content that is informative, useful, or entertaining. Inbound marketing campaigns are based on strategies that integrate content generation, SEO, and social media tactics. In Chapter 7, you will read more about how inbound marketers integrate content, SEO, and social media strategies in powerful marketing campaigns that deliver sales and profit. See **Figure 6.7.**

FIGURE 6.7 Inbound marketers use valuable content, search engine optimization, and social media to attract customers.

Black Hat versus White Hat SEO: Ethical Issues in Search Engine Optimization

Search engines regularly update their algorithms to improve results. Two well-known Google updates called Panda (released in 2011) and Penguin (released in 2012) were designed to improve the ranking of websites with quality content and downgrade poor-quality sites. Both updates are designed to defeat what are commonly referred to as "black hat SEO" tactics. People who employ black hat SEO tactics try to trick the search engine into thinking a website has high-quality content, when in fact it does not. With stronger detection systems now in place, websites that use these tactics (or even appear to use them) will be severely downgraded in Google's ranking system. Some examples of black hat SEO tactics are defined in the following list:

Link spamming—Generating backlinks for the primary purpose of SEO, not adding value to the user. Black hat SEOs use tricks to create backlinks. Some examples include adding a link to a page in the comments section of an unrelated blog post, or building sites called "link farms" solely for the purpose of linking back to the promoted page.

Keyword tricks—Black hat SEOs will embed several high-value keywords on pages with unrelated content to drive up traffic statistics. For instance, an e-commerce site might embed words like "amazon" (a word that frequently shows up in search queries) in an attempt to get listed on SERPs of people looking for amazon.com.

Ghost text—This tactic involves adding text on a page that will affect how a website is listed on SERPs. The text may not have anything to do with the real content of the page, or it may simply repeat certain words to increase the content density. The text is then hidden, usually by making it the same color as the background.

Shadow pages—Also called "ghost pages" or "cloaked pages," this black hat tactic involves creating pages that are optimized to attract lots of people. The pages, however, contain a redirect command so that users are sent to another page to increase traffic on that page.

These particular tactics are no longer effective as a result of updates to the Google ranking system. Most likely, other search engines have adopted similar measures. However, there will always be people who take shortcuts attempting to achieve higher SERP rankings. Businesses must be careful when hiring SEO consultants or agencies to make sure they do not use prohibited SEO techniques. When these actions are discovered, Google and other search engines will usually punish the business by dramatically reducing their visibility in search results.

Questions

1. Search engines use many different "clues" about the quality of a website's content to determine how a page should be ranked in search results. Explain how a search engine uses specific factors to determine the quality of a website's content.

2. SEO professionals strive to increase a Web page's PageRank score which is based on the quality and quantity of backlinks. Explain what a backlink is and why search engines use the PageRank score to determine the order in which websites are listed in SERPs.

3. Explain why the so-called black hat SEO tactics are ultimately short-sighted and can lead to significant consequences for businesses that use them.

4. What is the fundamental difference between on-page and off-page SEO factors?

5. Explain why providing high-quality, regularly updated content is the most important aspect of any SEO strategy.

6.3 Pay-Per-Click and Paid Search Strategies

In addition to organic listings, most search engines display paid or sponsored listings on their SERPs. These advertisements provide revenue for the search engine and allow it to offer Web search services to the general public for free. They also provide a way for smaller organizations with new websites to gain visibility on SERPs while waiting for their SEO strategies to produce organic results. Most major search engines differentiate organic search results from paid ad listings on SERPs with labels, shading, and placing the ads in a different place on the page. Some critics have complained that paid advertisements receive preferential page placement and are not clearly distinguished from organic listings. However, at the time of this publication, it is easy to distinguish ads from organic results on Google and Bing SERPs. Defenders of the search engine companies argue that since the paid ads make it possible for everyone to use search services for free, the preferential page placement is justified.

Creating a PPC Advertising Campaign

There are five steps to creating a PPC advertising campaign on search engines.

1. Set an overall budget for the campaign.
2. Create ads—most search engine ads are text only, but this is likely to change in the future.
3. Select keywords and other parameters associated with the campaign.
4. Set up billing account information.
5. Modify key words and ad copy based on results.

Search advertising allows businesses to target customers who are likely to purchase their products. They do this by selecting keywords that correspond to search queries that potentially identify someone as a customer. For instance, a company that sells women's purses may want to appear on a SERP when someone conducts a search using any of the following terms or phrases:

- Purse
- Handbag
- Women's purses
- Ladies' purses
- Designer purses
- Designer handbags

Google and other search engines provide advertisers with tools for evaluating the impact of different keywords or phrases. These tools typically display information about how often people use the word in a search and also recommend alternative words to consider using in the campaign. Advertisers "bid" on having their ads appear when someone searches on one of their keywords. Higher bids result in a greater probability that the ad will appear in search results associated with the keyword. However, this might also deplete the advertiser's budget more quickly. On the other hand, if a bid is too low, the ad might not appear at all. Keyword tools usually provide information about typical bid prices for each keyword or phrase. Smart advertisers start with a modest bid and increase it over time to achieve the ad placement rate they desire.

The likelihood of ad placement is also influenced by a **quality score** representing the search engine's estimate of how successful the ad will be. Quality scores are determined by factors related to ad relevance and user experience factors. Relevant ads closely match the intent of the user's search. The expected CTR indicates how likely the ad will be clicked on. The user's landing page experience is determined by things such as how relevant, transparent, and easy-to-navigate the page is. According to Google, quality scores are determined by several factors:

- Expected keyword CTR
- The past CTR of your URL
- Past effectiveness (overall CTR of ads and keywords in the account)
- Landing page quality (relevance, transparency, ease of navigation, etc.)
- Relevance of keywords to ads
- Relevance of keywords to customer search query
- Geographic performance—account success in geographic regions being targeted
- How well ads perform on different devices (quality scores are calculated for mobile, desktop/laptop, and tablets)

Relevant ads that produce sales are good for all parties. The search engine makes more money from clicked ads, the advertiser benefits from increased revenue, lower costs-per-click, and more favorable ad placement. When ads are relevant and landing pages are functional and contain relevant information, customers are more likely to find and purchase what they are looking for.

In addition to selecting keywords and setting bid prices, advertisers also set parameters for the geographic location and time of day they want the ad to appear. These factors allow for additional customer targeting designed to help advertisers reach the consumers most likely to purchase their products.

Companies need to consider the fit between ad content and landing page content and functionality. For instance, sometimes companies create product-oriented ads, but then link to the main page of their website instead of a page with information about the product in the ad. Other factors include landing page design, call to action (CTA) effectiveness, and quality of the shopping cart application. It does not make sense to spend money on a PPC campaign designed to drive consumers to an unattractive and dysfunctional website.

One of the attractive features of PPC ad campaigns is that managers can monitor results in real time and make adjustments to the campaign parameters if necessary. Advertisers frequently set up A/B tests to evaluate the relative effectiveness of two different ads. After a period of time, the advertiser checks to see which ad is producing better results and discontinues use of the less effective ad for the remainder of the campaign. Some advertisers run A/B tests throughout the campaign, constantly testing ad copy and other elements in the spirit of continuous improvement. You can learn more about advertising on the major commercial search engines by visiting the following websites:

- **Google** adwords.google.com
- **Bing** advertise.bingads.microsoft.com
- **Yahoo** advertising.yahoo.com

Metrics for Paid Search Advertising

In addition to more effective targeting, one of the key benefits of online advertising is the ability to evaluate its contribution to sales revenue more effectively. PPC advertisers use the following metrics to gauge the effectiveness of their campaigns:

Click-through rates (CTRs)   By themselves, CTRs do not measure the financial performance of an ad campaign. But they are useful for evaluating many of the decisions that go into a campaign, such as keyword selection and ad copy and ad attractiveness.

Keyword conversion   High CTRs are not always good if they do not lead to sales. Since the cost of the campaign is based on how many people click an ad, you want to select keywords that lead to sales (conversions), not just site visits. PPC advertisers monitor which keywords lead to sales and focus on those in future campaigns.

Cost of customer acquisition (CoCA)   This metric represents the amount of money spent to attract a paying customer. To calculate CoCA for a PPC campaign, you divide the total budget of the campaign by the number of customers who purchased something from your site. For instance, if you spent $1,000 on a campaign that yielded 40 customers, your CoCA would be $1,000/40 = $25 per customer.

Return on advertising spend (ROAS)   The campaign's overall financial effectiveness is evaluated with ROAS (revenue/cost). For example, if $1,000 was spent on a campaign that led to $6,000 in sales, ROAS would be $6,000/$1,000 = $6. In other words, for every dollar spent on PPC ads, $6 was earned.

Questions

1. What would most people say is the fundamental difference between organic listings and PPC listings on a SERP?
2. What are the five primary steps to creating a PPC advertising campaign on search engines?
3. In addition to the "bid price" for a particular keyword, what other factor(s) influence whether or not an advertisement will appear on a search results page? Why don't search engines use just the advertiser's bid to determine if an ad will appear on search results pages?
4. How do on-page factors influence the effectiveness of PPC advertisements?
5. What factors determine an ad's quality score?
6. Describe four metrics that can be used to evaluate the effectiveness of a PPC advertising campaign.

6.4 | A Search for Meaning—Semantic Technology

If there is one thing history has taught us, it is that the future is hard to predict. It might seem silly to predict what the future Internet will look like when it's clear so many people are having trouble understanding all the implications of the present Internet. However, forward-thinking businesses and individuals are beginning to plan for the next evolution which is sometimes called Web 3.0.

The current Web is disjointed, requiring us to visit different websites to get content, engage in commerce, and interact with our social networks (community). The future Web will use context, personalization, and vertical search to make content, commerce, and community more relevant and easier to access. With the addition of mobile technology, this Web will be always accessible.

- Context defines the intent of the user; for example, trying to purchase music, to find a job, to share memories with friends and family.

- Personalization refers to the user's personal characteristics that impact how relevant the content, commerce, and community are to an individual.
- Vertical search, as you have read, focuses on finding information in a particular content area, such as travel, finance, legal, and medical.

What Is the Semantic Web?

Semantic refers to the meaning of words or language. The **semantic Web** is one in which computers can interpret the meaning of content (data) by using **metadata** and **natural language processing** to support search and retrieval, analysis and information amalgamation from both structured and unstructured sources. Semantic technologies are being developed that will create a new, richer experience for Web users.

Tim Berners-Lee, creator of the technology that made the World Wide Web possible, is director of the *World Wide Web Consortium (W3C)*. This group develops programming standards designed to make it possible for data, information, and knowledge to be shared even more widely across the Internet. The result of these standards is a metadata language, or ways of describing digital information so that it can be used by a wide variety of applications.

Much of the world's digital information is stored in files structured so they can only be read by the programs that created them. With metadata, the content of these files can be labeled with tags describing the nature of the information, where it came from, or how it is arranged. At the risk of sounding too dramatic, metadata transforms a connected, but largely uninterpretable Web (network) of pages into a large database that can be searched, analyzed, understood, and repurposed by a variety of applications.

It is helpful to think about the semantic Web against the background of earlier Internet functionality (see **Table 6.2**). The early Internet allowed programmers and users to access information and communicate with one another without worrying about the details associated with the machines they used to connect to the network and store the information. The semantic Web continues this evolution, making it possible to access information about real things (people, places, contracts, books, chemicals, etc.) without knowing the details associated with the nature or structure of the data files, pages, and databases where these things are described or contained (Hendler & Berners-Lee, 2010). This will greatly expand the ways in which we search for and find information related to our needs and interests.

TABLE 6.2   Evolution of the Web

Web 1.0 (The Initial Web) A Web of Pages	Pages or documents are "hyperlinked," making it easier than ever before to access connected information.
Web 2.0 (The Social Web) A Web of Applications	New applications and technologies allow people to easily create, share, and organize information.
Web 3.0 (The Semantic Web) A Web of Data	Using metadata tags, artificial intelligence, natural language processing, and other semantic tools, computers can be used to access specific information across platforms and applications, regardless of the original structure of the file, page, or document. It turns the Web into a giant readable database.

The Language(s) of Web 3.0

The early Web was built using hypertext markup language (HTML). Web 2.0 was made possible, in part, by the development of languages like XML and JavaScript. The semantic Web utilizes additional languages that have been developed by the W3C. These include **resource description framework (RDF)**, **Web ontology language (OWL)**, and **SPARQL protocol and RDF query language (SPARQL)**. RDF is a language used to represent information about resources on the Internet. It will describe these resources using metadata **uniform resource identifiers (URIs)** like "title," "author," "copyright and license information." It is one of the features that allow data to be used by multiple applications.

As the acronym SPARQL implies, it is used to write programs that can retrieve and manipulate data stored in RDF format. OWL is the W3C language used to categorize and accurately identify the nature of things found on the Internet. These three languages, used together, will enhance the element of context on the Web, producing more fruitful and accurate information searches. The W3C continues its work, with input by programmers and the broader Internet community, to improve the power and functionality of these languages.

Semantic Web and Semantic Search

As you have read, the semantic Web is described by metadata, making it easier for a broad range of applications to identify and utilize data. One of the barriers to creating a semantic Web based on metadata, however, is the tagging process. Who will tag all the data currently on the Web? How can we be sure that such data will be tagged correctly? Will people purposely tag data incorrectly to gain some kind of advantage in the same way that black hat SEO tactics are used to mislead search engines?

Semantic search engines can be programmed to take advantage of metadata tags, but their usefulness would be very limited if that was the only way they could understand Web content.

Metadata tags, therefore, are just one approach used by semantic search engines to understand the meaning of online content. In addition to metadata tags, semantic search engines use a variety of other strategies to find meaning:

- Natural language processing
- Contextual cues
- Synonyms
- Word variations
- Concept matching
- Specialized queries
- Artificial Intelligence

Semantic search will seek to understand the context or intent of users looking for information in an effort to increase the relevance and accuracy of results (DiSilvestro, 2013). For instance, if a search engine understood the proper context of a search query containing the word "Disneyworld," it would know if the user was

- planning a vacation, or
- looking for a job at the theme park, or
- interested in the history of Disney World.

Semantic Search Features and Benefits
So what can semantic search engines do that is so much better compared to search engines that work solely on keyword matching? Grimes (2010) provides a list of practical search features based on semantic search technology.

Related searches/queries   The engine suggests alternative search queries that may produce information related to the original query. Search engines may also ask you, "Did you mean: [search term]?" if it detects a misspelling.

Reference results   The search engine suggests reference material related to the query, such as a dictionary definition, Wikipedia pages, maps, reviews, or stock quotes.

Semantically annotated results   Returned pages contain highlighting of search terms, but also related words or phrases that may not have appeared in the original query. These can be used in future searches simply by clicking on them.

Full-text similarity search   Users can submit a block of text or even a full document to find similar content.

Search on semantic/syntactic annotations   This approach would allow a user to indicate the "syntactic role the term plays—for instance, the part-of-speech (noun, verb, etc.)— or its semantic meaning, whether it's a company name, location, or event." For instance, a keyword search on the word "center" would produce too many results. Instead, a search query could be written using a syntax such as the following:

<organization> center </organization>

This would only return documents where the word "center" was part of an organization's name (e.g., Johnson Research Center or Millard Youth Center). Google currently allows you to do something similar to specify the kind of files you are looking for (e.g., filetype:pdf).

Concept search   Search engines could return results with related concepts. For instance, if the original query was "Tarantino films," documents would be returned that contain the word "movies" even if not the word "films."

Ontology-based search   Ontologies define the relationships between data. An ontology is based on the concept of "triples": subject, predicate, and object. This would allow the search engine to answer questions such as "What vegetables are green?" The search engine would return results about "broccoli," "spinach," "peas," "asparagus," "Brussels sprouts," and so on.

Semantic Web search   This approach would take advantage of content tagged with metadata as previously described in this section. Search results are likely to be more accurate than keyword matching.

Faceted search   Faceted search provides a means of refining or filtering results based on predefined categories called facets. For instance, a search on "colleges" might result in options to "refine this search by. . ." location, size, degrees offered, private or public, and so on. Many e-commerce websites provide users with faceted search features, allowing shoppers to filter search results by things like price, average rating, brand name, and product features.

Clustered search   This is similar to a faceted search, but without the predefined categories. Visit *Carrot2.org* to better understand this concept. After conducting a search, click on the "foamtree" option to see ways to refine your search. The refining options are extracted from the content in pages of the initial search.

Natural language search   Natural language search tools attempt to extract words from questions such as "How many countries are there in Europe?" and create a semantic representation of the query. Initially, this is what people hoped search engines would evolve toward, but Grimes wonders if we have become so accustomed to typing just one or two words into our queries that writing out a whole question may seem like too much work.

You may recognize some of these search enhancements when using popular commercial search engines like Google or Bing. That is because they have been building semantic technologies into their systems to improve user experience. You are encouraged to explore other search engines with semantic search features like **DuckDuckGo** and **SenseBot**.

Semantic Web for Business

What opportunities and challenges does the semantic Web hold for businesses? Perhaps the most immediate challenge faced by businesses is the need to optimize their websites for semantic search. Because search engines are responsible for directing so much traffic to business websites, it will be important that companies take advantage of semantic technologies to ensure they continue to remain visible to prospective customers who use search engines. While the details of semantic SEO are beyond the scope of this book, we can illustrate one important benefit of semantic website optimization. Websites optimized for semantic technology with metadata produce richer, more attractive listings on SERPs. Google calls these **rich snippets** (see **Figure 6.8**).

FIGURE 6.8   The Google search listing for this New York-based grocery chain is more attractive because it uses metadata from the business's website. (Google and the Google logo are registered trademarks of Google, Inc., used with permission.)

Note how detailed the organic search listing in Figure 6.8 is compared to a basic listing. These enhanced search listings are more visually attractive and produce greater CTRs.

Businesses need to stay up to date with advances in semantic search so that they can continuously optimize their sites to increase traffic from major search engines.

Questions

1. List five different practical ways that semantic technology is enhancing the search experience of users.
2. How do metadata tags facilitate more accurate search results?
3. Briefly describe the three evolutionary stages of the Internet?
4. Define the words "context," "personalization," and "vertical search." Explain how they make for better information search results.
5. What are three languages developed by the W3C and associated with the semantic Web?

6.5 | Recommendation Engines

A lot of times, people don't know what they want until you show it to them.
—Steve Jobs (quoted in *Business Week*, May 12, 1998)

Think about the challenge faced by large e-commerce websites like Amazon or Netflix. Brick-and-mortar retailers can capture people's attention in the store with eye-catching point-of-purchase displays or suggestive selling by store employees. However, these are not options for retail websites. They need an effective way of recommending their vast array of products to customers. Most e-commerce sites provide website search tools based on the technologies previously discussed in this chapter. Relying on customers to find products through an active search, however, assumes customers know what they want and how to describe it when forming their search query. For these reasons, many e-commerce sites rely on recommendation engines (sometimes called recommender systems). Recommendation engines proactively identify products that have a high probability of being something the consumer might want to buy. Amazon has long been recognized as having one of the best recommendation engines. Each time customers log into the site, they are presented with an assortment of products based on their purchase history, browsing history, product reviews, ratings, and many other factors. In effect, Amazon customizes their e-commerce site for each individual, leading to increased sales. Consumers respond to these personalized pages by purchasing products at much higher rates when compared to banner advertisements and other Web-based promotions. At Amazon, the recommendation engine is credited with generating 35% of sales (Arora, 2016).

Recommendation Filters

There are three widely used approaches to creating useful recommendations: content-based filtering, collaborative filtering, and hybrid strategies (Asrar, 2016).

Content-Based Filtering

Content-based filtering recommends products based on the product features of items the customer has interacted with in the past (**Figure 6.9**). Interactions can include viewing an item, "liking" an item, purchasing an item, saving an item to a wish list, and so on. In the simplest sense, content-based filtering uses item similarity to make recommendations. For instance, the Netflix recommendation engine attempts to recommend movies that are similar to movies you have already watched (see **IT at Work 6.2**). Music-streaming site Pandora creates its recommendations or playlists based on the Music Genome Project©, a system that uses approximately 450 different attributes to describe songs. These detailed systems for describing movies and songs enhance Netflix's and Pandora's positions in highly competitive industries because of their ability to offer superior recommendations to their customers.

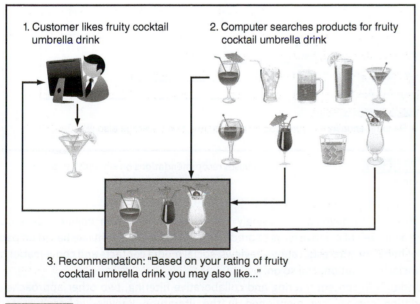

1. Customer likes fruity cocktail umbrella drink

2. Computer searches products for fruity cocktail umbrella drink

3. Recommendation: "Based on your rating of fruity cocktail umbrella drink you may also like..."

FIGURE 6.9   Content-based filtering produces recommendations based on similarity of product features.

IT at Work 6.2

Violent Nightmare-Vacation Movies and Other Fun Movie Genres at Netflix

Alexis Madrigal (2014) reverse-engineered Netflix's list of movie genres and was surprised to learn the company uses approximately 76,897 different ways to describe movies, creating the potential for some unusually specific movie recommendations. Christian Brown (2012) compiled a list of humorous and sometimes disturbing movie categories, a few of which are listed below:

10. Cerebral Con-Game Thrillers

9. Visually Striking Father–Son Movies

8. Violent Nightmare-Vacation Movies

7. Understated Independent Workplace Movies

6. Feel-Good Opposites-Attract Movies

5. Witty Dysfunctional-Family TV Animated Comedies

4. Period Pieces about Royalty Based on Real Life

3. Campy Mad-Scientist Movies

2. Mind-Bending Foreign Movies

1. More like *Arrested Development*

The fact that Netflix went to the trouble of creating so many detailed and descriptive labels suggests that a content-based filtering strategy is at use in the company's recommendation system.

Collaborative Filtering   **Collaborative filtering** makes recommendations based on a user's similarity to other people. For instance, when a customer gives a product a high rating, he or she may receive recommendations based on the purchases of other people who also gave the same product a high rating. Sometimes, websites will explain the reason for the recommendations with the message "Other people who liked this product also bought. . ." Many collaborative filtering systems use purchase history to identify similarities among customers. In principle, however, any customer characteristic that improves the quality of recommendations could be used (see **Figure 6.10**).

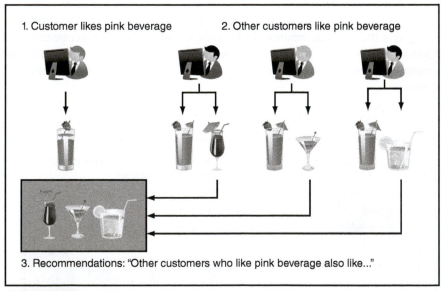

1. Customer likes pink beverage

2. Other customers like pink beverage

3. Recommendations: "Other customers who like pink beverage also like..."

FIGURE 6.10   Collaborative filtering bases recommendations on similarity to other customers.

In an effort to develop increasingly better recommendation engines, developers are exploring a number of creative ways to predict what consumers might like based on patterns of consumer behavior, interests, ratings, reviews, social media contacts and conversations, media use, financial information, and so on.

In addition to content filtering and collaborative filtering, two other approaches to recommendation engines are mentioned in the literature: knowledge-based systems and demographic systems. Knowledge-based systems use information about a user's needs to recommend products. This kind of system is useful for developing recommendations for products that consumers do not shop for very often. For instance, an insurance company may ask a customer a series of questions about his or her needs, and then use that information to recommend policy options. Demographic systems base recommendations on demographic factors corresponding to a potential customer (i.e., age, gender, race, income, etc.). While similarity to other customers might play a role in developing these recommendations, such systems are different from collaborative filtering systems that typically rely on information about a person's behavior (i.e., purchase, product ratings, etc.).

Systems are being developed that leverage big data streams from multiple sources to refine and enhance the performance of current systems.

Limitations of Recommendation Engines

While recommendation engines have proven valuable and are widely used, there are still challenges that must be overcome. Four commonly cited limitations are described as follows:

Cold start or new user   Making recommendations for a user who has not provided any information to the system is a challenge since most systems require a starting point or some minimal amount of information about the user (Adomavicius & Alexander, 2005; Burke, 2007). Tiroshi and colleagues (2011) have suggested consumers' existing social media profiles from sites like Facebook and Twitter could be used in situations where a website did not have sufficient information of its own to make recommendations.

Sparsity   Collaborative systems depend on having information about a critical mass of users to compare to the target user in order to create reliable or stable recommendations. This is not always available in situations where products have only been rated by a few people or when it is not possible to identify a group of people who are similar to a user with unusual preferences (Burke, 2007).

Limited feature content   For content filter systems to work, there must be sufficient information available about product features and the information must exist in a structured format so it can be read by computers. Often feature information must be entered manually, which can be prohibitive in situations where there are many products (Adomavicius & Alexander, 2005).

Overspecialization   If systems can only recommend items that are highly similar to a user profile, then the recommendations may not be useful. For instance, if the recommendation system is too narrowly configured on a website that sells clothing, the user may only see recommendations for the same clothing item he or she liked, but in different sizes or colors (Adomavicius & Alexander, 2005).

Hybrid Recommendation Engines

Hybrid recommendation engines develop recommendations based on some combination of the methodologies described above (content-based filtering, collaboration filtering, knowledge-based and demographic systems). Hybrid systems are used to increase the quality of recommendations and address shortcomings of systems that only use a single methodology. Burke (2007) identified various ways that hybrid recommendation engines combine results from different recommender systems. To illustrate the potential complexity and variation in hybrid systems, four approaches are listed below:

- **Weighted hybrid**   Results from different recommenders are assigned a weight and combined numerically to determine a final set of recommendations. Relative weights are determined by system tests to identify the levels that produce the best recommendations.

- **Mixed hybrid**   Results from different recommenders are presented alongside of each other.

- **Cascade hybrid**   Recommenders are assigned a rank or priority. If a tie occurs (with two products assigned the same recommendation value), results from the lower-ranked systems are used to break ties from the higher-ranked systems.

- **Compound hybrid**   This approach combines results from two recommender systems from the same technique category (e.g., two collaborative filters), but uses different algorithms or calculation procedures.

Recommendation engines are now used by many companies with deep content (e.g., large product inventory) that might otherwise go undiscovered if the companies depended on customers to engage in an active search.

To simplify our description of recommendation engines, most of the examples above have been based on the e-commerce sites recommending products to customers. However, this technology is used by many different kinds of business organizations, as illustrated in **Table 6.3**.

TABLE 6.3   **Examples of Recommendation Engine Applications**

Company	How It Uses Recommendation Engines. . .
Amazon	Recommends products using multiple filtering methods.
Netflix	Approximately 75% of Netflix movies are selected as a result of its recommendation system.
Pandora	This streaming music site creates playlists based on similarity to initial songs or artists selected by the user.
CNN, Time, Fast Company, Rolling Stone, NBCNews.com, Reuters, Us Weekly	These news and entertainment companies all use a recommendation engine (or "content discovery system") created by Outbrain.com to suggest additional articles related to the one site visitors initially viewed.
YouTube	YouTube uses a variation of Amazon's recommendation engine to suggest additional videos people might like to watch.
Goodreads	This social website for readers recommends books based on user ratings of books they have read.
Samsung	Uses recommendation engines built into its "smart TVs" to suggest television programming to viewers.
Facebook and LinkedIn	These social networking services use recommendation engines to suggest people that users may want to connect with.
Apple	Helps users find mobile apps they might enjoy.
Microsoft Xbox 360	Suggests new games based on what users have previously shown an interest in.
Tripadvisor	Recommends travel destinations and services based on destinations people have viewed or rated.
Stitch Fix	This fashion start-up uses a recommender system in conjunction with human stylists to select and ship clothing products to customers, before customers viewed or ordered them!

Questions

1. How is a recommendation engine different from a search engine?
2. Besides e-commerce websites that sell products, what are some other ways that recommendation engines are being used on the Web today?
3. What are some examples of user information required by recommendation engines that use collaborative filtering?
4. Before implementing a content-based recommendation engine, what kind of information would website operators need to collect about their products?
5. What are the four limitations or challenges that recommendation systems sometimes face?
6. What is a recommendation engine called that combines different methodologies to create recommendations? What are three ways these systems combine methodologies?

Key Terms

access control 172
backlinks 180
click-through rates (CTRs) 174
collaborative filtering 190
collection analysis module 169
content-based filtering 189
crawler control module 169
crawler search engines 168
dwell time 180
enterprise search 172
ghost text 181
hybrid recommendation engines 191
hybrid search engines 168
inbound marketing 180
indexer module 169
informational search 173
keyword conversion 184
keywords 169

link spamming 181
metadata 185
meta-search engines 168
navigational search 173
organic search listings 174
page repository 169
PageRank 180
paid search listings 174
pay-per-click (PPC) 174
petabyte 170
quality score 183
query interface 170
recommendation engines 173
resource description framework (RDF) 185
retrieval/ranking module 169
rich snippets 188
search engine 168
search engine marketing (SEM) 173

search engine optimization (SEO) 174
search engine results page (SERP) 166
semantic search engines 168
semantic Web 185
shadow pages 181
showrooming 175
social media optimization 174
SPARQL protocol and RDF query language (SPARQL) 185
spiders 168
structured data 172
transactional search 173
uniform resource identifiers (URIs) 185
unstructured data 172
vertical search engines 177
Web directories 168
Web ontology language (OWL) 185

Assuring Your Learning

Discuss: Critical Thinking Questions

1. Why is it important that businesses maintain a high level of visibility on SERPs?

2. Why are organic search listings more valuable than paid search listings for most companies over the long term? Even though organic search listings are more valuable, what are some reasons that companies should consider using PPC advertising as part of their search marketing strategies?

3. Why is relevant and frequently updated content a significant factor for companies concerned about their visibility on popular search engines? Does the quality of content impact organic results, paid results, or both? Explain.

4. Explain the differences between Web directories, crawler search engines, and hybrid search engines.

5. Why do search engines consider their algorithms for rank ordering Web page listings on SERPs to be trade secrets? What would be the consequences of publicizing detailed information about how a search engine ranks its results?

6. Why do consumer search engines like Google and Bing require vast amounts of data storage? How have they addressed this need? What environmental issues are associated with the way large technology companies operate their data storage facilities?

7. Explain why enterprise search technology is becoming increasingly important to organizations. Describe how enterprise search applications are different from consumer search engines in terms of their functionality, purpose, and the special challenges they must overcome.

8. Explain why people are much more likely to view and pay attention to product and service information in SERPs compared to traditional mass media advertising? What strategies are businesses adopting to take advantage of this trend?

9. Why is it easier to measure the return-on-investment of resources spent on search engine marketing compared to mass media advertising?

10. How has the widespread adoption of mobile devices impacted the SEO practices?

11. Identify at least five ways that Google has changed its algorithms in recent years to encourage website developers to do more than simply list keywords in an attempt to improve their ranking on search results.

12. The ultimate goal of Google, Bing, and other consumer search engines is to provide users with a positive user experience. What recommendations would you make to a website owner with regard to using website content to improve the site's rank on search result listings?

13. Why are "black hat" SEO techniques (see Section 6.2) considered unethical? Who is harmed by the use of such techniques? What are the consequences of using these questionable SEO tactics?

14. Explain how search engines determine if websites contain information relevant to a user's search inquiry.

15. Identify and describe the five steps to creating a PPC ad campaign.

16. How does an advertiser's bid and quality score determine the likelihood of PPC ad placement on SERPs? What are the factors that Google uses to determine an advertiser's quality score? Why does Google use the quality score instead of relying solely on the advertiser's bid?

17. Describe three metrics used by PPC advertisers to evaluate the effectiveness of their search ad campaign.

18. Identify the three things that SEO practitioners can optimize by making changes to on-page factors. What three things can SEO practitioners attempt to optimize by making changes to off-page factors?

19. Describe five ways that semantic search engines could enhance functionality for users. How will businesses benefit from the development of semantic search functions?

20. Recommender systems use different approaches to generating recommendations. Explain the difference between content-based filtering and collaborative filtering. Describe the kind of information required for each approach to work.

21. What are the alternatives to content-based filtering and collaborative filtering recommender systems? When is it most useful to use these alternatives?

22. Hybrid recommendation engines utilize two or more filtering strategies to create recommendations. Describe the four different approaches to creating a hybrid system.

Explore: Online and Interactive Exercises

1. Select a search query term or phrase based on a class assignment, a product you plan to purchase, or some area of personal interest. Use the query at each of the following search engines:

   a. Google.com

   b. Bing.com

   c. Yahoo.com

   d. DuckDuckGo.com

For each site, make the following observations:

   a. How relevant or useful are the websites listed on the first two pages of search results?

   b. What differences do you observe in terms of how the search engines list websites on the search results page?

   c. Do you see any indication that the search engine is using semantic technology to generate results (see "Semantic Search Features and Benefits" in Section 6.4)?

2. Visit the website for fitbit products at **fitbit.com** and familiarize yourself with the products and website content.

   a. Make a list of nonbranded keywords and phrases (i.e., doesn't contain the word "fitbit") that you would recommend fitbit use to optimize its pages so they show up in organic search listings.

   b. Based on your list of keywords and phrases, make a list of recommendations for content (i.e., articles, blog posts, information, etc.) that fitbit should add to its website to increase the chances that it will show up in organic search results. What keywords should be emphasized in the content you recommend?

3. Use an existing account, or sign up for an account, at one of the websites listed in Table 6.3. Make a list of the ways the website recommends its content, goods, or services to you. Based on your observations, are you able to determine what kind of recommendation system is in use by the website?

4. Pretend you are going to purchase an expensive item like a large flat-screen television or a major appliance from a national retailer like Best Buy or Sears. Using your mobile phone, attempt to find store locations, product information, and customer reviews. Next, install one of the popular shopping and price comparison apps listed below on your phone:

   • Red Laser

   • Amazon Price Check, or Flow (also by Amazon)

   • Barcode Scanner

   • Or, find a similar price-checking app at your mobile app store

   Now, go shopping (visit the store). While shopping, use your mobile app to find product reviews and make price comparisons of the products you find. Briefly describe your mobile shopping experience. How did the mobile technology help or hinder your shopping experience? What challenges does mobile technology pose for traditional retailers?

5. Pretend you are an SEO consultant for a local business or not-for-profit organization. Visit the organization's website to familiarize yourself with the brand, mission, products, services, and so on. Next, make a list of keywords or phrases that you think should be used to optimize the site for search engines. Rank-order the list based on how frequently you think the words are used in searches. Finally, go to **google.com/trends/explore** and enter your keywords or phrases, creating a graph that illustrates how often they have been used in search queries. Based on what you learn, what keywords or phrases would you recommend the organization use to optimize its site?

Analyze & Decide: Apply IT Concepts to Business Decisions

1. Perform a search engine query using the terms "data center" + "environmental impact." Describe the environmental concerns that large-scale data centers are creating around the globe and steps that companies are taking to address these concerns. Read about Google's efforts at **environment.google**. In your opinion, is Google making a satisfactory effort to minimize the negative impact of its business on the environment? Explain your answer.

2. Review the information in Section 6.1 about the three types of searches (informational, navigational, and transactional) that people conduct on search engines. Put yourself in the role of an SEO consultant for your college or university. Create a set of content and/or keyword strategies that you would recommend to your institution's leaders to increase the chances of appearing on SERPs resulting from prospective students conducting each kind of search.

3. Review the information about website relevance and credibility in Section 6.3. Next, generate a list of strategies or ways that a website owner might use to improve its ranking on search results pages by optimizing the site for relevance and credibility. For instance, if one of your factors is "site traffic," you might recommend that the website owner post links to the website on the company Facebook page to increase traffic. Or, you might recommend the website run a contest that requires people to visit the site to enter. This would increase traffic during the contest.

4. Traditional brick-and-mortar stores are increasingly frustrated by competition with online retailers. Online websites often have a cost advantage because they do not have to maintain physical storefronts or pay salespeople, and can use more efficient logistical and operational strategies. This sometimes allows them to offer better prices to consumers. With the emergence of recommendation engines, they appear to be gaining another advantage—the ability to suggest products to customers based on their past shopping history and personal characteristics. Pretend you are a senior manager for a national retail chain. How could your company make use of recommendation systems to suggest products to customers shopping in your store? Outline a creative approach to this problem that identifies the information you would need to collect, the in-store technology required, and the manner in which you would inform customers about the personalized recommendations generated by your system.

5. Select a consumer product or service for which there are at least three popular brand names. For example, you might choose the category "cell phone carriers," which includes Verizon, AT&T, Sprint, and T-Mobile. On the **Google.com/trends** page, type the brand names, separated by commas, into the search field at the top of the screen (e.g., Verizon, AT&T, Sprint, T-Mobile). The resulting chart will display the search query volume by brand, an indicator of how much interest each brand has received over time. Using the Google Trends data, answer the following questions.

Tip: Before answering the questions below, use Google's search engine to find articles on "how to interpret Google trends." This will help you better understand the Google trends report and make it easier to answer the following questions.

a. Using the date setting at the top of the *Google Trends* page, explore different periods of time. Briefly summarize how interest in each brand has changed over the last four years.

b. In the *Regional Interest* section, you can see how interest in each brand varies by country or city. In which countries and cities is each brand most popular?

c. In the *Related Searches* section, you will see a list of topics and query terms of interest to people who used one of the brand names in a search. How does the list of related topics change from one brand name to another? Do the topic and query term lists give you any insight into what kind of information people may be interested in relative to each brand?

d. Using a search engine, see if you can find market share data for the product or industry you researched on Google Trends. If you find this information, does there seem to be any relationship between search volume and market share for the brand names you explored?

Case 6.2

Business Case: Deciding What to Watch—Video Recommendations at Netflix

Netflix is the undisputed leader of video streaming services, accounting for more than half (53%) of U.S. video streaming subscriptions. Amazon Prime Video (25%) and Hulu (13%) are the company's largest competitors. Netflix is also the oldest company in this group, having originally started as a DVD by mail rental service. Unlike other companies that dominated the DVD rental business, Netflix successfully made the transition to on-demand video streaming by investing in new technology and redefining its business model. The service is now available in 190 countries and claims over 90 million subscribers globally.

Netflix executives credit the company's recommendation system for driving the "Netflix experience" and boosting profitability (Gomez-Uribe & Hunt, 2015; Raimond & Basilico, 2016). Surprisingly, the origin of the recommendation system dates back to 2000, when Netflix was still a DVD rental service. Recommendations during these early days were based largely on members' movie ratings. Ratings often reflect how people want to be perceived as opposed to how they act. For instance, rating data will tend to overemphasize how much people like documentaries and foreign language films, whereas behavioral metrics provide more accurate measures of how subscribers use the service. Today, when Netflix subscribers use the online service, they see recommendations generated by multiple algorithms that use descriptive information about the subscriber and their past viewing behavior (Gomez-Uribe & Hunt, 2015). Netflix claims that 75% of the activity on the service is a result of the recommendations it offers subscribers.

Netflix Analytics

Netflix enjoys a significant advantage over traditional television channels because the company collects information about how subscribers use the service. Netflix can make marketing and product decisions based on several behavioral metrics. You might be surprised at the details Netflix collects:

- The device you use (tablet, Roku, smart TV, etc.)
- Where (zip code) you watch from
- The days and times you watch
- When you pause, rewind, or fast-forward during viewing
- How you search—the words and phrases used, how long you search, etc.
- Whether or not you watch the credits following a show
- How many episodes of a series you watched
- Whether or not you watch all episodes in a series
- How long it takes you to watch all episodes in a series

- How many hours you spend using the service
- What movies and television shows you watch
- How often you use the service

In addition to making recommendations, Netflix uses the information to do the following:

- Identify subscribers who are likely to cancel the service
- Select new movies to add to their catalog
- Decide if a television show should be renewed for another season
- Identify movies and television shows to drop from the catalog
- Determine the days and times to recommend certain movies or shows
- Determine what to recommend immediately following the viewing of another movie or show
- Determine how to describe movies and shows (i.e., long vs. short descriptions)

Recommendation Algorithms at Netflix

The Netflix home screen can offer up to 40 rows of recommendations to a subscriber. Each row is generated by a different algorithm designed to personalize recommendations as well as determine the order in which movies and shows are listed. Each row is based on a different theme or rationale for the titles appearing in the row. Netflix even uses a Page Generation Algorithm to personalize the type of row-level recommendations and their order when creating the page. Some examples of the different recommendation rows include the following:

Genre Rows   Several of the rows appearing on the home page are based on movie or television show genres that Netflix believes the subscriber will be interested in based on past viewing behavior. Genre rows are generated by what Netflix calls its Personalized Video Ranker (PVR). The rows reflect three levels of personalization: (1) the selection of the genre, (2) the selection of specific titles within the genre, and (3) the ordering of the titles.

Continue Watching   Titles appearing in the *Continue Watching* row highlight episodic content that Netflix thinks a subscriber might want to return to. The *Continue Watching* ranker evaluates recently viewed videos for signals that a subscriber intends to resume watching or is no longer interested in the title. These signals include things like time since last viewing, point of abandonment (mid-program, end

of program), if other titles have been viewed since, and type of device used.

Because You Watched   The *Because you watched* (BYW) row is based on the similarity of recommended videos to past videos watched by the subscriber. The BYW row is determined by the Sims Ranker, which generates an ordered list of videos, based on similarity, for every title in the catalog. Various personalization cues are then used to further refine the subset of videos that actually appear in the row on the home page.

Top Picks   The goal of the *Top Picks* row is to feature Netflix's best guess as to the videos in its catalog that are most likely to be of interest to the subscriber. The *Top Picks* algorithm uses cues from the individual subscriber along with viewing trend information to recommend titles from among the most popular or top-ranked videos in the catalog.

Netflix believes that its recommendation system plays a significant role in user satisfaction and customer retention. A team of workers regularly updates the system with new algorithms and modifications to existing ones. Their ultimate goal is to generate such high-quality recommendations that subscribers will rarely have to search for videos to watch.

Questions

1. You read about four different types of recommendations that Netflix features on their home page. Think of a new type of recommendation row that Netflix could use and the kind of information or behavioral metrics that would be needed to generate your recommendations.

2. Based on the information in this case, would you say that Netflix primarily uses content-based filtering, collaborative filtering, or both? Explain your answer.

3. Netflix is expanding globally. When Netflix first enters a market, the recommendation system can face "cold start" or "sparsity" problems. Explain why this happens and suggests ways that Netflix might deal with these challenges.

4. What metrics do you think Netflix could use to identify subscribers who are likely to cancel the service?

5. Visit Netflix's Technology Blog **http://techblog.netflix.com**. Identify three challenges that the company faces in generating recommendations for its subscribers.

Sources: Compiled from Bulygo (2013b), Alvino and Basilico (2015), Gomez-Uribe and Hunt (2015), Arora (2016), Cheng (2016), Lubin (2016), Nicklesburg (2016), Raimond and Basilico (2016).

Case 6.3

Video Case: Power Searching with Google

This video case is a bit different from what you have seen in other chapters. Google has created two easy-to-follow video courses designed to teach you how to use search engines more effectively: Power Searching and Advanced Power Searching. Each course contains a series of videos that you can view at your own pace. Following each video, you

are shown a set of activities and small quizzes that you can use to test your knowledge. Start with the Power Searching course. Once you have mastered the basic skills discussed in that course, move on to the Advanced Power Searching course.

Visit Google's Search Education Online page powersearchingwithgoogle.com. On this page, you will see links for the two self-guided courses: Power Searching and Advanced Power Searching. Select the Power Searching link and begin viewing the course videos. After each video, do the related activities and test your knowledge with any online quizzes or tests that are provided. After you have completed the Power Searching course, go back and take the Advanced Power Searching course.

While it may take several days to complete both courses, we encourage you to do so. The time you invest in learning these power search techniques will pay off next time you need to use a search engine for a class- or work-related research project.

Question

1. Describe two or three search techniques you learned from these tutorial videos that you think will be particularly helpful.

References

Adomavicius, G. and T. Alexander. "Toward the Next Generation of Recommender Systems: A Survey of the State-of-the-Art and Possible Extensions." *IEEE Transactions on Knowledge and Data Engineering* 17, no. 6, 2005, 734–749.

Alvino, C. and J. Basilico. "Learning a Personalized Homepage." *techblog.netflix.com*, April 9, 2015.

Andrews, W. and H. Koehler-Kruener. "Magic Quadrant for Enterprise Search." *gartner.com,* July 16, 2014.

Anthony, S. "Microsoft Now Has One Million Servers–Less Than Google, But More Than Amazon, Says Ballmer." *extremetech.com*, July 19, 2013.

Arora, S. "Recommendation Engines: How Amazon and Netflix Are Winning the Personalization Battle." *martechadvisor.com*, June 28, 2016.

Asrar, S. "A Quick Look at Recommendation Engines and How the New York Times Makes Recommendations." *knightlab.northwestern.edu,* March 28, 2016.

Brown, C. "43 Increasingly Precise Netflix Custom Genre Recommendations." *TheAwl.com,* March 16, 2012.

Bulygo, Z. "How Mint Grew to 1.5 Million Users and Sold for $170 Million in Just 2 Years." *blog.kissmetrics.com,* November, 2013a.

Bulygo, Z. "How Netflix Uses Analytics to Select Movies, Create Content, and Make Multimillion Dollar Decisions." *blog.kissmetrics. com*, 2013b.

Burke, R. "Hybrid Recommender Systems." In Brusilovsky, P., A. Kobsa, and W. Nejdl (eds.), *The Adaptive Web*, pp. 377–408. Heidelberg: Springer-Verlag Berlin, 2007.

Candela, J. "Building Scalable Systems to Understand Content." *code. facebook.com*, February 2, 2017.

Cheng, R. "Netflix Leads a Streaming Video Market That's Close to Peaking." *cnet.com*, May 25, 2016.

Constine, J. "Facebook Sees 2 Billion Searches per Day, but It's Attacking Twitter not Google." *techcrunch.com,* July 27, 2016.

Delgado, J., L. Renaud, and V. Krishnamurthy. "The New Face of Enterprise Search: Bridging Structured and Unstructured Information." *Information Management Journal* 39, no. 6, 2005, 40–46. Business Source Premier. Online. February 28, 2014.

DiSilvestro, A. "The Difference Between Semantic Search and Semantic Web." *Search Engine Journal, July* 10, 2013.

eMarketer. "Yahoo Ad Revenue to Drop Nearly 14% This Year." *eMarketer.com*, March 23, 2016.

Gallagher, S. "The Great Disk Drive in the Sky: How Web Giants Store Big—and We Mean Big—Data." *Arstechnica.com,* January 26, 2012.

Glanz, J. "Google Details, and Defends, Its Use of Electricity." *The New York Times,* September 8, 2011.

Glanz, J. "The Cloud Factories: Power, Pollution and the Internet." *The New York Times,* September 22, 2012.

Gomez-Uribe, C. and N. Hunt. "The Netflix Recommender System: Algorithms, Business Value, and Innovation." *ACM Transactions Management Information Systems* 6, 4, Article 13, December 2015.

Google.com. "Algorithms." Accessed March 24, 2014.

Greene, K. "Mint Introduces Bill Pay, Helping Millions to Never Miss a Bill." blog.mint.com, December 13, 2016.

Grehan, M. "How Search Engines Work." Excerpted from *Search Engine Marketing: The Essential Best Practice Guide*. New York: Incisive Media, 2002.

Grifantini, K. "What It Takes to Power Google." *MIT Technology Review, September* 9, 2011.

Grimes, S. "Breakthrough Analysis: Two + Nine Types of Semantic Search." *InformationWeek.com,* January 1, 2010.

Hendler, J. and T. Berners-Lee. "From the Semantic Web to Social Machines: A Research Challenge for AI on the World Wide Web." *Artificial Intelligence* 174, 2010.

Jacobson, J. "Google: 129 Million Different Books Have Been Published." *PCWorld.com,* August 6, 2010.

Kraus, J. "The Advanced Guide to Facebook Graph Search." *sitepoint. com*, August 18, 2015.

Lubin, G. "How Netflix Will Someday Know Exactly What You Want to Watch as Soon as You Turn Your TV On." *Businessinsider.com*, September 21, 2016.

Madrigal, A. "How Netflix Reverse Engineered Hollywood." *The Atlantic, January* 2, 2014.

Miller, R. "Google Has Spent $21 Billion on Data Centers." *Datacenterknowledge.com,* September 17, 2013.

Newman, J. "6 Things You'd Never Guess About Google's Energy Use." *Techland.time.com,* September 9, 2011.

Nicklesburg, M. "Study: Amazon Video Is Now the Third-largest Streaming Service, Behind Netflix and YouTube." *geekwire.com*, June 22, 2016.

Oak, M. "How Does a Search Engine Work?" *buzzle.com,* June 5, 2008.

Obi-Azubuike, G. "Five SEO Strategies That Will Grow Your Business." *Linked.com/pulse*, February 4, 2016

Osher, M. "Finding Copyright Infringements of Your Artwork on the Internet." *MarianOsher.com,* February 9, 2014.

Prince, K.T. "Mint by the Numbers: Which User Are You?" *blog.mint. com*, April 6, 2016.

Prnewswire.com. "Growth of Big Data in Businesses Intensifies Global Demand for Enterprise Search Solutions, Finds Frost & Sullivan." January 24, 2013.

Raimond, Y. and J. Basilico. "Recommending for the World." *techblog. netflix.com*, February 17, 2016.

Schneider, D. "Under the Hood at Google and Facebook." *spectrum. ieee.org,* May 31, 2011.

Sullivan, D. "The Periodic Table of SEO Success Factors: 2015 Edition Now Released." *SearchEngineLand.com*, June 1, 2015.

Sullivan, L. "Report: Companies Will Spend $65 Billion on SEO In 2016." *MediaPost.com*, April 21, 2016.

Sukhraj, R. "How Mint Acquired Over 1.5 Million Users Without a Single Growth Hack." *Impactbnd.com,* June 17, 2015.

Sverdlik, Y. "Here's How Much Energy All US Data Centers Consume." *datacenterknowledge.com,* June 27, 2016.

Thomas, V. "Six Reasons to Break Out of Your Organization's Silos." *mangoapps.com,* September 24, 2013.

Tiroshi, A., T. Kuflik, J. Kay, and B. Kummerfeld. "Recommender Systems and the Social Web." In *Proceedings of the International Workshop on Augmenting User Models with Real World Experiences to Enhance Personalization and Adaptation (AUM)*, Girona, Spain, July 15, 2011. Ardissono, L. and T. Kuflik (eds.), Springer-Verlag Berlin, Heidelberg, 2012.

Venkatraman, A. "Global Census Shows Data Centre Power Demand Grew 63% in 2012." *Computerweekly.com,* October 8, 2012.

Walker, M. "Data Silos Obstruct Quest for Competitive Advantage." *datasciencecentral.com,* February 11, 2014.

Web 2.0 and Social Technology

CHAPTER OUTLINE

Case 7.1 Opening Case: Social Customer Service
Takes Off at KLM

7.1 Web 2.0—The Social Web

7.2 Social Networking Services and Communities

7.3 Engaging Consumers with Blogs and Microblogs

7.4 Mashups, Social Metrics, and Monitoring Tools

7.5 Enterprise 2.0: Workplace Collaboration and Knowledge Sharing

Case 7.2 Business Case: Facebook Helps Songkick
Rock the Ticket Sales Industry

Case 7.3 Business Case: AT&T's "It Can Wait"
Campaign against Distracted Driving

LEARNING OUTCOMES

7.1 Understand the key technologies that made Web 2.0 possible, and appreciate the opportunities and challenges that social media represents for business organizations.

7.2 Describe the features and capabilities of large social networking services.

7.3 Explain how blogs and microblogs facilitate communication on a global scale.

7.4 Describe how mashups, RSS technology, and monitoring tools are valuable to business organizations and individual users.

7.5 Describe how organizations and groups make use of new Web 2.0 collaboration tools and services.

Introduction

Everyone is talking about social media. Chances are you and your friends connect on social networking services or other forms of social media frequently. Every day, people discover new ways to share things with their network of friends through messaging, photographs, videos, and blogs. The digital-savvy, connected generation or millennials—teens and those in their early twenties—"get" social media, but might not be able to accurately define it or explain how companies use social technology to influence brand attitudes and consumer behavior. After you venture past the big brand names—Facebook, Twitter, YouTube, and LinkedIn—awareness of social media tools drops off quickly. Most social media use among Millennials is for recreational or entertainment purposes. There is little understanding of how social media can be used for marketing, recruiting, research, collaboration on projects, or personal branding.

Facebook has caught the attention of business organizations because the number of people who use the site is huge (and continues to grow!). Businesses are also exploring promotional opportunities on sites like Twitter, Pinterest, LinkedIn, and YouTube. Companies get 24/7 advertising, live interaction with customers and prospects, and targeted ads. Organizations are working feverishly to prompt consumers to engage—to like, tweet, comment, and share their brand experiences with others. And they are spending a lot of time doing just that. According to eMarketer (2016), U.S. companies will spend over $72 billion advertising on social networks, more than they spend on television ($71.29 billion).

In this chapter, you will learn what makes social media *social*. You will also learn about social media applications that have both personal and professional uses, and you will learn how business organizations make use of social media to gain competitive advantages in the marketplace.

Case 7.1 Opening Case

Lilja Kristjansdo/NordicPhotos/ Getty Images

Findlay/Alamy Stock Photo

Estelle Johnson/EyeEm/ Getty Images

Social Customer Service Takes Off at KLM

On April 14, 2010, an Icelandic volcano with a difficult name (Eyjafjallajökull) erupted, spewing volcanic ash several kilometers into the atmosphere and disrupting air travel for 10 million people across northwestern Europe for days. Like many other airlines in the area, KLM Royal Dutch Airlines was overwhelmed by stranded passengers seeking information by phone and e-mail. While some people waited on hold for hours trying to reach a call center, other passengers turned to social media to find answers.

Just a year before, KLM had launched an exploratory effort to figure out how the company could use social media. With a relatively new Twitter account and Facebook page, the company's social media team suddenly found themselves fielding questions from countless frustrated travelers. The team quickly set up a special social media

room, called in 100 reinforcements from other units in the company, and began responding around the clock to inquiries coming in on Facebook and Twitter. This marked the beginning of social customer service at KLM. Today, KLM employs over 235 social media service agents who respond each week to 15,000 questions or comments from customers in 13 different languages (Table 7.1).

Customer Service Is Not an Option

While KLM uses social media to run contests, entertain passengers, and promote the airline, customer service remains the clear priority for the social unit. The company believes that in today's fast paced, competitive environment, customers expect businesses to provide support services via social media. Companies that fail this test will suffer consequences.

TABLE 7.1	Opening Case Overview
Company	KLM Royal Dutch Airlines
Location	Headquartered in Amstelveen, KLM is the national airline of the Netherlands. KLM currently operates passenger and cargo service to 133 destinations in 70 countries around the world.
History	Founded in 1919, KLM is the oldest airline in the world still operating under its original name.
Social media	Customers can contact KLM on Twitter, Facebook, Facebook Messenger, and LinkedIn. The company publishes a blog and also maintains a presence on Pinterest, Google+, YouTube, and Instagram.
Customer service	KLM is credited with pioneering the use of social media for customer service. The company is widely recognized within the airline industry for providing excellent customer support.

Be Where Your Customers Are

A company's social media strategy can't be effective if they aren't using the same social channels as their customers. Over the years, KLM has expanded their social media coverage based on the platforms their customers use. In addition to Facebook and Twitter, customers can now contact KLM social agents from LinkedIn and Facebook Messenger. Agents can help customers book or change a flight, check-in, pick a seat, or assist with any problems that might occur. In addition, KLM **publishes a blog** and maintains a presence on Pinterest, Google+, YouTube, and Instagram.

One-Stop Shopping Means Social Revenue

The KLM model of customer service adheres to a one-stop shop principle. That means if a customer asks about changing their ticket, the social agent will look up the information and respond with a customized answer instead of just sending a link to the company's general terms and conditions Web page. The goal is to resolve the customer's issue through the social channel used to contact the company. After answering questions about flight times, pricing, and other details, KLM social agents provide a direct link to a payment page where customers complete their purchase. For many customers, the process is simply more convenient than purchasing through another channel.

"Move fast, break things, and don't be afraid to fail."

Karlijn Vogel-Meijer, Manager Social Media at KLM, explains that the company understands mistakes are bound to happen from time to time, especially if you're moving fast. The social unit has support from the top of the organization, giving it the freedom to try new things and innovate. As a result, KLM is considered a leader for the way its social customer service unit has pioneered the use of social media to support customers and maintain high levels of positive sentiment. It's hard to be innovative if you're always worried about making mistakes. As Vogel-Meijer says, "If you're afraid, you will stall." One of KLM's latest innovations is the use of artificial intelligence, a new technology that helps agents answer many routine questions they receive from customers.

Faster Response Times

As more companies gear up to engage customers through social media, customer expectations also increase. When customers contact a company about a problem, they not only expect an answer, they also want a response quickly. KLM strives to answer each customer within 30 minutes. At the top of KLM's Twitter page, the company posts the average response time and updates it every 5 minutes so even if things are taking a little longer, customers know when to expect a reply. By managing expectations, KLM minimizes customer frustrations.

Conclusion

KLM Royal Airlines is recognized around the world as the leader in social media customer service. Some airlines aren't prepared for the challenges associated with social media. For instance, when a disgruntled customer contacts a call center to make a complaint, only the customer and company know about the call. When a customer complains on social media, the world can see the complaint and how well the company works to resolve the problem. The social media customer service unit at KLM not only contributes to the company's high customer satisfaction and positive sentiment, but also to the bottom line. In 2015, KLM estimated that each social agent was responsible for approximately $170,000 in revenue. With 235 social agents, that translates into over $39 million.

Questions

1. Why does KLM think that Customer Service is the most important application of social media?
2. How does KLM determine which social media platforms to use?
3. Explain the reasoning behind KLM's ". . . don't be afraid to fail" philosophy.
4. KLM's "one-stop shop" model probably increases the time a social agent spends responding to a customer's inquiry. Why does the company use this approach?
5. Many airlines have yet to embrace the use of social media like KLM. What challenges do you think other airlines face when making the transition to using social media?

Source: Compiled from Baer and Brown (n.d.), ter Haar (2015), Koetsier (2015), Simson (2015), Azfar (2016), Hutchinson (2016), KLM (2016), Talkwalker. com (2017).

7.1 | Web 2.0—The Social Web

In your lifetime, there have been dramatic changes in the way people use the Internet. In the early 1990s, many people did not have regular access to the Internet, and those who did typically "dialed up" their network from a home or office telephone. Dial-up access meant long waits as content from Web pages "downloaded" onto the screen. Some users joked that the letters "www" in a Web address stood for "world wide wait." E-mail was the primary mechanism for communicating on the Internet. Online communities were often like public bulletin boards where all members of the community could read the messages that others posted. Websites were static, essentially online billboards for the businesses that created them. Online purchasing (e-commerce) was rare and risky because there were few safeguards in place to protect your credit card information. But all that has changed.

The Constantly Changing Web

Today, most of us access the Internet using wired or wireless broadband technology, consuming bandwidth that was unheard of a few years ago. We expect to be able to stream audio and video files, and watch feature-length films over wireless connections and mobile devices. We surf Web pages that constantly change their appearance in response to how we interact with them. While e-mail is still a common form of communication in business, young people tend to view it with disdain in favor of tweets, texts, or social networking sites like Twitter and Facebook. We keep track of our world, interests, and hobbies by reading blogs and online newspapers, and use a variety of tools and services for sharing them with others. In addition to consuming content, we add comments or reviews and signal our appreciation for the content by retweeting or clicking a "Like" button.

Increasingly, Internet users are becoming content creators—they write their own blogs, post videos on YouTube, share personal experiences on Facebook, and share pictures using sites like Flickr or Photobucket. E-commerce continues to grow and evolve, in some cases changing entire industries. E-books are now more popular than print books on sites like Amazon. More people purchase music from sites like iTunes or use streaming-music sites like Pandora or Spotify than purchase music on CDs. Sites like Travelocity and Orbitz have almost completely replaced traditional travel agencies and agents. Many people are more likely to use sites like eBay and Craigslist to get rid of unwanted household items instead of holding garage sales or placing classified ads in a local paper. One of the biggest changes in online retail is the use of social features by e-commerce sites. Most online retailers make use of customer reviews, customer ratings, and information sharing on social networks.

While there are many exciting examples of companies that have embraced the potential of **Web 2.0** technologies and the emerging social culture that characterizes our modern online experience, many businesses, agencies, and individuals have been slow to understand the challenges and opportunities created by the social Web. Smart managers are constantly evaluating how changes in social media and related technologies affect their business and industry. Businesses and business professionals must devote time and resources to consistently monitoring technological innovation and related changes in consumer behavior in order to remain relevant, taking advantage of potential opportunities to create competitive advantages when they arise.

Invention of the World Wide Web

The **World Wide Web (WWW)** was invented by Tim Berners-Lee and launched in 1991. Its use outside of scientific and academic circles was uncommon until the mid-1990s. Web access from homes was mostly via telephone lines, slow 56-kbps (kilobits per second) dial-up modems, and paid subscription network services such as CompuServe and America Online (AOL). Websites were primitive static designs that served as online billboards or postcards. You can view archived websites using the *Wayback Machine*. During that time, e-mail was viewed as a sophisticated communications tool that most people accessed at work or on college campuses, but not from home.

As the above description suggests, communication was primarily unidirectional. There were no easy-to-use conduits for widespread social interaction. The average user was the target or recipient of communications, not a creator.

A Platform for Services and Social Interaction

Now the Web is a platform for all kinds of activity—shopping, entertainment, news, education, research, and business processes like logistics and electronic funds transfer (EFT). Homes maintain **broadband** wireless networks to connect multiple users simultaneously to the Internet from computers, tablets, video game systems, and video-streaming devices like the Roku box. In addition to the aforementioned activities, new technologies gave rise to websites with features and services that make it easy for people to interact with one another. As a result, these services collectively are referred to as **social media**. While the applications that are labeled as Web 2.0 may simply be an extension of earlier advances, it is the change in user behavior that matters most to business organizations around the world. The new technologies dramatically increase the ability of people to interact with businesses and each other, sharing and finding information, and forming relationships. This perspective explains why Web 2.0 is often called the **social Web** (Table 7.2).

Web 2.0 a term used to describe a phase of World Wide Web evolution characterized by dynamic Web pages, social media, mashup applications, broadband connectivity, and user-generated content.

World Wide Web (WWW) a network of documents on the Internet, called Web pages, constructed with HTML markup language that supports links to other documents and media (e.g., graphics, video, audio, etc.).

Broadband refers to wide bandwidth technologies that create fast, high-volume connections to the Internet and World Wide Web.

Social media a collection of Web applications based on Web 2.0 technology and culture that allows people to connect and collaborate with others by creating and sharing digital content.

TABLE 7.2   Web 1.0 versus Web 2.0

Web 1.0—The Early Web	Web 2.0—The Social Web
Static pages, HTML	Dynamic pages, XML, and Java
Author-controlled content	User-controlled content
Computers	Computers, cell phones, televisions, PDAs, game systems, car dashboards
Users view content	Users create content
Individual users	User communities
Marketing goal: *influence*	Marketing goal: *relationships*
Data: single source	Data: multiple sources, for example, mashups

Emergence of Social Applications, Networks, and Services

Starting in 2000, a series of developments in the technology and business environment occurred that set the stage (infrastructure) for Web 2.0.

1. **Broad bandwidth (broadband)**   Internet access became faster and more widely available due to large-scale adoption of broadband technology. Website load times shrank from a minute to instantaneous. Huge bandwidth is required to support byte-intensive music downloads and streaming video and movie services. As residential broadband connections became common place and public broadband connections increased in coffee shops, malls, college campuses, and other community centers, people began to rely on applications that required fast, high-volume data connections. These broadband connections increased the overall attractiveness and accessibility of the Internet—laying the foundation for interactivity and the social Web.

2. **Sustainable business models**   After the dot.com bust in the late 1990s when many badly conceived Internet businesses failed, a new breed of business emerged. These businesses had realistic revenue models. Companies like Amazon, Google, eBay, and others began to demonstrate that it was possible to create e-commerce and consumer service sites that could generate revenue and become not only self-sustaining, but also profitable.

3. **New Web programming technologies**   New Web programming languages and technologies were developed that made it possible for programmers to create dynamic and feature-rich websites. In some cases, these new features and website capabilities created new business opportunities, which in turn led to increased demand for Web access. Increased Web usage then led to larger potential markets for businesses with successful revenue models. The businesses frequently reinvested earnings into expanding their technological capabilities in an effort to attract even more customers. This cycle of enhanced technological features leading to greater value for the consumer/Web user and then to more people using the Web continues today. Some of these new Web technologies are described in more detail in **Tech Note 7.1**.

4. **Application programming interfaces (API) and software development kits (SDK)**   One of the big differences between Web 1.0 and Web 2.0 is the extent to which business organizations are willing to share information (data) with other organizations and developers who are creating new programs or services. For instance, Google Maps might allow a restaurant review website like Yelp.com to use its mapping application to create a feature on the Yelp site showing restaurant locations on a map. Historically, businesses have been highly protective of their intellectual property and were generally unwilling to share it with other companies. However, many companies that emerged during the Web 2.0 era have come to recognize the benefits of certain types of sharing or collaboration with others. For instance, when Google makes part of its mapping program available to others, it increases the number of people using the Google product and expands its share of the marketplace. In turn, Yelp frequently makes some of its data available to companies developing new applications. For instance, Trulia is a real estate company that helps people find new homes.

They use information from Yelp.com to help their customers learn about businesses, restaurants, grocery stores, and other amenities in the neighborhood they are considering, without having to leave the Trulia website. Businesses have learned that when done right, sharing information often creates synergies that benefit all involved. From a technology standpoint, two programming tools make this data sharing possible: APIs and SDKs.

An API is a set of commands and programming standards used by developers to write applications that can communicate with other applications. In other words, it aids developers in determining how their applications can pass data back and forth with some other application.

An SDK is a bit more complex than an API. SDKs are a collection of software tools used by developers for writing applications that run on a specific device or platform. For instance, a Facebook SDK helps third-party developers write programs that will run on Facebook.

Businesses that share data with other companies usually write the APIs and SDKs that define the rules and restrictions for information sharing. In that way, they retain control over who uses their data and how it is used. If a developer simply needs to share data with another website, they will likely use an API created by the other website. If they are creating an application that will actually run on the other website, they will most likely use an SDK developed by the other website. Together, APIs and SDKs have fundamentally changed the degree to which businesses share their information resulting in a vastly improved and more useful World Wide Web.

While APIs and SDKs can either be proprietary (user pays a fee) or open source, most popular APIs are **open source**, which means that anyone can use them for free, although other conditions may be placed on their use. Visit **programmable Web.com** for a listing of popular APIs.

Tech Note 7.1

AJAX Technologies and APIs

AJAX technologies, or **asynchronous JavaScript and XML (AJAX)**, is a term referring to a group of technologies and programming languages that make it possible for Web pages to respond to users' actions without requiring the entire page to reload. AJAX makes it possible for Web developers to create small apps that run on a page instead of a server. This capability makes programs run much faster, eliminating a key source of frustration with the early Web. Another important programming development is the API, which acts as a software gateway programmers can use to pass data back and forth between two or more applications, platforms, or websites (see **IT at Work 7.1**). With AJAX and APIs, website programmers can import data from other sources to create new functions and features that we have come to associate with social media applications (see the discussion of mashups later in this chapter).

AJAX technologies include **JavaScript**, **extendable markup language (XML)**, **document object model (DOM)**, **hypertext markup language (HTML)**, **XMLHttpRequest**, and **cascading style sheets (CSS)**, all of which are defined in **Table 7.3**.

TABLE 7.3 AJAX Technologies for Web 2.0

Hypertext markup language (HTML): The predominant language for Web pages; it is used, along with CSS, to describe how things will appear on a Web page.

Cascading style sheets (CSS): A language used to enhance the appearance of Web pages written in a markup language.

Document object model (DOM): A programming API for documents. Programmers use it to manipulate (e.g., build, add, modify, delete, etc.) HTML documents.

Extensible markup language (XML): A set of rules and guidelines for describing data that can be used by other programming languages. It makes it possible for data to be shared across the Web.

JavaScript: An object-oriented language used to create apps and functionality on websites. Examples of JavaScript apps include pop-up windows, validation of Webform inputs, and images that change when a cursor passes over them.

XMLHttpRequest: A JavaScript object that serves as an API used by programs to retrieve data or resources from a URL without requiring a page load. It plays an important role in providing programmers with the ability to create dynamic and interactive Web pages and applications.

Sources: van Kesteren et al. (2014), techterms.com (2014), W3C (2015), Grigorik (2017) .

IT at Work 7.1

Myntra Leverages Facebook APIs and SDKs for Success in Mobile Fashion Sales

Myntra is India's largest fashion e-commerce company, serving millions of customers and featuring over 2,000 of the world's top fashion brands. The company generates sales of over 200,000 items from its mobile app on any given day. Myntra is recognized as being the world's first mobile-only e-commerce platform and reportedly sold $500 million in gross merchandise volume in FY2015–16. Using Facebook's Open Graph API and SDK, the company was able to install features that let customers easily post information to their Facebook pages without leaving the Myntra app. This makes it possible for the company to leverage the social network of each customer to increase brand awareness and interest in the marketplace.

Using Facebook's SDK, the company implemented Facebook Login for its app as well as developed programs to access customer insight data and a range of analytics about the performance of their Facebook ads, conversion channels, and the success of various customer retention strategies. As a result of these integrations with Facebook, Myntra experienced significant growth and credits Facebook for as much as 25% of its sales revenue. In addition, Myntra improved the effectiveness of ad targeting and reduced advertising costs after learning that customers who use Facebook Login to access the e-commerce app were 32% more likely to convert (make a purchase) than other customers.

Sources: "Myntra – Best of Fashion" at *developers.facebook.com.*

Why Managers Should Understand Web Technology

You might ask yourself why business managers who are not directly involved in managing an organization's website should be concerned about the underlying technology of Web 2.0 and social media. The answer is that these technologies determine website features and capabilities. In other words, they determine what is possible on the Web. Understanding how Web technology is evolving helps managers identify strategic opportunities and threats as well as the ways in which a company might develop sustainable competitive advantages in the marketplace. Therefore, it is important to monitor the ongoing development of APIs, Web development languages, and other technologies that affect the functioning of the Web.

APIs   For instance, APIs associated with Facebook determine the nature of apps that can be written to interact with core Facebook features. Major changes to the Facebook APIs are often rolled out to much fanfare because they define opportunities for developing new ways for users to create and share content on Facebook and across the Web, as described in IT at Work 7.1.

At Facebook's annual developer conferences in 2010 and 2011, founder Mark Zuckerberg made announcements about changes in Facebook APIs that would extend the social networking giant's presence across the Web through the use of social **plug-ins**, which are listed in **Table 7.4**. See the discussion of Open Graph in Section 7.2.

TABLE 7.4   Facebook Social Plug-Ins Used Across the Web

Plug-in	What It Does. . .
Like button	Shares pages from a website back to a user's Facebook profile with a single click.
Send button	Allows users to send content from a website to their Facebook friends.
Comments	This plug-in allows users to comment on a Web page's content using their Facebook profile and shows the activity to the user's friends in a newsfeed.
Embedded	Places content from any public Facebook post on to a website post or blog.
Facepile	This feature displays the profile photos of the people who have connected with a Facebook page or app.
Login button	Shows profile pictures of the user's friends who have already signed up for a Website in addition to a login button.

Source: Facebook (2014).

Plug-ins   Plug-ins are buttons or features on non-Facebook sites that interact with Facebook in some way. For instance, CNN.com might include a Recommend button on all its news articles. When a Facebook user presses the button, a link to the story is automatically created on the user's Facebook page. You don't have to be a Web programmer to follow and understand public announcements about API updates from Facebook, Google Maps, YouTube, Twitter, and other popular social media platforms. Using the monitoring tools discussed later in this chapter, you can stay informed about these changes and begin to assess how they will impact you as an individual, website developer, or business manager.

Communicating on the Web

Collectively, social media apps have shifted the locus of control for mass communications from large organizations to one shared with individual users. Now people as well as organizations control both the message and the medium. Instead of an organization broadcasting a single message to a mass audience, a massive number of conversations take place among any number of people and organizations.

No one has complete control over the message or the medium, yet everyone can play a part. The challenge for businesses today is to change mindsets and develop strategies that take advantage of social media. Instead of a focus on developing sophisticated ways of getting their message heard, companies must now develop sophisticated strategies for listening and responding to what their consumers are saying.

Because of the relatively low cost and ease of use, social media is a powerful force for democratization; the network structure enables communication and collaboration on a massive scale. **Figure 7.1** shows the emergence of mass social media. The figure compares traditional and social media and illustrates the new tools of social media, for example, blogs and **video blogs (vlogs)**, as being in the consumer's control. With traditional media, content is tightly controlled and brand messages are "pushed" out to users, often in the form of an ad interruption. With social media, users are frequently attracted or "pulled" to content that is interesting to them and they have greater freedom to decide if, when, and how they want to interact with such content.

Notice that traditional media content goes from the technology to the people, whereas in social media, people create and control the content.

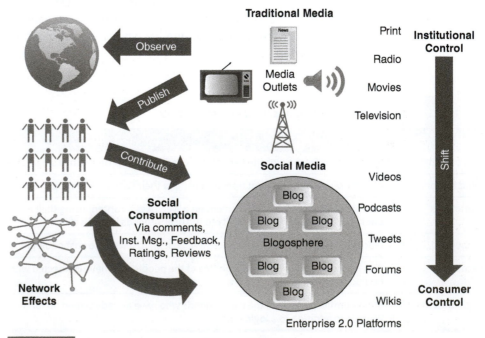

FIGURE 7.1   The emergence and rise of mass social media.

Social Media Applications and Services

Early descriptions of Web 2.0 would often identify the applications listed in **Table 7.5** as typical of social media. You will read more about each of these applications later in the chapter.

TABLE 7.5   Web 2.0 Applications

Application	Description
Social networking service	Online communities
Blogs	Online journals
Mashups/widgets/RSS	Web applications that pull data from various sources and display on another page to create new functionality
Social bookmarking/tags	An application for tagging or labeling online content for later retrieval
Wikis	A collaborative application that allows multiple people to create and edit online content
Sharing sites	Websites that make it easy for users to upload and share digital content like photos, videos, or music

Few applications fit neatly into these categories anymore because of **feature convergence**. For instance, Facebook started as a **social networking service (SNS)**, but now has features that span almost all of the categories in Table 7.5. It is a sharing site used by many to distribute photos. It is increasingly common for people to tag or label photos with the names of people in the picture, making it easy to find and display photos of individuals that have been saved in multiple locations on Facebook. Users can maintain blogs on their Facebook page and Facebook hosts thousands of apps that pull data from sources outside of the social network, making it a huge mashup app.

Likewise, YouTube started as a sharing site, making it easy for people to share video clips with others. However, YouTube now contains many features that make it difficult to distinguish from an SNS. The same is true of Flickr, a photo-sharing site that has really become a community platform for people interested in photography.

While some original social media applications are still present on the Web today, thousands of newer applications have sprung up and continue to blur the lines of the original social media application categories.

Social networking service (SNS) an online platform or website that allows subscribers to interact and form communities or networks based on real-life relationships, shared interests, activities and so on.

Social Media Is More than Facebook, YouTube, and Twitter

Many people think that social media is limited to a few iconic companies or brand names: Facebook, Twitter, YouTube, and LinkedIn. While those companies have certainly capitalized on the new technology and tend to dominate their respective market niches, social media is a term describing a range of technologies that are used across the Internet and are part of most websites you use today.

While you may be familiar with using social media for recreational purposes or communicating with friends and family, businesses use social technologies for a wide variety of other benefits:

- Collaboration
- Communication and engagement with customers (marketing)
- Image and reputation management (public relations)
- Communication and engagement with employees and partners (management)
- Talent acquisition and recruiting (human resources)
- Research and knowledge management
- Productivity and information utilities
- Fund raising

The following section lists some of the key elements of social media that distinguish it from other types of media.

Elements of Social Media: What Makes It Different?

In order to understand what makes the modern Web so different from its earlier incarnation, it is helpful to understand the differentiating features and benefits made possible by XML, Java Script, APIs, and related technologies.

User-generated content (UGC) In contrast to traditional media—TV, radio, and magazines—social media makes it possible for users to create and share their own content. Using social technologies, people share photographs, music, and video with the world. They express themselves using the written word in stories, articles, and opinion pieces that they publish on their own websites or other platforms. They rate products and write reviews. Many individuals and groups have become Internet celebrities as a result of the shows they created for YouTube. And because of YouTube's revenue-sharing policy, those that attract the largest audiences earn millions of dollars.

Content control Most content creation and sharing is done without editorial review. As a result, users decide for themselves what they want to create and share. Social technologies have shifted control of online content to a broad base of users. It is users who determine what content "goes viral" or becomes highly popular through sharing, not advertising agencies or companies with large advertising budgets.

Conversation With the advent of social media, a paradigm shift occurred in marketing communications from a broadcast (one-way) model to a conversation (two-way) model. Dialogue takes place in the form of one-to-one, one-to-many, and many-to-one formats. Social media websites contain features that allow people to talk back in a variety of ways.

Community (common values, culture) Many social media technologies ultimately result in the creation of communities. Like their offline counterparts, these online communities are made up of people who share a bond of common interests, values, norms, and even sanctions. Some communities are highly structured, whereas others may be more fluid and informal. As businesses learn to communicate on Web 2.0, some will attempt to create communities made up of consumers who have a strong interest in a particular brand. Social networking services lend themselves to this type of strategy, but brand communities can be developed around blogs, **wikis**, **sharing sites**, and many other types of social media applications.

Categorization by users (tagging) Newer Web technologies have begun to allow users to decide for themselves how to categorize and label information they find online. This has created the potential for powerful forms of collaboration and information sharing as well as alternative forms of information search (see the discussion of social bookmarking later in the chapter).

Real people (profiles, usernames, and the human voice vs. the corporate "we") Social media technologies allow people to express their individuality through the creation of online identities. In traditional media, communication and expression come from celebrities or corporate spokespersons. Web 2.0 provides people with the tools to create personal brands that characterize their personal, professional, or creative identity.

Connections (followers, friends, members, etc.) There are many ways to establish additional levels of connection and reflect some level of a relationship. You can become someone's friend on Facebook. Follow someone on Twitter. Subscribe to a person's blog. Perhaps just as important, these connections can be severed when one party wants to end the relationship.

Constant updating (real time, dynamic) Unlike the static Web of the 1990s, social technologies reflect our constantly evolving relationships, opinions, political views, religious beliefs, and values. The social Web is a constant stream of communications that never turns off and can sometimes be overwhelming. Popular examples of this characteristic include Twitter, Facebook Live, or Snapchat.

Content separated from form   Data from one source can be used or exported to other platforms. This allows users to organize and display content in ways they find most helpful. For instance, with a really simple syndication (RSS) aggregator, users pull content from a number of sources into a single location, making it easier to follow news stories and blog posts from multiple sites. Someone writing about local restaurants can pull content from food critics, customer comments, and map location information from a variety of sources and aggregate this information into a single site, making it easier for users to get a complete picture of a restaurant without having to surf around to different sites.

Equipment independence   Increasingly, people access the Web and social media from a variety of computers and mobile devices, including laptops, tablets, smartphones, video game systems, DVD players, and televisions. In the near future, you might access the Web from such home appliances as your refrigerator or even a kitchen countertop. (Check out the amazing new technology featured on videos by Corning Glass. Go to YouTube and search for "A Day Made of Glass" using the YouTube search engine.)

With Web 2.0, Markets are Conversations

As you have read, the availability of Web 2.0 applications is changing not only how people behave but also the way they think about things. This new way of thinking is captured in a provocative list of 95 statements called the **Cluetrain Manifesto** (Levine et al., 2000). Perhaps the fundamental principle of the Manifesto is described by its first thesis: *Markets are conversations*. Other excerpts from the Manifesto are listed in **Table 7.6**. Over time, successful companies will learn to engage customers in conversations as an alternative to the unidirectional or broadcast method of communication. While the Cluetrain Manifesto seemed idealistic, impractical, and revolutionary when it was first written in 2000, we are starting to see increasing examples of individuals and companies turning those principles into action.

TABLE 7.6   **Excerpts from the Cluetrain Manifesto**

Select Cluetrain Theses

- "Markets are conversations."
- These conversations enable powerful forms of social organization and knowledge exchange.
- People have figured out they obtain better information and support from one another than from vendors. So much for corporate rhetoric about adding value to commoditized products.
- Companies should realize their markets are often laughing. At them.

Source: Levine et al. (2000).

While many companies still struggle with the concept of *conversation,* Forrester researchers Charlene Li and Josh Bernoff (2008) describe a number of companies that recognize the power of what they call the **groundswell**, "a spontaneous movement of people using online tools to connect, take charge of their own experience and get what they need—information, support, ideas, products, and bargaining power—from each other". Li and Bernoff identify five key strategic priorities that companies should focus on to leverage the groundswell:

1. **Listening**   Monitoring what your customers say on social media. By listening to what customers say to your company and what they say to each other, organizations can gain valuable insights.

2. **Talking**   While listening is perhaps the most important priority, businesses still need to develop their message and communicate to their target audience(s).

3. **Energizing**   Using a variety of tactics, companies can create and maintain relationships with brand advocates who will support and promote the brand to their friends and followers on the Web. Energizing brand advocates is analogous to generating word-of-mouth communications in traditional marketing.

4. **Supporting** Using social media to deliver effective and convenient customer service is one way to support your customers. Some businesses create communities where customers can help each other with product-related issues and questions.

5. **Embracing** Many companies are utilizing social media to solicit new product ideas and suggestions for improving customer satisfaction from current customers. Managers are often surprised to learn that customers have great ideas for how the company can do better.

These groundswell strategies identify the most significant activities that companies should focus on with regard to using social media.

In the rest of this chapter, we describe a variety of social media applications that are growing in popularity. We highlight some of the most attractive features, and encourage you to explore them firsthand. Most are free, so they are easy to try. You are also encouraged to stay on top of new trends and applications by following online sources like Mashable, Social Media Today, and Social Media Examiner. The only way to truly understand the social media environment is to immerse yourself in it, experiencing it directly. We think it is both fascinating and fun, and hope you will too.

Questions

1. How has Web 2.0 changed the behavior of Internet users?
2. What are the basic tools or applications that characterize Web 2.0?
3. Why is Web 2.0 referred to as the social Web?
4. What are some of the benefits or advantages that Web developers gain from using AJAX technologies?
5. What are some of the most important messages for business organizations in the Cluetrain Manifesto?
6. What is feature convergence? Give some examples of this trend with regard to social media apps.

7.2 Social Networking Services and Communities

Online or **virtual communities** parallel physical communities, such as neighborhoods, clubs, and associations, except they are not bound by political or geographic boundaries. These communities offer several ways for members to interact, collaborate, and trade. Virtual or online communities have been around for a long time and predate the World Wide Web. The **Usenet** provided the initial platform for online communities by making it possible for users to exchange messages on various topics in public **newsgroups**, which are similar in many ways to online bulletin board systems. While the Usenet is technically not part of the Internet, much of its content can be accessed from Internet sites like Google Groups or subscription-based news services like **Giganews** and **Astraweb**.

Online communities can take many forms. For instance, some people view the blogosphere (all the blogs on the Web) as a community. **YouTube** is a community of people who post, view, and comment on videos. **Epinions** is a community of people who share their experiences and opinions about products and companies. **Flickr**, **Photobucket**, and similar sites are photo-sharing communities. **Wikipedia** is a community of people who create, edit, and maintain an online knowledge base. **Twitter** is a community, or perhaps several communities, of people who frequently exchange short, 140-character messages with one another about a variety of topics. Obviously, social networking sites like **Facebook** and **LinkedIn** are communities and have seen tremendous growth in recent years. People today spend a significant portion of their time on social networks (see **Figure 7.2**). For better or worse, social media has

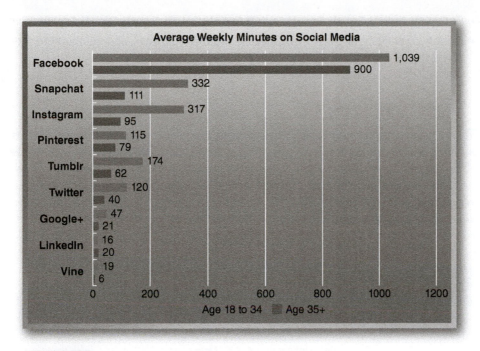

FIGURE 7.2   Data collected in 2016 illustrate that people spend more time on Facebook than any other social networking site. One of the newest social platforms, Snapchat, is already in second place across age groups, although younger people spend almost three times longer on the service than older people. (Adapted from comScore, 2016.)

changed the way we interact with others, how we communicate with companies and brands, how we learn about local and international events, and how we define relationships, reputation, privacy, group affiliations and status.

Social network analysis (SNA) is the mapping and measuring of relationships and flows between people, groups, organizations, computers, or other information- or knowledge-processing entities. The nodes in the network are the people and the groups, whereas the links show relationships or flows between the nodes. SNA provides a visual and a mathematical analysis of relationships. In its corporate communications, Facebook has begun using the term **social graph** to refer to the global social network reflecting how we are all connected to one another through relationships. Berners-Lee (2007) extended this concept even further when he coined the term **giant global graph**. This concept is intended to illustrate the connections between people and/or documents and pages online. Connecting all points on the giant global graph is the ultimate goal for creators of the **semantic Web**, which you read about in Chapter 6.

Online communities have received increasing attention from the business community. Online communities can be used as a platform for the following:

- Selling goods and services
- Promoting products to prospective customers; for example, advertising
- Prospecting for customers
- Building relationships with customers and prospective customers
- Identifying customer perceptions by "listening" to conversations
- Soliciting ideas for new products and services from customers
- Providing support services to customers by answering questions, providing information, and so on
- Encouraging customers to share their positive perceptions with others; for example, via word of mouth

Semantic Web   an extension of the World Wide Web that utilizes a variety of conventions and technologies that allow machines to understand the meaning of Web content.

- Gathering information about competitors and marketplace perceptions of competitors
- Identifying and interacting with prospective suppliers, partners, and collaborators (See the discussion of Enterprise 2.0 in the next section.)

The Power of the Crowd

In recent years, several companies have created online communities for the purpose of identifying market opportunities through crowdsourcing. **Crowdsourcing** is a model of problem solving, production and idea generation that marshals the collective talents of a large group of people. Using Web 2.0 tools, companies solicit, refine, and evaluate ideas for new products and services based on input from their customers. Business organizations that have implemented this approach include Fiat, Sara Lee, BMW, Kraft, Procter & Gamble, and Starbucks. See **Table 7.7** for a list of other examples.

TABLE 7.7	Examples of Crowdsourcing Websites
Category	**Crowdsource Websites**
R&D crowdsourcing	**InnoCentive**—Challenge Driven Innovation **Yet2**—Innovation and IP Marketplace **NineSigma**—Technology Problem Solving **Hypios**—Problem Solving for Advanced Technology
Crowdsourcing for marketing, design, and ideas	**Brand Tags**—Brand Identification from the Crowd **Guerra Creativa**—Logos and Designs **LeadVine**—Leads and Referrals **Challenge.gov**—Solutions to Government Problems
Crowdsourced product ideas	**Procter & Gamble**—Crowdsource Product Ideas for P&G **Quirky**—Community Sourced Product Ideas **CafePress**—Buy, Sell, Create Your Product
Crowdsourcing HR & freelance work	**Amazon Mechanical Turk**—"A Marketplace for Work" **Clickworker**—Cloud-based global workforce **Topcoder**—Crowd Coding
Crowdfunding websites	**ArtistShare**—New Artist Projects **Kickstarter**—Large, general crowdfunding site **GoFundMe**—For personal fundraisers **Crowdrise**—Funding for Inspiring Social Causes
Peer-2-peer websites	**Wikipedia**—Online Encyclopedia Produced by the People **Quora**—Answers from Experts, Amateurs and Insiders, Voted Up or Down **Yahoo Answers**—Another P2P Question & Answer Site **Diigo**—Crowdsourced Web Bookmarks, Tags, and More

Adapted from **Board of Innovation Crowdsourcing Examples.** See this page for additional examples.

Crowdfunding

More recently, businesses and entrepreneurs have turned to the crowdsourcing model to raise money for business start-ups or projects. A number of **crowdfunding** sites have become popular in recent years, including GoFundMe and Kickstarter. Each crowdfunding site is governed by different rules that establish the kinds of projects or organizations that can use them and the types of crowdfunding allowed on the site (**Table 7.8**). Crowdfunding sites

TABLE 7.8	Types of Crowdfunding
Donations	Often used by charities and political campaigns. Contributors do not receive anything tangible in exchange for their donation, just the knowledge that they are supporting a cause they like or believe in. (In some cases, contributors may be eligible for a tax write-off.)
Rewards	Contributors receive some kind of "perk" or thank-you gift. Often, it is something related to the project. For instance, people who contribute to a filmmaker's project may receive a copy of the finished work on DVD.
Credit	Contributors essentially make microloans to fund projects and expect to be repaid with interest.
Equity	Contributors make "micro investments" and receive a proportional ownership stake in the company. It is likely that regulatory agencies that oversee equities markets in the United States and other countries will establish rules governing or even restricting this type of crowdfunding.
Royalties	Contributors receive a percentage of the sales revenue generated by a project. For instance, people who contribute to a musician's recording project might receive royalties from the sale of the artist's music.

Sources: Outlaw (2013), Wikipedia (2014).

typically collect a percentage of the money raised, but even this can vary, so it is important to read the **terms of service (TOS) agreement** carefully before selecting a site to raise money on. See **Crowdfunding.com** for a list of the most popular sites.

Terms of service (TOS) agreement   a formal listing of the policies, liability limits, fees, user rights and responsibilities associated with using a particular service. Users are typically required to acknowledge they have read, understand, and agree to the TOS before they are allowed the service to use.

Social Networking Services

Social networking services represent a special type of virtual community and are now the dominant form of online community. With social networking, individual users maintain an identity through their profile and can be selective about which members of the larger community they choose to interact with. Over time, users build their network by adding contacts or friends. On some social networks, organizations create an identity by establishing discussion forums, group pages, or some other presence.

The number of SNSs has grown tremendously in recent years. It is expected that the social networking sector will segment and consolidate in the future just like other industries. Among general-purpose SNS platforms, Facebook is the clear leader with over 2 billion active users. Facebook's dramatic growth over the past decade has been unparalleled in the social media world (**Table 7.9**).

TABLE 7.9	Facebook Statistics
2 billion monthly active users as of July 5, 2017	
1.28 billion daily active users on average for March 31, 2017	
1.74 billion mobile monthly active users as of December 31, 2016	
1.15 billion mobile daily active users on average for December 2016	
Approximately 85.8% of daily active users are outside the United States and Canada	
Facebook owns several other companies including Instagram (mobile photo-sharing), WhatsApp (mobile messenger app), Oculus (virtual reality), Moves (activity log), and Masquerade (selfie filters)	
Over 2 billion people use one of Facebook's mobile messenger apps every month—Facebook Messenger or WhatsApp. That's in addition to the billions of active Facebook.com users	

Source: Facebook, Inc.

While SNS sites share some common features, they are not all alike. As the category matures, sites are differentiating themselves in a variety of ways:

- Target age group
- Geographic location of users
- Language
- Area of interest, for example, music, photography, gaming, travel
- Social versus professional networking (see **IT at Work 7.2**)
- Interface, for example, profile page, microblog, virtual world, emphasis on graphic versus text content

---

IT at Work 7.2

Recruiters Use Professional Networking Sites

Susan Heathfield, a human resources (HR) expert at About.com, maintains that it is no longer sufficient to post job openings on monster.com, Careerbuilder.com, and Craigslist.com. Job postings on these large sites often generate hundreds of applications from unqualified candidates. This can be overwhelming for recruiters and very inefficient. Instead, many have turned to professional networking sites like LinkedIn. Heathfield identified a number of specific ways that businesses recruiters use LinkedIn to increase their effectiveness:

- Identify potential candidates among their existing network of professionals.
- Ask their network to identify or recommend candidates for a position.
- Evaluate potential employees based on references and referrals from their existing network.
- Actively search for relevant keywords or qualifications in the profiles of LinkedIn users.
- Ask current employees to search among their LinkedIn networks for potential candidates.

- Post job openings on LinkedIn.
- Request introductions to potential candidates through their existing network of professionals.
- Use Inmail (the internal LinkedIn e-mail system) to contact potentially qualified individuals.

It is clear that recruiters have come to embrace LinkedIn as an effective and cost-efficient way of generating qualified candidates. As LinkedIn's global presence grows, this will provide an important benefit to companies who need to fill positions internationally.

IT at Work Questions

1. Why have monster.com, Careerbuilder.com, and Craigslist. com lost their effectiveness?
2. Why have HR departments turned to professional networking sites like LinkedIn?
3. Why is it so essential for career-minded workers to build a professional social network? What can this network do for you?

Source: Heathfield (2012).

Facebook Dominates Social Networking

Facebook was launched in 2004 by a former Harvard student, Mark Zuckerberg. Facebook features include Profile, News Feed, Messenger, Groups, Events, Photo and Video Sharing, Search and Pages (for individuals, groups, and organizations to create public profiles). Apart from these basic applications, users can add any of the millions of Facebook apps that have been developed by others. Today over 90% of users access the site from mobile devices instead of desktop computers and over 50% only access the site from a mobile device (see **Figure 7.3**).

Facebook pioneered the Newsfeed feature, a constantly updated stream of status updates and postings from a user's friends. Today the Newsfeed also contains sponsored posts (advertisements) as part of Facebook's growing advertising program. In late 2011, Facebook introduced another major revision to its site called Timeline. The Timeline app is designed to show the chronological progression of key events in a person's life as illustrated by his or her Facebook status updates, photos, songs listened to, bad haircuts, as well as changes in occupations, locations, relationships, and the like. The Timeline feature effectively curates all the content users share on the networking service. When it was initially launched, many users were surprised by

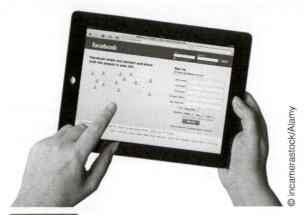

© incamerastock/Alamy

FIGURE 7.3   People are increasingly using mobile devices like smartphones and tablets to access Facebook and other social media sites.

what they felt was a radical interface change and were uncomfortable with how easy it became for others to access old, long forgotten posts and status updates. Facebook responded with privacy features that gave users greater control over who could view their content.

When Zuckerberg created Facebook, he had very strong social ambitions aimed at helping people connect to others on the Web. Facebook was initially an online social space for college and high school students. It started by connecting students to all others at the same school. In 2006 Facebook expanded to anyone 13 years or older with a valid e-mail address. The lack of privacy controls was among the biggest reasons why some business people resisted joining Facebook during its early years.

In 2008 Facebook introduced controls that allowed users to set different access levels to information for various groups of people in their network; for example, family, friends from school, friends from work, and so on. For instance, close friends might see your mobile phone number, music favorites, e-mail address, and so forth, while other friends might see only the basic information. Facebook is sometimes criticized for its approach to user privacy, highlighting an ongoing tension between the corporate goals of Facebook, which depends on a high level of access to user data, and the desire of individual users to control access to their personal information. See **IT at Work 7.3** for additional information about social media privacy issues.

Facebook has expanded to the rest of the world with the help of its foreign-language members: Engineers first collected thousands of English words and phrases throughout the site and invited members to translate those bits of text into another language. Members then rated translations until a consensus was reached. The Spanish version was created by about 1,500 volunteers in less than a month. The German version was created by 2,000 volunteers in less than 2 weeks. In early March 2008, Facebook invited French members to help out. They completed the translations in a few days. Facebook exists in over 100 different languages and approximately 85% of users reside outside of the United States and Canada. In May 2012, Facebook went public with its initial public offering (IPO), selling company shares on the NASDAQ stock exchange. It raised over $16 billion, making it the third largest ever IPO in U.S. history. While founder Mark Zuckerberg sold some 30 million shares during the offering (for $1.15 billion), he continues to own approximately 15% of the company. His net worth of over $56.7 billion places him among the 10 wealthiest people on the planet.

The Open Graph Initiative   A primary reason that Facebook expands is the **network effect**: More users mean more value. In April 2010, Zuckerberg announced Facebook's new initiative called **Open Graph**. The goal was to connect all the different relationships that exist on the Internet by linking websites to Facebook. Programmers at external websites were encouraged to include a Facebook "Like" button on their websites. That way, when a Facebook member visits the website, they can click "Like" and their relationship with that website will be reflected back on their Facebook page for friends to see.

Network effect   from the field of economics, the network effect explains how the perceived value of a product or service is affected by the number of people using the product or service.

IT at Work 7.3

Addressing Social Media Privacy Concerns

Privacy rights are too easily abused. Governments and industry associations are trying to control these abuses through legislation and professional standards, but they frequently fail to provide adequate protection. One of the most effective deterrents is fear of backlash from abuses that become public and cause outrage. So it is important to identify privacy issues that pertain to social media and specifically SNSs. Examples of privacy violations include the following:

- Posting pictures of people on social networking sites without their permission
- Tricking people into disclosing credit or bank account information or investing in "work at home" scams
- Sharing user information with advertisers without users' knowledge or consent
- Disclosing an employer's proprietary information or trade secrets on social networking sites
- Posting information on social networking sites that could compromise people's safety or make them targets for blackmail

Taking Control of Your Privacy

The most important thing that users can do to protect themselves is to understand that they are responsible for protecting their own information. The basic solution is common sense. Unfortunately, most social networking sites create the illusion of privacy and control. This sometimes can lull even the most vigilant users into making mistakes. Sites like Facebook make us feel like our information is only going to be seen by those we have allowed to become part of our network. Wrong. Listed below are common-sense guidelines:

- Do not post private data. Nothing, absolutely nothing you put on a social networking site is private. You should avoid posting personal information including full birth date, home address, phone number, and the like. This information can be used for identity theft.
- Be smart about who you allow to become part of your network. It is not uncommon for teenagers to "friend" hundreds of individuals on their Facebook accounts. With this many contacts, there is no way to protect profile or other information.
- Do not rely on current privacy policies or **terms of service (TOS) agreements**. Social networking sites change their privacy policies regularly. Many have accused Facebook of doing this specifically to wear down user vigilance with regard to maintaining desired privacy settings. Regularly review your social network service privacy policies explained in the TOS. Set your privacy settings at the level offering maximum protection—operating as if you have no privacy whatsoever.
- Minimize your use of applications, games, and third-party programs on social networking sites until you have carefully investigated them. They can expose you to malicious programs or viruses. Do not automatically click on links that look as if they were sent to you by members of your network.

IT at Work Questions

1. Which of these guidelines is the easiest to follow? Which is the toughest? Explain why.
2. Why is it recommended that you not post private data on a social network, even those with privacy settings?

Social Logins   Facebook also encourages other websites to allow people to use their Facebook username and password to sign in or create accounts. For instance, if you are a Facebook member and you visit **ESPN** (a sports news site) or **Yelp** (a local directory service), you can sign into the sites using your Facebook username and password. Facebook will then share your profile information with those sites. A number of services compete for social logins including Google+, Twitter, Yahoo, and LinkedIn. Toward the end of 2015, Facebook had the largest share of social logins (62%) followed by Google+ with 24% (Peterson, 2016).

Google Takes on Facebook with G+

Launched in June 2011, Google+, or G+, was the search engine giant's attempt to capture a share of the social networking market. Determining how well Google+ has performed takes a bit of calculation. Officially, there are over 2.5 billion G+ user accounts. But that figure is misleading because everyone that signs up for Google's popular e-mail service (Gmail) automatically gets a Google+ account. More realistic estimates of activity and users on Google+ suggest that the service probably has between 4 and 6 million users that engage, interact, and post publically (Gallagher, 2015). Having failed to meet early expectations for a big Facebook versus Google+ rivalry, one might wonder why the company continues to maintain the social platform. Some speculate that Google wants to maintain its position in social logins where it holds second place. Others have suggested that while few people actually use Google+, there is value in all those billions of profiles. The profiles, combined with the data you generate using other Google products, helps the company better understand your interests as well as how to effectively place ads in front of you as you surf the Web. Finally, the company does announce updates, improvements, and changes to Google+ from time to time. Given Google's tradition of regularly evolving products, perhaps the social network will emerge as something useful down the line. For now, Google hasn't given any indication that it is ready to close the doors on its social network (Pierce, 2015).

Be in the Now with Snapchat

Compared to social networks like LinkedIn (2003), Facebook (2004), YouTube (2005), and Twitter (2006), **Snapchat**, founded in 2011, is a relative newcomer to the social media big leagues. But that hasn't kept Snapchat from quickly becoming one of the most popular social platforms, second only to Facebook in terms of where people spend their time (see Figure 7.2). As Facebook's appeal among teens and young adults declines, the mobile-only Snapchat service has become the hot new social platform for an age group that some experts call *digital natives* or *The App Generation* because they were born after digital technologies became ubiquitous. Snapchat's core feature set can be described as a fun messaging app that emphasizes communication through pictures and videos instead of the text-based messages people have sent to each other for years. Snapchat's rapid growth during a relatively short life has been nothing but spectacular and mirrors in a way its most distinctive feature when compared to other social platforms—Snapchat picture and video messages self-destruct within 10 seconds after being viewed. When founder and CEO Evan Spiegel first pitched the concept to classmates at Stanford University, they frowned on disappearing picture idea, claiming nobody would use an app that couldn't save messages. On most other social platforms, it seems the goal is to curate or build a collection of photos, posts, and messages. Facebook even goes so far as to remind users of updates and pictures posted years ago, encouraging people to reshare the memories with others in their network. One of the post popular features on Twitter is the "retweet," or the act of forwarding an interesting tweet from someone to other people in your network. That's not allowed on Snapchat—no saving, no forwarding, no looking back through silly pictures that special someone sent you when your relationship was, well, less complicated. According to some of its most rabid fans, Snapchat is all about the "now." Most likely you've heard stories about people who spend hours cultivating their personal brand by sharing carefully retouched photographs of themselves, regularly posting witty status updates, and telling stories of doing "absolutely amazing things, all the time, with tons of friends." Snapchat seems to rebel against the rehearsed and unnaturally choreographed public images that people sometimes become obsessed with creating on other sites. Instead, Snapchat encourages users to have fun and be a little crazy while using the service. In the emerging Snapchat culture, spontaneous silliness is the norm. Some speculate that young people enjoy the app because it allows them to ignore all those warnings from parents, teachers, and future employers about posting incriminating images on social media. According to Snapchat, any consequences are likely to be short-lived, disappearing within 10 seconds. But while Snapchat's growing fan base might be enjoying the thrill of adding doggy noses and ears to selfies they just took with their friends at a party, senior leadership at the company is busy managing a host of serious issues. In 2012, Snapchat's daily user base of 10 million people were sharing about 20 million images a day. Fast forward to 2017, and the daily user base has grown to more than 160 million people sharing 2.5 billion snaps a day (snaps is a metric that counts both photographs and videos). With that kind of growth, the company must be continuously expanding its computing infrastructure, which, in turn, means arranging for venture capital funding and ultimately launching an IPO on March 2, 2017. Following its first day of trading, the app's parent company, *Snap, Inc.*, had a public market valuation of over $28 billion. While the company reported revenue of $404.5 million in 2016, like many start-up companies it still hasn't made a profit. Almost 98% of its revenue comes from advertising. While users have been quick to join the new social network, advertisers are still figuring out how Snapchat integrates with their overall promotion strategy. In addition, older social platforms obviously have advertising and promotional programs that advertisers already understand. As well, they have years of behavioral data and consumer insights that help advertisers accurately target prospective customers. In conclusion, while Snapchat is a hit with consumers, the business challenges facing the leadership team as they manage the company's growth, financing, infrastructure, and branding are monumental. Hopefully, the company's lively ghost logo will prove to represent the playful spirit in all of us and not the omen of a company that lived fast, but died young.

And Now for Something Different: Second Life

Avatars an icon, figure or visual representation of a person in computer games, simulations, virtual worlds or online discussion forms.

Second Life is a social network service unlike most others. What makes it unique is that it uses a 3D virtual world interface in which users, called *Residents*, are represented by **avatars**, or cyber bodies that they create (**Figure 7.4**).

Developed by Linden Research in 2003, Second Life lets residents communicate with others in the virtual world through chat or voice communications. Residents can create and trade things they make in Second Life, including virtual clothes, art, vehicles, houses, and other architectural structures. They can also earn money by providing services such as instruction in a foreign language or serving as a DJ in a virtual club. This has led to the evolution of a Second Life economy with its own currency, the Linden dollar (L$). While most of the economic activity remains in the Second Life world, there have been news reports of a few entrepreneurs who made considerable sums of real money. The most common businesses were operated by programmers and artists with the skills to make virtual objects that less talented residents were willing to pay real money for.

Between 2006 and 2008, there was a big spike in interest on the part of businesses that witnessed great potential in using Second Life. For example, IBM used it as a location for meetings, training, and recruitment. Musicians performed concerts to crowds in virtual amphitheaters, and to smaller audiences in virtual nightclubs and bars. American Apparel was the first major retailer to set up shop in Second Life. Starwood Hotels used Second Life as a relatively low-cost market research experiment in which avatars visit Starwood's virtual Aloft hotel. The endeavor created publicity for the company, and feedback on the design of the hotel was solicited from visiting avatars. This information was used in the creation of the first real-world Aloft hotel, which opened in 2008 (Carr, 2007). Starwood subsequently donated its Second Life property to a not-for-profit educational organization. Fashion and clothing manufacturers like Reebok, American Apparel, Adidas, and others used Second Life as a place to feature new clothing designs, setting up virtual stores where Second Life citizens could purchase digital clothing for their avatars. The hope was that awareness of fashion products on Second Life would spur interest and eventual purchase of real-world products. But efforts by these and

FIGURE 7.4 Second Life residents participate in a virtual world beauty contest sponsored by cosmetics manufacturer L'Oreal.

STR/Reuters - Images

other businesses, like 1-800-flowers, to get Second Life citizens to purchase real-world products through the virtual community proved disappointing. Many businesses that were quick to become part of the early excitement around Second Life eventually left the virtual world community.

The general consensus seems to be that we're still not ready for virtual world applications. Based on past experience, significant technological, social, cultural, and financial hurdles have to be overcome before virtual worlds like Second Life develop the kind of mass appeal that innovators predicted back in 2008. That said, there are signs that the virtual world concept may be entering a new phase of innovation. Second Life recently rolled out an upgraded **virtual reality** (VR) space called "Sansar" that takes advantage of new technology like the **Oculus Rift**, a VR headset that creates an immersive experience for users. Linden Labs, the company that operates Second Life believes the new VR technology will solve many of the in-world functionality problems that frustrated new users in the early days. This time, however, Linden Labs will have some competition. Philip Rosedale, the founder of Linden and Second Life has left that company and started a new "social VR" venture called **High Fidelity**. Rosedale's new company is also creating virtual world applications that make use of VR technology. He envisions an open-source platform where users can build their own virtual worlds connected to the worlds created by others, a type of virtual world social network.

Of course, given the history of virtual worlds up to now, it might be easy to dismiss claims and predictions about the potential of VR and virtual worlds if it weren't for the backing of companies like Facebook which invested close to $2 billion to acquire Oculus. Zuckerberg said that he believes the acquisition is a long-term bet on the future of social networking. Only time will tell if these new technologies represent the future of social networking (see Hay, 2015; Johnson, 2015; Kushner, 2017; Metz, 2017).

Private Social Networks

The ultimate niche community is the **private SNS**. Private SNSs use social technology to create a community restricted to members selected by the SNSs' owner. Private SNSs allow a greater degree of control over the network. Companies can easily monitor activity on their own SNS platforms and track conversations taking place about their brands and products. However, managing a private SNS requires considerably more time, attention, and resources than maintaining a presence on a general SNS. Organizations need to understand up-front that they are making a substantial commitment with this strategy.

Most colleges and universities have Facebook pages. In addition, many institutions have set up private SNSs to engage students even before they have started school there. Students typically gain access to these private SNSs when they are admitted to the institution. On the system, they can interact with admissions counselors, current students, and other admitted students. Interactions that occur on these networks set the stage for relationships and engagement that are simply not possible with e-mail and phone calls.

In 2008 Mercedes-Benz created two private SNSs designed to increase engagement with current and potential customers. The Mercedes Advisor network is for current Mercedes-Benz owners. GenerationBenz.com is a private network for prospective Mercedes owners. Membership in the network is limited to those who fit Mercedes' profile for younger luxury car buyers. Both of these communities provide the company with an opportunity to engage their target audiences directly. Members participate in market surveys and polls, provide feedback on prospective ad campaigns and product features, and participate in discussion groups with company managers. This provides valuable feedback to Mercedes as well as creates strong advocates for the company's luxury car brand.

While engaging customers on a private SNS can be time-consuming and potentially require significant staffing resources, the technological challenges associated with setting up a private SNS are relatively small. A number of companies offer a combination of free and subscription-based pricing for individuals or organizations wishing to create a private social network. Basic SNS sites can be set up fairly quickly for free. Search on "private social network services" for the latest information.

Future of Social Networking Systems

Social networking services are perhaps the most feature-rich applications of Web 2.0. It is expected that growth and innovation in this sector will continue as individual users and business organizations discover its power for building networks and relationships. We expect that Facebook will continue to dominate the field, but that smaller SNSs will stake out strong positions in niche markets using traditional market segmentation strategies that focus on the needs of specific geographic, cultural, age, or special interest segments. Finally, with the advent of VR technologies, more powerful computers, and large-capacity Web server installations, virtual worlds may become an exciting new platform for all types of social interaction in the future.

Questions

1. What are the major differences between SNSs and older online communities?
2. What is the basic difference between the social graph and Berners-Lee's concept of the Giant Global Graph?
3. Explain Facebook's Open Graph initiative and how it plans to expand its influence across the World Wide Web.
4. What are some potential ways that business organizations can take advantage of Second Life's unique virtual world interface?
5. Why would a business want to create a private SNS? What are some of the challenges associated with doing this?

7.3 | Engaging Consumers with Blogs and Microblogs

One of the problems with traditional media, like newspapers and magazines, is that editors and publishers decide what you should read. Often their decisions are based on what the masses will buy at the newsstands. Space is limited and barriers to getting published are high. News services frequently fail to devote sufficient space to complex issues or viewpoints that might challenge the financial or business interests of the publication's owners or advertisers. But with social media, anyone can write a column or article and publish it online for the world to read (see **IT at Work 7.4**).

Of course, this creates another potential problem: clutter. Blogging is so easy that even people who do not have much to say can publish their thoughts, opinions, and ideas. Readers need to be prepared to look at online content with a skeptical eye and find ways to judge the credibility of the material they find on social media.

In their simplest form, **blogs** are websites where people regularly post content. Some personal blogs are simply online diaries or journals where people share their thoughts, reflections, or an account of their life. Other blogs are more sophisticated and professional in format, resembling online newspapers or magazines. Because blogging technology has become so commonplace, you may not always realize you are reading a blog when accessing online content. Many organizations have integrated one of the blogging platforms discussed later with their website. Blogging tools make it easy for organizations to provide website visitors with frequently updated content on pages with titles such as "What's New," "Company News," or "Product Updates." As a result, you may be a frequent blog reader without realizing it!

Blogs contain content in a variety of digital formats including text, photographs, video, and music. People who create and maintain blogs are referred to as bloggers.

What Is the Purpose of a Blog?

Many professionals now blog as a way to establish their reputation and promote their business interests, or because they enjoy writing and sharing their viewpoints with others.

IT at Work 7.4

How to Create a Blog

Setting up a blog is relatively easy. Making the effort to regularly write and post content that others will find interesting is more challenging. The following steps outline the process of setting up a blog.

1. Create a plan. Successful blogging requires a certain degree of organization and discipline. You can address this part of the project by developing a plan at the outset. The plan should answer questions like these:

   a. What are you going to blog about? What will be the focus or topic of your blog?

   b. Identify your target audience. For whom are you writing?

   c. How often do you intend to update your blog? Some bloggers post new material daily, some weekly, and some just a few times a month. As a general rule, readers are more likely to follow blogs that are updated regularly. Avoid sporadic updates or only blogging when you feel like it. Successful bloggers frequently set up a publication schedule outlining topics and posting dates to keep themselves on track.

   d. Who else is blogging about the same topic? Identify bloggers you can interact with through your posts and comments on their blogs.

2. Determine if you will self-host your blog by purchasing a hosting plan and domain name (URL), or if your blog will use a free blogging service. Free services allow you to get up and running quickly and do not require any long-term commitments. This provides an easy, low-risk way to get started. While this might be the most convenient approach, you do not actually own your blog or the content you post there because it is on a domain owned by someone else. Your domain name in these situations is usually in the form of "myblogname.blogspot.com," which can appear less professional to some readers. Purchasing a hosting plan and domain name, however, is the better long-term strategy since it creates a unique identity for your blog.

3. Select a blogging platform (see the section below). This is the software that will provide the look and feel of your site and give you myriad features you can employ to build a successful blog. Standard features in most blog platforms include a comment section, RSS buttons so readers can subscribe to your blog, and share buttons so readers can post links to your blog on other social media sites (e.g., Twitter, Facebook, Digg, etc.).

4. Set up your blog. Once you've set up your hosting and platform arrangements, you will need to create the aesthetic design for your site. Most platforms make this easy with a multitude of template options that you can further customize to give your blog a unique look.

5. Get started. Now comes the challenging part, writing your posts and regularly updating your blog to attract readers. You can read blogs about blogging to get great tips and advice.

Corporate bloggers use the medium to tell stories about their brands and connect with customers.

On the surface, blogging appears to be a broadcast (one-to-many) communication tool. However, it can also be an effective tool for interactive dialogue. Many blogs utilize comment features, allowing readers to respond to blog posts, interacting with the blogger and other readers. Successful bloggers tend to comment on and link to other blogs in their posts, in effect maintaining a dialogue or conversation with other bloggers. These connections between blogs create what some refer to as the **blogosphere**, or a network of blogs. **IT at Work 7.5** lists a number of ways that organizations use blogs for marketing.

IT at Work 7.5

How Marketers Use Blogs and Microblogs

Blogs and microblogs provide individuals and organizations with a means to accomplish a variety of communications objectives. Marketers use blogs and microblogs to

- Develop relationships with independent bloggers, encouraging them to write positive stories about the brand, product, and company
- Engage members of the blogging community, via corporate blogs, by providing helpful and interesting information
- Tell the company's "story," position a product, create brand identity, and differentiate from the competition
- Engage customers and readers by soliciting comments and feedback about information provided in blog posts
- Drive traffic to the company website by using Twitter to announce recent updates to the company blog
- Inform current or prospective customers about positive blog posts featuring your product or company that were written by independent, third-party bloggers
- Encourage repeat visits to the company website through regular updates or new posts to the blog
- Have a celebrity or influential expert send a tweet with a promotional message about your brand using Twitter's new advertising program

Blogging and Public Relations

Some bloggers have become highly successful and have developed a large audience for their material. Many people approach blogging like a business and consider themselves "publishers," with the goal of generating enough readers or subscribers that they can make money from advertisers and ad agencies who will pay to display their ads on an individual blogger's site. Earlier in this chapter, you read about a set of groundswell social media strategies described by Charlene Li and Josh Bernoff. One of those strategies, *Energizing*, is accomplished when a business identifies a blogger whose audience matches its target market and persuades that person to write about the company's product. This is similar to a public relations manager sending a press release to a journalist, hoping he or she will write a news story about the company in the local paper. When a highly credible and influential blogger writes a positive story about your company, it can have a very positive impact on your brand's image. Bloggers can also have a negative impact if they write unfavorable posts about the company or its products. As a result, public relations professionals are learning how to identify and form positive relationships with influential bloggers with the goal of generating favorable coverage of the company and its products. Frequently, this will involve doing things like providing the blogger with information in advance of it being released to the public, providing access to company executives for interviews, sending the blogger samples of the company's product so that he or she can write about it from firsthand experience, and so on. For some companies, particularly those in the technology industry, building relationships with influential bloggers has become an important public relations strategy.

Reading and Subscribing to Blogs

The best way to gain an understanding of the blogging phenomenon is to simply start reading blogs. You can use search engines like Google or Yahoo to find blogs on all kinds of topics. Most blogs make it easy to subscribe using an RSS reader (see Section 7.4 later on in this chapter). Reading blogs is a great way to stay current on rapidly evolving topics related to technology and business.

Blogging Platforms

Blogging platform a software application used to create, edit, and add features to a blog. *WordPress* and *Blogger* are two of the most popular blogging platforms.

Selecting a **blogging platform** is an important decision when setting up a blog. Installing a platform when you are creating a blog is relatively easy. Converting to a new blogging platform after using another one for a while is not. Two of the most popular platforms are WordPress followed by Google's Blogger platform. Other blog platforms include TypePad, Movable Type, and Tumblr. The Tumblr platform is significantly different from traditional platforms in that it emphasizes easy posting of photos and light copy. As such, it is considered to be a microblogging platform and is discussed later in this chapter.

When choosing between WordPress and Blogger, WordPress is a feature-rich platform and offers greater control over site appearance (**Figure 7.5**). Blogger is simpler and easier to use, making it a more desirable choice for beginning bloggers who want to get up and running without becoming bogged down in technological issues. Blogger's affiliation with Google might also be attractive because of the potential for integration with other Google services. For instance, Blogger comes with a built-in analytics program that appears to share many similarities with Google Analytics, a stand-alone Web traffic-monitoring tool.

For now, begin by reading blogs about social media, information technology, and other topics that are of personal interest. Note how these blogs vary in terms of style, length, and appearance. Identify the features they offer readers for commenting on and sharing content. After you get a feel for how people blog, try setting up your own blog using Google's free platform and hosting service at **www.google.com/blogger**.

FIGURE 7.5   WordPress is one of the leading platforms for online blogs.

Microblogs

You may be a microblogger and not even know it! Microblogging is a way of sharing content with people by the regular, often frequent posting of short messages. Although people don't usually call it microblogging, perhaps the most common form of this social media activity occurs when you update your status message on Facebook. More often, however, the term is used to describe popular microblogging services like Twitter and Tumblr.

Most **microblog** content consists of text-based messages, although there appears to be an increase in people who are microblogging photos and video on Twitter and Tumblr. Tumblr has increased in popularity recently among younger Internet users because of its multimedia capabilities and ease of use.

Microblog   a blog that consists of frequent, but very brief posts containing text, pictures, or videos. Twitter is perhaps the most well-known example of a microblog.

Twitter

Twitter has grown in popularity over the last few years, becoming one of the world's largest communication platforms. According to Twitter, approximately 5 million messages, or **tweets**, are sent each day by over 310 million active monthly users (see **Figure 7.6**). People frequently attach descriptive keywords or **hashtags**, designated by the # sign, to their tweets to make them easier for others to find (e.g., #news, #politics, #fail).

Tweet   a brief 140-character message or post broadcast on Twitter, a microblogging service.

FIGURE 7.6   Twitter is a microblogging SNS that limits users to messages of 140 characters or less.

Twitter has played a significant role in both global and domestic events (Lee, 2013). In countries where the media is largely dominated by government control, Twitter has proven to be a valuable tool for activists engaged in organizing protests, debating political viewpoints, and broadcasting real-time information about significant events that might otherwise be ignored by the mainstream media. Twitter has become a primary channel for real-time updates on events and issues in politics, entertainment, social causes, and sports. In 2016, Twitter kept people informed about the #RIO2016 Olympics, #Brexit—Britain's separation from the European Union, the #BlackLivesMatter movement, news about the popular television show #GameofThrones, and, of course, the U.S. presidential #Election2016 where Twitter was used heavily by both candidates. For better or worse, President Donald Trump continues to use Twitter as a primary communications tool since winning the election. Because of Twitter's reach, most federal and state political leaders now use Twitter as a regular channel for communicating with their followers. For the same reason, most advocacy groups engage in what some call **hashtag activism**, using the service to maintain awareness levels about their cause as well as influence people's beliefs and attitudes on key issues. Twitter has even begun to influence investment decisions made on Wall Street. Financial research analysts have created algorithms that use the volume and sentiment of Twitter traffic to predict the future stock value of a company.

Twitter is attractive to individuals, groups, and organizations because it provides a direct link to the public, bypassing traditional mass media, which often acts as an information gatekeeper. Ironically, Twitter frequently influences what we see on traditional media. Journalists regularly use Twitter to broadcast breaking news stories. "Hashtag journalists" increasingly monitor Twitter to identify newsworthy events being tweeted (reported) by eyewitnesses and to gauge the public's interest in an event or issue by monitoring trending topics. Using Twitter to monitor public sentiment as well as influence public opinion has become an important skill for public relations professionals working for business and not-for-profit organizations. Organizations can no longer afford to ignore the conversations that take place on Twitter about their brands, products, and executives. Furthermore, public relations professionals must understand how to actively participate in these conversations or risk appearing aloof and out-of-touch.

Twitter is often used by consumers to complain about frustrations they are having with a company or its products. In response, some companies have adopted Twitter as a customer service channel, along with e-mail and telephone call centers (see Opening Case 6.1). When customer service representatives find people complaining about their brand or product, they can use the service to empathize with the customer's frustration and offer solutions for resolving the problem. Because conversations on Twitter are public, other customers can watch or "listen in" on interactions between an unhappy customer and a customer service representative and judge how effective the company is at solving problems. This can be a benefit or liability for organizations depending on how adept they are at communicating and resolving customer problems on Twitter.

Just a few years ago, many businesses appeared to be somewhat confused about how to incorporate the microblogging service into their communications strategy. That has changed. Over 65% of companies now use Twitter for marketing communications and are increasingly expanding their reach by encouraging employees to share relevant messages with their personal social networks. In addition to organic (unpaid) tweets, companies are spending close to $3 billion a year on **promoted tweets**, or paid ads sent out over the network. Twitter is viewed by many companies as a good way to reach people on mobile devices.

Like other social media tools, the best way to gain an understanding of Twitter is to use it. The official Twitter interface is simple and efficient, but a large segment of the **Twittersphere** uses third-party apps that have been developed to enhance the site's functionality and user experience. Some are considered essential tools in the life of the power Twitter user:

Twittersphere the universe of people who use Twitter, a microblogging service.

- **TweetDeck** is an advanced, split-screen app that allows users to view messages streaming from followers, people being followed, and people the user might wish to follow. It also makes it easy to quickly reply to incoming tweets, increasing the frequency of Twitter conversations. The TweetDeck interface makes it easy to participate in Twitter forums or online discussion groups similar to what takes place in a chat room. In 2011, this popular Twitter application was acquired by Twitter and continues to be a popular interface application for people accessing the service from a computer.

- **Dlvr.it** automates posts to Twitter and other social platforms published on a blog using RSS technology.
- **Twitterholic** is a service that ranks users by the number of followers, friends, and updates.

Many users believe Twitter is best suited for mobile devices like smartphones or tablets, which enable users to post spontaneous messages and updates regardless of their location. There are literally hundreds of third-party Twitter apps for computers and mobile devices, with more being written every day. You can find the most popular mobile apps by using an Internet search engine or searching your phone's app store.

How Do People and Businesses Use Twitter?

Think of Twitter as a social network where the dominant focus is on status updates. People tweet messages to their followers that they think will be of interest. While some businesses still struggle with ways to use Twitter effectively, many have adopted strategies that engage consumers, enhance brand image, and improve revenue. Examples include the following:

- Celebrities use Twitter to update loyal fans about their day-to-day activities.
- Social media experts like Jeremiah Owyang and Brian Solis use Twitter to share links to online material that people in their profession will find interesting.
- Companies use Twitter to update customers about new products and special offers.
- Mobile food service trucks in large cities use Twitter to update customers about their current and future locations.
- Businesses can advertise on Twitter using a variety of ad types including promoted tweets, promoted accounts, and promoted trends ads.
- News services like CNN and Mashable use Twitter as a "headline news" stream, sending links to news stories on their websites.
- Coupon and shopping services use Twitter to send daily deals and special offers to their followers.
- People use Twitter to send status updates to their friends, keeping others informed about their activities, sharing stories and links to online material they find interesting.
- Politicians use Twitter to communicate with their constituents, often linking to stories or material on their website that they believe will help support their positions on issues.
- Businesses can use Twitter to increase traffic to their website by tweeting links to information on the website that they think people will find interesting.

When users receive a tweet from someone they follow, they can "Reply" to the message, or **retweet** it by forwarding the message to everyone in their network. In this way, users engage in a dialogue of sorts with people they are connected to on the service. Tweets that are retweeted among many different users can go viral.

Tumblr Blogs

Tumblr is often described as a microblogging service because it makes the posting of multimedia content easy for users and allows them to update their blogs frequently. However, Tumblr blogs can include just as much text as a regular blog, although most who use the service emphasize photographs and video as the primary content. This emphasis on multimedia makes the Tumblr blogs more visually compelling. Tumblr is particularly popular among those who are blogging about things like fashion, entertainment, and the arts.

Questions

1. What is the difference between a blog and a microblog?
2. What is a blogging platform?
3. Why do marketers use blogs and microblogs?
4. What makes Twitter a more attractive communication channel than traditional media for many individuals and organizations?
5. How is Tumblr different from other types of blogging platforms?

7.4 | Mashups, Social Metrics, and Monitoring Tools

A **mashup** is a Web application that combines information from two or more sources and presents this information in a way that creates some new benefit or service. Using AJAX technologies and APIs, websites and applications can pull information from a variety of sources.

One of the most common examples of a consumer mashup that you are likely to encounter involves the integration of map data (from companies such as Google or MapQuest) with information like store names, locations, phone numbers, and consumer reviews from other websites.

By combining this information in a single location or application, users enjoy a powerful and visually compelling service. **ProgrammableWeb** maintains a helpful directory of mashups.

Enterprise mashups combine data from internal business sources (e.g., sales records, customer information, etc.) and/or information from external sources for enhanced usefulness and productivity. For instance, a bank may utilize an enterprise mashup to display a mortgage application from its own records, the property location on a Google map, and information from county government property tax records.

What Makes a Mashup Social

To begin with, many of the most popular APIs used in mashup apps are from social media sites. That means the data involved in the mashup are likely to be user-generated social information. The other reason mashups are considered social media is that they represent the power to separate content from form—allowing Web developers (and sometimes users) greater control over how information is displayed and used on the Web.

Mashups also represent a change in philosophy for content creators. Traditionally, a business that created content operated a closed system where it maintained almost complete control over the "product." On the social Web, content creators enjoy greater distribution by allowing others access to their digital information through an API. For instance, the Google brand name appears on thousands of websites due to its open-source mapping API. If Twitter did not have an open-source API, awareness and use of the service would be far less than it is today because users would have to go to the Twitter site in order to use it. By giving up some control, these content creators enjoy wider distribution and market penetration.

While the ability to create powerful mashup applications has not yet reached most individual Web users, it has decentralized control over how content is displayed and used, which is a key principle of Web 2.0 social technologies (Section 7.1). We anticipate that it will not be long before someone develops a technology that will make it easier for the average user to create his or her own custom mashup applications.

Mashup technology also represents a tremendous opportunity for new Web-based businesses with limited start-up capital. For example, the online directory and business review service, Yelp.com, uses the Google Maps API to make it easier for users to locate restaurants and bars in their area. In turn, Yelp has an API that allows sites like Zillow.com to use Yelp's information when displaying information about homes and neighborhoods to prospective real estate customers.

RSS Technology

Another technology that extends control of Web content beyond the creator is **really simple syndication (RSS)** (**Figure 7.7**). Traditionally, users had to visit multiple sites in order to view content at each location. This is potentially time-consuming and difficult for users who are interested in following several sources. RSS technology allows users to subscribe to multiple sources (e.g., blogs, news headlines, social media feeds, videos, and podcasts) and have the content displayed in a single application, called an "RSS reader" or "RSS aggregator." In effect, users can create a customized news and information site by personalizing how they want information from their news sources organized and displayed. Popular RSS aggregators include **Feedly**, **Digg Reader**, and **The Old Reader**. Many other free or freemium aggregators are available with a variety of features.

FIGURE 7.7   Many blogs use the RSS logo to identify the subscription link that readers use to import the blog's content to their RSS aggregator.

Social Monitoring Services

A fast-growing sector in the social technology field involves **social monitoring services**. Monitoring applications allow users to track conversations taking place on social media sites. The initial impetus for the growth of monitoring tools was the need for business organizations to better understand what people were saying about their brands, products, and executives (the "listening" part of the Groundswell Strategy model discussed in Section 7.1). Monitoring services can be used to identify industry experts, commentators, and opinion leaders who post regularly to social media sites. Once identified, public relations professionals can build relationships with these individuals and encourage them to become **brand advocates** who regularly portray the brand or company positively in their online writing and social media posts. See **IT at Work 7.6**.

In the next section, we describe two categories of social monitoring tools: subscription-based services and free monitoring services.

Subscription Monitoring Services   The most comprehensive social media monitoring tools require the user to pay a subscription or licensing fee. These tools not only monitor the social media environment for mentions of your brand or company name but also provide analytics and tools for measuring trends in the amount of conversation occurring, the tone or sentiment (e.g., positive, negative, neutral) of the conversation, and other important aspects

IT at Work 7.6

Businesses Monitor Social Activity. . .

- To identify brand advocates—people who repeatedly discuss a particular topic
- To find experts talking about technical or business topics
- To assess reputation or sentiment in the online community about a brand, person, or issue

- To understand customers by listening—identifying topics of interest to the online community
- To track trends in the volume or nature of online conversations
- To assess the relationship between marketing actions (e.g., product launch) and online conversations
- To identify potential problems with your brand's reputation before things get out of control

of the social interactions occurring online. Some of these tools are actually social media management platforms that help companies administer social media marketing campaigns and inbound marketing programs. The monitoring tools are just one of several features available in these enterprise-level applications.

Most high-end monitoring tools report information using a dashboard interface, which graphically represents the data it collects. Some of the most popular among these paid services include the following:

- **Salesforce's Social Studio (formerly Radian 6)**
- **Sysomos**
- **Cision**
- **Sprout Social**
- **Oracle Social Cloud**

While prices for these high-end monitoring services can vary widely (typically, hundreds of dollars a month), they are usually beyond the budget of individual users.

Free Monitoring Services
Fortunately, there are number of free monitoring tools that can be used by anyone. Some of these tools, like Twitter Search, are designed to monitor conversations on a single social media platform, while others, like Social Mention, are designed to provide feedback on activity across a number of social media platforms including Facebook, Twitter, and blogs. The following list provides a brief description of some free social monitoring services.

Social Mention
Our favorite free monitoring tool is **Social Mention**. This tool aggregates content from over 80 different social media sites including Facebook, YouTube, and Twitter. The best thing about Social Mention is that it provides users with four metrics that give insight into the nature of conversations taking place on the Web.

Users can generate these statistics daily for a particular topic (e.g., brand name, public figure, current event) and record them in a spreadsheet. Over a period of time, it becomes easy to see trends developing with regard to factors such as how many people are talking about a topic or how they feel about a topic. This is useful information for the social media marketer.

Social Mention Metrics

- **Strength**   The likelihood that a particular topic is being discussed on social media platforms
- **Passion**   The degree to which people who are talking about your brand will do so repeatedly
- **Sentiment**   The tone of the conversation; this metric helps you understand if people are feeling positive, negative, or neutral about the topic
- **Reach**   Measures the range of influence. It is the number of unique authors divided by the number of mentions.

Go to **www.socialmention.com** and explore what people are talking about with regard to current events, celebrities, popular products, or any other issue you are interested in. See what you can learn from the four metrics listed by the site.

Twitter Search   This tool on the Twitter website generates a list of recent tweets containing a specific word or phrase. You can use the search engine to generate a list of tweets containing keywords related to an issue, a brand name, a company name, elected official, and so on. If your goal is to measure the sentiment of the conversation about a particular topic or brand, you can accomplish this informally by simply scrolling through the messages to get a feel for what people are saying (see **twitter.com/search**).

If you want to do a more formal analysis, randomly sample, say, 100 tweets and manually categorize each as positive, negative, or neutral. Repeat this on a daily basis and you will be able to identify trends in the sentiment of online conversations over time. Companies can use Twitter search to identify users who are having problems or complaining about their product and take corrective action by responding to specific tweets.

Hootsuite   Hootsuite is a popular social media management platform with specific tools for engagement, publishing, analytics, monitoring, and advertising across multiple social media channels. Users can open a free account to explore the service and upgrade to a larger range of features for as little as $10/month. When fully configured, Hootsuite is similar to an enterprise-level system.

Google Alerts   Unlike the other tools listed above, Google alerts do not provide much in the way of metrics that describe social media activity. However, it is an extremely useful monitoring tool that conducts automated Google searches for new Web content. Searches can be general or specific to social content on blogs and discussion forums. Users receive regular e-mail updates with search results (see **www.google.com/alerts**). This tool is particularly useful for managers who need to be aware of any news stories, blog posts, and discussion forums where a particular product, brand name, company, or person is mentioned. It is great for monitoring competitive organizations. It is easy to use, and because the searches are automated, it is very convenient.

Social monitoring tools play an essential role in helping social media marketers gain insight into the conversations taking place on the Web. They represent a set of powerful tools in the arsenal of firms that seek to understand consumers, what they are interested in, what they are talking about, and what they are thinking. As such, it is important that you become familiar with these tools, their strengths and weaknesses.

Questions

1. Why are mashups considered part a social technology?
2. Describe a typical consumer mashup.
3. What is an RSS reader?
4. Describe the ways in which businesses can benefit from using social media monitoring tools.
5. Explain the difference between the Strength metric and the Sentiment metric reported by **www.Socialmention.com**.

7.5 | Enterprise 2.0: Workplace Collaboration and Knowledge Sharing

Working on a team project or coordinating the efforts of a work group or committee can be challenging. In addition to the normal challenges associated with teamwork, many organizations and their employees today are located in different locations across a region, a country, or the globe. Whether you are working with a group of fellow students on a class project, or a team of employees charged with developing a global marketing plan for your company's new brand, there are all kinds of factors that can be difficult to overcome for even the most dedicated groups.

In today's competitive environment, businesses must be agile, able to respond quickly to a rapidly evolving marketplace. Employees must be able to work collaboratively, communicate clearly, reach consensus, make decisions, and implement their action plans effectively. Many businesses use Intranets to deploy tools for employee collaboration and productivity. An **Intranet** is a password-protected network that uses the same Web-based technologies (e.g., browsers, Web pages, and hyperlinked text) found on the World Wide Web. Think of it as a private or internal Web. As organizations update their Intranets, employees can now take advantage of many social features they have become accustom to using on the World Wide Web. This trend is sometimes referred to as **Enterprise 2.0**. While employees may be familiar with the new technology, there is still a need to change work-related behaviors and organizational culture to maximize the benefit from these enterprise social technologies.

In this section, we review a number of social tools for collaboration that are available to everyone. Small businesses, startups, and nonprofits that lack resources to deploy modern Intranets can use these tools for increased productivity. Larger companies will use similar tools as part of their enhanced (Enterprise 2.0) Intranets.

Tools for Meetings and Discussions

Synchronous communication
dialogue or conversation that takes place in real time, without the long delays between exchanges that occur, for instance, in e-mail or discussion board conversations.

Dialogue or **synchronous communication** is an important part of the collaborative process. This can pose a challenge, however, for teams that cannot meet face to face. In the last few years, services like **Skype**, and **GoToMeeting** have become a popular way to make reasonably good-quality video calls between two or three people. **Fuze** and **Google+ Hangouts** are free video conferencing platforms that have the advantage of allowing up to 10 people to participate in a video conference (see **Figure 7.8**). Several other companies also offer free or low-cost video conferencing platforms with variations in performance quality and number of features. In addition to basic video conferencing features, some platforms offer the ability to share desktop views with other callers, which makes it possible to share presentations, spreadsheets, and documents just like you would in a face-to-face meeting.

Social Tools for Information Retrieval and Knowledge Sharing

When people work together as part of a group or team, they frequently need to share information with other members of the group. As you learned in Chapter 6, search engines like Google

© White House Photo/Alamy

FIGURE 7.8 On January 30, 2012, President Barack Obama participated in an online interview held through a Google+ Hangout, making it the first completely virtual interview from the White House.

and Bing are among the most frequently used tools on the Web. These large search engines now use information culled from social media sites to improve the relevance of SERP listings. In addition, some sites continuously update a real-time listing of trending search topics, providing users with another means of information retrieval based on the search behavior of the crowd.

While the most popular search engines use social media data as part of their search results ranking algorithm, the information retrieval process on Internet search engines is not particularly social. Over the last decade, some attempts have been made to personalize search results based on information from a user's social network. For instance, the names of people from your social network might appear alongside certain Web page listings if they visited a page, "liked" a page, or perhaps made a comment on a page. By and large that information is no longer provided on SERPs because of privacy concerns and the fact that it did not tend to result in an improved user experience. However, Internet search engines are not the only option available for information retrieval. Other services do a better job of integrating our social connections with social technology to create useful tools for information retrieval and knowledge sharing.

Discussion groups on SNSs can provide a forum for asking questions to groups of people. For instance, the American Marketing Association maintains a discussion group on LinkedIn that has over 52,000 members. Participants can ask questions and solicit input from other members of the group. Members can also monitor discussion groups, receiving periodic digests of group activity that can be scanned for material of interest. LinkedIn can be a particularly useful website for business professionals with questions that can be answered by experts or other business professionals. Facebook and Twitter also host topical discussion groups that can be a helpful resource for information. In addition to hosting different types of discussion groups, all three of these SNSs can serve as a platform or "virtual office" for the working group or team. For instance, a team can set up a private group page on LinkedIn and use it to communicate with one another as well as share information the team will need to conduct its work.

Q&A websites are very similar to discussion groups in that they provide a forum for people to ask questions and get answers from experts or knowledgeable professionals. There are literally hundreds of Q&A websites on the Internet and each site tends to target a different audience. Sites like Quora are considered high quality, general Q&A, which means that a wide array of topics are discussed on the site and the impact of disruptive users is limited by moderation, user profiles, website policy, and other controls that help maintain a constructive and useful environment. Reddit is another generalist Q&A site containing thousands of distinct discussion groups or "subreddits." The discussion groups on Reddit range from highly technical and professional to groups that engage in discussions and content sharing that most people would consider to be in extremely poor taste. But it is the lack of regulation and policing that appeals to a large portion of Reddit's audience, making it one of the top five most popular U.S. sites on the Web today. Another Q&A website likely to be useful to business professionals is StackExchange. This site is a collection of over 150 Q&A "communities" or groups where people share information. Many of these groups focus on programming and technology topics, but StackExchange also hosts communities for topics like Personal Finance & Money, Project Management, Personal Productivity, and Sustainable Living. Depending on the specific information needed, it is quite likely that some form of discussion group or Q&A website will prove useful in helping the group find answers to important questions in a timely manner.

Social search tools were discussed in Chapter 6 where you learned that many social networking sites like Facebook, YouTube, and Twitter have developed powerful search engines capable of finding information and multimedia content on their networks. These search tools have been largely overlooked by business professionals in favor of search engines like Google and Bing. However, for some topics, social media search engines may provide more timely and relevant information than Internet search engines.

Social Bookmarking Tools

Most Web browsers allow users to store links to online content by saving them to a list of favorites or bookmarks. This approach becomes cumbersome as more information is saved because lists grow long and difficult to use. Organizing bookmarks into folders helps a bit, but the folders tend to hide information and users can forget what folder they have stored information in.

Diigo, Delicious, Clipix, and Teamgum

Diigo, Delicious, Clipix, and Teamgum   **Social bookmarking** tools allow users to tag Web content with keywords of their choosing. Users can later retrieve those links by searching on one or more of these keywords. In addition to helping users retrieve the saved URLs of websites they want to return to, many social bookmarking sites can be used as an alternative search engine, helping users search for and discover Web content tagged by other users. This is what makes the bookmarking system "social." Information searches on these sites will produce different results than Google or Bing because the websites are categorized based on a **folksonomy** (folk taxonomy). In other words, humans tag websites differently than the computer algorithms used by Google or Bing, and that's why the search will generate a different and potentially more useful list of websites.

Delicious has a long history as a social bookmarking service. Founded in 2003, it was for many years the most popular application of its kind. Over the last decade however, its standing in the category has diminished as the company was bought and then sold several times. It appears that owners had trouble figuring out how to properly monetize the service. It is currently owned by Delicious Media, a joint venture between Domainer Suite, a website development company, and Science, Inc., an Internet technology investment company. While it continues to operate under its original brand name, Delicious, the company recently announced that its domain name would be changing back to the original, somewhat quirky spelling: **del.icio.us**.

In addition to developing new features that will attract social bookmarkers away from competing services, the company will have to reestablish its reputation and regain the trust of users who left Delicious during a turbulent time when it appeared the site would close down and leave users without a way to retrieve hundreds or thousands of bookmarks they had collected over a period of years. Today, the site continues to offer basic social bookmarking features. In addition, it appears the new management team is working on a business model where Delicious has become part of a sophisticated content/advertising/e-commerce network of publishers. Hopefully, the new strategy will allow the social bookmarking pioneer to become a successful company once again.

One of Delicious' competitors, **Diigo**, has developed several social bookmarking and collaboration tools, making it perhaps the best application in this category. On the Diigo platform, users can create either public or private groups for sharing Web content. Social tools on Diigo allow group members to comment on and discuss shared bookmarks as well as indicate their approval using a "Like" button. Diigo has a highlight tool that allows users to feature excerpts from Web pages for other members of the group and they can leave digital "sticky notes" with comments on websites for other members of the group to read. Public groups on Diigo can become quite large and take on the feel of an online community, with users contributing, liking, and commenting on bookmarks related to a particular topic.

While Diigo appears to be the most fully featured application in this category, two newer websites show strong potential for offering similar benefits. **Clipix** and **Teamgum** are social bookmarking sites that also allow users to tag Web content with their own keywords and phrases. Using the Teamgum application, users are encouraged to "Gum" (save) interesting Web content by clicking a small tab the program installs on your browser. The application makes saving and sharing images, videos and screenshots particularly easy. Teamgum also keeps everyone on the team updated about which members have viewed the shared content. Clipix users also tag content with their own keywords, but the application's user interface is almost completely visual, representing saved bookmarks as pictures. Diigo and Teamgum take a more traditional approach, using words to label the bookmarks with names and titles.

Folksonomy   a system of classifying and organizing online content into categories by the use of user-generated metadata such as keywords.

Content Creation and Sharing

Work groups and committees typically find it necessary to share documents and files as part of their collaborative efforts. In the past, a large amount of paper was consumed when everyone on the team was given a hard copy of the documents being used and discussed. With the advent of e-mail, workers began distributing documents electronically, which was perhaps the easiest way for working teams to share documents. Now business professionals are starting to experience the limitations of e-mail as a distribution and document storage system. It is not uncommon for successful business people to be overwhelmed by the volume of e-mail they receive each day. As a result, members of a team or work group will sometimes overlook an e-mail containing the latest version of an important document. Also, when documents are distributed via e-mail, it isn't always clear which team members are responsible for the different changes made to the original document. If the group determines that a previous version of the document is better than a later version, it isn't always easy to simply reverse the latest changes. And finally, some e-mail systems will reject the attachment of files that exceed a certain file size limit. This usually isn't a problem for text documents, but files containing pictures, sound, or other multimedia content can be problematic. Fortunately, today a number of different file-sharing and storage options are widely available.

Dropbox   **Dropbox** is a **cloud storage service** that makes it easy to access your documents from any of the devices you work on. Think of it as a shared hard drive for your computer, phone, and tablet computer. Dropbox also allows you to share files and folders with others, making it a great tool for document sharing. There are two Dropbox features that make it particularly attractive. First, saving files to Dropbox is just as easy as saving a file to your hard drive. Other cloud-based document services require you to manually upload and download files. Dropbox also maintains a version history record for documents, making it easy to see the changes made to a document and undo them if necessary. This is a great feature for teams working on collaborative writing projects. Dropbox prices its service based on the amount of storage space users anticipate needing. It also offers a free plan for people who will use less than 1 terabyte (1,024 gigabytes) of space. This makes Dropbox a good solution for students and small businesses. Business users will typically purchase a premium plan that provides for much more space, enhanced security, and account administrative features as well as API access, which will allow the company to integrate Dropbox with existing computer applications.

Box   Like Dropbox, **Box** is a cloud storage service but places greater emphasis on social tools and features, which make it a great choice for collaborating teams. Users can edit files stored on Box without downloading to their hard drives. Like many other social companies, Box has created an open-source API, allowing third-party developers to write applications for Box users that offer additional sharing and collaboration features. Over 60 such apps have been developed so far.

Wikis   While Dropbox and Box allow teams to collaborate on the creation of documents, a wiki allows teams to collaborate on the creation of Web pages. A wiki is a website that allows many people to add or update information found on the site. Wikis can be used as a work space for collaborative teams or they can become public websites built by groups of collaborators. The most popular wiki project is Wikipedia, the online encyclopedia (alexa.com, 2014). Businesses can create wikis for a particular product and allow employees and even customers to contribute information that will form a knowledge base resource for those who need information about the product.

There are many different sites like wikispaces.com and wikidot.com that offer free, basic wiki services to users. Wikis can be a particularly good way for a small business to distribute nonconfidential information to employees and business partners. Setting up a wiki is much easier than creating a full-featured website and it doesn't require anyone to administer the sharing of documents placed on the wiki.

Thanks to the features and benefits of social technology, teams and work groups today can communicate, conduct research, find information, and share results with others more easily than ever before. Videoconferencing in particular has enhanced our ability to converse and conduct meetings with people in distant locations. Social bookmarking services not only provide a better means of curating lists of websites we may want to return to someday, but these services also leverage the power of the crowd to index websites on the basis of human categorization, which can sometimes yield more useful results than the index systems of Web crawler search engines (see Chapter 6.) Finally, wikis and cloud-based services for document storage and sharing make it easier to save and organize our data. Many of these systems also provide features that facilitate collaboration among team or work group members improving organizational efficiency and productivity.

Questions

1. How can working teams use social media as an alternative to face-to-face meetings?

2. Why are social bookmarking services superior to the traditional method of saving "favorites" or "bookmarks" in a browser?

3. What are some ways you can use social media to solicit knowledge, information, and advice from experts on the Web?

4. What advantages do sites like Dropbox and Box have over e-mail as a way of sharing and collaborating on creating documents?

5. Why are search results generated on a social bookmarking site likely to be different from search results from Google or Bing?

Key Terms

application programming interface (API) 203
asynchronous JavaScript and XML (AJAX) 204
avatars 218
blogs 220
blogging platform 222
broadband 202
cascading style sheets (CSS) 204
cloud storage service 233
crowdfunding 212
crowdsourcing 212
document object model (DOM) 204
enterprise mashups 226
extendable markup language (XML) 204
feature convergence 207

folksonomy 232
giant global graph 211
hashtag activism 224
hypertext markup language (HTML) 204
Intranet 230
JavaScript 204
mashup 226
microblog 223
network effect 215
promoted tweets 224
really simple syndication (RSS) 227
semantic Web 211
sharing sites 208
social bookmarking 232

social media 202
social monitoring services 227
social network analysis (SNA) 211
social networking service (SNS) 207
social web 202
synchronous communication 230
terms of service (TOS) agreement 213
tweet 223
twittersphere 224
Usenet 210
Web 2.0 202
wiki 208
World Wide Web (WWW) 202
XMLHttpRequest 204

Assuring Your Learning

Discuss: Critical Thinking Questions

1. Explain the fundamental differences between Web 1.0 and Web 2.0.

2. Define social media and explain why how the use of social technologies fundamentally changed how people and organizations used the World Wide Web.

3. Compare the communication practices of organizations using the broadcast model versus the communication practices of organizations using a conversation model and Web 2.0 technologies.

4. What are the four primary factors described in the text that set the stage for Web 2.0 or the social Web that we enjoy today?

5. What is an API? Why should marketing professionals monitor changes in the access and functionality of APIs used by website and application developers?

6. Explain Facebook's Open Graph Initiative. How do Facebook's social plug-ins play a role in the Open Graph program?

7. Briefly describe each of the following kinds of social media:

    a. social networking service

    b. blog

    c. microblogging service

d. social bookmarking service

e. RSS reader

f. sharing communities

g. mashups

h. document storage and sharing site

8. Explain what is meant by "feature convergence" and how it is blurring the distinction between different types of social media platforms.

9. Each of the following was listed as an element of social media. Describe each and explain its role in shaping and defining the social Web.

a. user generated content

b. content control

c. conversation

d. community (common values, culture)

e. categorization by users (tagging)

f. real people

g. connections

h. constant updating

i. content separated from form

j. equipment independence

10. If you were looking for a job or wanted to build your reputation as an expert in some area related to marketing, what social media tools would you use for your personal branding strategy and why?

11. How can companies utilize social media collaboration tools to become more competitive?

12. Describe how mashups create new benefits and functionality from existing data or information.

13. Describe some common ways that marketers can benefit by using social media monitoring tools.

14. How will concern for individual privacy affect the growth and expansion of social networking services and other social Web applications?

Explore: Online and Interactive Exercises

1. Using online sources, research Facebook's Open Graph initiative. Make a list of "pros" and "cons" regarding these changes from the viewpoint of a Facebook user.

2. Using Google to find interesting and helpful blogs:

Step 1 First go to Google.com and enter a search word(s) or phrase related to the topic you are interested in.

Step 2 When the results page appears, click on the word "News" that appears under the left side of the search window. Then, click on the word "Tools" that appears under the right side of the search window.

Step 3 After you click Tools, a new row of filter words will appear. Look for the words "All news". Click on "All news" and select Blogs from the drop-down list. This will limit the SERP listings to blog Web pages.

Step 4 Find a blog or two that seem interesting and read a few posts. Leave comments in the response section (if available). See if the blog author or other readers reply.

3. Set up an account on two different RSS readers (e.g., Digg Reader and Feedly.com) and use them to subscribe to some blogs that are of interest to you (see question 2 above for how to find blogs). Prepare a report or presentation comparing the strengths and weakness of each application.

4. Using articles you can find online, prepare a report on the economic activity that takes place on Second Life. Describe how people make money in the virtual world and identify the opportunities and challenges associated with making a living via Second Life.

5. If you have an account on Twitter, download TweetDeck, an alternative interface for Twitter. Use TweetDeck and prepare a brief report on the advantages or disadvantages of using this program.

6. Visit the LinkedIn page for college students: *students.linkedin.com*. Using the information on this page, create a LinkedIn account and begin building your professional network. Search the Internet for additional tips on using LinkedIn to find jobs and prepare a brief report on your findings.

7. Using a search engine, find four examples of mashup applications. Prepare a report describing each one. If possible, identify the website(s) where data are pulled from to create the application.

8. Create an account on diigo.com, the social bookmarking site. Actively use it to tag and categorize Web pages that you want to remember for future viewing. Use the search engine on diigo.com to find pages that other users have tagged. Compare the effectiveness of your searches to similar searches using Google and Yahoo.

Analyze & Decide: Apply IT Concepts to Business Decisions

1. Use *socialmention.com* to evaluate the nature of conversations people are having about three telecommunications companies: AT&T, Verizon, and Sprint. Based on the four metrics provided by Social Mention, decide which company is viewed most favorably and least favorably by the marketplace. Using Twitter search, read a sample of tweets where people discuss the companies. Can you draw any conclusions as to specific reasons why the companies are viewed favorably or unfavorably?

2. Your boss would like you to recommend a free service for storing and sharing documents in the cloud. Create accounts at *Box.com* and *Dropbox.com*. Explore each service so that you understand how it works. Make a recommendation and provide your reasons for the service you select.

3. The supervisor of your department recently read a story about companies that use Second Life to conduct virtual meetings on the service. Create an account on Second Life and spend a few hours learning

how to use it. With a handful of other students, arrange to meet in Second Life for a brief discussion. Based on your experience, prepare a recommendation for your supervisor stating whether or not you think using Second Life for meetings would be a good idea. Justify your recommendation.

4. The marketing manager in your department just read a story about the rapid growth Snapchat, a relatively new social media app. Because your company sells fashion items to women in the 18- to 34-year-old age group, the manger thinks this may be a good platform for promoting your company's brand. You are asked to research the advertising and promotional opportunities on Snapchat and come up with a list of ways to promote your brand on the app. After visiting *snapchat.com/ads* to conduct your research, you might also want to use a search engine to find additional websites with information about advertising on Snapchat. After collecting your information, prepare a brief memo outlining your recommendations

Case 7.2

PeopleImages/DigitalVision/Getty Images

Business Case: Facebook Helps Songkick Rock the Ticket Sales Industry

Web 2.0 or social technology makes it possible for business to share information in mutually beneficial ways. Specifically, programming tools like APIs and SDKs make it possible for developers to create applications that will connect Facebook with other websites as well as applications that exchange data with applications on Facebook. For instance, Facebook has created several different programming tools that help organizations leverage the power social networking data for attracting and engaging customers. When IT and marketing managers understand the capabilities of Facebook's programs, they are better able to imagine the myriad ways to leverage the technology for engaging customers, promoting brands, enhancing brand reputations and reducing marketing expenses.

Songkick is the world's second largest seller of concert tickets, sending out over a million geo-targeted concert alerts each day via e-mail and push notifications. In a crowded industry of ticket sellers, Songkick's unique mission is to be the ". . . world's leading independent artist-ticketing and concert discovery platform." Their strategy is to treat artists with respect, providing multiple ways for musicians and bands to promote their music, grow their fan base, and provide a simple, cost–effective program for selling concert tickets. Their vision is simple, they want every show to sell out! For music fans, the mission is not just to sell you tickets to concerts you already know about, but to alert you to artists and events that you might not otherwise be aware of. As a business strategy, the company's mission and vision are inspirational, empowering and easy to understand. However, translating this simplicity into action requires a sophisticated combination of integrated technologies that rely heavily on APIs, SDKs, analytics programs, data sharing and social media.

For Songkick's customers to find value in the concert alerts they receive, the company must understand its customer base and be able to predict the kinds of shows people are most likely to be interested in. When customers create their Songkick account prior to purchasing tickets, they use Facebook's Login instead of filling out forms with lots of questions. This not only makes it easier to set up a Songkick account, but it gives the company access to a rich set of demographic and behavioral data that will later help them make personalized recommendations about artists and events. The *Facebook Login* feature is created by developers using the *Facebook SDK*, which provides tools programmer's use to integrate the login feature with their own platforms. Approximately 50% of Songkick's customers use the feature to create or log in to their account.

To further expand their understanding of customers and their behavior, Songkick's developers used the *Facebook SDK* and the *App Events Export API* to connect with the Facebook *Analytics for Apps* program. This provided Songkick with an in-depth view of its audience, their preferences, and behaviors associated with patterns of engagement and retention. Based on insights from *Analytics for Apps* program, Songkick was able to identify new features and services for their app that improved its value to customers. Finally, Songkick programmers used the *Facebook SDK* and APIs to integrate with the *Facebook App Ads* program. This program connected Songkick ads that appear on Facebook with the Songkick app, providing analytics and improving customer engagement. For instance, Songkick can use what Facebook calls *Deep Linking* with their ads. Deep Linking makes it easier for new app installers (customers) to reach the information that originally inspired them to try the service.

What this means in practice is that when a Facebook user sees a personalized Songkick ad promoting a Goo Goo Dolls concert, they will download and open the Songkick app, and be promptly taken to the app page for the Goo Goo Dolls concert, the reason they downloaded the app in the first place. Without Deep Linking, users would likely have to navigate several account setup and introductory screens before reaching the desired information. Deep Linking improves customer satisfaction, engagement, retention, and conversions.

As a result of Songkick's integration and data sharing with Facebook programs, the company experienced 7% more purchases by people using *Facebook Login* and a 15% increase in sales as a result of insights gained from *Analytics for Apps*. Furthermore, customers acquired from the Facebook network had a 35% higher lifetime value than customers acquired from other channels.

Questions

1. Why is Facebook motivated to share so much data about its users with other companies as well as creating ways for users to log in into other websites with their Facebook username and password?

2. What does Songkick gain by having customers use Facebook Login to create accounts and log in to their website or mobile app?

3. How does Facebook's Deep Linking program improve customer satisfaction and increased conversions (purchases)?

4. How did Songkick benefit from integrating its platform with Facebook's Analytics for Apps program?

5. How does Songkick use information it obtains from Facebook to effectively alert customers to artists and concert events they might not otherwise hear about? Couldn't they just as easily do that by sending information about all the upcoming concerts in a customer's geographic area?

Sources: For more information, see "Songkick Orchestrates a Sound Growth Strategy" at *developers.facebook.com* and *Songkick.com*.

Case 7.3

Business Case: AT&T's "It Can Wait" Campaign against Distracted Driving

Launched in 2010, AT&T has used the power of traditional and social media to change the way that people think and act about using their phones while driving. The *It Can Wait* campaign has grown over the years into a multipronged approach to reach new and experienced drivers from multiple age groups. Specific strategies that have been used during the life of the campaign so far include the following:

Online resource center   The campaign website (*itcanwait.com*) features downloadable resources and informational material for individuals, schools, and business organizations. The site also contains posters, educational guides, and fact sheets as well as links to videos and public service ads created for television. Recent additions to the site include an immersive, 360-view simulation of distracted driving, links to the DriveMode app (see below) and information about the organization's VR tour, which uses the VR technology to illustrate the dangers of distracted driving.

Traditional media   Campaign slogans "It can wait" and "No text is worth dying for" were incorporated into advertisements in print media, television, radio, and billboards. Television ads in particular were noted for their ability to convey the dramatic and emotional impact of fatal accidents resulting from distracted driving.

Social media   Multiple social media platforms were used to promote the campaign's message against distracted driving.

- Social buttons on the campaign's website are used to post anti-distracted-driving messages to a user's Facebook page and Twitter feed. These same messages provided links to the campaign website, encouraging people in the user's network to visit the site and learn more about the issue.

- The hash tag #ItCanWait has been appended to messages on Twitter and other social media platforms, resulting in over a billion impressions during the life of the campaign.

- Almost 130,000 people follow the campaign's Twitter handle, @ItCanWait. The campaign actively monitors and responds to tweets sent to @ItCanWait as well as messages with the #ItCanWait hashtag.

- Television ads and videos created specifically for social media have received over 6 million views on YouTube. A documentary about distracted driving by famed director Werner Herzog has over 3.3 million views on YouTube. Campaign advocates regularly share these videos with their social networks on Facebook, Twitter, and other social media platforms.

Online pledges   To further increase engagement with various audiences, people are encouraged to make a pledge on the campaign website to never engage in distracted driving. To increase public commitment to their pledges, people can post a "pledge picture" declaring their support of the #ItCanWait movement. So far, over 14 million people have made the pledge. After making their pledge, people can post it to Facebook and Twitter. Research has shown that people are more likely to follow through on public commitments.

The DriveMode app   AT&T created a smartphone app that allows users to customize auto-generated messages that are sent in response to any texts the user receives while driving. The app has been downloaded 10 million times. While the app receives generally positive reviews, comments on the apps download sites report a range of concerns including functionality issues that have caused users to abandon the app. AT&T also makes a commercial version of the app for business organizations that want to discourage employees from distracted driving during work.

Social support and advocacy All AT&T employees take the pledge and encourage every customer they speak with to take the pledge as well—that's 500,000 a day. In addition, the campaign has received public support from over 1,500 organizations across the United States and numerous celebrities have attended promotional events for the campaign and use their social media networks to express support for the campaign and its message.

VR Simulator The organization sponsors hundreds of events across the country each year where people have the opportunity to experience distracted driving in a 3D VR simulator developed by AT&T. Users sync their phones with the simulator, which then challenges them to operate a vehicle while reading and sending texts, with predictable outcomes.

The organization regularly collects data to evaluate the impact its efforts are having on distracted driving across the country. Some positive signs include the fact that more people are more aware of the dangers of texting and driving, and most people now agree that it is unsafe to text while driving. Preliminary research in a small number of states suggests a correlation between ItCanWait campaign activities and a reduction in distracted-driving-related accidents.

Questions

1. Visit the campaign website at *itcanwait.com*. After reviewing the website, describe which features you think are the most effective in terms of reducing the likelihood that people will engage in distracted driving.

2. Charlene Li and Josh Bernoff identified five key strategic priorities that companies should focus on to leverage the groundswell. Describe how the *It Can Wait* campaign has made use of the "Energizing" strategy described by Li and Bernoff.

3. Describe how the It Can Wait campaign has engaged in the "Listening" strategy described by Li and Bernoff.

4. Describe how the It Can Wait campaign has engaged in the "Talking" strategy described by Li and Bernoff.

5. Describe how the It Can Wait campaign has engaged in the "Supporting" strategy described by Li and Bernoff.

Sources: Herzog (2013), Schlackman (2014), AT&T (2016), Governors Highway Safety Association (2016), Kaker (2016).

References

alexa.com. "Alexa Topsites." June 5, 2014.

AT&T. "The AT&T Issue Brief Library: Promoting Safety." *about.att. com*, August 8, 2016.

Azfar, R. "KLM Pilots Artificial Intelligence-enabled Customer Service Responses on Social Media." *mobilemarketer.com*, October 3, 2016.

Baer, J. and A. Brown. (Hosts) "How a Volcano Created a World-Class Social Media Program for KLM Airlines" (Audio Podcast), *convinceandconvert.com*, n.d.

Berners-Lee, T. "Giant Global Graph." *Timbl's blog*, Decentralized Information Group, November 2007.

Carr, D. "Is Business Ready for Second Life?" *Baselinemag.com*, March 2007.

comScore. "2016 U.S. Cross Platform Future in Focus." *comScore. com*, 2016.

eMarketer. "US Digital Ad Spending to Surpass TV this Year." *eMarketer.com*, September 13, 2016.

Facebook. "Social Plugins." *developers.facebook.com*, June 10, 2014.

Gallagher, F. "How Many Users Does Google+ Really Have?" *techtimes. com*, May 6, 2015.

Grigorik, I. "Constructing the Object Model." developers.google.com, February 9, 2017.

Governors Highway Safety Association. "AT&T's It Can Wait." *ghsa. org*, 2016.

Hay, M. "Second Life Is Staying Alive." *good.is*, March 26, 2015.

Heathfield, S. "Use LinkedIn for Recruiting Employees." *Human resources.com*, accessed, August 12, 2012.

Herzog, W. "From One Second to the Next" Documentary Film, *YouTube.com*, August 7, 2013.

Hutchinson, A. "KLM Announces Facebook Messenger Integration – The Next Step for Messenger Commerce." *socialmediatoday.com*, March 30, 2016.

Johnson, E. "In the Shadow of Second Life, Virtual Reality Startups Say This Time It'll Work. Really." *recode.net*, July 31, 2015.

Kaker, R. "Campaign Analysis: 'It Can Wait'." *prezi.com*, April 13, 2016.

KLM. "KLM runs pilot with Artificial Intelligence provided by Digital-Genius." news.klm.com, September 29, 2016.

Koetsier, J. "KLM's 150 Social Media Customer Service Agents Generate $25M in Annual Revenue." *venturebeat.com*, May 21, 2015.

Kushner, D. "Beyond Second Life: Philip Rosedale's Gutsy Plan for a New Virtual-Reality Empire." *spectrum.ieee.org*, January 30, 2017.

Lee, D. "How Twitter changed the world, hashtag-by-hashtag." bbc.com, November 7, 2013.

Levine, R., C. Locke, D. Searls, and D. Weinberger. *The Cluetrain Manifesto: The End of Business as Usual*. Cambridge, MA: Perseus, 2000.

Li, C. and J. Bernoff. *Groundswell: Winning in a World Transformed by Social Technologies*. Cambridge, MA: Harvard Business Press, 2008.

Metz, R. "Second Life Is Back for a Third Life, This Time in Virtual Reality." *technologyreview.com*, January 27, 2017.

Outlaw, S. "What Type of Crowdfunding Is Best for You?" *Entrepreneur. com*, October 3, 2013.

Peterson, T. "Facebook Owns Social Login Scene, But Google's Creeping Up." *adage.com*, January 28, 2016.

Pierce, D. "Google+ as We Knew It Is Dead, But Google Is Still a Social Network." *wired.com*, March 2, 2015.

Schlackman, E. "Case Study: AT&T's 'It Can Wait' No Texting and Driving Campaign." sites.psu.edu, July 23, 2014.

Simson, M. "KLM Aims to Double Social Media ROI after €25 Million Haul in 2014." *runwaygirlnetwork.com*, February 7, 2015.

Talkwalker.com. "Social Media Analytics for KLM." n.d., Retrieved March 15, 2017.

techterms.com. "Javascript." June 10, 2014.

ter Haar, G. "What Has KLM Learned From 5 Years of Social Media Service?" *blog.klm.com*, April 17, 2015.

van Kesteren, A., J. Aubourg, J. Song, and H. Steen (eds.). "XML Http Request Level 1: W3C Working Draft 30 January 2014." *W3.org*, January 2014.

W3C. "XML Essentials." World Wide Web Consortium, *W3.org*, 2015.

Wikipedia. "Ajax (Programming)." June 10, 2014.

Wikipedia. "Crowdfunding." June 10, 2014.

CHAPTER 8

Retail, E-commerce, and Mobile Commerce Technology

CHAPTER OUTLINE	LEARNING OUTCOMES
Case 8.1 Opening Case: Macy's Races Ahead with Mobile Retail Strategies	
8.1 Retailing Technology	**8.1 Describe** how the concept of omni-channel retailing is changing the nature of shopping for consumers.
8.2 Business-to-Consumer (B2C) E-commerce	**8.2 Identify** five key challenges faced by online retail businesses in the Business-to-Consumer (B2C) marketplace.
8.3 Business-to-Business (B2B) E-commerce and E-procurement	**8.3 Identify** various ways that e-businesses are facilitating trade between buyers and sellers in the Business-to-Business (B2B) marketplace.
8.4 Mobile Commerce	**8.4 Understand** how mobile technologies are creating opportunities for new forms of commerce in established industries.
8.5 Mobile Transactions and Financial Services	**8.5 Recognize** how mobile payment methods benefit both consumers and retailers.
Case 8.2 Business Case: Chegg's Mobile Strategy	
Case 8.3 Video Case: Searching with Pictures Using MVS	

Introduction

This is both an exciting and challenging time to be a retailer. Traditional brick-and-mortar stores face increasingly intense competition from other traditional retailers as well as competitors in the online and mobile retail channels. Consumers, armed with mobile devices, have more information than ever before about products, prices, and alternative places to buy products. A particular source of frustration for traditional retailers is the practice of showrooming, where consumers visit a store to look at merchandise, seek information and advice from salespeople, maybe even try on clothes, and then leave the store to make their purchases online from a company that offers lower prices.

Online retailers also face significant challenges. Maintaining an e-commerce website requires ongoing investment in new technologies designed to enhance the online shopping experience, increase operational and logistical efficiency, as well as maintain high levels of customer satisfaction. Thanks to social media, dissatisfied customers now have numerous forums for informing others about frustrating experiences they might have with a company. It can be difficult meeting customer expectations that seem to grow more and more demanding every day.

Companies that are branching out into mobile commerce face challenges as well. For years, industry pundits have said that mobile commerce, or m-commerce, is going to be huge. But those predictions have failed to materialize for a number of reasons, leaving some to question their investments in mobile technology. However, there are signs that mobile devices have finally begun to make an impact on retailing in noticeable ways. Nevertheless, the question still remains whether or not this emerging channel will become as big a force as some have predicted for years. In this chapter, you will read about the forces that are shaping consumer shopping behavior and the ways that traditional, online, and mobile retailers are using technology to address the many challenges they face.

Barcode A machine-readable code consisting of numbers and a pattern of thick and thin lines that can be scanned to identify the object on which the code appears.

Showrooming The practice of examining products in a traditional retail store, sometimes with the help of a salesperson, and then purchasing the product online.

Quick response (QR) code A machine-readable code typically used to store a link to a URL or Web address that can be read by a mobile device.

Short message service (SMS) A technology used to send and receive text messages on mobile devices via a telecommunications network.

Case 8.1 Opening Case

Francesco Carta fotografo/Moment Open/Getty Images

Chris Ratcliffe/Bloomberg/Getty Images

KNSY/Corbis/Getty Images

Macy's Races Ahead with Mobile Retail Strategies

Mobile devices, particularly smartphones, have become a key tool in the arsenal of modern-day shoppers. Using **barcode** scanner apps, customers in brick-and-mortar retail stores can quickly compare prices with other stores and online retailers. They can access product information, check expert and consumer product reviews, and even purchase products from online retailers. This practice, called **showrooming**, represents a significant threat to many traditional retailers who continue to ignore the impact of mobile consumer behavior.

Showrooming is frustrating to retailers who bear the costs of providing sales support, product inventory and maintaining a store front, only to see customers purchase products at a lower price from an online retailer with lower overhead costs. At one point, Target asked several of its vendors to create special products, only sold in Target stores, in an attempt to stifle consumer comparison shopping via mobile devices (Zimmerman, 2012). But other retailers, recognizing the pervasive nature of mobile shopping trends, are developing strategies to embrace and engage the mobile shopper.

Department store giant Macy's is recognized as a pioneer when it comes to using mobile technologies to enhance the shopping experience of its customers (**Table 8.1**). The online trade magazine *Advertising Age*

says that Macy's is one of the most innovative when it comes to digital, social, and mobile technology (**Figure 8.1**). Macy's uses in-store displays to encourage customers to use mobile devices while shopping. The *Backstage Pass Program* is designed to enhance the in-store shopping experience at Macy's. Using **quick response (QR) codes** and **short message service (SMS)** technology, customers can easily access fun and informative 30-second videos that highlight the retailer's celebrity designers and fashion experts (see related videos at **youtube.com/Macys**). Mobile shoppers can access the videos by scanning the QR codes posted on displays in each department. Shoppers who do not have a QR code scanner can access the videos by texting a special keyword to Macy's using codes supplied on the displays. Backstage Pass is an example of what marketers call a **mobile display strategy**. It is supported by an integrated communications campaign involving traditional television and print media advertising. Macy's can measure customer interest in the program by tracking the number of times customers watch the videos. Based on the initial success of the program, Macy's increased spending on mobile display strategies by 70%.

Another key mobile strategy used by Macy's is the **SMS database strategy**, growing its list of customers who have opted in to receive discounts and special offers via text message. According to Martine Reardon, executive vice president of national marketing at Macy's, New York,

TABLE 8.1	Opening Case Overview
Company	Macy's, Inc.
The business	Macy's is a premier department store retailer with a significant online e-commerce website and mobile shopping app.
Product lines	Macy's department stores offer a range of products, including fashionable clothing, jewelry, footwear, furniture, bedding, small kitchen appliances, cookware, and other household goods.
Business challenges	Implementation of an omni-channel retail concept that allows consumers to freely and seamlessly engage with Macy's through a traditional storefront, e-commerce website, or mobile technology.
Digital technology	Macy's embraces technology to enhance the shopping experience through the use of QR codes and SMS text messaging, mobile videos to provide information about merchandise, and an SMS database for distribution of mobile coupons and marketing communications.
Taglines	"The Magic of Macy's," "Macy's, way to shop!"

© gpointstudio/Shutterstock

Augmented reality A technology that superimposes a computer-generated image onto an image of the real world to provide information or entertainment.

FIGURE 8.1 Macy's encourages shoppers to use mobile technology in its stores through a variety of strategies, including mobile videos that describe merchandise, benefits from mobile check-in, and fun augmented-reality apps.

the retailer is including SMS short codes in most of its printed coupons to encourage customers to opt in to receive coupons and other offers via text message. Macy's customers have responded well to these kinds of promotions, so growing the list of people who opt in to this program should be easy.

With its **mobile check-in strategy**, Macy's has partnered with Foursquare and Shopkick to create check-in programs that reinforce shopping behavior at retail outlets. Mobile customers using the Shopkick app on their phones receive points on their account just for visiting a Macy's store. They may also receive special offers from Macy's via the Shopkick app when they visit particular departments or scan featured merchandise. The points can be redeemed for restaurant vouchers, iTunes gift cards, and gift cards from a variety of participating retailers. Macy's partnered with Foursquare and a charitable foundation created by insurance company Aflac. For every consumer who checks-in at Macy's via the Foursquare app, Aflac donates $1 to its charity, The Aflac Cancer Center and Blood Disorders Service of Children's Healthcare of Atlanta. Aflac made the same offer to customers who checked in while watching Macy's famous Thanksgiving Day Parade, using an

entertainment check-in service called GetGlue.com (now called tvtag.com). These kinds of partnerships and programs not only reinforce store shopping behavior but also enhance Macy's positive brand reputation among target consumers.

Via the **mobile payment** strategy, customers can pay for products at Macy's using Google Wallet, a mobile payment app (**Figure 8.2**). At the register, customers simply tap their phones on a Near-Field Communications (NFC) device in order to transfer funds to Macy's. Google Wallet is one of several approaches to mobile payment competing to become the dominant alternative to traditional credit cards. Mobile payment is expected to become widespread in the near future as banks, retailers, and telecommunications companies gain experience with the technology. (Read more about mobile payment in Section 8.5.)

In an **augmented reality** strategy, during the Thanksgiving and Christmas holiday season, Macy's runs a program to benefit the Make-A-Wish Foundation. Over the past few years, Macy's has donated $1 for every customer who visits a store and "mails" a letter to Santa. In 2011, Macy's made that visit even more fun, inviting customers to take pictures of their children in special holiday displays using augmented reality apps

FIGURE 8.2 Customers at Macy's can pay for purchases with their smartphones by using a mobile wallet app.

that inserted one of the animated characters associated with the campaign into the picture. Pictures could then be uploaded into a holiday card template, shared by e-mail, or posted to the customer's Facebook page.

While other retailers are still trying to understand mobile consumer behavior, Macy's is already adapting to a new retail environment where increasing numbers of consumers are using handheld devices. It has shown that traditional brick-and-mortar retailers can enhance the in-store shopping experience using mobile technologies in a variety of ways.

Questions

1. Describe how each of Macy's mobile retail strategies enhances the in-store shopping experience for customers.

2. What will most customers think about Target's attempt to make mobile price comparison more difficult?

3. How does Macy's benefit from the use of location-based apps such as Foursquare and Shopkick?

4. Why is it important that Macy's get customers to "opt in" to its program before sending promotional text messages?

5. Does Macy's Backstage Pass Program really add value to the customer, or is it just a "gimmick" with short-term benefits?

6. Traditional retailers spend a considerable amount of money to maintain an inventory of products and provide salespeople to service in-store customers. Explain whether or not the practice of showrooming is unethical. What can retailers do to respond to the showrooming trend?

Sources: Compiled from Zimmerman (2012), Tsirulnik (2011), Macy's (2011), Johnson (2011), Kats (2012).

8.1 Retailing Technology

Life is not easy for managers in the retail sector these days. The challenges faced by retailers have never been more complex, frustrating, and fraught with peril. Consumers are demanding, price-conscious, and easily swayed by competitors. Technology is both a blessing and a curse. Countless new and innovative technology "solutions" to retailing problems are offered by a dizzying array of vendors. Many of the newest technologies promise to give retailers a competitive edge in the marketplace but are unproven. Budgets for technology are limited, and making the wrong decision can lead to financial consequences, operational failures, and lost customers. However, because of intense competition, retailers cannot afford to be too conservative, or they risk losing out to competitors with technologies that enhance the shopping experience, reduce costs, integrate sales channels, and improve recordkeeping, data collection, and analysis of key performance indicators (KPIs).

Keeping Up with Consumer Demands and Behavior

Understanding and responding to consumer needs and behavior is the key to survival for the modern retailer. The challenge, however, is increasingly complex as retailers are confronted with a number of difficult industrywide trends and changing consumer behavior (Galgey and Pattinson, 2013).

Empowered Price Sensitivity Consumers have always been concerned about price. In today's retail environment, the consumer is more empowered than ever to find the lowest price available for a product. Using the Web and mobile technology, consumers can look up information about alternative products and prices from a variety of local and online retailers using a mobile device. Retailers need clear strategies to respond to the empowered consumer by price matching or finding ways to offer greater value.

Nonlinear Search and Influence Patterns   The path by which consumers pursue purchases today is often varied and unpredictable. In simpler times, consumers were largely influenced by mass media advertising that drove them to brick-and-mortar stores for purchase. While things were perhaps never quite that simple, consumers today are influenced by a range of new communications channels including social media, mobile ads, e-mail, search marketing, and other digital communications.

Channel Hopping   Just as consumers are influenced by a greater number of communications channels, their options for purchasing products have increased. Consumers can now purchase products through traditional retailers, online, and via mobile devices and apps. Some experts are beginning to view social media as a potential retail channel called **social commerce**. For instance, Dell sells millions of dollars of refurbished computer equipment each year through its @delloutlet Twitter account. The manner in which consumers use each channel varies. Some consumers will use a brick-and-mortar store to gather information about a product but purchase it online. Others will do their research online but prefer to purchase the product through a traditional retailer. Some may plan to purchase the product at a store, but if they find that the product they want is not available, they will buy it from their mobile device while in the store. The many combinations of shopping channel, communications channel, and stage of the shopping process are enormous and make strategic planning a challenge. Modern retailers will increasingly rely on data analytics to distinguish patterns or trends in consumer shopping behavior across channels to identify the best ways to satisfy customer needs.

Digital Immigrants, Natives, and Dependents   Retailers have long been aware of the difference between digital immigrants and digital natives. **Digital natives** are the first generation to have grown up surrounded by digital devices (i.e., computers, smartphones, digital cameras, video recorders, etc.) and Internet connectivity. They are comfortable using technology to move easily between various retail channels to optimize their purchasing on price, convenience, and desire for instant gratification. **Digital immigrants**, however, are older, and although they are increasingly comfortable with technology, they fundamentally view retail channels as separate and distinct. They are much less likely than natives to incorporate mobile technology into their shopping behavior. **Digital dependents** represent the emerging generation of young people who are growing up in a world of broadband connections, constant connectivity, and related technology and become uncomfortable if they do not have access to it. This generation will place even greater demands on retailers, expecting to use technology to accomplish all facets of the shopping experience. Brick-and-mortar retailers will continue to play an important role in the lives of this generation, but they will expect in-store shopping to be fully integrated with the technology they have come to depend on.

Need for Convenience   As economic and social factors lead to more stressful lives, consumers will be looking for products and shopping channels that reduce the impact on their time and financial resources, while satisfying their demand for immediate gratification and desirable goods and services.

The Omni-Channel Retailing Concept

As the retailing world began to evolve as a result of digital technology and the Internet, new channels emerged that were initially thought to be separate and distinct. Most retailers and a fairly large segment of the consumer market still view online shopping (**e-commerce**) and **mobile commerce** (**m-commerce**) channels as competing with traditional brick-and-mortar stores.

As you read in the opening case, Target feels threatened by customers who showroom its stores using mobile devices. However, as businesses learn about the full potential of mobile and other digital technologies, the distinction between the newer channels and in-store retailing is beginning to blur. While most businesses currently operate their e-commerce and mobile channels separately from the traditional retail channel, it is expected that strategies integrating the customer experience across channels will emerge, resulting in what the National Retail Federation (2011) refers to as the **omni-channel retailing** approach.

As illustrated in **Figure 8.3**, many businesses operate separate retail channels. For instance, in-store product prices may be different from those the customer finds on the company's e-commerce website and direct mail catalog. Records of customer purchases from the e-commerce site may not be available to service personnel assisting the customer at the store level. But retail strategy is evolving. The ultimate goal is to offer consumers multiple brand-based "touchpoints" that leverage the strengths of each channel. For instance, a company with a truly integrated or omni-channel strategy might spark a customer's interest using mobile advertising or direct mail catalogs. The customer then visits a brick-and-mortar store to examine the product firsthand and speak to a salesperson. In-store purchases might be made using one of the mobile payment methods discussed later in this chapter. If the store does not have the particular size or color of the product desired, the customer might order it by accessing the store's e-commerce site with his or her smartphone by scanning a QR code placed strategically on an in-store display. The product would then be delivered through the mail. Product returns could be handled through the mail or returned to the store, depending on what is most convenient for the customer. Customer service reps in a call center would have a record of the customer's purchase regardless of which channel the transaction had been completed through. The omni-channel strategy will also take into consideration the potential impact of social media, whereby customers interact with the brand on sites such as Facebook or Twitter and share brand experiences with others in their social network.

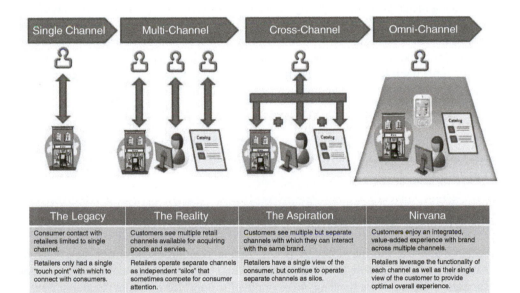

The Legacy	The Reality	The Aspiration	Nirvana
Consumer contact with retailers limited to single channel.	Customers see multiple retail channels available for acquiring goods and servies.	Customers see multiple but separate channels with which they can interact with the same brand.	Customers enjoy an integrated, value-added experience with brand across multiple channels.
Retailers only had a single "touch point" with which to connect with consumers.	Retailers operate separate channels as independent "silos" that sometimes compete for consumer attention.	Retailers have a single view of the consumer, but continue to operate separate channels as silos.	Retailers leverage the functionality of each channel as well as their single view of the customer to provide optimal overall experience.

FIGURE 8.3 Retail strategy is evolving toward an omni-channel approach (adapted from National Retail Federation, 2011).

Questions

1. Describe the factors that influence consumer shopping behavior today.
2. What does the concept of digital native, digital immigrant, and digital dependent help us to understand about people's use of technology during shopping activities?
3. Why are retailers likely to view technology as both a blessing and a curse?
4. Describe how an omni-channel retailer is likely to be different from a traditional, single-channel retailer?

8.2 Business-to-Consumer (B2C) E-commerce

During the late 1990s, the idea of purchasing things online was still a novel concept. People who purchased books and other low-priced items from websites were seen as innovators. Nowadays, shopping for things online and finding the best deal by comparing online prices with those in brick-and-mortar stores are common consumer behaviors. In the past decade, the variety of goods and services available through e-commerce sites has skyrocketed. If you look through older textbooks in the IT field, you will find authors predicting that e-commerce will only be successful with low-priced consumer goods. But we now know that this is simply not the case. People today purchase everything from toothpaste to cars and diamond rings online. E-commerce in the B2B sector is even larger than it is in the B2C marketplace.

Retail sales via online channels, financial services, travel services, and digital products (e.g., music- and movie-streaming services) are widely popular forms of B2C commerce. The most well-known B2C site is Amazon.com, whose IT developments received U.S. patents that keep it ahead of competition. Many of these are described in **IT at Work 8.1**.

Several of the leading online service industries are banking, trading of securities (stocks, bonds), and employment, travel, and real estate services.

Online Banking

Online banking includes various banking activities conducted via the Internet instead of at a physical bank location. Online banking, also called direct banking, offers capabilities ranging from paying bills to applying for a loan. Customers can check balances and transfer funds at any time of day. For banks, it offers an inexpensive alternative to branch banking. Transaction costs are about 2 cents per transaction versus $1.07 at a physical branch.

Most brick-and-mortar conventional banks provide online banking services and use e-commerce as a major competitive strategy. Customers are aware that if they bank exclusively with a brick-and-mortar institution, they may be missing out on high-paying investment options or competitive loan rates that easily undercut those of many traditional banking entities. For an illustration of how online banks operate differently than traditional banks, see **IT at Work 8.2**.

International and Multiple-Currency Banking

Electronic fund transfer (EFT)
A transfer of funds from one bank account to another over a computerized network.

International banking and the ability to handle trading in multiple currencies are critical for international trade. **Electronic fund transfer (EFT)** and electronic letters of credit are important services in international banking. An example of support for e-commerce global trade is provided by TradeCard (tradecard.com). TradeCard offers a *software-as-a-service (SaaS)* model that provides supply chain collaboration and a trade finance compliance platform.

Although some international retail purchasing can be done by giving a credit card number, other transactions may require cross-border banking support. For example, Hong Kong and Shanghai Bank (HSBC) has developed a special system, HSBCnet, to provide online banking in 60 countries. Using this system, the bank has leveraged its reputation and infrastructure in the developing economies of Asia to rapidly become a major international bank without developing an extensive new branch network.

Online Recruiting

Most companies and government agencies advertise job openings, accept résumés, and take applications via the Internet. The online job market is especially effective and active for technology-oriented jobs. While sites such as dice.com and monster.com can still be

IT at Work 8.1

Amazon.com's IT Patents Create Competitive Edge

Entrepreneur and e-commerce pioneer Jeff Bezos envisioned the huge potential for retail sales over the Internet and selected books for his e-commerce venture. In July 1995, Bezos started Amazon.com, offering books via an electronic catalog from its website. Key features offered by Amazon.com were broad selection, low prices, easy searching and ordering, useful product information and personalization, secure payment systems, and efficient order fulfillment. Early on, recognizing the importance of order fulfillment, Amazon.com invested hundreds of millions of dollars in building physical warehouses designed for shipping small packages to hundreds of thousands of customers.

Amazon has continually revised its business model by improving the customer's experience. For example, customers can personalize their Amazon accounts and manage orders online with the patented One-Click order feature. This personalized service includes an **electronic wallet (e-wallet)**, which enables shoppers to place an order in a secure manner without the need to enter their address, credit card number, and so forth, each time they shop. One-Click also allows customers to view their order status and make changes on orders that have not yet entered the shipping process. To emphasize its large inventory of books, Amazon obtained registered trademarks for its retail slogans: "Earth's Biggest Selection" and "If It's in Print, It's in Stock."

In addition, Amazon added services and alliances to attract more customers and increase sales. In January 2002, Amazon.com declared its first-ever profit during the 2001 fourth quarter; 2003 was the first year it cleared a profit in each quarter.

Amazon has heavily invested in its IT infrastructure and obtained patents for much of the technology that powers its website. The following list of patents gives a glimpse into the legal side of the e-commerce giant and explains why numerous major retailers, such as Sears and Sony, have used Amazon.com as their sales portal.

- 6,525,747: Method and system for conducting a discussion relating to an item
- 6,029,141: Internet-based customer referral system, also known as the Affiliate program
- 5,999,924: Method for producing sequenced queries
- 5,963,949: Method for data gathering around forms and search barriers

- 5,960,411: Method and system for placing a purchase order via a communications network (One-Click purchase)
- 5,826,258: Method and apparatus for structuring the querying and interpretation of semistructured information
- 5,727,163: Secure method for communicating credit card data when placing an order on a nonsecure network
- 5,715,399: Secure method and system for communicating a list of credit card numbers over a nonsecure network

Amazon launched the Kindle e-reader in 2007. Its success demonstrated the viability of the e-book market and led to the entry of numerous competitors, such as Barnes & Noble's Nook and the Apple iPad. E-books now account for about 30% of all books sold, and Amazon's share of the e-book market is 65% (Bercovici, 2014). Since 2011, Amazon has sold more e-books than print books (Miller and Bosman, 2011).

In mid-2010, Amazon started rolling out a software upgrade for Kindle, adding the ability for users to share e-book passages with others on Facebook and Twitter. The new social networking feature in Version 2.5 adds another Web link to the standard Kindle and the larger Kindle DX, as Amazon finds itself in an increasingly competitive market because of the iPad's features. The iPad is designed for reading digital books, watching online video, listening to music, and Web browsing, making it more of a tablet device than simply an e-reader. Amazon also created the Kindle app that can be used on a wide range of mobile devices, so now customers can purchase and read e-books from Amazon without having to purchase a Kindle reader.

Finally, as you read in Chapter 6, Amazon has been a pioneer in the development of recommendation engines designed to suggest products to customers based on their purchase history and shopping behavior. Amazon's recommendation system is considered among the best in the industry.

IT at Work Questions

1. Why is order fulfillment critical to Amazon's success?
2. Why did Amazon patent One-Click and other IT infrastructure developments?
3. How has Amazon adapted the Kindle to new technologies?
4. Why would other retailers form an alliance with Amazon.com?

Sources: Compiled from Gonsalves (2010), Rappa (2010), Bercovici (2014), Miller and Bosman (2011).

helpful, job seekers nowadays are employing a variety of social media tools, including the use of LinkedIn.com, to develop a network of contacts and establish an online reputation. A number of studies suggest that over 95% of recruiters use LinkedIn to identify prospective job candidates. Some candidates have used blogging as a way of creating a personal brand, establishing themselves as an expert in a particular area by sharing content that reflects their professional interests, expertise, and insight. For candidates that wish to employ this strategy without the hassle of maintaining their own personal blogs, LinkedIn provides a forum called LinkedIn Pulse. In many countries, governments must advertise job openings on the Internet.

Electronic wallet (e-wallet) A software application that can store encrypted information about a user's credit cards, bank accounts, and other information necessary to complete electronic transactions, eliminating the need to re-enter the information during the transaction.

IT at Work 8.2

Ally Bank – Building Trust and Confidence Online

A Crisis of Confidence in Consumer Banking

While the first Internet-only bank, or direct bank, appeared in the mid-1980s, it wasn't until around 2010 that these online institutions became mainstream. Some have attributed general consumer frustration resulting from the 2008 economic crisis with generating consumer interest in new, agile banking institutions that appear to be more responsive to consumer needs for convenience and customer support.

Banks have historically built their reputations on trust and consumer confidence that they would act ethically, protect consumers' money, and make customer interests a priority. However, the financial crisis of 2008 led to large-scale consumer mistrust and frustration with traditional banks and financial services companies. Banking is now considered one of the least trustworthy industries by consumers (Edelman, 2013, O'Connell, 2013). Consumers also believe that irresponsible behavior by banking organizations was a primary cause of the economic meltdown that led to high levels of unemployment and fiscal uncertainty in the United States and across the globe (The Financial Brand, 2013).

Many banks only made matters worse during this period when they instituted a number of business practices that further alienated consumers (O'Connell, 2013). During a time when consumers were already frustrated with financial institutions because of the economic crisis, many banks hiked interest rates on loans, reduced the interest rate they paid on consumer savings and checking accounts, made it more difficult for consumers to open credit accounts, imposed new types of fees on consumer services, and oftentimes failed to transparently disclose information about fees and interest rates in promotional messages and other forms of communication with consumers. As a result, consumer confidence in the banking industry dropped to an all-time low following the 2008 financial crisis (Gallup, 2014). See **Figure 8.4**.

In an effort to take advantage of widespread consumer frustration and dissatisfaction with traditional banking companies, a number of new, smaller, and more agile banks are moving to offer alternative approaches to consumer banking services. Ally Bank is a popular Internet-only bank that is widely recognized for its success in developing a business model with significant appeal to retail banking customers.

Overview of Ally Bank

Ally Bank, based in Midvale, Utah, is a subsidiary of Ally Financial, formerly GMAC, the financial unit of General Motors Corporation. Since its launch in 2009, Ally Bank has worked hard to create a public image that differentiates itself from business practices that caused consumers to mistrust and grow frustrated with traditional banks and financial service corporations. Ally's marketing communications messages emphasize that it:

- Puts customer needs first.
- Offers consumers smart banking alternatives with no hidden fees and higher interest rates on savings and investment accounts.
- Is friendly, transparent, and easy to work with, unlike large, fee-happy banks.
- Is new, innovative, fun and offers an attractive alternative to traditional banking corporations.

What Makes Ally Bank Different?

Apart from a brand image that differentiates Ally Bank from its competitors, the company uses technology to distinguish itself in three important ways:

1. The company is part of a growing group of Internet-only or direct banks. Instead of brick-and-mortar bank branches, Ally Bank's customers use the Web to access their accounts, make transactions, and monitor their funds.
2. Unlike other banks that have been slow to embrace social media, Ally Bank is recognized as a leader in the banking industry for its use of social media to engage consumers.
3. Ally Bank offers customers mobile banking apps to make doing business with the company even more convenient.

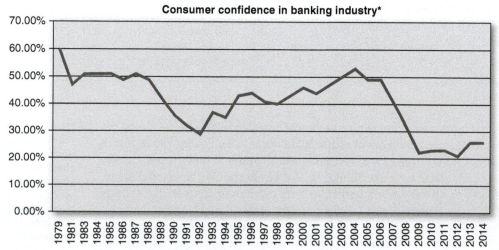

Consumer confidence in banking industry*

*percent of consumers who indicated a "great deal" or "quite a lot" of confidence in banks

FIGURE 8.4   Consumer confidence in the banking industry from 1979 to 2014. *Source:* Gallup, 2014.

Internet banks provide customers with the convenience of 24/7 banking services through the Web. Consumers access their account information using a computer, tablet, or smartphone. Deposits are made by scanning or photographing checks and transferring the image to the bank. Checks can also be mailed to the bank. Internet banks typically offer savings and checking accounts, certificates of deposit, retirement accounts, and various types of loans and mortgages. Because Internet banks do not bear the cost of maintaining physical branch offices, they often offer customers better interest rates and lower fees compared to traditional banks. To retrieve cash, customers use ATM machines. Many Internet banks reimburse customers for fees they incur when using the ATM machines of other banks.

Social Media

Traditional banks have been reluctant to utilize social media channels for engaging consumers for fear of violating long-standing banking regulations that govern disclosures and consumer privacy. Given the current level of consumer frustration, many banks are probably also hesitant about what their customers are likely to say about them through comments, ratings, and reviews on social media. This hesitation to embrace new media has created an opportunity for upstart banking organizations such as Ally Bank. Since the Internet bank lacks a physical presence, social media is the primary channel for interacting with customers in ways that promote trust, confidence, and loyalty, key ingredients for maintaining long-term financial relationships.

Ally Bank is recognized as an industry leader when it comes to its innovative use of social media. According to Smith (2014), Ally Bank excels in three areas of social media:

- Communicating the brand via social channels
- Using data to drive social marketing decisions
- Cross-platform integration of marketing strategies

Examples of Ally's social media marketing include using Twitter to offer personal finance advice. Ally has also teamed up with Bankrate.com to sponsor a monthly, hour-long TweetChat (discussion group) called #AllyBRchat, where participants discuss a range of personal finance issues. The firm's Facebook page is used to engage consumers with links to Ally's "Straight Talk Blog," opinion polls, and educational videos. On Ally Bank's YouTube channel, visitors will find installments of financial advice programs with titles such as "Ally Bank Financial Etiquette," "Discovering Retirement," and "Behind the Scenes with Kiplinger." Across all of these social platforms, Ally Bank offers consumers information, advice, and tools by posting over 1,500 pieces of content every month (Tejwani, 2012).

Ally Bank's Mobile Strategy

Ally Bank's adoption of mobile technology follows the bank's philosophy of putting the customer first and creating the most convenient ways for them to access and manage their money. According to Carrie Sumlin, a Digital Deposits Executive at Ally Bank, the company's goal with both mobile and Web technology is to make sure that all applications live up to the promise of transparency, simplicity, and ease of use (Yurcan, 2014). First introduced in April 2012, Ally's mobile apps offer a wide range of functionality including account management, bill payment, fund transfers to external banks, and a tool for finding ATM and cash-back locations. Managers at Ally Bank are constantly evaluating customer reaction to the mobile apps by monitoring how the apps are used, which devices are being used, and customer feedback collected through social media, Web-based consumer surveys, and calls to their customer service center.

Results

In a 2015 study of the top 100 banks, Ally Bank was ranked #1 for its use of social media. The study reported that Ally demonstrated the highest level of engagement compared to other banks. Customers found a series of posts about DeEtte Sauer, who became a competitive swimmer and adopted a healthier lifestyle after retiring, particularly interesting. The company used Facebook, Twitter, and YouTube videos to tell her story. More than 60,000 people responded to the series by liking, commenting, or sharing Ally Bank's posts. "Our goal was to engage consumers in a dialogue by featuring real-life retirees and their decisive financial turning points and actions that enabled their current retirement lifestyle," according to a bank spokesperson (McCormick, 2016).

Ally Bank was rated among the best in the nation by the Pew Charitable Trusts for its use of best disclosure practices, evidence that the company is succeeding in its goal to be transparent about fees and other information important to consumers (Malone, 2014).

Ally Bank is regularly recognized by organizations and publications such as Money Magazine, Huffington Post, Kiplinger, Forester Research, and Bank Tracker as being among the best banks in the industry, providing the best banking website, and providing an excellent customer experience. For an extensive list of awards and recognitions, see the Media Center—Awards and Recognitions page on the **Allybank.com** website.

Conclusion

Ally Bank is clearly an innovator and a disruptive competitor in an otherwise tradition-bound industry that has not always been responsive to consumer needs. The company has distinguished itself by its innovative, technology-driven approach to providing financial services, a provocative and engaging marketing and branding strategy, and an ability to communicate with consumers through social media channels. In the short time that Ally Bank has been in business, it has attracted over 825,000 customers, manages $45 billion in retail deposits, and achieves customer satisfaction levels of over 90% (Ally Financial, 2014). It is recognized as a leader in the direct banking segment of the consumer banking industry.

IT at Work Questions

1. Visit Ally Bank's Facebook page. Identify examples of how the company speaks in an authentic or real voice to its customers.

2. How has Ally Bank attempted to take advantage of negative consumer sentiment toward traditional banks in the industry?

3. As Ally Bank develops its mobile banking service, what guides the company's development of the necessary technological applications?

4. Visit Ally Bank's YouTube channel. After reviewing video clips of Ally's past advertising campaigns, how would you describe its brand image?

5. Visit Allybank.com and review the information about its banking services. Do you think that Internet-only banks will eventually attract a significant number of customers away from traditional banks?

Issues in Online Retailing

Despite the tremendous growth of online retailers, many face challenges that can interfere with business growth. Major issues include the following:

1. **Resolving channel conflict**   Sellers that are click-and-mortar companies, such as Levi's or GM, face a conflict with their regular wholesale and retail distributors when they circumvent those distributors by selling online directly to customers. (These distributors are other businesses that carry the company's product.) This situation is called **channel conflict** because it is a conflict between an online selling channel and physical selling channels. Channel conflict has forced some companies to limit their B2C efforts or not to sell direct online. An alternative approach is to try to collaborate in some way with the existing distributors whose services may be restructured. For example, an auto company could allow customers to configure a car online but require that the car be picked up from a dealer, where customers could also arrange financing, warranties, and service.

2. **Resolving conflicts within click-and-mortar organizations**   When an established company sells online directly to customers, it creates conflict with its own offline operations. Conflicts may arise in areas such as pricing of products and services, allocation of resources (e.g., advertising budget), and logistics services provided by the offline activities to the online activities (e.g., handling of returns of items bought online). To minimize this type of conflict, companies may separate the online division from the traditional division. The downside is that separation can increase expenses and reduce the synergy between the two organizational parts.

3. **Managing order fulfillment and logistics**   Online retailers face tough order fulfillment and **logistics** problems when selling online because of the need to design systems to accept and process a huge volume of small orders, to physically pick items from warehouse shelves and put them into boxes, to be sure that the correct labels are applied, and to accept returns. The return process is referred to as reverse logistics.

4. **Determining viability and risk of online retailers**   Many pure online retailers went bankrupt in the dot.com era, the result of problems with cash flow, customer acquisition, order fulfillment, and demand forecasting. Online competition, especially in commodity-type products such as CDs, toys, books, or groceries, became very fierce due to the ease of entry into the marketplace. As Porter's (2008) five competitive forces model explains, low entry barriers intensify competition in an industry. So a problem most new and established online retailers face is to determine how long to operate while you are still losing money and how to finance those losses.

5. **Identifying appropriate revenue (business) models**   One early dot.com model was to generate enough revenue from advertising to keep the business afloat until the customer base reached critical mass. This model did not always work. Too many dot.coms were competing for too few advertising dollars, which went mainly to a small number of well-known sites such as AOL, MSN, Google, and Yahoo. In addition, there was a "chicken-and-egg" problem: Sites could not get advertisers to come if they did not have enough visitors. To succeed in e-commerce, it is necessary to identify appropriate revenue models and modify those models as the market changes.

Online Business and Marketing Planning

Online marketing planning is very similar to any other marketing plan. It is not a best practice, though, and somewhat strange, to devise separate online and offline plans because that is not how customers perceive a business. Here are several online business and planning recommendations:

1. Build the marketing plan around the customer, rather than on products.
2. Monitor progress toward the one-year vision for the business in order to identify when adjustments are needed, and then be agile enough to respond.

Channel conflict   Competition between a manufacturer's distribution partners who sell through different channels. Channel conflict can occur at the wholesale, retail, or internal sales department level.

3. Identify all key assumptions in the marketing plan. When there is evidence that those assumptions are wrong, identify the new assumptions and adjust the plan.

4. Make data-driven, fact-based plans.

Questions

1. Describe how digital content and services can lead to significantly lower costs.

2. Why does channel conflict sometimes occur when companies sell their products through both traditional and online channels?

3. How has Amazon maintained its competitive edge?

4. Describe some of the ways that Ally Bank has become one of the most successful direct banks in the industry today.

5. Explain why retail banking has become one of the least trusted industries by consumers since the early 2000s.

6. List three online marketing planning recommendations.

8.3 | Business-to-Business (B2B) E-commerce and E-procurement

In **business-to-business (B2B)** markets, the buyers, sellers, and transactions involve only organizations. B2B comprises about 85% of e-commerce dollar volume. It covers applications that enable an enterprise to form electronic relationships with its distributors, resellers, suppliers, customers, and other partners. By using B2B, organizations can restructure their supply chains and partner relationships.

There are several business models for B2B applications. The major ones are sell-side marketplaces and e-sourcing (the buy-side marketplace).

Sell-Side Marketplaces

In sell-side B2B markets, there are basically two types of e-commerce: direct and marketplace. In direct e-commerce, organizations sell their products or services to other organizations from their own private website or one managed by a third party. This model is similar to the B2C model in which the buyer is expected to come to the seller's site, view catalogs, and place an order. In the B2B sell-side marketplace, however, the buyer is an organization. B2B marketplace e-commerce takes place on websites where the products of many different companies can be purchased. The marketplace model creates much greater competition for the companies that sell their products on the site and therefore creates an advantage for buyers. For this reason, some sellers prefer the direct model. A recent introduction of a B2B marketplace website is **Amazon Business**. **Alibaba** is a wholesaling e-commerce site that primarily sells products from Chinese manufacturers to other companies around the world.

In an attempt to avoid the cut-throat competition that can be produced by marketplace e-commerce sites, some B2B sellers are integrating back-office solutions to their direct e-commerce sites that add extra value to their buyers and create exit barriers for customers. For example, integrated B2B solutions can include things such as digital order writing for fields sales staff, automated order sync, which integrates orders with accounting or other administrative software, and integrations with Enterprise Resource Planning (ERP) systems. These integrated solutions can streamline the procurement process, saving the buyer time and money, giving them a reason to stick with a seller that offers these benefits.

Some B2B sellers such as **Dell Computer** use auctions extensively. In addition to auctions from their own websites, organizations can use third-party auction sites, such as **eBay**, to liquidate items. Companies such as **Overstock** help organizations to auction obsolete and excess assets and inventories.

B2B e-commerce websites are used by hundreds of thousands of companies. This strategy can be especially powerful for companies with superb reputations. The seller can be either a manufacturer (e.g., IBM), or a distributor (e.g., *avnet.com* is an example of a large distributor in IT), or a retailer (e.g., **Office Depot**). The seller uses e-commerce to increase sales, reduce selling and advertising expenditures, increase delivery speed, and reduce administrative costs.

E-Sourcing

E-sourcing refers to many different procurement methods that make use of an electronic venue for identifying, evaluating, selecting, negotiating, and collaborating with suppliers. The primary methods are online auctions, RFQ (request for quote) processing, and private exchanges. E-sourcing also applies to many other secondary activities, which add to the cycle time and transaction costs when performed using traditional methods. Secondary activities include trading partner collaboration, contract negotiation, and supplier selection.

E-Procurement

Corporate procurement, also called **corporate purchasing**, deals with the transactional elements of buying products and services by an organization for its operational and functional needs. Organizations procure materials to produce finished goods, which is referred to as **direct procurement**, and products for daily operational needs, which is referred to as **indirect procurement**. **E-procurement** refers to the reengineered procurement process using e-business technologies and strategies. Strategies and solutions linked to e-procurement have two basic goals:

- **Control costs** The first goal is to control corporate spending. Organizations want to spend intelligently for procurement activities to maximize the value of their spending, that is, to ensure that money spent to procure items results in procuring the right products at the best value. Corporate e-procurement constitutes a substantial portion of an organization's operational spending. For example, it is common for large manufacturing organizations to spend millions of U.S. dollars procuring products and services. Organizations thus design e-procurement systems to facilitate and control overall procurement spending.
- **Simplify processes** The second goal is to streamline the procurement process to make it efficient. Inefficiencies in the procurement process introduce delays in ordering and receiving items and tax internal resources.

The two goals of cost control and streamlining can be met in three ways:

1. Streamline the e-procurement process within an organization's value chain. Doing so reduces the number of employees needed to process purchasing, reduces the procurement cycle time to order and receive items, and empowers an organization's staff with enough information about the products and services to enable them to make intelligent decisions when procuring items.

2. Align the organization's procurement process with those of other trading partners, which belong to the organization's virtual supply chain. Alignment can be achieved by automating the process from end to end, including trading partner's systems, and simplifies the buying process. This enables suppliers to react efficiently to buyers' needs.

3. Use appropriate e-procurement strategies and solutions. Organizations analyze spending patterns in an effort to improve spending decisions and outcomes.

Electronic Data Interchange (EDI) Systems

Electronic data interchange (EDI) systems are typically set up by large companies for the efficient procurement of products from an assortment of established vendors. While EDI technologies predate large scale use of the Internet, most EDI systems now use the Internet as the primary method of transmitting data. EDI systems are designed as a way to efficiently exchange documents, eliminating many of the costs associated with processing paper documents. As such, they lend themselves to buyers and suppliers that need to convey information to each other in the form of purchase orders, invoices, bills of lading, customs documents, shipping status documents, payment documents, and so on. While EDIs use the Internet for data transmission, they are not accessible to the public. Instead, only approved or authorized vendors are given access to a company's EDI system.

Public and Private Exchanges

Exchanges are sites where many buyers and sellers conduct business transactions. They may be public or private, depending on whether or not they are open to the public. The two most common types of B2B online exchanges are vertical and horizontal exchanges. **Vertical exchanges** serve one industry (e.g., automotive, chemical), along the entire supply chain. **Horizontal exchanges** serve many industries that use the same products or services (e.g., office supplies, cleaning materials), although many exchanges sell a variety of wholesale goods, primarily to retail businesses.

1. **Vertical exchanges for direct materials**   These are B2B marketplaces where *direct materials*—materials that are inputs to manufacturing or specialized services such as health care—are traded, usually in *large quantities*. An example is PlasticsNet.com, a vertical marketplace for industry professionals.

2. **Horizontal exchanges**   These are many-to-many e-marketplaces for indirect materials, such as office supplies, light bulbs, and cleaning materials used by *any industry*. Because these products are used for maintenance, repair, and operations (MRO) (and not resold to generate revenue), these indirect supplies are called **MRO supplies**. Prices are fixed or negotiated in this systematic exchange. Examples include **Worldbid B2B Market**, **Global Sources** and **Alibaba.com**.

Another important facet of managing procurement is **demand management**—knowing or predicting what to buy, when, and how much. The best procurement cost is zero, when people are not buying what they do not need.

Questions

1. Briefly differentiate between the sell-side marketplace and e-sourcing.
2. What are the two basic goals of e-procurement? How can those goals be met?
3. What is the role of exchanges in B2B?
4. Explain why maverick buying might take place and its impact on procurement costs.

8.4 Mobile Commerce

In 1997, two Coca-Cola vending machines that accepted payment via SMS text message were installed in Helsinki, Finland. Ever since, industry experts and pundits have been predicting that mobile commerce was about to become "the next big thing" in marketing and the sale of consumer goods. Before we explore how mobile commerce has evolved since 1997, let us define some terms related to this topic:

Mobile commerce or m-commerce   The buying or selling of goods and services using a wireless, handheld device such as a cell phone or tablet (slate) computer.

Mobile e-commerce   The use of a wireless handheld devices to order and/or pay for goods and services from online vendors. *Example: Ordering a pair of shoes from Zappos.com using a mobile app, or purchasing music from iTunes from your iPod.*

Mobile retailing   The use of mobile technology to promote, enhance, and add value to the in-store shopping experience. *Example: Using a coupon on your cell phone when checking out at the Hard Rock Café, or "checking in" to a retail location using a mobile app from ShopKick.com or Foursquare.com.*

Mobile marketing   A variety of activities used by organizations to engage, communicate, and interact over Wi-Fi and telecommunications networks with consumers using wireless, handheld devices. *Example: Sending special offers to customers who have opted in to receive discounts via SMS text message or advertising a brand on a popular mobile game app such as Angry Birds.* For additional illustrations of mobile marketing, see **IT at Work 8.3**.

IT at Work 8.3

Angry Birds Make Mobile Game Developers Happy

Have you ever played popular mobile games such as Angry Birds, Candy Crush, or Pokémon Go? For years, games have been the most popular type of mobile app, second only to news apps. According to Business Insider, over 20% of the apps in Apple's App Store were mobile games, the largest category. While many apps in this category are free, 93% of app downloaders are willing to pay for game apps, compared to 76% for news apps. While the average time that people spend playing mobile games is only about 2 minutes a day, "core gamers," or the 20% that spend the most time playing, can log 1.6 hours a day or almost 12 hours a week. Revenue from the 2016 mobile game market is estimated to exceed $36 billion, and expect it to rise to over $52 billion by 2019.

To put this in perspective, in 2009, iOS and Android mobile gaming apps accounted for just 11% of the portable (handheld) gaming market dominated by Sony and Nintendo. By 2017, mobile games accounted for 37% of the overall gaming market. It is also the fastest growing segment (+21.3%) compared to PC games (+3.4%) and game consoles (+0.9%). Clearly, mobile gaming apps have become a disruptive force in the marketplace, displacing two historically strong companies who underestimated the potential of the mobile platform for gaming. Even more impressive is the fact that the aforementioned statistics are based on revenues produced by paid downloads and don't reflect the millions of free games downloaded every year. But even free games make money through advertising and in-app purchases. Some games, such as Angry Birds, become so popular that they generate additional revenue through sales of game-related merchandise (**Figure 8.5**).

FIGURE 8.5   Angry Birds was such a popular mobile game that it generated additional revenue from sales of clothing, plush toys, posters, lunch boxes, and even bed linens.

© Ian Dagnall/Alamy

IT at Work Questions

1. Why did established companies such as Nintendo and Sony fail to gain an early position in the growing mobile gaming market?

2. How are mobile games different from traditional video games? What advantages do mobile game apps have over traditional video games?

3. Gaming and social media are among the most popular mobile app categories in the United States. What do you think this says about the role of mobile devices in the lives of U.S. consumers?

4. Since many gaming apps are free, how do developers make money in this category?

5. From a business perspective, what evidence suggests that the mobile gaming market represents a significant marketplace?

Sources: Compiled from Meola (2016), Statista.com (2016), Asante (2012).

These four terms are not mutually exclusive. Mobile e-commerce, mobile retailing, and mobile marketing are all forms of mobile commerce. Mobile e-commerce emphasizes the use of mobile apps and mobile websites for carrying out transactions and does not necessarily involve interaction with a traditional retail store. **Mobile retailing**, on the other hand, emphasizes in-store shopping using a mobile device but could include situations where the customer ultimately orders from a website or mobile app. **Mobile marketing** is the term used to describe promotional strategies and tactics that encourage both mobile e-commerce and mobile retail. See **IT at Work 8.4** for examples of mobile marketing. This overlap is a reflection of the evolution toward the omni-channel retail concept discussed earlier in the chapter (see Figure 8.3).

Although there have been some interesting and even successful examples of m-commerce since 1997, predictions about mobile technology becoming a pervasive force in consumer retailing have proven overly optimistic over the years. There are several reasons why consumers and businesses have been slow to embrace m-commerce:

- Relatively primitive mobile devices (compared to modern smartphones and tablets)
- Concerns about privacy and security
- Slow network connection speeds
- Limited market size
- Limited and inconvenient mobile payment options
- Lack of technological standardization (devices, OSs, browsers, etc.)

However, many of these barriers have been reduced or eliminated. As you read in the previous section, the number of people who now own mobile devices, particularly smartphones, has grown dramatically. According to one widely quoted statistic, more people own cell phones today than own toothbrushes! Telecommunications carriers have expanded their coverage of populated areas using high-speed networks. Modern smartphones and tablet devices have features that make shopping via bright colorful screens fun and easy. Mobile devices have become the dominant way that people engage in some types of Internet activity, such as using social media, while other reports indicate that more people use mobile devices now than use personal computers. While security will always be an evolving concern, consumer comfort with completing transactions on mobile devices continues to grow. A number of mobile payment methods are emerging that are more convenient than traditional transaction methods. So after years of waiting, it appears that earlier predictions about m-commerce are finally starting to come true. In this section, we will describe some of the many ways businesses and consumers are using mobile technologies to buy and sell goods and services.

Information: Competitive Advantage in Mobile Commerce

Integrating mobile technology with a brand's retail and e-commerce strategy provides another important benefit to business: customer information and identification. When customers interact with a brand using a mobile device, information is collected about the customer that can be used to optimize the interaction. For instance, when customers use a brand's mobile app to shop for products, their shopping experience can be customized based on the company's knowledge of previous purchases, payment methods, product preferences, and even location.

In-Store Tracking In-store shopping experiences can be optimized through mobile technology that can track a customer's movement through a retail store. This is analogous to e-commerce sites that track the pages a customer looks at in order to better understand consumer interests and to make decisions about website design. Tracking how a customer moves through a store, noting what displays the customer looks at, or what departments the customer spends the most time in can be extremely helpful for understanding

IT at Work 8.4

Wireless Marketing and Advertising in Action

Industry analysts expect advertising in the mobile channel to heat up. Increasing numbers of smartphones, better browsers, enhanced GPS capabilities, and better ways of measuring advertising effectiveness are all factors powering this growth. The following are a few examples of wireless advertising in action.

Location-Based Marketing   Many apps that people use for shopping, travel, entertainment, and product/service reviews provide information useful to advertisers. In addition, many of these apps provide information about a user's GPS location while others employ a "mobile check-in" strategy. As previously discussed, many retailers are deploying in-store tracking with the use of apps. Advertisers can use this information to generate targeted in-app advertising messages, increasing the chances that the ads will lead to a purchase transaction.

Foursquare.com was one of the most popular apps in the emerging field of **mobile location-based marketing** and mobile advertising. It used social media and gamification to encourage users to share their location through mobile check-in. However, now that many other apps and social media platforms offer similar features, Foursquare has become less popular. But the number of companies using location-based marketing continues to increase.

Mobile Location-Based Marketing   A marketing strategy that uses information from a mobile device's GPS or customer's mobile check-in on a social network to determine the content of marketing communications they receive on the device (e.g., advertisements, coupons, special offers).

Another location-based mobile marketing app is Shopkick. When the **Shopkick** app is activated, users receive points when they visit a participating retailer. Retailers use the app to encourage and reward specific kinds of shopper behavior. Shopkick points are used to reward consumers for visiting specific locations in a store, purchasing products, scanning featured products, and even participating in brief surveys. Shoppers often receive targeted discounts and promotional offers when they are in a store. Shopkick users can trade in their points for restaurant vouchers, iTunes cards, or gift cards from participating retailers.

Augmented Reality (AR)   AR apps superimpose computer-generated graphic images on pictures of real things (e.g., people, rooms, buildings, roads, etc.). This technology can be used by advertisers in several ways. For instance, a mobile phone user might point his or her phone camera at an office building and activate an AR app that generates the logos of all food-service outlets (e.g., Starbucks, Subway, McDonalds) inside the building. Furniture retailer IKEA offers shoppers an AR app that allows them to project images of its products onto pictures of the rooms in their homes so they can "visualize" how the products will look. Legos and Converse also use AR to help customers visualize their products. Industry experts expect that AR advertising will grow as smartphone users become more familiar with the concept (see **Figure 8.6**). You can find several interesting examples of AR applications on YouTube. Simply go to YouTube and enter "augmented reality" in the search engine.

Jon Simon Feature Photo Service/NewsCom

FIGURE 8.6   IBM's augmented reality shopping app automatically delivers personalized coupons, customer reviews, and hidden product details (such as whether packaging is biodegradable) to smartphones as consumers browse store shelves. The app transforms marketing promotions from intrusions into services that customers welcome.

Mobile Search   Almost 60% of all Internet searches are conducted from a mobile device, and over half of all Web traffic comes from mobile devices. As a result, Google and other Internet search engines now use the performance of a company's mobile website as part of the criteria for ranking listing in search results. SEO specialists must now focus on a set of new factors for optimizing websites for mobile search to help companies maintain their status in search listings. Marketers need to think about context or how the things that people look for using a mobile device differ from the things they search for on a PC. For instance, 88% of all searches with the phrase "near me" come from mobile devices. This should then shape the content used on a company's mobile website to influence ranking by search engines and to provide the most useful information to consumers. Some companies, such as Yellow Pages, use location-based technology to create mobile directory apps that allow users to find services near their current location.

IT at Work Questions

1. Although the benefits of location-based apps for business are perhaps obvious, many previous attempts to get people to use apps that identify their location have met with limited results. Why do you think consumers are less enthusiastic about location apps and what would it take to prompt people to use a location-based app regularly?

2. What kind of information do you think people are most likely to search for with their smartphone? Based on your answer, what specific kinds of information should retailers make readily available on their mobile websites?

3. At present, AR apps are still relatively new and have not enjoyed high levels of adoption. What do you predict will happen with this technology? What applications of AR seem most interesting to you? What barriers will have to be overcome to get people to use this technology?

Sources: Compiled from Williams (2016), Gevelber (2016), *YellowPages.com*

individual consumer preferences as well as creating optimal store layout. Systems for tracking customers based on signals emitted from cell phones and other mobile devices are being deployed. However, stores must be cautious about how they use these systems because consumers generally respond quite negatively to the idea when asked. Consumers generally don't trust stores to keep their data private or secure. Recent news stories about data breaches involving credit card and other information at large retailers suggest there is reason for concern. Stores that use "opt-in" methods, receiving the customer's permission in exchange for some defined benefit, are more likely to get a positive reception. Those that opt in typically expect to receive discounts or some form of meaningful convenience benefit. Some will only agree to **in-store tracking** in exchange for free products. Consumer acceptance is sometimes accomplished through loyalty programs that offer discounts and special premiums to customers who opt in.

Not all tracking systems rely on user smartphones. Disney uses signal emitting wristbands to make everything in the Magic Kingdom more magical. The wristbands aid guests with hotel check-ins, replace tickets for park admission, make it easy to reserve times for popular rides, and even help Disney employees to deliver the correct dinners to hungry guests in large, crowded restaurants. Still, retailers and the makers of in-store tracking systems need to be concerned about consumer backlash related to this new technology since less magical applications are considered "creepy" by many shoppers. Therefore, it is important that brands involved in mobile e-commerce and mobile retailing have clear privacy statements and use an opt-in system to obtain permission from customers before tracking their online and offline shopping behaviors.

While relatively few businesses fully utilize mobile tracking and monitoring systems at present, as brands become more sophisticated with mobile technology, it is expected they will strive to gain a competitive advantage by using this information to provide better service, convenience, and a more personalized, enjoyable shopping experience, both online and in traditional stores.

Quick Response (QR) Codes In Japan, many products are tagged with QR codes. Consumers in that country frequently scan QR codes to access product information from a mobile device. Using a barcode scanner app and the camera feature of a mobile device, customers scan the QR code containing a link to an Internet Web page. You read in the case at the beginning of this chapter how Macy's uses QR codes on in-store displays to direct customers to promotional videos that feature its products. The QR code is supposed to be an easier alternative to typing a URL address into a **mobile browser** (see **Figure 8.7**). While QR codes have not been as popular in the United States as they are in Asia, marketers

Mobile location-based marketing A marketing strategy that uses information from a mobile device's GPS or customer's mobile check-in on a social network to determine the content of marketing communications they receive on the device (e.g., advertisements, coupons, special offers).

Mobile browser A Web browser that is optimized to display Web content effectively on a small mobile device such as a smartphone.

FIGURE 8.7 Smartphone users can scan QR codes that help them easily access product information on the Internet without the hassle of typing a URL code into a mobile browser.

have used them in print advertising and direct mail ads with some success. Charitable organizations use QR codes on the outside of direct mail solicitations. Scanning the code takes the user to a video explaining the mission of the organization and typically makes a more compelling request for a donation than is possible through print media. Additionally, responses to the QR code promotions can be tracked and used to evaluate program effectiveness.

Some experts believe, however, that QR code technology is never going to be as popular in the United States as it is in Asia. They cite studies reporting that many smartphone users simply do not know what to do with a QR code. Other research suggests users think that the scanning process is inconvenient or that QR codes frequently direct users to pages that do not really contain anything of interest. For QR codes to become something American consumers use frequently, businesses will have to prove that they help mobile users find content that is interesting and valuable. **Mobile visual search** technology is emerging as an alternative to QR codes. See Video Case 8.3 at the end of this chapter for additional information.

Mobile visual search engine A search engine that uses an image instead of a text-based query to search for information on the Web.

Mobile Entertainment

Mobile entertainment is expanding on wireless devices. Most notable are music, movies, videos, games, adult entertainment, sports, and gambling apps. For more information about the most popular mobile app category, mobile gaming, see IT at Work 8.3.

Sports enthusiasts enjoy a large number of apps and services on their mobile devices. Apps exist to check game scores; track news about specific athletes, teams, or sports; take part in fantasy team contests such as fantasy football; and participate in sports-oriented social networking services. A number of sports-related games such as mobile golf and sports trivia apps are widely available. There are even apps designed to provide tips and information for improving your own athletic performance. Apps are available to record workout times, schedule training exercises, record heart rates and a variety of other information related to athletic training. The iPhone even has an app that analyzes a person's golf swing and provides advice for improving performance.

ESPN is widely acknowledged as a leader in mobile marketing to the sports fan. It offers a number of popular branded mobile apps that deliver information and entertainment to its target audience. It also utilizes well-designed mobile websites and has a large database of fans that have opted in to receive sports-related news alerts sent to their phones via text messages.

Industry analysts predict that recent improvements in mobile devices will lead to an even bigger increase in the number of people who watch video clips, movies, and television programming on their mobile devices. The screen size of tablet computers make watching video programming more attractive than on a smartphone. However, the number of people viewing video on smartphones seems to be increasing as well as smartphone sizes increase. Popular fee-based video streaming services such as Netflix, Amazon, and Hulu now offer mobile apps for most mobile devices.

The iTunes Store, Google, and Amazon continue to be leading distributors of digital music, movies, TV shows, e-books, and podcasts available to consumers. Mobile users can also access music from digital streaming sites such as Pandora.com and Spotify.com. Both of these services offer free streaming music. Users can upgrade their accounts by paying a subscription fee, which then reduces the amount of advertising they are exposed to.

While still relatively small, the mobile gambling industry is expected to grow substantially over the next few years. Some predict that this type of mobile commerce could generate as much as $20 billion in the near future. Primary growth of this market is expected to take place in Japan and other Asian countries, such as horse racing in Hong Kong. Current laws in the United States prohibit most forms of online gambling; consequently, gambling via mobile devices is largely unavailable in the United States.

Many mobile apps are available for consumers interested in home-based entertainment activities. The Food Network offers an app with tips and recipes for fine dining and entertaining. **Martha Stewart** publishes articles about home entertainment and lifestyle apps while a number of bartending apps with numerous recipes for cocktails and party drinks can be found on iTunes and Google Play.

Hotel Services and Travel Go Wireless

In recent years, smartphones and other mobile devices have become essential travel aids. Most major airlines, hotel chains, and Internet travel agencies have developed mobile apps to help travelers manage their arrangements. Airlines frequently give passengers the option of receiving up-to-date information about their flights through an app or via SMS text messaging. Google Maps is perhaps one of the most popular apps used by travelers, particularly those traveling by automobile. Even AAA, the automobile club, has a mobile app that helps drivers plan their trips and an app for drivers who need roadside assistance. Other interesting mobile travel tools include apps that translate voice or text when traveling abroad, apps for finding nearby Wi-Fi hotspots, and apps created by a number of popular travel guides.

Most large hotel chains, independent hotels, and inns offer guests in-room, wireless high-speed Internet connections, although this is not always a free service. Some of these same hotels offer Wi-Fi Internet access in public areas such as the lobby and meeting rooms. Larger hotel chains have apps that allow guests to make reservations, check their bills, and locate hotel services using a mobile app. Starwood, Hilton, and other hotels have mobile check-in programs whereby guests use their mobile devices to gain access to their rooms. This makes it possible to check in to the hotel without having to stop first at the front desk. Most airlines now offer travelers the option of loading a boarding pass onto their mobile devices (see **Figure 8.8**).

FIGURE 8.8 Travelers use mobile apps to book reservations, find directions, and locate reviews and recommendations for a wide range of travel and hospitality services.

Mobile Social Networking

More people access social media from social apps than from personal computers now. As a result, Facebook and other popular sites have added mobile features in recent years to stay competitive. Some social media, such as the popular Snapchat platform, is entirely app based. Much as Web-based social networking, mobile social networking occurs in virtual communities. All of the most popular social networking sites offer apps that allow users to access their accounts from a smartphone or other mobile device, making social media a primary driver of growth in the mobile app industry.

Questions

1. Describe some of the ways that people are using mobile devices to shop for products and services.

2. What are some ways in which traditional brick-and-mortar retailers can use mobile technology to enhance a customer's in-store shopping experience?

3. List the types of mobile entertainment available to consumers.

4. List some ways that travelers and travel-related businesses are using mobile technology.

5. How are companies using QR codes to promote products and services to mobile consumers? Why are QR codes not as popular in the United States as they are in Asia and other parts of the world?

6. Explain why the mobile gaming market represents such a lucrative market opportunity.

8.5 Mobile Transactions and Financial Services

Mobile Payment Systems

Consumers use mobile devices for a wide range of shopping and other activities. As discussed in the case at the beginning of this chapter, shoppers are using mobile devices to compare prices, research products prior to purchase, and identify alternative product options and alternative retailers. Increasingly, mobile devices are becoming an attractive way to pay for products. Mobile payment is increasingly being accepted by retailers and is popular with consumers who now can use a variety of apps available on iTunes, Google Play, and from banks, credit card companies, and even smartphone manufacturers such as Samsung. Some forms of mobile payment represent an attractive option for consumers who do not have credit cards. Additionally, retailers may benefit from new payment options that carry lower transaction costs compared to what banks charge when credit cards are used. In 2016, approximately 38.4 million Americans will have used a mobile phone to purchase goods or services at least once in the preceding six months. That's only 19.4% of U.S. smartphone users; however by 2020, the figure is expect to increase to 33.1%. Proximity mobile payments, a common method based on RFID (Radio Frequency Identification) technology, are expected to reach $62.49 billion in 2017 and increase to more than $314 billion by 2020. RFID payment systems typically allow consumers to transfer payment authorization to a vendor by simply tapping on or passing their phone over the vendor's mobile payment terminal.

While most consumer mobile payment systems are based on the use of a smartphone and related technologies such as SMS text messaging, some companies are building mobile payment into wristbands, key fobs, watches, and similar wearables. Lyle and Scott, a Scottish knitwear brand, has even built mobile payment into a jacket (more specifically, the wrist cuff of the jacket).

As mobile commerce grows, a greater demand exists for payment systems that make transactions from mobile devices convenient, safe, and secure. A number of businesses have attempted to meet this demand using a variety of technologies. There are two basic transaction types of interest: using a mobile device for the online purchase of goods and services (e.g., ordering a book from Amazon.com) and for payment of goods and services in a traditional brick-and-mortar store. Here are examples of some approaches under development or in use today:

Charge to Phone Bill with SMS Confirmation This e-commerce payment solution is a lot easier than entering credit card and other information on a small mobile handheld device. It requires users to set up an account with a payment company such as zong. com. When completing an online transaction, users click the "ZONG–Buy with Mobile" button and enter their phone number. They receive an SMS text message with a secure

PIN number that they enter on the e-commerce website to complete the transaction. The amount of the charge is then added to the payer's phone bill, and the telecom carrier remits this amount to the payee. Telecom companies may deduct a service charge from the amount paid. Example: boku.com.

Near-Field Communications (NFC)   NFC is a high frequency form of RFID technology. Unlike other types of RFID technology, NFC devices are capable of both sending and receiving information with other NFC devices. At check-out, the mobile user simply passes or taps his or her phone on a merchant terminal and payment is transferred. Users receive an SMS text message confirmation. While Google Wallet has received considerable attention in the technology press, in part because of Google's power and influence in the industry, relatively few consumers can use this option. Only a small number of phones have the required NFC feature. Additionally, the program is only available to people with Citi MasterCard with PayPass or Google's prepaid credit card. However, the number of phones equipped with NFC technology is expected to increase, which in turn will increase mobile payment options based on NFC. Example: Google Wallet.

QR Code Systems   A number of companies are developing mobile payment systems that generate a QR code on the user's phone, which is, in turn, scanned by the retailer. Starbucks uses this approach with its mobile payment system (Tsirulnik, 2011). Customers create an account with Starbucks as part of the retailer's loyalty program and transfer money to a prepaid account. Upon check-out, a user activates the Starbucks app, which creates a barcode that can be scanned at check-out. The funds are then deducted from the user's account. With other QR code systems, the merchant has a QR code that the customer scans and then authorizes payment when a confirmation message appears. Several other retailers are adopting QR-code-based systems including: Walmart, Kohls, IKEA, and Chase Pay.

Credit Card 1 Webform   Using a mobile Web browser, the buyer makes online purchases by entering his or her credit card number and other identifying information just the way that person would if using a personal computer. This process can be cumbersome given the smaller screens and keyboards on most mobile devices, but it is an option.

Transfer of Funds from Payment Account Using SMS   (see **obopay.com** and **paypal. com**). Using this approach, the user creates an account at a company such as obopay.com and transfers money into it from a bank or credit card account. Using a mobile phone and SMS, the user can then transfer money to anyone else with a mobile phone number. The receiver must create an account at the payment company in order to retrieve the funds. Example: obopay.com, paypal.com.

Mobile Phone Card Reader   (see **Square.com** and **Paypal.com**). This novel approach requires mobile phone users to insert a small card reader into the audio jack of their mobile device. The card reader, which resembles a small cube (Square) or pyramid (PayPal), allows those with accounts at Square or PayPal to make or receive credit card payments without a merchant account.

Almost all of the payment systems thus described are illustrated by videos on Youtube.com. Interested readers are encouraged to view these video resources for a more complete explanation of how the different mobile payment systems work.

Wireless payment systems transform mobile phones into secure, self-contained purchasing tools capable of instantly authorizing payments over the cellular network. One advantage of many mobile payment systems over traditional credit card systems is the ability to handle **micropayments** or transactions involving relatively small sums of money. The ability to make micropayments allows individuals to use their mobile devices to do things such as purchase a beverage from a vending machine or make a payment to a municipal parking meter. Many cities in Europe, and a growing number in the United States, have adopted mobile phone payment systems for parking and report dramatic increases in revenue because of the reduction in loss due to theft and broken meters and the reduced expense associated with collecting cash from traditional meters.

Mobile Bill Payments   In addition to paying bills through wireline banking or from ATMs, a number of companies are now providing their customers with the option of paying bills directly from a cell phone. Western Union, HDFC Bank in India, Citibank, and several other institutions worldwide currently offer mobile bill payment services. This trend is proving particularly attractive to mobile users in developing countries where many people do not have bank accounts.

Mobile Banking and Financial Services

Mobile banking is generally defined as carrying out banking transactions and other related activities via mobile devices (**Figure 8.9**). The services offered include bill payments and money transfers, account administration and checkbook requests, balance inquiries and statements on an account, interest and exchange rates, and so on.

Banks and other financial institutions allow customers to use mobile devices for a wide range of services (see **Table 8.2**).

People access financial services using a combination of mobile media channels including SMS, mobile Web browsers, and customized apps. Mobile banking is a natural extension of online banking services, which have grown in popularity over the last decade.

Throughout Europe, the United States, and Asia, an increasing percentage of banks offer mobile access to financial and account information. In 2009, ABI Research evaluated 29 U.S. banks on accessibility of their mobile banking services. Six of the banks received top marks:

FIGURE 8.9   Mobile banking, stock trading, and payment services have increased in recent years.

TABLE 8.2   **Most Common Mobile Banking Services**

Account alerts, security alerts, and reminders
Account balances, updates, and history
Customer service via mobile
Branch or ATM location information
Bill-pay (e.g., utility bills) and delivery of online payments by secure agents and mobile phone client apps
Funds transfers
Transaction verification

Source: Mobile Marketing Association (2009).

BB&T, Eastern Bank, Fifth Third Bank, Northeast Bank, USAA, and Wells Fargo. Bank of America and Chase also received positive evaluations.

In Sweden, Merita Bank has pioneered many services, and the Royal Bank of Scotland offers mobile payment services. Banamex, one of Mexico's largest banks, is a strong provider of wireless services to customers. Many banks in Japan allow all banking transactions to be done via cell phone. Experts predict that growth in the mobile banking services sector could reach between 894 million and 1.5 billion customers globally by 2015. The Asia-Pacific region is expected to emerge as the predominant market for mobile banking services (berginsight. com, 2010, Global Industry Analysts, 2010).

Short Codes

Banks and financial service organizations have two basic options for providing mobile services. Smartphone users can download dedicated apps to conduct banking transactions. The other option is to provide service through SMS (text message) technology. As you know, text messaging is still widely popular, even with people who use smartphones. Many mobile financial services make use of short codes for sending SMS texts. A **short code** works similarly to a telephone number, except that it is only five or six characters long and easier to remember. Businesses lease short codes from the Common Short Code Association (CSCA) for $500 to $1,000 a month. The lower price is for randomly assigned codes, whereas companies that want a specific short code pay a higher monthly rate. Once a company has leased its short code, it can begin using that code in promotions and interactive exchanges with customers.

Short codes are used for a wide variety of SMS text services, not just financial services. For example, voting on the popular television show *American Idol* is done with short codes. Each contestant is assigned a specific short code, and viewers are encouraged to send text messages indicating which performer they like the best. The annual MTV Movie Awards also uses short code voting, which allows viewers to pick the winning entry in certain prize categories. On some telecommunications networks, ring tones are sold using short codes and SMS texts.

Security Issues

At present, the benefits associated with mobile banking seem to outweigh potential security threats. However, as the number of people who engage in mobile banking increases, the likelihood that criminals will target mobile financial activity is sure to grow as well. What kinds of threats exist to mobile banking? **Table 8.3** lists the most common mobile banking risks.

TABLE 8.3   Mobile Banking Security Risks
Cloning   Duplicating the electronic serial number (ESM) of one phone and using it in second phone, the clone. This allows the perpetrator to have calls and other transactions billed to the original phone.
Phishing   Using a fraudulent communication, such as an e-mail, to trick the receiver into divulging critical information such as account numbers, passwords, or other identifying information.
Smishing   Similar to phishing, but the fraudulent communication comes in the form of an SMS message.
Vishing   Again, similar to phishing, but the fraudulent communication comes in the form of a voice or voicemail message encouraging the victim to divulge secure information.
Lost or stolen phone   Lost or stolen cell phones can be used to conduct financial transactions without the owner's permission.

Sources: Compiled from Howard (2009), McGee (2008), and Mobile Marketing Association (2009).

Questions

1. What are the two basic technologies used for mobile banking and financial services?
2. Why have e-wallets not been widely adopted and what will makers of e-wallets need to do to make this payment method more attractive to consumers?
3. What are the most common types of mobile banking activities consumers perform?
4. What are the most common security risks associated with online retailers?
5. Research some of the mobile payment systems currently available to merchants and consumers.
6. What is a micropayment and why is it beneficial to consumers and businesses that mobile payment systems can process these types of transactions?

Key Terms

augmented reality   242
barcode   241
business-to-business (B2B)   251
channel conflict   250
corporate procurement   252
corporate purchasing   252
demand management   253
digital dependents   244
digital immigrants   244
digital natives   244
direct procurement   252
disruptive innovation   266
e-commerce   244
electronic fund transfer (EFT)   246

electronic wallet (e-wallet)   247
e-procurement   252
e-sourcing   252
horizontal exchanges   253
indirect procurement   252
in-store tracking   257
micropayments   261
mobile browser   257
mobile check-in strategy   242
mobile commerce   244
m-commerce   244
mobile display strategy   241
mobile location-based marketing   257
mobile marketing   255

mobile payment   242
mobile retailing   255
mobile visual search
engine   258
MRO supplies   253
omni-channel retailing   245
quick response (QR) codes   241
short code   263
short message service (SMS)   241
showrooming   241
SMS database strategy   241
social commerce   244
vertical exchanges   253

Assuring Your Learning

Discuss: Critical Thinking Questions

1. What is showrooming? Are customers who engage in it acting ethically? Provide reasons for your answer.

2. What are some creative and constructive ways for traditional retailers to respond to showrooming?

3. Describe the ways in which online retailer Amazon.com has acted strategically to maintain its position as a leading e-commerce site. What does this suggest about what it takes to be successful in e-commerce today?

4. How is Amazon's investment in the Kindle and e-books consistent with other trends in consumer behavior today?

5. Why is mobile technology potentially important to the banking industry? What consumer needs does it fulfill?

6. Identify and describe five key challenges faced by online retailers in the market today.

7. Why is the online B2B market so much larger than the online B2C market?

8. Explain the fundamental difference between vertical and horizontal exchanges in the online B2B market.

9. What is the difference between a direct and a marketplace B2B e-commerce website? Why do sellers find marketplace websites challenging?

10. What are the two primary goals of companies who engage in e-procurement and what strategies do they use to achieve those goals?

11. What is the purpose of an EDI procurement system?

12. How do direct B2B e-commerce sites attempt to make their sites more attractive to business buyers?

13. Why do you think that company employees engage in maverick buying? What can companies do to limit maverick buying?

14. Explain how mobile computing technology is being used by brick-and-mortar retailers to enhance the in-store shopping experience.

15. QR codes are very popular in Japan and other parts of Asia. Manufacturers place QR codes on product packages and advertisements, making it easy for consumers to access information about the products using a mobile device. Why do you think QR codes are not popular with U.S. consumers? Do you think QR codes will eventually become accepted by U.S. consumers? Why or why not?

16. How are people using mobile devices to conduct banking and other financial services?

17. Evaluate the various mobile electronic payment processes described in this chapter. Which one do you think is likely to emerge as the dominant method for mobile payment? Explain your answer.

18. What are some of the risks faced by consumers who use mobile devices for banking and other financial transactions?

19. What are the key benefits of using a mobile wallet? Do you think new improvements to this mobile application will make it more attractive to end-users?

20. How has mobile computing changed the retail shopping behavior of consumers?

21. Describe the mobile entertainment market and the ways people can use their mobile devices to have fun.

22. How do travelers use mobile technology when flying, using hotels, and traveling in foreign countries?

23. How is mobile computing creating an attractive opportunity for advertisers? Will consumers be receptive to this type of communication? Why or why not?

24. List some location-based services and explain their value to both businesses and mobile device users.

Explore: Online and Interactive Exercises

1. Assume that you are interested in buying a car. You can find information about financing and insurance for cars at autos.msn. com or autobytel.com. Decide what car you want to buy. Configure your car by going to the car manufacturer's website. Finally, try to find the car at autobytel.com. What information is most supportive of your decision-making process? Was the experience pleasant or frustrating?

2. Visit amazon.com and identify at least three specific elements of its personalization and customization features. Browse specific books on one particular subject, leave the site, and then go back and revisit the site. What do you observe? Are these features likely to encourage you to purchase more books in the future from Amazon.com? How does the "One-Click" feature encourage sales from mobile devices?

3. Read Google's new **privacy policy**. What types of information does Google collect about people who use its services? How can people either restrict or avoid having Google collect information about them? How does Google say it uses the information it collects about people who utilize its services?

4. Conduct a study on selling diamonds and gems online. Each group member investigates one company such as **Blue Nile**, **Diamond.com**, **Thai Gem Store**, **Tiffany**, or **The Jewelry Exchange**.

   a. What features are used in these sites to educate buyers about gemstones?

   b. How do the sites attract buyers?

   c. How do the sites increase trust in online purchasing?

   d. What customer service features are provided?

   e. Would you buy a $5,000 diamond ring online? Why or why not?

5. If you have a smartphone, download the shopping app Shopkick. com. Use the app for a few weeks and then prepare a report or presentation about your experience. Describe how Shopkick uses behavioral reinforcement to encourage specific kinds of shopping behaviors (e.g., store visits, looking for promotional products, participating in marketing surveys, etc.). Explain whether or not you think you will continue using this application.

Analyze & Decide: Apply IT Concepts to Business Decisions

1. What is the National Automated Clearing House Association (**NACHA**)? What is its role? What is the Automated Clearing House (**ACH**)? Who are the key participants in an ACH e-payment? Describe the "pilot" projects currently under way at ACH.

2. Use an Internet search engine such as Google or Bing to identify a list of online banks. Form teams and have each team research one of the banks. Each team should attempt to convince the class that its e-bank activities are the best.

3. As an independent IT contract worker, you must often arrange travel to and from your clients' places of business. You do not typically have time to always explore every travel website when planning travel, so you wish to identify the one that over time will work the best for you. Working in a small group of three to four people, use the Internet to explore the following travel sites: orbitz.com, travelocity.com, kayak. com, concierge.com, and expedia.com (search "online travel sites" for additional options). Select a handful of travel destinations and see how helpful each site is in terms of:

   a. Finding the lowest airfare.

   b. Identifying hotels for business travel.

   c. Recommendations for dining and other location-based services.

   d. Evaluate the site for its ability to aid in international travel arrangements.

   e. Availability and usefulness of travel tips, advisories, and other helpful information.

   f. Prepare a report comparing how each site performed in terms of its ease of use, helpfulness, and best overall deal. Which site would you recommend?

4. Using Youtube.com or any other video-sharing site, watch examples of AR mobile apps and promotional campaigns. Write a brief report describing your reaction to this new technology and predict if it will become more commonplace in the future.

Case 8.2

Business Case: Chegg's Mobile Strategy

Mobile technologies are considered a **disruptive innovation** because they have the capability of transforming traditional business practices by creating new value networks, spawning new markets, and eventually displacing earlier technologies. Popular examples of disruptive innovation include Apple's iTunes service that replaced music CDs with downloadable digital mp3 files. Netflix and other movie-streaming services disrupted the previous model of distributing movies on DVDs through brick-and-mortar retail outlets. Several companies are now exploring the use of mobile technologies as a disruptive innovation in the college textbook market.

End users (college students) have traditionally had very little power in the college textbook market. Textbook publishers promoted their products to college professors who decided what books are required for their courses. Competition at the retail level was for the most part nonexistent—students almost always had to purchase textbooks from a college bookstore or a used textbook from another student.

All that began to change, however, with the emergence of e-commerce. Nowadays, students have a range of options for purchasing new and used textbooks, renting textbooks, reading books online, or purchasing textbooks in an e-book format. Publishers and booksellers who once held fairly secure positions in the distribution channel now face competition from a variety of nonconventional sources, including online retailers (e.g., Amazon), C2C (consumer to consumer) e-commerce sites (e.g., Craigslist, eBay, half.com), and publishers who sell directly to students (e.g., Flatworld Knowledge).

Chegg.com

As part of this industry restructuring, **Chegg.com** began renting textbooks to students in 2007, creating an alternative to purchasing from college bookstores and online booksellers such as Amazon.com. While renting textbooks was an innovative approach at the time, Chegg managers realized that to remain competitive, they needed to position their company in a way that was not focused on a particular product form (e.g., printed textbook) or distribution method (e.g., retail bookstore). Instead, Chegg set out to create a learning network for students, offering a range of products and services through various channels that enhance students' educational experience. See **Table 8.4**.

Mobile technology has been a key component of Chegg's value strategy from the beginning. In 2009, just 2 years after entering the rental market, Chegg created a mobile website and an SMS-based service that made it possible for students to check rental prices for textbooks by texting the ISBN number of the book they were interested in. The following year, Chegg launched an app for iPhone and iPad users. Android users can still access services from the company's well-designed mobile site. In 2012, Chegg launched a cloud-based e-textbook reader designed to give students access to their textbooks from a wide range of mobile devices. While Chegg is not the first company to make textbooks available online, the e-textbook reader provides powerful features for highlighting text, taking notes, and checking word definitions. Users can view *Key Highlights* or material crowdsourced from the highlighting activities of other students using the reader. Finally, readers can access Chegg's *Always on Q&A Service*, where students ask questions about various academic subjects and often receive an answer back from subject matter experts within hours.

TABLE 8.4   The Chegg Learning Network

Purchase New/Used Textbooks
Online, mobile app, or mobile website
Renting Textbooks
Online, mobile app, mobile website, and bookstores and rental stands at select colleges
Homework Help Q&A
Online and mobile website
e-Textbooks
Cloud-based mobile textbook reader
Course Reviews, Grade Distributions, and Schedule Planning Tools
Online and mobile website

Source: Chegg.com (2012).

Despite Chegg's innovative and customer-oriented strategy, it faces an increasingly competitive marketplace. Well-funded competitors such as Amazon.com and Barnes & Noble now offer textbook rentals and e-textbooks with some of the same features as Chegg's reader. VitalSource is another online vendor offering digital content from major publishers such as Pearson, Cengage, McGraw Hill, and John Wiley & Sons (the publisher of this textbook). VitalSource provides a number of mobile apps for various devices as well as the capability to read texts through mobile browsers (no app download necessary). Finally, Apple has announced its desire to transform the textbook market in much the same way it changed the music business. However, the existing list of companies that are already practicing disruptive innovation may make it more difficult for Apple to have quite the same impact as it did in the music business.

Questions

1. Evaluate the mobile features of Chegg's textbook program. Does it offer services that are truly helpful to college students or are they just a gimmick?

2. Go to Chegg.com to view a demo of its e-textbook reader. After reviewing the service, evaluate whether the reader will motivate students to obtain their textbooks from Chegg instead of using alternative textbook suppliers.

3. How does Chegg's mobile price comparison service provide a benefit to college students? Do you think it helps to increase rentals and purchases from Chegg?

4. What other ways could Chegg use mobile technologies to provide further value to college students?

5. Using a mobile device, check the purchase and/or rental prices of the textbooks you are using this semester. Compare these with prices from alternative vendors (e.g., your college bookstore, Amazon.com, half.com, etc.). Prepare a table comparing your overall cost from each supplier. Based on your findings, do you plan to change the way you obtain textbooks in the future?

Sources: Chegg.com (2010), Conneally (2012), Wired Academic (2012), Crook (2009), Eldon (2012).

Case 8.3

Video Case: Searching with Pictures Using MVS

Earlier in the chapter, you read that U.S. consumers were not responding to QR code marketing with the same enthusiasm as Asian consumers. In response, some companies are experimenting with an alternative to QR codes called **mobile visual search (MVS)** technology. MVS is an image recognition technology that proponents claim will be more attractive to consumers.

With an MVS app, users scan the pictures they find on product labels, catalogs, or advertisements. This initiates a search function that returns information to the user. Depending on the MVS app used, the search information might be general in nature, similar to what you get when conducting a search on Google. Or, the app may return specific information, for instance, a page where the user can order the product. This technology has spawned a new industry of mobile visual search services that include companies such as BuzzAR, Blippar, and, of course, Google (see **Figure 8.10**).

FIGURE 8.10 Mobile visual search using Google's Goggle app.

Find and watch videos of three different MVS applications on YouTube or other video-sharing sites:

MVS Application/ Developer	Videos at YouTube.com
Goggles/Google	Search for "Google Goggles Experiment Video"
LTU Mobile	Search for "Shopgate–Mobile Shopping"
Blippar	Search for "Unlock the world around you - #DiscoverMore with Blippar"

You may find videos about other MVS apps by entering "mobile visual search" into the YouTube search engine. Get the latest news and information about MVS by searching on the phrase "mobile visual search" using Google or another search engine. Compare and contrast MVS with marketing strategies using QR codes.

Questions

1. If consumers begin to use MVS on a large-scale basis, how should businesses adjust their marketing practices to take advantage of this technology?
2. Based on the videos and additional research, how do the MVS services differ from one another?

References

Ally Financial. "Company Overview – CEO Letter." *media.ally.com*, May, 2014.

Asante, J. "Mobile Gaming Powers Up: '99 Cents Is the New Quarter.'" *NPR.org*, April 3, 2012.

Bercovici, J. "Amazon vs. Book Publishers, by the Numbers." *Forbes.com*, February 20, 2014.

Berginsight.com. "Berg Insight Predicts 894 Million Mobile Banking Users by 2015." April 2010.

Chegg.com. "Chegg.com Introduces Two New Ways for College Students to Easily Rent Their Textbooks." *PRNewswire*, August 11, 2010.

Conneally, T. "Everything You Need to Know about e-Textbooks before Apple Gets Involved." *Betanews.com*, January 17, 2012.

Crook, J. "Chegg Adds Mobile Components to Textbook Rental Service." *Mobile Marketer, August* 31, 2009.

Eldon, E. "Chegg Launches Mobile Reader for Online Textbooks." *Techcrunch.com*, January 18, 2012.

Edelman. "2013 Edelman Trust Barometer Reports Financial Services Is Least Trusted Industry Globally." *Edelman.com*, April 9, 2013.

Galgey, W. and S. Pattinson. "The Future Shopper: How Changing Shopper Attitudes and Technology Are Reshaping Retail." White paper, the Futures Company/Kanter Retail, 2013.

Gallup, Inc. "Confidence in Institutions 1973–2014," *Gallup.com*, Sept. 18, 2014.

Gevelber, L. "How to build your mobile-centric search strategy," thinkwithgoogle.com, March, 2016.

Global Industry Analysts. "Global Mobile Banking Customer Base to Reach 1.1 Billion by 2015." February 2010.

Gonsalves, A. "Amazon Kindle 2.5 Adds Social Networking." *Information Week,* May 3, 2010.

Howard, N. "Is It Safe to Bank by Cell Phone?" *MSN Money,* July 2009.

Johnson, L. "Macy's, Aflac Partner for Holiday Donation Campaign." *Mobile Commerce Daily,* November 29, 2011.

Kats, R. "Macy's Mobile Spend Up 70pc: FirstLook Keynote." Mobile Marketer, January 20, 2012.

Macy's. "Macy's Backstage Pass." Press release, February 2011.

Malone, C. "The Loyalty Storm Brewing for Banks, Wireless and Cable Companies." *Business2community.com*, September 15, 2014.

McCormick, E. "The Best Social Media Banks", bankdirector.com, April 15, 2016

McGee, B. "Mobile Banking Security–Phishing for Answers?" *Netbanker.com,* January 2008.

Meola, A. "Mobile gaming is about to become the undisputed king of the jungle" businessinsider.com, April 28, 2016.

Miller, C. and J. Bosman. "E-Books Outsell Print Books at Amazon." *New York Times,* May 19, 2011.

Mobile Marketing Association. "Mobile Banking Overview (NA)." January 2009.

National Retail Federation. "Mobile Retailing Blueprint: A Comprehensive Guide for Navigating the Mobile Landscape." January 4, 2011.

O'Connell, B. "Consumer Frustration Threatens Billions in Revenue at 10 Banks This Year." *TheStreet.com*, July 23, 2013.

Porter, M. "The Five Competitive Forces That Shape Strategy." *Harvard Business Review,* 86, no. 1 January 2008, pp. 86–104.

Rappa, M. "Case Study: Amazon.com." *DigitalEnterprise.com,* 2010.

Smith, C. "Trio of Online Banks Dominate Social Media Channels." *Thefinancialbrand.com*, April 28, 2014.

Statista.com. "Weekly time spent playing games on selected devices according to gamers in the United States as of December 2016," December, 2016.

Tejwani, A. "One Bank that Got Social Media right – Ally Bank (Case Study)." *Sociallycharged.com*, Sept. 17, 2012.

The Financial Brand. "Majority of Americans Still Hold a Grudge Against Banks." *thefinancialbrand.com*, April 8, 2013.

Tsirulnik G. "Macy's Is 2011 Mobile Marketer of the Year." *Mobile Marketer,* December 9, 2011.

Williams, M. "Augmented reality gets practical: Here's how Hololens could transform car buying." *PCWorld.com*, March 31, 2016.

Wired Academic. "Chegg Trots Out Its HTML5 E-Textbook Reader, Challenging Inkling, Cengage, Kno, et al." January 28, 2012.

Yurcan, B. "Ally Bank's Mobile Strategy." *Banktech.com*, April 18, 2014.

Zimmerman, A. "Showdown Over 'Showrooming': Target Asks Vendors for Help Keeping Comparison Shoppers." *Wall Street Journal*, January, 23, 2012.

CHAPTER 9

Functional Business Systems

CHAPTER OUTLINE

LEARNING OBJECTIVES

Case 9.1 Opening Case: Ducati Redesigns Its Operations

9.1 Business Management Systems and Functional Business Systems

9.1 Describe various types of functional systems and how they support managers and workers at the operational level.

9.2 Production and Operations Management Systems

9.2 Define how manufacturing, production, and transportation information systems enable organizational processes and support supply chain operations and logistics.

9.3 Sales and Marketing Systems

9.3 Explain how sales and marketing information systems support advertising, market research, intelligence gathering, getting products and services to customers, and responding quickly and efficiently to customers' needs.

9.4 Accounting, Finance, and Regulatory Systems

9.4 Describe how accounting, auditing, and finance application systems meet compliance mandates, help deter fraud, and facilitate capital budgeting and forecasting.

9.5 Human Resource Systems, Compliance, and Ethics

9.5 Analyze how human resources information systems (HRIS) improve business-to-employee (B2E) communications, workforce productivity, and compliance with federal employment laws; discuss ethical issues related to the use of HRIS data.

Case 9.2 Business Case: HSBC Combats Fraud in Split-Second Decisions

Case 9.3 Video Case: United Rentals Optimizes Its Workforce with Human Capital Management

Introduction

Every business is managed through multiple business functions, each responsible for managing certain aspects of the business. The finance function is responsible for acquiring capital needed for research and development (R&D) and other investment processes. The marketing function is responsible for product promotion and pricing, identifying target customers, and improving the customer experience (CX). The operations function plans and coordinates all the resources needed to design, manufacture, and transport products. The IT function is responsible for the technology infrastructure, data management, and social, mobile, and cloud services. Accounting manages assets and meets compliance mandates. Human resource (HR) recruits, trains, and develops a talented workforce. These business functions involve complex processes that depend on access to data, collaboration, communication, and data analysis to pinpoint what must be done and employees' workflows to make that happen.

While most attention is on external interests—customers, competitors, and partners—they are only part of the solution. Business success also depends on internal factors—the efficiency and effectiveness of managers, employees, core business processes and functions. A wide range of specialized technologies, such as Salesforce.com and eXtensible Business Reporting Language (XBRL) for financial reporting, support problem-solving, decision-making, and compliance. Ultimately, data from functional systems are used by enterprise applications, including business intelligence (BI), e-commerce, customer relationship management (CRM), and supply chain management (SCM), as shown in **Figure 9.1**.

Business is messy, sometimes chaotic. Resolving those situations requires human creativity, critical thinking, and judgment—all of which relate back to corporate culture, training, and empowerment of employees. The technology and software applications described in this chapter are designed to help employees and managers make better decisions and improve efficiency and performance in the functional areas of a typical business organization.

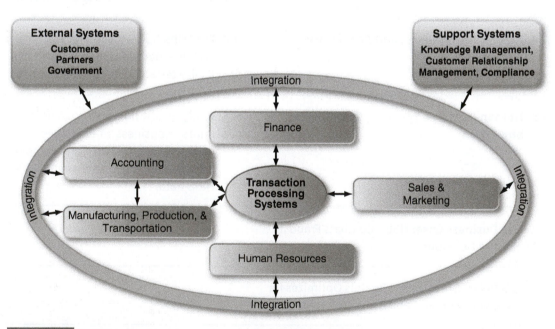

FIGURE 9.1 Data from functional area ISs support enterprise applications.

Case 9.1 Opening Case

Reuters/Alamy Stock Photo

Andrey Kekyalyaynen/Alamy Stock Photo

Fred MacGregor/Alamy Stock Photo

Ducati Redesigns Its Operations

Company Overview

Ducati Motor Holding manufactures motorcycles known worldwide for their precision engineering, lightning speed, and sleek design and for customers who are passionate about their motorcycles (Table 9.1). Six models make up the product lines, with prices starting at $15,000 to the $90,000 Superleggera Superbike, which produces up to 200 HP at the crankshaft. Ducati is owned by Audi through its Italian subsidiary Lamborghini. Its 2013 net sales were $518 million.

Awards

In March 2014, Ducati received five awards at the annual Motorrad des Jahres (Motorcycle of the Year) event in Stuttgart, Germany. Ducati's Multistrada and Diavel were awarded Motorcycle of the Year in the Allrounder and Cruiser categories, respectively (Figure 9.2). Ducati's models are benchmarks in innovative design and technology.

Product Lines

In addition to six motorcycle brands, the company sells parts, apparel, accessories, and other items to create the Ducati experience. Dealers

TABLE 9.1	Opening Case Overview
Company	Ducatiusa.com and Ducati.com
	Founded in 1926, the company has 1168 employees.
	Ducati's main factory site and headquarters are located in Bologna, Italy, with an additional assembly factory in Thailand.
Industry	Racing-inspired motorcycles characterized by "Desmodromic" performance engines and innovative design and technology.
Product lines	Four models: Diavel, Hypermotard, Monster, Superbike, and SuperSportter.
Digital technology	New dealer communication application for mobile devices called DCS or Ducati Communication System. The interface lets dealers easily find, send, and receive all the information they need to place orders and track them through production and delivery. The high-performance global communication system serves more than 5,500 users worldwide in seven languages.
Business challenges	Because of competition and tough economic conditions worldwide, motorcycle dealerships had to offer customers better value and after-sales services.

© imageBROKER/Alamy

© Johnrob/iStockphoto

FIGURE 9.2 Ducati's Multistrada and Diavel were awarded Motorcycle of the Year in 2014 in their class for their innovative design and technology.

need to be familiar with thousands of products and customization options for their customers.

Business Challenges

Companies worldwide were faced with tougher competition and economic conditions after the financial meltdown in 2008. And as global manufacturers, geography was a marketing challenge.

Internally, its sales staff struggled with conflicting or outdated data on product inventory, availability, and ordering time schedules. The source of the problem was multiple communication systems and data silos that were not coordinated.

To resolve these challenges and grow the business, Ducati focused on the following:

1. Improving the sales process
2. Engaging the customer in the design of its motorcycles
3. Decreasing the cost of operations

The plan was to redesign dealer operations, business processes, and communication tools to align them with leading industry practices.

Partnership with Accenture and Apple

Ducati selected Accenture to help redesign operations and processes and to roll out a new integrated communication application for its dealers worldwide. Ducati equipped its sales network with iPads and developed a custom in-house app called DCS or Ducati Communication System. The DCS app gives dealers a single point of access to Ducati's back-end systems. The DCS is an SAP-based interface used by dealers to easily find, send, and receive data necessary to place orders through a point-of-sale (POS) device and then to track orders through the production and delivery processes. (SAP is a global software company that specializes in Enterprise Resource Program (ERP) applications.)

Authorized dealers receive updates directly through the Apple App Store. They also have access to a configurator app on their iPads to configure a customer's dream motorcycle. An e-mail detailing the customized motorcycle and accessories is then sent to the customer. Dealers communicate in real time with colleagues and complete the sale without delay.

Intuitive User Experience

The familiar user experience was designed to be the same for desktop computers, iPads, and iPhones.

Cristiano Silei, vice president of Global Sales at Ducati, said: "It was clear from the start that iPad was the right device. It's the simplicity, the immediate usability. Everyone understands how it works in just a few minutes."

Visiting a dealership is a very emotional experience for customers. Dealers want to make the experience unforgettable. According to Silei, the iPad helps gives the future Ducati owner a richer experience.

In addition to providing real-time sales support, the DCS app on iPad acts as a training interface to keep dealers updated on Ducati's evolving product line. A change management program helped dealers transition smoothly from the old solution to DCS. DCS was quickly embraced by Ducati dealers, whose positive feedback included comments such as "It's a game changer" and "a great time saver."

Performance Improvements

Ducati's high-performance global DCS was deployed in 88 countries across four continents. DCS serves more than 5,500 users worldwide in seven languages. By leveraging dealer communication, Ducati is able to capture and consolidate local and global sales activity, spare parts, warranty, and service activity. As a result:

- Ducati is able to capture and consolidate local and global sales activity, spare parts, warranty, and service activity, improving the company's ability to respond daily to changing consumer demand.
- Dealers run all parts of their business and have a robust tool to execute their operational, growth, and customer objectives.
- Dealers respond more quickly to customer demands and market conditions, making each dealership easier for customers to do business with.
- Dealers are equipped with leading practices for their processes to help them better serve customers in a simple, streamlined manner.

The dealer system is one of the most innovative and effective user experiences in the industry. It is user-friendly and sleek and reinforces Ducati's brand.

Questions

1. What pressured or motivated Ducati to implement new digital technology?
2. What costs could Ducati cut? What costs could it not cut? For example, could Ducati cut its R&D budget? Explain your answers.
3. Why did Ducati need to improve communications with dealers?
4. Explain the capabilities and benefits of the DCS.
5. Why was it important to implement a change management program?
6. What other factors contributed to the success of DCS? Explain their contributions.
7. Visit the Apple iPad store at apple.com/ipad and search for "Ducati." Review the Ducati Communication System app. Explain how the DCS app gives the future Ducati owner a richer experience.

Sources: Compiled from Ducati websites (2014), LexisNexis company profiles (2014), Apple.com (2014), Accenture.com (2014).

9.1 Business Management Systems and Functional Business Systems

In this section, we will provide an overview of two types of information systems (ISs) that support different areas or activities in an organization. Business Management Systems (BMS) are ISs designed to support planning and the implementation process across the entire organization. Functional Business Systems (FBSs) are ISs designed to improve the efficiency and performance of a specific functional area within the organization.

Business Management Systems (BMSs)

BMSs aid leadership teams by using technology to improve cross-functional collaboration, clarify the relationship between steps in the planning and implementation process, assign responsibilities, and monitor progress toward objectives and outcomes. BMSs typically employ a variety of visual aids (e.g. flowcharts, dashboards, process charts) to communicate alignment of strategies, goals, objectives, and tactics as well as the metrics selected to measure performance and progress. Typical features or modules in a BMS include the following:

- Definition of Organizational Mission
- Identification of Strengths, Weakness, Opportunities, and Threats (SWOT Analysis)
- Establishing Goals and Measurable Objectives
- Defining Strategies and Key Performance Indicators (KPIs)
- Articulation of Tactical or Action Plans—Assigning Responsibilities and Time Tables
- Monitoring and Reporting Progress and Performance

Planning occurs at three levels of the organization—strategic, managerial, and operational, as illustrated in **Figure 9.3**. Managers at each level operate with a different time frame, which transitions from long term (a few years) at the strategic level to "in the moment" (daily) at the operations level.

For the organization to be fully effective, operational, tactical, and strategic plans and goals must be aligned. That is, they must be consistent, mutually supportive, and focused on achieving the enterprise's **mission**. BMSs help optimize organizational performance by aligning the planning and activities at each of these three levels.

Mission defines the organization's purpose and what it hopes to achieve.

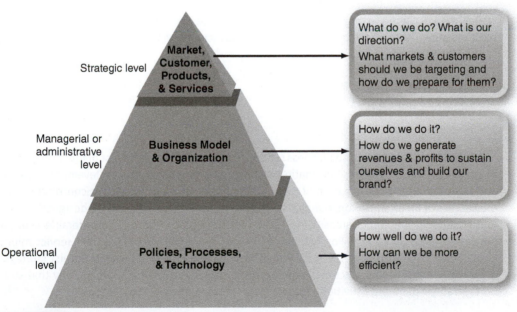

FIGURE 9.3   Three organizational levels, their concerns, and strategic and tactical questions, planning, and control.

Management Levels

Strategic planning is a top management activity that establishes goals and objectives, identifies strategies, allocates resources, and aligns operational activity for achieving desired outcomes. **Strategic plans** are visionary and future-oriented. As part of the strategic planning process, companies conduct a SWOT analysis of their strengths, weaknesses, opportunities, and threats. Data from external sources—the economy, markets, competitors, and business trends—are used in a BMS to evaluate opportunities and threats. Data from internal sources

Strategic plan is a document used to communicate the company's goals and the actions needed to achieve them.

are captured in a BMS to provide insight into a company's financial, human, marketing, and production resources and capabilities. Many BMSs employ Application Programming Interfaces (APIs) that allow companies to import data from sources from FBSs and other sources outside the system for use in the strategic planning process. (You read about APIs in Chapter 7 and the role they play in the development of Web 2.0 and social media.) Over time, strategic plans are reexamined and adjusted as elements of the internal and external environment change. Good BMSs anticipate the need to change plans, goals and outcomes and possess functionality that allows organizations to make these changes without undue difficulty.

At the **tactical level**, mid-level managers design business processes, procedures, and policies to implement strategic plans.

At the **operations level**, managers and supervisors work closely with the workforce and customers. They are on the "front lines" so to speak, ensuring that employees have the resources necessary to carry out their roles and ensuring that customers are well-served and satisfied with their experience. They depend on detailed data in real time or near real time to do their jobs, get work done, and close the deal. They need to track work schedules and employee performance; inventory levels, sales activity, and order fulfillment; production output and delivery schedules; and resolve disruptions or deviations from expected outcomes. In many companies today, operations-level managers and employees use handheld technologies to both gather data and receive real-time reporting on the processes they are responsible for. Decision-making is mostly immediate or short term because decisions are made to close the deal or control ongoing activities and operations. Feedback and control are vital to identify deviations from goals as soon as possible in order to take corrective action. Data captured or created within the company are most important at this level.

Business Functions vs. Cross-Functional Business Processes

FBSs are ISs designed to improve an organization's efficiency and performance in a functional business area. Traditional functional business areas include the following:

- Finance and Accounting
- Production/Operations & SCM
- Marketing and Sales
- HR Management

In addition, managers and business scholars frequently expand this list of functional areas to include Strategic Planning, Information Technology & Support, Business Development, R&D, and Customer Service. While each of these additional areas make important contributions to the success of an organization, our goal in this chapter will be to describe ISs designed for the four traditional functional areas listed earlier. In some cases, there is considerable overlap between areas on both lists. For instance, business development and customer service might easily be considered part of the marketing and sales function. While we do not list strategic planning as a traditional functional area, we have described BMSs as a technology that supports strategic planning activities.

Cross-Functional Coordination and Integration
Originally, ISs were designed to support the accounting function. Systems for other functions were rolled out later. This fragmented roll-out approach created data silos where information was effectively trapped in one functional area of the business and could not support cross-functional business processes. For example, accounting systems record sales, payments, customer profile information, product pricing, promotional expenses, and so on. To effectively evaluate the impact of past promotional activities and pricing decisions, the marketing department must be able to analyze the relationship between the product's price, promotional expenditures, and sales volume during a specific time period. In addition, the marketing unit might need to analyze the revenue generated by each customer to determine how the salesforce should prioritize accounts. However, if this information is trapped in the accounting system, it may not be available to

the marketing unit. In some cases, employees in marketing may not be granted access to the accounting system, or even more problematic, the system may only be programmed to use the data for creating standard accounting reports and statements and might not permit retrieval of information in ways that are useful to the marketing department or other units in the company.

In today's fast-paced, competitive business environment, departments or functions must be able to coordinate in the development of strategic plans and the performance of operations-level actions. FBSs that do not support cross-functional collaboration are an impediment to organizational success. Workflows and data flows between departments that are not coordinated result in delays, errors, poor customer service, and higher costs. When FBSs do allow for cross-functional coordination, it becomes possible for the company to monitor and evaluate progress toward goals and objectives established during the strategic planning process. It also becomes easier to identify problems or barriers to achieving objectives and develop solutions to those problems.

The data requirements of operations-level units are extensive and relatively routine because they have fixed sources of input and tasks that follow **standard operating procedures (SOPs)**. Functional area ISs help companies and employees adhere to SOPs, which are often easily automated. SOPs are an integral part of a quality control (QC) system because they provide individuals with information to perform jobs properly. A key benefit of SOPs is that they minimize variation and promote quality through consistent implementation of a process or procedure within the organization, even if there are temporary or permanent personnel changes. For example, SOPs are written for handling purchase orders, order fulfillment, customer complaints, recruitment and hiring, emergency response, and disaster recovery. Data that are lost or compromised have financial implications. As such, it is critical that businesses have SOPs to maintain three related data properties in company ISs:

> **Standard operating procedures (SOPs)** are a set of written instructions on how to perform a function or activity. SOPs provide the framework for complex processes to be managed more effectively.

Data security   Data security refers to the protection of data from malicious or unintentional corruption, unauthorized modification, theft, or natural causes such as floods. The purpose of data security is to maintain data integrity.

Data validity   Data validation involves tests and evaluations used to detect and correct errors, for instance, mistakes that might occur during data entry in fields such as customer name and address.

Data integrity   Data integrity refers to the maintenance of data accuracy and validity over its life cycle including the prevention of unintended modification or corruption.

Transaction Processing Systems

Transaction processing is information processing that is divided into distinct, undividable operations called transactions. While transaction processing certainly applies to the financial transactions that take place in a business (i.e., the data generated by a store cash register), transaction processing is used in the FBSs of all areas. For example:

- **Production/Operations**   The tracking of materials or component parts as they enter and exit a warehouse or manufacturing facility.
- **Marketing and Sales**   Management of sales orders and order fulfillment.
- **Human Resources**   Processing of payroll and employee records.
- **Finance/Accounting**   Processing of credits and debits to a customer's checking account at a bank.

Transaction processing systems (TPSs) are software and/or hardware technologies that collect, monitor, store, process, and distribute transactional data according to certain criteria referred to as the **ACID test**, which is short for atomicity, consistency, isolation, and durability:

- **Atomicity**   If all steps in a transaction are not completed, then the entire transaction is canceled. For example, if you transfer funds from your savings account to your checking account, a debit is made to savings, while a credit is made to the checking account. If one of these actions fails, the other is not allowed to occur, effectively canceling the transaction.

- **Consistency**   Only operations that meet data validity standards are allowed. For instance, systems that record checking accounts only allow unique check numbers for each transaction. Any operation that repeats a check number will fail in order to maintain accuracy in the database. Network failures can also cause data consistency problems.

- **Isolation**   Transactions must be isolated from each other. For example, bank deposits must be isolated from a concurrent transaction involving a withdrawal from the same account. Only when the withdrawal transaction is successfully completed will the new account balance be reported.

- **Durability**   Backups by themselves do not provide durability. A system crash or other failure must not cause any loss of data in the database. System failures can occur for any number of reasons including human error, computer virus or an attack by computer hackers, hardware failure, or natural disasters. Durability is achieved through separate transaction logs that can be used to recreate all transactions from a known checkpoint. Other ways include the use of recovery manager programs that utilize a range of solutions including cloud-based database mirrors that replicate the database on another server.

Real Time and Batch Processing

Transactions can be processed in two ways: batch processing and real time. Batch processing involves the collection of transactional data over some period of time, and then all of the transactions are processed as a batch at one time. The opposite of batch processing is real-time processing where transactions are processed as they occur, which means that account balances and other related counts are kept up to date. For instance, when you purchase two tickets to a show at a Broadway theater, not only is the count of remaining tickets immediately reduced by two, but also the specific seats indicated on your tickets are blocked off so that the ticketing system doesn't sell your seats to someone else.

Online Transaction Processing Systems

Increasingly, organizations today are employing **Online Transaction Processing Systems (OTPS)**. These are TPSs that employ client server systems that allow transactions to run on multiple computers on a network, processing transactions in real time. Data are accessed directly from the database, and reports can be generated automatically (**Figure 9.4**).

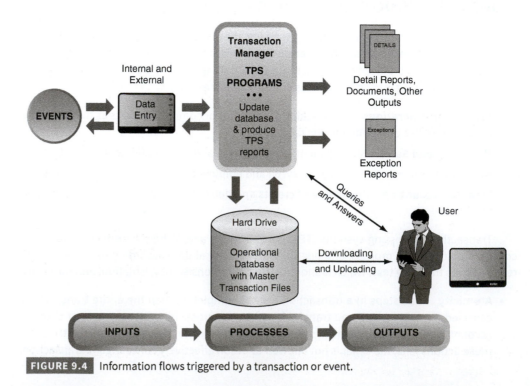

FIGURE 9.4   Information flows triggered by a transaction or event.

Questions

1. Explain the purpose of BMSs.
2. Define what an SOP is and give an example.
3. Explain each component of the ACID test.
4. Explain the differences between batch and real-time processing.
5. Explain the relationship between TPSs and FBSs.

9.2 Production and Operations Management Systems

Historically, the production and operations area focused primarily on activities within the company related to the manufacture of products and services. Considerable emphasis was placed on increasing product quality and reducing manufacturing costs, believing that these were critical factors in business success. More recently, businesses have developed a broader perspective, understanding that customer value is a more critical success factor. Significant advances in customer value require more than just improvements in product quality and reduced costs. In addition, because of globalization, many companies began outsourcing tasks traditionally performed by the company. As a result, SCM was adopted as a way to coordinate all of the factors that contribute to customer value, including supplier relationships, logistics, inventory management across the supply chain, order fulfillment, and so on. In some companies, manufacturing simply became a supply chain factor that could be performed internally, outsourced or both, as conditions in different markets evolved (see **Figure 9.5**). As a result, production and operations

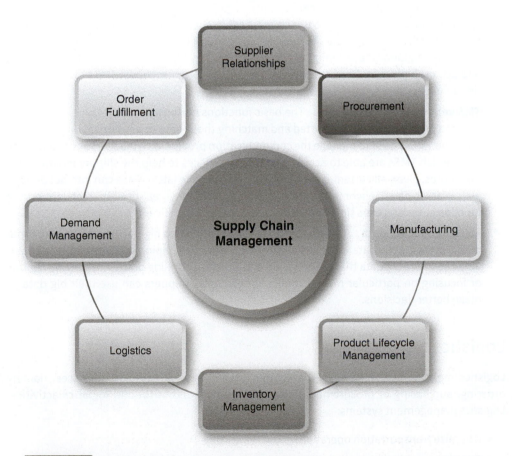

FIGURE 9.5 Companies recognize that careful management of supply chain processes is critical for success in the highly competitive global economy.

are sometimes viewed in the larger context of SCM, and ISs have been developed to support organizations with traditional production and operations management (POM) as well as SCM processes. It is not always clear if a function such as logistics is part of a company's production and operations process or part of the company's supply chain. Oftentimes, the way a function is managed will depend on if the company is responsible for the function or if it outsources the function, relying on supply chain partners. In either case, production operations management and SCM ISs both play a critical role in managing these important functions and facilitating coordination between different divisions within an organization or between the organization and its partners. In this section, we will describe FBSs commonly associated with POM. As you will read in Chapter 10, some of these process are also considered part of SCM and supported by SCM ISs.

Transportation Management Systems

Transportation management systems (TMSs) are relied on to handle transportation planning, which includes shipping consolidation, load and trip planning, route planning, fleet and driver planning, and carrier selection. TMSs also support vehicle management and accounting transactions.

Four trend factors contributing to the growth of TMS are as follows:

1. **Outdated transportation systems need to be upgraded or replaced**   Many systems were installed over 10 years ago—before tablet computers and mobile technologies had become widespread in business. They are considered legacy (old) systems, and are inflexible, difficult to integrate with other newer systems, and expensive to maintain.

2. **Growth of intermodal transport**   Intermodal transportation refers to the use of two or more transport modes, such as container ship, air, truck, and rail, to move products from source to destination. Many more companies are shipping via intermodals, and their older TMSs cannot support or deal with intermodal movement, according to Dwight Klappich, a research vice president for Gartner.

   When brick-and-mortar manufacturers began selling online, for example, they learned that their existing TMSs were inadequate for handling the new line of business. Shippers that expand globally face similar challenges when they try to manage multiple rail, truck, and ocean shipments. Thus, there is a growing need for more robust TMSs to handle multidimensional shipping arrangements.

3. **TMS vendors add capabilities**   The basic functions performed by a TMS include gathering data on a load to be transported and matching those data to a historical routing guide. Then the TMS is used to manage the communication process with the various carriers. New feature-rich TMSs are able to access information services to help the shipper identify optimal routes, given all current conditions. For example, the latest TMSs can interact directly with market-data benchmarking services. An automated, real-time market monitoring function saves shippers time and errors and cuts costs significantly.

4. **TMSs handle big data**   Transportation tends to generate a high volume of transactional data. Managing the data is not easy. TMS vendors are developing systems that make valuable use of the big data that are collected and stored. By drilling down into specific regions or focusing on particular market trends, for example, shippers can use their big data to make better decisions.

Logistics Management

Inbound logistics   refers to receiving inventory.

Outbound logistics   refers to shipping inventory.

Logistics management deals with the coordination of several complex processes, namely ordering, purchasing or procurement, **inbound logistics**, and **outbound logistics** activities. Logistics management systems:

- Optimize transportation operations.
- Coordinate with all suppliers.

- Integrate supply chain technologies.
- Synchronize inbound and outbound flows of materials or goods.
- Manage distribution or transport networks.

These systems enable real-time monitoring and tracking of supply chain shipments, schedules, and orders.

Inventory Control Systems

Inventory control systems are important because they minimize the total cost of inventory while maintaining optimal inventory levels. Inventory levels are maintained by reordering the quantity needed at the right times in order to meet demand. POM departments keep **safety stock** as a hedge against **stockouts**. Safety stock is needed in case of unexpected events, such as spikes in demand or longer delivery times. One of the crucial decisions involved in inventory management is weighing the cost of inventory against the cost of stockouts. Stockouts of materials and parts can slow or shut down production while stockouts of final products result in reduced sales. Both of these situations can have significant short and long-term financial consequences that need to be balanced against the potential savings associated with lower inventory levels.

Managing inventory is important to profit margins because of numerous costs associated with inventory, in addition to the cost of the inventory. Inventory control systems minimize the following three cost categories:

- **Inventory carrying costs**
- **Inventory ordering costs**
- **Cost of shortages**

To minimize the sum of these three costs (see **Figure 9.6**), the company must decide when to order and how much to order. One inventory model that is used to answer both questions is the **economic order quantity (EOQ)** model. The EOQ model takes all costs into consideration.

> **Inventory control systems** are stock control or inventory management systems.
>
> **Safety stock** is extra inventory used as a buffer to reduce the risk of stockouts. It is also called buffer stock.
>
> **Stockouts** inventory shortage arising from unexpected demand, delays in scheduled delivery, production delays, or poor inventory management.

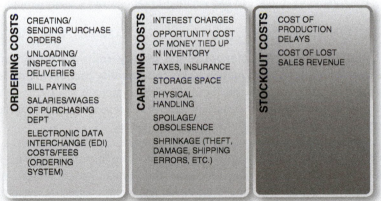

INVENTORY COSTS

ORDERING COSTS	CARRYING COSTS	STOCKOUT COSTS
CREATING/ SENDING PURCHASE ORDERS	INTEREST CHARGES	COST OF PRODUCTION DELAYS
UNLOADING/ INSPECTING DELIVERIES	OPPORTUNITY COST OF MONEY TIED UP IN INVENTORY	COST OF LOST SALES REVENUE
BILL PAYING	TAXES, INSURANCE	
SALARIES/WAGES OF PURCHASING DEPT	STORAGE SPACE	
	PHYSICAL HANDLING	
ELECTRONIC DATA INTERCHANGE (EDI) COSTS/FEES (ORDERING SYSTEM)	SPOILAGE/ OBSOLESENCE	
	SHRINKAGE (THEFT, DAMAGE, SHIPPING ERRORS, ETC.)	

FIGURE 9.6   Inventory Control Systems help companies balance inventory ordering and carrying costs against the costs inventory shortages.

Just-in-Time Inventory Management Systems **Just-in-time (JIT)** and lean manufacturing are two widely used methods or models to minimize waste and deal with the complexity of inventory management. Minimizing inventory costs remains a major objective of SCM.

JIT inventory management attempts to minimize holding costs by not taking possession of inventory until it is needed in the production process. With JIT, costs associated with carrying large inventories at any given point in time are eliminated. However, the trade-off is higher ordering costs because of more frequent orders. Because of the higher risk of stockouts, JIT requires accurate and timely monitoring of materials' usage in production.

Everything in the JIT chain is interdependent, so coordination and good relationships with suppliers are critical for JIT to work well. Any delay can be very costly to all companies linked in the chain. Delays can be caused by labor strikes, interrupted supply lines, bad weather, market demand fluctuations, stockouts, lack of communication upstream and downstream in the supply chain, and unforeseen production interruptions. In addition, inventory or material quality is critical. Poor quality causes delays, for example, fixing products or scrapping what cannot be fixed and waiting for delivery of the reorder.

JIT was developed by Toyota because of high real-estate costs in Tokyo, Japan, which made warehousing expensive. It is used extensively in the auto manufacturing industry. For example, if parts and subassemblies arrive at a workstation exactly when needed, holding inventory is not required. There are no delays in production, and there are no idle production facilities or underutilized workers, provided that parts and subassemblies arrive on schedule and in usable condition. Many JIT systems need to be supported by software. JIT vendors include HP, IBM, CA, and Steven Engineering.

Despite potential cost-saving benefits, JIT is likely to fail in companies that have the following:

- Uncooperative supply chain partners, vendors, workers, or management.
- Custom or non-repetitive production.

Lean Manufacturing Systems
In a **lean manufacturing system**, suppliers deliver small lots on a daily or frequent basis, and production machines are not necessarily run at full capacity. One objective of lean manufacturing is to eliminate waste of any kind, that is, to eliminate anything that does not add value to the final product. Holding inventory that is not needed very soon is seen as waste, which adds cost but not value. A second objective of lean manufacturing is to empower workers so that production decisions can be made by those who are closest to the production processes.

Oracle, Siemens, and other vendors offer demand-driven lean manufacturing systems. As any IS, JIT needs to be justified with a cost–benefit analysis. And all JIT success factors apply to lean manufacturing. For example, JIT requires that inventory arrive on schedule and be of the right quality. For companies subject to bad weather or labor strikes, lean manufacturing may not be suitable.

Quality Control Systems
Manufacturing quality control (QC) systems can be stand-alone systems or part of an enterprise-wide **total quality management (TQM)** effort. QC systems provide data about the quality of incoming materials and parts, as well as the quality of in-process semifinished and finished products. These systems record the results of all inspections and compare actual results to expected results.

QC data may be collected by sensors or radio frequency identification (RFID) systems and interpreted in real time, or they can be stored in a database for future analysis. Reports on the percentage of defects or percentage of rework needed can keep managers informed of performance among departments. KIA Motors introduced an intelligent QC system to analyze customer complaints, so it could more quickly investigate and make corrections.

Other Production/Operations Technologies
Many other areas of production/operations are improved by ISs and tools. Production planning optimization tools, product routing and tracking systems, order management, factory layout planning and design, and other tasks can be supported by POM subsystems. For example, a Web-based system at Office Depot matches employee scheduling with store traffic patterns to increase customer satisfaction and reduce costs. Schurman Fine Papers, a manufacturer/retailer of greeting cards and specialty products, uses special warehouse management software to improve demand forecasting and inventory processes. Its two warehouses efficiently distribute products to over 30,000 retail stores.

Computer-integrated Manufacturing and Manufacturing Execution Systems

Computer-integrated manufacturing (CIM) systems control day-to-day shop floor activities. In the early 1980s, companies invested greatly in CIM solutions even though they were complex, difficult to implement, and costly to maintain. They had required the integration of many products and vendors.

Prior to CIM, production managers were given many pieces of information such as time, attendance, receiving reports, inspection reports, and so on to figure out how to accomplish production tasks. The information was frequently late, rarely current or reliable, voluminous, and extremely difficult to assimilate. CIM helps production managers better use information to execute manufacturing plans.

Manufacturing execution systems (MESs) manage operations on the shop floors of factories. Some MESs schedule a few critical machines, while others manage all operations on the shop floor. Functions of MES programs include the following: compiling a bill of materials, resource management and scheduling, preparing and dispatching production orders, preparing work-in-progress (WIP) reports, and tracking production lots. For instance, an MES can schedule and track each step of the production phase of a particular job and then print out the bill of materials for the operator and the production steps to complete at each phase. It repeats this process for each operator and each step until a particular job is complete.

CIM and MES are very similar concepts, but there are differences. MES typically refers to a broader infrastructure compared to CIM. MES is based much more on standard reusable application software, instead of custom-designed software programs on a contract-by-contract basis. MES tries to eliminate the time and information gap of early years on the shop floor by providing the plant with information in real time. Corporate business functions are given timely plant information to support business planning decisions. For the most part, the term CIM is more commonly used and will be used in the rest of this section.

Today's CIM systems provide scheduling and real-time production monitoring and reporting. CIM data-driven automation affects all systems or subsystems within the manufacturing environment: design and development, production, marketing and sales, and field support and service. CIM systems can perform production monitoring, scheduling and planning, statistical process monitoring, quality analysis, personnel monitoring, order status reporting, and production lot tracking. The manufacturer BAE has implemented CIM.

MESs are generally installed on-premises, but cloud-based solutions are becoming available. MES is a subset of enterprise resource planning (ERP) systems, which you will read about in Chapter 10.

BAE Systems Uses CIM in Its Combat Aircraft Facility   BAE Systems is a global company headquartered in London, England, engaged in the development, delivery, and support of advanced defense, security, and aerospace systems. BAE is among the world's largest military contractors.

In September 2010, BAE opened a titanium-machining facility to manufacture components for the F-35 Lightning II combat aircraft. It took 10 months to complete the facility, during which time engineers at BAE considered a number of ways to ensure that it would be able to accommodate the high throughput of titanium military aircraft parts cost-effectively. According to Jon Warburton, BAE's F-35 program manager, after conducting a thorough examination of numerous potential manufacturing solutions, the BAE team finally decided to deploy a highly automated CIM system (Wilson, 2011). The CIM system ensures that titanium parts for the aircraft can be manufactured on a JIT basis. To do so, it coordinates the orders received at the plant, as well as the movement of raw materials and tooling, and optimizes the use of the machine tools.

A key element of the CIM strategy was the deployment of two **flexible manufacturing systems (FMSs)** that can accommodate the manufacture of different parts at different volumes. When an order for a part is received, the data relating to it are passed to the FMSs, which schedule the manufacture of a part in the most expedient way by examining the current workload across each of eight machine tools. Each FMS can store up to 1,000 cutting tools in a racking system ready to be loaded into the machine tools. A series of twin robot systems deliver the stored cutting tools into each machine, as well as replenishing any worn tools. The biggest challenge faced by the team in the development of the facility was to ensure that the FMS and the machine tools communicated effectively with one another and with BAE's CIM system.

Reasons Why Companies Invest in CIM   The benefits of CIM are as follows: (1) It simplifies manufacturing technologies and techniques, (2) automates as many of the manufacturing processes as possible, and (3) integrates and coordinates all aspects of design, manufacturing, and related functions. CIM is comprehensive and flexible, which is especially important in the redesign or elimination of business processes. Without CIM, it may become necessary to make large investments to change existing ISs to fit new processes.

Questions

1. What is the function of SCM in an organization?
2. What trends are contributing to the growing use of TMS?
3. Define logistics management.
4. What are the three categories of inventory costs?
5. What are the objectives of JIT?
6. Explain the difference between EOQ and JIT inventory models.
7. What is the goal of lean manufacturing?
8. What is CIM?

9.3 | Sales and Marketing Systems

As a result of the Internet and other technology, significant changes have occurred in the field of marketing over the last decade. Not only has technology created entire new service and product categories, but also many traditional marketing functions including product development, pricing, distribution, and promotion have changed. ISs and digital networks that have emerged in the last 10–15 years have resulted in new revenue streams, new business models, new retail, promotion and distribution channels, and entirely new industries. **IT at Work 9.1** describes such an example. In general, sales and marketing systems support the following:

- Digital advertising
- Social media monitoring and promotions
- Sales and customer support
- Automated ad placement and media buying
- Market research
- Intelligence gathering
- Distributing products and services to customers
- Order tracking
- Online and mobile order processing
- Online and mobile payment methods

Many of these systems are depicted in **Figure 9.7**. Chapters 7, 8, and 10 covered or will discuss sales and marketing systems and strategies, including e-commerce and CRM. This chapter, specifically this section, focuses on data-driven marketing and the capabilities of sales and marketing ISs.

IT at Work 9.1

Google Customer Surveys

Google Customer Surveys is a service that publishers can use to generate revenues from their online content. The service is an alternative to having a paywall for online news content. For example, when users visit the websites of partners such as the *New York Daily News* and *Texas Tribune*, they find several articles partially blocked. To continue reading the full article, they have to answer a question or micro-survey provided by Google.

Adweek

Adweek's editors, reporters, and designers spend a lot of time analyzing how digital technology transforms businesses and the people they cover. They needed to monetize their digital assets to keep the brand profitable. To that end, *Adweek* partnered with Google on

a new Web-based revenue play. By answering a single marketing question per day, readers receive full access to Adweek.com and reporting, analysis, and video.

Market Research

One or two market research multiple-choice questions are asked, for instance, "Which types of candy do you usually buy for your household?" Possible answers: none, chocolate, hard candies, gummies, toffees. Advertisers pay Google to host the surveys, and the sites receive 5 cents per response from Google. To minimize the possibility that people select untruthful answers leading to poor-quality data, Google makes the questions as engaging as possible. And if users start to just answer the first question on each page, or answer too quickly, the program notices that behavior and forces readers to answer new questions.

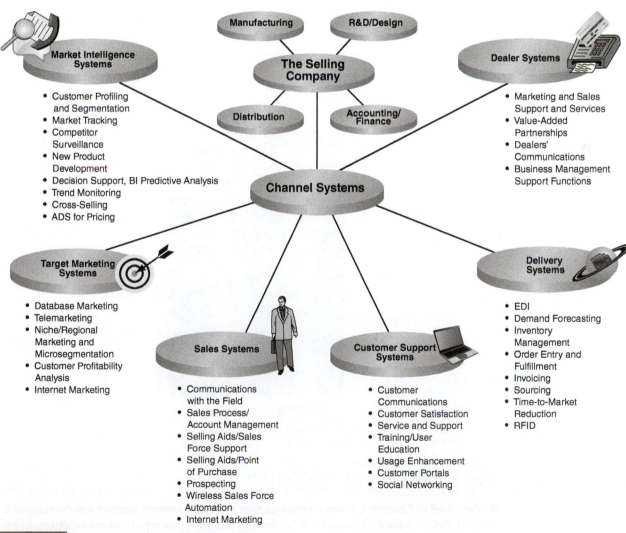

FIGURE 9.7 Sales and marketing systems and subsystems.

Data-Driven Marketing

Data-driven, fact-based decision-making increasingly relies on data that are *hot*—impacting the business or potential customer right now or in real time. One use of hot data is pay-per-click (PPC) website advertising that "appears" on the screens of consumers' devices based on their location, behavior, interests, or demographic information. Unlike search engine PPC ads that appear based on the user's keyword searches, website ads use data about the person to determine whether the ad should appear. This capability creates opportunities for highly targeted advertising programs. For example, Facebook members self-report data about their location, age, interests, and so on. Based on these data, advertisers can request that their ad be pushed to Facebook members who fit a specific profile based on demographic, geographic, or behavioral factors.

Sales and Distribution Channels

Marketers need to determine the optimal ways to distribute their products and services through a combination of electronic, mobile, and physical channels. For example, integrating a PPC advertising campaign with other online and offline advertising initiatives generally provides the best overall results.

Here are representative topics relating to sales and distribution channels:

- In Macy's stores and many other retailers, customers can check current sale prices on digital screens with barcode readers.
- Customers use Exxon Mobil Speedpass to fill their tanks by waving a token, embedded with an RFID device, at a gas-pump sensor. Then the RFID starts an authorization process, and the purchase is charged to the debit or credit card linked to the account.
- Home Depot and many supermarkets installed self-check-out machines. Self-service kiosks cut labor costs for retailers and can reduce customers' check-out times, as shown in **Figure 9.8**.

© Marmaduke St. John/Alamy

FIGURE 9.8 Self-check-out kiosks reduce labor costs.

Social Media Customer Service

As described in Chapter 7, many companies now employ customer support representatives to monitor social media platforms such as Twitter and Facebook to identify customers with questions or who are frustrated because of a problem they are having with a product or service. These social media customer service representatives are trained to offer support and solutions to customer problems in order to retain the customer's loyalty and demonstrate the brand's commitment to customer satisfaction. Failure to respond to these customers has public consequences, since by definition, social media tends to be a public forum and both the customer's complaint and the company's response can be viewed by other people using the social media platform. On the other hand, companies that have learned how to handle these situations stand to benefit by demonstrating their responsiveness to a wide audience of prospective customers. As with more traditional forms of customer service, such as call centers, social customer service engagement is recorded in a customer service IS so that performance metrics, volume and type of complaint can be analyzed.

Marketing Management

The following are some representative examples of how marketing management is being accomplished.

Pricing of Products or Services

Sales volume as well as profits are determined by the prices of products or services. Pricing is a difficult decision, particularly during economic recessions. ISs used in conjunction with data collected from online markets are able to help companies maximize profits using a variety of yield management practices. For instance, online retailers can personalize the Web pages shown to individual customers and display a combination of products and prices customized to entice that customer to make a purchase. The automated decisions about what products and prices to display to a customer are determined by a complex algorithm based on the customer's previous purchases, Web viewing history, activity on social media, and product searches. While airlines have been charging different ticket prices for the same flight for years, the practice is now employed by many different businesses as part of a mass-customization strategy made possible by information and computing technologies. Another example of technology-driven pricing and promotional strategies includes flash sales designed to engage customers and trigger a quick spike in sales. Flash sales work by offering customers an incredible deal for a very short time, usually announced via mobile text message, e-mail, or social media.

Salesperson Productivity

The performance of salespeople is collected in the sales and marketing TPS and used to compare performance along several dimensions, such as time, product, region, and even the time of day. Actual current sales can be compared to historical data and to expectations. Multidimensional spreadsheet software facilitates this type of analysis.

Sales productivity can be boosted by Web-based call centers. When a customer calls a sales rep, the rep can look at the customer's history of purchases, demographics, services available where the customer lives, and more. This information enables reps to provide better customer service.

Sales automation software is especially helpful to small businesses, enabling them to rapidly increase sales and growth. One leading software is Salesforce.com, which is a CRM application that is offered as a software as a service (SaaS). You will read about Salesforce.com in detail in the CRM section of Chapter 10.

Profitability Analysis

In deciding on advertising and other marketing efforts, managers need to know the profit contribution or profit margin (profit margin = sale price − cost of good) of certain products and services. Profitability metrics for products and services can be derived from the cost-accounting system. For example, profit performance analysis software available from IBM, Oracle, SAS, and Microstrategy is designed to help managers assess and improve the profit performance of their line of business, products, distribution channels, sales regions, and other dimensions critical to managing the enterprise. Several airlines, for example, use automated decision systems to set prices based on profitability.

Marketing activities conclude the primary activities of the value chain. Next, we look at the functional systems that are *support activities,* also called *secondary activities*, in the value chain: accounting, finance, and HR management.

9.4 | Accounting, Finance, and Regulatory Systems

Accounting and finance departments control and manage cash flows, assets, liabilities, and net income (profit). Financial accounting is a specialized branch of accounting that keeps track of a company's financial transactions and prepares financial statements, such as balance sheets and **income statements**. Investors, regulators, and others rely on the integrity and accuracy of external financial statements. Accounting must comply with generally accepted accounting principles (GAAP) and the **Financial Accounting Standards Board (FASB)**.

Corporations whose stock is publicly traded must also comply with the reporting requirements of the Securities and Exchange Commission (SEC), a regulatory agency of the U.S. government. Using standardized guidelines, the transactions are recorded, summarized, and presented in a financial report or financial statement such as an income statement or a balance sheet. However, the objective of financial accounting is not simply to report the value of a company. Rather, its purpose is to provide sufficient and accurate information for others to assess the value of a company for investment or other purposes.

Income statement summarizes a company's revenue and expenses for one quarter of a fiscal year or the entire fiscal year. It is also known as a P&L (profit and loss) or earnings statement.

Financial Accounting Standards Board (FASB) establishes financial accounting and reporting standards for public and private companies and not-for-profit organizations.

Financial Disclosure: Reporting and Compliance

As part of an organization's compliance obligations, the accounting function must attest (verify) that there are no material weaknesses in internal controls. A weakness in an internal control is a major cause of fraud, which is also known as white-collar crime. The prevention, detection, and investigation of financial fraud are needed to reduce the risk of publicly reporting inaccurate information. High-profile examples of **financial misrepresentations** are Bernard L. Madoff Investment Securities (2008), Lehman Brothers (2008), Enron (2001), and many related to the subprime mortgage crisis. **Table 9.2** describes three of the worst accounting fraud cases of all time. The FBI investigates white-collar crime and reports on the subject at its website FBI.gov.

Financial misrepresentation occurs when a company has intentionally deceived one or more other parties.

Accounting Software Packages
Accounting software is a foundational technology for many companies, and as a business grows, powerful and effective accounting solutions are critical. Most accounting software packages offer the same basic features necessary for managing finances: accounts receivable (A/R), accounts payable (A/P), general ledger, billing and invoicing, purchase and sales orders, and reporting. In addition to basic functionality, the top accounting solutions offer additional features to give users more power, flexibility, and customization. Often, accounting solutions are closely integrated with enterprise systems, such as ERP systems that include an extensive accounting module.

Many providers offer cloud-based solutions. SaaS accounting software solutions include the features of traditional systems, with the added benefit of anytime, anywhere accessibility and updating.

TABLE 9.2   Three of the Worst Accounting Scandals of All Time

Company and Fraudsters	Damages	How They Did It	Penalties
Bernie Madoff Investment Securities LLC (2008) Bernie Madoff, his accountant David Friehling, and CFO Frank DiPascalli	Tricked investors out of $64.8 billion through the largest Ponzi scheme in the history.	Investors were paid returns out of their own money or money from other investors—rather than from profits.	150 years in prison for Madoff + $170 billion restitution. Prison time for Friehling and DiPascalli.
Lehman Brothers (2008) Lehman executives and the company's auditors, Ernst & Young	Hid over $50 billion in loans disguised as sales.	Allegedly sold toxic assets to Cayman Island banks with the understanding that they would be bought back eventually. Created the impression that Lehman had $50 billion more in cash and $50 billion less in toxic assets than it actually had.	Forced into the largest bankruptcy in U.S. history.
Enron (2001) CEO Jeffrey Skilling and former CEO Ken Lay	Shareholders lost $74 billion, thousands of employees and investors lost their retirement accounts, and many employees lost their jobs.	Kept huge debts off its balance sheets.	Lay died before serving time; Skilling received 24 years in prison. The company filed for bankruptcy. Arthur Andersen was found guilty of fudging Enron's accounts.

Financial Disclosure   The SEC's financial disclosure system is central to its mission of protecting investors and maintaining fair, orderly, and efficient markets. Since 1934, the SEC has required financial disclosure in forms and documents. In 1984, the SEC began collecting electronic documents to help investors obtain information, but those documents made it difficult to search for and find specific data items. To eliminate that difficulty and improve how investors find and use information, the SEC now requires public companies, called filers, to submit their financial reports as *tagged interactive data files* (FASB.org, 2012) formatted in **eXtensible Business Reporting Language (XBRL)**. In addition, data in the reports must be tagged according to standards established by the Financial Accounting Securities Board (FASB). Each year, FASB updates the list of over 15,000 computer readable tags known as the **GAAP Financial Reporting Taxonomy**. Annual updates reflect changes in accounting standards and other enhancements designed to improve the reporting process and usability.

XBRL Tagging   XBRL is a language for the standards-based exchange of business information between business systems. Each item, such as cash or depreciation expense, is tagged with descriptive metadata or labels, such as calendar year, audited/unaudited status, currency, and so on, as defined by the GAAP Financial Reporting Taxonomy. The taxonomy is like a data dictionary that defines financial concepts and the relationships between various types of data that might be included in a financial report. The XBRL language and data tags make it possible for the reports to be read by any software that includes an XBRL processor. Interactive (tagged) data make it easier for investors to analyze and compare the financial performance of public companies, increasing the efficiency and transparency of reporting processes and the ability to consolidate financial data from different operating systems. Prior to XBRL, reports were noninteractive. Investors who wanted specific data had to manually search lengthy corporate annual reports or mutual fund documents. As more companies use interactive data, sophisticated analysis tools used by financial professionals are now available to average investors.

Creating XBRL documents does not require XML computer programming. As requirements for XBRL reporting become increasingly common around the world, more vendors are developing software products for marking up reports, tagging data, submitting reports to various recipients, as well as receiving and analyzing tagged data from other sources. **Figure 9.9** shows how XBRL documents are created. XBRL helps companies:

- Generate cleaner data, including written explanations and supporting notes.
- Produce more accurate data with fewer errors that require follow-up by regulators.
- Transmit data more quickly to regulators and meet deadlines.
- Increase the number of cases and amount of information that staffers can handle.

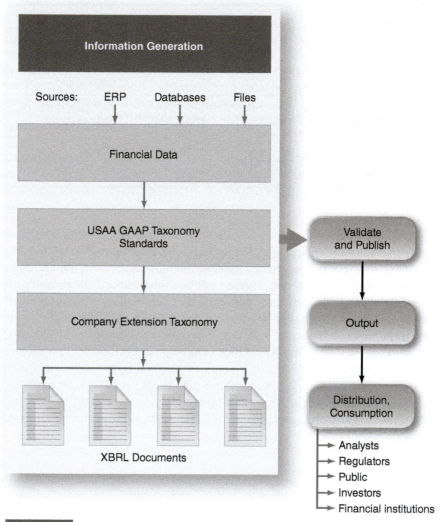

FIGURE 9.9 Overview of the creation of XBRL documents.

XBRL Reporting Compliance In addition to the public companies required by the SEC to submit their financial reports as XBRL documents, other businesses are being required to use XBRL-formatted reporting. For instance, the SEC requires mutual funds to submit risk return summaries in XBRL format, and banks in the United States must submit certain types of XBRL reports to the Federal Deposit Insurance Corporation (FDIC). Globally, regulators in many other countries require companies to file reports using XBRL. When international firms file XBRL reports, they will oftentimes use the International Financial Reporting Standards (IFRS) Taxonomy created by the International Accounting Standards Board (IASB). We anticipate that XBRL reporting will increase over time as regulatory agencies, investors, and organizations responsible for setting accounting standards increasingly argue that XBRL reporting is good for both business and the economy.

Fraud Prevention and Detection

Fraud is a crime with severe financial consequences, as you observed in Table 9.2. Fighting fraud is an ethical duty—and essential to public trust and the integrity of a company's brand. **Insider fraud** is a term referring to a variety of criminal behaviors perpetrated by an organization's employees or contractors. Other terms for this crime are **internal, employment, or occupational fraud**.

Why Fraud Occurs   Fraud occurs because internal controls to prevent insider fraud—no matter how strong—will fail on occasion. **Fraud risk management** is a system of policies and procedures to prevent and detect illegal acts committed by managers, employees, customers, or business partners against a company's interests. Although each corporation establishes its own specific procedures, fraud risk management involves assessing a company's exposure to fraud; implementing defenses to prevent and detect fraud; defining procedures to investigate, prosecute, and recover losses from fraud. Analyzing why and how fraud could occur is as important as detecting and stopping it. This analysis is used to identify necessary corporate policies to deter insider fraud and fraud detection systems when prevention fails.

Fraud Risk Factors   Factors that increase a company's exposure to fraud are illustrated in **Figure 9.10**. ISs are implemented to harden it against these factors. Companies make themselves targets because of the interaction of these four factors:

1. A high level of trust in employees without sufficient oversight to verify that they are not stealing from the company
2. Relying on informal processes of control
3. A mindset (belief) that internal controls and fraud prevention systems are too expensive to implement
4. Assigning a wide range of duties for each employee, giving them opportunities to commit fraud

FIGURE 9.10   Factors that make companies targets for fraud.

When a small manufacturer was the victim of theft of intellectual property, the computer network logs identified the computer that had been used to commit the alleged crime. But there was no way to connect that computer to one specific individual. A manager's conviction that he knew who had perpetrated the crime was not sufficient evidence. The lesson learned was that the internal control—*separation of duties*—is important not only to fraud prevention but also to fraud prosecution and recovery of losses. At the company, employees had shared computer accounts, so they were not able to link the fraud to the person who committed it.

Designing effective fraud response and litigation-readiness strategies (postincident strategies) is crucial to be able to do the following:

- Recover financial losses.
- Punish perpetrators through lawsuits, criminal charges, and/or forfeited gains.
- Stop fraudsters from victimizing other organizations.

History has shown that if the punishment for committing fraud is not severe, the fraudster's next employer will be the next victim, as described in **IT at Work 9.2**.

Trying to keep fraud hidden can mean either *doing nothing* or simply firing the employee. These approaches to dealing with fraud are not sustainable because they erode the effectiveness of fraud prevention measures and produce **moral hazard**—that is, they take the risk out of insider fraud.

One of the most effective fraud prevention techniques is the perception of detection and punishment. If a company shows its employees that it can find out everything that every employee does and will prosecute to the fullest extent anyone who commits fraud, then the feeling that "I can get away with it" drops drastically (Johnson et al., 2011). The Catch-22 is that companies may have limited resources that hinder a proper fraud diagnosis or forensic accounting investigation, even though they cannot afford unrecoverable losses either.

IT at Work 9.2

Serial Fraudster

A dental practice with $4 million in annual revenues had fired its bookkeeper after a tax audit revealed to the owners that she had been stealing over $100,000 per year for at least four years. The bookkeeper was responsible for all accounting duties and financial reporting for tax purposes. Her work was not inspected closely by external auditors or the owners. No internal control systems, for example, controls that would prevent checks being written to bogus vendors or employees, were implemented.

The classic **red flags** or fraud indicators—lavish vacations, jewelry, and cars that she could not afford—were evident, but ignored by the owners/managers. The bookkeeper was a "serial fraudster," having defrauded at least two prior employers: a religious organization and a nonprofit where she had worked as a volunteer.

The defrauded medical practice decided to keep the incident quiet, so it did not take legal action against the bookkeeper. That turned out to be a mistake because the bookkeeper used that situation to her advantage. She filed a wrongful termination lawsuit. For several reasons, including not being able to collect evidence (lax internal controls enabled the bookkeeper to destroy evidence), the practice settled the lawsuit by paying her over $5,000. In effect, the fraudster had turned to extortion, knowing that the practice was unprepared to fight back. Inarguably, she must be defrauding her current employer.

IT at Work Questions

1. How was the fraud detected?
2. How long had it been going on?
3. What were the red flags that suggested that the bookkeeper was living beyond her means?
4. What mistakes were made in the handling of the fraud?
5. In your opinion, did the dental practice have an ethical responsibility to prosecute the fraudster?

Financial Meltdowns Triggered by Fraud In the early 2000s, the U.S. business economy was significantly impacted by fraud scandals that involved senior executives at a number of major corporations. Lawmakers believed that the scope of the crimes destroyed the public's confidence in the country's financial systems and markets. A number of laws were passed that heightened the legal responsibilities of corporate management to actively guard against fraud by employees, established stricter management and reporting requirements, and introduced severe penalties for failure to comply. As a result, fraud management became a necessary functional process. These frauds played a role in the SEC's rule for XBRL data reporting.

Internal Controls In companies with lax accounting systems, it is too easy for employees to misdirect purchase orders and payments, bribe a supplier, or manipulate accounting data. When senior managers are involved in a fraud, preventing fraud is extremely tough. Consider Bernie Madoff, who committed a record-setting fraud scheme for many years even after the Sarbanes–Oxley Act was passed in 2002 to help prevent financial fraud.

In a much smaller but still serious fraud case involving a New York-based nonprofit, a volunteer was responsible for counting cash receipts at the annual fundraiser. The volunteer had performed this task for 30 years. One year, an accountant was assigned to assist the volunteer with the count. The volunteer offered the accountant a "cut" of the cash in exchange for her silence about the theft.

Strong internal controls, which depend on IT for their effectiveness, consist of the following:

- **Segregation of duties** tops the list of best practices in control procedures. When handling a company's assets, the work of managers and employees needs to be subject to approval or authorization. For example, any attempt to issue a check to a vendor not in the database of approved vendors will be prevented by the accounting IS.

- **Job rotation** More than one person should be familiar with each transaction cycle in the business wherever possible. Rotation of jobs helps prevent overreliance on a single individual—and is a way to expose fraudulent activities.

- **Oversight** Management—whether a single owner or a team of individuals—must monitor what is actually happening in the business. Auditing ISs are part of a strong oversight function. Unannounced periodic walk-throughs of a process or review of how things are really being done can reveal existing or potential problem areas.

- **Safeguarding of assets** is essential to a fraud prevention program. Access to networks, financial systems, and databases must be controlled with strong passwords and other security measures. Similarly, bank checks, petty cash funds, and company credit cards need to be locked up when not in use.

- **IT policies** Understand your IS. Heavy reliance on IT staff can open up opportunities for fraud. Establish a computer use policy and educate employees on the importance of securing information. Strictly enforce the use of separate logins and keep passwords confidential.

Auditing Information Systems

Fraud can be easy to commit and hard to detect. Just ask any auditor. The problem is worse in government and nonprofit entities that have inadequate accounting and internal control systems. The problem is so bad at the federal level that auditors have been unable to express an opinion on the fairness of the consolidated financial statements of the United States. For example, space agency NASA had been unable to explain about the $565 billion in year-end adjustments to its books. It could be bad accounting, fraud, waste, or abuse. Without adequate records, no one really knows. This amount is astounding, especially when one considers that the combined cost of fraud at Enron and WorldCom was less than $100 billion in shareholder equity.

Because the physical possession of stolen property is no longer required and it is just as easy to program a computer to misdirect $100,000 as it is $1,000, the size and number of frauds have increased tremendously. Auditing ISs aid auditors in the analysis of large amounts of financial data and accounting records to uncover fraud as well as unintentional accounting errors.

Financial Planning and Budgeting

The management of financial assets is a major task in financial planning and budgeting. Financial planning, similarly to any other functional planning, is tied to the overall organizational planning and to other functional areas. It is divided into short-, medium-, and long-term horizons, much as activities planning. Accounting ISs help companies create and manage budgets, improving the organization's ability to monitor performance and quickly identify departures from planned financial activity when they occur.

Knowing the availability and cost of money is a key ingredient for successful financial planning. Especially important is projecting cash flows, which tells organizations what funds they need and when and how they will acquire them. In today's tough economic conditions with tight credit and limited availability of funds, this function has become critical to most companies' survival.

Inaccurate cash flow projection is the #1 reason why many small businesses go bankrupt. The inability to access credit led to the bankruptcy of investment bank Lehman Brothers in September 2008.

Budgeting The best-known part of financial planning is the annual budget, which allocates the financial resources of an organization among participants, activities, and projects. The budget is the financial expression of the enterprise's plans. Management allocates resources in the way that best supports the mission. IT enables the introduction of financial logic and efficiency into the budgeting process. Several software packages, many of which are Web-based, are available to support budget preparation and control.

Capital budgeting is the process of analyzing and selecting investments with the highest return on investment (ROI) for the company. The process may include comparing alternative investments, for example, evaluating private cloud vs. public cloud computing options.

The major benefits of using budgeting software are that it can reduce the time and effort involved in the budget process, explore and analyze the implications of organizational and environmental changes, facilitate the integration of corporate strategic objectives with operational plans, make planning an ongoing continuous process, and automatically monitor exceptions for patterns and trends.

Forecasting As you read, a major reason why organizations fail is their inability to forecast and/or secure sufficient cash flow. Underestimated expenses, overspending, financial mismanagement, and fraud can lead to disaster. Good planning is necessary, but not sufficient, and must be supplemented by skillful control. Control activities in organizations take many forms, including control and **auditing** of the ISs themselves. ISs play an extremely important role in supporting organizational control, as we show throughout the text. Specific forms of financial control are discussed in the next section.

Financial Ratio Analysis A major task of the accounting/finance department is to watch the financial health of the company by monitoring and assessing a set of financial ratios. These ratios are also used by external parties when they decide whether to invest in an organization, extend credit, or buy it.

The collection of data for ratio analysis is done by the TPS, and computation of the ratios completed through financial analysis models. Interpretation of ratios and the ability to forecast their future behavior require expertise, which is supported by decision support systems (DSSs).

Profitability Analysis and Cost Control Companies are concerned with the profitability of individual products or services, product lines, divisions, or the financial health of the entire organization. Profitability analysis DSS software allows accurate computation of profitability and allocation of overhead costs. One way to control cost is by properly estimating it. This is done by using special software. For example, Oracle Hyperion Profitability and Cost Management software is a performance management app that provides insights into costs and profitability. This app helps managers evaluate business performance by discovering the drivers of cost and profitability and improving resource alignment. Sophisticated business rules are stored in one place, enabling analyses and strategies to be shared easily across an enterprise.

Questions

1. What is eXtensible Business Reporting Language (XBRL)?
2. Why does the SEC mandate data disclosure, whereby data items are tagged to make them easily searchable?
3. What is insider fraud? What are some other terms for insider fraud?
4. What is fraud risk management?
5. What four factors increase the risk of fraud?
6. Explain how accounting ISs can help deter fraud.

9.5 | Human Resource Systems, Compliance, and Ethics

Companies cannot simply hire a great workforce. They have to find, recruit, motivate, and train employees to succeed in their workplace. Retaining high-performance people requires monitoring how people feel about the workplace, their compensation, value to the company, and chances for advancement—and maintaining workplace health and safety.

HR is a field that deals with employment policies, procedures, communications, and compliance requirements. Effective HR compliance programs are a necessity for all organizations in today's legal environment. HR needs to monitor workplace and employment practices to ensure compliance with the Fair Labor Standards Act (FLSA), Occupational Health & Safety Agencies (OSHA), and the antidiscrimination and sexual harassment laws. Seven other employment laws to protect against discrimination are listed in **Table 9.3**.

TABLE 9.3   **HR Monitors Compliance with Antidiscrimination Employment Laws**

Title VII of the Civil Rights Act of 1964	Prohibits discrimination on the basis of race, color, religion, national origin, and sex. It also prohibits sex discrimination on the basis of pregnancy and sexual harassment.
Civil Rights Act of 1966	Prohibits discrimination based on race or ethnic origin.
Equal Pay Act of 1963	Prohibits employers from paying different wages to men and women who perform essentially the same work under similar working conditions.
Bankruptcy Act	Prohibits discrimination against anyone who has declared bankruptcy.
Americans with Disabilities Act	Prohibits discrimination against persons with disabilities.
Equal Employment Opportunity Act	Prohibits discrimination against minorities based on poor credit ratings.
Age Discrimination in Employment Act (ADEA)	Prohibits discrimination against individuals who are age 40 or above.

Career Insight 9.1

Compliance Is Good Business

While carrying out day-to-day operations or trying to hit targets, managers may lose sight of the big picture. A narrow focus can lead to serious compliance and regulatory violations, which can do permanent damage to the brand and expose managers to criminal charges. Crossing the line is a crime.

According to the U.S. Department of Justice (DOJ) *Federal Prosecution of Corporations (1999)*:

Corporations are "legal persons," capable of suing and being sued, and capable of committing crimes. Under the doctrine of *respondeat superior,* a corporation may be held criminally liable for the illegal acts of its employees, directors, officers, and agents.

In all cases involving wrongdoing by corporate agents, prosecutors should consider the corporation, as well as the responsible individuals, as potential criminal targets.

Source: justice.gov.

HR Information Systems

Effective human resource information systems (HRISs) reduce the workload of the HR department. PeopleSoft Human Capital Management, which is one of the market-leading HRISs, provides a global foundation for HR data and improved business processes.

HRISs have been moved to intranets and clouds—wherein HR applications are leased in SaaS arrangements. Using intranets, HR applications have shifted many routine tasks to employees who log in to manage their retirement benefits, payroll deductions, direct deposits, health-care benefits, and the like. When employees manage their own HR services, HR professionals can focus on legal and compliance responsibilities, employee development, talent management, hiring, and succession planning.

Benefits of SaaS for HR   Three real-world examples illustrate the benefits of tying SaaS to global HR transformation efforts:

- A global medical device manufacturer needed to create an independent HR system as it divested from its parent company. Cloud computing was at the core of its new global HR delivery model, which reduced the demand on internal business and IT resources. The company was able to establish fully independent HR operations within 10 months.
- A national nonprofit foundation with a fast-growing employee population wanted to improve the effectiveness of HR operations. The organization selected a cloud-based solution, which dramatically improved time to value without overstretching internal IT resources. Because little front-end investment was required, the foundation hit its budget target.
- A global entertainment company needed a learning management system that could deliver content varying from instructor-based training to 30-second video how-to snippets. It chose to deploy a new learning management system in the cloud. With this approach, it quickly got the new system up and running.

Figure 9.11 illustrates how IT facilitates the work of the HR department. The figure summarizes the role HR plays in acquiring and developing talented people in organizations.

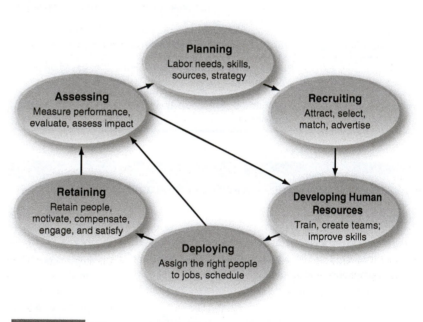

FIGURE 9.11   HR management activities.

Recruitment   Recruitment is the process of finding potential employees with the skills and talent needed by the company, testing them, and deciding which ones to hire. Most companies are flooded with applicants, but might still have difficulty finding the right people. LinkedIn is a primary social media site for recruitment and headhunters. Some reports suggest that over 90% of U.S. companies use LinkedIn as their primary source of identifying job candidates. HR managers using LinkedIn must become familiar with the website's search tools for finding candidates that meet certain criteria for the position they are trying to fill. Using the advanced search features, HR managers can develop search queries that screen user profiles on the basis of things such as current job title, current industry, seniority level, and years of education. Keywords can be used to find candidates with specials, training, or experience. Job hunters should consider the search strategies HR professionals are likely to use when searching for candidates and include information in their profiles that will increase the chances of being included in search results.

Management and Employee Development

Once recruited, employees become part of the corporate HR talent pool, which needs to be maintained and developed. Several activities supported by IT include the following.

Performance Evaluation Employees are evaluated periodically by their immediate supervisors. Peers or subordinates may also evaluate others. Evaluations are usually recorded on paper or electronic forms. Using such information manually is a tedious and error-prone job. Once digitized, evaluations can be used to support many decisions, ranging from rewards to transfers to layoffs. For example, Cisco Systems is known for developing an IT-based human capital strategy. Many universities evaluate professors online. The evaluation form appears on the screen, and the students fill it in. Results can be tabulated in minutes. Corporate managers can analyze employees' performances with the help of intelligent systems, which provide systematic interpretation of performance over time. Several vendors provide software for performance evaluation, such as HalogenSoftware.com and Capterra.com.

Training and Human Resources Development Employee training and retraining are important activities of the HR department. Major issues are planning of classes and tailoring specific training programs to meet the needs of the organization and employees. Sophisticated HR departments build a career development plan for each employee. IT can support the planning, monitoring, and control of these activities by using workflow applications.

HR Planning, Control, and Management

In some industries, labor negotiation is an important aspect of HR planning, and it may be facilitated by IT. For most companies, administering employee benefits is also a significant part of the HR function. Here are several examples of how IT can help.

Personnel Planning and HR Strategies The HR department forecasts requirements for people and skills. In some geographical areas and for overseas assignments, it may be difficult to find particular types of employees. In such cases, the HR department plans how to locate sufficient HR or develop them from within.

Benefits Administration Employees' contributions to their organizations are rewarded by salary/wage, bonuses, and other benefits. Benefits include those for health and dental care as well as contributions for pensions. Managing the benefits system can be a complex task, due to its many components and the tendency of organizations to allow employees to choose and trade off benefits. In large companies, using computers for self-benefits selection can save a tremendous amount of labor and time for HR staff.

Providing flexibility in selecting benefits is viewed as a competitive advantage in large organizations. It can be successfully implemented when supported by computers. Some companies have automated benefits enrollments. Employees can self-register for specific benefits using the corporate portal or voice technology. Employees self-select desired benefits from a menu. Payroll pay cards are now in use in numerous companies, such as Payless Shoes, which has 30,000 employees in 5,000 stores. The system specifies the value of each benefit and the available benefits balance of each employee. Some companies use intelligent agents to assist employees and monitor their actions.

Employee Relationship Management In their effort to better manage employees, companies are developing human capital management, facilitated by the Web, to streamline the HR process. These Web applications are more commonly referred to as employee relationship management. For example, self-services such as tracking personal information and online training are very popular in ERM. Improved relationships with employees result in better retention and higher productivity.

Ethical Challenges and Considerations HRIS applications raise ethical and legal challenges. For example, training activities that are part of HRM may involve ethical issues in recruiting and selecting employees and in evaluating performance. Similarly, TPS data processing and storage deal with private information about people, their performance, and so forth. Care should be taken to protect this information and the privacy of employees and customers.

The federal law related to workplace substance abuse, the Drug-Free Workplace Act of 1990, requires employers with federal government contracts or grants to ensure a drug-free workplace by documenting and certifying that they have taken a number of steps. Dealing with alcoholism and drugs at work entails legal risks because employees have sued for invasion of privacy, wrongful discharge, defamation, and illegal searches. Employment laws make securing HR information necessary for the protection of employees and the organization.

Questions

1. What are the key HR functions?
2. What are the benefits of moving HRISs to intranets or the cloud?
3. What concerns have deterred companies from implementing SaaS HR?
4. How can companies reduce the cost of recruiting qualified employees?
5. Describe IT support for HR planning and control.
6. What are ethical issues related to HRM applications?

Key Terms

ACID test 275
auditing 292
capital budgeting 292
computer-integrated manufacturing (CIM) 281
economic order quantity (EOQ) 279
eXtensible Business Reporting Language (XBRL) 287
Financial Accounting Standards Board (FASB) 286
financial misrepresentation 286
flexible manufacturing systems (FMSs) 281
fraud risk management 289
GAAP Financial Reporting Taxonomy 287
inbound logistics 278

income statement 286
insider fraud 289
internal employment or occupational fraud 289
inventory control systems 279
just-in-time (JIT) 279
lean manufacturing system 280
manufacturing execution systems 281
manufacturing quality control (QC) systems 280
mission 273
moral hazard 290
online transaction processing systems (OTPS) 276

operations level 274
outbound logistics 278
red flag 290
safety stock 279
standard operating procedures (SOPs) 275
stockouts 279
Strategic plans 273
strategic planning 273
tactical level 274
total quality management (TQM) 280

Assuring Your Learning

Discuss: Critical Thinking Questions

1. Discuss the need for sharing data among functional areas.

2. How does waste increase costs? Give three examples.

3. What is the value of lean manufacturing?

4. What is the objective of EOQ?

5. What are the risks of JIT?

6. Explain the value of being able to respond to hot data.

7. Push-through ads use data about a person to determine whether the ad should appear. What marketing opportunities does this capability create?

8. Explain why the SEC requires that filers use XBRL.

9. How can internal controls help to prevent fraud?

10. How do companies allow themselves to become targets for insider fraud?

11. What are the benefits of prosecuting an employee who has committed fraud against the company?

12. Why might a company not want to prosecute a fraudster?

13. Explain moral hazard. Give a fraud-related example.

14. Fraudsters typically spend the money they steal on luxury items and vacations. Explain why these items are red flags of fraud.

15. What are three examples of strong internal controls?

16. Discuss how IT facilitates the capital budgeting process.

17. Discuss the role IT plays in auditing.

18. Explain the role and benefits of SaaS in HR management.

19. How does digital technology improve the recruitment process?

Explore: Online and Interactive Exercises

1. Visit the Oracle website at **www.oracle.com**.

   a. Search for "Peoplesoft."

   b. Select *Human Capital Management* and review the HR applications. Describe three benefits of PeopleSoft Human Capital Management.

   c. Return to the Peoplesoft site. Select *Financial Management*. Describe how PeopleSoft Financial Management reduces costs.

2. Search for a video or demo that explains EOQ. Explain the formula.

3. Finding a job on the Internet is challenging; there are almost too many places to look. Visit two recruiting sites, for example, careerbuilder.com and LinkedIn.com. What benefits do these sites provide to you as a job seeker?

4. Examine the capabilities of two financial software packages: Prepare a table that clearly compares and contrasts their capabilities.

5. Review Salesforce.com. What functional support does the software provide?

Analyze & Decide: Apply IT Concepts to Business Decisions

1. Research and analyze a major corporate fraud.

   a. Identify the company and explain when and how the fraud occurred, who was involved, and damages.

   b. How was the fraud detected?

   c. Describe any red flags associated with the fraud.

   d. Visit SAS.com and search "SAS fraud management." Explain how SAS fraud management could have helped prevent the fraud.

Case 9.2

Business Case: HSBC Combats Fraud in Split-second Decisions

With billions of dollars, corporate reputations, customer loyalty, and criminal penalties for noncompliance at stake, financial firms must outsmart fraudsters. Detecting and preventing fraudulent transactions across many lines of business (checking, savings, credit cards, loans, etc.) and online channels require comprehensive real-time data analytics to assess and score transactions. That is, each transaction has to be analyzed within a split second to calculate the probability that it is fraudulent or legitimate.

A big part of a bank's relationship with customers is giving them confidence that they are protected against fraud and balancing that protection with their need to have access to your services.

HSCB Overview

HSBC is a commercial bank known by many as the "world's local bank." HSBC is a United Kingdom-based company that provides a wide range of banking and related financial services. The bank reported a pretax profit of $6.8 billion in the first quarter of 2014 (1Q 2014). It has 6,300 offices in 75 countries and over 54 million customers.

Fighting Fraudulent Transactions

HSBC was able to reduce the incidence of fraud across tens of millions of debit and credit card accounts. The bank implemented the latest Fraud Management software from SAS. The software includes an application programming interface (API) and a real-time transaction scoring system based on advanced data analytics. Using the Fraud Management app, HSBC has reduced its losses from fraudulent transactions worldwide and its exposure to increasingly aggressive threats. The antifraud solution is live in the United States, Europe, and Asia, where it protects 100% of credit card transactions in real time.

Scenario

Consider this scenario. A credit card transaction request comes in for the purchase of $6,000 in home appliances. The bank has a moment to decide to approve the transaction or reject it as potentially fraudulent. Two outcomes are possible:

- **Legitimate purchase rejected** When a legitimate purchase is rejected, the customer might pay with another card. The bank loses the fee income from the purchase and the interest fee. Risk of account churn increases.

- **Fraudulent purchase accepted** When a fraudulent purchase is accepted, a legitimate customer becomes a victim of a crime. The bank incurs the $6,000 loss, the cost of the fraud investigation, potential regulatory scrutiny, and bad publicity. Chances of recovering any losses are almost zero.

With trillions of dollars in assets, HSBC Holdings plc is a prime target for fraud. Fighting all forms of fraud—unauthorized use of cards for payment and online transactions and even customer fraud—has risen to the top of the corporate agenda. Fraud losses are operating costs that damage the bottom line.

As required by regulations, HSBC has implemented policies to segregate duties, create dual controls, and establish strong audit trails to detect anomalies. In addition, the bank has antifraud technology, which includes SAS Fraud Management, to monitor and score the millions of daily transactions. It is the cornerstone of these efforts.

Fraud Management

In 2007, HSBC's first SAS implementation went live in the United States, which was their largest portfolio with 30 million cards issued there. All transactions were scored in real time. Detection rates on debit ATM transactions have been very effective. HSBC has updated its Fraud Management solution multiple times as newer technology and threats emerged.

Of course, financial fraud morphs to avoid new detection methods, so antifraud models have a very short shelf life. Once HSBC closes up one loophole, thieves devise new threats to exploit other potential vulnerabilities. To counteract threats, fraud-monitoring algorithms and scoring models require constant refreshing.

Questions

1. Analyze the reasons to invest millions of dollars to detect and prevent fraudulent transactions. In your evaluation, do a cost–benefit analysis to show why the investment cost is worthwhile.

2. Review the two outcomes of the fraud scenario. Assess the business implications of each of the following two goals. Explain why these goals are conflicting.

   a. To minimize rejecting legitimate purchases by authorized customers

   b. To minimize the risk of making customers victims of fraud

3. The Fraud Management solution is based on a scoring model. For example, assume that the scores range from 1 to 10, with 10 being the highest probability that the transaction is fraudulent. What cutoff score would you use to decide to approve a purchase? What cutoff score would you use to decide not to approve a purchase? If those cutoff scores are not the same, how do you suggest those falling between scores be treated?

4. Why are approval decisions made in a split second? Would customers tolerate a brief delay in the approval process if it reduced their risk of identity theft? Explain your answer.

5. Research ATM or other banking transaction fraud. How has a financial firm been defrauded or harmed?

Sources: BusinessWire (2011), SAS.com (2014), Reuters (2014), YouTube video "HSBC Relies on SAS for Comprehensive Fraud Detection."

Case 9.3

Video Case: United Rentals Optimizes Its Workforce with Human Capital Management

Visit Oracle.com and search "United Rentals Optimizes Workforce." Click on the video link to "United Rentals Optimizes Its Workforce with Oracle HCM." Watch the video. Describe the key benefits of its HR software. Visit Forbes.com and search for the article "10 Trends Driving the Mandate for Modern HCM" posted on February 7, 2014.

Questions

1. Typically, the importance of the HR function is overlooked, or at least overshadowed by accounting and finance, which manage cash and other financial assets. In your opinion, is HCM software as important as accounting software? Explain your answer.

2. Briefly describe three of the key trends driving HCM and how they relate to the HR software benefits at United Rentals.

References

Accenture.com. "Ducati Motor Holding S.p.A: SAP Dealer Communication System." 2014.

Apple.com. "Ducati." 2014.

BusinessWire. "SAS Fraud Management Speeds Real time Processing Boosts Detection and Prevention." June 15, 2011.

Ducati Motor Holding S.p.A. 2014. http://www.ducatiusa.com/index.do

fasb.org. "US GAAP Financial Reporting Taxonomy." 2012.

Johnson, P., L. Volonino, and I. Redpath. "Fraud Response and Litigation-Readiness Strategies for Small and Medium Businesses: A Handbook on How to Prepare for Litigation, Prosecution & Loss Recovery in Response to Insider Fraud." *IFP.org*, November 2011.

Justice.com, 2014.

Oracle.com. 2014.

Reuters. "HSBC Holdings plc Company Profile." 2014. http://www.reuters.com

Salesforce.com. 2014.

SAP.com. 2014.

SAS.com. "Reduce Losses from Fraudulent Transactions." http://www.sas.com

sec.gov. 2014

Wilson, D. "Manufacturing Technology: Hard Work." *The Engineer* 33, April 25, 2011.

xbrl.sec.gov. 2014.

CHAPTER 10

Enterprise Systems

CHAPTER OUTLINE	LEARNING OBJECTIVES
Case 10.1 Opening Case: 3D Printing Drives the "Always-On" Supply Chain	
10.1 Enterprise Systems	**10.1 Name** the different types of enterprise systems and explain how they differ from legacy systems.
10.2 Enterprise Resource Planning	**10.2 Describe** the functions of enterprise resource planning (ERP) systems, implementation risks, and how ERP investments are justified.
10.3 Supply Chain Management	**10.3 Explain** the planning and forecasting, sourcing and purchasing, and distribution support provided by supply chain management (SCM) systems.
10.4 Customer Relationship Management	**10.4 Describe** customer relationship management (CRM) systems and their role in customer acquisition, retention, and customer lifetime value.
10.5 Enterprise Social Platforms	**10.5 Identify** the leading enterprise social platforms (ESPs) and discuss how they impact collaboration in an organization.
Case 10.2 Business Case: Lowe's Fresh Approach to Supply Chain Management	
Case 10.3 Video Case: Procter & Gamble: Creating Conversations in the Cloud with 4.8 Billion Consumers	

Introduction

An important challenge for business leaders is how to seamlessly integrate their data existing in the many different types of information systems (ISs), such as TPS, MIS, DSS, and EIS, to better meet the needs of their customers and achieve business objectives.

This dilemma is widespread in the business community since many enterprises who have been in business for over 25 years are still using antiquated, siloed mainframe computers and software implemented 20–30 years ago. These systems are difficult and expensive to maintain, update, integrate, and **interface** securely with leading-edge business apps. When companies decide to update their IT infrastructure, they must invest in tightly integrated **enterprise systems** that offer seamless data handling between all the different types of systems and are easier to secure. With these enterprise-level system, companies are able to operate at optimal efficiency levels and make better informed decisions consistent with the corporate strategy. Enterprise systems fall into three primary categories: **Enterprise resource planning (ERP)**, **supply chain management** (SCM), and **customer relationship management (CRM)**. These enterprise systems are integrated by their connection to central data repositories that enable them to synchronize and share corporate data from all departments and functional areas so that employees can view enterprisewide data. A fourth category of an enterprise level system—enterprise social platforms(ESPs)—is a relative newcomer to the enterprise system portfolio. ESPs are designed to facilitate collaboration and communication among employees of an organization.

In this chapter, you will learn about the benefits, limitations, and risks of investing in and implementing cross-functional enterprise systems and business apps that support business strategy, managers, and employees—and how these systems affect relationships with suppliers, vendors, and customers. In the opening case, you will learn how strategic technology, such as 3D printing, can drive the changing demands of business processes that are supported by enterprise systems.

Enterprise systems are cross-functional and interorganizational systems that support the business strategy.

Supply chain management (SCM) is the efficient management of the flows of material, data, and payments among the companies in the supply chain, from suppliers to consumers.

3D printing Also known as additive manufacturing, builds objects layer-by-layer to create real-world objects.

Case 10.1 Opening Case

© Stefano Tinti/Shutterstock

monkeybusinessimages/ iStock/ Getty Images

3D Printing Drives the "Always-On" Supply Chain

It is widely agreed that 3D printing is destined to transform almost every major industry and change the way we live, work, and play in the future. When MHI and Deloitte identified eight technologies that are driving the always-on supply chain, their list included 3D printing, and Gartner predicts that 3D printer will necessitate a rethinking of assembly line and supply chain processes as it expands to meet demand in more industry sectors. Goldman Sachs and McKinsey made similar predictions (see **Figure 10.1**).

The worldwide revenue of the 3D printing industry is expected to reach $12.8 Billion by 2018 and exceed $21 Billion by 2020. With **3D printing**, computer-created digital models are used to create real-world objects such as cars, toys, jewelry, food, spare parts, prosthetic devices, organ tissues, and more. **Table 10.1** lists and explains the features and benefits of 3D printing.

For several decades, 3D printing has been used by manufacturers to reduce research and development (R&D) costs. 3D printing builds products layer by layer, using an **additive manufacturing** process that has less overhead costs and allows for more complex designs. Using this technology, engineers rapidly created a physical prototype of a new design. The prototype is then used to test the quality of the design and to check for defects.

Impact on The Supply Chain

3D printing is revolutionizing how companies offer their products. The process of creating a product in traditional manufacturing is widely different from 3D printing. Most parts are built by removing layers of material (cutting, drilling, sanding, etc.), which results in the part's final form. But with 3D printing, layers of materials are added to each other by applying heat or chemicals to create a finished product. Compared to traditional manufacturing and prototyping methods,

---

According to global investment management from GOLDMAN SACHS

3D printing is 1 of 8 technologies that are going to creatively destroy how companies do business

---

IT Research firm Gartner predicted:

3D printing of nonliving medical devices such as prosthetic limbs, combined with past population growth and insufficient healthcare in emerging markets, is likely to cause an explosion in demand for the technology

---

Global Research firm McKinsey forecasted:

3D printing is 1 of 12 disruptive technologies that could deliver major economic impact to the global economy by 2025

Global Research firm MHI/Deloitte forecasted:

There will be an evolution of 3D printing supply chain applications, increasing adoption rates.

FIGURE 10.1 Strong forecasts for 3D printing made by leading research and investment management firms—Goldman Sachs, Gartner, McKinsey, and MHI/Deloitte.

TABLE 10.1 Overview of 3D Printing

What is 3D printing? How does it work?	3D printing, also known as additive manufacturing, builds objects layer by layer. Traditional manufacturing typically uses a subtractive process, whereby materials are cut, ground, or molded to create an object.
What enterprise systems are impacted by 3D printing?	The potential for 3D printing to revolutionize ERP (enterprise resource planning) and SCM (supply chain management) means business and IT professionals must develop a framework for evaluating its impact.
Where is 3D print technology used?	3D technology is being used by consumer-product designers, automotive manufacturing engineers, medical and dental labs for building prototypes, replacement parts, and customized products on demand. Retailers and manufacturers are evaluating applications of 3D printing.
What factors are limiting widespread use?	3D printing has not yet reached the point where its cost, speed, and scalability can compete with traditional manufacturing.

3D printing offers high levels of customization, reduced costs for complex designs, and lower overhead costs for short-run parts and products. Capabilities of 3D printing hardware are expanding, and costs have dropped dramatically. They will be able to build larger components with greater precision or resolution at higher speeds and lower costs. Forecasts indicate that 3D printing is becoming a viable alternative to traditional manufacturing processes in a growing number of applications. Instead of using ink cartridges that are currently used in printer, 3D printing uses a wide range of materials, including advanced nickel alloys, carbon fiber, glass, conductive ink, electronics, pharmaceuticals, and biological materials.

According to McKinsey, 3D printing will have an impact on consumer sectors that place a premium on highly customizable products, for example, footwear, toys, and jewelry. McKinsey estimates that by 2025, sales of 3D-printed products in these three industries alone may reach $550 billion per year.

The following examples show the potential of 3D printing.

Hardware Stores

When customers shop for replacement parts, the store could use a 3D printer with all the pattern specifications to print onsite and on-demand. Hardware stores could slash their inventory and store sizes and improve customer service.

Defense

Troops in the field and their equipment require regular maintenance. Having a 3D printer at small supply post in the field rather than at a larger base far away alters the ability to complete maintenance and repair and provide a **supply chain** in combat.

Health Care

Hospitals use expensive equipment, such as magnetic resonance imaging (MRI) scanners. Downtime spent waiting for onsite repair is expensive. A technician who was guided remotely by the manufacturer could diagnose and fix the problem immediately by 3D-printing the MRI scanner replacement part onsite.

The outlook for medical use of 3D printing is growing at an extremely rapid pace as specialists are beginning to utilize 3D printing of 3D-printed implants and prosthetics. For example, hip surgery done with a 3D-printed titanium implant and bone stem cell graft has been conducted in the United Kingdom. The hip part was designed using the patient's CT scan, thereby matching the patient's exact specifications and measurements. Even more radical is the potential for complex and controversial **3D bioprinting** of human tissue and organs. Scientists are already 3D-printing organ tissue. Organovo, a San Diego, CA, forward-thinking medical company, recently announced plans to develop 3D bioprinted human liver tissues for direct transplantation into patients, and Russian scientists have bioprinted a thyroid gland using stems as an "ink." Although printing whole human organs for surgical transplants is still years away, the technology is rapidly developing. The ethical arguments and challenges of bioprinting will be discussed in Chapter 14.

Reproduction of Vintage Car Components

In 1969, Ferrari introduced one of its most masterful race cars—the 312P. But parts for that vintage car do not exist. To rebuild an engine, a special aluminum alloy was poured into a cast, which was created by 3D printing. The new engine block and engine rebuild were completed in record time. 3D printing is by far the most efficient method for reproducing components that are no longer available. Often, it is the only way to reproduce certain components quickly and at reasonable cost.

Aerospace Manufacturing

GE is using additive manufacturing to make fuel nozzles for its next-generation Leap engines that will power the new Boeing 737 and Airbus A320 jets. The fuel nozzles will be 25% lighter and 5 times more durable. Since there are 20 nozzles in each engine, the weight savings for each aircraft are significant. In addition, the FAA recently cleared GE Aviation's first 3D-printed jet engine part to fly! Another aerospace application is the combustion chamber liners that are being printed using selective laser melting by NASA.

Industrial Design

Large industrial group Siemens explains that 3D printing allows its designers to imagine shapes that would be impossible to create through older techniques. The use of additive manufacturing has radically speeded up prototyping of Siemens's gas turbine blades, from 20 weeks to 48 hours. Additive manufacturing has also cut the cost of tooling and materials. For example, a piece can have all of its holes incorporated into it with precision because it is built up from powder rather than being expensively drilled afterward. Siemens hopes to cut the cost of some parts by 30%.

Manufacturing On-Demand

The ability to manufacture replacement parts on-demand using 3D printers is expected to transform after-market services and restructure industries. Smaller facilities with 3D printers onsite could replace large regional warehouses. The supply of service parts might even be outsourced: Small fabricators located, for example, at airports, hospitals, or major manufacturing venues could make these parts for much of the equipment used onsite, with data supplied directly by the manufacturers.

Questions

1. Compare and contrast the predictions made by Goldman Sachs, Gartner, MHI/Deloitte, and McKinsey on the impact of 3D printing.

2. Discuss the differences between the traditional linear supply chain and the always-on supply chain.

3. Explain how the manufacturing supply chain will be changed by 3D printing.

4. In what situations is 3D printing most valuable?

5. Explain why medical use of 3D printing is growing at an extremely rapid pace.

6. Name four industries in which 3D printing is changing the supply chain.

7. Do you consider 3D printing an important technology? Explain.

Sources: Compiled from Fine (2014), Bourne (2014), *The Engineer* (2014), Cole (2014), MHI and Deloitte (2016), Gartner.com (2016) and 3dprinting.com (2017).

10.1 | Enterprise Systems

An Enterprise system is a large-scale application software package that supports business processes, information flows, reporting, and data analytics in complex organizations. Enterprise systems not only integrate systems within the organization but also link organizations with their suppliers, business partners, and customers. While enterprise systems are considered a boon to many organizations seeking to integrate a host of disparate, siloed ISs, they can also disrupt an organization as they change the way in which data is stored and accessed and lead to resistance as demonstrated in Opening Case 10.1.

There are four types of enterprise systems typically implemented to improve business processes and functions through integration (**Table 10.2**). These are as follows:

- Enterprise resource planning (ERP)
- Supply chain management (SCM)
- Customer relationship management (CRM)
- Enterprise Social Platforms (ESPs)

3D bioprinting is the medical application of 3D printing to produce living tissue and organs. Biotech firms are using 3D printing for tissue engineering applications where organs and body parts are built using inkjet techniques. Layers of living cells are deposited onto a gel medium and slowly built up to form three-dimensional structures.

TABLE 10.2	Enterprise Systems and Their Functions	
Name	**Acronym**	**Function**
Enterprise resource planning	ERP	Integrates an enterprise's internal applications, supports its external business processes, and links to its external business partners.
		Integrate business processes, including supply chains, manufacturing, financial, human resources, budgeting, sales, and customer service.
		Used primarily in the manufacturing industry
Supply chain management	SCM	Supports the steps in the supply chain—procurement, sourcing, manufacturing, storage, inventory control, scheduling, order fulfillment, and distribution.
		Improves decision making, forecasting, optimization, and analysis.
Customer relationship management	CRM	Helps create a total view of customers to maximize share-of-wallet and profitability.
		A business strategy to segment and manage customers to optimize customer lifetime value (CLV).
Enterprise Social Platforms	ESP	Enhances social networks, both within the enterprise and across key members of the enterprise's supply and distribution chains. An important method for enhancing communication, coordination, and collaboration for business purposes.

Core business processes include accounting, finance, sales, marketing, human resources, inventory, productions, and manufacturing.

Enterprise systems, such as ERP, SCM, and CSM are integrated by their connection to a central data repository that enables them to sync and share the latest data, as illustrated in **Figure 10.2**. For example, the integration of ERP and SCM improves inventory management and supply chain performance. Another advantage of these enterprise systems is that **core business processes** can be automated for consistency and efficiency.

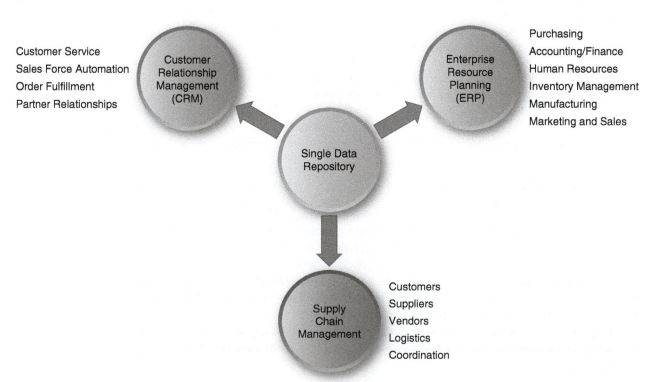

Customer Service
Sales Force Automation
Order Fulfillment
Partner Relationships

Customer Relationship Management (CRM)

Purchasing
Accounting/Finance
Human Resources
Inventory Management
Manufacturing
Marketing and Sales

Enterprise Resource Planning (ERP)

Single Data Repository

Supply Chain Management

Customers
Suppliers
Vendors
Logistics
Coordination

FIGURE 10.2 Integration of enterprise systems is achieved via access to shared data.

In contrast, ESPs focus on communication and collaboration within the company and are a relative newcomer to the suite of enterprise systems in which companies are investing. Each of these types of enterprise systems is discussed in greater detail later in this chapter.

Implementation Challenges of Enterprise Systems

Implementing an enterprise system is complex, time-consuming and typically requires the help of a consulting firm, vendor, or **value-added reseller (VAR)**. Integrating legacy systems with cloud-based applications is complex, as described in **Tech Note 10.1**. Much of the complexity is due to getting new apps or system modules to **interface** with existing or legacy systems that are several generations older.

> **Value-added reseller (VAR)** customizes or adds features to a vendor's software or equipment and resells the enhanced product.
>
> **Interface** means to connect to and exchange data with apps and systems.

Tech Note 10.1

Data Transfers to Mainframes

Enterprise systems require data transfers—often to mainframes. Designing enterprise-level systems involves a variety of components that had been implemented on mainframes, midrange computers, networks, or cloud environments. In most large enterprises, mainframes are the workhorse systems that run the majority of business transactions. In contrast, customer interfaces through customer service; ERP, CRM, and SCM apps; websites; and business-to-business (B2B) interactions are usually on distributed systems or in the cloud. Many times seemingly well-planned projects fail and require extensive reworking because integration issues had not been properly planned.

Some enterprises choose to avoid the challenges of integration by creating a new system that replaces the full functionality of the old one. This option is the most expensive, difficult, and risky. An advantage is that this option offers a longer-term solution that is agile to respond to changing business needs. Despite that potential pay-off, complete replacement requires a large up-front investment for development, poses difficulties in duplicating behavior of the **legacy system**, and increases the risk of complete software project failure.

Investing in Enterprise Systems

Companies tend to migrate to an enterprise solution when they need to consolidate their disparate systems, such as when limitations caused by their existing legacy systems interfere with performance or the ability to compete. **IT at Work 10.1** is an example. Here are major reasons why companies replace parts of their legacy systems or supplement them with enterprise systems. It is important to realize that many companies do not have the resources to replace all their legacy systems.

> **Legacy systems** are older information systems (ISs) that have been maintained over several decades because they fulfill critical needs.

- **High maintenance costs**   Maintaining and upgrading legacy systems are some of the most difficult challenges facing chief information officers (CIOs) and IT departments.
- **Inflexibility**   Legacy architectures were not designed for flexibility. These huge systems cannot be easily redesigned to share data with newer systems, unlike modern architectures.
- **Integration obstacles**   Legacy systems execute business processes that are hardwired by rigid, predefined process flows. Their hardwiring makes integration with other systems such as CRM and Web-based applications difficult and sometimes impossible.
- **Lack of staff**   IT departments find it increasingly difficult to hire staff who are qualified to work on mainframes and applications written in languages no longer used by the latest technologies.
- **Cloud**   The cloud has lowered up-front costs. Cloud-based enterprise systems can be a good fit for companies facing upgrades to their legacy ERP and other enterprise systems.

IT at Work 10.1

Organic Valley Does Business Better with Enterprise System

Organic Valley Family of Farms is the largest U.S. cooperative (co-op) of organic farmers and one of the nation's leading organic brands. The co-op represents over 1,300 family farms in 34 states and Canada. Its mission is to keep small and midsized farmers farming. Organic Valley produces over 200 organic foods, including organic milk, soy, cheese, butter, eggs, produce, juice, and meats, which are sold in supermarkets, natural foods stores, and food co-ops and as ingredients for other organic food manufacturers nationwide. One of the biggest challenges for Organic Valley had been managing growth in the face of increasing competition from larger companies.

Need to Consolidate Disparate Systems

Organic Valley needed to consolidate its disparate systems into one enterprise solution to improve operating efficiencies and maintain the high quality of its line of perishable food products. The company had been doing planning using spreadsheets; separately, it completed its financials, order management, and inventory on an enterprise system designed for discrete manufacturing. As operations expanded, it needed to make a major leap in business systems.

Organic Valley also needed a solution with enough flexibility and versatility to manage the company's dairy, produce, meat, and egg lines of business, all of which have different and unique requirements.

Use of a Consultant and Vendor

Organic Valley hired a consultant during the selection process to help identify the most important functions and features, such as shelf-life management and expiration date management. Based on these requirements, three possible vendors were identified. Organic Valley and its consultant agreed that the solutions offered by the vendor Infor best fit its business.

Doing Business Better

The company now has one integrated system to support all business processes across all of its lines of business. With the Infor enterprise solution, Organic Valley is much more agile on the technical side, and this has given it the ability to support rapid business growth. The company projects savings of $2 million per year through improved supply chain planning and other operational efficiencies.

IT at Work Questions

1. Why did Organic Valley need an enterprise system?
2. What factors contributed to the successful implementation and outcomes? Explain their importance.
3. Enterprise systems are expensive. What factor helped justify the investment?
4. Using spreadsheets for planning is rather common. Why do you think companies use stand-alone spreadsheets for planning?

Implementation of Best Practices

Best practices for implementing enterprise systems involve changes in the management of processes, people, and existing systems. Three situations where changes are needed are as follows:

1. **Redesign of business processes** Processes need to be simplified and redesigned so that they can be automated, either totally or partially. Tasks that are no longer necessary are removed from the processes.

2. **Changes in how people perform their jobs** Jobs and how they are performed will change to accommodate the new processes. Enterprise systems require retraining users whose productivity will drop initially as they adjust to a new way of doing their jobs.

3. **Integration of many types of information systems** Integrating ISs is necessary so that data can flow seamlessly among departments and business partners. Automated data flows are essential to productivity improvements.

A best practice is to examine the inefficiencies in existing processes to find ways to improve or significantly simplify the process. For example, manual document-intensive processes such as order entry and billing create major headaches for workers. These processes require users to manually review documents for approval, enter data from those documents into a back-office system, and then make decisions. Automated order entry systems track customer orders from the time of initial order placement through the completion of those orders and perform back-order processing, analysis, invoicing, and billing.

Common ways to overcome implementation complexity are to lease or license enterprise systems from vendors and to access cloud-based enterprise systems.

Enterprise Systems Insights

Here are three other insights related to enterprise systems to better understand the current state of enterprise systems and their potential.

1. One of the IT department's most important roles is to provide and support applications that enable workers to access, use, and understand data. These applications need to be tightly aligned with well-defined and well-designed business processes—a standard that few enterprises are able to achieve.

2. Customer loyalty helps drive profits, but only for customers who are profitable to the company. Many companies do not know how to recognize or encourage the kind of customer loyalty that is worth having. Using data about buying behaviors (e.g., amount spent per month; purchase of high-margin products; return activity; and demands for customer service) helps a company identify its loyal customers and which ones are profitable.

3. Companies worldwide spend billions of dollars in the design and implementation of enterprise systems. Huge investments are made in ERP systems from vendors such as SAP, Oracle JD Edwards, Sage ERP, EVO~ERP, Infor, and NetSuite to create an integrated global supply chain. Interorganizational ISs play a major role in improving communication and integration among firms in a global supply chain.

Questions

1. Explain the purpose of an enterprise system.
2. Describe the three types of enterprise systems.
3. What is customer lifetime value (CLV)?
4. What is a value-added reseller (VAR)?
5. What are two challenges of legacy systems?
6. Why do companies migrate to enterprise systems?
7. Explain the challenges of enterprise system implementation.
8. Explain the three types of changes needed when an enterprise system is implemented.

10.2 Enterprise Resource Planning (ERP)

To understand what an ERP does, it helps to think about all of the various processes needed to run a business. These might include inventory and order management, finance and accounting, human resources (HR), CRM, SCM, and e-commerce. ERP software integrates all these various functions into one complete system to streamline processes and information across the entire organization.

The central feature of all ERP systems is a shared database that supports multiple functions used by different business units so that employees in different divisions, such as accounting and sales, can rely on the same information for their different purposes.

ERP software also offers some degree of synchronized reporting and automation. Instead of forcing employees to maintain separate databases and spreadsheets that have to be manually merged to generate reports, some ERP solutions allow staff to pull reports from a single system. For instance, with sales orders automatically flowing into the financial system without any manual rekeying, the order management department can process orders more quickly and accurately, and the finance department can close the books faster. Other common ERP features include a portal or dashboard to enable employees to quickly understand metrics of the firm's KPIs.

Brief History of ERP

ERP originated in the 1990s as a means to integrate accounting, finance, HR, marketing, and other critical business functions. ERPs were devised to help managers run a business. Ideally, each business function would access a centralized database instead of data silos. In many cases, the ERP was bought, installed, and configured by a vendor who supplied the entire suite of applications, or modules, for manufacturing, distribution, retail, and service organizations. Early ERPs ran on client–server architectures and custom-designed apps that accessed the shared database servers.

Then, similarly to most modern business software, ERP systems migrated to a Web-based architecture. Users accessed the ERP via a Web browser from within the company or accessed it externally via the Internet using a secured encrypted virtual private network (VPN).

ERP Today ERP is now a mature technology, whose core components have not changed much. What has changed are the way ERPs are deployed—on-premises, in the cloud, or as a managed service—and users' expectations. The latest ERP solutions are designed with a focus on social collaboration, deployment flexibility, faster response, and accessibility from mobile devices. They have touch-enabled user interfaces designed to work with all touch-screen devices. New apps and mobile add-ons enable the following:

- Sales associates to process orders, take payments, and collect signatures with an iPad app
- Field technicians to provide customer service from anywhere
- Marketing to manage every aspect of ongoing customer relationships using a smartphone app
- Production to access to the real-time information needed to reduce stockouts and excess inventory
- Customers to access, pay, and view invoices online

The worldwide ERP software market grew $82.1 billion in 2015 (Pang, 2016). SAP remained the ERP market leader in ERP licenses, maintenance, and subscription revenues. SAP accounted for 6% of the market share, FIS Global was next with a share of 4%, followed by Oracle and Fiserv, which were tied for third at 3%.

Technology Perspective

From a technology perspective, ERP is the software infrastructure that links an enterprise's internal applications and supports its external business processes. Departments stay informed about what is ongoing in other departments that impact its operations or performance. Knowing about problem situations and being able to work around them saves time and expense and preserves good customer relations. For example, using ERP, a manufacturer shares the database of parts, products, production capacities, schedules, backorders, and trouble spots. Responding quickly and correctly to materials shortages, spikes in customer demand, or other contingencies means that small initial problems are solved instead of allowing them to be amplified down the line.

Figure 10.3 demonstrates how an ERP fits into an enterprise's IT infrastructure. The core ERP functions are integrated with other systems or modules, such as SCM and CRM. An **enterprise application integration (EAI)** layer enables the ERP to interface with legacy apps. EAI is middleware that connects and acts as a go-between for applications and their business processes.

Acquiring an ERP ERPs are not built in-house or built using proprietary software because the costs and time to do so would be staggering. Typically, ERP systems are acquired by purchasing or leasing in a Software-as-a-Service (SaaS) arrangement. (You will read more

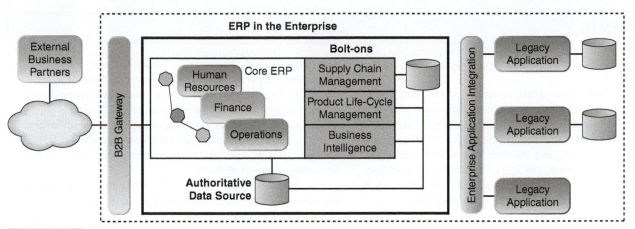

FIGURE 10.3   Overview of the complexity of ERP and its interfaces with other enterprise systems (U.S. Army Business Transformation Knowledge Center, 2009).

about IS sourcing and contracts in Chapter 12.) All ERPs must be customized to the company's specifications. Here are two examples of how ERP acquisitions can be customized:

1. **Boers & Co Fine Metalworking** in the Netherlands has been manufacturing fine mechanical parts, high-precision assembly, and sheet metal products for over 100 years. The company implemented Epicor ERP to access real-time data for everything from the shop floor to finance. All business operations from the front office through production, receiving and shipping, to order entry and cash receipts are handled by the ERP.

2. **Peters Ice Cream** in Australia had been under the ownership of food giant Nestlé and was working under its ERP. That ERP was not tailored for the specific needs of an ice cream company and did not interface well with Peters' legacy systems. Peters' network of freezers extends throughout Australia, and to get the ice cream flavors where they were needed when they are needed, it was essential that information on stock levels and deliveries be accurate and in real time. Peters selected Infor's M3 QuickStep for Food and Beverage ERP solution because 70% of the necessary business processes were already preconfigured within it. With preconfigured business processes, Peters was able to implement its new ERP system in eight months.

Enlisting the help of an experienced ERP consultant can greatly increase the chances of a successful ERP implementation (see **Career Insight 10.1**).

Career Insight 10.1

ERP Consultant: What Skills do you Need?

According to the Bureau of Labor Statistics, the role of ERP Consultant is becoming a high-demand job in the U.S. economy. ERP consultants currently earn a median pay of $80,802 and can demand top income of $143,306 (*payscale.com*).

What do ERP consultants do all day? They write design specifications ad estimates for programs, based on requirements; participate in decision making to optimize and improve IT management; analyze and understand existing software, and assist technical teams using change management and technical skills.

What specific skills do ERP consultants need? According to **Morgan McKinley**, a large online recruiting service, if you envision

becoming an ERP consultant, you will need to have the following experience and skills:

1. Business Process Analysis experience including requirements gathering, ability to identify defects and stakeholder management

2. Excellent organizational skills including ability to deal with ambiguity, juggle multiple priorities, and meet goals and deadlines

3. Exceptional interpersonal skills and the ability to influence people

4. Ability and willingness to share knowledge as a trainer or mentor to end-users

Implementing an ERP is often a complex, long-term, and challenging project for an ERP consultant, as described in **IT at Work 10.2**.

IT at Work 10.2

Agency Replaced 50 Legacy Systems with an ERP

A large European public sector agency processes 200 million payments every year. Its finance and HR systems were a complex combination of 50 legacy systems that had evolved over time without a plan. Technical support for the outdated legacy systems was no longer available, and the few remaining internal developers were near retirement. The agency had to replace this legacy architecture with an ERP system that could process the hundreds of millions of payments and support more than 70,000 users.

In the first phase of the ERP implementation project, the scope and budget of the ERP were approved, vendor proposals were evaluated, and a contract with the selected vendor was negotiated. These activities took almost a year to complete. Then a roll-out strategy was developed wherein the legacy systems were replaced by ERP modules and new data stores. Replacing legacy systems with ERP requires migrating databases and applications. The roll-out strategy was planned to minimize risk by ensuring that the agency met its strict legal requirements of having one leading accounting system at all times.

Implementing the ERP system across the agency took 2.5 years and was delivered on time and budget and at the desired quality level. Extensive planning, executive support, experienced consultants, and ERP-informed vendor selection were key success factors.

Another important aspect of acquiring and successfully implementing an ERP is the vendor selection process (**Tech Note 10.2**).

Tech Note 10.2

Selecting an ERP Vendor

The two largest vendors of ERPs are SAP and Oracle. The website **top10erp.org** provides comparisons of top ERP vendor products, provide free demos of the software, and offers prices quotes for the different offerings.

To simplify and reduce the cost of the ERP software evaluation, comparison, and selection processes, an annual event called the ERP Vendor Shootout (**erpshootout.com**) is held and geared toward ERP selection teams and decision-makers for companies with manufacturing, distribution, or project-oriented requirements.

Four Rules for Selecting an ERP ERPs are complex, but they are becoming more user-friendly. Other options are hosted ERP solutions, such as ERP SaaS, and cloud-based ERP. Still, ERPs are expensive, time-consuming implementations that require a lot of planning. Four rules to consider when selecting an ERP solution or software package are listed in **Table 10.3**.

TABLE 10.3   ERP Selection Rules

Selection Rule	Description
1. **Select** an ERP solution that targets the company's requirements	ERP packages are tailored for organizations based on their size and industry. Midmarket solutions have more sophisticated capabilities than packages for small businesses; large enterprise packages are the most complex. It is important to choose an ERP that can support critical functions of the organization, such as accounting or inventory management
2. **Evaluate** potential ERP vendors' strengths and weaknesses	Check how many customers each vendor has; its financial health (you do not want to select a vendor on the brink of bankruptcy); experience in the specific industry, and how the ERP can scale as the company grows
3. **Meet** with each vendor and get a hands-on demo of its ERP solutions	Demos allow employees to experience the usability of each ERP module and how well the ERP would support business processes
4. **Calculate** ERP's total cost of ownership (TCO)	The cost of the ERP or the monthly SaaS fee is only the beginning of the calculation. The TCO also includes implementation, customization, management services, training, additional hardware and networks, additional bandwidth for a Web-based product, and IT staff

Achieving ERP Success

Managers and other decision makers tend to think that if an enterprise system works for leading companies, it will work for them as well. But that is not true. In fact, several of the best companies have suffered devastating consequences that led to multimillion dollar losses, bankruptcy, or lawsuits. Most often, the ERP is eventually fixed and remains in use, which gives the false impression that the ERP was successful from the start.

The success of an ERP depends on organizational and technological factors that occur prior to, during, and after its implementation. Knowing what to do and what not to do are important. Both the successes and failures teach valuable lessons as well, as you will learn in this section.

Be aware that reading vendor white papers and viewing Webcasts or demos may give you a biased view of the benefits of ERP software. You need to conduct your own research to learn the full story behind an enterprise system implementation. Problems may be skipped over or ignored. While blogs and YouTube posts may be good sources of objective data, many vendors have blogs and YouTube videos that are designed to appear neutral, when in fact they are not.

ERP Disasters and Failures

ERP implementations are complex—and risky. Planning, deploying, or fine-tuning these complex business software systems for your company is such a large undertaking that such projects fail more than 50% to 70% of the time. Those are not encouraging statistics. ERP failures have made it impossible to ship products and, at the extreme, have led to bankruptcy. Many ERP projects have ended up in litigation, the headlines, and out-of-court settlements. Dell canceled an ERP system after spending two years and $200 million on its implementation. Hershey Food Corp. filed highly publicized lawsuits against its ERP vendors for a failed implementation. The following ERP failures have led to lawsuits against vendors or consulting firms. Unfortunately, lawsuits do not result in a successful ERP implementation.

ScanSource vs. Avanade—"bait-and-switch"

A half-million lines of custom code were not enough to produce a viable Microsoft Dynamics AX ERP system for point-of-sale and RFID products distributor ScanSource, according to a lawsuit filed by ScanSource against Avanade. AX is one of four ERP products sold under the Dynamics brand and is aimed at larger companies. The project was estimated to cost $17 million and take 11 months, but the cost estimate grew to a staggering $66 million, and it failed to "go live" after three years. Avanade misrepresented the skills of its consultants in order to win the contract; then sent in a continually changing cast of consultants without the expertise to do the job or familiarity with AX—hence, the allegation of "bait-and-switch" tactics.

ScanSource terminated the contact with Avanade and hired another company to fix the problems at an additional cost of $58 to $72 million.

Dillard's, Inc. vs. JDA Software Group—unmet obligations

Dillard's alleged that i2 failed to meet obligations regarding two software-license agreements for which the department store had paid $8 million. JDA Software Group Inc. was ordered to pay $246 million in damages.

FoxMeyer Drugs vs. SAP and Andersen Consulting—"bankruptcy bound"

FoxMeyer Drugs was a $5B company and the nation's largest distributor of pharmaceuticals before its ERP failure that led to a $500M lawsuit against SAP and Andersen Consulting. FoxMeyer's ERP could not process the transactions needed to supply its customers with their orders. FoxMeyer had been processing 425,000 invoice lines per day on its legacy software. The company's ERP was limited to 10,000 invoice lines per day. This quickly decreased order processing capability, sent the company into bankruptcy protection, and ultimately shut down the business. Implementation was troubled almost from the start. Despite warnings from Woltz Consulting, during the early stages of the project, that a schedule for the entire implementation to be completed in 18 months was totally unrealistic, FoxMeyer went ahead with the vendor's planned implementation.

The lesson to be learned is that when it comes to ERP selection, you either get it right or pay the price for years to come!

ERP Success Factors In order to successfully implement an ERP, you need to know the factors that increase the likelihood of ERP success and minimize the risk of problems. Many managers assume that success or failure depends on the software and, furthermore, that a failure is the fault of the software that is purchased or licensed. In reality, 95% of a project's success or failure lies in the hands of the company implementing the software, not the software vendor.

The results of a survey to identify the factors ERP experts considered most important to successful ERP projects are shown in **Figure 10.4**.

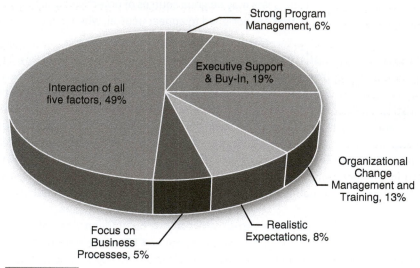

Most Important Factors for ERP Project Success

FIGURE 10.4 Experts identify the combination of factors needed for ERP success.

Nearly half of the experts indicated that the failure of any one of the factors significantly increases the risk of ERP failure.

The following recommendations explain why ERP success depends on several key factors being met:

1. **Focus on business processes and requirements** Too often, companies get caught up in technical capabilities or platforms on which the ERP runs. But compared to business processes, none of this really matters. What matters is how managers want business operations to run and what the key business requirements are. Once management and IT have defined them, they can intelligently choose the software, modules, and vendor that fit their unique business needs.

2. **Focus on achieving a measurable ROI** Developing a business case to get approval from upper management or the board of directors is essential, but not sufficient. Establish key performance measures, set baselines and targets for those measures, and then track performance after going live. The performance results are proof of how well the ERP meets the expectations that had been listed in the business case.

3. **Use a strong project management approach and secure commitment of resources** An ERP project depends on how it is managed. Responsibility for the management of the ERP implementation project cannot be transferred to vendors or consulting firms. Because of the business disruption and cost involved, ERP projects require the full-time attention and support of high-profile champions on the key functions for a long period of time, from 6 to 12 months on average. It is also known that ERP projects cannot be managed by people who *can be spared*. They must be managed by people who are *indispensable* personnel. Without powerful champions and an adequate budget (discussed next), expect the ERP to fail. Project management will be covered in Chapter 13.

4. **Obtain strong and continuing commitment from senior executives**   Any project without support from top management will fail. No matter how well run a project is, there will be problems such as conflicting business needs or business disruptions that can only be resolved by someone with the power and authority to cut through the politics and personal agendas.

5. **Take sufficient time to plan and prepare before starting the project**   An ERP vendor's motive is to close the deal as fast as possible. The company needs to make sure it correctly defines its needs and what it can afford to achieve in order to intelligently evaluate and select the best vendor. Do not be rushed into a decision. Too often, companies jump right into a project without validating the vendor's understanding of business requirements or their project plan. The principle of "measure twice, cut once" applies to vendor selection. The more time the company spends ensuring that these things are done right at the start, the lower the risk of failure and the less time spent fixing problems later. Filing a lawsuit against a vendor is not a fix. Lawsuits are both expensive and risky and contribute nothing to the company's performance.

6. **Invest in training and change management**   Another key principle to understand is that when you design an ERP, you redesign the organization. ERP systems involve dramatic change for workers. ERPs lose value if people do not understand how to use them effectively. Investing in training, change management, and job design are crucial to the outcome of any large-scale IT project.

Questions

1. What are the three ways ERP can be deployed?
2. Briefly describe the latest ERP features and add-ons.
3. Describe ERP from a technology perspective.
4. What types of situations are best suited to investing in an ERP?
5. List and briefly describe three of the ERP implementation success factors.
6. Describe causes or factors that contribute to ERP failure.

10.3 Supply Chain Management Systems

The journey that a product travels, as shown in **Figure 10.5**, is called the **supply chain**. It is a network of raw material suppliers, distributors, manufacturers or assemblers, order fulfillment and logistic providers, and retailers that participate in the production, delivery, and sale of a product to the customer. The supply chain is like a pipeline composed of multiple companies that coordinate activities to differentiate themselves from their competitors.

Supply chains vary significantly depending on the type, complexity, and perishability of the product. For example, in a simplified sense, the food supply chain begins with the livestock or farm, moves to the manufacturer, then through the distribution centers and wholesalers to the retailer and final customer.

Supply chain starts with the acquisition of raw materials or the procurement (purchase) of products and proceeds through manufacture, transport, and delivery—and the disposal or recycling of products.

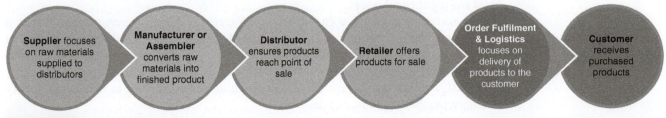

FIGURE 10.5 Build a Supply Chain.

Supply chain management (SCM) is the efficient management of the flows of material, data, and payments among the companies in the supply chain, from suppliers to consumers. SCM systems are configured to achieve the following business goals:

- To reduce uncertainty and variability to improve the accuracy of forecasting.
- To increase control over processes to achieve optimal inventory levels, cycle time, and customer service.

An example of how supply chains are managed to achieve business goals is discussed in IT at Work 10.3.

IT at Work 10.3

Managing the U.S. Munitions Supply Chain

Munitions Supply Chain Management

The Joint Munitions Command (JMC) is a major part of the U.S. Army Materiel Command (AMC). Munitions are the weaponry hardware, vehicles, and equipment and their ammunition. JMC supports U.S. warfighters by managing the *munitions supply chain* to get the right munitions at the right place at the right time. JMC manufactures, procures, stores, and transports tanks, weaponry, howitzers, and other munitions as well as bullets, artillery shells, and other ammunition to locations worldwide. Much like a military hierarchy, the munitions supply chain follows a predictive and linear model of logistics to meet "readiness goals and minimize overall costs" (Haraburda, 2016).

Supply Chain Challenges

JMC provides bombs and bullets to America's fighting forces—all services, all types of conventional ammunition from 500-pound bombs to rifle rounds. JMC manages plants that produce more than 1.6 billion rounds of ammunition annually and the depots that store the nation's ammunition for training and combat.

Clearly, managing the munitions supply chain is extremely complex and critical. Similarly to other supply chains, it depends on good relationships among suppliers in the network, the quality of supplier information, and communication channels.

JMC Improves Battle Readiness at Reduced Cost

JMC's project began with a focus on efficiency but has resulted in increased warfighting readiness at reduced cost. After transforming operations, integrating its supply chain, and improving data management, JMC is now better able to rapidly supply U.S. forces with the highest-quality munitions when they need them and to cut transportation costs up to 50%—a significant savings per year. These improvements were made possible as a result of greater asset visibility (tracking and monitoring), better forecasting and decision-making capabilities, communication, and collaboration along the supply chain.

IT at Work Questions

1. Explain the role of the munitions supply chain.
2. Discuss how JMC ensures that soldiers receive the highest-quality ammunition, on time, and where needed.
3. Why would improvements in munitions SCM also improve warfighting readiness?
4. What factors impact the ability to manage the munitions supply chain?
5. For the JMC, where does the munitions supply chain start and where does it end?
6. Is munitions SCM unique, and if so, why? Or, is it similar to the management of any supply chains? Explain your position.

Sources: Compiled from Butler et al. (2016) and Haraburda (2016).

SCM systems allow organizations to manage supply chains, vendor relationships, and distribution channels to better manage resources and improve efficiency. Businesses benefit from an SCM by identifying inefficiencies in supply and distribution channels, optimizing warehouse storage, and automating purchases. Software solutions in this category allow businesses to integrate multiple tools into an existing system or a single software suite to manage supply chain and logistics processes.

For example, SCM suites, such as *Streamline Shipping* and *Supply Vision*, manage the entire SCM process, while other products focus on specific processes within the supply chain. For example, *JDA Demand Planning* focuses on giving users data for inventory and revenue forecasts and helping decision-makers plan for the future, *Dr. Dispatch* manages orders, inventory data, SCM, and customer service, and *eSellerHub* allows companies to manage and track inventory, purchasing, sales, and deliveries.

Managing the Flow of Materials, Data, and Money

Supply chains involve the flow of materials, data, and money. Descriptions of these three main flows are as follows:

1. **Material or product flow**   This is the movement of materials and goods from a supplier to its consumer. For example, Ford supplies dealerships that, in turn, sell to end-users. Products that are returned make up what is called the **reverse supply chain** because goods are moving in the reverse direction.

2. **Information flow**   This is the movement of detailed data among members of the supply chain, for example, order information, customer information, order fulfillment, delivery status, and proof-of-delivery confirmation. Most information flows are done electronically, although paper invoices or receipts are still common for noncommercial customers.

3. **Financial flow**   This is the transfer of payments and financial arrangements, for example, billing payment schedules, credit terms, and payment via **electronic funds transfer (EFT)**. EFT provides for electronic payments and collections. It is safe, secure, efficient, and less expensive than paper check payments and collections.

Supply chain links are managed. Think of the chain in terms of its links because the entire chain is not managed as a single unit. A company can only manage the links it actually touches. That is, a company will manage only partners who are one-back and one-up from them in the supply chain.

Order Fulfillment and Logistics

The order fulfillment process demonstrates how these "flows" work and link together the various parts of the supply chain. **Order fulfillment** depends on the type of product/service and purchase method (online, in-store, catalog, etc.). For example, a customer who has ordered a new appliance via the Sears.com website needs to receive it as scheduled, with assembly and operating instructions, and warranty and return information. The customer can receive a paper manual with the product or download the instructions from Sears' website.

Order fulfillment is a part of **back-office operations**, such as accounting, inventory management, and shipping, and is closely related to **front-office operations** or customer-facing activities. The key aspects of order fulfillment are the delivery of materials or products at the right time, to the right place, and at the right cost.

Logistics entails all the processes and information needed to move products from origin to destination efficiently. The order fulfillment process is part of logistics.

Order fulfillment is the set of complex processes involved in providing customers with what they ordered on time and all customer services related to on-time delivery of a product.

Back-office operations support the fulfillment of orders.

Front-office operations such as sales and advertising are visible to customers.

Steps in the Order Fulfillment Process

The order fulfillment process starts when an order is received and includes the following nine activities that are supported by SCM software or are automated:

Step 1: Make sure that the customer will pay   Depending on the payment method and prior arrangements with the customer, verify that the customer can and will pay and agrees to the payment terms. This activity is done by the finance department for B2B sales or an external company such as PayPal or a credit card issuer such as Visa for business-to-customer (B2C) sales. Any holdup in payment may cause a shipment to be delayed, resulting in a loss of goodwill or a customer. In B2C, the customers usually pay by credit card, but with major credit card data theft at Target and other retailers, the buyer may be using a stolen card.

Step 2: Check in-stock availability and reorder as necessary   As soon as an order is received, the stock is checked to determine the availability of the product or materials. If there is not enough stock, the ordering system places an order, typically automatically using electronic data interchange (EDI). To perform these operations, the ordering system needs to interface with the inventory system.

Step 3: Arrange shipments When the product is available, shipment to the customer is arranged (otherwise, go to Step 5). Products can be digital or physical. If the item is physical and available, packaging and shipment arrangements are made. Both the packaging/shipping department and internal shippers or outside transporters may be involved. Digital items are usually available because their "inventory" is not depleted. However, a digital product, such as software, may be under revision, and thus unavailable for delivery at certain times. In either case, information needs to flow among several partners.

Step 4: Insurance The contents of a shipment may need to be insured. Both the finance department and an insurance company could be involved, and again, information needs to be exchanged with the customer and insurance agent.

Step 5: Replenishment Customized orders will always trigger a need for some manufacturing or assembly operation. Similarly, if standard items are out of stock, they need to be produced or procured. Production is done in-house or outsourced.

Step 6: In-house production In-house production needs to be planned, and actual production needs to be scheduled. Production planning involves people, materials, components, machines, financial resources, and possibly suppliers and subcontractors. In the case of assembly and/or manufacturing, several plant services may be needed, including collaboration with business partners. Production facilities may be located in a different country than the company's headquarters or retailers. This may further complicate the flow of information.

Step 7: Use suppliers A manufacturer may opt to buy products or subassemblies from suppliers. Similarly, if the seller is a retailer, such as in the case of Amazon.com or Walmart.com, the retailer must purchase products from its manufacturers. In this case, appropriate receiving and quality assurance of incoming materials and products must take place.

Once production (Step 6) or purchasing from suppliers (Step 7) is completed, shipments to the customers (Step 3) are arranged.

Step 8: Contacts with customers Sales representatives keep in contact with customers, especially in B2B, starting with the notification of orders received and ending with notification of a shipment or change in delivery date. These contacts are frequently generated automatically.

Step 9: Returns In some cases, customers want to exchange or return items. The movement of returns from customers back to vendors is *reverse logistics*. Such returns can be a major problem, especially when they occur in large volumes.

Innovations Driving Supply Chain Strategic Priorities

Always-on supply chain is an integrated set of supply networks characterized by a continuous, high-velocity flow of information and analytics creating predictive, actionable decisions to better serve the customer 24/7.

Technology is changing the traditional supply chain into a digitized, 24/7 supply chain, referred to as "always-on" supply chain. Supply chain executives are leveraging digital technologies and business innovations to manage the increasing complexity of today's global **always-on supply chain**. In the past, supply chains were linear and companies tackled supply chain challenges primarily by focusing on internal cost reduction and improved operational efficiency. But traditional approaches are less effective as supply chains become longer and more interconnected, and there are higher stakeholder expectations and more sources of risk. Always-on supply chains are more connected, intelligent, scalable, and agile. Sensors that enable data collection and advancements in computing power have improved predictive analytics. Supplemental tools, such as automation and wearables, are creating digital, continuously operating supply chains and an interconnected network of supply chain workers.

Recently, *MHI*, an international trade association that has influenced materials handling and logistics within the supply chain industry and Deloitte released their 2016 MHI Annual Industry Report focused on the significant changes occurring in SCM driven by technological innovations. Based on responses from 900 respondents, in large and small companies across a wide range of sectors, the report revealed that eight technologies are dramatically impacting the supply chain and the people who run them. These eight technologies that can either increase competitive advantage or disrupt an organization are as follows:

- Robotics and automation
- Inventory and Network Optimization Tools
- Sensors and automatic identification
- Predictive Analytics
- Wearables and mobile technology
- Driverless vehicles and drones
- Inventory and network optimization tools
- Cloud computing and storage
- 3D printing

Robotics and automation
Robotics and automation are revolutionizing supply chains across the globe. As technology becomes smarter, faster, and cheaper, it is being called upon to do more. Robots are increasingly able to demonstrate "human" capabilities and traits such as sensing, dexterity, memory, and trainability. They are being integrated into supply chains, taking on more human-oriented tasks, including picking and packaging, testing or inspecting products, and assembling electronics.

Inventory and Network Optimization Tools
Route planning, product flow path analysis, and asset optimization help companies streamline operations, improve inventory control, gain visibility, manage risk, and reduce costs. The ability to deploy assets and position inventory well is critical to delivering the right service at the right cost. Inventory and network optimization are powerful decision-support tools to model end-to-end supply chain costs and trade-offs. An equipment manufacturer who had excess inventory across its distribution network, as a result of lead-time discrepancies between similar parts from the same supplier, high variability of transportation lead times, and a highly complex product portfolio, constructed an integrated parts management framework consisting of inventory analytics and optimization, sales and customer insights, supply insights, and a parts business plan to reduce product and transportation costs and improve product placement and inventory balance.

Sensors and Automatic Identification
Sensors are a means of delivering computing and communications power to everyday devices and businesses. The data they generate can lead to better business models and increased visibility in supply chains. By collecting data from objects, then communicating and aggregating that data into information that is presented to users, sensors can help users reach decisions about how to make, move, or change those objects. For example, by positioning a network of sensors throughout its plants, an automobile company can measure humidity in its buildings. If readings rise about those acceptable for paining vehicle bodies, the next car body on the line will automatically be routed to a different step of the manufacturing process that is not adversely affected by the humidity in the building. This process change reduces costs of repainting and downtime on the line.

Predictive Analytics
Some of the most effective applications of predictive analytics focus on predicting patterns associated with consumer behavior. For example, retailers and consumer goods companies with millions of customers have effectively mined big data from social media to find and keep new customers. In the supply chain arena, predictive modeling allows managers to manage inventory better, plan more reliable transportation networks, and reduce variability in lead times. This can enhance service levels, lower costs, and improve the bottom line.

Wearable and Mobile Technology   Wearable technologies are devices incorporated into clothing and accessories that can be comfortably worn. These devices perform many of the same computing tasks as mobile phones and laptop computers and frequently can out-perform them. Enterprise wearables from smart glasses to voice-directed hands-free wearable scanners and real-time views of every touchpoint within the supply chain are improving worker safety and increasing transparency within the supply chain and avoid potential bottlenecks. Increasing numbers of companies are piloting the use of smart glasses within their supply chains. One company used them to implement "vision picking" in their warehouse where displays on the smart glasses showed the task information during the pick process, including aisle, product location, and quantity. As a result, staff worked much faster and reduced errors, increasing efficiency by 25%.

Driverless Vehicles and Drones   Driverless vehicles and drones use a variety of technologies, including sensors, cameras, and advanced driver assistance systems, to handle some or all functions of operating a vehicle. Drones can deliver significant value to businesses by improving supply chain operations. Companies can transform their operations by using drones to monitor functioning of plants, maintain security, and provide real-time data about a facility's surroundings. One large U.S. retailer has asked for permission to test drones for making deliveries to customers in its parking lots and at customers' homes. The retailer also wants to use the aerial technology enabled by drones to check on its buildings, warehouses, and distribution centers. The retailer has tested drones inside its facilities but now wants to do outdoor tests. To do that, it needs FAA permission.

Cloud Computing and Storage   Cloud computing and storage plays a critical role in the improvement of SCM by supporting an enterprise's efforts to share data with multiple, geographically dispersed partners. Benefits of cloud computing in the supply chain include improved collaboration among supply chain partners, cost-effective use of staff resources, and the ability to adapt to changing business needs quickly.

3D Printing   Additive manufacturing could revolutionize production processes and have far-reaching future implications for product supply chains. A global aerospace and defense company deployed electronic beam melting, a 3D printing technology, and reduced production costs for aerospace components by 50% while still maintaining functionality and performance.

The main message of the report was that business leaders embrace these new and emerging technologies that can provide improvements in supply chain visibility, reduce costs and enhance customer service, and determine how best to apply them to their specific supply chain requirements. MHI and Deloitte recommend using a test-and-learn approach to gain familiarity with the new technologies before investing and to share their insights between participants within their supply chains. The major barriers to adopting these innovative technologies in the supply chain are lack of clear business case to justify investment, lack of talent to utilize the technology effectively, and cultural aversion to risk.

Questions

1. What is a supply chain?
2. List four functions carried out by companies in a supply chain.
3. List and describe the three main flows being managed in a supply chain.
4. Describe SCM.
5. What are steps in the order fulfillment?
6. Explain logistics.
7. What are the top two strategic priorities of SCM executives?
8. What are the two major barriers preventing innovation in the supply chain?
9. What are the top innovative digital technologies impacting SCM?

10.4 | Customer Relationship Management Systems

Similarly to ERP and SCM systems, CRM is a widely used and mature technology that can be deployed on-premises or on-demand as a service or SaaS. The fierce competition among the big four CRM vendors—Salesforce.com, SAP, Oracle, and Microsoft—motivates innovation. Numerous successful CRM implementations have helped transform the business, increased profit, and strengthened customer loyalty. CRM can provide managers with a 360-degree view of the customer relationship, enable real-time responses, and improve sales productivity and predictability. However, CRM technology cannot transform or improve anything on its own.

A recent survey conducted by Forrester revealed that technology and strategy are necessary, but not sufficient to ensure CRM project success. A total of 414 business professionals thought that business performance improvement actually depends on a combination of the right people, processes, strategy, and technology. See **Figure 10.6** to see how well you can estimate the percentage they attributed to each of these four factors.

Changes in people's behavior, their commitment, attitude toward the mandatory change as well as process improvements make the difference between better bottom lines or a $100 million write-off. Buying the most suitable CRM is like buying a Ferrari or Porsche. You will not win any races simply because you bought a sports car.

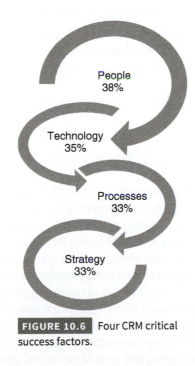

FIGURE 10.6 Four CRM critical success factors.

How are CRM Apps Different from ERP? Why are they Different?

ERP and CRM have to interface and share data. They are similar from a technology perspective—sold in modules, offered on site or in the cloud, and must share data. ERPs often requires tight business rules and user practices—that those in accounting, finance, and HR tend to be accustomed to by their professions. For example, they must comply with generally accepted accounting principles (GAAP), the Securities Exchange Commission (SEC), labor laws, or legal requirements. But sales and marketing are the primary users of CRM—and they tend not to be accustomed to inflexible rules of conduct. They are accustomed to creativity and closing the deal, for instance. If the CRM does not support them their way, they can reject it—and cause total system failure.

Why Does CRM Matter? CRM systems play the major role in customer experience (CX), and good CX helps to retain customers. However, not all customers are worth retaining. Customers can be unprofitable. Imagine having 20,000 customers. How would you determine the **customer lifetime value (CLV)** of each customer and continue to recompute their value? The point is that data analytics, sophisticated predictive analytics, and business intelligence (BI) are needed to determine CLV; then business rules need to specify how to treat or manage customers based on their value score.

Intelligently managing relationships with customers can increase revenues and net profits significantly. Similarly to managing inventory and supplier relationships, effective CRM is data-driven, complex, and continuously changing. The growth of mobile sales channels and social networking makes recognizing customers across multiple touchpoints complex. In addition, many companies have customer data in multiple, disparate systems that are not integrated—until they implement CRM systems.

CRM Technology Perspective

From a technology perspective, CRM refers to the methodologies and software tools to leverage customer data in order to achieve the following:

- Identify the appropriate CX for customers.
- Predict and prevent attrition (loss) of a customer, unless he or she is not worth retaining.
- Acquire new customers who are most likely to become profitable.
- Up-sell (sell more profitable products/services) or cross-sell (sell additional products/services) to unprofitable customers to move them to a profit position.
- Reduce inefficiencies that waste advertising dollars.

The top CRM vendors include: OnContact, Salesforce, SalesNexus, NetSuite TeamWox, and worksbooks.com.

Customer Acquisition and Retention

CRM technologies help marketing managers run effective campaigns, promotions, commercials, and advertisements to attract new customers, or to increase sales to existing customers, or to do both. Attracting and acquiring new customers are expensive activities: for example, it costs banks roughly $100 to acquire a new customer. Newly acquired customers are unprofitable until they have purchased enough products or services to exceed the cost to acquire and service them. Therefore, retaining customers that generate revenues in excess of the costs (e.g., customer service, returns, promotional items, and the like) is critical. The purpose of loyalty or frequent purchase programs offered by online retailers, coffee shops, airlines, supermarkets, credit card issuers, casinos, and other companies is to track customers for CRM purposes and build customer loyalty to improve financial performance. Loyalty programs rely on data warehouses and data analytics torecognize and reward customers who repeatedly use services or products. The 1-800-Flowers loyalty program is described in **IT at Work 10.4**.

CRM for a Competitive Edge

According to management guru Peter Drucker, "Those companies who know their customers, understand their needs, and communicate intelligently with them will always have a competitive advantage over those that don't" (Drucker, 1969). For most types of companies, marketing effectiveness depends on how well they know their customers: specifically, knowing what their customers want, how best to contact them, and what types of offers they are likely to respond to positively. According to the *loyalty effect*, a 5% reduction in customer attrition can improve profits by as much as 20%. Customer-centric business strategies strive to provide products and services that customers want to buy. One of the best examples is the Apple iPhone and iPod—devices that customers were willing to camp out on sidewalks to buy to guarantee getting one

IT at Work 10.4

1-800-Flowers.com Uses Data Mining for CRM

1-800-Flowers.com is an Internet pioneer. Online sales are a major marketing channel in addition to telephone and fax orders. Competition is very strong in this industry. The company's success was based on operational efficiency, convenience (24/7 accessibility), and reliability. However, all major competitors provide the same features today. To maintain its competitive edge, the company transformed itself into a customer-centric organization, caring for more than 15 million customers.

The company decided to cultivate brand loyalty through customer relationships based on detailed knowledge of customers. How is this accomplished? SAS software spans the entire decision-support process for managing customer relationships. Collecting data at all customer touchpoints, the company turns those data into knowledge for understanding and anticipating customer behavior, meeting customer needs, building more profitable customer relationships, and gaining a holistic view of a customer's lifetime value. Using SAS Enterprise Miner, 1-800-Flowers.com sifts through purchasing data to discover trends, explain outcomes, and predict results so that the company can increase response rates and identify profitable customers. In addition to selling and campaign management, the ultimate goal is to make sure that when a customer wants to buy, he or she continues to buy from 1-800-Flowers.com and cannot be captured by a competitor's marketing. Their objective is not just about getting customers to buy more. It is about making sure that when they decide to purchase a gift online or by phone, they do not even think of going to the competition.

Data mining software helps the company identify the many different types of customers and how each would like to be treated. Customer retention has increased by over 15% since this approach was adopted.

IT at Work Questions

1. Why is being number one in operation efficiency not enough to keep 1-800-FLOWERS.COM at the top of its industry?
2. What is the role of data mining?
3. How is the one-to-one relationship achieved in such systems?

on the day of their release. In contrast, companies with product-centric strategies need to create demand for their products, which is more expensive and may fail.

Common CRM Mistakes: How to Avoid Them

According to Gartner, the CRM market reached $26.3 billion in 2015 after several years of strong growth. Given that level of investment, companies obviously want to get as much value as possible out of their systems. It is unfortunate, then, that so many of them make mistakes in selecting and implementing CRM software. There are a number of CRM mistakes that must be avoided. Five of these CRM mistakes and actions that need to be taken to avoid them are explained in **Table 10.4**.

TABLE 10.4 **CRM Mistakes and Avoiding Them**

CRM Mistakes	How to Avoid The Mistakes
Putting IT department in charge of the CRM project instead of the business users	The hands-on business users need to champion and lead the project initiative, with IT playing a supporting role. CRM is a software project whose success relies on users' input, which helps ensure that they actually will use it. Unlike other apps, salespeople do not have to use CRM. If the system is underused, companies will see only limited improvements.
Not getting the CRM requirements right by not involving key business stakeholders from the outset	CRM implementations need buy-in from the users and other business stakeholders, who can spread enthusiasm. Frequent communication about the project is important to engaging them in a meaningful way.
Making mobile CRM strategy an afterthought	Consider mobility a priority in the CRM project from the outset. Putting an existing CRM on mobile devices is a bad plan.
Taking wrong approach to CRM training	Make sure that the interface is intuitive enough that most users will not need hands-on training. When people sit in a classroom for an hour, they will only retain 5 minutes of what they hear. A learning program during lunch that focuses on one or two lessons is a much more effective adoption strategy.
Underestimating users' resistance to change	Users will not tolerate poorly designed systems. Frustrating users is a fast track to failure, or at a minimum, suboptimal results.

Source: All (2014).

Example of a Failed CRM Citizen National Bank's experience is an example of a failure that then replaced its CRM vendors and became a success. The lessons learned, at a cost of $500,000, were as follows:

- Be absolutely clear on how the CRM application will add value to the sales process.
- Determine if and why salespeople are avoiding CRM.
- Provide incentives for the sales team to adopt CRM.
- Find ways to simplify the use of the CRM application.
- Adjust the CRM system as business needs change.

Justifying CRM

One of the biggest problems in CRM implementation is the difficulty of defining and measuring success. Many companies say that when it comes to determining value, intangible benefits are more significant than tangible cost savings. Yet, companies often fail to establish quantitative or even qualitative measures in order to judge these intangible benefits.

A formal business plan must be in place before the CRM project begins—one that quantifies the expected costs, tangible financial benefits, and intangible strategic benefits, as well as the risks. The plan should include an assessment of the following:

- **Tangible net benefits** The plan must include a clear and precise cost–benefit analysis that lists all the planned project costs and tangible benefits. This portion of the plan should also contain a strategy for assessing key financial metrics, such as ROI, net present value (NPV), or other justification methods.
- **Intangible benefits** The plan should detail the expected intangible benefits, and it should list the measured successes and shortfalls. Often, an improvement in customer satisfaction is the primary goal of the CRM solution, but in many cases, this key value is not measured.
- **Risk assessment** The risk assessment is a list of all of the potential pitfalls related to the people, processes, and technology that are involved in the CRM project. Having such a list helps to lessen the probability that problems will occur. And, if they do happen, a company may find that, by having listed and considered the problems in advance, the problems are more manageable than they would have been otherwise.

Tangible and Intangible Benefits Benefits typically include increases in staff productivity (e.g., more deals closed), cost avoidance, revenues, and margin increases, as well as reductions in inventory costs (e.g., due to the elimination of errors). Other benefits include increased customer satisfaction, loyalty, and retention.

Questions

1. Explain the four critical success factors for CRM.
2. Why does CRM matter?
3. Discuss how CRM impacts customer acquisition and retention.
4. According to Peter Drucker, what does marketing effectiveness depend on?
5. Give three reasons why CRM fails.
6. How can CRM be justified?

10.5 Enterprise Social Platforms

In Chapter 7, you learned how organizations use social media to connect with their customers, vendors, and partners to promote their business. Within an organization, enterprisewide communication and collaboration are equally important to help enable business leaders enhance productivity, teamwork, and employee satisfaction. Using an ESP by employees can connect and collaborate, stay informed, build relationships, and share documents and data. Collecting real-time data and closing the gap between globally distributed teams can be critical to an organization's performance. With quick access to corporate knowledge through an ESP, organizations can resolve issues sooner, minimize costs, and attain a competitive advantage. Whether its answering questions or sharing ideas, the open forum provided by an ESP flattens corporate hierarchies and motivates employees to share their opinions and creative thoughts.

Enterprise social platform is a private, company-owned social media software application that promotes social connectivity and collaboration with an organization and enhances productivity and employee satisfaction.

Growth of Enterprise Social Investments and Markets

In March 2016, the Boston Consulting Group prediction that social investment spending would soon easily and overwhelmingly surpass its current level of $211.6 million came to fruition when social media investment platform Big Society Capital reported that its investment value had already reached $1.6 billion.

Greater interest in ESPs can be attributed to three factors (**Figure 10.7**):

- **Knowledge management**   To capture and reuse knowledge within the enterprise
- **Collaboration**   Maintain human connections across a disparate workforce
- **Employee pressure**   Pressure from workers to use the social technologies they prefer to use

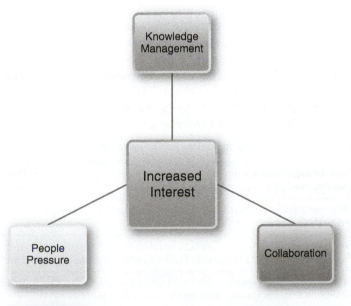

FIGURE 10.7   Main Reasons for Greater Interest in Enterprise Social Platforms.

This increased use of ESPs reflects a trend toward more informal communication at work as more companies seek to integrate and embed social media into primary enterprise solutions to support business-critical decisions and create more social workflows as an alternative to existing formal communication channels.

Sharepoint

SharePoint was initially released by Microsoft in 2001, and in 2016, 78% of Fortune 500 firms were using it. SharePoint is difficult to define because it is not a single software program, but rather a platform for multiple kinds of programs and apps. The platform is a back-end system that links employees' computers and mobile devices to make it easy to communicate and to synchronize their efforts. At companies that have their SharePoint on-premises, they are now considered legacy systems. SharePoint in the **Microsoft Cloud** is the later version.

SharePoint has the following social capabilities.

Microsoft Cloud provides a hybrid infrastructure and capabilities to manage enterprise apps and data.

Intranet and Extranet Intranets are the internal-facing sites everyone in a company logs into to find news, announcements, scheduled tasks, and access to files and data. Dashboards are customized by department and role to control access. SharePoint also provides tools for setting up employee social network platforms and company wikis. SharePoint can be used to set up a secure, access-controlled extranet site to share with external partners in the supply chain, contractors, and so on.

Documents SharePoint provides a shared space to store documents, so they are not siloed on any one person's hard drive or device. Documents stored on SharePoint can be accessed by anyone in the company—unless the administrator has limited access. SharePoint enables coworkers to work simultaneously on a single document, save previous versions, and track updates.

Collaboration and Business Intelligence An ESP makes it easy for users to stay up to date and to coordinate their efforts on projects from any desktop or mobile device and to discover patterns and insights into enterprise data.

Yammer Smart companies connect their employees' desire to contribute and interact with peers with their own need to get timely feedback from the trenches. Red Robin, discussed in **IT at Work 10.5**, learned the benefits of **Yammer** for entry-level employees. Six recommendations for realizing business value from enterprise social networking are listed in **Table 10.5**.

Yammer is "Facebook for business." The platform has features similar to Facebook likes, newsfeeds, threaded conversation, and direct messaging. This private social channel helps employees, partners, and customers communicate; exchange information; and collaborate across departments, locations, and business apps.

TABLE 10.5 **Recommendations to Realize Business Value from Enterprise Social**

1. **Make sure that management is listening** Leaders and decision-makers need to monitor social chatter to keep informed and respond promptly.

2. **Provide visible feedback and rewards** Employee participation is largely driven by the desire to be recognized by peers and managers.

3. **Brand the social network** Employees want to feel that the company is behind the initiative. At Red Robin, for example, renaming Yammer to Yummer connected employees to the brand.

4. **Identify and leverage change agents** Start with those employees most eager to participate, especially Millennials who are looking for recognition and purpose.

5. **Introduce competitions and games** Experience shows that people are more likely to engage when they are having fun.

6. **Make the rules of engagement simple** Do not overengineer or control the social network. Make it easy to enroll and participate.

IT at Work 10.5

Red Robin Transforms Its Business with Yammer

Red Robin Gourmet Burgers, Inc. is a casual dining restaurant chain serving an innovative selection of high-quality gourmet burgers in a family-friendly atmosphere. In 2015, revenues were $1.26 billion, representing an increase of 9.7% over 2014. Revenue at comparable restaurants had increased only 5.4%.

Front-Line Staff Know Customers Best

In retail and restaurants, front-line employees understand the CX far better than managers in remote corporate offices. Yet, companies often do not pay close attention to their front-line staff. Corporate culture is part of the reason, but a lot has to do with the absence of a channel for employees to be heard. With over 29,000 employees working in 538 restaurants in 49 states, Red Robin's new management team decided to give front-line employees a voice. In 2010, the company invested in enterprise social networking, in part, to reduce the high cost of employee turnover that is common in the restaurant business. The premise of the project was to enable employees to provide insight into management about consumer preferences. In terms of food quality, employees would document the popular menu items and any modifications made to them by customers.

Engaging Employees with Yammer

Newly hired Senior VP of Business Transformation and CIO Chris Laping believed that the company's workers—87% are **Millennials**—were searching for meaning. So engaging these workers in a meaningful way would create the atmosphere that strengthened employee loyalty.

Laping selected Yammer as the private social channel for employees, partners, and customers. The free version of Yammer was initially rolled out as a social experiment, to see if employees would engage. A few employees were invited to join Yammer. After they were urged to invite colleagues, membership spread quickly. Eventually, two Yammer networks emerged at Red Robin: namely *Yummer*, a network for restaurant managers, regional managers, and corporate office members to exchange information and answer questions from field staff; and *Yummversity*, a network for training employees. Yummer gave a voice to the silent front-line workers at Red Robin. Prior to Yammer, these employees would pass information up the company management chain, but they rarely received feedback on the information or what was done in response to it.

Better Burgers through Yummer and Yummversity In 2012, Red Robin introduced a new menu item, the Tavern Double burger. It did not receive customer feedback via Facebook, as expected. However, restaurant servers and regional managers posted what they heard from customers on Yummer. Managers at headquarters monitor Yummer, so they immediately knew the burger recipe needed to be adjusted.

They were able to respond with an updated menu within 4 weeks at much lower cost. Prior to Yammer, this feedback loop took 6 to 12 months and involved running expensive focus groups and surveys, hiring outside consultants, scheduling review sessions, and generating reports.

Mining Employees' Ideas

"Blueprint Project" was a CEO-led initiative to uncover the best employee idea to cut expenses and not negatively impact CX. A $1,000 prize was announced, and thousands of employees contributed ideas. The winning entry was submitted by a Seattle location manager who proposed replacing disposable kid beverage cups with reusable ones. According to Laping, this minor change was "a six figure savings for the organization."

IT at Work Questions

1. Why are employees a source of valuable information? In your opinion, why are employees an untapped resource at many companies?

2. How does Yammer capture BI from employees?

3. Explain Yummer and Yummversity. Why would employees want to use them?

4. What is the expected benefit of naming the ESP, as Red Robin had done?

5. How did Red Robin motivate its employees to contribute to the enterprise social net?

6. How did the restaurant reduce employee turnover?

Sources: Compiled from redrobin.com (2017), Keitt (2014), Lavenda (2014), and *MarketWatch* (2016).

At the first ever YamJam Conference in 2012, Yammer's CEO and founder introduced the new platform **Enterprise Graph**—calling it an enhanced way for business to be more social. Enterprise Graph tries to show how users are related to one another. It enables developers and customers to seamlessly connect people, conversations, and data across all their business services. With Enterprise Graph, Yammer solves the **social network sprawl** problem, which is when businesses end up interacting with multiple social networks inside their own company. The objective is to develop a standard that brings everything together and works off the same database.

Millennials is the term used to describe people born between the early 1980s and the early 2000s.

Office Graph and Oslo App
Microsoft's newer project, code-named Oslo, builds on the concept of the Enterprise Graph. One of the significant features of Yammer is how it maps the relationships between people and information by simply recording likes, posts, replies, shares,

and uploads. Microsoft applied these capabilities to Office with **Office Graph**. Office Graph uses signals from e-mail, social conversations, documents, sites, instant messages, meetings, and more to map the relationships between people and concepts. By tapping into Office Graph, Oslo provides a natural way for users to navigate, discover, and search people, information, and knowledge across the enterprise.

Oracle's Social Network

Oracle's social enterprise network connects processes, professionals, and enterprise apps in one place. Users can update CRM leads, communicate in real time, and search for key experts on the network. The social net also makes sharing files and information easy with sales teams and company members. Employees can work on documents together in real time, while having the option to access them anytime. Conversations and CRM data on the network can be accessed through Microsoft Outlook and mobile devices.

Jive

Jive's ESP provides tools for communication, sharing, and content creation to make social media monitoring and engagement easier. The platform features activity streams that keep employees updated and a text editor for users to create, review, and edit documents as a team.

Jive also has an enterprise search engine that offers social graph analytics and insight into make searching easier. Users can search across their customer network and SharePoint as well. Employees can also create blogs and custom attention streams to track specific people, projects, or groups.

Chatter

Chatter is an add-on to Saleforce.com, a CRM tool. As with all other ESPs, Chatter offers companies their own private network while pushing updates and news in real time to user feeds. The software offers smart search, which places items an employee frequently uses higher in the search list.

Similarly to many enterprises, if someone was trying to solve a problem or get feedback on a presentation, he or she would send out a global e-mail. Some people would reply to everyone, some would just reply to the sender, the e-mail thread gets jumbled—and quickly becomes a mess. With Chatter, the problem-solving process becomes a conversation rather than a series of disjointed e-mails. People can interact and spark new ideas. There is no confusion over which is the latest version of a document. Other employees can be brought into the conversation using the @ function. The whole process is just a much smarter way of working.

Chatter customer groups let users work with external customers, vendors, and partners, with the option of limiting what they can see and access. Private groups can also be set up when employees need to work on sensitive projects with certain colleagues.

Business processes can be approved from within a Chatter feed along with vacation requests or hiring decisions.

The features of ESPs will continue to evolve and disrupt existing applications and the future of work.

Questions

1. What are the basic functions of an ESP?
2. What are the capabilities of SharePoint?
3. In what ways can enterprises realize value from Yammer or other enterprise social?
4. How do Office Graph and Enterprise Graph support collaboration?
5. How does Chatter enable workers to solve problems?

Key Terms

3D bioprinting   303
3D printing   301
additive manufacturing   301
always-on supply chain   316
back-office operations   315
core business processes   304
customer lifetime value (CLV)   320
customer relationship
management (CRM)   301
electronic funds transfer (EFT)   315
enterprise application integration (EAI)   308

enterprise graph   325
enterprise resource planning
(ERP)   301
enterprise social platform   323
enterprise systems   301
front-office operations   315
interface   301
legacy systems   305
logistics   315
Microsoft Cloud   324
millennials   325

office graph   326
order fulfillment   315
reverse supply chain   315
SharePoint   324
social network sprawl   325
supply chain   313
supply chain management   301
value-added reseller (VAR)   305
Yammer   324

Assuring Your Learning

Discuss: Critical Thinking Questions

1. *Consider the following scenario:* In the 1990s, hard disk drive (HDD) makers were among the first industries to move production to lower-cost countries. Beginning in Singapore, these companies shifted manufacturing operations to China and Thailand, in search of ever-lower labor costs. Since then, Thailand has become the second-largest maker of hard drives and a major supplier of parts to the industry worldwide. With the catastrophic Thai floods in the fall of 2011, the industry faced shortages of over 30 million drives per quarter. Some executives at HDD companies were forced to explain a glaring oversight: Why had they had relied so heavily on a supplier in a country located in a high-flood risk area?

Also consider that: By the end of the 1990s, most supply chains had become lean by minimizing their inventories and reducing waste and

could schedule deliveries across the globe with incredible precision. Supply chain speed and flexibility were impressive. Products that should take months to procure and manufacture were promised within days of customer requests.

a. What SCM lessons can be learned from the experiences of HDD makers?

b. What are the risks of highly efficient and lean supply chains?

c. Could one catastrophic supply chain event wipe out years of profits or market share? Explain your answer.

d. In your opinion, when do cost savings outweigh the risks?

e. In your opinion, when are cost savings outweighed by the risks?

Questions for Discussion & Review

1. The vast majority of supply chain professionals agree that one of the biggest barriers to successful collaboration is a slow *issue resolution* process. This has been identified as a systemic problem related to quality of information flow, in terms of both the granularity (level of detail) and timeliness of data shared. In addition, almost all supply chain professionals agree that rapid problem resolution is part of good collaboration. True collaboration can be defined in terms of speed, both in problem-solving and in organizational learning. Many also indicate that speed of response in truly collaborative relationships is twice as fast or faster, with learning curve improvements more than 50% greater than in noncollaborative trading partner relationships.

a. Discuss why supply chain partners may not be able to resolve issues quickly. Consider *information flows* in your discussion.

b. What impacts might slow problem (issue) resolution have on the supply chain?

c. Based on your answer to (a), discuss which enterprise systems could speed up problem resolution.

d. What is meant by learning curve improvements?

2. In your opinion, what might limit the growth of 3D printing?

3. Distinguish between ERP and SCM software. In what ways do they complement each other? Why should they be integrated?

4. State the business value of enterprise systems and how they can be used to manage the supply chain more effectively.

5. What problems are encountered in implementing ERP systems?

6. Find examples of how two of the following organizations improve their supply chains: manufacturing, hospitals, retailing, education, construction, agribusiness, and shipping. Discuss the benefits to the organizations.

7. It is claimed that supply chains are essentially "a series of linked suppliers and customers; every customer is in turn a supplier to the next downstream organization, until the ultimate end-user." Explain this statement. Use a diagram.

8. Discuss why it is difficult to justify CRM.

9. A supply chain is much more powerful in the Internet marketplace. Discuss how Internet technologies can be used to manage the supply chain.

Explore: Online and Interactive Exercises

Visit each of the following enterprise vendor websites. Write a brief report on the latest features of their enterprise systems, platforms, apps, or solutions.

1. SharePoint
2. Yammer
3. Oracle
4. Salesforce
5. SAP

Analyze & Decide: Apply IT Concepts to Business Decisions

1. Select an enterprise system vendor. Search and read a case study of one of the vendor's customers. Summarize the case and identify the benefits of the implementation.

2. Assess the costs and benefits of a cloud CRM. A large food-processing company would like to determine the cost–benefit of installing a CRM app in a private cloud. Create a report that contains these analyses:

   a. Calculate the tangible costs and benefits in a spreadsheet using the data provided.

   b. List two intangible benefits of moving to the cloud.

   c. Estimate the value of those two benefits and include them in your spreadsheet prepared for Question 1.

   d. List two risks associated with the CRM app if it were moved to a public cloud.

Data

Tangible Costs

- CRM in private cloud: $35 per user per month
- Technical support and maintenance: $250 per month
- Total number of users: 100 (90 salespeople and 10 supervisors)
- Training of 90 salespeople for five days: productivity loss $200 per day per person
- Training of five supervisors: productivity loss $300 per day per person
- Additional hardware, networks, and bandwidth: $15,000 per month

Tangible Benefits

- Increase in average sales revenues = $6,000 per month per salesperson
- Increase in sales revenues from an improvement in customer retention = $5,000 per month
- Gross profit from sales revenues = 20 percent

Case 10.2

Business Case: Lowe's Fresh Approach to Supply Chain Management

Lowe's Inc. is a retail company based out of Mooresville, NC, specializing in the sale of hardware, home appliances, and building materials. With over 285,000 employees, the company can serve nearly 15 million customers each week from over 1,800 stores in the United States, Canada, and Mexico. Lowe's provides both products and services to their customers, using the input–transformation–output (ITO) model. The ITO model is the center function of the supply chain that successful companies, such as Lowe's, use. With over 7,500 suppliers, Lowe's is able to decrease reliance on vendors and focus on providing its own method of customer and product relationship management.

Commitment to Customers

A large aspect of Lowe's supply chain is its commitment to ensuring that relationships with customers are maintained throughout the life cycles of the products the customers purchase. The two ways Lowe's upholds the commitment are "installed sales" and the "extended protection plans and repair services." Providing service for purchased products over the lifetime of the product is called "product lifecycle management" or PLM. PLM has become important from a supply chain standpoint as warranties and guarantees are becoming more popular. Lowe's gives extended warranties and allows customers to request repairs and replacements along with installation of the products.

A New Approach to Retailing

In addition to meeting customer needs in the store and through the installation services it offers, Lowe's has employed a method of reaching the mobile and online customer called Omni-Channel retailing: creating a consistent experience for customers on mobile apps, websites, and in the stores, since online retailing is becoming more effective because so many consumers "window shop" online. Omni-Channel retailing makes every method of purchasing universal. This is where Lowe's sets itself apart in the hardware market with its ability to engage technology and the internet of things in its operations. A significant contributor to the success of this model is that Lowe's controls 80% of its products in its own distribution channel. When coupled with Omni-Channel, Lowe's provides its customers products and services at the lowest cost and the highest convenience. Customers are able to order directly from Lowe's distribution centers, effectively eliminating the middle man, and to order products and services from the app, website, or physical store.

Enhancing the Customer Experience

In effort to beat out its competitors, Lowe's rolled out Holoroom, its virtual reality system that allows customers to visualize potential home improvement projects in the kitchen and bathroom. Customers of 19 U.S. stores, mainly in the Bay Area, were able to move products around in virtual rooms and see how they interact together. Customers wear a virtual reality headset and select items from a library of Lowe's products and place them in the virtual environment to determine if they are desirable to place in one's house. Beyond visualizing product placement in one's house, the customers are able to employ different design patterns and paint colors.

To make the system personalized, customers first enter the dimensions of their rooms into Lowe's website or mobile app using the MyLowes feature. Using the dimensions as a template, Lowe's gives potential project and product recommendations to customers using the feature. This feature has proved to be extremely successful in attracting more customers to Lowes.

Questions

1. How does Lowe's provide quality products and services through its supply chain system?
2. What is Lowe's approach to product lifecycle management?
3. Why does Lowe's focus so strongly on CRM?
4. What is Lowe's view on technology in its processes?
5. How does Omni-Channel retailing further connect Lowe's to the customer?

Sources: Compiled from lowes.com (2017), Soni (2016a), Soni (2016b), and Marxentlabs (2017).

Case 10.3

Video Case: Procter & Gamble: Creating Conversations in the Cloud with 4.8 Billion Consumers

The decline of traditional marketing channels forced changes in CRM transformation at Procter & Gamble (P&G). P&G's cloud environment allows for all consumer data to be in one location for fresh, relevant relationships with 4.8 billion consumers as they transition from one product to the next over the course of their lifetimes.

Visit **Teradata.com** and search for the video entitled "Procter & Gamble: Creating Conversations in the Cloud with 4.8 Billion Consumers." Watch the video and answer the following questions:

Questions

1. How does P&G maintain an ongoing dialog with a customer?
2. What were P&G's data challenges?
3. What is 1, Consumer Place? Where is it?
4. In your opinion, how does P&G try to maximize CLV?

References

3dprinting.com. 2017.

All, A. "8 Common CRM Mistakes, and How to Avoid Them." *Enterprise Apps Today,* February 20, 2014.

Bourne, A. "What Does 3D Printing Mean for ERP?" *Manufacturing.net,* January 29, 2014.

Butler, D, et al. "Identifying Efficiencies in the Supply Chain for Training Ammunition." *Rand Corporation,* 2016.

Cole, B. "Gartner Report Finds Slow Growth in Global ERP Market." *SearchManufacturingERP.com,* May 16, 2014.

Drucker, P.F. *The Age of Discontinuity.* New York: Harper & Row. 1969.

Fine, R. "What Role Does 3D Printing Play in an ERP-Managed Manufacturing Process?" *Toolbox.com,* May 21, 2014.

Gartner.com. "Gartner Says Uses of 3D Printing Will Ignite Major Debate on Ethics and Regulation." January 29, 2014. *Gartner.com.*

goldmansachs.com. "The Search for Creative Destruction." March 24, 2014. *goldmansachs.com.*

Haraburda, S. "Transforming military support processes from logistics to supply chain management." U.S. Army, February 29, 2016.

Keitt, T. "Case Study: Red Robin Builds an Agile Customer-Centric Culture with Yammer." *Forrester*, June 20, 2014.

Lavenda, D. "How Red Robin Transformed Its Business with Yammer." *Fast Company*, February 6, 2014.

lowes.com. 2017.

MarketWatch. "RRGB." December 5, 2016.

Marxentlabs. "Lowe's Holoroom, Virtual Reality for Retail." http://www .marxentlabs.com/ar-videos/lowes-holoroom-3d-augmented-reality-virtual-room-home-improvement/

MHI and Deloitte. "Accelerating Change: How Innovation is driving digital, always-on supply chains – The 2016 MHI Annual Industry Report" 2016. https://www.mhi.org/publications/report

Pang, A. "Top 10 ERP Software Vendors and Market Forecast 2015-2020." *Apps Research & Buyer Insight*, June 28, 2016.

redrobin.com. 2017.

Soni, P. "How Lowe's is Leveraging its Omni-Channel Opportunity." *MarketRealist*, January 27, 2016a.

Soni, P. "Will Lowe's Holoroom Virtual Reality Push Attract More Customers?" *MarketRealist*, January 27, 2016b.

The Engineer. "Patient Receives 3D Printed Titanium Hip." May 19, 2014.

U.S. Army Business Transformation Knowledge Center, 2009 army .mil/armyBTKC.

CHAPTER 11

Data Visualization and Geographic Information Systems

CHAPTER OUTLINE

Case 11.1 Opening Case: Safeway and PepsiCo Apply Data Visualization to Supply Chain

11.1 Data Visualization and Learning

11.2 Enterprise Data Mashups

11.3 Digital Dashboards

11.4 Geospatial Data and Geographic Information Systems

Case 11.2 Visualization Case: Are You Ready for Football?

Case 11.3 Video Case: The Beauty of Data Visualization—Data Detective

LEARNING OBJECTIVES

11.1 Describe how data visualization applications and interactive reports support learning and business functions.

11.2 Explain how data mashup applications streamline the process of integrating diverse data sources and information feeds to support data needs that cannot be anticipated.

11.3 Describe how companies optimize operations with the help of dashboards. Explain how enterprise dashboards are built and how they leverage real-time data and people's natural ability to think visually.

11.4 Assess the business applications and benefits of geospatial data and geographic information systems.

Introduction

The concept of using pictures or graphics to understand data has been around for centuries—from seventeenth century maps and graphs to the invention of the pie chart in the early 1800s. In recent years, technology has brought the art and science of data visualization to forefront, and it is changing the corporate landscape.

Historically, data analytics was performed by statisticians, programmers, and data scientists who rarely interact directly with the business. However, easier-to-use data visualization, dashboard, and mashup technologies have changed this "experts-only" approach to data analysis and presentation. Data analytics are being pushed out into the business by advances that make it possible for employees at most levels of the organization to analyze data in a meaningful way. Vendors of enterprise-level analytics are also upgrading their visualization and reporting platforms previously designed for use by the statistical experts.

In Chapter 3, you learned about big data analytics, data mining, and business intelligence (BI) and how they are being used to enhance performance, productivity, and competitive advantage in organizations around the globe. In this chapter, we expand on these topics to introduce you to the latest in data visualization, visual discovery, dashboards, mashups, and geographic information systems (GISs). We also introduce you to another important concept— **geospatial data** and how companies are incorporating geospatial data and GISs into their customer relationship management (CRM), supply chain management (SCM), BI, and other related enterprise activities

Several tools discussed in this chapter enable you to be self-sufficient. Drag-and-drop, automation, "show me" wizards, and easy-to-use dashboards enable you to develop your own interactive data visualization apps and dashboards. Reducing dependency on IT staff has a long history. For example, at one time, managers did not analyze data with spreadsheets, but now Excel expertise is expected. Vendors offer academic alliances to enable universities to teach their software in MBA and undergraduate business courses. Tableau Desktop, QlikView, TIBCO Spotfire, and IBM's SPSS Analytic Catalyst enable business users to perform the kind of advanced analysis that could only have been performed by expert users of statistical software a few years ago.

Geospatial data is data that has an explicitly geographic component, ranging from vector and raster data to tabular data with site locations.

Case 11.1 Opening Case

REUTERS/Alamy Stock Photo

Matt Cardy/Stringer/Getty Images

Richard Levine/Alamy Stock Photo

Safeway and PepsiCo Collaborate to Reduce Stock Outages using Data Visualization

If there's one activity that is central to retail operations, it's inventory management. Striking just the right balance between enough and not too much stock puzzles even those retailers who are regarded as inventory management experts. So, when PepsiCo suggested to Safeway that they try using data visualization software to improve forecasting and inventory management, Safeway leaders jumped at the chance!

Enhancing Supply Chain Visibility

In an effort to improve awareness and sharing of POS data and data about product orders, inventory levels, demand forecasts, transportation, and logistics, Safeway implemented data-sharing programs with PepsiCo and other key vendors using data visualization techniques (**Figure 11.1** and **Table 11.1**). This type of improved data visibility can result in increased sales and millions of dollars in reduced

costs along the entire supply chain—from raw material to delivery to end customer.

Safeway's Data Visibility program was already forward thinking, so when they partnered with PepsiCo's 360° Retail execution program, Safeway's teams were equipped to improve an already lean supply chain. But to further improve their supply chain, Safeway needed an altogether different way to view the data. So, when Deloitte Consulting offered to partner with PepsiCo and Safeway to provide an effective way to interpret massive amounts of data at its Highly Immersive Visual Environment (HIVE), they were very interested.

Excel-based analytics

In the past, when Safeway wanted answers about stockouts, managers used spreadsheets to gather and compile inventory data and see how stockouts trended across the company. With spreadsheets, managers could discover general trends over time, but they could not identify trends across a specific brand or universal product code (UPC). Trends

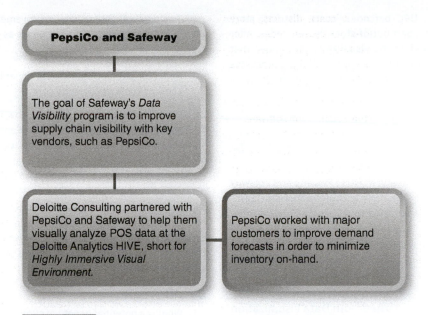

FIGURE 11.1 Deloitte Consulting partnered with PepsiCo and Safeway to help them analyze massive amounts of point-of-sale (POS) data at its state-of-the-art visualization center called HIVE.

TABLE 11.1   Opening Case Overview

Business	**Safeway**, headquartered in Pleasanton, CA. has 197,000 employees and 1,368 stores in the United States and Canada. Safeway, Inc., reported revenue of $36.3 billion in 2015.
	PepsiCo, Headquartered in Purchase, NY. has 263,000 employees across operations in over 200 countries and territories in Europe, Sub-Saharan Africa; in Asia, Middle East, and North Africa. PepsiCo reported a net revenue of $63 billion in 2015.
Products Lines	PepsiCo—food, snacks and beverages
	Safeway—food and drug retailers
Business challenges	Inventory management is critical in retail operations—and a challenge throughout the supply chain.
Digital Technology	**HIVE**—a physical environment where people can examine the latest analytics approaches themselves using their own data offered by Deloitte Consulting
Taglines	**PepsiCo**—"You Got the Right One Baby"
	Safeway—"Ingredients for Life"

about each brand required more data than could be represented in rows and columns of a spreadsheet. These spreadsheet limitations ultimately led the company to try data visualization. To initialize the project, representatives from Safeway and PepsiCo traveled to Deloitte's HIVE in Washington, DC, for a day-long design session to analyze many terabytes of data.

HIVE

Deloitte's HIVE is a research lab that measures and studies the interactions between business analytics technologies and real-world data. The applications used at the HIVE to develop real-world business solutions are translated into portfolios that are intuitive to understand. Deloitte hosts business leaders who want to understand business analytics better in sessions tailored to address their specific business

challenges (Curtis, 2013). At the HIVE, executives get help with analytics tools using their own data.

The HIVE gathers together a wide range of the latest analytics technologies from all over the world. In a very short amount of time, executives can learn what might otherwise have taken months of meetings, demonstrations, and business pitches. You can find out more about the HIVE in the video "**Deloitte Analytics HIVE**".

Data Visualization at the HIVE

PepsiCo and Safeway participants collaborated to understand how to reduce the "number of days of supply" from their supply chain while maintaining service levels—a project that would save PepsiCo and Safeway millions of dollars each year! During their HIVE session, they built data visualizations to explore questions about stockouts.

The data included brands, UPC barcodes, costs, districts, store numbers, out-of-stock scans, and out-of-stock reason codes. After Safeway and PepsiCo decided on the visualization technique that best represented their supply chain, they designed three processes to operationalize it. The three processes they chose to design were as follows:

1. How to feed the huge data sets into the visualization software
2. The best ways to display the data visually
3. How to gather feedback

Within 40 days after their session at HIVE, PepsiCo and Safeway were able to implement their initial data visualization with dashboards and drill-down capabilities, then spent another 20 days refining it. Employing these data visualization techniques led to greatly improved performance and reduced the frequency of stockouts at Safeway. In some areas, managers were able to increase accuracy by 35%!

What PepsiCo and Safeway Learned from Data Visualization and Dashboards

Safeway identified the stores experiencing the most stockouts and their root causes. For example, it learned a disproportionate number of stockouts were occurring at a store on Catalina Island. The store is in a resort area where the tourist traffic causes uneven demand. Safeway adjusted its supply chain strategy to address uneven demand patterns.

Safeway also discovered that they were sending multiple and conflicting forecasts to their vendors from various departments. Safeway changed the way the company creates and communicates forecasts with its suppliers.

Two significant operational improvements at Safeway from discoveries made through data visualization are as follows:

1. Improved forecast accuracy by 35%
2. Reduced on-hand warehouse inventory, which cut inventory carrying costs significantly

PepsiCo also benefited because now it has incredible, near real-time access to the movement of every PepsiCo item, at every Safeway store, every day. Moreover, Pepsi recognizes that communicating data in an effective manner is important as Generation Z is increasingly becoming a large proportion of the customer base and workforce. The new players in the workforce need visuals that abbreviate information but still provide thorough analysis to make quicker decisions. Pepsi's experience at Deloitte have allowed it to develop a mobile app for cross-team collaboration and data publication, derive consistent information from customer surveys, and more accurately segment and attract different consumer markets.

Questions

1. What is a potential benefit of supply chain visibility?
2. What was the limitation of Excel-based data analytics at Safeway?
3. What makes Deloitte's HIVE unique in its approach to data analysis?
4. What steps did Safeway and PepsiCo undertake to arrive at their data visualization solution?
5. What were the two operational improvements at Safeway?
6. Name one way in which PepsiCo benefited from the partnership with Safeway?

Sources: Compiled from Deloitte (2016), Pathak (2015), pepsico.com (2017), safeway.com/ShopStores/Our-Story.page (2017).

11.1 Data Visualization and Learning

Data visualization is the presentation of data in a graphical format to make it easier for decision-makers to grasp difficult concepts or identify new patterns in the data.

Drill down is searching for something on a computer moving from general information to more detailed information by focusing on something of interest, for example, quarterly sales—monthly sales—daily sales.

Data visualization harnesses the power of data analytics and adds a visual display to capitalize on the way our brains work. You've probably heard the saying "A picture is worth a thousand words"—interactive displays, charts with **drill down** capability, and **geospatial data** analysis do just that and are some of the many ways companies can present data to enhance decision-making. For example, maps can tell a much more compelling story than words or numbers, as shown in **Figure 11.2**, by effective use of visual cues. Organizational decision-makers rely on visual cues to grasp and process huge amounts of information.

Visualizing data can save a business money, help communicate important points, and hold customer attention. Data visualization is important because of the way the human brain processes information. Using pie charts, histograms, or bar graphs to visualize large amounts of complex data is much easier than poring over spreadsheets or reports. Data visualization is a quick, easy way to convey concepts in a universal manner—and you can experiment with different scenarios by making slight adjustments.

Data visualization software can be extremely powerful and complex, similarly to Deloitte's HIVE platform. At the other continuum are tools with simple, point-and-click interfaces that do not require any particular coding knowledge or significant training. Most non-data-scientist-friendly tools have interactive elements and can pull data from Google

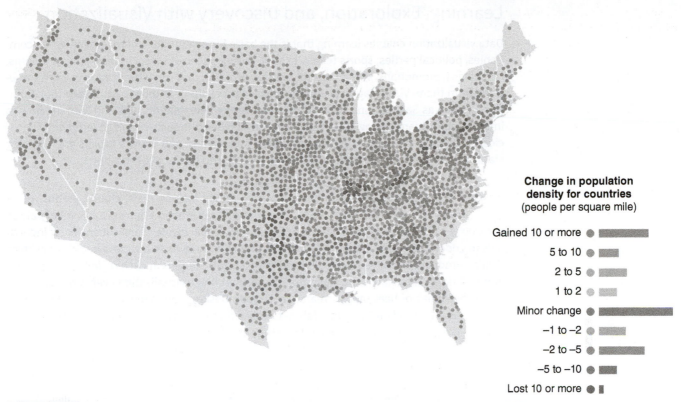

**Change in population
density for countries**
(people per square mile)

Gained 10 or more
5 to 10
2 to 5
1 to 2
Minor change
−1 to −2
−2 to −5
−5 to −10
Lost 10 or more

FIGURE 11.2 U.S. Census Bureau map shows easily identifiable changes in county population density. Different colors are used to indicate areas that gained and lost population. Intensity of color indicates extent of gain/loss.

Docs, Excel spreadsheets, Access databases, and other sources that most business people work with already. Some useful business applications for data visualization include the following:

- Identifying areas that need attention or improvement
- Clarifying which factors influence customer behavior
- Helping understand which products to place where
- Predicting sales volumes

First, we'll explore different technologies that fall into the data analytics category, as shown in **Figure 11.3**. Vendor packages usually offer tools in more than one category. In general, **reporting tools** generate BI that shows what has already happened in a business. **Analytical tools** show what might or could happen in the future. Later sections discuss information delivery and data integration.

Information Delivery
- Dashboards
- Interactive reports

Data Analytics
- Data visualization
- Data discovery
- Geospatial & GIS

Data Integration
- Data mashups
- GIS

FIGURE 11.3 Tools and technologies in this chapter fall into three related categories.

Learning, Exploration, and Discovery with Visualization

Data visualization enables learning that is the basis for continuous improvement. When companies, political parties, sports teams, or fund-raising agencies invest in marketing programs, campaigns, promotions, special events, or other projects, they use visualization to learn something from them. Visualization is also used as a data explorer and **data discovery** tool. Companies, such as Safeway and PepsiCo, are discovering new relationships and learning how to improve performance using data visualization in all types of industries and governmental agencies. Enterprise visualization apps for Androids, Apple iPads, and Surface tablets are replacing static business reports with real-time data, analytics, and interactive reporting tools.

Examples of Visuals Examples of visualizations include dials, charts, graphs, timelines, geospatial maps, and heat maps. The tricolor heat map in **Figure 11.4** instantly alerts the viewer to critical areas most in need of attention. Visual displays make it easier for individuals to understand data and identify patterns that offer answers to business questions such as "Which product lines have the highest and lowest profit margins in each region?" Interactivity and drill-down capabilities are standard features that make visualization even more valuable. Two other types of heat maps, created in Tableau Desktop, are shown in **Figure 11.5**; both heat maps are based on the same data set. Notice that the way in which the data are visually displayed depends on what you want to learn or convey.

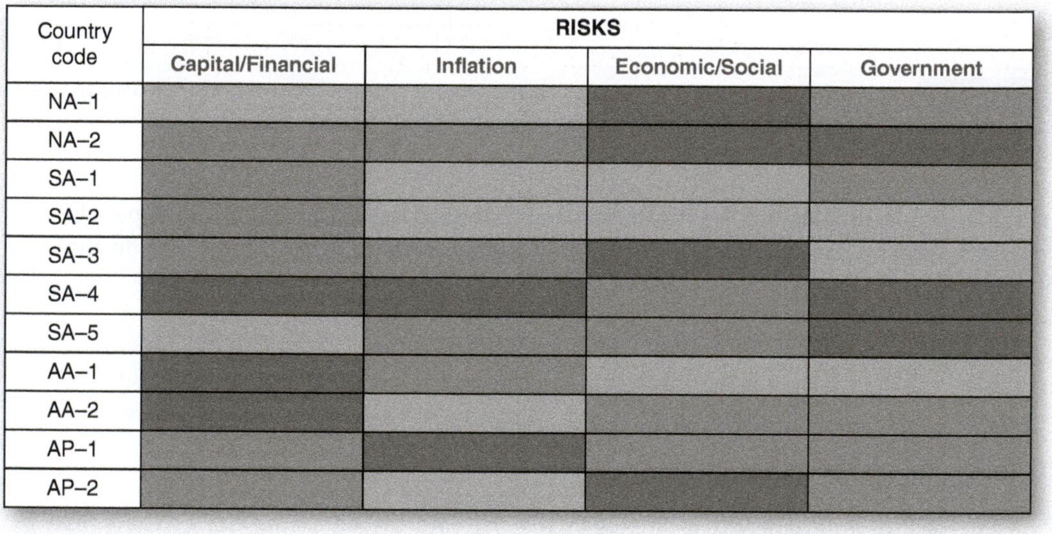

Country code	RISKS			
	Capital/Financial	Inflation	Economic/Social	Government
NA–1				
NA–2				
SA–1				
SA–2				
SA–3				
SA–4				
SA–5				
AA–1				
AA–2				
AP–1				
AP–2				

FIGURE 11.4 This heat map uses three colors to convey information at a glance. The heat map is like a spreadsheet whose cells are formatted with colors instead of numbers.

Human expertise is an essential component of data visualization (see **Figure 11.6**). A common mistake organizations make is to invest in the analytics foundation—tools, quality data, data integration, touch screens—but overlook the most crucial component, which is the users' ability to interpret the visual reports and analyze them correctly.

Data Discovery Market Separates from the BI Market

According to Gartner Research, the data analytics market has split into two segments: the traditional BI market and the newer data discovery market. Data discovery software had previously been viewed as a supplement to traditional BI platforms. Now it is a stand-alone alternative to BI. This split occurred because today's data discovery technologies provide greater data exploration and ease of use to help users find answers to "why" and "what if" questions through self-service analytic apps. The split is another example of pushing analytics onto the computers of business workers. **IT at Work 11.1** describes the trend at IBM.

Product Cate...	Product Sub-Category	Region			
		Central	East	South	West
Furniture	Bookcases	73	−10,151	−22,417	−676
	Chairs & Chairmats	37,920	33,583	34,026	44,409
	Office Furnishings	26,293	14,523	25,121	30,941
	Tables	−19,777	−50,677	26,172	−16,990
Office Supplies	Appliances	22,950	16,812	26,986	31,276
	Binders and Binder Accessories	73,951	71,420	69,530	92,273
	Envelopes	10,825	7,482	19,182	11,222
	Labels	2,429	4,041	3,479	3,740
	Paper	11,047	13,510	10,997	10,433
	Pens & Art Supplies	2,781	2,856	1,397	518
	Rubber Bands	−174	−238	156	178
	Scissors, Rulers and Trimmers	−1,765	−1,179	−2,903	−1,953
	Storage & Organization	−68	−7,233	11,836	−2,018
Technology	Computer Peripherals	11,971	14,808	30,475	37,280
	Copiers and Fax	513	67,254	63,598	35,997
	Office Machines	38,876	47,277	129,060	61,377
	Telephones and Communication	79,393	73,715	78,985	84,860

(a)

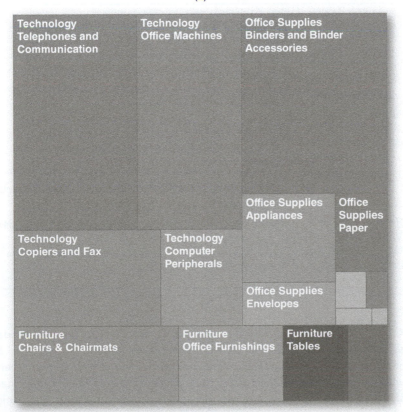

(b)

FIGURE 11.5   These heat maps represent the same data set using different colors (usually red and green) and color intensity to show the profitability of three product categories and their subcategories. In (a), data labels show detailed profit, while in (b), the area of each segment is used to make comparisons.

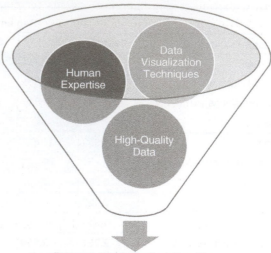

Patterns, trends, and relationships
Context to understand what numbers represent
& how to interpret them
Action to be taken

FIGURE 11.6 Data visualization, human expertise, and high-quality data are needed to obtain actionable information.

IT at Work 11.1

IBM Tackles Big Data Discovery

As one of the world's leading technologies corporations, IBM consistently takes advantage of opportunities to increase its market share in the computing and data analytics realm. In addition to hosting data storage platforms, IBM produces ways for customers to analyze data more effectively. Its most recent development is a service package of application programming interfaces (APIs) called the Watson Discovery Service. Watson is intended to decrease the amount of time analysts have to spend organizing and cleaning data and allow them to focus on making data-driven decisions.

The most prevalent issue in data analytics is the struggle to standardize and organize data in a way that makes information usable. Steve Lohr of the New York Times claims that analysts spend 80% of their time cleaning and organizing data for use (Lohr, 2014). The Watson Discovery Service solves this problem by standardizing

and categorizing data and making it available for query by the user. The most impressive aspect of the new service is its ability to accurately analyze text sources on a "massive scale" (Forrest, 2016). This allows employees of any level to gather the most important information from numerous sources without having to manually research each source individually.

IT at Work Questions

1. How is IBM's approach to big data unique?

2. Why is a data organization service so vital to data analysis?

3. What makes the Watson Discovery Service attractive to companies?

4. Do you think the service will make data analysis more accurate?

Sources: Lohr (2014) and Forrest (2016).

Analytics/Visualization Vendors Respond to Demand Smaller data visualization vendors are competing head-on with BI megavendors IBM, Oracle, and SAS. For example, vendors DOMO, QlikView, Birst, Tableau, Sisense, and others are adding enterprise features with each new release. SAS is one of the leaders in the data visualization space. SAS® Visual Analytics uses intelligent autocharting to help business analysts and nontechnical users create the best possible visual based on the data that is selected. The visualizations make it easy to see patterns and trends and identify opportunities for further analysis. The SAS® LASR™ Analytic Server feature executes and accelerates analytic computations through in-memory processing. The combination of high-performance analytics and an easy-to-use data exploration interface enables different types of users to create and interact with graphs and charts to better understand and derive more value from their data faster than ever.

Others, such as Qlik, are integrating inference engines to replace the query-based approach, which divorces data from its context. Using an inference engine, users can input as much information as they have, and the software not only will search for the information provided but also will make associations with all other data that is related to the information provided.

These vendors continue to focus on business users of all levels and backgrounds. For example, Jeff Strauss, BI architect at Allstate Insurance Company, explained that Allstate invested in Tableau data discovery tools, so users throughout the organization could do their own analysis rather than rely on the IT department. Tableau has built a large following with its easy-to-access dashboards.

Data Discovery Offers Speed and Flexibility
Data discovery is expected to take on a greater role in corporate decision making. Companies are investing in the latest data discovery solutions largely because of their speed and flexibility. Experts and novices can collect data quickly from disparate sources and then explore the data set with easy-to-use interactive visualizations and search interfaces (**Figure 11.7**). Drill-down paths are not predefined, which gives users more flexibility in how they view detailed data.

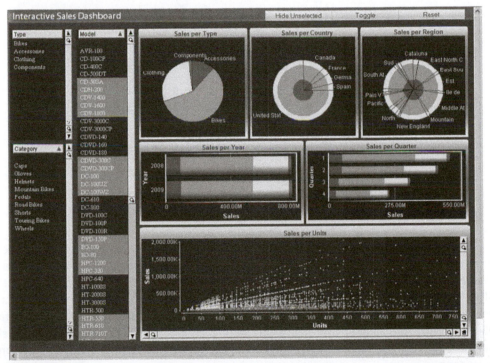

FIGURE 11.7 Data discovery tools allow users to interact with multiple corporate data sources.

A powerful feature of data discovery systems is their ability to integrate data from multiple data stores and identify data types and roles. See **Tech Note 11.1**. While data are being loaded into the program, the software automatically extracts and organizes them by data type. Software may also extract and organize terms from unstructured content, such as texts, e-mail, and PDFs, and create tag clouds. **Figure 11.8** shows an example of a Word cloud that give users a quick way to evaluate the most aspects of SCM and start to make discoveries.

Big Data Visualization Challenges
The speed, size, and diversity of big data brings new challenges to visualization. One challenge is how to display the results of data discovery in a meaningful way that is not overwhelming. For example, you may need to collapse and condense the results to display graphs and charts in a way that decision makers are accustomed to viewing. Results may also need to be available quickly on mobile devices, and users may want to be able to easily explore the data on their own in real time.

Tech Note 11.1

Understanding Data Types and Roles

Data types and roles are fundamental components that affect how visualizations behave. Each field in any data source has an associated data type. For example, a field that contains customer names has a string (text) data type, and a field that contains price information usually has a numeric data type. To visualize data QlikView, Tableau—or in any analytics or BI tool, for that matter—you need to understand dimensions and measures.

- **Dimensions** Dimensions contain discrete or categorical data, such as a region (e.g., Northeast, Southwest), product category, product subcategory, product name, supplier, size,

date, and zip code. Dimensions often become labels in the data visualization.

- **Measures** A measure is a calculation based on numeric data, such as profit, margin, quantity sold, speed, and miles. The calculation always returns one single value that summarizes all relevant records. The calculation is called an **aggregation**. As in spreadsheets, there are several aggregation functions: Sum(), Count(), Average(), Min(), Max(), and so on. Key performance indicators (KPIs) of interest might include monthly revenue, number of orders, quantity on hand, and total cost. A measure is always based on an aggregation.

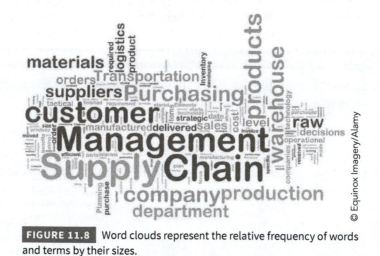

FIGURE 11.8 Word clouds represent the relative frequency of words and terms by their sizes.

Another issue associated with big data is the speed within which traditional architectures and software can process the data. If the data are not processed in a timely manner, the data may not be accurate or useful, for example, stock market data. For example, IBM SPSS integrates three visualization tools to handle big data—*Netezza*, *InfoSphere BigInsights*, and *InfoSphere Streams*—to provide comprehensive analytics capabilities in the big data platform. *Netezza* is a high-performance data warehouse whose data can be used for model building, scoring, and model refresh; *InfoSphere BigInsights* is an enterprise-ready distribution of Hadoop.

How Is Data Visualization Used in Business?

The ultimate goal of data analytics is to drive profits, and often that depends on learning how to manage assets, such as inventory, or engage customers in a smarter way. Collecting data is relatively easy. Making sense of that data is not. Here are examples of how companies and/or entire industries are using data visualization and interactivity to improve decision speed and performance often with mobile displays.

The latest data visualization software addresses issues associated with processing big data by speeding up data discovery and returns the visualization within an appropriate time-frame, in an easy-to-understand format. BI and data visualization vendors are working to assist business analysts and nontechnical users in determining how best to display these massive amounts of data.

Quick Detection and Decisions in Stock Markets Wall Street firms, traders, wealth managers, risk analysts, and regulators rely on their ability to process and capitalize on market anomalies in real time. Because of the demanding pace of their decisions, capital market professionals use visualization for risk analysis, pretrade and posttrade checks, compliance monitoring, fraud detection, client profitability analysis, research and sales, and portfolio performance. Vendor Aqumin provides real-time visual interpretation solutions for the financial services industry. Aqumin's OptionVision enables traders, risk managers, and market participants to spot opportunities, risk, and market changes. AlphaVision for Excel enables visual interpretation capabilities directly within the Microsoft Excel platform, and AlphaVision for Bloomberg is developed for professional portfolio managers, traders, and risk analysts and is connected directly to the Bloomberg Terminal to leverage data provided by Bloomberg.

The Chicago Board Options Exchange (CBOE), Gain Capital, JP Morgan, hedge funds, and other asset management firms not only need data visualization but their executives and investors expect the quality and excitement of visuals to make sense of dry financial data.

Improving the HR Function ADP Corporation is one of the largest payroll service providers in the world, with data on 33 million workers. When payroll processing company ADP rolled out data visualizations with predictive analytics to improve its human resource (HR) function, it was surprised by what it found. After organizing the information and funneling it through an analysis program, the HR department found that ADP would soon face a serious retirement problem. To mitigate its foreseeable future talent gaps, ADP constructed new training programs to prepare the next generation of workers.

Prompt Disaster Response by the Insurance Industry The effectiveness of an insurer's response to a devastating hurricane or other catastrophic event depends on its ability to combine large amounts of data to fully understand the impact. Leading insurers are using Web-based data visualization and analysis technologies to better manage their responses to major disasters. In the days and weeks after a disaster, insurers face analysis and reporting bottlenecks. Analysts capable of creating maps and reports work frantically to respond to requests for information. Because new data continue being generated even after the event, the data have a short life span and reports need to be regenerated and redistributed.

For example, when an earthquake occurs, workers throughout an insurance company access a Web-based (cloud) data app to visualize and analyze the impact. Users quickly determine which properties were subject to specific shake intensities and can visually build analyses on their own, rather than waiting for a report.

Data Visualization Tools

A number of vendors offer data visualization software. The following list describes a few of these. Many of these vendors offer a free trial of their software on the websites.

- **SAS Visual Catalyst** has an intelligent autocharting feature that automatically presents the most appropriate visualization of a specified data set based on the amount and type of data being analyzed. By building hierarchies "on the fly," interactively exploring data, and displaying data in different ways to answer specific questions or solve new problems, these new data visualization products relieve the user of constantly having to rely on assistance from the IT department when they want to change the ways in which the data is displayed. For example, if you have a billion rows of data, it would be impossible to see so many data points on a scatter plot. However, a box plot would convey the information that you need.

- **Birst** combines capability, scale, and data governance that IT needs with the agility, speed, and usability of consumer-grade desktop tools. Birst's adaptive user experience offers users a wide range of self-service, data analysis, and presentation options, and its cloud architecture allows users to instantly share findings and data across its supply chain.

- **QlikView** distinguishes itself from other BI tools through its unique inference engine that automatically maintains data associations. The inference engine works much the same as the human brain, in that when it "thinks" of a data set, it is reminded of all things related to it. Qlikview also offers a simple, Google-like search that works in an associative manner, producing results for the phrase and also for things commonly related to the phrase. For example, if a user wants contact information for a salesperson in an organization, and only knows the product that the salesperson specializes in but didn't know the person's name or the company, Qlikview could produce the desired results.

- **IBM SPSS Analytic Catalyst** has made sophisticated analytics accessible. Analytic Catalyst enables business users to conduct the kind of advanced analysis that had been designed for experts in statistical software. The software fast tracks analytics by identifying key drivers, selecting an appropriate model, testing it, and then explaining the results in plain English. See the YouTube video titled "IBM SPSS Analytic Catalyst" for an overview. The tool condenses the analytic process into three steps: data upload, selection of the target variable (the dependent variable or outcome variable), and data exploration. Once the data are uploaded, the system selects target variables and automatically correlates and associates the data. Based on characteristics of the data, Analytic Catalyst chooses the appropriate method and returns summary data rather than statistical data. On the initial screen, it communicates the so-called top insights in plain text and presents visuals, such as a decision tree in a churn analysis. Once the user has absorbed the top-level information, he or she can drill down into top key drivers. This enables users to see interactivity between attributes.

- **IBM Watson Analytics** is a cloud-based data visualization tool that guides data exploration, automates predictive analytics, and enables effortless creation of dashboards and infographics.

- **Tableau** is one of the easier data discovery tools to implement, requiring just basic database information to connect it to the target data sources. With a new in-memory database engine, such tools are developing the power to perform big data analytics. Despite data visualization advancements, data integration between data sources can still be very challenging.

- **Roambi Analytics** is a leading mobile reporting and data visualization app designed for iPads and iPhones. The app can take data from most sources, including Box, Google Docs, spreadsheets, BI systems, databases, and Salesforce.com, and transform them into interactive data visualizations. Roambi has a worldwide customer base of Global 500 companies and small and medium businesses across industries, including telecommunications, biotechnology, pharmaceuticals, consumer technology, and packaged goods.

Questions

1. How does data visualization contribute to learning?
2. How do heat maps and tag clouds convey information?
3. Why are data visualization and discovery usage increasing?
4. Give two examples of data visualization for performance management.

11.2 Enterprise Data Mashups

Enterprise data mashup the combination of data from various business systems and external sources without relying on the middle step of ETL (extract, transform, and load) into a data warehouse or help from IT.

Enterprise data mashups combine business data and applications from multiple sources—typically a mix of internal data and applications with externally sourced data, SaaS (software as a service) and Web content—to create an integrated experience. Mashups, in general, became popular because of social and mobile technology. The ability of enterprise mashups to quickly and easily consolidate data and functionality that is normally spread across several applications, onto a single Web page or mobile device screen, offers real business opportunities for companies of all shapes and sizes around the world.

Enterprises use mashups as quick, cost-effective solutions to a range of issues. Because mashups use preexisting technology, they do not require a huge investment and can be developed in hours rather than days or weeks.

Data mashups are becoming an increasingly important tool for businesses of all sizes by allowing users to gain new insights and spot trends within data. While combining disparate data sources is common for a data mashup, even if there is only a single data source, a mashup can be made by combining data in a way that is not anticipated. End users and analysts who rely on dashboards and drill-down capabilities benefit from greater access to data, but the mashups remain behind the scene and invisible. Interactive dashboards and drillable reports can be rapidly built based on mashed-up data. **Tech Note 11.2** discusses dashboard software. Heat maps and tree maps can be created as data visualizations in mashups.

Tech Note 11.2

Adaptive Discovery Dashboard Software

Software vendor Adaptive Insights offers *Adaptive Discovery,* next-generation finance, and operations software built for the cloud. The software is widely used by businesses, nonprofits, government, and universities. Several users are Boston Scientific, Goodwill, Arizona Cardinals, Coca-Cola, Blue Cross/Blue Shield, AAA, Mayo Clinic, and DHL.

The Adaptive Suite consists of Budgeting and Forecasting that can increase financial planning and analysis productivity by more than 705: faster Financial Reporting that allows management to slice and dice financial data and drill down into details with self-service reporting on the Web or using Microsoft Office, and dashboards and analysis tools that track business metrics and KPIs faster and tell a story with the data.

Hortonworks, an open-source data company, uses Adaptive Planning to track new hires and prospects. Dan Bradford, Hortonworks' VP of Finance, noted that when using it "The ability to change a headcount assumption and have it globally run through our entire business model to see the impact on payroll taxes or personnel allocations is instantaneous."

Hortonworks built its business on innovation, so it sought a financial management solution that shared the same mindset. That's why it turned to Adaptive Planning. With the click of a button, a user could drill down into KPIs and forecast the impact of employee growth. The visibility elevated financial management beyond just tracking labor and managing expenses. This newly gained proficiency with data visualization gave Hortonworks a competitive edge in a landscape of continuous innovation in the open-source data market.

For organizations, mashup apps decrease IT implementation costs over traditional, custom software development (discussed in Chapter 12) and significantly simplify business workflows—both increase the ROI (return on investment) of mashup implementations.

Point-and-click dashboard building is a common feature in data mashups. These mashup technologies provide visually rich and secure enterprise apps created from live data. They provide the flexibility to combine data from any enterprise app and the cloud regardless of its location. Users can build apps and dashboards that can be displayed on the Web and mobile devices.

Mashup Architecture

Technically, a data mashup is a technique for building applications that combine data from multiple sources to create an integrated experience. As techniques for creating mashups became easier, companies started using them to build enterprise mashups that supported their business models. Tech-savvy managers realize that they can use mashup apps with their existing data and external services to provide new and interesting views on the data.

Figure 11.9 shows the general architecture of an enterprise mashup app. Data from operational data stores, business systems, external data (economic data, suppliers; information, competitors' activities), and real-time news feeds are integrated to generate an enterprise mashup.

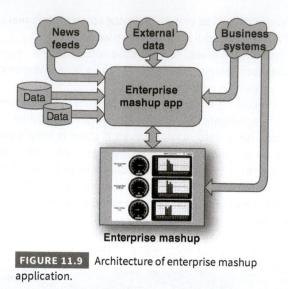

FIGURE 11.9 Architecture of enterprise mashup application.

Why Do Business Users Need Data Mashup Technology?

Business users have a hard enough time identifying their current data needs. It is not realistic to expect them also to consider all the new sources of data that might be made available to them and the analyses they might do if they had access to that data. With traditional BI and data warehousing systems, data sources have to be identified, and some understanding of data requirements and data models is needed.

Realizing that there will always be data needs that cannot be anticipated, the question is whether IT should be in the middle of supporting those requests? Providing business users with self-service enables them to meet their needs more quickly. They also have the opportunity to explore and experiment.

Enterprise mashups improve operational efficiency, optimize the sales pipeline, enhance customer satisfaction, and drive profitability. Within government, mashups have positively impacted strategic areas such as citizen engagement and satisfaction, financial transparency, project oversight, regulatory compliance, and legislated reporting. A summary of enterprise mashup benefits is given in **Table 11.2**.

TABLE 11.2 **Enterprise Mashup Benefits**

- Dramatically reduces time and effort needed to combine disparate data sources.
- Users can define their own data mashups by combining fields from different data sources that were not previously modeled.
- Users can import external data sources, e.g., spreadsheets and competitor data, to create new dashboards.
- Enables the building of complex queries by nonexperts with a drag-and-drop query building tool.
- Enables *agile BI* because new data sources can be added to a BI system quickly via direct links to operational data sources, bypassing the need to load them to a data warehouse.
- Provides a mechanism to easily customize and share knowledge throughout the company.

Enterprise Mashup Technology

Mashup technology leverages investments in both BI tools and interactive technologies. BI systems are very good at filtering and aggregating huge data volumes into information. With mashup technology, for example, users can filter down the data based on their needs so that only the information needed is provided by the available data services. **Tech Note 11.3** describes mashup self-service.

Tech Note 11.3

Mashup Self-Service

Many BI systems are designed by the IT department and based on inflexible data sources. The result is a bottleneck of end-user change requests as business needs and data sources change. The solution is self-service mashup capabilities.

Using data mashup apps, nontechnical users can easily and quickly access, integrate, and display BI data from a variety of operational data sources, including those that are not integrated into the existing data warehouse, without having to understand the intricacies of the underlying data infrastructures or schemas.

In an enterprise environment, mashups can be used to solve a wide variety of business problems and day-to-day situations. Examples of these types of mashups are as follows:

1. **Customer** A customer data mashup that provides a quick view of customer data for a salesperson in preparation for a customer site visit. Data can be pulled from internal data stores and Web sources, such as contact information, links to related websites, recent customer orders, lists of critical situations, and more.

2. **Logistics** A logistics mashup that displays inventory for a group of department stores based on specific criteria. For example, you can mash current storm information onto a map of store locations and then wire the map to inventory data to show which stores located in the path of storms are low on generators.

3. **Human resource** An HR mashup that provides a quick glance at employee data such as profiles, salary, ratings, benefits status, and activities. Data can be filtered to show custom views, for example, products whose average quarterly sales are lower than last quarter.

Questions

1. Sketch or describe the architecture of an enterprise mashup application.
2. What is an enterprise data mashup?
3. What are the functions and uses of enterprise mashups?
4. Explain why business workers may need data mashup technology.
5. What are the three benefits of mashup technology to the organization?

11.3 Digital Dashboards

A **digital dashboard** provides in-depth business analysis while providing a real-time snapshot of productivity. The digital dashboard emerged in the 1970s from the different report formats produced by decision support systems. As more and more companies moved to the Web some 20 years later, digital dashboard systems were developed to combine data reporting and facilitate smooth business operations and decisions. When done well, a digital dashboard is a tool that helps an organization efficiently develop analytical goals and strategies.

Digital dashboards pull data from disparate data sources and feeds to report KPIs and operational or strategic information on intuitive dashboards and interactive displays (**Figure 11.10**).

Table 11.3 lists typical metrics displayed on dashboards by function. An executive dashboard displays a company's performance metrics, which are automatically updated in real time (every 15 minutes) based on custom programming and connectivity with existing business systems. Dashboards improve the information synthesis process by bringing in multiple, disparate data feeds and sources, extracting features of interest, and manipulating the data, so the information is in a more accessible format. Users no longer need to log into multiple applications to see how the business is performing.

Digital dashboard is an electronic interface used to acquire and consolidate data across an organization.

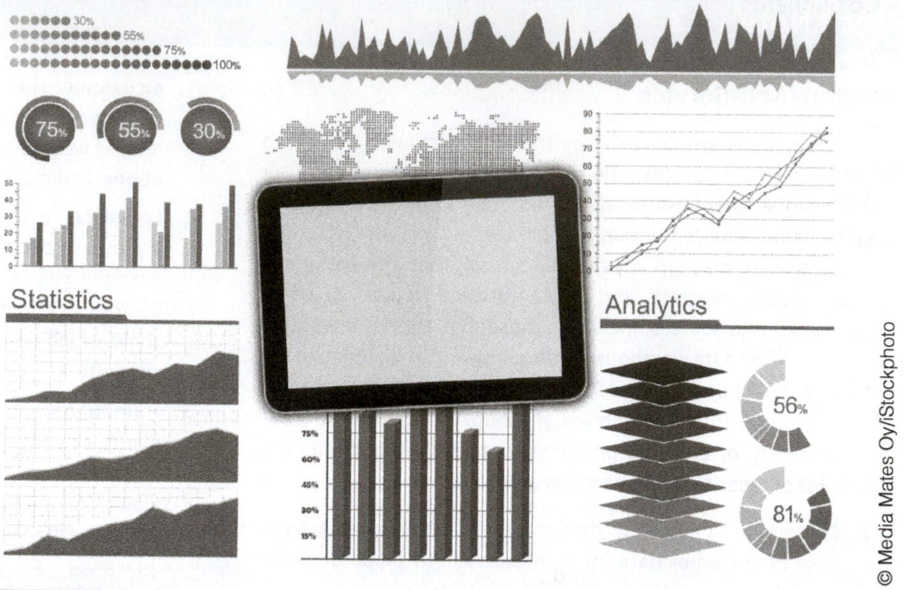

© Media Mates Oy/iStockphoto

FIGURE 11.10 Dashboards pull data from disparate data sources and feeds, manipulate the data, and display the metrics.

TABLE 11.3 Metrics Displayed on Dashboards by Function

Dashboard Type	Metrics
Financial performance	• Net income • Cash balance, actual vs. expected • Profit, current month projection • Changes in A/R and A/P
E-commerce	• Daily website visitors by traffic source • Trend of mobile vs. tablet traffic • Location where visitors are located • Top referring websites • Top keywords referring traffic • Revenue per website visitor
Revenue	• Sales per day per channel • How revenue is trending • Days with the strongest sales, weakest sales • Products selling the best, worst
Sales team	• Sales by lead source; which leads are most and least effective • Number of leads and proposals per salesperson • Proposal close percentage • Salesperson closing percentages • Where in the conversion funnel customers are being lost. Conversion funnels are paths that prospective customers take before they become paying clients
Advertising	• Number of leads generated by advertising; which advertising is most and least effective • Cost per lead, by advertising source • Advertising expense, as a percent of sales • Which advertising sources directly lead to sales
Order fulfillment	• Number of products manufactured, reworked • On-time completion percent • Changes in inventory levels • Percent of on-time delivery per week, month

Components of dashboards are as follows:

- **Design** The visualization techniques and descriptive captions to convey information so that they are correctly understood. Infographics are widely used because they convey information in interesting and informative designs.
- **Performance metrics** KPIs and other real-time content displayed on the dashboard. All dashboard data should reflect the current value of each metric.
- **API** APIs connect disparate data sources and feeds to display on the dashboard. The alternative is for users or IT to manually enter data to the dashboard. Dashboards created in this manner tend to fail because of the risk of incomplete, outdated, or wrong data, which users learn not to trust.
- **Access** Preferred access is via a secure Web browser from a mobile device.

Dashboards are Real Time

Dashboards are often mistakenly thought of as reports consisting of various gauges, charts, and dials, but the purpose of business dashboards is much more specific and directed. The purpose of dashboards is to give users a clear view of the *current* state of KPIs, real-time alerts, and other metrics about operations. Dashboard design is a critical factor because business users need to be able to understand the significance of the dashboard information at a glance and have the capability to drill down to one or more levels of detail. Having real time, or near real time, data is essential to keep users aware of any meaningful changes in the metrics as they occur and to provide information for making decisions in real time. Users can take corrective actions promptly.

It's easy to see in **Figure 11.11** how color-coded displays can quickly inform the user of the status of KPIs.

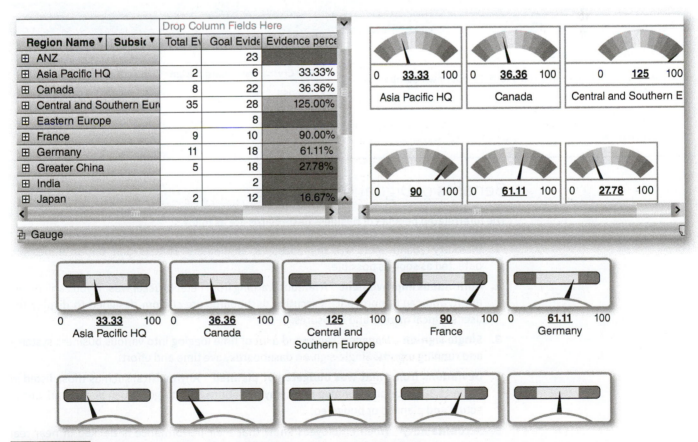

FIGURE 11.11 Dashboards are designed to meet the information needs of their users.

How Operational and Strategic Dashboards Work

Dashboards are custom programmed to automatically and securely pull, analyze, and display data from enterprise systems, cloud apps, data feeds, and external sources. They work by connecting to business systems, such as accounting software, ERP, CRM, SCM, e-mail systems, website analytics programs, and project management software via APIs. **IT at Work 11.2** describes dashboards in action at Hartford Hospital. **Tech Note 11.4** lists vendors that offer free trials of dashboard software.

IT at Work 11.2

VA Employs Digital Data Dashboards

In December, 2016, the Department of Veterans Affairs (VA) launched a new website to raise awareness of the Agency's Digital Health Platform (DHP)—a cloud-based approach to integrating veterans' health data to produce real-time, analytics-driven personalized care.

The VA has been historically inefficient at managing the health information and care of veterans. The new website (**http://www.oit.va.gov/specialreports/dhp/index.html**) explains the purpose of the DHP, provides a detailed overview of how the DHP works and provides "user stories" of veterans who have benefits from the comprehensive digital dashboard that enables customized care. The DHP is used to gain recommendations for care and analysis on potential or existing health issues. Instead of providers having to respond to health issues as they arise, the DHP makes preventive care a priority and easy to implement.

A fact sheet published by the VA says "DHP leverages a network of application programming interfaces (APIs) to integrate military and commercial health data, while unifying VA's data stores, connecting patient to provider in real-time, and predicting the most successful care to provide a better experience to the veteran" (U.S. Department of Veterans Affairs, 2016).

IT at Work Questions

1. What benefits do veterans get as a result of the digital dashboard approach to health care?

2. Why would the VA implement a digital dashboard instead of staying with their traditional approach to processing electronic health records?

Sources: Compiled from Verton (2016), Slabodkin (2016), and U.S. Department of Veterans Affairs (2016).

Tech Note 11.4

Free Trial Dashboards

A few vendors that offer free trials to build your own dashboards are as follows:

- Dundas
- GrowThink
- MicroStrategy
- SAP Crystal Dashboard Design
- Sisense

Benefits of Digital Dashboards

The interrelated benefits of business dashboards are as follows:

1. **Visibility**   Blind spots are minimized or eliminated. Threats and opportunities are detected as soon as possible.

2. **Continuous improvement**   A famous warning from Peter Drucker was "if you can't measure it, you can't improve it." Executive dashboards are custom designed to display the user's critical metrics and measures.

3. **Single sign-on**   Managers can spend a lot of time logging into various business systems and running reports. Single-sign-on dashboards save time and effort.

4. **Deviations from what was budgeted or planned**   Any metrics, such as those listed in Table 11.3, can be programmed to display deviations from targets, such as comparisons of actual and planned or budgeted.

5. **Accountability**   When employees know that their performance is tracked in near real time and can see their results, they tend to be motivated to improve their performance.

Questions

1. Describe business dashboards and their functions.
2. Why do you think dashboards must be in real time and customized for the executive or manager?
3. How do business dashboards differ from other types of visual reports?
4. Explain the components of dashboards.
5. What are benefits of dashboards?

11.4 Geographic Information Systems and Geospatial Data

Every day millions of decisions are made using **geographic information systems** (GISs). A GIS connects data with geography to understand *what* belongs *where*. For example, it's really difficult to visualize the locations of towns by their latitude and longitude coordinates listed in a spreadsheet, but it's easy to know where they are when you show these positions on a map (**Figure 11.12**).

Geographic information system (GIS)   is a computer-based tool that captures, stores, manipulates, analyzes, and visualizes geographic data on a map.

name	latitude	longitude
Seattle	47.5700	−122.3400
New York	40.7500	−73.9800
Miami	25.7876	−80.2241
Los Angeles	33.9900	−118.1800
Dallas	32.8200	−96.8400
Washington DC	38.9072	−77.0365

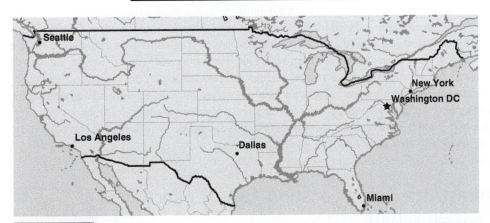

FIGURE 11.12   Longitude and Latitude Coordinates on a spreadsheet are much more difficult to visualize than when they are displayed on a map.

GIS is not just about mapping data, government, businesses, and individuals find GIS useful in solving everyday problems using **geospatial data**. For example, GIS can connect to location-tracking devices and apps. GIS software can link **geospatial data**—*where things or people are and where they are going*—with descriptive data—*what things are like or what customers are doing*. GIS's ability to track customers' movement and behavior in real space enables new strategies for marketing, retail, and entrepreneurship. Their ability to track products along the supply chain also offers opportunities in logistics and order fulfillment.

Collecting home and work addresses only paints a static picture of consumer locations. Their movements over time are not tracked. Data that are organized by zip code only cannot reveal customers' habits. By integrating GISs, businesses can more effectively solve problems such as organizing sales territories, pinpointing optimal locations, finding customers, managing campaigns, and delivering services. Geospatial data can also map competitors' actions.

Geocoding

In many cases, locations are already in existing data stores, but not in a format suitable for analytics. A simple process called **geocoding** can convert postal addresses to geospatial data that can then be measured and analyzed. By tapping into this resource, decision-makers can use the geographic or spatial context to detect and respond to opportunities.

Case in Point: GM General Motors (GM) spends a staggering $2 billion a year on marketing. In the past, it shotgunned its ads at the general public. Now, it maps out which types of households will buy new cars, more accurately determines locations where people buy certain models, and channels its ads specifically to those areas. As a result, GM spends less money to generate higher sales.

GM managers use ESRI's ArcGIS software to view local demographics, location characteristics, regional differences, and the competitive brand environment to determine how a given dealership should be performing compared to actual results. The GIS makes it possible for GM to isolate demand, target its marketing efforts to local preferences, and position its dealerships to improve sales. With the intelligence provided by the GIS, GM has increased sales despite cutting the advertising budget.

GIS Is Not Your Grandfather's Map

Unlike a traditional flat map, a GIS-generated map is made up of many layers of information that provides users different ways to view a geographic space (**Figure 11.13**).

Imagine for a moment that you are a regional sales manager who needs to view sales data for one of your 75 stores distributed throughout the State of South Carolina. On a flat map of South Carolina, if you looked at retail store #50, you would see the name of the store and a dot showing where it is located on the map. However, if you view a GIS map of the United States on your computer, smartphone, or tablet, you can hover over South Carolina and when you click on retail store #50, up pops the store's location, store manager's name and phone number, weekly and monthly revenue, product categories, a photo of the storefront, and a virtual tour. As a highly paid, busy regional sales manager, this saves you time and your company money, increasing organizational effectiveness and efficiency.

Infrastructure and Location-Aware Collection of Geospatial Data

The infrastructure needed to collect geospatial data continues to expand. Cellular and Internet service providers, sensors, Google Earth, GPS, and RFID systems know the location of each connected user or object. Foursquare, Google Maps, and other mobile apps rely on GPS locations. With the Shopkick app, Macy's can track a shopper's every move within one of its stores and send the shopper notifications about deals and items of interest. iBeacon is a feature available in iOS 7 devices that uses a low-power Bluetooth transmission to broadcast a user's location. iBeacon allows Apple, or app developers leveraging Apple technology, to track users inside buildings where satellite transmissions may not reach.

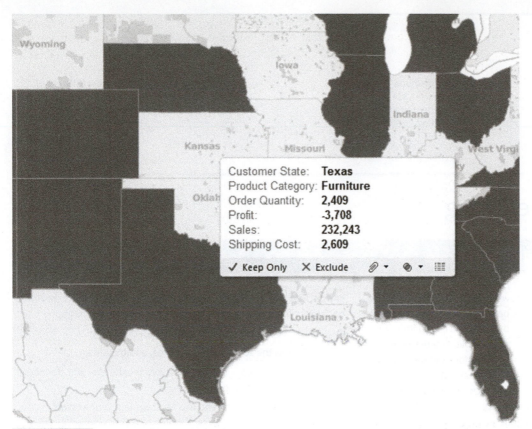

Customer State: **Texas**
Product Category: **Furniture**
Order Quantity: **2,409**
Profit: **-3,708**
Sales: **232,243**
Shipping Cost: **2,609**

✓ Keep Only   ✕ Exclude

FIGURE 11.13 An example of a GIS-generated map. By hovering over a state, such as Texas, another layer of sales and financial data appears.

Similarly to Macy's, businesses can motivate customers to download a location-tracking app. Using GIS can help businesses target their customer markets more effectively and dynamically by engaging with them in real time.

Applying GIS in Business

GIS tools have made significant contributions to decision making in finance, accounting, marketing, and BI. Business applications include the following:

- Analysts can pinpoint the average income in areas where the highest performing stores are established.
- Retailers can learn how store sales are impacted by population or the proximity to competitors' stores.
- A retail chain with plans to open a hundred new stores can use GIS to identify relevant demographics, proximity to highways, public transportation, and competitors' stores to select the best location options.
- Food and consumer products companies can chart locations of complaint calls, enabling product traceability in the event of a crisis or recall.
- Sales reps might better target their customer visits by analyzing the geography of sales targets.

With current GIS, geospatial, and geocoding technologies and platforms, GISs can be easily incorporated and managed within data analytics and visualization software.

With the GIS moving into the cloud, developers of enterprise applications based on SAP, Microsoft Office, SharePoint, MicroStrategy, IBM Cognos, and Microsoft Dynamics CRM are using it to create a wide range of mobile applications.

Key Terms

aggregation 340	digital dashboard 345	geographic information system (GIS) 349
analytical tools 335	drill down 334	geospatial data 332
data discovery 336	enterprise data mashup 342	reporting tools 335
data visualization 334	geocoding 350	

Assuring Your Learning

Discuss: Critical Thinking Questions

1. How people use, access, and discover data in business is being actively disrupted by tablets, which had been designed for consumers. Users have higher expectations for data displays and capabilities. Boring, static graphs and pie charts are unacceptable. Discuss how performance management—the monitoring of KPIs, for example—may be improved by providing managers with data visualizations. Now consider the opposite. In your opinion, would lack of data visualization hurt the ability to manage performance?

2. Lots of data are available to retailers to make good decisions—loyalty programs, Web analytics, and POS data. However, there is a big gap between having data and being able to leverage them for real-time decision-making. How can enterprise mashups close this gap?

3. Visit SAS.com and search for Visual Data Discovery.

   a. Review the screenshots, features, and benefits.

   b. In your opinion, what are the two most important benefits of this data discovery tool?

   c. Would you recommend this tool? Explain your answer.

4. Explain how executive dashboards can lead to better business insights. What are the limitations of dashboards?

Explore: Online and Interactive Exercises

1. **Periscopic** is a socially conscious data visualization firm that specializes in using IT to help companies and organizations facilitate information transparency and public awareness. From endangered species, to politics, to social justice, it is the goal of Periscopic to engage the public and deliver a message of responsibility and action. Its philosophy and tagline are "do good with data."

   a. Visit **http://periscopic.com** and explore its recent work.

   b. Discuss how data are used to do good.

   c. How effective is Periscopic's approach to public awareness and social justice?

2. Visit **TIBCO Spotfire** and click "Demos" and "Demo Gallery."

   a. Select and watch one of the demos.

   b. Describe the data visualizations features in the demo.

   c. Explain the benefits of the application or analytics.

3. Visit the **Analysis Factory**

   a. Click Gallery and then select Custom Solutions.

   b. View one demo, such as Performance Trends, Fusion Charts, Manufacturing Performance, and Sales Map Dashboard.

   c. Create a table listing all of the customer solutions for which you tried the demo in the first column. In the second column, list the departments or functions each customer solution supports. In the third column, list the types of visualizations used in each solution.

   d. In the team report, discuss how dashboards can impact the quality of business decisions.

Analyze & Decide: Apply IT Concepts to Business Decisions

1. Qlik offers a complimentary e-book entitled "Turn your Excel Reports into Stunning Dashboards." Download the e-book. Write a report about what you learned.

2. Visit **IBM's Watson Analytics Event Center** any Thursday at 3 pm ET to take a Tour of Watson Analytics. Write a report on what you learned.

3. Visit the website of software provider **Microstrategy**

   a. Click "Explore the Product."

   b. Click "Browse Solutions."

   c. Scroll down to choose an industry that interests you. Click on that Industry and "Learn More."

   d. Click "Watch the Video."

   e. Write a report describing what you learned.

Case 11.2

Visualization Case: Are You Ready for Football?

Nothing inspires passionate comments among sports fans like pre-season predictions. Brett McMurphy's data visualization looks at how teams ranked in different polls. Visit **www.tableausoftware.com** and search using "ready for football." You will see the Preseason Polls & Returning Starters visualization. (a) Interact with the Preseason Polls & Returning Starters visualization. (b) Select various filters and observe the changes. (c) Download the workbook by clicking the Download button at the lower right corner of the display. View and interact with two other sports-related visualizations, for example, CBS Sports Defensive Matchup Tracker, Fantasy Closers, and Premier League Points Leaders. Download each. Click the Business and Real Estate Gallery. View and interact with two data visualizations in the gallery. Download each.

Questions

1. Which visualization was the easiest to understand at a glance? Explain.

2. Which visualization was the most difficult or complicated to understand easily? Explain.

3. What are the benefi ts and potential drawbacks of interactive visualizations?

Case 11.3

Video Case: The Beauty of Data Visualization—Data Detective

TED stands for technology, entertainment, and design. Visit TED.com and search "data visualization." Select "Making Sense of Too Much Data" and find "David McCandless: The beauty of data visualization." The video and transcript are available. In his TED talk, The Beauty of Data Visualization, David McCandless says that data visualization gives us a second language—the language of the eye.

Questions

1. Explain what McCandless means by language of the eye.

2. What are the examples of language of the mind?

3. What happens when language of the eye and language of the mind combine?

4. What did David McCandless say about information design?

IT Toolbox

Create Your Own Digital Dashboard

Visit software provider **Sisense**. Sign in, start your free trial, and build your first dashboard in minutes.

References

Curtis, K. "Deloitte Hosts PepsiCo and Safeway at the HIVE (Highly Immersive Visual Environment)." *GMAOnline.Org*. 2013. gmaonline.org

Deloitte CIO Journal. "Data Visualization Helps Safeway Keep Shelves Stocked." *The Wall Street Journal*. December 3, 2013.

Deloitte. "Deloitte Analytics Labs." 2016. Retrieved December 22, 2016 from https://www2.deloitte.com/us/en/pages/deloitte-analytics/solutions/deloitte-analytics-labs.html.

Forrest, C. "IBM launches Watson Discovery Service for big data analytics at scale." *TechRepublic*, December 16, 2016.

Lohr, S. "For Big-Data Scientists, 'Janitor Work' Is Key Hurdle to Insights." *New York Times*, August 17, 2014.

Pathak, S. "How PepsiCo sweetens up consumer insights." *Digiday*, June 8, 2015.

pepsi.com. 2017.

safeway.com/ShopStores/Our-Story.page. 2017.

Slabodkin, G. "VA lays out plans for cloud-based Digital Health Platform." *HealthData Management*, December 16, 2016.

U.S. Department of Veterans Affairs. "Digital Health Platform." 2016. Retrieved December 27, 2016 from http://www.oit.va.gov/library/dhp/DHP_factsheet.pdf.

Verton, D. "VA Launches New Site for Digital Health Platform." *MeriTalk*, December 8, 2016.

CHAPTER 12

IT Strategy, Sourcing, and Strategic Technology Trends

CHAPTER OUTLINE

LEARNING OBJECTIVES

Case 12.1 Opening Case: Intel Reaps Rewards from Its Sustainable IT Strategy

12.1 IT Strategic Planning

12.1 Understand IT strategic planning and its link to competitive advantage.

12.2 Aligning IT with Business Objectives for Competitive Advantage

12.2 Explain the value of aligning the IT strategy with the business strategy.

12.3 IT Sourcing Strategies

12.3 Describe the balanced scorecard methodology and how it functions as a road map for strategic planning.

12.4 Balanced Scorecard

12.4 Explain how organizations identify strategic technology trends to help achieve their strategic vision and list the five steps to technology scanning.

12.5 Strategic Technology Trends

Case 12.2 Business Case: Cisco IT Improves Strategic Vendor Management

Case 12.3 Data Analysis: Third-Party versus Company-Owned Offshoring

Introduction

IT strategy is a plan of action to create an organization's IT capabilities for maximum and sustainable value in the organization.

As you have learned throughout this book, organizational performance depends on the quality and responsiveness of its IT infrastructure and information systems. **IT strategy** shapes the direction of IT investments over the next one to five years to maximize business value and shareholder wealth. As all strategies, IT strategy defines priorities, a road map, budget, and investment plan—and must align with and support the **business strategy**. Deciding on a strategy entails making decisions about a future that can only be imagined. According to Roger L. Martin's article in *Harvard Business Review*: "True strategy is about placing bets and making hard choices. The objective is not to eliminate risk but to increase the odds of success" (Martin, 2014). Strategy making is uncomfortable because it is about taking risks and facing the unknown. Economic and technical experts agree that the extent to which an organization can achieve **business–IT alignment** (BITA) heavily influences its chances of success and sustainability.

Creating an IT strategy takes into consideration the acquisition, implementation, maintenance, and disposal of all IT assets needed to meet current and future organizational objectives along with methods to monitor, measure, and control how well the IT plan is working. An IT strategic plan also includes an operating plan for acquiring or providing new technology and services. The **operating plan** defines how to execute the IT strategic plan: for example, deciding on **in-house development** or **sourcing** options such as managed services, cloud computing, or software as a service (SaaS). Strategies are measured and evaluated continuously and revised annually during the strategic planning process. Some of these measures are quantifiable, and others are not. A tool that is used to evaluate both financial and nonfinancial metrics of an IT strategy is the balanced scorecard (BSC). The BSC provides a much more comprehensive assessment of a company's performance than solely relying on numbers on a profit/loss statement.

Another important component of the IT strategy is the acquisition of newly emerging strategic technologies. Strategic technologies can change the way that a business operates and are important differentiators in determining future directions of a company in the digital economy.

In this chapter, we will discuss the components of an IT strategy, the benefits an IT strategy offers, how a BSC helps evaluate the effectiveness of an IT strategy. You will also learn the advantages of discovering and implementing strategic technologies to ensure sustainability. But first, let's take a look at a best-practice IT Strategic Planning Process that Intel developed.

Business strategy sets the overall direction of a company, defines how a business will achieve its mission, goals, and objectives, and specifies the necessary financial requirements, budgets, and resources.

Business–IT alignment refers to applying IT in an appropriate and timely way that is consistent with business strategies, goals, and needs.

Case 12.1 Opening Case

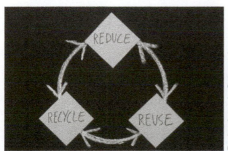

Pedro Antonio Salaverria Calahorra/Alamy Stock Photo

Justin Sullivan/Getty Images News/Getty Images

makromedya/Getty Images

Intel Reaps Rewards from Sustainable IT Strategy

Company Overview

Intel is the largest manufacturer of PC microprocessors and the holder of the x86 processor architecture patent—the microprocessors used in more than 80% of personal computers worldwide. Based in Santa Clara, CA, Intel supplies processors to Apple, Lenovo, HP, and Dell. Intel also manufactures communication and computing devices such as motherboard chipsets, network interface controllers, integrate controllers, flash memory, graphics chips, and embedded processors. Over 90% of all new services at Intel are deployed to the cloud.

Intel operates in 46 countries. Intel has almost 100,000 employees at over 300 sites worldwide, including 12 manufacturing and 6 assembly/test sites.

Intel's Journey to Sustainable IT

Intel has a track record of taking a proactive approach to issues related to sustainability both economically and environmentally. Reducing–reusing–recycling is an important part of Intel's business strategy and long-term goal. From an economic standpoint, Intel has mitigated risks, saved costs, protected brand recognition, and developed new products and market opportunities. From an environmental perspective, Intel has addressed climate issues, diversity in the workforce, employee safety, set up an ethical work environment, conducted supply chain audits, and established and supported community service volunteer programs.

Sustainable IT is one of the main drivers of Intel's sustainability program. Chief information officer (CIO) Diane Bryant seized the opportunity for IT to play a key role in enabling Intel to achieve its corporate sustainability goals when the chief executive officer (CEO) Paul Otellini's announced his ambitious goal to reduce environmental impacts in key areas including energy efficiency, water conservation, and a 20% emissions reduction, Bryant committed IT to help the business deliver their objectives through the use of Sustainable IT to reduce environmental impacts of IT operations and help transform the overall Intel organization by the following:

- Aligning all IT processes and practices with the core reduce, reuse, and recycle principles of sustainability
- Identifying innovative ways to use IT in business processes to delivery sustainability benefits across the enterprise

To better manage sustainability initiatives and effect change within IT and across Intel, Bryant established the IT Sustainability Program Office (SPO). The task of the SPO was to develop a sustainability strategy to educate and provide leadership to the organization on the principles and importance of sustainable business practices. First, necessary metrics, strategies, and processes were defined and implemented internally. To do this, they focused on the

core metric of carbon footprint (CO_2) reduction, as well as reducing water, energy, and other resource consumption, and adopted internal IT goals to manage Intel's IT energy footprint and contribute to energy reduction.

Moving forward, the SPO's key challenge was to embed a sustainability focus in decision-making activities and best practices throughout Intel's daily business activities and transform sustainability from a program to a mind-set. The process that Intel has used to achieve its Sustainable IT strategy is explained next.

Intel's Six-Step IT Strategic Planning Process

Intel used a six-step IT Strategic Planning process that closely aligns IT investments and solutions to strategic planning at the corporate level. This **business–IT alignment** was achieved by bringing together a variety of perspectives from senior management, IT, and business groups in the planning stage as shown in steps 1 through 4 in **Figure 12.1**. To minimize time demands, the strategic planning team engaged subject matter experts at critical points instead of involving them at every step of the process.

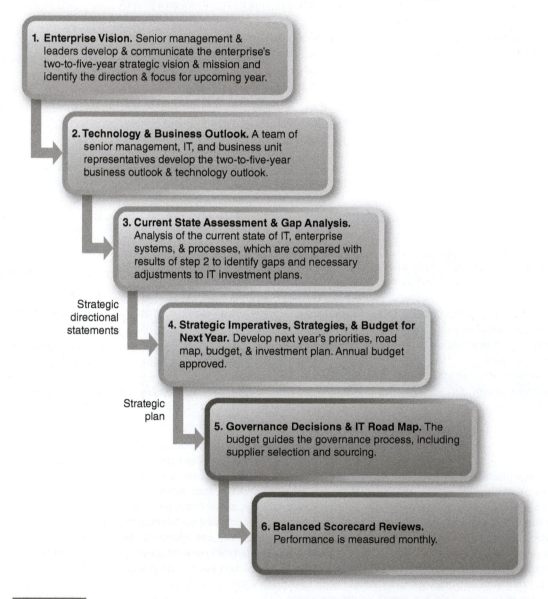

1. **Enterprise Vision.** Senior management & leaders develop & communicate the enterprise's two-to-five-year strategic vision & mission and identify the direction & focus for upcoming year.

2. **Technology & Business Outlook.** A team of senior management, IT, and business unit representatives develop the two-to-five-year business outlook & technology outlook.

3. **Current State Assessment & Gap Analysis.** Analysis of the current state of IT, enterprise systems, & processes, which are compared with results of step 2 to identify gaps and necessary adjustments to IT investment plans.

Strategic directional statements

4. **Strategic Imperatives, Strategies, & Budget for Next Year.** Develop next year's priorities, road map, budget, & investment plan. Annual budget approved.

Strategic plan

5. **Governance Decisions & IT Road Map.** The budget guides the governance process, including supplier selection and sourcing.

6. **Balanced Scorecard Reviews.** Performance is measured monthly.

FIGURE 12.1 Model of Intel's six-step IT strategic planning process. Planning phase: steps 1 to 4. Decision-making phase: step 5. Measuring and evaluation phase: step 6.

The activities in the planning, decision making, measuring, and evaluation phases flow naturally from one step to the next. The business and IT strategic plans are evaluated and adjusted annually to keep pace with rapid changes in the industry. Characteristics of Intel's strategic planning process are summarized in **Table 12.1**.

TABLE 12.1	Characteristics of Intel's Corporate and IT Strategic Planning Process
Integrated	Intel IT activities are synchronized with the company's strategic direction. By tightly linking Intel IT to the corporate planning process, the IT function has strengthened its credibility throughout Intel and earned the position of a trusted partner.
Holistic	The strategic planning process aligns IT investments with Intel's business direction and consolidates expertise and ideas from across Intel IT.
Sustainable	As new strategies are implemented, a common practice is to "look up" every 2 or 3 years and ask, "What's next?" Instead of replacing the plan every 2 to 3 years, Intel uses a different approach. To keep pace with changes in the environment, the team looks at the plan every year to determine if anything shifted in its environment. If a shift has occurred and affected its business, the IT plan is updated as needed.

Benefits of Intel's Sustainable IT Strategy

Intel has reaped many benefits from establishing a Sustainable IT Strategy both economically and environmentally. Examples of some of these benefits are presented in **Table 12.2**.

Since its inception, Intel has also earned a number of awards and recognitions for its Sustainable IT strategy including the InfoWorld Green 15 award and numerous recognitions for innovation. In January 2016, Corporate Knights (the magazine for Clean Capitalism) reported the results of the 2016 Global 100 Most Sustainable Corporations in the World index. Intel earned a spot in that prestigious list thanks to Bryant's Sustainable IT strategy that embedded sustainability within IT and the business.

Clearly, Intel's IT strategic planning approach has improved Intel's agility, performance, and sustainability. It has provided a clear and credible direction for the enterprise and supports consistent decision-making at all levels of the business.

Intel's experience demonstrates that an effective strategic planning process is critical to an enterprise's long-term success and health and support consistent decision-making at all levels of the business. Each

TABLE 12.2	Intel's Sustainable IT Strategy Benefits
IT Initiative	**Benefit**
Videoconferencing	Reduce carbon footprint by 22,000 tons of CO_2
	Save $25 million by reducing travel hours by 57,000 hours
Reduce number of data centers	Lower data center power consumption
Increase server utilization	Reduced servers by 25%—save energy and cost of equipment
Pin code on printers	Reduced paper waste—save resources and $$$
Electronic newsletter "Digital Edge"	Raise employee awareness of sustainability goals and progress being made
Power management program	Reduce PC energy consumption

enterprise has its own way of conducting the strategic planning process and approach that fits its own culture and leadership style. For those companies that haven't yet established a Strategic Planning Process, or aren't reaping the sought after rewards from an already established process, Intel's IT Strategic Planning Process provides an excellent model to follow.

Questions

1. What are the three phases in Intel's IT strategic planning process? Describe the steps in each phase.

2. Intel formulates a 2-to-5-year strategic plan. Given this time frame, why is the plan reviewed and evaluated every year?

3. Given the frequency of the planning process, what is done to minimize demands on people's time?

4. How is Intel's IT strategic plan measured and evaluated?

5. What makes the process sustainable?

6. How does the IT strategy support the short-term (1-year) business strategy?

7. In what ways does Intel's IT strategic planning process impact the company's commitment to sustainability?

Sources: Compiled from Curry and Donnellan (2014); Krishnapura et al. (2014); Corporate Knights (2016) and intel.com (2017).

12.1 | IT Strategic Planning

IT strategy focuses on the technology needs of a business. Setting an IT strategy and creating an IT strategic plan is an important part of managing IT. Industry, sector, and specific competitive environments along with prevalent technology trends all shape IT strategy. IT strategy directs investments in social, mobile, analytics, cloud, and other digital technology resources. To create an effective IT strategy, a CIO must have a clear understanding of the business strategy and the environment in which the business exists to create, maintain, and sustain a competitive advantage and business value for the organization.

Strategy addresses fundamental issues such as the company's position in its industry, its available resources and options, and future directions. A strategy addresses questions such as the following:

- What is the long-term direction of the business?
- What is the overall plan for deploying resources?
- What trade-offs are necessary? What resources will need to be shared?
- What is the company's position compared to that of its competitors?
- How does a company achieve competitive advantage over rivals in order to achieve or maximize profitability?

Strategic planning is a series of processes in which an organization selects and arranges its businesses or services to keep the organization healthy or able to function even when unexpected events disrupt one or more of its businesses, markets, products, or services.

It's important to remember that IT **strategic planning** is not just a one-time activity. It is an ongoing iterative process that focuses on the **value drivers** in core process areas in order to make targeted improvements.

Value Drivers

Value driver enhances the value of a product or service to consumers, creating value for the company. Advanced IT, reliability, and brand reputation are examples.

Long-term strategic planning starts with a clear understanding of the factors that create significant value and that work together with other factors to drive future revenue and profit at or above their current rates. These factors are **value drivers**.

In order to create business value, you must identify value drivers and link them to daily activities. For example, it is not enough to identify *cost* as a key value drive. Cost is almost always a value driver, but for this factor to be useful, you need to drill down to the activities that impact cost. The general types of business value drivers are explained in **Table 12.3**. Drivers can have a limited life span. Their value can diminish due to chances in the economy or industry, at which time they are replaced with relevant ones.

Value drivers are considered in the strategic planning process and the BSC methodology.

TABLE 12.3 Three General Types of Business Value Drivers

Type of Business Value Drivers	Definitions	Examples
Operational—Shorter-term factors	Factors that impact cash flow and the cash generation ability through increased efficiency or growth	Cost of raw materials, cost of providing service, cost per mile, sales volume, sales revenue
Financial—Medium-term factors	Factors that minimize the cost of capital incurred by the company to finance operations	Debt level, working capital, capital expenditures, day's receivables, bad debt expense
Sustainability—Long-term factors	Survival factors; factors that enable a business to continue functioning consistently and optimally for a long time	Government regulations, industry standards, federal and state environmental laws, privacy and security regulations

IT Strategic Plan Objectives

The four objectives of IT strategic plans are to:

1. Improve management's understanding of IT opportunities and limitations
2. Assess current performance
3. Identify capacity and human resource requirements
4. Clarify the level of investment required

Various functions in the organization—such as manufacturing, R&D (research and development), and IT—are the most successful when their strategies are forward looking. Forward looking means that they carry out strengths, weaknesses, opportunities, and threats (SWOT) analysis to create their future rather than react to challenges or crises. Additionally, IT implementations that require new infrastructure or the merging of disparate information systems can take years. Long lead times and lack of expertise have prompted companies to explore a variety of IT strategies.

IT and Business Disconnects

According to a survey of business leaders by PwC Advisory, 87% of business leaders believe that IT is critical to their companies' strategic success, but not all of them work with IT to achieve that success. Less than 50% of business leaders reported that the IT function was very involved in the strategic planning process. When the IT strategy was not aligned with the business strategies, there was a higher risk that the IT project would be abandoned before completion. About 75% of companies abandoned at least one IT project and 30% abandoned more than 10% of IT projects for this reason. There are several possible reasons why a high percentage of IT projects are abandoned—the business strategy changed, technology changed, the project was not going to be completed on time or budget, the project sponsors responsible did not work well together, or the IT strategy was changed to cloud or SaaS.

The fundamental principle to be learned is that when enterprise strategies change, the IT strategies need to change with them. Both strategies are dynamic—to adapt to opportunities and threats.

Corporate and IT Governance

Business and IT strategies depend on shared IT ownership and shared IT governance among all senior managers. When an IT or any type of failure causes harm to customers, business partners, employees, or the environment, then regulatory agencies will hold the CEO accountable—and the public will as well. A high-profile example is BP CEO Tony Hayward, who was held accountable to Congress for "The Role of BP in the Deepwater Horizon Explosion and Oil Spill," the rig explosion that killed 11 workers and caused the subsea oil gusher that released 60,000+ barrels per day into the Gulf of Mexico. Hayward's attempts to claim ignorance of the risks and use the SODDI ("some other dude did it") defense does not get him or any CEOs off the hook. *A company can outsource the work, but not the responsibility for it.*

Because of the interrelationship between IT and business strategies, IT and other business managers share responsibility in developing IT strategic plans. Therefore, a governance structure needs to be in place that crosses organizational lines and makes senior management responsible for the success of key IT initiatives.

Reactive Approach to IT Investments Will Fail

Few companies today could realize their full potential business value without updated IT infrastructures and services. Yet many companies still struggle to make the right IT decisions and investments in order to leverage relatively new IT trends—cloud computing and SaaS, big data, analytics, social, and mobile. Making IT investments on the basis of an immediate need or threat—rather than according to IT strategy—might be necessary at times, but reactive approaches result in incompatible, redundant, expensive to maintain, or failed systems. These IT investments tend to be patches that rarely align with the business strategy.

Two of the biggest risks and concerns of top management are (1) failing to align IT to real business needs and, as a result, (2) failing to deliver value to the business. Since IT has a dramatic effect on business performance and competitiveness, the failure to manage IT effectively seriously impacts the business.

IT Strategic Planning Process

IT strategic planning is a systematic process for determining what a business should become and how it can best achieve that goal, as you read in Opening Case 12.1. Typically, an organization will evaluate its full potential using SWOT analysis (**Tech Note 12.1**) and then will decide how to allocate resources to develop critical capabilities. In practice, competing agendas, tight budgets, poor interdepartmental communication, and politics can turn strategic planning discussions into bar room brawls—if they are not well managed.

Tech Note 12.1

SWOT Analysis

The SWOT analysis is a useful tool in developing and confirming the goals of the corporate and IT strategies.

The SWOT analysis begins with the evaluation of internal **strengths** and **weaknesses** in your organization, followed by an examination of the external **opportunities** and **threats** that may affect the organization based on the market and the overall environment of the organization. Examples of some of the strengths, weaknesses, opportunities, and threats commonly experienced by organization are shown in **Figure 12.2**.

SWOT analysis is the most useful when it is completed in the early stages of the strategic planning process. In the **IT Toolbox** at the end of this chapter, you will learn how to conduct a SWOT analysis of a business and of yourself.

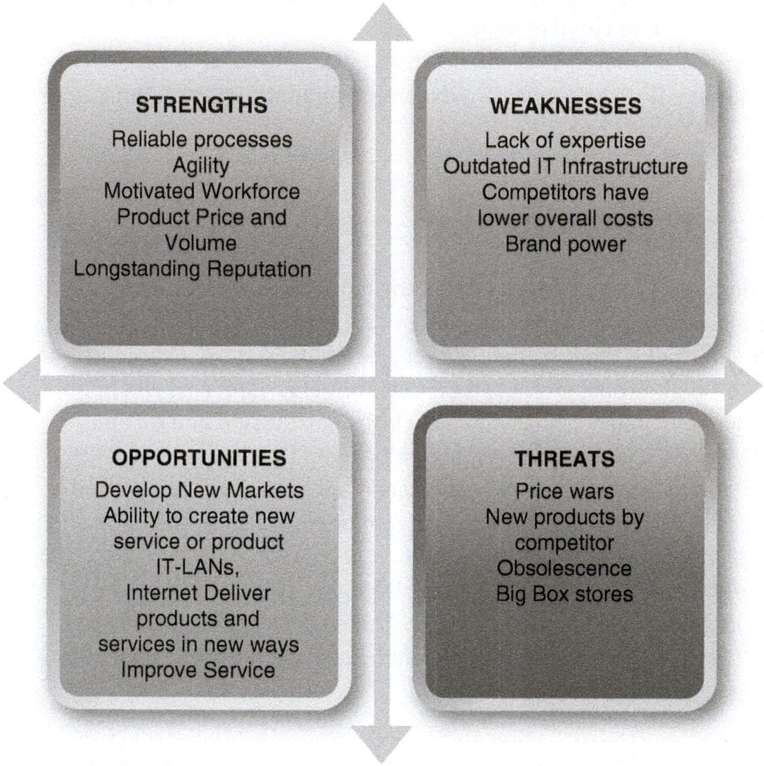

STRENGTHS
Reliable processes
Agility
Motivated Workforce
Product Price and
Volume
Longstanding Reputation

WEAKNESSES
Lack of expertise
Outdated IT Infrastructure
Competitors have
lower overall costs
Brand power

OPPORTUNITIES
Develop New Markets
Ability to create new
service or product
IT-LANs,
Internet Deliver
products and
services in new ways
Improve Service

THREATS
Price wars
New products by
competitor
Obsolescence
Big Box stores

FIGURE 12.2 SWOT analysis consists of a realistic evaluation of internal strengths and weaknesses and external opportunities and threats.

Generally speaking, during strategic analysis, an organization scans and reviews the political, social, economic, and technical environments of an organization. For example, any company looking to expand its business operations into a developing country has to investigate that country's political and economic stability and critical infrastructure. In this case, strategic analysis would include reviewing the U.S. Central Intelligence Agency's (CIA) *World Factbook*.

The *World Factbook* provides information on the history, people, government, economy, geography, communications, transportation, military, and transnational issues for 266 world entities. Then the company would need to investigate competitors and their potential reactions to a new entrant into their market.

Equally important, the company would need to assess its ability to compete profitably in the market and impacts of the expansion on other parts of the company. For example, having excess production capacity would require less capital than if a new factory needed to be built.

CIOs undertake IT strategic planning on a yearly, quarterly, or monthly basis. A good IT planning process helps ensure that IT aligns, and stays aligned, within an organization's business strategy. Because organizational goals change over time, it is not sufficient to develop a long-term IT strategy and not re-examine the strategy on a regular basis. For this reason, IT planning is an ongoing process. The IT planning process results in a formal IT strategy or a reassessment each year or each quarter of the existing portfolio of IT resources.

Recall that the focus of an IT strategy is on how IT creates business value. Typically, annual planning cycles are established to identify potentially beneficial IT services, to perform cost–benefit analyses, and to subject the list of potential projects to resource allocation. **Figure 12.3** illustrates the IT strategic planning process.

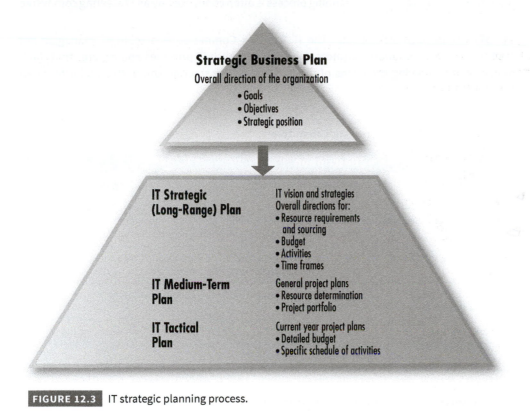

Strategic Business Plan
Overall direction of the organization
- Goals
- Objectives
- Strategic position

IT Strategic (Long-Range) Plan
IT vision and strategies
Overall directions for:
- Resource requirements and sourcing
- Budget
- Activities
- Time frames

IT Medium-Term Plan
General project plans
- Resource determination
- Project portfolio

IT Tactical Plan
Current year project plans
- Detailed budget
- Specific schedule of activities

FIGURE 12.3   IT strategic planning process.

The planning process begins with the creation of a strategic business plan. The *long-range IT plan*, sometimes referred to as the *strategic IT plan*, is then based on the strategic business plan. The IT strategic plan starts with the IT vision and strategy, which defines the future concept of what IT should do to achieve the goals, objectives, and strategic position of the firm and how this will be achieved. The overall direction, requirements, and sourcing—either outsourcing or insourcing—of resources, such as infrastructure, application services, data services, security services, IT governance, and management architecture; budget; activities; and time frames are set for three to five years into the future. The planning process continues by addressing lower-level activities with a shorter time frame.

The next level down is a *medium-term IT plan*, which identifies general project plans in terms of the specific requirements and sourcing of resources as well as the **project portfolio**. The project portfolio lists major resource projects, including infrastructure, application services, data services, and security services, that are consistent with the long-range plan. Some companies may define their portfolio in terms of applications. The **applications portfolio** is a list of major, approved information system projects that are also consistent with the long-range plan. Expectations for sourcing of resources in the project or applications portfolio should be driven by the business strategy. Since some of these projects will take more than a year to complete and others will not start in the current year, this plan extends over several years.

The third level is a *tactical plan*, which details budgets and schedules for current-year projects and activities. In reality, because of the rapid pace of change in technology and the environment, short-term plans may include major items not anticipated in the other plans.

The planning process just described is currently practiced by many organizations. Specifics of the IT planning process, of course, vary among organizations. For example, not all organizations have a high-level IT steering committee. Project priorities may be determined by the IT director, by his or her superior, by company politics, or even on a first-come, first-served basis.

The deliverables from the IT planning process should include the following: an evaluation of the strategic goals and directions of the organization and how IT is aligned; a new or revised IT vision and assessment of the state of the IT division; a statement of the strategies, objectives, and policies for the IT division; and the overall direction, requirements, and sourcing of resources. The entire strategic planning process is often conducted by an IT steering committee.

IT Steering Committees The IT Steering Committee is a team of managers and staff that represents various business units that establish IT priorities and ensures that the IT department is meeting the needs of the enterprise. The steering committee major tasks are listed in **Table 12.4**.

TABLE 12.4 **Tasks of Steering Committee**

Task	Description
Set the direction	In linking the corporate strategy with the IT strategy, planning is the key activity.
Allocate scarce resources	The committee approves the allocation of resources for and within the information systems organization. This includes outsourcing policy.
Make staffing decisions	Key IT personnel decisions involve a consultation-and-approval process made by the committee, including outsourcing decisions.
Communicate and provide feedback	Information regarding IT activities should flow freely.
Set and evaluate performance metrics	The committee should establish performance measures for the IT department and see that they are met. This includes the initiation of SLAs.

The success of steering committees largely depends on the establishment of IT *governance*, formally established statements that direct the policies regarding IT alignment with organizational goals and allocation of resources.

12.2 Aligning IT with Business Objectives

The goal of a good **IT strategy** is to achieve **business–IT alignment**. IT strategy should be an integral part of business planning, otherwise strategic systems would be developed in a piecemeal manner and wouldn't contribute to strategic vision or enable organizations to respond to market changes (**Figure 12.4**). Therefore, a primary focus of a firm's IT strategy for its systems or business IT applications should be to align them with the business needs and use them to achieve strategic benefits.

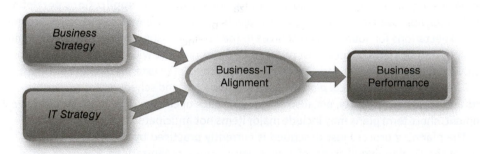

FIGURE 12.4 The role of aligning IT strategy with business strategy to achieve organizational strategic objectives is still one of the most important challenges that IT executives face.

Alignment allows a firm to make the most of its IT investments and increase profitability by attaining accord between its business strategies and plans. Even though firms instinctively expect benefits from IT alignment, many of them are resistant to achieving alignment.

Alignment is a complex management activity and calls for extensive communication and collaboration between IT and corporate leaders. Business–IT alignment can be improved by focusing on the following activities:

1. **Commitment to IT planning by senior management**   Senior management commitment to IT planning is essential to success.

2. **CIO is a member of senior management**   The key to achieving business–IT alignment is for the CIO to attain strategic influence. Rather than being narrow technologists, CIOs must be both business and technology savvy. The skill set of CIOs is outlined in **Table 12.5**.

3. **Understanding IT and corporate planning**   A prerequisite for effective business–IT alignment for the CIO is to understand business planning and for the CEO and business planners to understand their company's IT planning.

4. **Shared culture and good communication**   The CIO must understand and buy into the corporate culture so that IS planning does not occur in isolation. Frequent, open, and effective communication is essential to ensure a shared culture and keep everyone aware of planning activities and business dynamics.

5. **Multilevel links**   Links between business and IT plans should be made at the strategic, tactical, and operational levels.

TABLE 12.5   **CIO Skills to Improve Business–IT Alignment**

- **Political savvy**   Effectively understand managers, workers, and their priorities and use that knowledge to influence others to support organizational objectives.
- **Influence, leadership, and power**   Inspire a shared vision and influence subordinates and superiors.
- **Relationship management**   Build and maintain working relationships with coworkers and those external to the organization. Negotiate problem solutions without alienating those impacted. Understand others and get their cooperation in nonauthoritarian relationships.
- **Resourcefulness**   Think strategically and make good decisions under pressure. Can set up complex work systems and engage in flexible problem resolution.
- **Strategic planning**   Capable of developing long-term objectives and strategies and translating vision into realistic business strategies.
- **Doing what it takes**   Persevering in the face of obstacles.
- **Leading employees**   Delegating work to employees effectively; broadening employee opportunities; and interacting fairly with employees.

The first step in achieving business–IT alignment is to understand business objectives and how IT capabilities can best support business requirements; this way strategic planning will ensure that maximum IT dollars are spent on creating business value for the organization. It's important for IT to understand where the organization is headed and how technology can help it achieve its goals. Aligning technology with business processes is becoming increasingly important due to the pace of change in technology and the business. From business strategy planning to execution, digital technology has become the foundation for everything enterprises do.

Questions

1. What is business–IT alignment?
2. Describe how business–IT alignment helps a company achieve its goals.
3. Name the five activities that need to be focused on to improve business–IT alignment.

Achieving and Sustaining a Competitive Advantage

A well-thought-out and executed IT strategy that aligns with the business to develop, source, and put in place technology that best supports business processes and goals can give an organization a **competitive advantage** in the marketplace.

In business, as in sports, companies want to win—customers, market share, position in the industry. Basically, this requires gaining an edge over competitors by being first to take advantage of market opportunities, providing great customer experiences, doing something well that others cannot easily imitate, or convincing customers why it is a more valuable alternative than the competition.

Competitiveness relies heavily on IT **agility** and **responsiveness**. The benefit of IT agility is that it enables organizations to take advantage of opportunities faster or more effectively.

Closely related to IT agility is **flexibility**. For example, mobile networks are flexible—able to be set up, moved, or removed easily, without dealing with cables and other physical requirements of wired networks. Mass migration to mobile devices from PCs has expanded the scope of IT beyond traditional organizational boundaries—making location practically irrelevant.

IT agility, flexibility, and mobility are tightly interrelated and fully dependent on an organization's IT infrastructure and architecture, as discussed in Chapter 2.

Once an enterprise has developed a competitive edge, it can only be maintained and sustained by continually pursuing new and better ways to compete. Maintaining a competitive advantage requires forecasting trends and industry changes and figuring out what the company needs to do to stay ahead of the game. It demands continuously tracking competitors and their future plans and promptly taking corrective action. It's important to remember that while IT plays a key role in competitive advantage, that advantage is short-lived if competitors quickly duplicate it.

Two of the most widely used methodologies associated with gaining, maintaining, and sustaining a competitive edge are the **Competitive Forces Model** and **Value Chain Model**. Both of these are discussed next.

Competitive advantage is an edge that enables a company to outperform its average competitor in ways that matter to its customers.

Agility means being able to respond quickly.

Responsiveness means that IT capacity can be easily scaled up or down as needed, which essentially requires cloud computing.

Flexibility means having the ability to quickly integrate new business functions or to easily reconfigure software or apps.

Porter's Competitive Forces Model Michael Porter's **competitive forces model**, also called the **five-forces model**, is a simple but powerful strategic planning tool for understanding the strength of an organization's competitive position in its current environment and in the environment into which it's considering moving. Professor Porter discusses his model in detail in a **13-minute YouTube video from Harvard Business School**.

The model assumes that there are five important forces that determine competitive power in a business situation and influence a company's position within a given industry and the strategy that management chooses to pursue. Other forces, including new regulations, which affect all companies in the industry and have a rather uniform impact on each company in an industry, are not included in the model.

The Five Forces According to Porter, five major forces in an industry affect the degree of competition, which impact profit margins and ultimate profitability (**Figure 12.5**). While each of the five forces need to be assessed individually, it's their overall interaction that determines potential competitive advantage. For example, while profit margins for pizzerias may be small, the ease of entering that industry draws many new entrants. Conversely, profit margins for delivery services may be large, but the cost of technology needed to support the service is a huge barrier to entry into the market.

The five industry (or market) forces are as follows:

1. **Threat of entry of new competitors** Industries that have large profit margins attract entrants into the market to a greater degree than industries with small margins. The same principle applies to jobs—people are attracted to higher-paying jobs, provided that they can meet the criteria or acquire the skills for that job. In order to gain market share, entrants usually need to sell at lower prices as an incentive. Their tactics can force companies already in the industry to defend their market share by lowering prices—reducing

profit margin. Thus, this threat puts downward pressure on profit margins by driving down prices.

This force also refers to the strength of the **barriers to entry** into an industry, which is how easy it is to enter an industry. The threat of entry is lower (less powerful) when existing companies have ITs that are difficult to duplicate or very expensive. Those ITs create barriers to entry that reduce the threat of entry.

2. **Bargaining power of suppliers**   Bargaining power is high where the supplier or brand is powerful, such as Apple, Microsoft, and auto manufacturers. Power is determined by how much a company purchases from a supplier. The more powerful company has the leverage to demand better prices or terms, which increase its profit margin. Conversely, suppliers with very little bargaining power tend to have small profit margins.

3. **Bargaining power of customers or buyers**   This force is the reverse of the bargaining power of suppliers. Examples are Walmart and government agencies. This force is high when there are few large customers or buyers in a market.

4. **Threat of substituting products or services**   Where there is product-for-product substitution, such as Kindle for Nook, there is downward pressure on prices. As the threat of substitutes increases, the profit margin decreases because sellers need to keep prices competitively low.

5. **Competitive rivalry among existing firms in the industry**   Fierce competition involves expensive advertising and promotions, intense investments in R&D, or other efforts that cut into profit margins. This force is most likely to be high when entry barriers are low, the threat of substitute products is high, and suppliers and buyers in the market attempt to control it. That is why this force is placed in the center of the model.

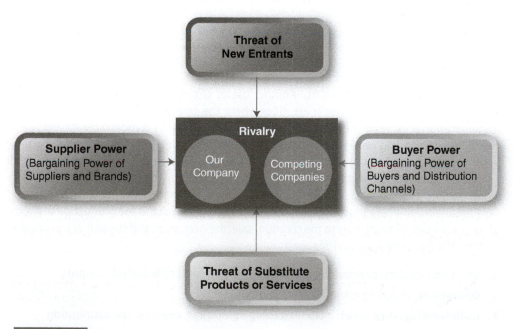

FIGURE 12.5   Porter's competitive forces model.

The strength of each force is determined by the industry's structure. Existing companies in an industry need to protect themselves against these forces. Alternatively, they can take advantage of the forces to improve their position or to challenge industry leaders or move into a new industry. The relationships between the forces are shown in Figure 12.5.

Companies can identify the forces that influence competitive advantage in their marketplace and then develop their strategy. Porter (1985) proposed three types of strategies—cost leadership, differentiation, and niche strategies. In **Table 12.6**, Porter's three classical strategies are listed first, followed by a list of nine other general strategies for dealing with competitive advantage. Applying the right kinds of technology support can enhance each of these strategies.

TABLE 12.6 Strategies for Competitive Advantage

Strategy	Description
Cost leadership	Produce product/service at the lowest cost in the industry.
Differentiation	Offer different products, services, or product features.
Niche	Select a narrow-scope segment (market niche) and be the best in quality, speed, or cost in that segment.
Growth	Increase market share, acquire more customers, or sell more types of products.
Alliance	Work with business partners in partnerships, alliances, joint ventures, or virtual companies.
Innovation	Introduce new products/services; put new features in existing products/services; develop new ways to produce products/services.
Operational effectiveness	Improve the manner in which internal business processes are executed so that the firm performs similar activities better than its rivals.
Customer orientation	Concentrate on customer satisfaction.
Time	Treat time as a resource, then manage it, and use it to the firm's advantage.
Entry barriers	Create barriers to entry. By introducing innovative products or using IT to provide exceptional service, companies can create entry barriers to discourage new entrants.
Customer or supplier lock-in	Encourage customers or suppliers to stay with you rather than going to competitors. Reduce customers' bargaining power by locking them in.
Increase switching costs	Discourage customers or suppliers from going to competitors for economic reasons.

Porter's Value Chain Model Another useful strategic management tool is Porter's Value Chain. The Value Chain Model identifies where the greatest value exists in an organization and how that value can be increased. Understanding how your company creates value and identifying ways to add even greater value are essential in developing a competitive strategy. Porter proposed a general-purpose value chain that any organization can use to examine all of its activities and their relationships to each other. These activities fall into two major categories: primary and support.

Primary activities are those business activities directly involved in the production of goods. Primary activities relate directly to the creation, sale, maintenance, and support of a product of services. The five **primary activities** are as follows:

1. **Inbound logistics**, or acquiring and receiving of raw materials and other inputs
2. **Operations**, including manufacturing and testing
3. **Outbound logistics**, which includes packaging, storage, delivery, and distribution
4. **Marketing and sales** to customers
5. **Services**, including customer service

Primary activities usually occur sequentially, from 1 to 5. As work progresses, value is added to the product in each activity. To be more specific, incoming materials (1) are processed (in receiving, storage, etc.) in activities called inbound logistics. Next, the materials are used in operations (2), where significant value is added by the process of turning raw materials into products. Products need to be prepared for delivery (packaging, storing, and shipping) in the outbound logistics activities (3). Then marketing and sales (4) attempt to sell the products to customers, increasing product value by creating demand for the company's products. The value of a sold item is much larger than that of an unsold one. Finally, after-sales service (5), such as warranty service or upgrade notification, is performed for the customer, further adding value.

A variety of support activities feed into one or more of the primary activities. The four **support activities** are as follows:

1. The firm's infrastructure, accounting, finance, and management
2. Human resources (HR) management
3. Technology development, and research and development (R&D)
4. Procurement, or purchasing

Each support activity can be applied to any or all of the primary activities. Support activities may also support each other, as shown in **Figure 12.6**.

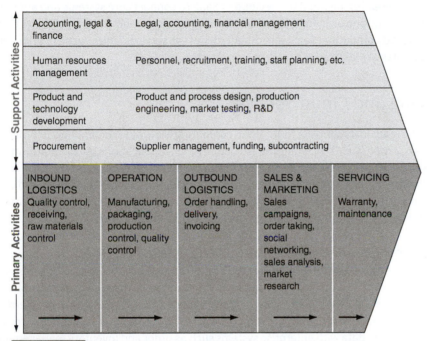

FIGURE 12.6   Porter's value chain. The arrows represent the flow of goods, services, and data in an organization.

Questions

1. What are the three categories of value drivers?
2. Why do reactive approaches to IT investments fail?
3. What is the goal of business–IT alignment?
4. Why is IT strategic planning revisited on a regular basis?
5. What are the functions of a steering committee?
6. Describe the IT strategic planning process.
7. Explain how a good IT strategy can help companies gain a competitive advantage in the marketplace.
8. What are the five competitive forces in Porter's five forces model?

12.3 IT Sourcing Strategies

IT strategy guides the investment decisions and decisions on the development, acquisition, and/or implementation of information systems. These strategies fall into two broad categories:

1. **In-house development**, in which systems are developed or other IT work is done in-house, possibly with the help of consulting companies or vendors. Typically, ITs that provide

competitive advantages or that contain proprietary or confidential data are developed and maintained by the organization's own in-house IT function.

2. **Sourcing**, in which systems are developed or IT work is done by a third party or vendor. There are many versions of sourcing, which had been called **outsourcing**. Work or development can be sourced to consulting companies or vendors that are within the same country, which is referred to as **onshore sourcing**. Or the work can be sourced offshore to other countries. Sourcing that is done offshore is also called **offshoring**. Other options are to lease or to purchase ITs as services. Cloud computing and SaaS have expanded sourcing options significantly.

When legacy systems could no longer provide the functionality needed to solve the businesses' problems, companies migrated to the cloud or SaaS to connect core systems and apps. At most companies today, one or more types of outsourcing arrangements are part of their IT strategy, including cloud computing, SaaS, and other types of "as services" introduced in prior chapters. How these Xaas are sourced is a topic of high interest.

Sourcing and Cloud Services

As you have read, in its simplest form, cloud computing is a way for companies to procure technology *as a service (XaaS)*, including infrastructure (IaaS), applications (AaaS), platforms (PaaS), and business processes, via the Internet. IT resources no longer depend on capital investments and IT developers to own that resource. IT capabilities can be sourced, scaled on, and delivered on demand without physical location, labor, or capital restrictions. As a result, an enterprise's cloud strategy plays a role in its sourcing strategy and business growth.

Integrating Cloud with On-Premises Systems While the concept of cloud is simple, an enterprise's **cloud strategy** tends to be quite complex. Cloud is being adopted across more of the enterprise, but mostly in addition to on-premises systems—not as full replacements for them. Hybrid solutions create integration challenges. Cloud services—also referred to as **edge services**—have to integrate back-to-core internal systems. That is, edge services have to connect and share data with enterprise systems such as order and inventory management, ERP, CRM, SCM, legacy financial, and HR systems and on mobile and social platforms.

Edge service is a term that refers to a cloud service.

Tactical Adoption versus Coordinated Cloud Strategy Deploying cloud services incrementally results in apps and services that are patched together to create end-to-end business processes. This is a short-sighted **tactical adoption approach**. While this approach may have been sufficient in the recent past, cloud services are increasingly more sophisticated and numerous. Tactical approaches will cause difficult integration problems—as occurred with adoption of ERP, mobile, social, and big data systems. Cloud adoption needs to occur according to a coordinated strategy. Given the ever-changing cloud services, it will be tough to know how to design a sustainable cloud strategy. For example, a new class of cloud offerings is being built around business outcomes instead of as point solutions. In effect, this would be business outcomes as a service.

Determining cloud strategies and lease agreements that best support business needs may require hiring cloud consultants, such as Accenture, Booz Allen, Deloitte, Gartner, HP, IBM, or others.

Cloud Strategy Challenges From the outset, the top challenges about migrating to the cloud revolved around cybersecurity, privacy, data availability, and the accessibility of the service. The newer challenges relate to cloud strategy, including integration of cloud with on-premises resources, extensibility, and reliability of the cloud service. **Extensibility** is the ability to get data into and out of the cloud service. These cloud service challenges need to be addressed before deciding on sourcing solutions.

For example, when Nestlé Nespresso S. A. transitioned from a traditional coffee shop to an online distributor in the single-serving coffee machine category, Nespresso needed to replace its complex ERP. By deploying a cloud integration platform, Nespresso has integrated its ERP, warehouse management systems, and ordering tool. Nespresso now leverages its cloud and traditional IT solutions.

In another case, social network LinkedIn migrated to cloud services to support sales and CRM; it began by using noncustomized, out-of-the-box capabilities (Main and Peto, 2013). As the company grew rapidly, the standard cloud services could no longer support the lines of business. Business processes increasingly needed to be integrated with ERP and proprietary systems to generate sales leads. LinkedIn switched to a cloud-based integration platform that is able to connect its lead generation, financial, and CRM systems and its proprietary apps and data warehouse. Integrating cloud and on-premises systems gives salespeople a single view of the data they need to do their jobs.

Outsourcing Challenges   The migration was far from perfect at first, and hard lessons learned early helped achieve impressive results eventually. Six lessons that eBay learned were as follows:

1. **Manage change** by securing the commitment of senior leaders in an overt fashion and by recognizing subtle cultural differences that can undermine initial transition efforts.

2. **Assess organizational readiness** for a transition from a mental and technical standpoint and set realistic expectations and manage them actively.

3. **Anticipate risks and formulate a plan for mitigating them**, beginning with a strategy for dealing with "loss-of-control" threats, both real and imagined.

4. **Build project management infrastructure** that recognizes the "process of transition" needs to be managed as carefully as processes being transitioned. Mapping how the AP process should look posttransition and how it will be managed end to end and by whom is important.

5. **Create a governance mechanism** that can discreetly collect feedback from the transition project manager and provide formal executive oversight and guidance. Form an executive steering committee that includes two senior managers from each organization and representation from all business units impacted by the outsourcing.

6. **Properly define how success will be measured,** both qualitatively and quantitatively. Identifying the right benchmarks for success and vigilantly measuring efforts against them over time are critical. eBay continued to outsource—transitioning its global vendor/supplier maintenance and general ledger activities.

Factors Driving Outsourcing

Enterprises choose outsourcing for the reasons shown in **Table 12.7**.

TABLE 12.7   Reason Why Organizations Outsource IT functions

Generate revenue
Increase efficiency
Gain agility to respond to changes in the marketplace
Allow enterprise to focus on core competencies
Cut operational costs
Greater acceptance of offshoring as an IT strategy
Cloud computer and SaaS are proven effective IT strategies
Differentiate themselves from competitors
Reduce burden on internal IT department

Outsourcing Risks and Hidden Costs

As companies find that their business strategy is increasingly tied to IT solutions, the concerns about outsourcing risks increase. Risks associated with outsourcing are as follows:

Shirking The vendor deliberately underperforms while claiming full payment, for example, billing for more hours than were worked and/or providing excellent staff at first and later replacing them with less qualified ones.

Poaching The vendor develops a strategic application for a client and then uses it for other clients.

Opportunistic repricing When a client enters into a long-term contract with a vendor, the vendor changes financial terms at some point or overcharges for unanticipated enhancements and contract extensions.

Breach of contract by vendor The vendor fails to carry out the terms of the outsourcing agreement.

Inability of vendor to deliver as promised Sometimes outsourcers represent themselves as being more skilled than they actually are and they are unable to deliver the products or services that are promised in the outsourcing agreement.

Vendor lock-in In the event that the outsourcing relationship does not go well, it can be difficult to get out of the outsourcing agreement.

Loss of Control over data Once the data is on the outsourcers servers, the organization has little control over how and when that data can be accessed and by whom.

Lower employee morale IT employees may feel devalued as a result of development and services being performed by an outside source.

Depending on what is outsourced and to whom, an organization might end up spending 10% above the budgeted amount to set up the relationship and manage it over time. The budgeted amount may increase anywhere from 15 to 65% when outsourcing is sent offshore and the costs of travel and cultural differences are added in.

Offshoring

Another IT strategy is to offshore IT development and services. Offshoring of software development has become a common practice due to global markets, lower costs, and increased access to skilled labor. About one-third of Fortune 500 companies outsource software development to software companies in India. It is not only the cost and the technical capabilities that matter. Several other factors to consider are the business and political climates in the selected country, the quality of the infrastructure, and risks such as IT competency, human capital, the economy, the legal environment, and cultural differences.

Duke University's *Center for International Business Education and Research* studied actual offshoring results. According to their study, Fortune 500 companies reduced costs by offshoring—63% of the companies achieved over 30% annual savings and 14% of them achieved savings over 50%. The respondents were overwhelmingly satisfied with their offshore operations. Three-quarters (72%) said their offshore implementations met or exceeded their expected cost savings. Almost one-third of the respondents (31%) achieved their service level goals within the first five months of their contracts while 75% did so within 12 months. The study concluded that "offshoring delivers faster results than average domestic improvement efforts." Even though these are very general results, offshoring success stories ease the fears about the risks of offshoring.

Based on case studies, the types of work that are not readily offshored include the following:

- Work that has not been routinized.
- Work that if offshored would result in the client company losing too much control over critical operations.

- Situations in which offshoring would place the client company at too great a risk to its data security, data privacy, or intellectual property and proprietary information.
- Business activities that rely on an uncommon combination of specific application domain knowledge and IT knowledge in order to do the work properly.

Outsourcing Life Cycle

Regardless of the services an organization wants to outsource, such as manufacturing, data center, applications management, call center, business process, or supply chain, there are multiple ways to approach outsourcing. As with any significant transformation of an organization's business model, it is always best to follow an organized and methodical approach. The exact approach chosen will be determined by many things, including the following:

- An organization's familiarity with outsourcing in any areas other than the one being currently considered
- What currently exists in-house that can be used as a foundation for the outsourcing process
- Level of outsourcing sophistication of the procurement and legal groups
- Whether an organization is just exploring the possibilities of outsourcing or has definite outsourcing objectives

The Five-Phase Outsourcing Life Cycle   Jeff Richards of CIO Professional Services proposes a five-phase outsourcing life cycle, comprising a total of 12 distinct stages (Richards, 2016).

Depending on an organization's maturity, changing business conditions, or recognition of new information, it can choose to enter or exit the outsourcing life cycle at any point in the process. Just be aware that each entry or exit point has associated risks, costs, and benefits.

Here is a "top level" description of each phase of the outsourcing life cycle shown in **Figure 12.7**:

- **Phase 1**   This is the preparatory phase, where you assess opportunities and develop your overarching strategy and process- or geography-specific business cases for outsourcing.
- **Phase 2**   In this phase, you prepare and issue the request for proposal (RFP), evaluate the proposals that are submitted, and select a service provider.
- **Phase 3**   Once a service provider has been selected, the next step is to develop and negotiate the contract that will serve as the framework for your relationship with your new business partner.
- **Phase 4**   Once the contract is in place, it's time to plan and execute the service transition. This is the point at which all of your and the service provider's efforts either come to fruition or go off the track. Time invested in Phases 1 to 3 will mitigate that risk.
- **Phase 5**   Finally, with everything in place, the last phase is all about the ongoing management of the Service Level Agreements (SLAs) and the service provider relationship.

Using this type of phased outsourcing strategy, organization can optimize what, where, and when they acquire IT assets and services.

Tech Note 12.2 discusses a sourcing challenge and solution.

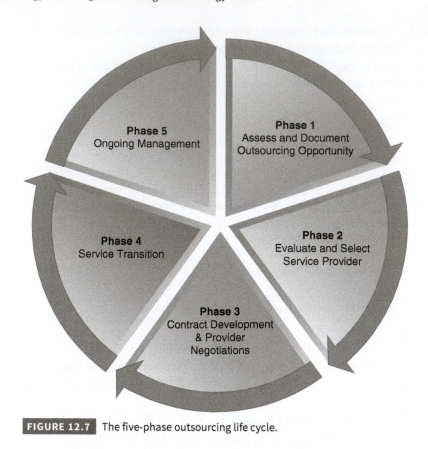

FIGURE 12.7   The five-phase outsourcing life cycle.

Tech Note 12.2

Managing Sourcing Arrangements and SLAs

Sourcing creates its own set of challenges. Companies that have multiple outsourcers face the challenge of managing all of these relationships. As companies increase outsourcing activities, a gap is created in their organizational structures, management methods, and software tools. At that point, companies turn for help to an **outsource relationship management (ORM) company**. ORMs provide automated tools to monitor and manage the outsourcing relationships. ORMs monitor and manage SLAs. The SLA must be managed because it serves as both the blueprint and warranty for the outsourced arrangement.

This example shows the importance of managing SLAs. A U.S. transportation company needed to make cuts immediately to its IT operating budget to reverse cost overruns. The company had a long-standing outsourcing agreement with a top-tier service provider, but it had not implemented effective SLAs to control costs. As a result, it had outsourced 750 terabytes of data at an annual cost of more than $20,000 per terabyte, an overinvestment that contributed to runaway IT outsourcing expenditures of $225 million a year. A company-wide budget shortfall forced the IT division to cut $36 million from its 2016 budget—without harming quality of service. The CIO had to re-examine its data and infrastructure needs and take a more informed, proactive role in managing the relationship with its service provider.

Today, the critical question is no longer whether cloud computing will be a fundamental deployment model for enterprise systems, such as ERP and SCM. Rather, the question is "How can companies profit from the capabilities that cloud computing offers?"

Organizations use a combinations of IT Strategies:

- in-house
- onshore or domestic sourcing
- offshoring
- cloud computing
- SaaS

Managing IT Vendor Relationships

When sourcing IT projects, the starting point in building a positive and strong vendor relationship is vendor selection. If a company makes a bad selection or enters into a vaguely worded service contract, most likely the software, app, or implementation will fail, and the vendor will not be able to resolve the problems fast enough, if at all. Failures are usually followed by lawsuits.

Finding and Selecting a Vendor   To minimize interpersonal or technical conflicts with IT vendors, businesses need to thoroughly research the vendor. It is very important to ask questions about the services and products the vendor will provide and get as many specifics as possible. Also take the time to verify the vendor's claims about its products and check all references to make sure that the vendor has a proven track record of success. When selecting a vendor, two criteria to assess first are experience and stability:

- Experience with very similar systems of similar size, scope, and requirements. Experience with the ITs that are needed, integrating those ITs into the existing infrastructure and the customer's industry.
- Financial and qualified personnel stability. A vendor's reputation impacts its stability.

Of course, for innovative IT implementations, vendors will not have experience and one major failure—and the lawsuit that follows—can create instability. If those criteria are not met, there is no reason to further consider the vendor.

Research by McKinsey indicates that a majority of technology executives want to have stronger relationships with their IT suppliers, but they often act in ways that undermine that goal. In fact, many corporate customers lose out on the potential benefit of close relationships by an overemphasis on costs instead of value. Ideally, a customer/vendor relationship is a mutually beneficial partnership, and both sides are best served by treating it as such.

Vendors often buy hardware or software from other vendors. In order to avoid problems with the primary IT vendor, check secondary suppliers as well. Ask the primary vendor how they will deliver on their promises if the secondary vendors go out of business or otherwise end their relationship.

Ask for "Proof of Concept" or A Trial Run   A **proof of concept (POC)** is a vendor demonstration of a product to see how or how well it works. Requesting a "proof of concept" of a vendor product, puts the old adage "it worked in development" to the test in a production environment to ensure that the product under consideration prove can deliver as promised. The results of a POC need to be measurable for use in the decision-making process. For example, a certain performance level may be used as a threshold for acceptance of a product.

A **trial run**, or pilot, is a little different. In this scenario, a vendor may offer the option to let you test their products or services in a pilot study or a small portion of the business to verify that it fits the company's needs.

In either case, if the vendor demo or test adds value on a small scale, then the system can be rolled out on a larger scale. If the vendor cannot meet the requirements, then the company avoids a failure.

Proof of concept (POC) is a vendor demonstration of a product to see how or how well it works.

Trial run is when a vendor product or service is tested in a pilot study or limited area of the business to confirm its usefulness to the company.

Contracts: Get Everything in Writing

SLAs are designed to protect the service provider, not the customer, unless the customer takes an informed and active role in the provisions and parameters.

By making both parties aware of their responsibilities and when they may be held liable for failing to live up to those responsibilities, a strong SLA can help prevent many of the disruptions and dangers that can come with sourcing or migrating to the cloud. The provisions and parameters of the contract are the only protections a company has when terms are not met or the arrangement is terminated. No contract should be signed without a thorough legal review.

There is no template SLA, and each cloud solution vendor is unique. Certainly, if a vendor's SLA is light on details, that alone may be an indicator that the vendor is light on accountability. Additionally, if a sourcing or cloud vendor refuses to improve its SLAs or negotiate vital points, then that vendor should not be considered.

Questions

1. What contributes to the complexity of a cloud strategy?
2. How does tactical adoption of cloud services differ from a coordinated cloud strategy?
3. What is onshore sourcing?
4. What are the major reasons for sourcing?
5. What types of work are not readily outsourced offshore?
6. When selecting a vendor, what two criteria need to be assessed?
7. What is the risk of putting too great an emphasis on cost when selecting or dealing with an IT vendor?
8. What needs to be done before signing a contract with an IT vendor?
9. Why would a company want to invest in strategic technologies?

12.4 Balanced Scorecard

Traditionally, the typical business objective could be summed up simply as *to make a profit*. As a result, performance metrics have typically been based on quantitative measures such as the following:

- P&L (profit and loss) reports: revenue, expenses, net profit
- Cash flow statements: enough cash to pay its current liabilities
- Balance sheets that reflected the overall status of finances at a certain date

Lagging indicators confirm what has happened. They evaluate outcomes and achievements.

These financial metrics are called **lagging indicators** because they quantify past performance. As such, they represent historical information and are not ideal tools for managing day-to-day operations and planning.

Today, many managers are frustrated by the inadequacies of traditional quantitative performance measures and have completely abandoned financial measures. However, the majority of managers do not want to have to choose between financial and operational measures. Instead, they want a balanced presentation of measures that allow them to view the company from several perspectives simultaneously.

During a year-long research project with 12 companies at the leading edge of performance measurement, Robert Kaplan and David Norton developed a "balanced scorecard," a new performance measurement system that gives top managers a fast but comprehensive view of the business. The BSC includes financial measures that tell the results of actions already taken. And it complements those financial measures with three sets of operational measures that drive future financial performance: customer satisfaction, internal business processes, and the organization's ability to learn and improve. With the help of a BSC, managers can take a 360° perspective of the performance of their organization by translating their company's strategy and mission statements into specific goals and measures.

The Balanced Scorecard

Balanced scorecard is a strategic management methodology for evaluating performance based on both financial and nonfinancial metrics.

The **balanced scorecard** provides companies with a blueprint for selecting strategic measures to improve performance and facilitate strategy implementation by enhancing strategic awareness and closer business–IT alignment.

In 1992, Kaplan and Norton introduced the concept of a BSC in their *Harvard Business Review* (HBR) article, "The Balanced Scorecard – Measures that Drive Performance" (Kaplan and Norton 2008).

Kaplan and Norton compared the BSC to the screens and indicator displays in an airplane cockpit. They explained that during the complex task of flying an airplane, pilots need detailed information about fuel, air speed, altitude, bearing, and other indicators that summarize the current and predicted environment. Reliance on one instrument can be fatal. Similarly, the complexity of managing an organization requires that managers be able to view performance in several areas simultaneously. A BSC or a balanced set of measures provides that valuable information. What was novel about BSC in the 1990s was that it measured a company's performance using a multidimensional approach of **leading indicators** as well as lagging indicators.

Leading indicators predict future events to identify opportunities

The BSC is typically used at the end of the strategic planning process to review performance on a regular basis. For example, in the opening case, Intel took a BSC approach to measure its business performance in the final step of its six-step IT strategic planning process.

Using the Balance Scorecard

The BSC can be used to translate strategic plans and mission statements into a set of **business objectives** and performance metrics that can be quantified and measured to evaluate how well objectives are being achieved.

Business objectives are the building blocks of strategy.

Objectives set out what the business is trying to achieve. They are action-oriented statements that define the continuous improvement activities that must be done to be successful, that is, achieve a return on investments (ROI) of at least 10% in 2017. Well-thought-out objectives should meet the five "SMART" criteria shown in **Figure 12.8**.

The BSC is widely accepted as one of the most influential management ideas of the past 75 years. Using the **balanced scorecard** methodology, performance is measured and evaluated from four different perspectives to ensure that limited resources are invested to achieve the highest possible ROI. These perspectives are as follows:

1. **Financial**   To succeed financially, how should we appear to our investors and shareholders?
2. **Customer**   To achieve our vision, how should we provide value to our customers?
3. **Business processes**   To satisfy our shareholders and customers, what business processes must we focus on and excel at?
4. **Innovation, learning, and growth**   To achieve our vision, how will we sustain our ability to innovate, learn, change, and improve?

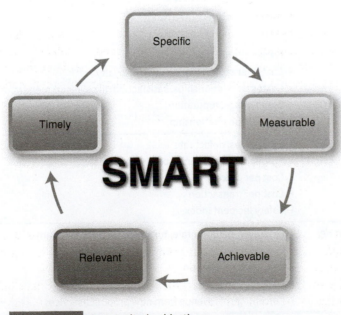

FIGURE 12.8   Smart criteria objectives.

The BSC method is "balanced" because it does not rely solely on traditional financial measures. Instead, it balances financial measures with three forward-looking nonfinancial measures, as shown in **Figure 12.9**.

The BSC is not a template that can be applied to business in general or even to an entire industry. Different market situations, product strategies, and competitive environments require different scorecards. Business units need to devise customized scorecards to fit their mission, strategy, technology, and culture. Some examples of measurement criteria that can be used within each of these perspectives are shown in **Table 12.8**.

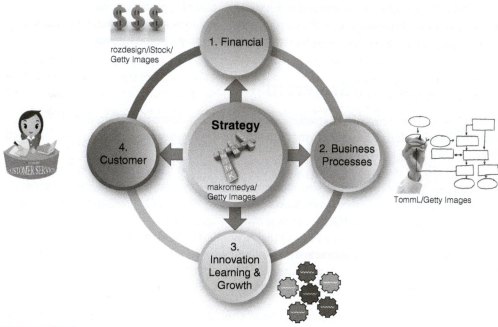

rozdesign/iStock/Getty Images

makromedya/Getty Images

TommL/Getty Images

FIGURE 12.9 Balanced Scorecard (BSC) uses four metrics to measure performance—one financial metric and three nonfinancial metrics.

TABLE 12.8	Examples of Balanced Scorecard (BSC) Measurement Criteria
Perspective	**Examples of Measurement Criteria**
Financial	• Revenue and revenue growth rates • Earnings and cash flow • Asset utilization • Project profitability
Customer	• Market share • Customer acquisition, retention, loyalty • Customer relationships, satisfaction, likes, recommendations, loyalty • Brand image, reputation • Price–value relationship
Internal business processes	• Cycle times, defect rate • Production throughput, productivity rates • Cost per process • Cost per transaction • Safety Incident Index
Innovation, learning, and growth	• Employee skills, morale, turnover, capacity for change • IT capabilities • Employee motivation • R&D • Percentage of revenue from new products/services

Companies use BSCs to improve their strategic planning process by the following:

- Clarifying or updating a business strategy
- Linking strategic objectives to long-term targets and annual budgets
- Integrating strategic objectives into resource allocation processes
- Increasing companywide understanding of the corporate vision and strategy

Applying the BSC

BSC converts senior management priorities into visible, actionable objectives by identifying ways to measure progress against agreed-upon targets.

Assume that a low-cost airline bases its profitability on the following interrelated factors: lower costs, increased revenue, percent of flights departing and arriving on time, competitive pricing, maximum fly time or minimal time jets are on the ground, and the ability of the ground crew to learn to do their jobs faster. Objectives, measures, and targets are diagrammed and detailed in **Figure 12.10**.

Using the results of the BSC methodology, management teams have an agreed-upon set of objectives and measures that are used to identify and set targets and the actions to achieve them that are appropriate for the company's business model.

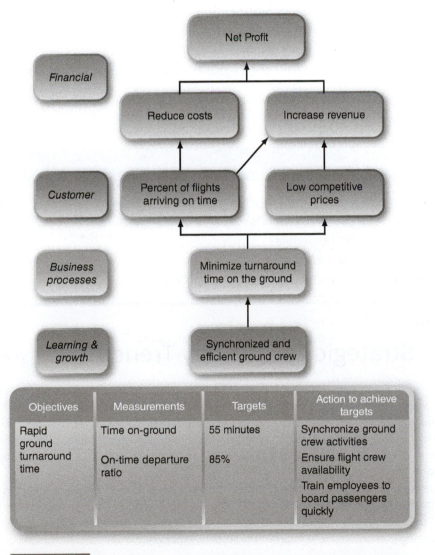

Objectives	Measurements	Targets	Action to achieve targets
Rapid ground turnaround time	Time on-ground	55 minutes	Synchronize ground crew activities
	On-time departure ratio	85%	Ensure flight crew availability
			Train employees to board passengers quickly

FIGURE 12.10   Overview of a low-cost airline's BSC objectives, measures, targets, and actions to achieve targets.

Consider JetBlue and Southwest Airlines—both compete to a large extent on price. Yet JetBlue allows one free checked bag while Southwest allows two free checked bags. Now consider the value drivers—time the jet sits on the ground and on-time arrivals. The time it takes to board passengers impacts the ability to take off, which in turn impacts on-ground time and arrival time. Since JetBlue has assigned seats, the terminal crew can control boarding starting at the back of the plane to minimize bottlenecks in the aisle. In contrast, Southwest has open seating, which typically occurs from the front of the jet and can clog the aisle. Now the differing free-baggage policies make sense because the more baggage brought on board, the longer boarding tends to take. By allowing two free checked bags, Southwest attempts to reduce carry-on bags in order to offset the extra time needed for the open-seating boarding process.

By measuring how well targets for on-ground times and arrival times are achieved, both airlines can determine if their actions are optimal or need to be revised. Based on these examples, it is easier to understand the processes involved in the BSC methodology, which start with the business vision and strategy. The general steps include the following:

1. Identify performance metrics (as in Table 12.4) that link vision and strategy to results—financial performance, operations, innovation, employee performance.
2. Select meaningful objectives (Figure 12.10).
3. Select effective measures and targets (Figure 12.10).
4. Determine the actions needed to achieve the targets (Figure 12.10).
5. Implement necessary tracking, analytics, communication, and reporting systems, including sensors, data visualization, mashups, and dashboards via social and mobile channels.
6. Collect, analyze, and compare performance data with targets.
7. Revise actions to improve performance gaps and take advantage of new opportunities.

BSC is used to clarify and update the strategy, align the IT strategy with the business strategy, and link strategic objectives to long-term goals and annual budgets.

Questions

1. How did the BSC approach differ from previous measurement approaches?
2. How does the BSC approach "balance" performance measurements?
3. What are the four BSC perspectives?
4. Give an example of each BSC metric.
5. How does BSC help align IT strategy with business strategy?

12.5 Strategic Technology Trends

Strategic technology has the potential to make significant impacts on an organization's long-term plans, programs, and initiatives.

To gain the competitive advantage they need to flourish, companies need to strategically invest in emerging **strategic technology** to widen their set of core competencies and help them differentiate themselves in the market, expand their existing market, or move into different markets. This might include technologies with a high potential for disruption of the business, end-users, or IT; the need for a major investment; or the risk of being a late adopter of the technology.

Every year, Gartner, Inc. highlights top technology trends that will be strategic for most organizations at the Gartner Symposium/ITxpo. Gartner's top 10 strategic technology trends for 2017 are described in **Table 12.9. IT at Work 12.1** describes how ESSA Academy in England used strategic technologies to improve the student experience.

TABLE 12.9   **Top 10 Strategic Technology Trends**

Trend	Strategic Technology	Description/Examples
1	Artificial Intelligence and Machine Learning	Robots, autonomous vehicles, consumer electronics
2	Intelligent Apps	Virtual personal assistant (VPA), Virtual customer assistant (VCA)
3	Intelligent Things	Drones, smart appliances
4	Virtual and Augmented Reality	Immersive consumer and business content—mobile, wearables, Internet of Things, sensor-rich environments
5	Digital Twin	Dynamic software model of a physical thing of system that relies on sensor data. Used to proactively repair and plan for equipment service, mfg. processes, operate factories, predict equipment failure
6	Blockchain and Distributed Ledgers	Chains sequentially grouped value exchange transactions—in bitcoins or other tokens—and records them across a peer-to-peer network. Music distribution identity identification, title registry, supply chain.
7	Conversational System	Connection points will expand and greater cooperative interaction between devices will emerge creating foundation for a new continuous and ambient digital experience
8	Mesh App and Service Architecture (MASA)	Mobile apps, web apps, desktop apps, and IoT apps link to a broad mesh of backend services to create what users view as one "application."
9	Digital Technology Platforms	Basic building blocks (IS, customer experience, analytics and intelligence, IoT, and business ecosystems) for a digital business. A critical enabler to become a digital business.
10	Adaptive Security Architecture	IoT creates new vulnerabilities that will require new remediation tools and processes.

IT at Work 12.1

Strategic Technology Changes a Failing School to "Good"

Five years ago, ESSA Academy was a failing school. Now it is known as the first school in Britain to buy touch-screen devices for all its students. As a result, it has turned the fortunes of the school, its students and teachers around and advises schools from Afghanistan to Australia on how to teach with technology.

Situated in Bolton, Lancashire, England, ESSA Academy has 845 students aged 11–16 years. The school has designed its own curriculum based on its own vision of learning.

As part of a whole school approach to transforming the learning environment, school–student relationship, and relationships between students, teachers, and parents, ESSA administrators had a vision. Abdul Chohan, a director of the academy, wanted to use technology to create an environment in which students could enjoy learning and use computers for something other than playing games. He also wanted to encourage teachers to embrace new ways of understanding planning, classroom activities, and the learning process.

Inspired by this vision of a modern school, the ICT coordinator turned to strategically using consumer level technology rather than educational solutions. The idea of giving expensive electronics to its mostly poor, ethnic-minority students was derided when the plans were announced in the local press. People saw it as a gimmick—a bribe to get students to come to the school.

From the start, ESSA's strategy involved the parents who made the new technology "family technology." In this way, parents were able to share the learning experiences with their children "anytime, everywhere." And, teachers developed materials from lessons accessible from iTunesU and combined this with the use of apps and digital tools available on the iPad.

The latest development has been for Chohan to use iTunes U to curate content collaboratively and turn that content into textbooks that students can reference online rather than buying physical textbooks. This innovative approach enables ESSA students to create, develop, and share resources in a collaborative way to further enhance their learning.

The gamble paid off—in 2015, 54% of ESSA's graduating students achieved high scores on exit exams, a statistic that is above the national average. The move toward Cloud technology, where most of the resources and communications between students, teachers, and parents are digital, has resulted in cost savings for most school departments and a feeling of liberation from physical constraints. Students are more motivated and engaged. There is a sense of enjoyment in learning to use their own technology, and students who have been encouraged to get involved in the new initiative are finding new apps to use in different classes—an activity that teachers highly value.

IT at Work Questions

1. At what point in the initiative do you think students, parents, and teachers should be involved?

2. Why do you think the initiative was successful?

3. What different strategic technologies could Chohan consider?

Sources: Compiled from Lee (2015); Pipe (2016) and **www.essaacademy.org (2017).**

Strategic Technology Scanning

To achieve their corporate vision, organizations need to have a structured process in place to identify suitable strategic technologies. In an era of rapid technological change, technology scanning is a critical strategic activity for any organization. To enhance their IT strategy, every organization needs to continually scan for emerging technologies. Understanding the performance improvements provided by new technologies, such as cost savings or service improvements, can range from incremental to revolutionary. Certain strategic technologies can create a basis for significant improvements, while other technologies may address relatively narrow needs and opportunities.

To be most effective, it's useful to establish a structured approach to strategic technology scanning. The five steps listed in **Table 12.10** provide a framework to guide technology scanning activities.

TABLE 12.10 **Five Steps to Technology Scanning**

Step	Activity
1. General Technology Search	Conduct a very broad review of new and emerging technologies that might be beneficial to the organization
2. Technology Mapping	Conduct structured investigations into an organization's performance capabilities and identify the points of leverage for technological developments related to cost, reliability, safety, or capacity (for all competing modes)
3. Systems Modeling	Develop and maintain a set of models that can be used to evaluate technological improvements as they affect specific aspects of the organization
4. Customer Requirements Analysis	Investigate the requirements of selected groups of customers and identify new ways of doing business; estimate resulting customer benefits in cost, speed, reliability, safety, and capacity
5. Analysis of Specific Technologies	Examine specific technologies identified as having potential for enhancing performance

Finding Strategic Technologies

One approach to finding possible strategic technologies is to look at what is going on at major research centers and technology industry conferences, such as COMDEX, IBM Inter-Connect, Google Next, Adobe Summit, and HIMSS. Another approach is to look for entirely new areas of technology that are emerging based on fundamental advances in the technology industry, such as Internet of Things (IoT), **digital mesh**, artificial intelligence, and cybersecurity.

Digital mesh is an expanded set of end points used to access applications, gather information, or interact with people, social communities, government, and businesses to ensure instant connection and response to build experience. Examples include smart devices, wearables, consumer and home electronic devices.

Investing in Strategic Technologies Once appropriate new strategic technologies have been identified and assessed, companies need to strategically invest in emerging technologies. Although this might include technologies with a high potential for disruption of the business, end-users, or IT; the need for a major investment; or the risk of being a late adopter of the technology, it is money well spent. Through the purchase of emerging strategic technologies, organizations can gain the competitive advantage they need to flourish, widen their set of core competencies, expand their existing market, or move into different markets.

Key Terms

agility 364
applications portfolio 361
balanced scorecard 374
barriers to entry 365
business objectives 375
business–IT alignment 355
business strategy 355
cloud strategy 368
competitive advantage 364
competitive forces model 364
digital mesh 380
edge service 368
extensibility 368
five-forces model 364
flexibility 364

in-house development 355
IT strategic planning 359
IT strategy 354
lagging indicators 374
leading indicators 375
offshoring 368
onshore sourcing 368
operating plan 355
opportunities 360
outsourcing 368
outsource relationship management (ORM)
  company 372
primary activities 366
project portfolio 361
proof of concept (POC) 373

responsiveness 364
sourcing 355
strategic planning 358
strategic technology 378
strategy 358
strengths 360
support activities 367
tactical adoption approach 368
threats 360
trail run 373
value chain model 364
value driver 358
weaknesses 360

Assuring Your Learning

Discuss: Critical Thinking Questions

1. What are the three value drivers for a major retail store, such as Macy's or Sears? Do any of them have a limited life span? Explain.

2. What directs investments in social, mobile, analytics, cloud, and other digital technology resources?

3. What are the four objectives of IT strategic plans?

4. What might be some reasons why companies use sourcing instead of in-house development?

5. In your opinion, what are the benefits of onshore sourcing?

6. What are the benefits and disadvantages of offshoring work/jobs to other countries, for example, to China or India?

7. Describe the IT strategic planning process.

8. If there are conflicting priorities and disagreements among members of the IT steering committee, how might they be resolved?

9. Review IT at Work 12.1. Why do you think strong collaborators achieved better results?

10. Why is the BSC methodology "balanced"?

11. Why are financial metrics lagging indicators?

12. Why has tactical adoption of IT become a risky approach compared to a coordinated cloud strategy?

13. Why are strategic technologies important to strategic planning?

14. Give three examples of strategic technologies and how they can influence organizational performance.

Explore: Online and Interactive Exercises

1. Visit Accenture.com and search for "outsourcing." Describe the IT outsourcing services offered by Accenture. Do the same for Deloitte at deloitte.com, Ernst & Young at ey.com, KPMG at kpmg.com, or PricewaterhouseCoopers at pwc.com. Create a table that compares the outsourcing services of two of these consulting firms.

2. Visit the Government Technology website at govtech.com. Search for "managing successful vendor relationships." Prepare a list of recommendations based on what you learn.

3. Visit the IBM website and search for "balanced scorecard." Identify and describe its BSC software product.

4. Search for a YouTube video featuring Harvard Business School's Robert Kaplan and the BSC. List three lessons learned from Kaplan, the title of the video, and its URL.

Analyze & Decide: Apply IT Concepts to Business Decisions

1. Vinay Gupta, President and CEO of Janeeva, which sells software to help companies manage outsourcing relationships, gave this advice (Bloomberg Businessweek, 2013):

    I would strongly encourage business owners to visit the vendor's facilities. There are a lot of fly-by-night operators, so you want to make sure you have touched and seen the facility before you hand them your business – I would do at least a 30-day free pilot with the provider. You want to see if it is a good fit and find out who you will be interacting with on a day-to-day basis.

    Not all companies follow this advice.

    a. Discuss why companies would take these precautions when setting up an outsourcing relationship.

    b. Discuss why companies would not take these precautions when setting up an outsourcing relationship.

2. Research legal websites discussing SLAs. Compile a list of recommendations, including what to do and what to avoid.

3. Netflix streams videos on TVs, personal computers, and smartphones using cloud services from Amazon Web Services (AWS). Its model is a direct challenge to traditional content distributors, which are limited by physical distribution and network broadcasting. In contrast, Netflix capitalizes on low cost and virtually unlimited cloud capacity to deliver content on demand almost anywhere. In 2011, Netflix's subscriber base surpassed that of Comcast, the largest cable provider in terms of subscribers, to become one of the largest video content distributors in the nation. Research Netflix to learn more about its position in the industry in the on-demand economy and explain how it is currently using cloud technologies to create business value. Research another company in the media and entertainment space—for example, Roku or Hulu. Compare the cloud strategies of the competitor to Netflix.

Case 12.2

Business Case: Cisco IT Improves Strategic Vendor Management

With more than 35,000 employees and hundreds of locations, each Cisco office has many complex requirements. Although Cisco uses its own products whenever possible, it still has an annual spend of $500 million for IT products and services from other companies.

The Problem

Working with local suppliers, Cisco encountered a number of issues. It was difficult to get formal contracts, support wasn't always there when needed, and there were often disagreements over prices and warranties. Their somewhat haphazard way of soliciting bids resulted in little or no emphasis on aligning with corporate strategy. Cisco needed to unify its vendor management process to gain greater control and reduce costs.

The Solution

Cisco created the Cisco Vendor Management Organization (VMO)— a new global IT group within Cisco—to manage strategic vendors to supply hardware infrastructure, software, storage, telecom services, and outsourced services. The VMO was also tasked with providing expertise in process and business development, asset management, and vendor engagement in keeping with Cisco's corporate strategy.

The Outcome

With standard contracts in place worldwide, Cisco could now manage existing contracts and negotiate new ones more easily. Thanks to the efforts of the VMO, Cisco saved $33 million through the first three quarters after its inception and $64 million over the life of the contracts put in place during that time! Cisco has also reduced its number of vendors and has consolidated contracts with a small number of strategic vendors to give them more business and reduce Cisco's paperwork. Cisco also works with its strategic vendors to help them develop skills and relationships to increase their value and position in the market, and Cisco is receiving the same type of support from its strategic vendors.

By centralizing its outsourcing contracts, Cisco saves $11 million per quarter.

Lesson Learned

When it comes to vendors, less is more: working with a few number of strategic vendors that help a company fulfill its business strategy. This, in turn, creates a tighter connection between the business and IT and results in closer alignment between the two strategies, saving time and money.

Questions

1. What mistakes did AstraZeneca make?

2. What mistakes did IBM make?

3. Why are outsourcing contracts for 5 or more years?

4. Why do you think two major corporations could make such mistakes?

5. Do you think the initial SLA was doomed to fail? Explain your answer.

6. What provisions in the new SLAs protect AstraZeneca and the vendors?

7. Why would parties prefer to use an arbitrator instead of filing a lawsuit in court?

Sources: Compiled from Cisco on Cisco (2017) and Gruman (2007).

Case 12.3

Data Analysis: Third-Party versus Company-Owned Offshoring

Major companies, such as Citigroup, had wholly owned offshore service centers. Those types of company-owned offshore centers are called captive models. Captive offshoring models reduce the risk of offshoring. A recent study from the Everest Research Institute estimated the costs of third-party offshoring and captive offshoring. The estimates are as follows.

Create a spreadsheet that totals the average cost of each model for each cost item. For example, average the annual salary based on the range for third parties and also the captives. Then calculate the total cost of ownership (TCO) of each model. The difference is the cost of risk.

Full-time equivalents (FTEs) are used to standardize labor costs since workers may be part time or full time. For example, two part-time workers equal one FTE. The estimates are given in terms of FTEs, so the conversion is already done.

Question

1. Based on your results, how much does the captive offshoring model allow for risk? The answer is the difference between the TCOs of the two models.

	Third-Party Offshoring Model	Captive Offshoring Model
Office space: annual rental cost per square foot (assume 10,000 square feet of office space)	$11 to $13	$14 to $16
Base salary costs of workers (assume 1,000 FTEs)	$7,770 to $8,200	$9,500 to $10,300
General management staff for every 1,000 FTEs	12 to 14	16 to 18
General management salary	$55,000 to $65,000	$70,000 to $90,000
Travel and housing costs per FTE	$280 to $320	$900 to $1,060

IT Toolbox

SWOT Analysis

As discussed in the chapter, the primary purpose of the SWOT analysis is to identify and assign significant factors that affect the business to one of the four categories to analyze where it stands in the market and help guide an organization's strategic planning process.

Don't worry about elaborating on the nature of the strengths, weaknesses, opportunities, and threats; bullet points are sufficient at this stage of the analysis. Just capture the factors that are relevant in each of the four areas using two or three words to describe them.

After listing factors in all four areas, compare your lists side by side to get an overall picture of how the businesses is performing and what issues need to be addressed. Create four prioritized lists by prioritizing the issues by importance and ease of implementation by asking yourself "What needs to and can be addressed now?" and "What can and will have to wait until later?"

Finally, review the prioritized lists by asking:

1. How can we use our strengths to take advantage of the opportunities identified?
2. How can we use these strengths to overcome the threats identified?
3. What do we need to do to overcome the identified weaknesses to take advantage of the listed opportunities?
4. How can we minimize our weaknesses to overcome the identified threats?

When you have your finalized lists, the SWOT analysis is ready to guide the process of developing corporate and IT strategies. The value of a SWOT analysis depends on how well the analysis is performed. To gain the greatest value from performing a SWOT, carrying out the SWOT early on in the strategic planning process and following these rules helps:

- Be realistic about the strengths and weaknesses of your organization.
- Be realistic about the size of the opportunities and threats.
- Be specific and keep the analysis simple or as simple as possible.
- Evaluate your company's strengths and weaknesses in relation to those of competitors (better than or worse than competitors).
- Expect conflicting views because SWOT is subjective, forward-looking, and based on assumptions.

Have fun with a Personal SWOT

To identify the actions you can take to best meet the requirements of the job or promotion you are seeking, conduct a personal SWOT analysis. To help you understand yourself, picture yourself as a competitive product in the marketplace and list your strengths, weaknesses, opportunities, or threats from the perspective of a prospective "customer," that is, employer. Comparing your strengths and weaknesses to job requirements will help you identify gaps, prepare you to be the best candidate for the position you are seeking, and alert you to issues that could arise in the interview process.

References

Bloomberg Businessweek. "Outsourcing Advice from the Pros." September 2, 2013. images.businessweek.com/ss/09/02/0213_outsourcing/10.htm

Cisco on Cisco. "Business Management Case Study: How Cisco IT Improved Strategic Vendor Management," http://www.cisco.com/en/US/about/ciscoitatwork/case_studies/business_management_dl1.html, accessed on July 17, 2017.

Corporate Knights. "2016 Global 100 Results." *Corporate Knights, The Magazine for Clean Capitalism*, Winter 2016 Issue, p. 1.

Curry, E. and B. Donnellan. "Implementing Sustainable IT Strategy: The Case of Intel," *Journal of Information Technology Teaching Cases*, v. 4, pp. 41–48. 2014.

essaacademy.org. 2017.

Gruman, G. "Why you should create a vendor management office." CIO from IDG 2007.

intel.com. 2017.

Kaplan, R. S. and D. P. Norton, "Mastering the Management System." *Harvard Business Review* 86, no. 1, January 2008.

Krishnapura, S., S. Achuthan, B. Barnard, L. Vipul, R. Nallapa, S. Rungta, and T. Tang. "Intel's Data Center Strategy for Business Transformation." *Intel White Paper.* January 2014.

Lee, J. "This Bolton School was Failing – until it gave each pupil an iPod." *The Telegraph*, January 2015.

Main, A. and J. Peto. "Cloud Orchestration." *Tech Trends 2014.* Deloitte University Press (http://dupress.com/). 2013.

Martin, R. L. "The Big Lie of Strategic Planning." *Harvard Business Review*, January–February 2014.

Pipe, M. "Seven Ideas for Using Education Technology," *SecEd*, July 2016. Accessed from: http://www.sec-ed.co.uk/best-practice/seven-ideas-for-using-educational-technology/

Richards, J. "Introduction to the Outsourcing Lifecycle." *CIO Professional Services*, July 2016. Accessed from: http://ciops.com/blog/163-introduction-to-the-outsourcing-lifecycle#.WMAzMVwsBVo

CHAPTER 13

Systems Development and Project Management

CHAPTER OUTLINE	LEARNING OBJECTIVES
Case 13.1 Opening Case: Denver International Airport Learns from Mistakes Made in Baggage-Handling System Project	
13.1 The Systems Development Life Cycle (SDLC)	**13.1 Describe** the activities that occur in each of the phases of the systems development life cycle (SDLC) and identify the four types of system conversion strategies.
13.2 Software Development Methodologies	**13.2 Describe** and compare the different systems development methodologies.
13.3 Project Management Fundamentals	**13.3 Understand** the five phases of the project management life cycle, and explain the role of the triple constraint in project management.
13.4 Initiating, Planning, and Executing Projects	**13.4 Describe** the activities of the initiating and planning phases of the project management life cycle and the tools and techniques used.
13.5 Monitoring, Controlling, and Closing Projects	**13.5 Describe** the activities of the monitoring/controlling and closing phases of the project management life cycle and the tools and techniques used. Explain why projects fail, and describe the conditions under which an ongoing project should be cancelled.
Case 13.2 Business Case: Steve Jobs' Shared Vision Project Management Style	
Case 13.3 Demo Case: Mavenlink Project Management and Planning Software	

Introduction

As an informed user of IT, it's important to know how organizations develop information systems (ISs) and manage IT projects. A basic understanding of the principles of systems development will enable you to spot mistakes and make suggestions during the development process to increase the success of the project. As you learned in Chapter 12, systems can be acquired in a number of different ways. The way a system is sourced often depends on the number and skill level of IT professionals who are employed in an organization. Regardless of the manner in which systems are acquired, most companies use the **systems development life cycle (SDLC)** to guide them through the process.

And, all systems development projects have to be managed. When companies develop or build new products, services, markets, enterprise systems, or apps, they typically use a project management approach. Project management is a structured methodology to plan, manage, and control the completion of a project throughout its life cycle. The project life cycle starts with an idea or concept and project plan. If the project is approved, then the project team proceeds to perform the tasks and deliver the **project**. As part of closing the project, participants conduct a **post mortem** to document lessons learned in order to improve future projects.

Project management and an appropriate system development process help to get the IT project delivered on time, within budget, and according to specifications. But, IT projects are inherently risky. In a recent survey, PricewaterhouseCoopers reported that only 55% of digital projects were completed according to specifications, that is, set out to do what they said they would do (Konrad, 2017). To minimize risk of failure, the project needs to be rigorously planned, evaluated, and monitored. Weekly status meetings, communication, and reporting are critical to find out about potential problems as far in advance as possible and fix them to avert a crisis. Project management is gaining in importance for all types of projects because of technology complexity, tighter budgets, tougher competition, and shorter time-to-delivery requirements. In short, companies cannot afford project failures or delays.

Case 13.1 Opening Case

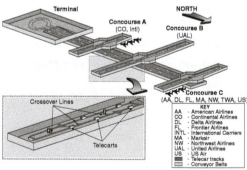

Denver International Airport Learns from Mistakes Made in Failed Baggage-Handling System Project

This classic project management case illustrates almost every possible project management mistake and the lessons that were learned from it. It documents a project disaster that occurred in the development of the baggage-handling system at Denver International Airport (DIA) in the late 1980s and early 1990s. The failure of the baggage-handling system propelled DIA into newspaper headlines across the country, and people joked that if you were flying to Denver, you had to go to Chicago to pick up your luggage! To this day, it remains the classic example of how not to conduct a project.

The purpose of the DIA project was to create the most advanced automated handling of baggage in the world by integrating baggage handling at all three concourses into a single system. The terms "most advanced, automated, and integrated" clearly indicate that the system was going to be extremely complex, risky, and subject to delays. Unfortunately, an unrealistic schedule was planned and the project approved despite the fact that experts warned that the project was infeasible and that any delay would postpone the opening of Denver's new state-of-the-art international airport.

As a result of the project's failure, the newly completed international airport designed to service multiple major airlines remained idle for 16 months while engineers dealt with the complexities of the baggage-handling system. During that time, the project had to be scaled down from the original project plan to servicing all concourses to servicing only one concourse. The system was working, but only in segments. Only baggage handling on outbound flights for one concourse was automated. Instead, baggage to/from other concourses had to be handled using a manual tug-and-trolley system that was quickly built when key players finally acknowledged that the automated system would never meet its goals. The problem appeared to be with the software required to get different systems to talk to each other.

The delay resulted in an additional $560 million to build DIA and a U.S. Securities and Exchange Commission probe into whether Denver officials had deliberately deceived bondholders about how equipment malfunctions would affect the opening of DIA. In addition, at least one major airline that was scheduled to occupy DIA pulled out, resulting in one entire concourse remaining unused for several years. The cost of maintaining the empty airport and interest charges on construction loans also cost the city of Denver $1.1 million per day throughout the delay. Ten years after its implementation, the automated baggage-handling system was scrapped because it still did not work correctly.

The System

DIA's $200 million baggage-handling system was designed to be state of the art. Conventional baggage-handling systems are manual, and each airline operates its own system. DIA wanted an automated one-baggage-system-fits-all configuration that it could lease back to multiple airlines.

The system would consist of 100 computers, 56 laser scanners, conveyor belts, and thousands of motors. The system would contain 400 fiberglass carts, each carrying a single suitcase through 22 miles of steel track. Operating at 20 miles per hour, the system would deliver 60,000 bags per hours from dozens of gates. The system was designed to carry luggage from airplane to baggage carousel in less than 10 minutes. The goal was that the luggage would be waiting at the carousel for deplaning passengers. No more waiting for baggage at the end of a long trip—so customer satisfaction would soar.

The baggage-handling system would be centered on track-mounted cars that slow down, but don't stop, as a conveyor ejects bags onto their platform. A scanner reads the bar-coded label and transmits the data through a programmable logic controller to an RFID tag on a passing car. In this way, the car knows the destination of the bag it's carrying, as does the computer software that routes the car to its destination. Imagine thousands of driverless taxi cabs in New York City being controlled by a computer as they pick up and dispatch passengers throughout the streets.

The Team

The city of Denver selected two companies to assist in the project management process. Greiner Engineering—an engineering, architecture, and airport planning company—and Morrison-Knudsen Engineering—a design-construction organization. The City of Denver, Greiner, and MKE made up the project management team that coordinated schedules, controlled costs, managed information, and administered approximately 100 design contract, 160 general contractors, and more than 2,000 subcontractors.

What Went Wrong

DIA's baggage-handling system was a critical component in the city of Denver's plan to construct a new state-of-the-art airport that would position Denver as an air transportation hub. By automating baggage handling, aircraft turnaround time was to be cut to as little as 30 minutes. Faster turnaround meant airlines could minimize on-ground time, which would be DIA's competitive advantage.

Following is the timeline of the major events and project management mistakes:

- November 1989: DIA construction work starts.
- **Ignored experts**   In 1990, the City of Denver hired Breier Neidle Patrone Associates to do a feasibility analysis to build a fully integrated baggage system. Reports advised that complexity made the project unfeasible. Experts from Munich airport advised that the much simpler Munich system had taken two full years to build and that it had run 24/7 for 6 months prior to opening to allow bugs to be ironed out.
- Summer 1991: A decision is made to go ahead with the DIA project and the DIA project management team asked for bids for the automated baggage-handling system.
- **Underestimated complexity**   Fall 1991: Of the 16 companies included in the bidding process, only 3 responded. None could complete the project in time for the October 1993 opening. All three bids were rejected, and the urgent search for a company that would meet the deadline continued.
- **Poor planning and impossible expectations**   In April 1992, DIA went to contract with BAE Systems to complete the project in time for the October 1993 opening—ignoring expert evidence that the timeline was impossible to achieve.
- **Lack of due diligence**   Contract terms between DIA and BAE and project specifications were hammered out in only three meetings. The rush to contract ignored the feasibility analysis. The pressure to move quickly drove them to skip critical due-diligence steps.
- **Excluded key stakeholders**   BAE and the airport project management team excluded key stakeholders—the airlines that had contracted with DIA—during the negotiations. Excluding stakeholders from discussions in which key project decisions are made is always a losing strategy.
- **Scope creep**   1992–1993: Numerous changes in the scope of the project are made. For instance, Continental Airlines requested ski equipment handling facilities be added to its concourse, and the scope of the baggage-handling system expanded from handling only Concourse "B" baggage to handling baggage for the entire airport.
- **Ignored interface design**   The baggage-handling system had to interface with the airport. That is, because the design of the building was started before the baggage system design was known, the designers of the physical building only made general allowances for where they thought the baggage system

would go. The allowance of spaces in which the baggage system would operate represented the interface between the design of DIA and the baggage system. To make effective decisions about how to design DIA, the DIA designers should have worked with experts in designing the baggage system. DIA had sharp corners that required turns that baggage carts cannot navigate. To keep carts from falling off the rails, the speed of the system had to be decreased to 30 cars per minute. This change frustrated passengers who had to wait inordinately long times to pick up their baggage, thus eliminating DIA's competitive advantage of fast baggage turnaround time.

Lessons Learned

Despite the fact that they are 6 months into formal negotiations for the project, as of March 7, 2017, DIA officials are still not ready to ink the deal with the bid team for a massive planned renovation of Jeppesen Terminal. Although 6 months was the length of time allotted for negotiations as part of a "predevelopment agreement," DIA spokesman Heath Montgomery said airport officials are still working out project details and design that could be worth hundreds of millions of dollars. When asked how much longer it would take to complete the deal, Montgomery declined to estimate how soon the two sides would propose a full development agreement for public scrutiny and said "We have the ability to stretch it out as long as we need to." Under the council-approved predevelopment contract, DIA CEO Kim Day can extend the negotiations period by up to six additional months without council approval.

Conclusion

From a project management perspective, the baggage-handling system was doomed from the start. Nobody knew how to design the baggage-handling system or realized the complexity of the software requirements. The decision to proceed with a single integrated system at DIA knowing that the deadline could not be met, not considering possible risks and making other irrational decisions, contributed heavily to project failure.

As a result, the DIA baggage-handling project was a spectacular failure that teaches us a lot about project communication and scope creep and has become the classic example of how not to manage a project. And, at DIA, the massive project failure has led to better project management practices.

Questions

1. In what ways did the baggage-handling project fail?

2. What red flags indicated that the baggage-handling project was likely to be a failure?

3. Which red flags were ignored in the DIA automated luggage-handling project?

4. Why do you think each of these best practice and red flags were ignored?

5. In your opinion, who are the ones responsible for the failure of this important project?

Sources: Calleam.com (2008), Grimes (2013), Coolman (2014), Perkins (2014), and Murray (2017).

13.1 System Development Life Cycle

ISs are driven by a number of factors including the need for improved services, reduced costs, stronger controls, better performance, more and better information, and support for new products and services. They are developed by people who are technically qualified, business oriented, and highly motivated. Systems developers must be good communicators with strong analytical and critical thinking skills.

The SDLC is a multiple-stage approach used by IT professionals to develop high-quality ISs from planning and analysis through support and maintenance. The SDLC provides a framework for a number of different systems development methodologies (discussed later in the chapter). Typical SDLC activities include gathering the user requirements, determining budgets, creating a logical systems design, creating a physical systems system, building and testing the system, writing detailed user and developer documentation, training users, and maintaining the system. The activities performed during systems development vary depending on the size and complexity of the system.

Stages of the SDLC

The SDLC consists of five stages, shown in **Figure 13.1**. The SDLC stages are planning, analysis, design, implementation/testing, and support/maintenance. Each stage consists of well-defined tasks based on the scope of the project. The SDLC is an iterative process, not a linear one. This means that when results from one stage are assessed, they can be revised, if needed, and a previous stage can be revisited before continuing on to the next stage.

Systems Planning
To begin the SDLC, a business unit submits a systems request based on a business need and systems planning begins (Figure 13.1). The systems request begins the planning process by describing the problem or desired changes. The purpose of the planning stage is to perform a preliminary investigation and to find out if the request is feasible.

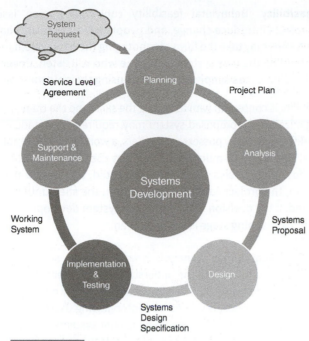

FIGURE 13.1 Systems development life cycle.

A feasibility study determines the probability of success of a proposed system and provides a rough assessment of its technical, economic, organizational, and behavioral feasibility. The feasibility study is critical to the system development process because, when done properly, the study can prevent companies from making expensive mistakes, such as those experienced at DIA in the opening case, where systems are created that will not work, that will not work efficiently, or that people cannot or will not use. The Census Bureau case in IT at Work 13.1 is another useful example. The various feasibility analyses also give the stakeholders an opportunity to decide what metrics to use to measure how a proposed system meets their objectives.

- **Technical feasibility**   Technical feasibility determines if the required technology, IT infrastructure, data structures, analytics, and resources can be developed and/or acquired to solve the business problem. Technical feasibility also determines if the organization's existing technology can be used to achieve the project's performance objectives.

- **Economic feasibility**   Economic feasibility determines if the project is an acceptable financial risk and if the company can afford the expense and time needed to complete the project. Economic feasibility addresses two primary questions: Do the benefits outweigh the costs of the project? Can the project be completed as scheduled?

Management can assess economic feasibility by using cost–benefit analysis and financial techniques such as time value of money, return on investment (ROI), net present value (NPV), and breakeven analysis. ROI is the ratio of the net income attributable to a project divided by the average cost of resources invested in the project. NPV is the net amount by which project benefits exceed project costs, after allowing for the cost of capital and the time value of money. Breakeven analysis calculates the point at which the cumulative cash flow from a project equals the investment made in the project.

Calculating economic feasibility in IT projects is rarely straightforward. Part of the difficulty is that some benefits are intangible. For a proposed system that involves big data, real-time analytics, or 3D printing, there may be no previous evidence of what sort of financial payback can be expected.

- **Legal and organizational feasibility**   Are there legal, regulatory, or environmental reasons why the project cannot or should not be implemented? This analysis looks at the company's policies and politics, including impacts on power distribution and business relationships.

- **Behavioral feasibility** Behavioral feasibility considers human issues. All system development projects introduce change, and people generally resist change. Overt resistance from employees may take the form of sabotaging the new system (e.g., entering data incorrectly) or deriding the new system to anyone who will listen. Covert resistance typically occurs when employees simply do their jobs using their old methods.

Behavioral feasibility is concerned with assessing the skills and the training needed to use the new IS. In some organizations, a proposed system may require mathematical or linguistic skills beyond what the workforce currently possesses. In others, a workforce may simply need to improve their skills. Behavioral feasibility is as much about "can they use it" as it is about "will they use it."

Go/no-go Decision A determination to proceed with or abandon a plan or project.

After the initial feasibility analysis has been completed, a **go/no-go decision** is reached. If it is a no-go decision, the project can be revised. put on the shelf until conditions are more favorable, or discarded. If the decision is "go," then the system development project proceeds. The deliverable from the planning stage is a Project Plan.

Systems Analysis

Requirements analysis is critical to the success of the project. The purpose of systems analysis is to analyze and understand the problem identified in the planning stage by gathering user requirements. This can be accomplished by observing how the business process that the system will support is carried out, interviewing users, sending out a questionnaire, or applying knowledge gleaned in developing similar systems. During this stage, process models are created to establish the **logical design** of the system and explore alternative solutions to create the system. The deliverable from the systems analysis stage is the Systems Proposal.

Logical design lists and describes all the information resources (data and processes) and the scope of duties and responsibilities of consumers of the information involved in the operation of the new system. It is business focused and always precedes physical design.

System development practitioners agree that the more time invested in planning and analyzing the current system, business problem, or opportunity and understanding problems that are likely to occur during development, the greater the probability that the new system will be a success.

Systems Design

In the systems design stage, system developers utilize the design specifications to create the user interface and establish data requirements. They also develop the **physical design** of the system by determining and acquiring the hardware and software needed to carry out the logical design of the system. Next, they create user and system documentation. During the design stage, management and user involvement is critical to ensure that business requirements are being met. The deliverable from the design stage is the System Design Specification.

Physical design transforms business requirements into a specific technological solution by identifying all physical servers and major technical components that will be used to support the desired business outcome.

Implementation and Testing

Implementation, or deployment, is the process of converting from the old system to the new system. During this stage of the SDLC, the system is actually put in place and tested. There are four ways that the new system can be installed. We call these the four "Ps" of systems conversion: plunge, parallel, pilot, and phased.

In the **plunge**, or direct, conversion, the old system is cut off and the new system is turned on at a specified time. This type of conversion is the least expensive, but it is the riskiest if the new system does not work as planned.

In a **parallel** conversion, the old system and the new system operate concurrently for a specified period of time. That is, both systems process the same data at the same time, and the outputs are compared. This type of conversion is the most expensive but least risky.

A **pilot** conversion introduces the new system in one location, or with one group of people, to test it out. After the new system works properly, it is rolled out to the entire organization.

A **phased** conversion introduces components of the new system, such as individual modules, in stages. Each module is assessed, and, when it works properly, other modules are introduced until the entire new system is operational.

One the system is up and running, testing verifies that apps, interfaces, data transfers, and so on work correctly under all possible conditions. Testing requires a lot of time, effort, and expense to do properly. However, the costs and consequences of improper testing, which could possibly lead to a system that does not meet its objectives, are enormous.

Finally, users are trained in the use of the system and provided with the user documentation created during the design stage. The deliverable from the implementation and testing stage is the new working system.

Support and Maintenance Once the new system's operations are stabilized, *audits* are performed during operation to assess the system's capabilities and determine if it is being used correctly. Maintenance must be kept up rigorously at all times. Users of the system should be kept up to date concerning the latest modifications and procedures.

This phase also involves supporting users in their use of the system according to any service level agreements (SLAs) that may be in place. The deliverable from the support and maintenance stage is the SLA.

Since most ISs need to be updated significantly or replaced after several years of operation, systems development is a repetitive process as maintenance turns into the development of a new system.

Questions

1. What are the five stages of the SDLC?
2. Name the deliverables from three of the five SDLC stages.
3. Explain the purpose of feasibility tests and why they are important in developing ISs.
4. Is the systems development process a linear or a cyclical process? Explain.
5. Name the four system conversion methods.

13.2 Systems Development Methodologies

While there is only one SDLC, there are many different methods associated with creating ISs. The major systems development methodologies are waterfall, object-oriented, and agile. Each of these are explained next.

Waterfall Model

The **Waterfall Model** was the first SDLC model to be used widely in systems development (**Figure 13.2**). Sometimes known as "structured analysis," the Waterfall Model is a *sequential, predictive approach*. It is very simple to use and understand, but is quite inflexible. Using the Waterfall Model, each phase of the SDLC must be completed before the next phase can begin.

Waterfall Model is a sequential, predictive systems development methodology that is simple to use and understand, but inflexible.

FIGURE 13.2 Waterfall Method.

There is no opportunity to go back to a previous stage and no overlapping in the phases. Recordkeeping is extremely important in the Waterfall method to keep everything on track within each clearly defined stage according to the project plan.

The Waterfall Model is particularly useful for small systems, short-term projects, when it is very unlikely that requirements will change and when there are no ambiguous requirements. A disadvantage of developing a system using the Waterfall Model is that it doesn't allow for much reflection or revision. This can be problematic since users are notorious for seeing opportunities for changing or adding features during development.

Object-Oriented Analysis and Design

Object-oriented (O-O) is an iterative systems analysis and design methodology that emphasizes modularity and reusability.

Unlike the sequential predictive Waterfall Model, **object-oriented (O-O)** is an *iterative, adaptive* systems analysis and design method. O-O analysis and design is a popular approach for systems development that emphasizes modularity and reusability and encourages better communication between analysts, developers, and users. The introduction of the O-O approach in the 1970s marked a radical change in systems development. In O-O analysis, entities that interact with each other are grouped together to create a model that accurately represents the purpose of the new system using terminology that is close to that used in the users' every day work.

O-O views a system as a collection of modular objects that encapsulate data and processes. Objects are such things as people, things, transactions, and events. For example, in a college admissions system, objects of interest might include student, course, and major. By keeping data and processes together, developers save time and avoid errors by using reusable program modules that have been tested and verified. And, the iterative nature of O-O allows changes to be made along the way.

A large part of O-O analysis is the unified modeling language (UML) and use cases. UML uses a set of symbols to graphically represent the various components and relationships within a system and is used primarily to support O-O analysis and develop object models. Use cases are a simple to construct and easy to understand graphical representation of the existing system early on in the systems development process and reflect user requirements for the new system in later models.

Use-case diagram is a graphic depiction of the major elements (use cases) within a system and it environment.

Use-case description is a text-based list of actions or steps that detail the interactions between users and the system needed to achieve the goal of the system.

Use-Case Model Use cases show business events, who or what objects initiated the events, and how the system responds to the events. A use case has two parts: **use-case diagram**, which is a visual summary of several related use cases within a system; and a **use-case description**, which is a text-based description of the business event and how users will interact with the system to accomplish the task (**Figure 13.3**).

Using O-O analysis and design methods to develop systems can potentially produce more reliable and useable systems. The O-O approach promotes a better understanding of a system, making information easier to use and reuse throughout a system, and developing a system that can be easily modified or changed to make maintenance easier. It also helps reduce the complexity of the systems development process.

Agile Methodology

Agile is a very flexible iterative, incremental systems development methodology that overcomes the disadvantages of the Waterfall model.

The **Agile** methodology is the most flexible of all systems development methodologies. Agile uses an *iterative, incremental approach* to overcome the disadvantages of the sequential Waterfall Model. The goal of Agile is to deliver software components early and often through a highly iterative process. Developers begin with a simplistic project design and begin to work on small modules. The Agile methodology addresses the problems of rapid change occurring in the on-demand economy, such as changes in market forces, system requirements, and project staff. Agile methodologies minimize risk by breaking down the project into small manageable chunks called iterations and puts a strong emphasis on real-time communication and teamwork.

In doing so, Agile focuses on the collaboration and communication skills of its participants. For example, instead of Agile managers creating a structured contract with the project sponsor, they focus on creating a collaborative relationship. Using Agile, the emphasis is on competency

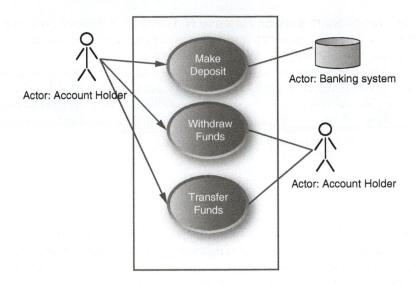

Use case name	States the use case name. Typically, the name expresses the objective or observable result of the use case, such as "Withdraw Cash" in the case of an ATM machine.
Brief description	Describes the role and purpose of the use case. i.e., Make Deposit
Actor(s)	Names of actor(s) involved in the use case. i.e., Account holder, banking system
Typical flow	Describes the ideal, primary steps involved in this use case.
Alternative flows	Describe exceptions or deviations from the basic flow, such as how the process works when the actor enters an incorrect user ID and the user authentication fails.
Special requirements	Specify any nonfunctional requirement that is specific to a use case but is not specified in the text of the use case flow of events. Examples of special requirements include: legal and regulatory requirements; application standards; quality attributes of the system, including usability, reliability, performance, and supportability; operating systems and environments; compatibility requirements; and design constraints.
Preconditions	A state of the system that must be present before a use case is performed, i.e., what triggers the use case?
Post conditions	A list of possible states for the system immediately after a use case is finished.
Assumptions	List the gaps in your information for this use case. What (if anything) did you have to assume when completing the description?

FIGURE 13.3   An object-oriented use-case model has two parts: the use-case diagram and the use-case description. Here's a simple example of an account holder interacting with a banking ATM.

rather than process where reaching the goal is more important than how you get there. As a result, teams in rigid organizations find it difficult to adjust to the fluidity of the Agile method.

The Agile process has four stages, sometimes called tracks, shown in **Figure 13.4**. These stages (warmup, construction, release, and production) have many simultaneously occurring activities that cause them to be much less structured than activities in other types of systems development methodologies. So much so that some feel that a method as flexible as Agile shouldn't even have stages.

Advantages of using Agile include ease of making changes, adding features, and incorporating client feedback and early identification of glitches in the system. Disadvantages include requirement of a good project manager and the absence of a definitive plan at the beginning of the SDLC that can cause the final product to be significantly different from that originally intended.

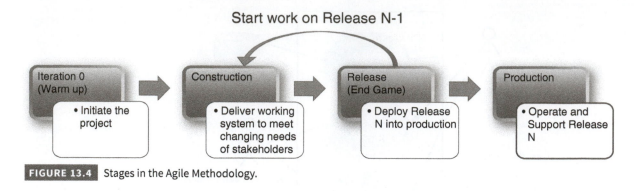

FIGURE 13.4 Stages in the Agile Methodology.

Created by the Agile Alliance, Agile systems development is the umbrella term used for a number of different software development methods including scrum and extreme programming. These are discussed next.

Scrum

Sprints is a set period of time during which specific work has to be completed and made ready for review. Traditionally, a sprint lasts 30 days.

Scrum is a framework that consists of small self-organizing, cross-functional Scrum Teams who work together to produce small pieces of a system iteratively and incrementally in **sprints** to maximize opportunities for feedback. At the end of each sprint, project priorities are evaluated, and acceptance tests are run and evaluated. These short sprints allow for errors to be found and customer feedback that can be incorporated into the design before the next sprint is run. Every day, a 15-minute Daily Scrum is held to synchronize activities and create a plan for the next 24 hours.

The Scrum approach is centered around three tenets: *transparency* (sharing a common understanding of the work), *inspection* (users must be able to frequently inspect Scrum output and progress), and *adaptation* (if an inspection reveals one or more deviation outside of acceptable limits, it must be adjusted as quickly as possible to minimize further deviation).

Extreme Programming

Extreme programming is a pragmatic systems development to Agile development that emphasizes business results first and takes an incremental approach to building software, using continual testing and revision.

Using **Extreme programming**, software is developed in small pieces that make little sense on their own, but when put together, they form a system—somewhat like putting jigsaw pieces together to complete a jigsaw puzzle. The first step in developing a system using extreme programming is to create user stories in which use requirements are documented to understand what the user wants the system to do. Next, acceptance tests are conducted to make sure that the system produces the results that the user wants. Gaining verification of the functionality by the user in this way shifts the responsibility to the user. Finally, after user approval, small releases are delivered. Extreme programming works because it creates good communication between developers and users, designs are simple and efficient, feedback is obtained at every step of the project, and the methodology adapts well to changes.

The DevOps Approach to Systems Development

DevOps is a set of processes that encourages collaboration between system developers, operators and testers.

The latest development methodology to emerge is **DevOps**—short for software DEVelopment and IT OPerations. DevOps is a set of processes that emphasize *collaboration between software developers, operators, and* testers involved in the development and operations of ISs. The popularity of Agile and its increased number of releases led to the creation of a DevOps way of thinking. When a system is delivered that doesn't work the way user wants it to, there is a saying that the system "worked in development."

Gaps in communication and understanding between development, operations, and testing personnel can lead to this type of situation. DevOps was developed to address this gap in communication and collaboration and create a culture where building, testing, and delivery of a system can happen quickly, frequently, and reliably (**Figure 13.5**). The goal of DevOps is to lower the failure rate of new releases, shorten lead time between fixes, enable shorter time to market and mean time to recovery.

FIGURE 13.5   DevOps

Organizations that use DevOps have reported significant benefits such as shorter time to market, improved customer satisfaction, better product quality, more reliable release, improved productivity and efficiency, and the ability to build the right product.

Unlike other systems development methodologies, DevOps requires a change in organizational culture to bring together somewhat incompatible departments such as IT operators, developers, and testers who have different motivations. To build this type of culture, organizations are using team-building and engagement activities such as games, trust activities, and seminars.

Questions

1. Name the different types of systems development methodologies.
2. What the is the main difference between the Waterfall method and the Agile method?
3. Why is it important for an organization to be flexible when developing ISs?
4. Why is the concept of DevOps appealing to organizations?

13.3 Project Management Fundamentals

Many organizations today have a new or renewed interest in **projects** and **project management**. The world as a whole spends nearly 25% of its gross product on projects of all kinds, and more than 16 million people view project management as their profession. Organizations can benefit from using a formal project management approach to carry out their IT projects in the following ways:

- Better control of financial, physical, and human resources (HR)
- Improved customer relations
- Short development times
- Lower costs
- High quality and increased reliability
- High profit margins
- Improved productivity
- Better internal coordination
- Higher worker morale

Projects   is a temporary endeavor undertaken to create a unique product, service, or result.

Project management   is the application of knowledge, skills, tools, and techniques to project activities to meet project requirements.

What Is a Project?

Unlike day-to-day operations, that is, work performed to sustain business, projects end when their objectives have been reached or the project has been terminated. Projects can range from small to large and can take anywhere from a few hours to many years to complete. For example, a small software development team may add a new feature to an in-house software application for the marketing department, or a college decides to upgrade its technology infrastructure to provide wireless Internet access across the whole campus.

Regardless of size or length of time they take to complete, all projects require a variety of resources and have a primary sponsor who usually provides the direction and funding for the project. And, every project involves certain elements of risk. The typical characteristics associated with a project are shown in **Table 13.1**.

TABLE 13.1   Distinguishing Characteristics of Projects
A project has these characteristics.
• Clearly defined scope, deliverables, and results
• An estimated time frame or schedule that is subject to a high degree of uncertainty
• An estimated budget that is subject to a high degree of uncertainty
• The requirement of extensive interaction among participants
• Tasks that may compete or conflict with other business activities, which makes planning and scheduling difficult
• Risky but with a high profit potential or benefits

Program   is a set of related projects.

Portfolio   is the entire set of projects within a department or organization.

While many business managers do not manage projects, almost everyone will be a member of a project team at some time during their career. As such, you'll need to understand the basics of project management. Project management has evolved from being project-centric to three distinct management levels: project, **program** and **portfolio** management. Although the terms project management and program management are sometimes used synonymously unlike projects, programs don't always have a single, clearly defined deliverable or a finite time horizon.

A fundamental difference between programs and projects is the pattern of activities over time requiring programs be managed differently, typically demanding more than planning, tracking, and controlling projects. Similarly, for projects to drive business goals, portfolio managers require a holistic view of programs and projects to improve ROI and attain strategic alignment.

Choosing Projects

Business case   is a presentation or document that outlines the justification for the start-up and funding of a project.

Enterprises face the challenge of choosing which investments will add most value in a business and how to allocate scarce resources to competing projects. Typically, a senior manager composes a **business case** that identifies an opportunity, problem, or need and the desired business outcomes of the project. Since not all projects are viable and not all viable projects can be funded, the business cases are reviewed. In the review process, projects compete for approval and funding.

Project analysis methods are used to prioritize proposed projects and allocate the budget for maximum return. Budgeting decisions apply to all business investments, such as construction to increase manufacturing capacity, entering new markets, modernizing retail stores, R&D, and acquiring IT, apps, and enterprise systems. Investments in IT for marketing or manufacturing innovations compete head-on with investments needed to comply with new laws and regulations in finance, accounting, HR, and cybersecurity.

When companies are evaluating projects they need to examine them holistically to see how they will help the company achieve its mission—that is, all projects currently proposed or running should be assessed to identify investment synergies. This approach is known as **project portfolio management (PPM)**. PPM is a set of business practices to manage projects as a strategic portfolio. PPM ensures the alignment of programs and projects with organizational objectives. Executive management needs to review portfolios and programs, determine why projects are or are not necessary, see where money is spent, prioritize projects, stage the start of new projects, spread resources appropriately, and then keep tabs on progress.

PPM establishes a path from the concept through successful project completion. Without the necessary data, management is incapable of making informed decisions to approve the "right" new projects and to shut down projects with no hope for success:

- Map proposed projects to organizational strategies.
- Assess the value that a proposed project brings to the company.
- Assess the complexity of proposed projects.
- Prioritize project proposals for project selection.

The Triple Constraint

There are three aspects of a project that must always be carefully managed by the project manager as he/she works with project sponsors, the project team, and other stakeholders to meet the project objectives and produce the project **deliverables**. This is called the **triple constraint**.

The triple constraint (**Figure 13.6**) refers to three core knowledge areas that must be managed effectively for successful completion and closure of any project.

> **Deliverable** is any measurable, tangible, verifiable outcome, result, or item that is produced to complete a project or part of a project. Examples might be hardware, software, planning documents, or meeting minutes.
>
> **Triple constraint** is the combination of the three most significant elements of any project: scope, time and cost. It is also known as the iron triangle.

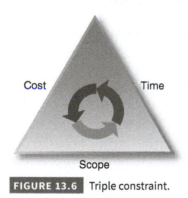

FIGURE 13.6 Triple constraint.

1. **Scope** The project scope is the specification of what the project is supposed to accomplish—its outcomes or deliverables. Scope is measured in terms of the project size, goals, and requirements.

2. **Time** A project is made up of *tasks*. Each task has a start date and an end date. The duration of a project extends from the start date of the first task to the finish date of the last task. Time needed to produce the deliverables is naturally related to the scope and availability of resources allocated to the project.

3. **Cost** This is the estimation of the amount of money that will be required to complete the project. Cost itself encompasses various things, such as resources, labor rates for contractors, risk estimates, and bills of materials, and so on. All aspects of the project that have a monetary component are made part of the overall cost structure. Projects are often approved based on cost.

These three constraints are closely interrelated so that a change in any one of the three constraints manifests a change in the other two. Ignoring the potential repercussions of adjusting the scope, time, or cost of a project will lead to problems and may cause the project to fail.

The Project Management Framework

Not using a best-practice project management approach within the systems development life cycle is the biggest IT project mistake a business can make. **Tech Note 13.1** provides good advice on this topic. Project management helps keep projects on schedule and on budget.

A good project management plan identifies anticipated costs early on to develop a realistic budget. Using resource conflict solutions, project managers can minimize the effect of funding a new project on operating capital by optimizing the allocation of workers. Coordinating tasks and clearly identifying goals or deliverables within phases reduce inefficiencies in time management that can result in being over budget.

Tech Note 13.1

Six Basic Systems Development Guidelines

1. Always develop a project plan.
2. Involve all stakeholders and listen carefully to them at all stages of the project.
3. Encourage teamwork and commitment to the project.
4. Use project management tools to identify tasks and milestones.
5. Perform accurate cost/benefit analysis.
6. Remain flexible.

The PMI® Project Management Body of Knowledge (PMBOK 5e) is the definitive guide for managing projects of all types. Developed by the Project Management Institute, a highly regarded international project management association, the PMBOK is a framework that guides project managers through the five phases that they refer to as process groups, while addressing 10 areas involved in best-practice project management.

Five Phases of the Project Management Life Cycle The five phases of project management are: Initiating, Planning, Executing, Monitoring/Controlling, and Closing (**Figure 13.7**). Each of these five phases consists of a number of procedures that need to be completed to achieve a successful project outcome and produce a number of documents to pass on to the next stage. There are a total of 47 procedures that may be performed during the project management life cycle, depending on the scope and complexity of the project. These procedures, inputs, outputs, and tools and techniques used to produce them are discussed in detail in Sections 13.4 and 13.5 of this chapter.

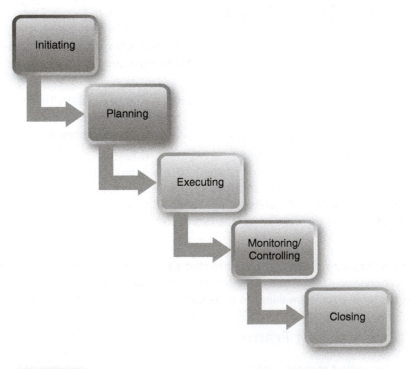

FIGURE 13.7 The five phases of the project management life cycle. All projects, IT or otherwise, move through five phases of the project management life cycle.

Ten Knowledge Areas of Project Management   To efficiently and effectively move through each phase of the project management life cycles, project managers must manage 10 knowledge areas that impact the completion of any project. Four of these knowledge areas are referred to as "core" areas, one is referred to as "integrating," and five are "support" areas (**Figure 13.8**).

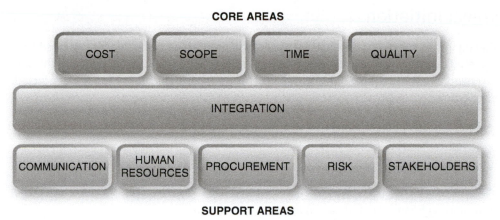

FIGURE 13.8   Ten Knowledge Areas of Project Management.

The knowledge areas that a project manager has to manage, monitor, and control make sense when you think about what you need to pay attention to when completing a project. Let's take a simple example of organizing a tailgating party. Before you start, you have to know the **scope** of the tailgating event you want to organize, how much **time** you have before the event needs to begin, and how much it will **cost** to achieve the desired outcome. Now, you'll want to make sure that everyone has a good time, so you'll want to make sure that you understand what's involved in creating and delivering a **quality** product. Once these areas of the project are understood, you'll need some support—**communication** will tell you how, when, and with whom to communicate, **human resources** will help you focus on who should be involved in the planning, execution, and monitoring of the event, a knowledge of HR will help you find the **people** that you need to organize the event, and **procurement** will help you find suppliers for items that you haven't already got, and you'll have to consider **risk**, just in case it rains or the game is cancelled. Lastly, but certainly not least, you'll need to make sure that you understand how to handle all the people interested in the tailgating event, that is, your **stakeholders**.

Successful project managers consistently apply the PMBOK framework to bring in high-quality results and bring projects in on time and on budget. In the next section, you will learn how to apply the project management framework in managing projects.

Scope   is the body of work that needs to be completed within a project to achieve a desired outcome.

Questions

1. What distinguishes a project from day-to-day operations?
2. What are the three components of the triple constraint?
3. What are the five process groups in the project management life cycle?
4. Why is it important to use a structured project management approach to IT projects?

13.4 Initiating, Planning, and Executing Projects

While all phases of the project management life cycle need to be carefully planned and executed, the first two phases of the project management life cycle are particularly important. If the existing business environment and needs of project stakeholders are not considered and the project is not planned well, it is very unlikely that it will achieve its objectives. Walking through the project management life cycle stage by stage and learning about the tools and techniques that project managers use in each stage is a good way to understand the mechanics of project management.

Project Initiation

Initiating involves deciding on what the project will produce and what work tasks need to be performed in order to achieve the desired outcome. To do this, you must understand the business environment and the way it works. Some of the key activities in the initiating stage include the following:

- Analyzing business requirements
- Identifying stakeholders and their roles
- Identifying stakeholder needs
- Evaluating business processes
- Reviewing financial reports and budgets
- Conducting a feasibility analysis
- Choosing a project manager
- Setting up the project team

During the initiating stage, you will create a number of documents to define the new project. Often a feasibility study (similar to the one described in the earlier part of this chapter) is performed and/or a business case is developed.

Preparing a Business Case
Projects start with an idea that is explained in a business case. To justify a project, a project manager, senior executive, or sponsor prepares a convincing business case for consideration.

Statement of Work (SOW)
If the business case is accepted, a **statement of work (SOW)** is prepared. The SOW is written as a definitive statement, which means that it defines the project plan but does not offer any options or alternatives in the scope. The project plan in the SOW is reviewed; a go or no-go decision is made; if a go decision is made, the project is initiated.

Templates is a sample document that already has some details in place.

Templates are often used to create many of the project management documents, including the business case and the SOW. The IT Toolbox at the end of this chapter contains a Business Case and SOW Template representative of those typically used in the Initiating stage.

Project Charter
An essential part of the initiating stage is the preparation of a **project charter** (Figure 13.9).

The project charter specifies the scope of the project, gives the project manager authority over the project, provides summary milestones, specifies the project budget, and identifies the source of project funding. Most importantly, the project charter formally approves the project so that it can progress to the Planning stage.

Once the business case has been reviewed and the project has received initial approval to proceed, it's time to move on to the next and much more complex phase of the project.

Project Planning

The Planning stage further clarifies the project objectives and plans all of the necessary activities to complete the project. The Planning stages focuses on time, schedule, costs, and allocation of resources. A project plan will be developed that addresses each of these items along with any associated risks that might occur during the execution and implementation of the project. Planning activities include following:

- Identifying project deliverables
- Identifying tasks that need to be performed to complete the project

---

Project Charter
ABC COMPANY
ACCOUNTS PAYABLE PROJECT

This Charter formally authorizes the Accounting Project Team to develop and implement a new accounts payment system for use in ABC Company's accounting group. A project plan will be developed and submitted to the Project Sponsor for approval. The project plan will include: scope statement; schedule; cost estimate; budget; and provisions for scope, resource, schedule, communications, quality, risk, procurement, and stakeholder management as well as project control. All resources will be assigned by the Project Sponsor, Tony Golembesky, National Accounts Director.

Project Scope

The purpose of the Accounts Payable project is to improve the timeliness and accuracy of accounts payable. This project meets ABC's need for improved efficiencies across all departments by reducing accounts payable cycle time and minimizing staffing required for accounts payable operations. The project deliverables shall include accounting system design, all coding, testing, implementation of an integrated system for use with existing IT infrastructure, and a user's guide. The objectives of the Accounts Payable project are to reduce accounts payable cycle time by 20% and reduce accounts payable staffing by 15%. High level risks for this project include ensuring implementation is completed without impacting ongoing accounts payable operations and ensuring there are no issues with migrating accounts from the legacy system to the new system. Success will be determined by the Project Sponsor once the system is implemented and one full accounts payable cycle has been completed that meets the objectives with no variances.

Milestone Schedule

The project plan will be submitted and approved in accordance with the milestone schedule below. Upon approval of the project plan resources will be assigned to the project and work will commence within five business days. The Project Sponsor must approve any schedule changes which may impact milestones. A detailed schedule will be included in the project plan.

The high level milestone schedule is:

Feb 1, 2017 – Project Plan Complete and Approved

Mar 31, 2017 – Accounts Payable Design Completed

May 31, 2017 – Coding Completed

June 30, 2017 – Testing Completed

July 31, 2017 – Beta Testing Completed

Sept 30, 2017 – Implementation Completed

Oct 15, 2017 – One Accounts Payable Cycle Complete and Project Completion

Project Budget

The budget for the Accounts Payable project is $730,000. The project is to be funded through the Accounting Technology Budget.

Sponsor Acceptance

Approved by the Project Sponsor

_____ Date: _____

Tony Golembesky, National Accounts Director

FIGURE 13.9 A Sample Project Charter.

- Developing a list of tasks, called a Work Breakdown Structure (WBS) to show the dependencies between the tasks
- Creating a schedule to carry out the task listed on the WBS
- Determining resources need to complete the project tasks
- Obtaining cost estimates for resources such as materials, equipment, and people
- Preparing a project budget
- Identifying potential risks and formulating appropriate responses to problems that could occur during the project

The WBS and Risk Register are two important documents that are prepared during the Planning stage along with plans that consider how to manage each of the 10 knowledge areas.

Work Breakdown Structure (WBS)   The **work breakdown structure (WBS)** is a list of tasks that identify all work or activities that need to be performed, the order in which the work will be performed. An example of a WBS is shown in **Figure 13.10. Figure 13.11** shows a screenshot of a WBS (left side) developed using Microsoft Project. All project resources—people, equipment, facilities—are managed according to the tasks listed in the WBS.

Milestones   The WBS breaks a project down into the tasks or activities that must be performed and defines the order in which they will be performed, to produce the deliverable or part of a deliverable at each milestone. Project **milestones** are very important scheduling and status devices because they enable the project manager to measure progress as the project proceeds through its planned life cycle. Lack of milestones has been a contributing factor in many project failures. Each milestone typically represents a deliverable (100% complete), but it may also signify the percent complete, such as 50% complete.

Milestones are used to manage the project work effort, monitor results, and report meaningful status to project stakeholders.

- **Milestone Example**   Assume that you are the project manager of a project for a client who wants to post a creative project on Kickstarter.com to raise funds using **crowdfunding**. You visit Kickstarter.com and do requirements analysis. You determine that you need to produce five deliverables: (1) a video, (2) a set of photos and illustrations, (3) a script that

Crowdfunding is raising funds for a project from the public, or *crowd*, via the Web.

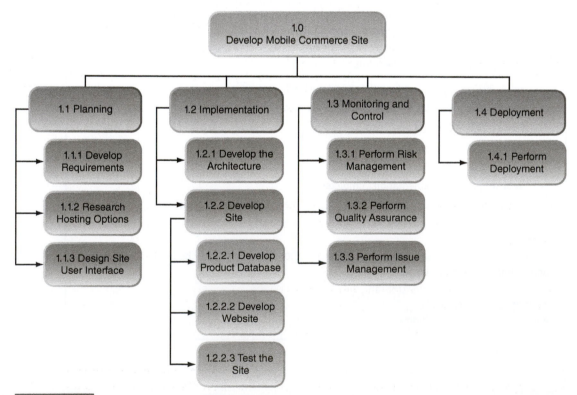

FIGURE 13.10   One segment of the WBS for a mobile commerce site project.

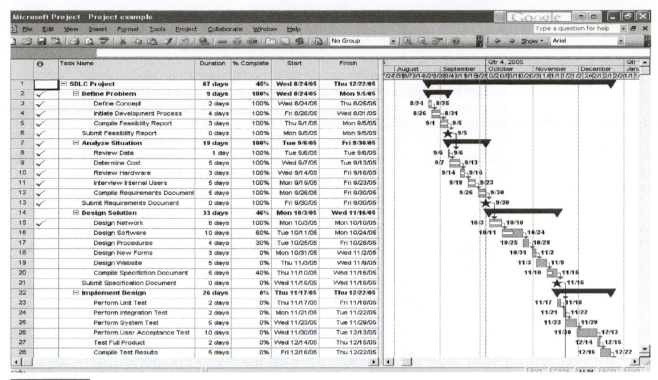

FIGURE 13.11   Microsoft Project screenshot of WBS (left side) and Gantt chart (right side).

explains why the creative project deserves funding, (4) a set of pledge categories and rewards to backers, and (5) the final site with all deliverables uploaded to Kickstarter.com and tested. Each deliverable represents a milestone in your project plan. You then rely on your milestone schedule to verify that the project is on track or to warn of the need for corrective action. Milestones should be natural, important control points in the project and easy for everyone to recognize.

Risk Register   During a project, many known and unknown risks can occur. Consideration of these risks needs to occur early in the project life cycle, during the Planning stage. The **Risk register** also lists the source of each risk, how you will respond to each risk, and the name of the person responsible for addressing the risk.

    When the planning stage has been successfully completed, the project may be approved, sent back to the drawing board to be revised, or may be thrown on the rubbish heap and rejected. If it's approved, the real work of the project can begin.

> **Risk register**   lists all known risks and their source, an estimation of unknown risks and the response to be taken to each risk.

Project Execution

It's during the executing phase of project management that the project team starts work on the actual project deliverable. Key activities listed on the WBS are carried out and the project plan produced in the planning stage is put into action. Activities performed in the Executing stage include the following:

- Allocating resources to tasks listed on the WBS
- Communicating and coordinating with key stakeholders
- Performing the tasks listed on the WBS
- Reporting progress that has been made in regular meetings

Gantt Chart   A **Gantt chart** is a bar chart that is used to show the timeline of the project schedule, as shown on the right side of Figure 13.10. On a Gantt chart, the start and finish dates of all tasks and milestones appear as bars whose length represents its duration. Gantt charts

> **Gantt chart**   is a horizontal bar chart that graphically displays the project schedule.

are multipurpose visualization tools that are used in planning, executing, and monitoring phases and enable the project manager to prepare at-a-glance status reports.

Cost Estimation

While costs are not technically part of the WBS, the projects' estimated cost can be calculated from the WBS. Each task or activity has a start date and duration, which determine its finish date. For example, if a task starts on Monday, November 2, and takes eight work days (excluding weekend days) to complete, the finish date is Wednesday, November 11. Assume that the resources—people, equipment, and materials—needed to complete the task and their costs are known. Project management software computes the cost of the project based on labor time (duration) of each task in the WBS and the cost of labor or other resource.

Responsibility Matrix

If a resource is listed on the WBS, that means they are responsible for at least one project task. A **responsibility matrix** shows who has primary responsibility and who has support responsibility for each activity listed on the WBS. **Table 13.2** is an example of a responsibility matrix.

Responsibility matrix lets everyone know who is responsible for completion of tasks.

TABLE 13.2 Responsibility Matrix Showing Primary and Support Responsibilities for WBS Tasks

WBS ID	Activity	Level of Responsibility				
		Anna	Bart	Beth	Fred	Don
1.1	Storyboard video		S		P	
1.2	Recruit volunteers to act in video		S	P		
1.3	Record video segments				P	S
2.1	Select five photographs and images	P				S
2.2	Crop and edit photos	S				P

P = primary responsibility, S = support responsibility

13.5 Monitoring/Controlling and Closing Projects

Once the project work has begun, it's time to start monitoring performance, collecting feedback, and putting controls in place to correct any variances from the original project plan and eventually formally closing out the project.

Project Monitoring and Controlling

Project Monitoring and Controlling include tracking, reviewing, and managing the progress and performance of the project along with managing any necessary changes.

Monitoring and controlling occur continuously while the project work is being executed, so it overlaps with Project Execution. These processes, described in Figure 13.11, depend on the baseline, milestones, responsibility matrix, and other elements from the planning stage. They keep the project team informed of project status and help them cope with challenges they encounter. Except for short, simple projects, there are going to be risks and changes that need to be kept under control and documented.

Monitoring depends on prompt and candid feedback from the project team, as you read in the opening case. In-person visits, reports, and records are also monitoring methods. Project control depends on systems and decision rules for managing variances between the project's scope, cost, schedule, and quality and the realities of project implementation.

Throughout the project, the work must be tracked against the schedule to ensure that the project is on track. Doing this helps identify variances from the baseline target early so they can be addressed before the gap between actual and expected performance becomes too great. In this way, cost overruns and risk can be minimized and the probability of completing the project on time and on budget is maximized. Feedback is very important in this stage. While monitoring identifies problems, feedback enables controls to be put in place to "stop the bleeding." Activities during the Monitoring/Controlling stage include the following:

- Measuring extent and timing of task completion
- Comparing actual versus expected performance on all tasks
- Collecting feedback
- Taking appropriate action to correct problems and address issues
- Making report reports to appropriate stakeholders
- Documenting progress and updating the project plan, as needed

Project Status Report
To monitor the progress of a project, project status reports will be prepared and reviewed to check on the progress of the project. Status reports are typically prepared once a week. Status reports include a summary of the project status vis-à-vis planned performance; work planned; work completed; work planned; open issues; open risks; status of project milestones and deliverables; open change requests; project key performance indicators (KPIs); schedule status and cost status.

Scope Creep
During the project, it is almost guaranteed that requests will be made that change the scope of the work required to produce the project deliverable. **Scope creep** refers to the growth of the project, which might seem inconsequential—at least to the person who is requesting that change. It is absolutely imperative that any change to the scope of the project explicitly include compensating changes in the budget, the deadline, and/or resources. Consider the following scenario.

The project scope is to build a new online accounting application capable of processing at least 1000 expense reports (in multiple currencies) per day, which has a budget of $200,000, and is expected to last three months. After the project is started, the scope expands to include processing of thousands of sales commissions per day. The project manager needs to renegotiate the project's duration and budget for the added functionality, testing, and user training, making sure that any requested change, no matter how small, is documented and accompanied by approval.

IS design is highly susceptible to scope creep for many reasons. Intended users ask for additional features. People who were not intended users ask to be included. Technology changed from the time the business case was written and system development began. The actions of a competitor, supplier, or regulatory agency triggered additional requests for functionality. Because scope creep is expensive, project managers impose controls on changes requested by users. These controls help to prevent *runaway projects*—system development projects that are so far over budget and past deadline that they must be abandoned, typically with large monetary loss.

> **Scope creep** is the piling up of small changes that by themselves are manageable but in aggregate are significant.

Integrated Change Control
Quite often, changes occur as the project proceeds. Changes tend to have a trickle-down effect because of task dependencies and shared resources. For example, consider the following three activities from Table 13.2:

1.1 Storyboard a video.

1.2 Recruit volunteers to act in the video.

1.3 Record video segments.

Activity 1.3 is dependent on the completion of activities 1.1 and 1.2. Video recording cannot start until after the video has been storyboarded and actors are available.

Integrated change control processes help to manage the disruption resulting from requested changes and corrective actions across the project life cycle (**Figure 13.12**). **Integrated**

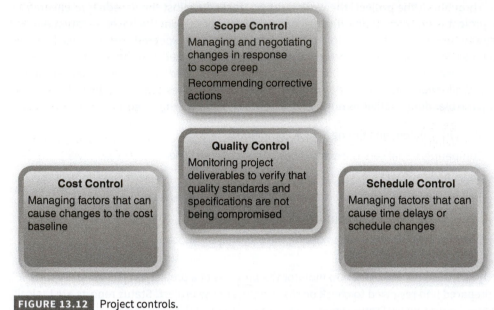

change control processes are always documented and saved in the event of project failure or lawsuits related to the failure. These documents are needed to defend decisions—what did and did not happen, such as the following:

- Approved change requests
- Rejected change requests
- Updates to the project plan
- Updates to the scope
- Approved corrective and preventive actions
- Approved defect repair
- Validated defect repair

Critical path is the shortest time possible to complete all tasks required to finish the project. A delay of any task on the critical path will delay the project.

Critical Path Analysis All projects have a **critical path** that extends the length of the project and determines the shortest path along which all projects tasks must be completed in order to finish the project. Project management software shows the critical path on the Gantt chart, as in **Figure 13.13**. Each task or activity on the critical path is called a **critical task** or

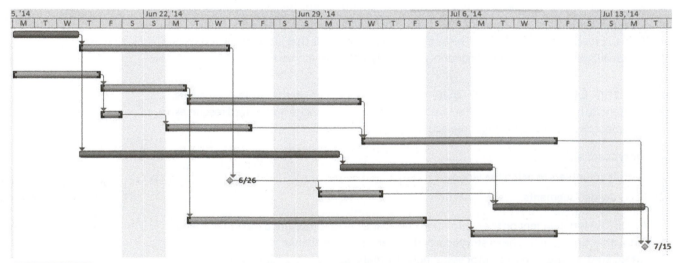

FIGURE 13.13 The critical path is shown as red bars. The critical path consists of all tasks from project start to finish that must be completed on time in order for the project to finish on time.

activity. Critical tasks must finish on schedule because delays will delay the project unless something is done to compensate. While it may seem that adding new people to a project is an obvious solution, in fact, it may initially slow it down. If any noncritical tasks get delayed enough, they could go critical, so both critical and noncritical paths need to be monitored.

Project Baseline Plan When the project plan is finalized and accepted, the accepted plan becomes the **baseline** or master plan. The baseline is used for monitoring and controlling. Any change to the baseline is a deviation, or **variance**, to the plan—and it needs to be documented. Using project management software, you can save the WBS as the baseline. From then on, deviations will automatically be documented as variances from the baseline, as shown in **Figure 13.14**.

Baseline is a specification of the project plan that has been formally reviewed and agreed upon. It should be changed only through a formal change control process.

Once all work has been monitored and controlled and the project deliverable has been completed, it's time to move on to the final phase of the project management life cycle and formally close the project.

Work			
Scheduled:	680 hrs	Remaining:	581.2 hrs
Baseline:	528 hrs	Actual:	98.8 hrs
Variance:	152 hrs	Percent complete:	15%

Costs			
Scheduled:	$14,104.00	Remaining:	$11,751.60
Baseline:	$10,624.00	Actual:	$2,352.40
Variance:	$3,480.00		

Task Status		Resource status	
Tasks not yet started:	7	Work resources:	4
Tasks in progress:	9	Overallocated work resources:	4
Tasks completed:	0	Material resources:	0
Total tasks:	16	Total resources:	8

FIGURE 13.14 Work and cost variances from the agreed-upon project baseline are documented by project management software.

Project Closing or Post Mortem

At closing, the project manage declares the project complete. In keeping with the saying, "It ain't over until the fat lady sings," project closing can't occur until the stakeholders are satisfied with the final project deliverable and have formally accepted the project. Closure of the project also requires that the project manager, with the help of the project team, conducts a **Post mortem** of the project to identify the things that went right and the things went wrong.

Post mortem is a method for evaluating project performance, identifying lessons learned, and making recommendations for future projects.

Activities that occur during closing include the following:

- Delivering the final project deliverable
- Obtaining and documenting formal stakeholder acceptance of the project deliverable
- Documenting and archiving all project documents

- Documenting "Lessons Learned" to inform upcoming projects
- Formally releasing all resources

Lessons Learned Report   An important document that is created during Project Closing is the **Lessons Learned report**. The Lessons Learned enables future project teams to learn from the project team's positive and negatives experiences. The Lessons Learned identify the reasons the project was successful or not, strengths and weaknesses of the project plan, how problems were detected and resolved, and how the project was successful in spite of them.

Here are three common lessons learned that are frequently documented during the project closing phase.

- **Communication is King**
  The most important skill that a project manager can learn is good communication. Timely, frequent, and targeted communication to all key stakeholders is paramount to keeping a project on track. Make sure that you communicate early and often to the right people in the right way!

- **Set Realistic and Detailed Project Plans with Adequate Time and Resources**
  Projects are subject to unanticipated and uncontrollable events, so they need to have slack time built into the schedule and budget. However, project teams can be pressured to cut project costs. In response, they might reduce the time and budget allocated to training, testing, and change management. These cuts result in poor quality and low user acceptance.

- **Encourage Timely Feedback and Be Willing to Listen**
  All projects encounter difficulties. Make sure that employees know they will not be punished for raising concerns, even if other project members deny that problems exist. Fear blocks the flow of useful information.

- **Manage Risk with Regular Project Status Reviews**
  For the most part, no one likes formal project reviews, but they are necessary to identify and address current and potential problems.

Why Projects Fail

An important part of project management is knowing when to declare an ongoing project a failure. Take for example, the case of a Fortune 500 company that learned that six of its major projects were in trouble two months into a new project. In each case, it *seemed* as though the project failed overnight without warning. The CIO felt blindsided and executive management wanted to know who and what was to blame. The company's **project management office (PMO)** was asked to explain.

During the investigation, the PMO learned that the project staff felt strong but subtle pressure to keep problems to themselves. The six failing projects had executive sponsors who were politically powerful and known to attack people who delivered bad news. So, rather than report that their project was in trouble, staff worked harder, hoping to recover from missed deadlines, but deadlines were still missed.

Sometimes, the only right way to fix a project is to cancel it. If a project suffers from one or more of conditions listed in the following scenario, it has reached a point where its feasibility must be critically re-examined. It is very difficult to kill any project when millions of dollars have been spent to date—even when it is clearly the right decision.

The project is behind schedule. The scope changes almost daily. There were too few milestones identified during the planning stage to be able to monitor progress. Too many, or the wrong, resources were allocated. Because of the lack of regularly scheduled meetings, the project manager has no information on what the team members are working on at any given time. The team members are not communicating

Project management office (PMO) is an organizational group responsible for coordinating the project management function throughout an organization.

because they know that the project is on its deathbed and are afraid to say so. Many people in the company also know that the project is in trouble, except for senior management.

The money already spent on the project, or **sunk costs**, should not be considered in the decision to cancel. The only relevant cost, from a financial point of view, is whether the total value from continuing is greater than the total cost of doing so. **IT at Work 13.1** describes a real-world case of a project out of control.

Sunk cost is a cost that has already been incurred and cannot be recovered.

IT at Work 13.1

U.S. Census Project Out of Control

U.S. Secretary of Commerce Carlos M. Gutierrez issued the following official statement explaining (in an obscure way) why the Census Bureau was scrapping its $600 million project. The project plan was to develop a system for collecting census data using 500,000 hand-held devices. The Census Bureau had contracted to use handheld devices from Harris Corp., but mismanagement, cost overruns, and poor planning caused the project to be cancelled.

According to a U.S. Census Press Release:

Multiple internal and external reviews have identified continuing Census challenges across a number of areas, including adequate planning over key systems requirements, key technology requirements, specification of operational control system characteristics and functions and regional center technology infrastructure. . . . Gutierrez said that the Census Bureau will need an additional $2.2 to $3.0 billion in funding over the next five years to meet the replan needs. . . . The life cycle cost for the Reengineered 2010 Census was estimated at $11.8 billion in the FY 2009 Budget Request, including $1.8 billion for the American Community Survey which replaced the long-form. The new estimated life cycle cost for the 2010 Census is $13.7 to $14.5 billion.

In summary, the Census Bureau had planned to issue more than 500,000 handhelds to temporary employees to collect personal data on Americans who do not return census forms in the mail. The handhelds were being developed under a $600 million contract awarded to Harris Corp., in 2006. Stumbling over this multibillion-dollar plan for a high-tech census, the government reverted to counting the nation's 300 million people the old-fashioned way: with paper and pencil. Poor management—not poor technology—caused the government to spend an additional $3 billion for the next census.

Was the Failure a Surprise?

Senator Susan Collins, ranking member of the Committee on Homeland Security and Governmental Affairs, was not surprised by the failure. "This committee is unfortunately no stranger to tales of federal projects and contracts that have gone awry, often at a heavy cost in taxpayer funds," she said. Collins listed the usual failure reasons:

- poorly defined initial requirements and
- inability or unwillingness of management to control "requirements creep" and cost overruns.

Something larger than poor project management was at work. It was the failure of top management in the Bureau to assess and mitigate the risks inherent in such a major project. "It should be noted that the problems with this contract seemed apparent to everyone except the Census Bureau," said Senator Tom Coburn (D-Oklahoma).

Analysis of the Handheld Project Failure

The 2010 census was to have been the first true high-tech count in the nation's history. The Census Bureau had awarded a contract to purchase 500,000 of the computers, plus the computer operating system, at a cost of more than $600 million. The contract ballooned to $1.3 billion, even though the Bureau scaled back its purchase to only 151,000 handheld computers. The higher expenditure was due to cost overruns and new features ordered by the Census Bureau on the computers and the operating system. Gutierrez blamed many of the problems on "a lack of effective communication with one of our key contractors."

Census officials were being blamed for doing a poor job of spelling out technical requirements to the contractor, Harris. In addition, the handhelds proved too complex for some temporary workers who tried to use them in a test in North Carolina, and the devices were not initially programmed to transmit the large amounts of data necessary.

Harris spokesman Marc Raimondi said the cost of the contract increased as the project requirements increased: "The increased funding is required to cover additional sites, equipment, software and functions added by the bureau to the program."

Representative Alan Mollohan, chairman of the appropriations subcommittee, said the Census Bureau and Harris "contributed to today's crisis." The Census Bureau's failure to address problems with the computers early on has "turned the crisis into the emergency that we now face."

IT at Work Questions

1. What went wrong?
2. What should have been done that was not done?
3. Where any problems unforeseeable?
4. Consider the statement: "hope is not a plan." Does the statement apply to this project failure? Explain why or why not.
5. What are the similarities between the U.S. Census project failure and the DIA automated baggage-handling project failure?

IT Project Management Mistakes

Managing IT projects to ensure a successful outcome has become more important than ever in the on-demand economy (Stackpole, 2013). In closing, it's useful to understand the factors that appear to consistently contribute to project failure. The Center for Project Management that helps IT organizations implement effective project management came up with a list of the seven most common IT project management mistakes that can cause a project to fail. Unfortunately despite all the available project management education, the "Seven Deadly Sins of Project Management" are still being made (Symonds, 2014). They are the following:

1. Failing to stick to a project process architecture
2. Treating half-baked ideas as projects
3. Missing or ineffective leadership
4. Employing underskilled project managers
5. Inadequately tracking the project's tasks, milestones, and resource usage
6. Failing to fix problems as soon as they are detected
7. Failing to engage in PPM

Career Insight 13.1

IT Project Management Jobs

Project management is a high-level skill and a demanding career choice. The most successful upper-level project managers typically have an MBA or other business degree, a recognized project management certification, and financial background to plan and manage the project budget.

A sample job description for an IT project manager is as follows:

Responsible for the coordination and completion of projects within the information technology department. Oversees all aspects of projects and project budgets. Sets deadlines, assigns responsibilities, and monitors and summarizes progress of project. Builds and maintains working relationships with team members, vendors, and other departments involved in the projects. Prepares reports for upper management regarding status of project. Requires a bachelor's degree, 2 to 4 years of experience, and knowledge of project management software. MBA is preferred. Leads and directs the work of others. A wide degree of creativity and latitude is expected. Typically reports to a senior manager or head of a unit/department.

Questions

1. What processes help to ensure that the impacts resulting from requested changes and corrective actions are managed across the project life cycle?
2. What happens when a task on the critical path is delayed?
3. What are the three attributes that must be managed effectively for successful completion and closure of any project?
4. Why are lessons learned from a completed project identified?
5. Why is the evaluation of a project's success or failure somewhat subjective?
6. What are three best practices to keep projects on track?
7. Why are IT projects high susceptible to scope creep?

Key Terms

agile 392
baseline 407
business case 396
communication 399
cost 399
critical path 406
critical task 406
crowdfunding 402
deliverable 397

DevOps 394
extreme programming 394
Gantt chart 403
go/no-go decision 390
human resources 399
integrated change control 405
lessons learned report 408
logical design 390
milestones 402

object-oriented (O-O) 392
people 399
physical design 390
portfolio 396
post mortem 407
procurement 399
program 396
projects 395
project charter 400

project management   395
project management office (PMO)   408
project portfolio management (PPM)   396
quality   399
responsibility matrix   404
risk   399
risk register   403
scope   399

scope creep   405
sprints   394
stakeholders   399
statement of work (SOW)   400
sunk cost   409
systems development life cycle (SDLC)   386
time   399
templates   400

triple constraint   397
use-case description   392
use-case diagram   392
variance   407
Waterfall Model   391
work breakdown structure (WBS)   402

Assuring Your Learning

Discuss: Critical Thinking Questions

1. Business cases take a long time to research and write. As a result, they are also time-consuming to review. Explain why business cases require so much effort and detail.

2. What risks might the use of project portfolio management (PPM) minimize? Do you think PPM can guarantee honest and unbiased project approvals or not? Explain your position.

3. Do you think that projects that are needed to comply with regulations, such as the international anti-money-laundering (AML) laws that require firms to *know your customer* (KYC), should undergo the same approval requirements as discretionary projects, such as in manufacturing or marketing? Explain your reasons.

4. Why should each deliverable be made a milestone?

5. Why is the critical path an important monitoring tool?

6. How does diagramming the triple constraint as a triangle clearly demonstrate how time, scope, and cost are interrelated?

7. Refer to the Center for Project Management's list of seven IT project management mistakes. Select two of these mistakes and explain how they contribute to project failure.

8. Why should the go/no-go decision be made more than once in a project's life cycle?

9. If a project is started without a documented baseline, what risks might the project and project team face?

10. Explain how control activities are, in effect, risk management activities.

11. Why is it tough to ignore sunk costs when evaluating a failing project?

12. Why are IT projects so susceptible to scope creep?

13. What leads to a runaway project?

14. What feasibilities are needed prior to IT project approval?

15. Explain the stages of the SDLC.

Explore: Online and Interactive Exercises

1. ProjectLibre is the open-source replacement of Microsoft Project. Visit the ProjectLibre website at **www.ProjectLibre.org**.

    a. Download the free software.

    b. Assume that you are the project manager on a project of your choice that you are able to manage. Several project examples are delivering a tailgate party for 50 people, remodeling a kitchen, creating a YouTube video for advertising a new product, or implementing a new cloud accounting IS.

    c. Use the software to plan a project of your choice. Create a WBS and Gantt chart.

2. Research and compare the current top three open-source project management tools. What are their limitations?

3. Research the three project management vendors' software packages and find a review of each one. Write a report that compares the features of the packages, including prices, and that summarizes the reviews.

4. Assume that you are a member of a project team working on a project with a six-month timeline. The materials your team needs to complete their first set of tasks will arrive three days later than their promised delivery date. The delay has a 10% chance of delaying completion of the project. You know that no one will tell the project manager of the delayed delivery because it is the first month of the project so it does not seem important enough to report. Would you inform the project manager of the delay? Explain your decision. Now assume that you did not report the delay and such delays happened in each month afterward. What would you do and when? In your opinion, should the entire team present these problems? Explain your decisions.

Analyze & Decide: Apply IT Concepts to Business Decisions

1. You are the project manager and need to compose a SOW for clients who want you to develop a Kickstarter.com site for their project, as discussed in the chapter.

   a. Start off by composing a SOW using a standard SOW template that you found and downloaded from the Internet.

   b. Use **Tom's Planner** or other free Gantt chart software to create a Gantt chart for your project.

   c. Assume that after your clients review your SOW and Gantt chart, they request that you discount the price 20%. Based on the triple constraints, how would you respond?

2. Explore project management software on vendors' websites. Select a single project management package, download the demo,

and try it. Make a list of the important features of the package. Be sure to investigate its cloud and collaboration features. Report your findings.

3. Managing a project with Microsoft Project is often the approach to IT project management, but many users prefer to use Microsoft Excel instead. The main reasons are that MS Project is too expensive, wastes too much time to set up and keep updated, and is tough to use. The debate between Excel and Project has valid arguments for either approach. Research the reviews of Excel and MS Project as project management tools. When is each software appropriate for use?

Case 13.2

Business Case: Steve Jobs' Shared Vision Project Management Style

Steve Jobs (1955–2011) cofounded Apple Inc. and reinvented the PC, music players, phones, tablets, and digital publishing (**Figure 13.15**). He is regarded as technology industry's most notable luminary. He continuously managed remarkably innovative projects—extremely successful ones as well as many failures. Although widely recognized as a marketing and technology guru, Jobs was largely successful because of his project-based approach for managing his business and producing new products. His approach to executing projects ultimately changed the business world. Jobs's *shared vision* project management style offers lessons to help managers focus and motivate their team to get projects completed on schedule.

Shared Vision and Accountability

A significant part of what made Jobs successful was his persistent push to keep projects moving while communicating with his team to ensure that they were working toward the shared vision. He stressed accountability and did not let anyone slide on that principle. He got to know everyone on the team and actively inspired them.

Guy Kawasaki, Apple's chief evangelist and liaison to the Mac developer community, said Jobs appreciated great work. He was well known for giving employees feedback—publicly telling them if they were great or lousy. His bluntness infuriated some people but also motivated them to either do their best or leave.

Communication

Structure, understanding, and inspiration depend on the one irreplaceable management skill: communication. Part of what made Jobs so successful was his constant push to keep projects moving

FIGURE 13.15 Steve Jobs, CEO and founder of Apple Computers and Pixar boss, was one of the greatest project managers.

EdStock/iStockphoto

while communicating with his team to ensure that they were working toward a shared vision. He held regular meetings to avoid wasting time with long e-mail chains and having to address the same concerns multiple times.

Do Not Just Listen—Understand

There is a big difference between listening and understanding. Jobs made sure that he understood everyone on his team and that they understood him. This is done by making people demonstrate that they understand and not simply asking them if they understand. When everyone confirms that they are on the same page, they will keep moving forward.

Questions

1. Steve Jobs shows the importance of people skills. Explain Jobs' way of motivating people. For example, did he try to get everyone to like him? Did he try to get everyone to get along with each other?

2. Why did Jobs' approach to project management work so well for him?

3. What lessons can project managers learn from Jobs?

4. Research Steve Jobs' management style from reputable sources. What did you learn about how people reacted to Jobs' style?

5. Create a checklist of effective project management practices.

Sources: Darton Group (2012), Isaacson (2012), and Kimbrell (2014).

Case 13.3

Demo Case: Mavenlink Project Management and Planning Software

Although some organizations still use Excel to manage their projects, Excel is not an ideal tool in larger projects. Instead, organizations achieve far greater project management productivity and efficiency using one or more of the hundreds of different products designed specifically to assist in project management. These project management software packages fall into the three main categories shown in Table 13.3.

TABLE 13.3 **Project Management Software**

Category	Application	Cost	Example Products
Low-end tools	Single or small project well	$200 per user	
Mid-range Tools	Multiple projects and users	$200–$1,000 per user	
High-end tools	Large projects	Typically licensed on a per-user basis	Microsoft Enterprise Project Management

Project management software and apps continue to be improved with advanced features and integration with other technology. The decision on which project management software to use depends on the company's needs, size of business, and industry. Cloud-based or online project management applications are popular choices.

Mavenlink is a vendor that provides easy-to-follow video tutorials and online project management resources through the World's First Unified Project Delivery Cloud. With Mavenlink, you can track project timelines, collaborate on tasks, manage team activities, and integrate with Google Apps, QuickBooks, and Salesforce from a single workplace environment.

Visit Mavenlink's website **http://Mavenlink.com**. Read about the company and its project management products. Search for the Mavenlink Tutorial by Michelle on YouTube and watch the video. (The video runs for 12:54 minutes.)

Questions

1. What Mavenlink features support project planning?

2. What Mavenlink features support project monitoring and control?

3. How does Mavenlink support change management supported?

4. If you were a project manager, would you choose Mavenlink to manage your projects? Explain.

IT Toolbox

Project Management Templates

One of the tools typically used by project managers is a set of templates. Templates, or standardized forms, are usually created by an organization's PMO in larger firms or senior project manager in a small firm. Templates serve two main purposes. (1) Templates standardize the content of documents across all projects. (2) Templates minimize time and effort required of project managers and portfolio managers in creating and reviewing the multitude of documents used in project management.

A full set of project management templates organized by stages of project management life cycle are available online from **Project Management Docs**. Go to their website and check them out.

Following are two templates for documents prepared during Project Initiation. These easy-to-use Business Case and SOW templates will help get you started on your project management journey.

Business Case Template

Project Overview Statement

Executive Summary

Project Name:

Department:

Date:

Author(s):

Project Manager(s):

Executive Sponsor(s):

Describe the pertinent facts of the project in a clear and concise way.

PROJECT BUSINESS CASE

Project Overview

Describe what is involved in executing the project.

Business Issue/Opportunity

Describe expected benefits and how the project fits within the company's business strategy and contributes toward its goals and objectives.

Project Business Goal

Clearly identify the opportunity, need, or problem facing the company and why the project is necessary. Discuss the drivers that have triggered the project proposal and link them to the business need.

Primary Project Objectives

List and describe the objectives of the project.

1. *Objective 1*
2. *Objective 2 . . .*
3. *Objective n . . .*

Project Benefits and Cost–Benefit Analysis

Describe the key benefits from implementing this project.

1. *Benefit 1*
2. *Benefit 2 . . .*
3. *Benefit n . . .*

Based on the costs established for each option, describe how those costs are weighed against the benefits. Conduct the cost–benefit analysis for each option taking into account costs, benefits, and risks.

PRIMARY PROJECT DELIVERABLES

Milestone 1

1. *Deliverable name: Description of the deliverable*
2. *Deliverable name: Description of the deliverable*

n. *. . .*

Milestone *n*

1. *Deliverable name: Description of the deliverable*
2. *Deliverable name: Description of the deliverable*

n. *. . .*

Project Interdependencies and Inputs

Explain other projects in process or planned that have a relationship to this proposed project. List inputs that other projects may have to this project development.

- *[input]*
- *[input]*
- *[input]*

Project Assumptions and Constraints

List and describe all underlying technical, environmental, and resource availability assumptions upon which the project and benefits are based. List and describe constraints that can come from external or internal factors.

Project Risks

Describe known risks that apply to this project.

PROJECT KEY PERFORMANCE INDICATORS

List and describe project KPIs or critical success factors.

Project Duration Estimates and Deliverables		
Project Milestone	**Date Estimate**	**Confidence Level**
Project Start Date		[High/Medium/Low]
Milestone 1		[High/Medium/Low]
Milestone n		[High/Medium/Low]
Project Completion Date		[High/Medium/Low]

APPROVALS

Prepared by

_____
Project Manager

Approved by

_____
Project Sponsor

_____
Executive Sponsor

_____
Client Sponsor

Statement of Work Template

Date	[Insert date]
Client	[Insert client's name]
Job Name	[Insert project name]
Requested by	[Insert client sponsor's name]
From	[Insert project manager's name]
Summary and Objectives	A high-level description of the project and objectives
Project Scope	Description of the project scope, deliverables, and the process for how it will be performed
Schedule and Work Breakdown Structure (WBS)	List of tasks in sequential order, resources allocated to each task, and schedule
Cost or Pricing	Description of the cost (pricing) for all types of resources—labor costs, materials, equipment, overhead expenses; discussion of payment terms, including a payment schedule and if payments are based on a milestone/deliverable or a schedule, if appropriate
Key Assumptions	A crucial part of an SOW—any assumptions made when scoping and estimating the project need to be documented

Acceptance

The client named below verifies that the terms of this statement of work are acceptable. The parties hereto are each acting with proper authority of their respective companies.

_____   _____
Company name   Company name

_____   _____
Full name   Full name

_____   _____
Title   Title

_____   _____
Signature   Signature

_____   _____
Date   Date

References

Calleam Consulting Ltd. "Case Study – Denver International Airport Baggage Handling System – An Illustration of Ineffectual Decision Making." *www.Calleam.com*. 2008.

Coolman, A. "Lessons Learned from Project Failure at Denver International Airport: Why Checking Bags is still a Pain." *Wrike*, https://www.wrike.com/blog/lessons-learned-from-project-failure-at-denver-international-airport-why-checking-bags-is-still-a-pain/ 2014.

Darton Group. "Steve Jobs and Lessons for Project Managers." *DartonGroup.com*, January 2, 2012.

Grimes, R. A. "11 Signs Your IT Project Is Doomed." *Computerworld.com*, May 6, 2013.

Isaacson, W. *Steve Jobs*. New York: Simon & Schuster, September 2012.

Kimbrell, G. "Four Project Management Lessons You Can Learn from Software Engineers." *Forbes*, January 31, 2014.

Konrad, A. "Business Leaders Are Losing Ground in 'Digital IQ' New PwC Study Finds." *Tech in the Cloud*, February 28, 2017.

Murray, J. "DIA and Bid Team are Closer to Reaching Deal on Massive Terminal Project, Spokesman says." *The Denver Post*, June 20, 2017.

Perkins, B. "Bart Perkins: How to Keep Projects on Track." *Computerworld.com*, April 21, 2014.

Stackpole, B. "Why Project Management in IT Is More Important Than Ever." *State Tech Magazine*, September 25, 2013.

Symonds, M. "The Seven Deadly Sins of Project Management." *The Project Management Hut*, January 17, 2014.

U.S. Census, 2008. *census.gov*

CHAPTER 14

IT Ethics, Privacy, and Sustainability

CHAPTER OUTLINE	LEARNING OBJECTIVES
Case 14.1 Opening Case: Lessons Learned: How Google Glass Raised Risk and Privacy Challenges	
14.1 IT Ethics	**14.1 Discuss** the importance of IT ethics and issues related to technology-related unethical behavior.
14.2 Privacy and Civil Rights	**14.2 Understand** privacy issues associated with organizational use of personal information.
14.3 Technology Addictions and Focus Management	**14.3 Describe** how technology use can lead to obsessive behavior and impact the ability to focus.
14.4 ICT and Sustainable Development	**14.4 Understand** how the increasing use of IT and social media dependence affect global warming and other sustainable development issues.
Case 14.2 Business Case: Android Auto and CarPlay Keep Drivers Safe, Legal, and Productive	
Case 14.3 Video Case: IT Ethics in the Workplace	

Introduction

Several of today's toughest ethical and social challenges did not even exist at the start of this decade. The latest social, mobile, cloud, and information management technologies are powerful forces. While businesses, governments, and users greatly benefit from their use, they may have harmful effects—not all of which are obvious yet. For example, what is the effect of people spending their personal and professional lives in a state of continuous disruption or partial (distracted) attention?

Are you prepared to deal effectively with ethical challenges and corporate responsibilities that social, mobile, big data, and analytics technology create in business? Anecdotal research suggests that individuals often do not even recognize when ethical issues are present. If people cannot recognize them, then it is hard to imagine how they could act responsibly.

This chapter will make you aware of IT ethics, risks, legal responsibilities, and sustainability controversies. These issues are examined within the context of civil rights, employment laws, regulations, research findings, and case examples. Of course, even those guidelines cannot provide easy answers to social discrimination, the demise of privacy, distractions, piracy, and theft of intellectual property, and what the latest digital devices are doing to quality of life. There are no easy fixes, clear-cut judgments, answers, or solutions. As managers, you need to be able to recognize ethical issues and tip the balance toward better responsible conduct in the workplace.

Case 14.1 Opening Case

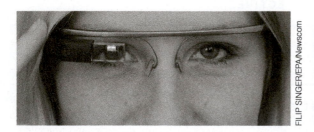

FILIP SINGER/EPA/Newscom · Lisa Werner/Alamy Stock Photo · maxkabakov/Getty Images

Lessons Learned: How Google Glass Raised Risk and Privacy Challenges

Although Google Glass is now "broke" (Bilton, 2015), some interesting privacy and ethical issues are worth remembering about this revolutionary technology. When Google Glass was unveiled, it was considered the gadget most sought out by everyone, from nerds and chief executives to chefs and fashionistas. It was the must-have toy that was going to set the gold standard for a new class of wearable computers.

Time Magazine named it one of the best inventions of 2012, and Google Glass got its own 12-page spread in Vogue magazine. There was even an episode of "The Simpsons" TV show that was devoted to Google Glass in which Homer called them "Oogle Goggles" (Bilton, 2015). But, there were some serious risk and privacy issues associated with Google Glass use that Google had not foreseen.

For example, when California Highway Patrol (CHP) officer Keith Odle pulled over Cecilia Abadie for speeding along Interstate 15 in San Diego, Odle noticed that Abadie was wearing Google Glass. He ticketed her for speeding and for being in violation of the distracted-driving law. California Vehicle Code Section 27602 bans people from driving while video screens are operating in the front of the vehicle, except for mapping displays such as GPS and other built-in screens. Abadie, a software developer, was one of the explorers who were pilot testing Google Glass before its later release to the public.

The **CNET website** reported that Abadie's alleged violation "does pose a thorny legal question that police, judges and drivers will have to face as these wearable devices become more prevalent" (Whitney, 2013).

Distracted Drivers or Informed Drivers?

Wearing computer-in-eyewear could be a distracted-driving violation according to the traffic code if the eyewear was on while Abadie was driving. The CHP officer had seen the light from Abadie's Glass screen. However, her defense attorney claimed that the Glass activated when she looked up at the officer during the stop but was not on when she was driving. The California judge dismissed her ticket saying that the CHP officer failed to prove that the Glass was in operation when the driver was stopped.

One side argues that driving with a wearable computer is as risky as texting or watching TV while driving. The opposing side claims that the advantages of Glass outweigh any risks. They cite the DriveSafe app that detects when drivers are falling asleep and wakes them up—making driving safer. **Figure 14.1** shows a number of views and opinions surrounding Google Glass. When the case came up for hearing, Commissioner John Blair threw out both charges against Abadie, stating there was insufficient evidence to prove beyond a

Violation of distracted driving traffic codes	Technology is inherently neutral. Misuse by users creates social risk so users bear the responsibility.
If Glass distracts drivers and causes traffic accidents, then Google has a responsibility to address this issue.	A Glass wearer in a movie theater was detained by a U.S. Immigration and Homeland Security Investigations unit, which targets piracy.
Glass violates the *right to be left alone*. The facial recognition app, *NameTag*, allows Glass wearers to scan faces of strangers against known face databases.	The *DriveSafe* app detects when drivers are falling asleep and wakes them up—making driving safer.

FIGURE 14.1 Diverse views and arguments about the consequences of wearing Google Glass.

reasonable doubt that the Google Glass was turned on at the time that Abadie was driving.

Product Liability, Risk, And Responsibility Controversy

This case triggered many debates over the responsibility and business risk of digital technology products hitting the market. Here are several debated issues:

- *Google Glass may redefine the boundaries of companies' product liability*. Certainly, individuals have the responsibility to drive safely at all times. Does Google also bear responsibility for potential harm caused by Glass users?

- The *United Nations (U.N.) Guiding Principles on Business and Human Rights* was unanimously endorsed by the Human Rights Council in 2011. It states that companies must "avoid causing or contributing to adverse human rights impacts through their own activities, and address such impacts when they occur." Glass constitutes Google's "own activities"; therefore, according to the United Nations, if Glass distracts drivers and causes traffic accidents, then Google has a responsibility to address this issue. The possible legal and ethical question is whether or not technology companies are obligated to inform users that there may be social risks (risks to others) from using their products in plain language—similar to warnings of side effects of medications.

- *Do technology companies bear any responsibility for the social risks of how consumers or buyers use their products?* Lawmakers are worried about what drivers will do with the Internet at their eyeballs.

- A common argument is that technology is inherently neutral. Misuse by users creates social risk, so users bear the responsibility. Opponents argue that technology companies must manage the social risks that they contribute to or cause.

Driving violations are only one example of the effects of Glass on the legal system. Additionally, Glass is only one example of intersection of new devices and ethical, legal, and social responsibility. Similarly to other new digital technologies, the device is influencing a wide range of legal issues, including copyright infringement, privacy, and piracy. The legal system is reactive and slower moving than IT—and may not be prepared for upcoming challenges.

Copyright, Piracy, and Privacy Infringement

Since it is worn instead of held, Glass can record events less obtrusively than smartphones do. Wearers who want to take photos simply wink with their right eye. Google Glass also can be outfitted to prescription lenses, which introduces another issue since when the Glass is needed for correct vision.

Example 1: Piracy and Theft of Intellectual Property

In January 2014, a man in Columbus, Ohio, who was wearing prescription Google Glass was pulled out of an AMC theater about an hour into watching the movie *Jack Ryan: Shadow Recruit*. He was detained by agents from the U.S. Immigration and Customs Enforcement's Homeland Security Investigations unit, which targets piracy. After the interrogation, the agents hooked the Glass up to a computer and saw that all it was storing were personal family photos. Why and how did agents show up so quickly? AMC issued the following statement to address why it called the agency (Taylor, 2014):

> [M]ovie theft is something we take very seriously, and our theater managers contact the Motion Picture Association of America anytime it's suspected. . . . At AMC Easton 30 last weekend, a guest was questioned for possible movie theft after he was identified wearing a recording device during a film. The presence of this recording device prompted an investigation by

the MPAA, which was on site. The MPAA then contacted Homeland Security, which oversees movie theft. The investigation determined the guest was not recording content.

An AMC representative explained that wearing a device that was capable of recording video, which could then be used to pirate movies, was not allowed at movies. Certainly the motion picture industry has the right to protect its products against piracy via wearable devices that can record movies in stealth. Do owners of wearables have comparable rights? Which of these conflicting rights should override the other? Now consider a similar example.

Example 2: Privacy Invasions

Privacy invasions by people wearing Google Glass who take photos or shoot video instantaneously are another violation. Some entertainment and dining places, including a restaurant in Seattle, have banned people who wear the devices. In some states, wearers who give Glass the command to record could potentially violate wiretapping laws. Should people who are out relaxing and enjoying themselves be subject to being recorded without their consent or knowledge? Whose rights should override in these cases?

Purpose of Google Glass Conflicts with Privacy of Others

In Google's view, the whole purpose of Glass is to have it on all the time. That is the Glass business model. The more the devices are worn, the more profitable they are. Google's response to privacy and piracy violations is that Glass is designed with explicit signals, such as the screen lighting up, to alert others when someone is taking a picture or recording video. In your opinion, is a lit screen sufficient protection?

The devices make it harder for nonwearers to remain anonymous. A facial recognition app, NameTag, allows Glass wearers to scan faces of strangers against known databases of faces. Google officially bans facial recognition apps on Google Glass. Does that ban have any meaning? Will people figure out how to get around it?

This opening case introduces current ethical challenges and competing rights decisions. Your answers to the questions within the case may change once you start to wear technology—or suffer because of others who do.

Questions

1. Imagine you had an app that monitors your surroundings and tells you when you are about to crash into something. In your opinion, should the use of that app while driving be legal or illegal? Explain your reasoning.

2. Individuals who become accustomed to capturing their lives with wearable devices could end up violating privacy, copyright, or piracy laws without realizing it. Research each of these laws and give a description of each.

3. Use what you learned in Question #2 to give three examples of how such a violation could occur. Why might these violations be practically impossible to prevent or prove?

4. Do you think that wearables similar to Google Glass should be illegal? Explain your answer.

5. Do you agree with the United Nation's position on corporate responsibility? Explain your answer.

6. Visit the SearchEngineWatch.com site. Search for "6 Funny Google Project Glass Parody Videos." Watch the original video named "Project Glass: One day. . ." Imagine how human interaction might change if a majority of people spent the day wearing Glass. Describe how you see interaction changing.

Sources: Compiled from Bader (2014), Perry (2014), Davis (2014), Taylor (2014), and Bilton (2015).

14.1 IT Ethics

We are in an age where technology is capturing and processing the details of everything we do through our interconnected devices in real time. Organizations view this as the ultimate way to predict who, where, and when customers will buy their products and what their future products should look like to be attractive. In the case of employees, organizations can predict how they will behave in different situations. On the one hand, this can lead to responsible conduct that benefits both organizations and their customers or employees, and on the other hand, it can lead to irresponsible conduct on the part of organizations who are eager to garner as much information as they possibly can, regardless of its negative impact.

Ethical versus Unethical Behavior

Any discussion about ethical behavior related to data and digital devices raises more questions than answers. Does the availability of data justify their use? Should shoppers be able to keep their buying habits private? Can people keep their entertainment, online gaming, and other legal activities confidential? Do media have the right to publish or post highly private text messages of politicians and celebrities? Questions about data access, collection, mining, tracking, monitoring, privacy, and profiling are examples of IT capabilities that have ethical considerations.

IT services and products are integral to the working of essentially every organization. Unethical and risky behavior by IT personnel can have far-reaching and negative impacts on organizations, industries, and society. As you read in Chapter 5, security breaches occur not only because of cyberattacks by hackers or APTs, but also by unethical or negligent IT employees who can bring entire industries to a halt by delaying or shutting down operations. Consider the situation where a database of health-care electronic records (first introduced in Chapter 3) is compromised. If vital medical data disappear or are unavailable when and where needed, patient care can be adversely affected.

From a societal perspective, people are naturally hesitant about using an organization's Internet-based and e-commerce services if they have concerns about the integrity of these systems. And, students graduating from college may be affected by IT hiring freezes imposed by companies who have encountered unethical employees in their IT departments.

And, in the development of software, some risky behaviors can be intentionally or inadvertently introduced by their developers.

Sometimes, the power of information and analytics is taken too far. This widely cited case of Target's questionable practice of predicting people's behavior using data analytics discussed in **IT at Work 14.1** is just one example.

Mobile Apps and Risky Behavior   According to app security analytics firm Appthority's *App Reputation Report* (2014), 93% of the top 200 free apps for iOS and Androids exhibited at least one risky behavior. However, so did 89% of the top 200 paid apps. Just about every app requires that you click "yes" on the user agreement, which gives your consent to use your data. Types of risky behaviors are shown in **Table 14.1**.

TABLE 14.1	Mobile App Risky Behaviors
Location Tracking	
Accessing device's address book or contact list	
Identifying user or phone unique identifier (UDID)	
Recording in-app purchases	
Sharing data with ad networks and analytics companies	

IT at Work 14.1

Predicting People's Behavior: Were Target's Big Data Analytics Tactics Too Invasive?

An angry man went into a Target store near Minneapolis insisting on talking to a manager. He handed a Target promotion that had been mailed to his teenage daughter to the manager, saying: "My daughter got this in the mail. She's still in high school, and you're sending her coupons for baby clothes and cribs? Are you trying to encourage her to get pregnant?" The confused manager had no idea what was going on. The mailer had been sent by Target and addressed to the man's daughter, and it contained specials for maternity clothing and nursery furniture. A few days later, he called the father to apologize again. Instead, the father apologized to the manager, explaining that he had since learned that his daughter was pregnant.

Inferences Based on Purchasing Data

How did Target know? Target knew by recognizing changes in the daughter's buying habits caused by a significant life event.

Using big data, models of buying habits, predictive analytics, and her purchase history, Target had figured out, with about 87% certainty, that she was pregnant. Target informed her family before she did. A lesson that Target discovered fairly quickly is that knowing about pregnancies in advance upsets people and can be a public relations disaster (Ellenberg, 2014). While Target assures compliance with all privacy laws, not breaking the law does not mean it is in the company's best interest to invade customers' privacy.

How Does Target Make Such Accurate Predictions?

Target assigns all customers a guest ID number that is linked to their credit card, name, e-mail address, and social media profile. The guest IDs become a bucket to store everything they have bought as well as demographic data. The demographic data linked to the guest ID include age, marital status, number of kids, address, how long it takes to drive to the store, estimated salary, whether the person moved recently, other credit cards, and visited websites. Using its own predictive models, Target identifies customers who are pregnant.

Why Does Target Invest in Predictive Analytics?

Target's strategy is to capture a greater share of spending on baby items by being first to reach and promote to prospective parents. Waiting for public birth records is too late because by then, parents are bombarded with offers and incentives from competing companies. Not everyone appreciates Target's strategy.

IT at Work Questions

1. Is Target's data mining and predictive analytics a success, a failure, or both? Explain your answer.
2. How does Target create profiles of customers?
3. Is Target's "pregnancy predictor" a long-term competitive advantage? Explain.
4. How can this predictor upset families who receive the promotions?
5. How does Target make such accurate predictions?
6. Why does Target invest in predictive analytics?

Mobile apps, such as Twitter, Foursquare, and Instagram, routinely gather information from personal address books and other places on your phone. Apple admits that any app that gathers a user's information without its permission is a violation of the law. Fortunately, Apple and Androids can only monitor apps available through the Apple Store and Google Play. However, there are countless third-party apps that are unregulated. If a user has an app that allows a company to access data on his or her phone and that phone is linked to the company's network, then privacy violations will happen.

Google's Street View Wi-Spy Snooping Scandal Google's Street View cars drove along U.S. streets—and later in Europe, Canada, Mexico, and everywhere else—collecting a stream of images to feed into Google Maps. Google's engineers realized that the cars could be used for **wardriving**—driving around sniffing out and mapping the physical location of the world's Wi-Fi routers. Wardriving is also a hacking technique, an invasion of privacy, and an information security risk.

Wardriving the act of searching for Wi-Fi wireless networks by a person in a moving vehicle using a laptop or smartphone.

Creating a database of Wi-Fi hotspot locations would make Google Maps more useful on mobile devices. Mobiles without GPS chips could use the database to approximate their physical location, and GPS-enabled devices could use the system to speed up their location-monitoring systems. When Google was building its system, a few start-ups had already created their own Wi-Fi mapping databases. However, Google was not only recording the location of people's Wi-Fi routers. When a Street View car encountered an **open Wi-Fi network**—a non-password-protected router—it recorded *all the digital traffic traveling across that router*. That is, when the car was within range of someone's open router, Google captured personal data, including login names and passwords, the full text of e-mails, Internet histories, people's medical conditions, online dating searches, streaming movies, and all other traffic.

Open Wi-Fi network an unprotected Wi-Fi network found particularly in public places where you don't know who else could be on the network.

According to the FCC (Federal Communications Commission) report, French investigators reviewed the data Google collected and found "an exchange of emails between a married woman and man, both seeking an extra-marital relationship" and "Web addresses that revealed the sexual preferences of consumers at specific residences." The sniffing stopped only when regulators discovered the practice. Google denied any wrongdoing.

The FCC posted the following on its website: "Google's behavior also raises important concerns. Whether intentional or not, collecting information sent over Wi-Fi networks clearly infringes on consumer privacy."

The FCC determined that Google's actions were not technically illegal because snooping on unencrypted wireless data is not prohibited by the Wiretap Act. Given that Google manages so much of our personal data, this privacy invasion is an example of irresponsible conduct.

The story did not end with the FCC's decision. The FCC's investigation into Google's mapping project was itself investigated. The renewed attention followed release of a mostly unredacted version of the FCC's findings in the case. The unredacted findings appear to contradict Google's claim that it inadvertently intercepted "payload data," or the content of individuals' Internet communications, in the process of gathering information from Wi-Fi networks across the globe for the Street View project. The document shows that, during preparations for the Street View effort, a Google engineer shared e-mails with colleagues at the firm revealing that he designed software for the project that was capable of collecting payload data. The new revelations have prompted **Consumer Watchdog**, a Washington-based advocacy group, to call for a hearing by the Senate Judiciary Subcommittee on Privacy, Technology, and the Law.

Tech-Savvy Individuals and Scalpers Exploit Artificial Intelligence

Artificial intelligence (AI) was designed to make our lives better and more efficient, but that is not always the case. For example, buying event tickets online is more stressful and near impossible in some instances than ever before due to AI.

Tech-savvy individuals create macros, which are computing apps that allow users to input one instruction that coincides with a long list of instructions to be completed automatically by the program, to instantly and automatically buy as many tickets to popular events and shows as possible. Acting alone or in collaboration with "scalpers," they resell the tickets at immensely inflated prices since the original tickets are sold out (Heritage, 2016).

One example of this type of unethical behavior was evident in tickets sales for Canadian hip-hop star Drake's February 5, 2017 concert in Greenwich, United Kingdom. To the consternation of many Drake fans who had roused themselves from sleep to have a chance to buy a ticket, the concert sold out online almost immediately. With original ticket prices ranging from 55 to 132 euros, the scalpers sold tickets for up to 800 Euros. It is estimated that one macro developer profited more than 25 million euros using this method.

Texting While Driving
Texting while driving is comparable to driving under the influence (DUI), according to safety experts. Several studies indicate that the use of mobile devices is a leading cause of car crashes. At any given moment, more than 10 million U.S. drivers are talking on handheld cell phones, according to the National Highway Traffic Safety Administration (NHTSA). Why is this a problem? Mobiles are a known distraction, and the NHTSA has determined that driver inattention is a primary or contributing factor in as many as 16% of all police-reported traffic accidents, and teen drivers are distracted by a mobile device while driving 25% of the time (Scopatz and Zhou, 2016). This does not include the thousands of accidents not reported to the authorities.

In most or all states, distracted driving carries mandatory fines. For example, in California and New York State, drivers charged with this crime face fines and have their driving license suspended. If driving while distracted causes injury or death to others, violators face jail time.

3D Printing and Bioprinting—Additive Manufacturing Dilemmas
Another trendy technology that has sparked ethical and other debates is the 3D printer and 3D bioprinting. Actual and planned applications include heart valves and other human organs (Martin, 2014). In 2014, surgeons used a 3D-printed model of a baby's skull in an intricate

surgery to correct a serious birth defect. Bioprinting of aortic valves and 3D bioprinting technology have been used by researchers at Cornell University to fabricate living heart valves that possess the same anatomical architecture as the original valve.

In 2015, 3D-printed airway splints for babies with tracheobronchomalacia, which makes the tiny airways around the lungs prone to collapsing, were successfully tested in three children between the ages of 3 months and 16 months (Hendricks, 2016). 3D technology may seem like a win-win with no dark side or ethical challenges. Unfortunately, that is not true.

Despite benefits, the medical application of bioprinting to produce living tissue and organs is expected to spark major ethical debates about whether lives are being saved or redefined (McRae, 2016). 3D-bioprinted human organs may be subject to conflicting religious, political, moral, and financial interests. The 3D printing of nonliving medical devices, such as prosthetic limbs, is expected to be in high demand because of longer life spans and insufficient levels of health care in various countries. A major hurdle is determining who is legally responsible for ensuring the quality of the resulting organs and devices? Without medical malpractice insurance covering these new applications, they cannot proceed.

According to a study by sustainable design strategist and Berkeley mechanical engineering expert Jeremy Faludi, 3D printers can exert impacts on the environment worse than those of standard manufacturing (Martin, 2014). The carbon footprint depends on what is being made and the type of printer used to make it. 3D printers use a lot more energy than conventional milling machines. 3D printers can use 100 times more electricity to produce a part than would have been used to produce the same part by nonadditive manufacturing.

Gartner (2016) predicts very strong growth in the 3D printer market with Greater China, emerging Asia/Pacific, and mature Asia/Pacific regions experiencing a combination of high 3D printer shipments and high growth rates through 2020. The growth will be driven by private-sector and public-sector organizations who recognize the threat that 3D printing poses to industries that don't get onboard and continue to rely on conventional manufacturing technologies. As the use of 3D printing accelerates, so will the debates about the ethical challenges it poses.

Competing Responsibilities

Most major retailers, from supermarket and drug store chains to major investment banks, rely on predictive analytics to understand consumer shopping habits and their personal habits to market more efficiently (IT at Work 14.1). In these cases, there are competing interests and trade-offs relating to privacy. There is also no clear-cut framework for deciding what is ethical and what is not. The personal privacy–public security debate is a prime example. Typically, privacy invasion is considered unethical. An ethically conscious corporate attitude sounds politically correct, but managers also have a responsibility to stakeholders. Monitoring may be (or seem to be) the responsible thing to do, and with intense competition, marketers naturally want to use every tool or technique to gain an edge or nullify a risk.

Globalization, the Internet, and connectivity have the power to undermine moral responsibility because it becomes relatively easy to ignore harm. Despite the challenges and lack of clear answers, ethics is important because relying on the law alone to safeguard civil rights and society is insufficient. The law has its limits in large part because it changes so slowly.

Questions

1. By avoiding illegal conduct, do companies also act responsibly? Explain your answer.
2. What types of companies can benefit from predicting people's behavior?
3. When is predicting people's behavior a violation of privacy? Give an example.
4. When is predicting people's behavior *not* a violation of privacy? Give an example.
5. What are the ethical challenges attached to 3D printing and 3D bioprinting?
6. Research the current debate about 3D printing and 3D bioprinting.

14.2 Privacy and Civil Rights

We do not live in a world without consequences and boundaries. Yet many people act as though they do, as the privacy paradox points out.

Privacy and the New Privacy Paradox

Privacy is the right to self-determine what information about you is made accessible, to whom, when, and for what use or purpose. Privacy means we have freedom of choice and control over our personal information, including what we do not want shared with or used by others. Unauthorized disclosure of personal information is normally considered a **breach of privacy**, although what is *unauthorized* and what is *personal information* are matters of dispute, particularly when it is online.

While privacy is still the social norm, a person's privacy is based to a large extent on what choices that person has made. The amount of shared personal information is a decision that individuals make over their lifetime. This is a critical concept because online content can persist for an entire lifetime. Private content that uninhibited teenagers with bad judgment posted or sent cannot be made to disappear when they apply for jobs requiring security clearance or intense background checks—or run for public office.

Users of social sites often claim that they are concerned about their privacy. At the same time, they disclose their highly personal lives, even content that is incriminating or illegal, in their profiles or posts. The **privacy paradox** refers to this phenomenon where social users are concerned about privacy, but their behaviors contradict these concerns to an extreme degree.

Facebook membership has increased despite Facebook founder Mark Zuckerberg's frequent changes to default privacy settings to allow everyone to see and search for names, gender, city, and other information. Zuckerberg's position is that people "have really gotten comfortable not only sharing more information and different kinds, but more openly and with more people." It is well known that Zuckerberg has a multibillion-dollar commercial interest in the elimination of online privacy, so trusting Facebook's privacy policies exemplifies the privacy paradox.

In a 2016 national privacy and security survey, Pew Research found that 64% of Americans have personally experienced a major data breach (**Figure 14.2**) and approximately 50% do not

---

Breach of privacy is the loss of, unauthorized access to, or disclosure of, personal information.

Privacy paradox refers to the competing demands of social media where users are concerned about privacy, but their willingness to disclose personal information does not mirror these concerns.

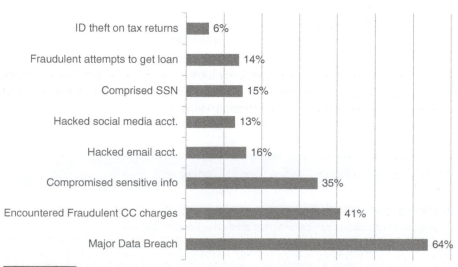

FIGURE 14.2 Major data breaches reported by 1,040 adult Americans in 2016 Pew Research privacy and security study.

trust the federal government or social media sites to protect their personal data even though they frequently neglect cybersecurity bet practices in their own personal lives (Olmstead and Smith, 2017). Unfortunately, 49% of the 1,040 adult Americans who took the study said that they feel their personal information is less secure than it was 5 years ago, and Americans aged 50+ were especially likely to feel that the privacy of their personal information was at risk. Fifty-eight percent in this older age group expressed this opinion compared with 41% of those in the 18–49 year age group.

This may be accounted for by the fact that social sites have become so embedded in the social lives of younger users that they disclose information about themselves even though these sites do not provide adequate privacy controls. The consequences of the privacy paradox are far reaching.

Social Media Recruiting

The use of social media is pervasive in today's workplace. Employers use social media for multiple reasons: to engage employees, to share knowledge among employees, and for recruitment and hiring of new employees. When the Society for Human Resource Management (SHRM) surveyed its members, they found that 84% of organizations are currently recruiting new talent via social media and another 9% are planning to use it in the near future (SHRM, 2016). They also reported that over one-third of the organizations represented have taken steps to leverage mobile recruiting to target smartphone users.

Social Tools for Recruiting and Background Checks
In order to cast a wide net for potential candidates, social media are used in **social recruitment**. However, improper use of information scraped from these sites may be discriminatory and illegal. The problem starts with members who post age, race, gender, and ethnicity information—or enable it to be learned from content on their sites. To the extent that employers conduct a social media background check on job candidates, these are three best practices. **Figure 14.3** shows the job levels that are typically recruited through social media (SHRM, 2016).

Social recruitment refers to use of social media to find, screen, and select job candidates.

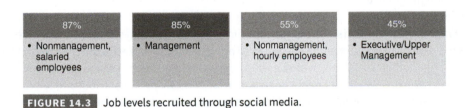

FIGURE 14.3   Job levels recruited through social media.

Recruiting through social media often involves searching information the job candidate did not want considered or that is illegal to use in the hiring process. To guard against this, it's advisable for companies to carry out the following steps:

1. Have either a third party or a designated person within the company who does not make hiring decisions do the background check.

2. Use only publicly available information. Do not friend someone to get access to private information.

3. Do not request username or passwords for social media accounts.

The National Conference of State Legislatures has passed summary legislation preventing employers from requesting passwords to personal Internet accounts to get or keep a job. To date, 25 states have enacted such laws. Other states have such laws pending, and there are several proposals before Congress to do the same on a federal level.

Social Recruiting and Social Stalking   Recruiters see LinkedIn as the world's largest resume database. Depending on how job candidates control their privacy and how much they reveal through check-ins and posts, recruiters learn a great deal of information that should not be used in their decision to interview, recommend, or hire someone. A 2016 Jobvite survey reported that 92% of all participating recruiters used social media in their outreach and that 87% said that they found LinkedIn to be the most effective way to vet candidates during the hiring process. Facebook, Twitter, blogs, and other forms of social media are also used.

Recruiters are also social stalkers! Almost half of the recruiters in the Jobvite survey said that they regarded photos of alcohol consumption and marijuana use on social networks negatively. And, interestingly were also negatively influenced by bad spelling in social media posts! Facebook members who expose too much information about themselves through social posts are vulnerable to employers and recruiters who use social content in the hiring process. Although laws forbid the use of certain types of social media information, it's hard to monitor its effect on hiring practices.

And job seekers fight back in response to these somewhat questionable recruiting practices. Jobvite reported that 23% of job seekers have modified their privacy settings on their Facebook pages and 10% on LinkedIn. In addition, 13% of job seekers have deleted some content on their Facebook pages and 10% said they'd changed content on their LinkedIn page (Jobvite, 2016).

EEOC (Equal Employment Opportunity Commission) enforces federal laws prohibiting discrimination in employment.

Protected Classes and Information   According to the **Equal Employment Opportunity Commission** (EEOC, 2014), discriminatory practices are prohibited. Title VII of the Civil Rights Act of 1964, the Age Discrimination in Employment Act of 1967 (ADEA), the Americans with Disabilities Act of 1990 (ADA), and Genetic Information Nondiscrimination Act of 2008 (GINA) make it illegal to discriminate in any aspect of employment, including recruitment, hiring, and firing. GINA, the latest of these laws, was passed when results from the Human Genome Project started raising ethical dilemmas. **Protected classes** is a term used in these laws to describe characteristics that cannot be targeted for **discrimination** and harassment. Protected classes include age, disability, gender, religion, genetic information, race, national origin, and pregnancy.

Protected classes are characteristics identified by law that cannot be used in the hiring process.

If information about protected classes is used to weed out candidates, it can lead to **corporate social media discrimination**. Discrimination is not always black and white because it is prejudicial treatment that may be tough to prove. Although job applicants might not know whether or not their social media profiles had been screened, they have several ways of finding out. For instance, an applicant might be tipped off after receiving a suspicious friend request or by talking with current employees and hiring managers who disclose the information—either purposely or accidentally—during the interview.

Discrimination is biased or prejudicial treatment in recruitment, hiring, or employment based on certain characteristics, such as age, gender, and genetic information, and is illegal in the United States.

Enterprises that have not implemented formal processes for the use of social media in recruiting and selection may put themselves at risk of legal complaints because of inconsistent practices.

Legal Note: Civil Rights

Civil rights are protected by federal law. If a person's civil rights are interfered with by another, the person can seek legal action for the injury. Examples of civil rights are freedom of speech, press, and assembly; the right to vote; and the right to equality in public places. Discrimination occurs when the civil rights of an individual are denied or interfered with because of their membership in a particular group or class. Various jurisdictions have enacted statutes to prevent discrimination based on a person's race, sex, religion, age, previous condition of servitude, physical limitation, national origin, and, in some instances, sexual orientation.

Competing Legal Concerns

Two competing legal concerns are discrimination and negligent hiring (discussed briefly earlier).

- **Discrimination**   Most employers have stringent employment policies that prevent their recruiters and hiring managers from learning potentially discriminatory information about candidates. Visiting a person's social media sites, however, clearly creates the opportunity to view large amounts of information going against these nondiscriminatory practices.

- **Negligent hiring**   Employers must consider the potential risk of a **negligent hiring** or negligent retention lawsuit related to social networking profile information. It is possible that if a workplace violence incident occurred and the attacker's public social networking profile contained information that could have predicted that behavior, the employer may be held liable for negligence in not using readily available information during the hiring decision.

Negligent hiring   is the hiring of an employee when the employer knew or should have known about the employee's background which, if known, indicates a dangerous or untrustworthy character.

Examples and a discussion of these issues follow.

Discrimination via Social Media Scenario   Imagine that an employer reviews a candidate's activity on social media platforms and discovers the following information about him.

1. The candidate checks in via Foursquare at Woodsman Gym once or twice a day usually around 7 a.m., noon, or 6 p.m.

2. His Facebook album is filled with party photos, showing what might be considered excessive drinking.

3. His resume suggests that he is in his early 30s, but his social profile about high school indicates that his real age is late 40s.

4. His posts describe his religious beliefs and customs, family's serious medical conditions, financial stress, and desire to spend as much time as possible snowboarding.

5. He makes fun of and posts insulting cartoons of people who follow a dress code at work.

The Federal Trade Commission (FTC) has ruled that companies that research how you spend your personal time, hobbies, and so on, do not violate your privacy. Party photos might not show illegal behavior, but when posted on a social network, they could influence a potential employer's evaluation of a job applicant as well as disclose information about race, gender, age, and other protected characteristics.

As many other job seekers, this candidate is posting, tweeting, and blogging information he would not want a recruiter or prospective employer to know about. If he is rejected because of his age, religion, or genetic condition, the company has committed social media discrimination and is very likely in violation of other laws.

Reducing the Risk of Negligent Hiring   In the past, employment law attorneys dealt with this risk by advising companies to avoid using social media in their hiring and recruitment process to avoid legal risk. However, that proposal is not realistic. By opting out of social media, recruiting firms lose a productive way to find candidates, which could cost them millions of dollars. Additionally, background checks must be conducted. Almost all employers do some form of background screening in order to avoid the risk of negligent hiring. Negligent hiring is a claim made by an injured party against an employer who knew or should have known about an employee's background that indicates a dangerous or untrustworthy character. Employers have a legal obligation to make the best effort to protect their employees and customers when

they hire. Steps companies can take to balance the competing risks of negligent hiring and social discrimination are as follows:

1. **Ask candidates to sign a disclosure statement**   Let candidates themselves disclose information found on social media. Explain to them the reason for the disclosure statement.

2. **Create a standard process and document it**   A consistent and well-documented process is needed to ensure and show compliance if there is an EEOC employment investigation.

3. **Avoid coercive practices**   Make sure that recruiters do not pressure applicants to disclose protected information via social media by requiring them to disclose passwords or relax privacy settings for purposes of review by the employer.

4. **Training**   This may sound like a no-brainer, but training and repeated reminders are important to emphasize that management intends to be in compliance with laws and regulations related to social recruiting.

Financial Organizations Must Comply with Social Media Guidelines

The Federal Financial Institutions Examination Council (FFIEC) released guidelines entitled *Social Media: Consumer Compliance Risk Management Guidance* to help financial institutions effectively manage the current risks caused by the use of social media. The activities of financial institutions are regulated by consumer protection and compliance laws. These institutions must take steps to protect their reputations and their clients—very similar to the steps that HR departments must take to comply with EEOC guidelines (EEOC, 2014). Key social media guidelines for financial institutions are listed in **Table 14.2**.

TABLE 14.2   **Key Social Media Guidelines for Financial Institutions**

Guidelines	Issue	Solution
Institute policies to comply with advertising, communications, and other consumer protection laws	No policies in place; need a social media risk assessment tool.	Implement social policies to prevent issues such as spam. For example, staff should know how to react when a customer posts confidential information such as a bank number on their social profiles.
Use monitoring tools	Financial institutions have added social channels that can expose their brand to additional feedback.	Use social monitoring tools to identify issues that may cause a negative reaction and respond quickly. The use of social monitoring tools also helps banks refute inaccurate statements, protecting their brand reputation.
Train employees	Whether or not employees represent your brand on social media, their public social comments may be seen to reflect the financial institution.	The best way to reduce risk is to train employees on how to use social networks professionally.

Companies expose themselves to harsh sanctions by federal agencies when they violate the privacy policies that their customers rely upon. Unlike social discrimination, these cases are rather easy to detect and prosecute. For example, the FTC charged SnapChat for, in effect, deceiving its customers with its bogus disappearing messages services. The FTC scrutinizes business practices to regulate "unfair and deceptive trade practices." The FTC has been focused on curtailing deceptive practices, even if unintentional, by businesses engaged in online commerce. While businesses should always ensure that their online advertisements are truthfully conveyed, a business with a social media presence should take particular note of the FTC's recent efforts concerning online privacy, security, and advertising. **IT at Work 14.2** describes such a case.

IT at Work 14.2

SnapChat Lied about Disappearing Messages and Privacy

FTC Chairwoman Edith Ramirez stated, "If a company markets privacy and security as key selling points in pitching its service to consumers, it is critical that it keep those promises" (Fitzpatrick and Kibel, 2014).

SnapChat Fined for Violating Its Own Privacy Policies and Misleading Users

The FTC charged SnapChat with violating its promises of "disappearing messages." According to the FTC's complaint:

1. SnapChat's mobile app allows consumers to send and receive photo and video messages known as snaps. SnapChat falsely marketed its app as a service for sending disappearing photo and video messages. Before sending a snap, the sender has to designate a period of time that the recipient will be allowed to view the snap.

2. Despite SnapChat's claims, the FTC contended that several methods exist by which a recipient can use tools outside of the app to save both photo and video messages, allowing the recipient to access and view the photos or videos indefinitely. For example, when a person receives a video message, the app stores the video file in a location outside of the app's sandbox. Sandbox is the app's private storage area on the device that other apps cannot access.

3. Until October 2013, a recipient could connect his or her mobile device to a computer and use simple file browsing tools to locate and save the video file. Although this method for saving video files was widely publicized as early as December 2012, the FTC contended that SnapChat did not mitigate this flaw until October 2013.

4. SnapChat misrepresented its data collection practices by transmitting geolocation data from users of its Android app despite its privacy policy saying that it did not track or access these data.

5. SnapChat collected contact data from users' address books without notice or consent and continued to do so without notifying users or obtaining their consent until Apple modified its operating system to provide notice with the introduction of iOS 6.

6. SnapChat's failure to secure its "Find Friends" feature resulted in a security breach that enabled attackers to compile a database of 4.6 million SnapChat usernames and phone numbers.

Settlement

SnapChat settled FTC charges alleging false promises of disappearing messages and failure to protect consumer data. Under the terms of its agreement with the FTC, SnapChat is prohibited from misrepresenting the extent to which it maintains the privacy, security, or confidentiality of users' data. SnapChat must implement a comprehensive privacy program that will be monitored by an independent privacy professional for the next 20 years.

IT at Work Questions

1. Which SnapChat claims of privacy protection were false?

2. Assume that users relied on SnapChat's state privacy policies and claims about how the app worked. What potential risks did SnapChat users face?

3. If you had used the SnapChat app to send disappearing messages, what would you do when you learned of SnapChat's false claims?

4. Do you think the consequences SnapChat faced as part of its settlement with the FT are harsh enough to deter false claims? Explain.

Questions

1. What is privacy of information?
2. What is the phenomenon where social users are concerned about privacy but their behaviors contradict these concerns?
3. What is the use of social media to find, screen, and select job candidates?
4. Rejecting a job candidate because of concerns about the person's health from information on his or her Facebook page is an example of what?
5. Age, disability, gender, religion, and race are examples of what?
6. Why are the legal concepts of discrimination and negligent hiring competing demands on a business?

14.3 Technology Addictions and Focus Management

Technologies in the digital age blur work, social, and personal time. IT keeps people connected with no real off switch. Tools that are meant to improve the productivity and quality of life in general can also intrude on personal time.

The complexity of a connected life will increase as we move to the new era of nanosensors and devices, virtual spaces, and 3D social networks exchanging zillions of bytes of data. Managers and workers need to consider ethical and social issues, such as quality of life and working conditions. Individuals will experience both positive and negative impacts from being linked to a 24/7 workplace, working in virtual teams, and being connected to handhelds whose impact on health can be damaging. A 2016 study by nonprofit organization Common Sense Media found that always being connected is a borderline obsession for many people. According to the study, 50% of American teens may suffer from FOMO, or the fear of missing out, and *disconnect anxiety*—feelings of disorientation and nervousness when deprived of Internet or wireless access for a period of time (Wallace, 2016).

Many people live and work in a state of continuous partial attention as they move through their day—loosely connected to friends and family through various apps on mobile and wearable devices. Consider what devices you use to stay informed and how often you glance at them. You might not have noticed the gradual increase in the amount of data and information that you receive or check routinely until one day they seem to overwhelm your time. How many more things do you check today compared to a year ago? How long can you go without checking your devices without experiencing anxiety? When do you put down your mobiles and concentrate on one thing at a time? Your answers may indicate digital or connectivity overload and your tolerance for distractions.

The time between a new device or app going from *must have* to *cannot function without* is rather short. This situation is not limited to only digital natives. Studies show that adults are just as distracted as teenagers, which can also be confirmed with a casual glance at offices, airports, cafes, and other public gathering places.

Digital Distractions and Loss of Focus

People do not need to be reminded how their lives are being taken over by tweets, texts, e-mail, social media, and annoying electronic static. Business users are more likely to suffer from too much data, rather than from data scarcity. This condition, known as **cognitive overload**, interferes with our ability to focus and be productive.

How big is this problem and how much does it cost? Some researchers estimate that distraction costs hundreds of billions of dollars a year in lost productivity. Gloria Mark, a professor of informatics at the University of California, Irvine, says a worker distracted by a Web search that goes rogue or a new text or tweet can take about 25 minutes to return to the task at hand and get focused again (Dumaine, 2014). Digital distraction and lack of focus in the workplace are getting the attention of senior management. When Inc. called the CEOs of technology companies Instagram, Box, and Zumba, they confirmed that the lack of focus on the job is a big concern for them.

Focus Management

Senior management at Google, SAP, Instagram, Box, and Zumba are experimenting with new ways to diminish cognitive overload in order to help their employees stay focused. For example, at Google, employees take courses that help to sharpen their attention skills. The founders of Zumba and Box have developed their own methods to carve out focus time, such as putting aside large blocks of time to think undisturbed.

The Importance of Being Able to Focus   Nobel Prize-winning neuroscientist Eric Kandel wrote in his book *In Search of Memory* that only by intensely concentrating can a person link new ideas and facts "meaningfully and systematically with knowledge already well-established in memory" (Kandel, 2006). He explained the importance of mental discipline to successful performance. If your mind is free of distraction, your mind is better able to absorb data, interactions, and trends and synthesize the new information with what you already know. As a result, you are more likely to come up with innovative ideas. If you are multitasking or are trying to function with only partial attention, your ability to synthesize information may be compromised.

Researchers at the Communication Between Humans and Interactive Media Lab at Stanford University studied digital distraction and focus. Researchers gave the same three cognitive tests to two different groups of test subjects:

1.   **Media (high) multitaskers**   Forty-nine subjects who spent a lot of time searching the Internet, gaming online, watching TV, and hanging out on social media sites.
2.   **Low multitaskers**   Fifty-two subjects who spent less time online and multitasked significantly less often.

Ten years ago, many believed that the Internet sharpened cognitive skills. Gaming required fast thinking and good motor skills. In contrast to widely held assumptions, the subjects who were heavy online users scored poorly on the cognitive test. One explanation for their poor performance was that they had attention deficits—less control over their attention. Because of their inability to concentrate for long, they were not able to distinguish important information from trivia. Researchers continue to study whether chronic media multitaskers are born with an inability to concentrate or are damaging their cognitive control by willingly taking in so much at once. Science also shows that the best strategy to improve focus is to practice doing it.

Michael Merzenich, a neuroscientist, gave a biological explanation of the impacts of multitasking on focus ability. He explained that the more you focus, the more your brain releases a chemical called noradrenaline, which helps you concentrate on the task at hand.

The American Psychological Association disagrees saying that "Although switch costs may be relatively small, sometimes just a few tenths of a second per switch, they can add up to large amount when people switch repeatedly back and both between tasks. Thus, multi-tasking may see efficient on the surface, but may actually take more time in the end and involve more error" (Wrike, 2015). Even brief mental blocks created by shifting between tasks can cost as much as 40% of someone's productive time—that's 16 hours out of every work week!

In our hyperconnected world, people are always on—collaborating, communicating, and creating—and not always aware of how technology impacts them or the environment. Today's connected lifestyles will further harm the environment unless corrective actions are taken such as those listed in **Figure 14.4**.

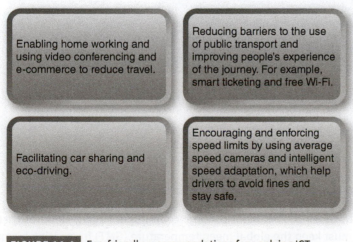

FIGURE 14.4   Eco-friendly recommendations for applying ICT.

Learning how to harness ICT to develop the next generation of critical, thoughtful thinkers who are respectful of the environment is the challenge we need to meet.

Questions

1. What are the several potential causes of cognitive overload?
2. What are the consequences of constant distractions?
3. When a person is distracted, how long does it take to return to the task at hand and get focused again?
4. Why are senior managers interested in focus management?
5. What is the difference between the performance of high and low multitaskers on cognitive tests?
6. How can multitaskers improve their ability to focus?

14.4 ICT and Sustainable Development

Sustainability grows more urgent every year as carbon emissions contribute to climate changes that are threatening quality of life—and possibly life itself. For example, every day people watch hundreds of millions of hours on YouTube and generate billions of views. Statistics about LinkedIn, Twitter, and other social media services also show phenomenal growth. Almost all of these network activities are powered by the burning of fossil fuels.

Being profit-motivated without concern for damage to the environment is unacceptable. Society expects companies to generate a profit and to conduct themselves in an ethical, socially responsible, and environmentally sustainable manner. Four factors essential to preserving the environment are shown in **Figure 14.5**.

skegbydave/iStockphoto

FIGURE 14.5 The four "Rs" of environmental sustainability.

Global Temperature Rising Too Much Too Fast

At the United Nations' 2009 climate conference in Copenhagen, climatologists estimated that countries must keep the global mean temperature (GMT) from rising by more than 2°C (3.6°F) above the preindustrial GMT in order to avoid profound damage to life on the earth

(**Tech Note 14.1**). Damage includes water and food scarcity, rising sea levels, and greater incidence and severity of disease. Only three years later, GMT had already increased by 0.7°C or 1.3°F. In 2012, IEA chief economist Faith Birol warned that this trend is perfectly in line with a temperature increase of 6°C by 2050, which would have devastating impacts on the planet. Since 2005, the Prince of Wales' Corporate Leaders Group on Climate Change has lobbied for more aggressive climate legislation within the United Kingdom, the European Union, and internationally. It holds that carbon emission reductions between 50% and 85% are necessary by 2050 to prevent the global temperature from rising too much too fast because of the greenhouse effect.

Tech Note 14.1

NASA's Greenhouse Gas Emission Warnings

According to **NASA**, carbon dioxide (CO_2) and other **greenhouse gases (GHGs)** trap the sun's heat within the earth's atmosphere, warming it and keeping it at habitable temperatures. Scientists have concluded that increases in CO_2 resulting from human activities have thrown the earth's natural carbon cycle off balance, increasing global temperatures and changing the planet's climate.

The main international treaty on climate change is the United Nations Framework Convention on Climate Change (UNFCCC). The

UNFCCC has proposed that future global warming should be limited to below 2°C (3.6°F) relative to the preindustrial level. Analysis suggests that meeting the 2°C target would require annual global emissions of GHG to peak before the year 2020 and decline significantly thereafter, with emissions in 2050 reduced by to 50% compared to 1990 levels.

Analyses by the United Nations Environment Programme and International Energy Agency warn that current policies are too weak to achieve the 2°C target.

IT and Global Warming

Global warming refers to the upward trend in GMT. It is one of the most complicated issues facing world leaders. **Figure 14.6** shows the relationship of fossil fuel, soil, water, atmosphere, and other elements in the carbon cycle. Even though the global carbon cycle plays a central role in regulating CO_2 in the atmosphere and thus the earth's climate, scientists' understanding

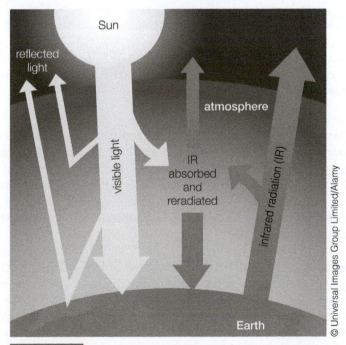

FIGURE 14.6 Greenhouse gases absorb infrared radiation (IR) emitted from the earth and reradiate it back, thus contributing to the greenhouse effect.

of the interlinked biological processes that drive this cycle is limited. They know that whether an ecosystem will capture, store, or release carbon depends on climate changes and organisms in the earth's biosphere. The biosphere refers to any place that life of any kind can exist on the earth and contains several ecosystems. An ecosystem is a self-sustaining functional unit of the biosphere; it exchanges material and energy between adjoining ecosystems. Global warming occurs because of the greenhouse effect, which is the holding of heat within the earth's atmosphere. GHGs such as CO_2, methane (CH_4), and nitrous oxide (N_2O) absorb infrared radiation (IR), as diagrammed in **Figure 14.7**.

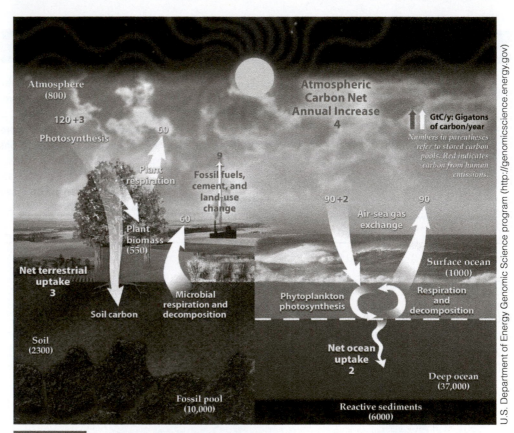

FIGURE 14.7 Carbon cycle. The Orbiting Carbon Observatory-2 was launched in July 2014. The observatory is NASA's first satellite mission dedicated to studying CO_2, which is a critical component of the earth's carbon cycle driving changes in the earth's climate. CO_2 is also the largest human-produced GHG. Courtesy of genomicscience.energy.gov.

The IT industry sector is called the information and communications technology, or ICT, in emission reports. ICT has certainly supported economic growth in developed and developing countries and transformed societies, businesses, and people's lives. But what impacts do our expanding IT and social media dependence have on global warming? How can business processes change or reduce GHGs? And what alternative energy sources can be used to power the increasing demands for connectivity? Listed next are several reports and initiatives to help answer these questions.

Global e-Sustainability Initiative and the SMART 2020 Report The Climate Group's SMART 2020 Report is the world's first comprehensive global study of the IT sector's growing significance for the world's climate. On behalf of the Global e-Sustainability Initiative (**GeSI**), Climate Group found that ICT plays a key role in reducing global warming. Transforming the way people and businesses use IT could reduce annual human-generated global emissions by 15% by 2020 and deliver energy efficiency savings to global businesses of over 500 billion euros or $800 billion. And using social media, for example, to inform consumers of the grams (g) of carbon emissions associated with the products they buy could change buyer behavior and ultimately have a positive eco-effect. Similarly to food items that display calories and grams of fat to help consumers make healthier food choices, product labels display the CO_2 emissions generated in the production of an item. By 2020, not only will people become more connected, but things will as well—an estimated 50 billion machine-to-machine connections in 2020. A benefit of machine-to-machine connections is that they can relay data about climate changes that make it possible to monitor our emissions.

Recommended Actions for the IT Sector   Analysis conducted by management consultants McKinsey & Company concludes the following:

- The IT sector's own footprint of 2% of global emissions could double by 2020 because of increased use of tablets, smartphones, apps, and services. To help, rather than worsen, the fight against climate change, the IT sector must manage its own growing impact and continue to reduce emissions from data centers, telecom networks, and the manufacture and use of its products.
- IT has the unique ability to monitor and maximize energy efficiency both within and outside of its own industry sector to cut CO_2 emissions by up to 5 times this amount. This represents a savings of 7.8 Gt of CO_2 per year by 2020, which is greater than the 2010 annual emissions of either the United States or China.

The SMART 2020 Report gives a picture of the IT industry's role in addressing global climate change and facilitating efficient and low-carbon development. The role of IT includes emission reduction and energy savings not only in the sector itself, but also by transforming how and where people work. The most obvious ways are by substituting digital formats—telework, videoconferencing, e-paper, and mobile and e-commerce—for physical formats. Researchers estimate that replacing physical products/services with their digital equivalents would provide 6% of the total benefits the IT sector can deliver. Greater benefits are achieved when IT is applied to other industries. Examples of those industries are smart building design and use, smart logistics, smart electricity grids, and smart industrial motor systems.

Global Warming: A Hot Debate   Does our society have the capacity to endure in such a way that the 9 billion people expected on the earth by 2050 will all be able to achieve a basic quality of life? The answer is uncertain—and hotly debated. As you read, many scientists and experts are extremely alarmed by global warming and climate change, but other experts outright deny that they are occurring.

This debate may be resolved to some degree by NASA. A NASA spacecraft was designed to make precise measurements of CO_2 in the earth's atmosphere. The Orbiting Carbon Observatory-2 (OCO-2) was launched in July 2014. The observatory is NASA's first satellite mission dedicated to studying CO_2, a critical component of the earth's carbon cycle that is the most prevalent human-produced GHG driving changes in the earth's climate (Figure 14.7).

OCO-2 is a new tool for understanding both the sources of CO_2 emissions and the natural processes that remove CO_2 from the atmosphere and how they are changing over time. The mission's data will help scientists reduce uncertainties in forecasts of how much CO_2 is in the atmosphere and improve the accuracy of global climate change predictions.

According to NASA, since the start of the Industrial Revolution more than 200 years ago, the burning of fossil fuels and other human activities have led to an unprecedented buildup in GHGs. Human activities have increased the level of CO_2 by more than 25% in just the past half century.

It is possible that we are living far beyond the earth's capacity to support human life. While sustainability is about the future of our society, for businesses, it is also about return on investment (ROI). Businesses need to respect environmental limits, but also need to show an ROI.

Sustainability Through Climate Change Mitigation   There are no easy or convenient solutions to carbon emissions from the fossil fuels burned to power today's tech dependencies. But there are pathways to solutions, and every IT user, enterprise, and nation plays a role in **climate change mitigation**. Climate change mitigation is any action to limit the magnitude of long-term climate change. Examples of mitigation include switching to low-carbon renewable energy sources and reducing the amount of energy consumed by power stations by increasing their efficiency. There have been encouraging successes. For example, investments in research and development (R&D) to reduce the amount of carbon emitted by power stations for mobile networks are paying off. A breakthrough in the design of signal amplifiers for mobile technology will cut 200 megawatts (MW) from the load of power stations, which will reduce CO_2 emissions by 0.5 million tonnes a year (Engineering and Physical Sciences Research Council, 2014).

Mobile, Cloud, and Social Carbon Footprint No one sees CO_2 being emitted from their Androids or iPhones. But wired and mobile networks enable limitless data creation and consumption—and these activities increase energy consumption. Quite simply, the surge in energy used to power data centers, cell towers, base stations, and recharge devices is damaging the environment and depleting natural resources. It is critical to develop energy systems that power our economy without increasing global temperatures beyond 2°C. To do their part to reduce damaging carbon emissions, some companies have implemented effective sustainability initiatives.

Sustainability Initiatives Communications technology accounts for approximately 2% of global carbon emissions; it is predicted that this figure will double by 2020 as end-user demand for high-bandwidth services with enhanced quality of experience explodes worldwide. Innovative solutions hold the key to curbing these emissions and reducing environmental impact.

Network service providers as well as organizations face the challenges of energy efficiency, a smaller **carbon footprint**, and eco-sustainability. To deal with these challenges, wired and wireless service providers and companies need to upgrade their networks to next-generation, all-IP infrastructures that are optimized and scalable. The network must provide eco-sustainability in traffic transport and deliver services more intelligently, reliably, securely, efficiently, and at the lowest cost.

For example, Alcatel-Lucent's High Leverage Network (HLN) can reduce total cost of ownership (TCO) by using fewer devices, creating an eco-sustainable choice for service providers. Fewer devices mean less power and cooling, which reduces the carbon footprint. HLN can also handle large amounts of traffic more efficiently because the networks are intelligent, sending packets at the highest speed and most efficiently.

Technology to Transform Business and Society

People hold the power to shape and apply technology to create positive change, improve lives, and transform business and society. According to Paul Daugherty, Accenture's Chief Technology and Innovation Officer, "The pace of technology change is breathtaking, bringing about the biggest advancements since the dawn of the Information Age. As technology transforms the way we work and live, it raises important societal challenges and creates new opportunities. Ultimately, people are in control of creating the changes that will affect our lives, and we're optimistic that responsive and responsible leaders will ensure the positive impact of new technologies." (Accenture, 2017).

IoT in Developing Nations An important technology that is helping developing nations harness the power of data to make crucial decisions about agriculture, health care, education, and infrastructure is the Internet of things (IoT).

Although data is sparse in some developing nations, big data can be gathered from surrounding nations to find correlations in the information. Joseph Alhadeff, Chair of the ICC Commission on the Digital Economy, says "For sustainable development, the reason why this technology has application in developing countries is that it can be used for any problem that requires data to help solve it. Internet of Things is really an enabling technology in terms of usability. Even basic deployments can be transformative for populations" (ICC, 2016).

People-First Approach to Technology   Each year, Accenture publishes its *Technology Vision* (Accenture, 2017), an analysis of key IT trends that are expected to disrupt business and society over the next 3 years. According to *Vision 2017*, taking a **people-first approach** by empowering people with more human technology will allow organizations to improve performance by redefining their relationship with customers and employees from provider to partner. This will require organizations to change the way they develop their business models and provide technology that support them to promote social responsibility.

People-first approach   ensures that technology meets the needs of the users by involving the users at every stage of systems development.

A comparison of the disruptive technologies highlighted by Accenture's Technology Visions 2015, 2016, and 2017, listed in **Table 14.3**, illustrates the trend toward a *people-first* approach to technology.

TABLE 14.3   **Comparison of Accenture's Top Five Disruptive Technologies 2015–2017**

Vision 2015	Vision 2016	Vision 2017
Internet of Me	Intelligent Automation	Artificial Intelligence as the new User Interface
Outcome Economy	Liquid Workforce	Design for Humans
Platform Evolution	Platform Economy	Ecosystems as Macrocosms
Intelligent Enterprise	Predictable Disruption	Workforce Marketplace
Workforce Reimagined	Digital Trust	The Unchartered

An explanation of *Vision 2017's* five IT trends that have the most potential to transform business and society over the next three years follows:

TREND 1: AI is the new UI   AI is coming of age, tackling problems both big and small by making interactions simple and smart. AI is becoming the new user interface (UI), underpinning the way we transact and interact with systems. Seventy-nine percent of survey respondents agree that AI will revolutionize the way they gain information from and interact with customers.

TREND 2: Design for Humans   Technology design decisions are being made by humans, for humans. Technology adapts to how we behave and learns from us to enhance our lives, making them richer and more fulfilling. Eighty percent of executives surveyed agree that organizations need to understand not only where people are today, but also where they want to be—and shape technology to act as their guide to realize desired outcomes.

TREND 3: Ecosystems as Macrocosms   Platform companies that provide a single point of access to multiple services have completely broken the rules for how companies operate and compete. Companies don't just need a platform strategy, they need a rich and robust ecosystem approach to lead in this new era of intelligence. Already, more than one-quarter (27%) of executives surveyed reported that digital ecosystems are transforming the way their organizations deliver value.

TREND 4: Workforce Marketplace   The number of on-demand labor platforms and online work-management solutions is surging. As a result, leading companies are dissolving traditional hierarchies and replacing them with talent marketplaces, which in turn is driving the most profound economic transformation since the Industrial Revolution. Case in point: Eighty-five percent of executives surveyed said they plan to increase their organization's use of independent freelance workers over the next year.

TREND 5: The Uncharted   To succeed in today's ecosystem-driven digital economy, businesses must delve into uncharted territory. Instead of focusing solely on introducing new products and services, they should think much bigger—seizing opportunities to establish rules and standards for entirely new industries. In fact, 74% of the executives surveyed said that their organization is entering entirely new digital industries that are yet to be defined.

Next Wave of Disruption Will Be More Disruptive

High-performing business leaders now accept that their organizations' future success is tied to their ability to keep pace with technology. Accenture reports that its clients tell them that technology is more important than ever to their business success. But today, the biggest IT innovations will not be in the technology tools themselves, but in how they are designed with people in mind. It is widely agreed that a people-*first* approach is the key to any organization's digital success.

Questions

1. Why do some experts warn that carbon emission reductions between 50% and 85% are necessary by 2050?
2. What contributes to the rise of global mean temperature?
3. What is the greenhouse effect?
4. How does the use of mobile devices contribute to the level of greenhouse gases?
5. What is ICT's role in global warming?
6. Why is global warming hotly debated?
7. What is the role of IT in sustainable development?
8. Why is it important for organizations to take a *people-first* approach to IT?

Key Terms

breach of privacy   424
carbon footprint   436
civil rights   426
climate change mitigation   436
cognitive overload   430
corporate social media discrimination   426

discrimination   426
Equal Employment Opportunity Commission   426
greenhouse gases (GHGs)   433
negligent hiring   427
open Wi-Fi network   421

people-first approach   437
privacy   424
privacy paradox   424
protected class   426
social recruitment   425
wardriving   421

Assuring Your Learning

Discuss: Critical Thinking Questions

1. Why will companies and recruiters continue to engage in social recruiting?

2. Visit two or more social media sites and review information that people have posted about themselves—or their friends have posted about them. What types of protected class information did you find? Give examples.

3. When organizations source their hiring to recruiting firms, how might that increase or decrease the risk of social media discrimination?

4. How has IT changed the way you communicate in the last two years?

5. What changes do you predict in the way we communicate with each other in future?

6. In your opinion, how does multitasking impact your performance?

7. How does the use of mobile devices contribute to the level of greenhouse gases?

8. What is ICT's role in global warming?

9. How do mobile devices contribute to carbon emissions?

10. Discuss the ethical issues of anytime–anywhere accessibility.

11. What health and quality-of-life issues are associated with social networks and a 24/7 connected lifestyle?

12. Is distracted driving an unsolvable problem? Explain.

Explore: Online and Interactive Exercises

1. Social media discrimination is now a serious consideration for employers.

   a. Research recruiting service providers and vendors. Select two of them.

   b. Review the website of each service or vendor.

   c. Describe the features they provide to defend against negligent hiring.

   d. Do each of them protect against social discrimination? Explain your answer and give examples.

2. Visit the Nokia website **https://networks.nokia.com/blog/2015/new-digital-deal-earths-climate**

   a. Read about Alcatel-Lucent's "New Digital Deal for the Earth's Climate."

   b. Describe how the company has made major investment to address the issue of network power consumption.

   c. Explain how the company is enabling a low-carbon economy. What is its most significant contribution to sustainability?

Analyze & Decide: Apply IT Concepts to Business Decisions

1. Refer to the discrimination scenarios in this chapter. For each scenario, explain whether or not it should be used in the hiring decision.

2. In your opinion, what is the meaning of *responsible conduct* with respect to the use of social media for screening purposes?

3. Do you agree with the FTC's 2011 rule that states that searches by hiring companies into how you spend your personal time, hobbies, and the like do not violate your privacy? Explain.

4. Clerks at 7-Eleven stores enter data regarding customers' gender, approximate age, and so on, into a computer system. However, names are not keyed in. These data are then aggregated and analyzed to improve corporate decision-making. Customers are not informed about this, nor are they asked for permission. What problems do you see with this practice?

5. Discuss whether cognitive overload is a problem in your work or education. Based on your experience, what personal and organizational solutions can you recommend for this problem?

6. The State of California maintains a database of people who allegedly abuse children. (The database also includes names of the alleged victims.) The list is made available to dozens of public agencies, and it is considered in cases of child adoption and employment decisions. Because so many people have access to the list, its content is easily disclosed to outsiders. An alleged abuser and her child, whose case was dropped because there was insufficient evidence to warrant further investigation or prosecution, but whose names remained on the list, sued the State of California for invasion of privacy. Debate the issues involved. Specifically:

   a. Who should make the decision or what criteria should guide the decision about what names should be included and what the criteria should be?

   b. What is the potential damage to the abusers (if any)?

   c. Should the State of California abolish the list? Why or why not?

Case 14.2

Business Case: Android Auto and CarPlay Keep Drivers Safe, Legal, and Productive

We've all done it—driving while talking on our smartphone and perhaps texting. But, in more and more states across the United States, it is becoming illegal to do one or both. While one technology can tempt us to break the law, new mobile apps, such as Google's Android Auto and Apple's CarPlay, can help us stay on the right side of the law. And, these new apps are a boon to business. For example, salespeople, project managers, insurance adjusters, and tradespeople who spend much of their time driving between customer locations can now safely make the most of their driving time and increase their productivity.

If you buy a car today, it will probably come with some kind of touch-screen computer onboard: basically, an embedded table computer that runs some kind of operating system, with software provided by the car manufacturer and their suppliers. Unfortunately, since car manufacturers are not in the software business, these onboard computers aren't designed very well and don't have the user-friendly interface that smartphones do. As a result, many people still resort to using their handheld mobile devices (Amadeo, 2015). Android Auto and CarPlay have easy-to-use, safety-focused user interfaces with a heavy emphasis on voice commands and the look and feel of the mobile devices that are already familiar to you.

Android Auto

Android Auto is a projected interface that runs on an Android phone and is beamed to the car screen when it's hardwired through a USB connection. Google worked with the NHTSA and other government agencies to design an interface that follows best safety practices for computing while driving. The result is larger touch targets, bigger text that can been seen "at a glance," a focus on voice commands, and an overall greatly simplified interface (Amadeo, 2015).

Third-party apps on Android Auto are limited to Media and Messaging apps—nothing else is allowed. Developers can't make an app interface. Third-party apps can only plug into Google's UI template. This means there are only a few apps that currently work with Android Auto. These include Spotify, Skype, and WhatsApp. The reason for the third-party limitations is compliance with the hundreds of car infotainment safety regulations worldwide to ensure user safety.

At Google, every Android app get heavily reviewed by Google's new Play Store moderation team and inspected by "real, living humans" to ensure that even the limited amount of customizations don't break any safety guidelines. This includes making to ensure that the app isn't distracting and making sure that everything has good contrast to make it easily read. At Google, safety is paramount and Android Auto even has a "parked mode" interface. For example, Google Maps has a keyboard that can only be activated when the care is in park.

Android Auto is currently available on selected models of cars manufactured by Buick, Cadillac, Chevrolet, GMC, Honda, Hyundai, Kia, Mercedes-Benz, Volkswagen, and Volvo (Popely, 2016).

CarPlay

CarPlay is the Apple iPhone version of an in-car integration system. It lets drivers perform voice-enabled and touch-screen control of making and answering calls, text messaging, and playing music. Plug your iPhone in via a lightning cable, and you can control everything through Siri natural voice language assistant, capacitive or resistive touch and knobs, dials and buttons that work the built-in display. Originally named "iOS in the Car," the service supports third-party music apps such as Pandora, Spotify, and iHeartRadio.

A fascinating aspect of CarPlay is its AI capabilities. The software works with Maps and scans through user data, such as calendar, contacts, texts, or e-mails, to anticipate destinations to pull up driving directions, traffic conditions, and ETA. CarPlay also anticipates drivers' needs by plotting driving routes based on their schedule and normal routine. With this feature, Apple has made its biggest push into predictive services.

CarPlay debuted on the $302,450 Ferrari FF and has since trickled down to lower-priced cars. Currently, it is offered by numerous car manufacturers. A list of automobile manufacturers that offer CarPlay can be found on Apple's website **www.apple.com/ios/carplay/available-models**

Questions

1. Using privacy concepts introduced in this chapter, identify the ways in which Android Auto and CarPlay can violate a user's privacy.

2. Consider the privacy paradox. How does that principle relate to users' reactions to Android Auto CarPlay?

3. Getting a customer hooked on Android Auto or CarPlay technology means that the company is positioned to expand on it out of the vehicle, especially in the areas of wearables and home appliances. How might the integration of data from your car, smartphone, wearables, and home appliances impact your privacy?

4. If you were thinking of buying a car that had CarPlay, would you have any concerns about CarPlay's predictive analytics capabilities? Explain.

Case 14.3

Video Case: IT Ethics in the Workplace

In the digital age, most organizations are tracking employee activity in all kinds of ways in an effort to become more productive.

Some are measuring keystrokes or using programs that can tell supervisors when a keyboard has been idle for 15 minutes. Others use keywords to flag which websites employees visit—and block ones that aren't related to work—or are checking employees' e-mails and instant messages to make sure that they don't contain inappropriate or proprietary material.

Indeed, nearly every aspect of work is now measurable in some way: Hours are tracked via security badges and fingerprint scanners, locations are monitored using GPS, and certain employee activities are captured by digital camera and video.

While it's clear that employers *can* measure nearly everything employees do, the question for many is whether they should. To find out, it's important for companies to have a clear sense of what they hope to accomplish—and to be forthcoming and transparent in their communication with employees. When employee monitoring is done poorly,

businesses may find that what they hoped to gain in productivity is undermined by what they lose in engagement and trust.

Visit YouTube and search for the video "*Ethics in the Workplace to IT – Team 8.*" Answer the following questions.

Questions

1. Why do you think employers monitor their online behavior at work?

2. Name the policies the company has put in place in regard to ethics in the workplace.

3. What monitoring technologies does the company use to keep track of sites employees access.

4. Do you think it's ethical for employers to monitor sites that employees access?

5. Which is more expensive—firing an employee or putting policies in place for employees to follow?

Source: Katz (2015).

IT Toolbox

The Ten Commandments of Computer Ethics

Commitment to ethical conduct is expected of everyone who interacts with IT, whether they are IT professionals or users. The Computer Ethics Institutes Institute offers the Ten Commandments of Computer Ethics to help reinforce ethical behavior. The commandments were created as a set of standards to guide and instruct people in the ethical use of computers. The International Information System Security Certification Consortium (ISC) uses the commandments as a foundation for its own ethics rules. They are an excellent foundation upon which to model your technology-related ethical behavior.

1. Thou shalt not use a computer to harm other people.
2. Thou shalt not interfere with other people's computer work.
3. Thou shalt not snoop around in other people's computer files.
4. Thou shalt not use a computer to steal.
5. Thou shalt not use a computer to bear false witness.
6. Thou shalt not copy or use proprietary software for which you have not paid.
7. Thou shalt not use other people's computer resources without authorization or proper compensation.
8. Thou shalt not appropriate other people's intellectual output.
9. Thou shalt think about the social consequences of the program you are writing or the system you are designing.
10. Thou shalt always use a computer in ways that ensure consideration and respect for your fellow humans.

Print this out, post it somewhere you can see it every day, and let it serve as a tool to guide your online behavior to enhance your work and social interactions.

References

Accenture. "Technology Vision 2017: Amplify You: Technology for People" 2017. https://www.accenture.com/t20170321T032507_w_/us-en/_acnmedia/Accenture/next-gen-4/tech-vision-2017/pdf/Accenture-TV17-Full.pdf#view=FitH

Amadeo, R. "Android Auto Review: A Beautiful, but Beta Alternative to Awful OEM Solutions." *Cars Technica*, June 23, 2015. https://arstechnica.com/cars/2015/07/android-auto-review-a-beautiful-but-beta-alternative-to-awful-oem-solutions/

Appthority. *App Reputation Report*. Summer 2014. *appthority.com/resources/app-reputation-report*

Bader, C. "The Risks and Responsibilities of Tech Innovation." *MIT Sloan Management Review*, June 10, 2014.

Bilton, N. "Why Google Glass Broke." *The New York Times*, February 4, 2015.

Davis, W. N. "Google Glass is already causing legal experts to see problems." *ABA Journal Law News*. April 1, 2014.

Dumaine, B. "The Kings of Concentration." *Inc. Magazine*, May 2014.

EEOC. "Social Media Is Part of Today's Workplace but Its Use May Raise Employment Discrimination Concerns." Press release, *EEOC.gov*, March 12, 2014.

Ellenberg, J. "What's even creepier than Target guessing that you're pregnant?". Slate. 2014. http://www.slate.com/blogs/how_not_to_be_wrong/2014/06/09/big_data_what_s_even_creepier_than_target_guessing_that_you_re_pregnant.html

Engineering and Physical Sciences Research Council. "New Design for Mobile Phone Masts Could Cut Carbon Emissions." April 22, 2014.

Fitzpatrick, A. and G. Kibel. "Technology, Digital Media and Privacy Alert." *Inside Counsel*, June 17, 2014. insidecounsel.com/2014/06/17/technology-digital-media-and-privacy-alert

Gartner. "Gartner Says Worldwide Shipments of 3D Printers to Grow 108 Percent in 2016." *Gartner Newsroom*, October 13, 2016. http://www.gartner.com/newsroom/id/3476317

Hendricks, D. "ED Printing is Already Changing Health Care." *Harvard Business Review*, March 4, 2016.

Heritage, Stuart. "How bots ruined everything: from Drake to diets." *The Guardian*, October 30, 2016.

ICC. "Expert opinion: How technology can catalyze sustainable development." October 17, 2016.

Jobvite. "Job Seeker National 2016 Study: Where Job Seekers Stand on the Economy, Job Security and the Future or Work". *Jobvite* 2016.

Kandel, E.R. *In Search of Memory*. New York, NY: W. W. Norton & Company, 2006.

Katz, L. "Monitoring Employee Productivity: Proceed with Caution." *HR Magazine*, July 1, 2015.

McRae. R. "Bioprinting Human Organs: Saving Life or Redefining it? 2016. http://blogs.kentplace.org/bioethicsproject/2016/02/08/bioprinting-of-organs-what-does-this-mean-for-our-future-and-how-should-we-regulate-it/

Martin, G. "So 3-D Printers May Be Nifty and Trendy, But Environmentally Friendly? Not Necessarily." *California Magazine of UC Berkeley*, March 11, 2014.

Olmstead, K. and Smith, A. "Americans and Cybersecurity." *PewResearch Center*, 2017.

Perry, T. "Woman wearing Google Glass found not guilty of distracted driving." *LA Times*. January 16, 2014.

Popely, R. "Which 2016 Cars Have Android Auto?". *Cars.com*, October 1, 2016 https://www.cars.com/articles/which-2016-cars-have-android-auto-1420681175443/.

Scopatz, R. A. and Zhou, Y. "Effect of electronic device use on pedestrian safety: A literature review." *National Highway Traffic Safety Administration*, April 6, 2016.

SHRM. "Using Social Media for Talent Acquisition – Recruitment and Screening" 2016. https://www.shrm.org/hr-today/trends-and-forecasting/research-and-surveys/Pages/Social-Media-Recruiting-Screening-2015.aspx

Taylor, J. "Feds Interrogate Man Wearing Google Glass in Movie Theater." *BetaBeat.com*, January 21, 2014.

Wallace, Kelly. "Half of teens think they're addicted to their smartphones." *CNN*, July 29, 2016.

Whitney, L. "Google Glass Wearer Challenges Distracted Driving Charge." *CNET.com*, December 4, 2013.

Wrike. "The High Cost of Multi-tasking: 40% or Productivity Lost by Task Switching." September 2015.

3D bioprinting It is the medical application of 3D printing to produce living tissue and organs. Biotech firms are using 3D printing for tissue engineering applications where organs and body parts are built using inkjet techniques. Layers of living cells are deposited onto a gel medium and slowly built up to form three-dimensional structures.

3D printing Also known as additive manufacturing, builds objects layer-by-layer to create real-world objects.

Adware A software that embeds advertisements in the application. It is considered a legitimate alternative offered to consumers who do not wish to pay for software.

Agile A very flexible iterative, incremental systems development methodology that overcomes the disadvantages of the Waterfall model.

Agility Being able to respond quickly.

Always-on supply chain An integrated set of supply networks characterized by a continuous, high-velocity flow of information and analytics creating predictive, actionable decisions to better serve the customer 24/7.

Application program interface (API) An interface is the boundary where two separate systems meet. An API provides a standard way for different things, such as software, content, or websites, to talk to each other in a way that they both understand without extensive programming.

Attack vector A path or means by which a hacker can gain access to a computer or network server in order to deliver a malicious outcome.

Augmented reality A technology that superimposes a computer-generated image onto an image of the real world to provide information or entertainment.

Avatars An icon, figure or visual representation of a person in computer games, simulations, virtual worlds or online discussion forms.

Back-office operations They support the fulfillment of orders.

Balanced scorecard A strategic management methodology for evaluating performance based on both financial and nonfinancial metrics.

Barcode A machine-readable code consisting of numbers and a pattern of thick and thin lines that can be scanned to identify the object on which the code appears.

Baseline A specification of the project plan that has been formally reviewed and agreed upon. It should be changed only through a formal change control process.

Big data An extremely large data set that is too large or complex to be analyzed using traditional data processing techniques.

Big data analytics Process of examining large and varied data sets to identify hidden patterns and correlations, market trends, customer preferences and other useful information to enable better business decisions.

Blogging platform A software application used to create, edit, and add features to a blog. *WordPress* and *Blogger* are two of the most popular blogging platforms.

Bluetooth A short-range wireless communications technology.

Breach of privacy The loss of, unauthorized access to, or disclosure of, personal information.

Broadband Wide bandwidth technologies that create fast, high-volume connections to the Internet and World Wide Web.

Business case A presentation or document that outlines the justification for the start-up and funding of a project.

Business intelligence (BI) A set of tools and techniques for acquiring and transforming raw data into meaningful and useful information for business analysis purposes in the forms of reports, dashboards, or interactive visualizations.

Business objectives The building blocks of strategy.

Business process management It consists of methods, tools, and technology to support and continuously improve business processes.

Business strategy Sets the overall direction of a company, defines how a business will achieve its mission, goals, and objectives, and specifies the necessary financial requirements, budgets, and resources.

Business–IT alignment Refers to applying IT in an appropriate and timely way that is consistent with business strategies, goals, and needs.

Centralized database Stores all data in a single central compute such as a mainframe or server.

Channel conflict Competition between a manufacturer's distribution partners who sell through different channels. Channel conflict can occur at the wholesale, retail, or internal sales department level.

Click-through rates (CTRs) Percentage of people who click on a hyperlinked area of a SERP or Web page.

Cloud service Any computing resource that is provided over the Internet on demand.

Competitive advantage Edge that enables a company to outperform its average competitor in ways that matter to its customers.

Computer networks Set of computers connected together for the purpose of sharing resources.

Core business processes They include accounting, finance, sales, marketing, human resources, inventory, productions, and manufacturing.

Crawler control module A software program that controls a number of "spiders" responsible for scanning or crawling through information on the Web.

Critical infrastructure Systems and assets, whether physical or virtual, so vital to the a country that the incapacity or destruction of such systems and assets would have a debilitating impact on security, national economic security, national public health or safety, or any combination of those matters.

Critical path The shortest time possible to complete all tasks required to finish the project. A delay of any task on the critical path will delay the project.

Crowdfunding Raising funds for a project from the public, or *crowd*, via the Web.

Cyberthreat A threat posed by means of the Internet (a.k.a. cyberspace) and the potential source of malicious attempts to damage or disrupt a computer network, system, or application.

Data analytics Technique of qualitatively or quantitatively analyzing a data set to reveal patterns, trends, and associations that often relate to human behavior and interactions, to enhance productivity and business gain.

Database Collection of data sets or records stored in a systematic way.

Database management system (DBMS) Software used to manage the additions, updates, and deletions of data as transactions occur, and to support data queries and reporting. They are online transaction-processing (OLTP) systems.

Data breach The *successful retrieval* of sensitive information by an individual, group, or software system.

Data Describe products, customers, events, activities, and transactions that are recorded, classified, and stored.

Data governance The control of enterprise data through formal policies and procedures to help ensure data can be trusted and are accessible.

Data incident An *attempted* or *successful* unauthorized access to a network, system, or application; unwanted disruption or denial of service; unauthorized use of a system for processing or storage of data; changes to system without the owners knowledge, instruction, or consent.

Data management The management of the flow of data from creation and initial storage to the time when the data become obsolete and are deleted.

Data silo Stand-alone data stores. Their data are not accessible by other ISs that need it or outside that department.

Data visualization Presentation of data in a graphical format to make it easier for decision-makers to grasp difficult concepts or identify new patterns in the data.

Deliverables Any measurable, tangible, verifiable outcome, result, or item that is produced to complete a project or part of a project. Examples might be hardware, software, planning documents, or meeting minutes.

DevOps A set of processes that encourages collaboration between system developers, operators and testers.

Digital dashboard An electronic interface used to acquire and consolidate data across an organization.

Digital mesh An expanded set of end points used to access applications, gather information, or interact with people, social communities, government, and businesses to ensure instant connection and response to build experience. Examples include smart devices, wearables, consumer and home electronic devices.

Digitization The process of transforming any kind of activity or information into a digital format that can be collected, stored, searched, and analyzed electronically—and efficiently.

Dirty data Poor-quality data that lacks integrity and cannot be trusted.

Discrimination A biased or prejudicial treatment in recruitment, hiring, or employment based on certain characteristics, such as age, gender, and genetic information, and is illegal in the United States.

Distributed database Stores portions of the database on multiple computers within a network.

Drill down Searching for something on a computer moving from general information to more detailed information by focusing on something of interest, for example, quarterly sales—monthly sales—daily sales.

Edge service A term that refers to a cloud service.

EEOC (Equal Employment Opportunity Commission) It enforces federal laws prohibiting discrimination in employment.

Electronic fund transfer (EFT) A transfer of funds from one bank account to another over a computerized network.

Electronic records management system (ERMS) This system consists of hardware and software that manage and archive electronic documents and image paper documents; then index and store them according to company policy.

Electronic wallet (e-wallet) A software application that can store encrypted information about a user's credit cards, bank accounts, and other information necessary to complete electronic transactions, eliminating the need to re-enter the information during the transaction.

Enterprise data mashup Combination of data from various business systems and external sources without relying on the middle step of ETL (extract, transform, and load) into a data warehouse or help from IT.

Enterprise data warehouses (EDWs) Data warehouse that integrates data from databases across an entire enterprise.

Enterprise systems Cross-functional and interorganizational systems that support the business strategy.

Exabyte One quintillion bytes (1,000,000,000,000,000,000 Bytes) which is the equivalent of 1,000 petabytes of data or 7 trillion online video clips. Five Exabytes is equal to all words ever spoken by human beings.

Extreme programming A pragmatic systems development to Agile development that emphasizes business results first and takes an incremental approach to building software, using continual testing and revision.

Financial Accounting Standards Board (FASB) It establishes financial accounting and reporting standards for public and private companies and not-for-profit organizations.

Financial misrepresentation It occurs when a company has intentionally deceived one or more other parties.

Flexibility Means having the ability to quickly integrate new business functions or to easily reconfigure software or applications.

Folksonomy A system of classifying and organizing online content into categories by the use of user-generated metadata such as keywords.

Fraud A nonviolent crime in which fraudsters use deception, confidence, and trickery for their personal gain.

Front-office operations Operations such as sales and advertising that are visible to customers.

Gantt chart A horizontal bar chart that graphically displays the project schedule.

Geographic information system (GIS) A computer-based tool that captures, stores, manipulates, analyzes, and visualizes geographic data on a map.

Geospatial data Data that has an explicitly geographic component, ranging from vector and raster data to tabular data with site locations.

Go/no-go Decision A determination to proceed with or abandon a plan or project.

Hacking Broadly defined as intentionally accessing a computer without authorization or exceeding authorized access. Various state and federal laws govern computer hacking.

Hacktivist Short for hacker-activist or someone who performs hacking to promote awareness for or otherwise support a social, political, economic, or other cause. Hacking an application, system, or network without authorization, regardless of motive, is a crime.

Inbound logistics Refers to receiving inventory.

Income statement Summarizes a company's revenue and expenses for one quarter of a fiscal year or the entire fiscal year. It is also known as a P&L (profit and loss) or earnings statement.

Information Data that have been processed, organized, or put into context so that they have meaning and value to the person receiving them.

Information management The use of IT tools and methods to collect, process, consolidate, store, and secure data from sources that are often fragmented and inconsistent.

Information Systems (ISs) A combination of information technology and people's activities using the technology to support business processes, operations, management, and decision-making at different levels of the organization.

Informed user A person knowledgeable about information systems and IT.

Intellectual property A work or invention that is the result of creativity that has commercial value, including copyrighted property such as a blueprint, manuscript, or a design, and is protected by law from unauthorized use by others.

Interface To connect to and exchange data with apps and systems.

Internet of Things (IoT)   Network of physical objects or "things" embedded with electronics, software, sensors, and network connectivity, that enables these objects to collect and exchange data.

Internet Protocol (IP)   Method by which data are sent from one device to another over a network.

Inventory control systems   Stock control or inventory management systems.

IP address   A unique identifier for each device that communicates with a network that identifies and locates each device. An IP address is comparable to a telephone number or home address.

IPOS   The cycle of inputting, processing, outputting, and storing information in an information system.

IP Version 4 (IPv4)   Has been Internet protocol for over three decades, but has reached the limits of its 32-bit address design. It is difficult to configure, it is running out of addressing space, and it provides no features for site renumbering to allow for an easy change of Internet Service Provider (ISP), among other limitations.

IP Version 6 (IPv6)   The most recent version of the Internet Protocol. IPv6 is replacing IPv4. IPv6 has a 128-bit address and allows 7.9×10^{28} times as many addresses as IPv4, which provides about 4.3 billion addresses.

IT strategy   A plan of action to create an organization's IT capabilities for maximum and sustainable value in the organization.

Knowledge   Adds understanding, experience, accumulated learning, and expertise as they apply to a current problem or activity, to information.

Lagging indicators   They confirm what has happened. They evaluate outcomes and achievements.

Leading indicators   They predict future events to identify opportunities

Legacy systems   They are older information systems (ISs) that have been maintained over several decades because they fulfill critical needs.

Logical design   It lists and describes all the information resources (data and processes) and the scope of duties and responsibilities of consumers of the information involved in the operation of the new system. It is business focused and always precedes physical design.

Malware   Refers to hostile or intrusive software, including computer viruses, rootkits, worms, trojan horses, ransomware, and other malicious programs used to disrupt computer or mobile operations, gather sensitive information, gain access to private computer systems.

Mashup   A general term referring to the integration of two or more technologies.

Mega trends   Forces that shape or create the future of business, the economy, and society.

Microblog   A blog that consists of frequent, but very brief posts containing text, pictures, or videos. Twitter is perhaps the most well-known example of a microblog.

Microsoft Cloud   Provides a hybrid infrastructure and capabilities to manage enterprise apps and data.

Milestones   They are used to manage the project work effort, monitor results, and report meaningful status to project stakeholders.

Millennials   Term used to describe people born between the early 1980s and the early 2000s.

Mission   Defines the organization's purpose and what it hopes to achieve.

Mobile browser   A Web browser that is optimized to display Web content effectively on a small mobile device such as a smartphone.

Mobile location-based marketing   A marketing strategy that uses information from a mobile device's GPS or customer's mobile check-in on a social network to determine the content of marketing communications they receive on the device (e.g., advertisements, coupons, special offers).

Mobile visual search engine   A search engine that uses an image instead of a text-based query to search for information on the Web.

Near-field communication (NFC)   Enables two devices within close proximity to establish a communication channel and transfer data through radio waves.

Negligent hiring   The hiring of an employee when the employer knew or should have known about the employee's background which, if known, indicates a dangerous or untrustworthy character.

Network effect   From the field of economics, the network effect explains how the perceived value of a product or service is affected by the number of people using the product or service.

Object-oriented (O-O)   An iterative systems analysis and design methodology that emphasizes modularity and reusability.

On-demand economy   The economic activity created by technology companies that fulfill consumer demand through the immediate provisioning of products and services.

Online transaction processing (OLTP) systems   Designed to manage transaction data, which are volatile.

Open Wi-Fi network   An unprotected Wi-Fi network found particularly in public places where you don't know who else could be on the network.

Order fulfillment   Set of complex processes involved in providing customers with what they ordered on time and all customer services related to on-time delivery of a product.

Outbound logistics   Refers to shipping inventory.

Packet   A piece of a message that is collected and re-assembled with the other pieces of the same message at their destination. To improve communication performance and reliability, each larger message sent between two network devices is often subdivided into packets.

Page repository   A data structure that stores and manages information from a large number of Web pages, providing a fast and efficient means for accessing and analyzing the information at a later time.

People-first approach   It ensures that technology meets the needs of the users by involving the users at every stage of systems development.

Petabyte   A unit of measurement for digital data storage. A petabyte is equal to one million gigabytes.

Physical design   It transforms business requirements into a specific technological solution by identifying all physical servers and major technical components that will be used to support the desired business outcome.

Portfolio   The entire set of projects within a department or organization.

Post mortem   A method for evaluating project performance, identifying lessons learned, and making recommendations for future projects.

Privacy paradox   Refers to the competing demands of social media where users are concerned about privacy, but their willingness to disclose personal information does not mirror these concerns.

Program   A set of related projects.

Project   It is a well-planned sequential series of tasks to achieve a result. Projects have a defined beginning and end, a scope, resources, and a budget. Projects are approved before they are funded and allocated resources.

Project management   Application of knowledge, skills, tools, and techniques to project activities to meet project requirements.

Project management office (PMO)   An organizational group responsible for coordinating the project management function throughout an organization.

Projects   Temporary endeavors undertaken to create a unique product, service, or result.

Proof of concept (POC) A vendor demonstration of a product to see how or how well it works.

Protected classes Characteristics identified by law that cannot be used in the hiring process.

Query Ad hoc (unplanned) user request for specific data.

Quick response (QR) code A machine-readable code typically used to store a link to a URL or Web address that can be read by a mobile device.

Ransomware A type of malware that is designed to block access to a computer system until a sum of money has been paid.

Responsibility matrix Lets everyone know who is responsible for completion of tasks.

Responsiveness Means that IT capacity can be easily scaled up or down as needed, which essentially requires cloud computing.

Risk Probability of a threat successfully exploiting a vulnerability and the estimated cost of the loss or damage.

Risk register Lists all known risks and their source, an estimation of unknown risks and the response to be taken to each risk.

Safety stock Extra inventory used as a buffer to reduce the risk of stockouts. It is also called buffer stock.

Scope The body of work that needs to be completed within a project to achieve a desired outcome.

Search engine An application for locating Web pages or other content (e.g., documents, media files) on a computer network. Popular Web-based search engines include Google, Bing, and Yahoo.

Search engine marketing (SEM) A collection of online marketing strategies and tactics that promote brands by increasing their visibility in SERPs through optimization and advertising.

Semantic Web An extension of the World Wide Web that utilizes a variety of conventions and technologies that allow machines to understand the meaning of Web content.

Short message service (SMS) A technology used to send and receive text messages on mobile devices via a telecommunications network.

Showrooming The practice of examining products in a traditional retail store, sometimes with the help of a salesperson, and then purchasing the product online.

Social media A collection of Web applications based on Web 2.0 technology and culture that allows people to connect and collaborate with others by creating and sharing digital content.

Social networking service (SNS) An online platform or website that allows subscribers to interact and form communities or networks based on real-life relationships, shared interests, activities and so on.

Social recruitment Refers to use of social media to find, screen, and select job candidates.

Spiders Also known as crawlers, Web bots, or simply "bots," spiders are small computer programs designed to perform automated, repetitive tasks over the Internet. They are used by search engines for scanning Web pages and returning information to be stored in a page repository.

Sprints A set period of time during which specific work has to be completed and made ready for review. Traditionally, a sprint lasts 30 days.

Spyware A tracking software that is not designed to intentionally damage or disable a system. For example, an employer may install spyware on corporate laptops to monitor employee browsing activities, or an advertiser might use cookies to track what Web pages a user visit in order to target advertising in a marketing campaign.

Standard operating procedures (SOPs) A set of written instructions on how to perform a function or activity. SOPs provide the framework for complex processes to be managed more effectively.

Stockouts Inventory shortage arising from unexpected demand, delays in scheduled delivery, production delays, or poor inventory management.

Strategic plan A document used to communicate the company's goals and the actions needed to achieve them.

Strategic planning A series of processes in which an organization selects and arranges its businesses or services to keep the organization healthy or able to function even when unexpected events disrupt one or more of its businesses, markets, products, or services.

Strategic technology The potential to make significant impacts on an organization's long-term plans, programs, and initiatives.

Structured query language (SQL) A standardized query language for accessing databases.

Sunk cost A cost that has already been incurred and cannot be recovered.

Supply chain management (SCM) Efficient management of the flows of material, data, and payments among the companies in the supply chain, from suppliers to consumers.

Supply chain Starts with the acquisition of raw materials or the procurement (purchase) of products and proceeds through manufacture, transport, and delivery—and the disposal or recycling of products.

Synchronous communication Dialogue or conversation that takes place in real time, without the long delays between exchanges that occur, for instance, in e-mail or discussion board conversations.

Templates A sample document that already has some details in place.

Terms of service (TOS) agreement A formal listing of the policies, liability limits, fees, user rights and responsibilities associated with using a particular service. Users are typically required to acknowledge they have read, understand, and agree to the TOS before they are allowed the service to use.

Trial run When a vendor product or service is tested in a pilot study or limited area of the business to confirm its usefulness to the company.

Triple constraint The combination of the three most significant elements of any project: scope, time and cost. It is also known as the iron triangle.

Trojan horse A program that appears harmless, but is, in fact, malicious.

Tweet A brief 140-character message or post broadcast on Twitter, a microblogging service.

Twittersphere Universe of people who use Twitter, a microblogging service.

Use-case diagram A graphic depiction of the major elements (use cases) within a system and it environment.

Use-case description A text-based list of actions or steps that detail the interactions between users and the system needed to achieve the goal of the system.

Value-added reseller (VAR) Customizes or adds features to a vendor's software or equipment and resells the enhanced product.

Value driver It enhances the value of a product or service to consumers, creating value for the company. Advanced IT, reliability, and brand reputation are examples.

Wardriving The act of searching for Wi-Fi wireless networks by a person in a moving vehicle using a laptop or smartphone.

Waterfall Model A sequential, predictive systems development methodology that is simple to use and understand, but inflexible.

Web 2.0 A term used to describe a phase of World Wide Web evolution characterized by dynamic Web pages, social media, mashup applications, broadband connectivity, and user-generated content.

Wi-Fi The standard way computers connect to wireless networks.

Wisdom A collection of values, ethics, moral codes, and prior experiences that form an evaluated understanding or common-sense judgment.

World Wide Web (WWW) A network of documents on the Internet, called Web pages, constructed with HTML markup language that supports links to other documents and media (e.g., graphics, video, audio, etc.).

Yammer It is "Facebook for business." The platform has features similar to Facebook likes, newsfeeds, threaded conversation, and direct messaging. This private social channel helps employees, partners, and customers communicate; exchange information; and collaborate across departments, locations, and business apps.

Zettabytes One sextillion bytes (1,000,000, 000,000,000,000,000 Bytes) which is approximately equal to 1,000 Exabytes.

Organization Index

A

AAA, 259
ABC Company, 401
Accelerating Medicines Partnership, 86
Accenture, 6, 437–438
ACCOR Hotels, 27
Accuweather, 112
Adaptive Insights, 343
Adidas, 218
ADP Corporation, 341
Adweek, 283
Aflac Cancer Center, 242
Airbus A320 jets, 303
Air New Zealand, 27
Airbnb, 2–4, 5
Alcatel-Lucent, 436
Alibaba, 251
Ally Bank, 248–249
Amazon, 5, 112, 113, 131, 175, 189, 192,
        203, 247, 258
Amazon Web Services (AWS), 14, 57
AMC (U.S. Army Materiel Command), 419
American Apparel, 218
American Express (AMEX), 12, 96
American Marketing Association, 231
American Nazi groups, 140
Andersen Consulting, 311
Anonymous (hacktivist group), 139, 140
Anthem Insurance, 131
Apple, 49, 148, 175, 192, 365
Apple Watch, 14
Appthority, 420
Aqumin, 341
Argo Corporation, 89
Arthur Andersen, 153
Asia–Pacific bank, 77
Association for Information and Image
        Management (AIIM), 94
Association of Records Managers and
        Administrators (ARMA), 94
AT&T, 108, 110
AV firm Symantec, 140
Avanade, 311

B

BAE Systems, 281
Banamex, 263
Bank of America, 263
BB&T, 263
Bernard L. Madoff Investment
        Securities, 286, 287
Bing, 168
Bitcoin, 129, 137, 177
Blogger platform, 222
Blood Disorders Service of Children's
        Healthcare of Atlanta, 242
Bloomberg, 341
BMW, 212
Boers & Co Fine Metalworking, 309
Booz Allen, 368
Bolsa de Comercio de Santiago, 31
Boston Consulting Group, 323
Box, 233, 430

BP, 359
Breier Neidle Patrone Associates, 387

C

CA, 280, 303
California Highway Patrol (CHP), 418
California Pizza Kitchen (CPK), 35
Capital One, 81
Careerbuilder.com, 214
Carlsberg, 27
CarMax, Inc., 93–94
Caterpillar, Inc., 120
Center for International Business Education
        and Research (Duke University), 370
Center for Project Management, 410
Central Intelligence Agency (CIA), 140
Centre for Therapeutic Target Validation
        (CTTV), 86
Chase, 263
Chase Pay, 261
Chegg.com, 266
Chicago Board Options Exchange (CBOE), 341
Chinese electronics manufacturer
        Foxconn, 140
Cisco, 144
Citibank, 27, 262
Citizen National Bank, 322
Climate Group, 434
Clipix, 232
Cloud Standards Customer Council, 53
CNN, 192
Coca-Cola, 66–68, 253
Combined Systems, Inc., 139
Comcast, 108
Common Short Code Association (CSCA), 263
Consumer Watchdog, 422
Cornell University, 423
Craigslist, 202

D

Delicious, 232
Dell, 10, 244
Deloitte, 316
Denver International Airport (DIA), 386–388
Diigo, 232
Dillard's, Inc., 311
Disney, 257
Dow Chemical, 21
Dropbox, 143, 233
Ducati, 271–272

E

Eastern Bank, 263
eBay, 5, 131, 202, 203, 252
Eli Lilly & Co., 86
Enron, 286, 287
Epicor, 309
Epinions, 210
ESPN, 258
ESSA Academy, 379
E*Trade, 112
European Bioinformatics Institute (EBI), 86
Experian, 131
Exxon Mobil, 284

F

Facebook, 112, 144, 192, 200, 207
Fast Company, 192
Federal Communications Commission
        (FCC), 108
Federal Deposit Insurance Corporation
        (FDIC), 288
Federal Trade Commission (FTC), 150
Ferrari, 303
Fiat, 212
Fifth Third Bank, 263
First Wind, 88
FitBit, 12, 14
Ford Motor Company, 119
FoxMeyer Drugs, 311

G

Gain Capital, 341
Gartner, Inc., 378
GlaxoSmithKline, 86
Global Payments, Inc., 128
Goldman Sachs, 89, 301
Goodreads, 192
Google, 112, 145, 168, 175, 183, 187,
        203, 419, 421
Google Analytics, 143
Greiner Engineering, 387
Grubhub, 5, 12

H

Harris Corp., 409
HDFC Bank in India, 262
Heinz, 27
Hershey Food Corp, 311
Home Depot, 284
Honda, 27
Hong Kong and Shanghai Bank (HSBC), 246
HP, 280
Hulu, 258

I

IBM, 31, 72, 218, 280, 285, 336, 338
IKEA, 261
Infinity Insurance, 89
InnoCentive, 21
Intel, 355–357
InnoCentive, 21
Instagram, 42
International Accounting Standards Board
        (IASB), 288

J

JDA Software Group, 311
JD Edwards, 307
JetBlue Airlines, 378
Jive, 326
Johnson & Johnson, 86
Joint Munitions Command (JMC), 314
JP Morgan, 27

K

KIA Motors, 280
Kickstarter, 212
KLM Royal Dutch Airlines, 200
Kohls, 261

Konica Minolta, 27
Korean Pharmaceutical Information Center, 131
Kraft, 212

L
Lee, 212
Lehman Brothers, 286, 287
LG, 27
Liberty Wines, 60
Linden Labs, 219
LinkedIn, 20, 131, 192, 200, 207
L'Oreal, 218
LulzSec, 139
Lyle and Scott, 260

M
McDonald's, 89
McKinsey, 301, 302, 373
Mercedes-Benz, 219
Merita Bank, 263
Microsoft, 72, 175, 365
Microsoft Xbox 360, 192
Microstrategy, 285
Mint.com, 166–167
Morrison-Knudsen Engineering, 387
Myntra, 205

N
National Aeronautics and Space Administration
    (NASA), 291, 435
National Archives and Records Administration
    (NARA), 94
National Climatic Data Center, 49
National Security Agency's (NSA) data
    center, 49
NBCNews.com, 192
Netflix, 192, 258
Nintendo, 254
Northeast Bank, 263

O
obopay.com, 261
Office Depot, 252
Office of Syria's president, 140
1-800-Flowers, 219, 320, 321
Optus, 27
Oracle, 72, 285, 338
Organic Valley Family of Farms, 306
Organovo, 303
Overstock, 252
Oxford University, 86

P
P. F. Chang's China Bistro,
Pandora, 189, 192
Payless Shoes, 295
PayPal, 134

paypal.com, 261
Pebble, 14
PepsiCo, 332–334, 336
Peters Ice Cream, 309
Pfizer Inc., 86
Philippine Commission on Elections, 139
Procter & Gamble (P&G), 120, 212
Prykarpattyaoblenergo Control Center
    (PCC), 141

Q
Qantas, 27

R
Rackspace, 57
Red Robin Gourmet Burgers, Inc., 325
Reebok, 218
Reliance, 375
Reuters, 192
Rolling Stone, 192
Royal Bank of Scotland, 263

S
Safeway, 332–334, 336
Salesforce.com, 54, 57, 143, 270, 285, 319,
    342
Samsung, 192, 260
San Diego, 303
SAP, 311
Sara, 212
SAS, 285, 338
ScanSource, 311
Schurman Fine Papers, 280
Seamless, 12
Sears, 112
Second Life, 218–219
Selinko,
Shyp, 2, 18
Siri, Inc., 148
Skyhook, 27–28
SnapChat, 208, 217–218
Sony, 102–103, 131, 254
Southwest Airlines, 378
Starbucks, 212
Starwood Hotels, 218
Steven Engineering, 280
Stitch Fix, 192
Surgery Center of Baltimore, 96

T
Target, 202, 241, 244,
Target Discovery Institute, 86
TaskRabbit, 2
Teamgum, 232
Teradata, 72
Time, 192
Tin Eye, 176

Toyota, 280
TradeCard, 246
Travelocity, 82
Tripadvisor, 192
Trulia, 203–204
Tumblr, 222, 223, 225
Turkish General Directorate of Population and
    Citizenship Affairs, 131
Twitter, 4, 112, 143, 200, 207, 223–225

U
Uber, 2–4, 5, 18, 49
Unilever, 112, 120
University of Cincinnati, 96
U.S. Army Materiel Command (AMC), 314
U.S. Census Bureau, 335
U.S. Chamber of Commerce, 148
U.S. Department of Justice (DOJ), 129
U.S. Office of Personnel Management,
    131
U.S. Immigration and Customs
    Enforcement, 419
U.S. National Institutes of Health (NIH), 86
U.S. National Security Agency (NSA), 171
Us Weekly, 192
USAA, 263

V
Vanderbilt University Medical Center
    (VUMC), 62
Verizon, 108, 129
Virgin Money, 27
VUMC (Vanderbilt University Medical Center), 62

W
Walmart, 89, 120, 261
Warner Music, 118
WebEx, 143
Wellcome Trust Sanger Institute, 86
Wells Fargo, 263
Western Union, 262
WhatsApp, 49
Wikis, 233
The Wild Feathers, 118
Woolworths, 27
WordPress, 222, 223
World Wide Web Consortium (W3C), 185

Y
Yahoo, 129, 131, 168
Yellow Pages, 256
YouTube, 192, 200, 207

Z
Zappos, 254
zong.com, 260
Zumba, 430

Name Index

A

Alhadeff, Joseph, 436
Alspach, Loddie, 45

B

Baratov, Karim, 129
Belan, Alexsey, 129
Belsky, Scott, 12
Berners-Lee, Tim, 185, 202
Bernoff, Josh, 209, 222
Bezos, Jeff, 247
Bhargava, Hemant, 129
Bippert, Doug, 68
Birol, Faith, 433
Blair, John, 418
Boland, Michael, 3
Bradford, Dan, 343
Bryant, Diane, 355

C

Cerf, Vinton, 111
Cheah, Michael, 108
Chenault, Ken, 12
Chohan, Abdul, 379
Coburn, Tom, 409
Columbus, Louis, 84

D

Daugherty, Paul, 436

F

Faludi, Jeremy, 423
Friedman, Eric, 12

G

Gibbon, Kevin, 18
Goldman, Jonathan, 20
Gonzalez, Joaquin, 122
Gordon, Gregg, 20
Gutierrez, Carlos M., 409

H

Hansen, Eric, 89
Hayward, Tony, 359
Heathfield, Susan, 214
Hinssen, Peter, 2
Hoffman, Reid, 20

I

Ingham, Francis, 162
Iñigo de la Serna, 122

J

Jobs, Steve, 412

K

Kandel, Eric, 431
Kaplan, Robert, 374
Klappich, Dwight, 278
Kremez, Vitali, 129

L

Laping, Chris, 325
Lay, Ken, 287
Li, Charlene, 209, 222
Lieberthal, Kenneth G., 149
Lohr, Steve, 338

M

Madoff, Bernard L., 286, 287
Madoff, Bernie, 290
Madrigal, Alexis, 190
Mark, Gloria, 430
Martin, Roger L., 355
McClelland, Matt, 31
Merzenich, Michael, 431
Mitnick, Kevin, 134
Mollohan, Alan, 409

N

Norton, David, 374

O

Obama, Barack, 230
Odle, Keith, 418
Otellini, Paul, 356
Owyang, Jeremiah, 225

P

Park, James, 12
Patzer, Aaron, 167
Porter, Michael, 364

R

Raimondi, Marc, 409
Ramirez, Edith, 429
Reardon, Martine, 241
Richards, Jeff, 371
Rogers, Mike, 149
Rosedale, Philip, 219

S

Silei, Christiano, 272
Silliman, Craig, 129
Skilling, Jeffrey, 287
Solis, Brian, 225
Strauss, Jeff, 339
Sumlin, Carrie, 249

T

Tomlinson, Ray, 111

V

Vogel-Meijer, Karlijn, 201

W

Warburton, Jon, 281
Wheeler, Tom, 108

Z

Zuckerberg, Mark, 205, 214–215, 424
Zulpo, Scott, 19

Subject Index

3G, 110
4G, 110
5G, 110
802.11a, 115
802.11ac, 115
802.11b, 115
802.11g, 115
802.11n, 115

A
Acceptable use policy (AUP), 158
Access control, 148, 152, 172
Accounting cycle fraud, 151
Accounting, finance, and regulatory systems
   auditing information systems, 291
   financial disclosure, 286–288
   financial planning and budgeting, 291–292
   financial ratio analysis, 292
   fraud prevention and detection, 289–291
   profitability analysis and cost control, 292
ACID test, 275
Active data warehouse (ADW), 81–82
Additive manufacturing process, 301
Ad hoc report, 34
Administrative controls, 152
Advanced persistent threat (APT), 139
Advanced search, 176
ADW (active data warehouse), 81
Adware, 135
Age Discrimination in Employment Act
   (ADEA), 293
Aggregation, 340
Agile methodology, 392–394
Agility, 11, 364
AJAX (asynchronous JavaScript and XML), 204
Always-on supply chain, 316
American Idol, 263
Americans with Disabilities Act, 293
Analytical tools, 335
Android Auto, 439–440
Anonymous, 139
Anti-money laundering (AML), 158
Antivirus software, 146
Anything as a service (XAAS), 55–58
API, See Application program interface (API)
Application architecture, 41
Application controls, 154
Application program interface (API)
   for Alexa, 113
   defined, 111, 112
   Google Maps, 125
   value chain, in business, 112
   Web 1.0 and Web 2.0, 203, 205
Application service provider (ASP), 105
Applications portfolio, 361
Application virtualization, 59
App Reputation Report, 420
APT (advanced persistent threat), 139
Artificial intelligence (AI), 422
ASP (application service provider), 105
Assets, 139
Asynchronous JavaScript and XML (AJAX), 204

Atomicity, 275
Attack, 135
Attack vector, 138
Auditing, 148, 292
Auditing information systems, 155
Augmented reality (AR), 242, 256
AUP (acceptable use policy), 158
Authentication, 148
Automated API, 112
Avatars, 218

B
Backdoors, 134
Backlinks, 180
Back-office operations, 315
Balanced scorecard (BSC)
   defined, 374
   examples of measurement criteria, 376
   IT strategy, 355
   JetBlue and Southwest Airlines, 378
   leading indicators, 375
   low-cost airline, 377
   metrics, 376
   perspectives, 375
   smart criteria objectives, 375
Bandwidth
   broad, 203
   capacity, 106, 107
   digital, 106
   media, 106
Bankruptcy Act, 293
Barcode, 241
Barriers to entry, 23, 365
Baseline, 407
Batch processing, 33
Behavioral feasibility, 390
Big data, See also data analytics
   and decision models, 68
   defined, 15, 83
   as a service, 58
Big data analytics
   defined, 84
   industrial project relies on, 88
   for revitalizing McDonald's, 98–99
Biometric control, 148
BITA, See Business–IT alignment (BITA)
Bitcoin payments, 177
Black Book model, 68
Black hat
   defined, 133
   vs. white hat, 181
Blogging
   platform, 222
   and public relations, 222
   Tumblr, 225
   Twitter, 223–225
Blogosphere, 221
Blogs, 220
Bluetooth, 115
Bot herder, 136
Botnets, 136
Bots, 168

Breach of privacy, 424
Bribery, 151
Bring your own apps (BYOA), 143
Bring your own device (BYOD), 142–143
Broadband, 202
Broad bandwidth, 203
BSC, See Balanced scorecard (BSC)
Business analytics, 68
Business architecture, 41
Business case, 396, 412–413
Business continuity
   ERM for, 95
   planning, 149
Business-driven development approach, 92
Business impact analysis (BIA), 163
Business intelligence (BI)
   architecture and analytics, 93–94
   business benefits of, 92
   with business strategy, 92–93
   competitive analytics practice, 93–94
   data selection and quality, 92
   defined, 20, 69, 91
   electronic records management system
      (ERMS), 94
   legal duty to retain business records, 94
Business–IT alignment (BITA)
   CIO skills, 363
   competitive advantage (See Competitive
      advantage)
   defined, 355
   organizational strategic, 362
Business management systems (BMSs), 273
Business model, 3
Business objectives, 375
Business process
   automation, 10
   defined, 9
   gaining competitive advantage, 11–12
   improving business processes, 9–10
   software support for, 13
Business process management (BPM)
   defined, 10, 13
   software support for, 13
Business process reengineering (BPR)
   defined, 10
   eight phases of, 11
Business record, 94
Business strategy, 355
Business success
   company growth and valuation, 4
   search technology for, 168–177
Business-to-business (B2B)
   defined, 15, 251
   electronic data interchange (EDI)
      systems, 253
   e-procurement, 251–253
   e-sourcing, 252
   public and private exchanges, 253
   sell-side marketplaces, 251–252
Business-to-consumer (B2C)
   international and multiple-currency
      banking, 246

Business-to-consumer (B2C) (*Continued*)
  marketing planning, 250–251
  online banking, 246
  online business, 250–251
  online recruiting, 246–247
  online retailing, issues in, 250
Business value, creation, 88–89

C
Campus area network (CAN), 104
Capacity bandwidth, 106
Capital budgeting, 292
Carbon footprint, 436
CarPlay, 440
Cascading style sheets (CSS), 204
Centralized database
  defined, 67, 73
  vs. distributed, 74
Change data capture (CDC), 80
Channel conflict, 250
Channel hopping, 244
Channel service unit/data service units
    (CSU/DSU), 105
Chatter, 326
Chicago Board Options Exchange (CBOE), 341
Chief information officer (CIO), 355,
    357, 360, 363
Chief technology officers (CTOs), 19
Ciphertext, 148
Circuit switching, 111
Cisco, 382
Civil rights, 426
Civil Rights Act of 1966, 293
Click-through rates (CTRs), 174
Climate change mitigation, 435–436
Cloaked pages, 181
Cloud computing
  cloud infrastructure, 54
  defined, 14, 52
  infrastructure issues, 55
  selecting cloud vendor, 52–54
Cloud service agreements (CSAs), 53
Cloud services
  anything as a service (XaaS) models, 55–58
  and cloud service agreements (CSAs), 53–54
  data as a service (DaaS), 57
  defined, 17, 55
  infrastructure as a service (IaaS), 57
  platform as a service (PaaS), 57
  service models, 58
  software as a service (SaaS), 56–57
  vendor management, 53–54
  virtualization, 58–60
  and virtual machines (VMs), 58–60
Cloud storage service, 233
Cloud vendors, 52–54
Cluster area network (CAN), 104
Clustered search, 187
COBIT (Control Objectives for Information and
    Related Technology), 155
COBIT 5, 156–157
CoCA (cost of customer acquisition), 184
Cognitive overload, 430
COIT (consumerization of information
    technology), 143
Collaborative filtering, 190
Collection analysis module, 169
Command and control (C&C) channel, 144
Communication, 399
Competing legal concerns, 427

Competitive advantage
  business process (*See* business process)
  competitive forces model, 364–366
  defined, 364
  gaining, 11–12
  IT agility and responsiveness, 364
  mobile commerce, 255–258
  in mobile commerce, 255–258
  value chain model, 367–368
Competitive forces model, 364–366
Computer Fraud and Abuse Act (CFAA), 43
Computer-integrated manufacturing (CIM)
  BAE Systems uses in, 281–282
  defined, 281
  reasons why companies invest in, 282
Computer networks, 104
Concept search, 187
Confidentiality, integrity, or availability
    (CIA), 130
Conflict of interest, 151
Consistency, of data, 276
Consumer banking, 248
Consumer behavior
  mobile impact, 241
  on-demand economy, 4
  predictive analytics, 317
  retailing technology, 243–244
Consumer demands, 243–244
Consumerization of information technology
    (COIT), 143
Consumer watchdog, 422
Content-based filtering, 189
Content control, 208
Content creation, 232–234
Content sharing, 232–234
Contract hackers, 134
Control Objectives for Information and Related
    Technology (COBIT), 155
Core business processes, 304
Corporate culture, 36–37
Corporate governance, 151
Corporate IT infrastructures, 51
Corporate procurement, 252
Corporate purchasing, 252
Corporate social media discrimination, 426
Cost, 398
Cost–benefit analysis, 163, 389
Cost control, 292
Cost efficiencies, 8
Cost estimations, 404
Cost leadership strategy, 366
Cost of customer acquisition (CoCA), 184
Covert resistance, 390
Crawler control module, 169
Crawler search engines, 168, 169–170
Credit card 1 Webform, 261
Crimeware, 132
Critical infrastructure, 140
Critical path, 406
Critical success factor (CSF), 10
Critical task, 406
CRM, *See* Customer relationship
    management (CRM)
Cross-functional business process, 9, 274–275
Cross-functional coordination and
    integration, 274–275
Crowdfunding, 212, 403
Crowdsourcing, 212
Customer-centric business models, 47
Customer experience (CX), 7, 270, 320

Customer lifetime value (CLV), 320
Customer relationship management (CRM)
  competitive edge, 320–321
  critical success factors, 319
  customer acquisition and retention, 320, 321
  customer experience, 320
  defined, 301
  vs. ERP, 319
  failure, 322
  functions, 303, 304
  mistakes, 321
  risk assessment, 322
  tangible net benefits, 322
  technology perspective, 320
Customer satisfaction, 26
Customer value analytics (CVA), 84
Cyberattack
  BYOD, 142–143
  critical infrastructure attacks, 140–141
  "high-profile" and "under-the-radar"
      attacks, 139–140
  identity theft, 142
  IP theft, 141
  social media attacks, 144
Cyber defense
  do-not-carry rules, 148–149
  fraud, strategies for, 153–154
  industry standards, 157
  IT governance frameworks, 155–157
  IT security defense-in-depth model, 157–159
  mobiles, minimum security defenses for, 148
  risk management, 155–157
Cyber risk management
  business continuity planning, 149
  government regulations, 149–150
  IT defenses, 146–149
Cybersecurity program, 147
Cyberthreats
  attack vectors, 138
  defined, 131
  denial-of-service (DoS), 137
  face and future of, 130–138
  hacking, 133–134
  insider and privilege misuse, 137
  intentional threats, 132
  miscellaneous errors, 138
  physical theft/loss, 138
  social engineering, 134–137
  sources of, 132
  unintentional threats, 132–133
  web-based threats, 134–137
Cycle time, 22

D
DaaS (data as a service), 56, 57
Dashboards
  defined, 12
  FitBit's competitive strengths, 12
Data, 30
Data analytics
  analytics vendor rankings, 90–91
  creation business value, 88–89
  data and text mining, 88
  defined, 3, 83, 84
  human expertise and judgment are
      needed, 85–88
  people's behavior, 420, 421
  text analytics procedure, 90
Data as a service (DaaS), 56, 57
Database, 33, 69

Database management system (DBMS)
  and data warehousing vendors, 72–73
  defined, 70
  functions, 71
  trend toward NoSQL systems, 72
  vendor rankings, 72–73
Data breach
  defined, 62, 130
  impact of, 129
  type of, 131
Data centers
  data virtualization, 50
  defined, 38, 48–50
  evolution of, 52
  integrating data to combat data, 50–52
  software-defined data center (SDDC), 50–52
Data consistency, 70
Data deduplication, 80
Data discovery, 83–91, *See also* Data analytics
  market, 336
  tool, 336, 339
Data entity, 79
Data errors, 79
Data failure, costs of, 63
Data governance
  characteristics of, 47
  and cost control, 46–47
  defined, 46
  enterprisewide, 46
  implementation, 63
  maintaining data quality, 46–47
  master data, 46–47
  and master data management (MDM), 46–47
Data incident, 130
Data integrity, 275
Data latency, 70
Data life cycle, 77–78
Data management
  Coca-Cola strategically to retain customers
    and reduce costs, 66–67
  database management systems and
    SQL, 69–72
  data breaches, 62
  DBMS and data warehousing vendors, 72–73
  and decision models, 68
  defined, 69
  enterprise, 67–68
  faulty data, 62
  sustaining business performance, 68
Data marts, 80
Data mining, 88
Data ownership and organizational
    politics, 76–77
Data principles, 77–78
Data quality, control of, 73
Data science, 20
Data security, 275
Data silo, 43
Data silos, 43
Data tampering, 137
Data validity, 275
Data virtualization, 50, 59
Data visualization
  analytical tools, 335
  apps, 332, 335
  Birst, 341
  in business, 340–341
  challenges, 339–340
  data analytics, 332
  data discovery tools, 339, 340

defined, 334
  drill down capability, 334
  Google Maps API, 125
  heat map, 336, 337
  human expertise, 336, 338
  IBM SPSS analytic catalyst, 342
  IBM tackles big data discovery, 336, 338
  IBM Watson analytics, 342
  learning, 336
  maps, 334, 335
  QlikView, 342
  reporting tools, 335
  Roambi analytics, 342
  Safeway and PepsiCo, 332–334
  SAS Visual Catalyst, 341
  Tableau, 342
  vendors, 338–339
Data warehouses
  building, 80–81
  defined, 67, 80
  industrial applications, 82
  prepare EDW data analytics, 80
  real-time support from ADW, 81–82
Data warehousing vendors, 72–73
DBMS (database management system), 70
Decision model, 68
Decision support systems (DSS)
  defined, 32
  structured decisions, 34–35
Declarative language, 70
Defend Trade Secrets Act (DTSA), 141
Deliverables, 9, 397
Deloitte Analytics HIVE, 333
Demand management, 253
Demodulator, 105
Denial-of-service (DoS), 137
Denver International Airport (DIA)
    project, 386–388
Desktop virtualization, 59
Detached search vendors, 173
DevOps, 394–395
Digital bandwidth, 106
Digital business models, 6–7
Digital dashboards
  benefits of, 348
  components of, 347
  defined, 345
  disparate data sources, 345, 346
  free trial dashboards, 348
  at Hartford Hospital, 348
  metrics, 345, 346
  PepsiCo and Safeway, 334
  real time, 347
Digital dependents, 244
Digital immigrants, 244
Digital mesh, 380
Digital natives, 244
Digital technology, impacts of, 2
Digitization, 15
Direct procurement, 252
Dirty data
  costs and consequences, 75–76
  defined, 26, 75
Discrimination, 426, 427
Disruptive innovation, 266
Distributed database, 73
Distributed denial-of-service (DDoS),
    132, 135, 137
Dlvr.it, 225
Document object model (DOM), 204

Dodd–Frank Wall Street Reform and Consumer
    Protection Act of 2010, 46
Do-not-carry rules, 148–149
DSS (decision support systems), 32
Durability, of data, 276
Dwell time, 180

E

EA, *See* Enterprise architecture (EA)
EAI (enterprise application integration), 308
E-commerce, 244
Economic feasibility, 389
Economic order quantity (EOQ), 279
Edge service, 368
EDI (electronic data interchange), 120
EFT (electronic funds transfer), 246, 315
EISs (executive information systems), 32, 39
Electronic data interchange (EDI), 120, 253
Electronic funds transfer (EFT), 246, 315
Electronic records management system (ERMS)
  benefits, 95
  for business continuity, and compliance, 95
  defined, 94
  for disaster recovery, 95
  practices, 94–95
Electronic wallet (e-wallet), 247
Embezzlement, 151
Empowered price sensitivity, 243–244
Encryption, 148
Enterprise 2.0
  content creation and sharing, 232–234
  for information retrieval, 230–231
  knowledge sharing, 230–234
  meetings and discussions, tools for, 230
  social bookmarking tools, 231–232
  workplace collaboration, 230–234
Enterprise application integration (EAI), 308
Enterprise architects, 42
Enterprise architecture (EA)
  components of, 41
  defined, 26
  developing enterprise architecture
    (EA), 41–42
  IT infrastructure *vs.* architecture, 38
  maintain sustainability, 38–40
Enterprise data management, 67–68
Enterprise data mashups
  Adaptive Discovery Dashboard Software, 343
  architecture, 343, 344
  business users, 344
  defined, 226
  self-service, 344, 345
Enterprise data warehouses (EDWs), 80
Enterprise Graph, 325
Enterprise resource planning (ERP)
  Boers & Co Fine Metalworking,
    Netherlands, 309
  consultant, 309, 310
  vs. CRM, 319
  defined, 301
  disasters and failures, 311–312
  functions, 303, 304
  history of, 308
  overview of, 308, 309
  Peters Ice Cream, Australia, 309
  selection rules, 310
  success factors, 312–313
  vendor selection process, 310
Enterprise resource planning (ERP)
    systems, 251

Enterprise risk management (ERM), 155
Enterprise search
  defined, 172
  security issues in, 172
  structured *vs.* unstructured data, 172
  vendors, 173
Enterprise social platforms (ESPs)
  Chatter, 326
  defined, 301
  functions, 303, 304
  growth of, 323–324
  Jive, 326
  Oracle's social network, 326
  SharePoint, 324–326
Enterprise systems
  core business processes, 304
  CRM, 303, 304, 319–322
  ERP, 303, 304, 307–313
  ESPs, 303, 304, 323–326
  implementation of, 306
  insights, 307
  interface, 305
  legacy systems, 305, 306
  SCM (*See* Supply chain management (SCM))
  value-added reseller (VAR), 305
Enterprisewide IT architecture, 26
E-procurement, 252
Equal Employment Opportunity Act, 293
Equal Employment Opportunity Commission
    (EEOC), 426
Equal Pay Act of 1963, 293
ERP, *See* Enterprise resource planning (ERP)
E-sourcing, 252
ESPs, *See* Enterprise social platforms (ESPs)
ETL (extract, transform and load), 80
Eventual consistency, 70
Exabyte, 114
Exception report, 34
Executive information systems (EISs), 32, 39
Extendable markup language (XML), 204
Extensibility, 368
EXtensible Business Reporting
    Language (XBRL)
  defined, 287
  reporting compliance, 288
  tagging, 287–288
External transactions, TPS, 32
Extract, transform and load (ETL), 80
Extranet, 105
Extreme programming, 394

F

Faceted search, 187
Fault tolerance, 72, 148
Faulty data, 62
Feature convergence, 207
Federal Communications Commission
    (FCC), 422
Federal Financial Institutions Examination
    Council (FFIEC), 428
Federal Trade Commission (FTC), 427, 429
Feedback, 28
Filetype, 176
Financial Accounting Standards Board
    (FASB), 286
Financial disclosure
  accounting software packages, 286
  defined, 287
  XBRL reporting compliance, 288
  XBRL tagging, 287–288

Financial misrepresentation, 286
Financial ratio analysis, 292
Firewall, 148
Five-forces model, 364
Fixed-line broadband, 108
Flexibility, 11
Flexible manufacturing systems (FMSs), 281
Focused search, 176
Focus management, 430–432
Folksonomy, 232
Formal processes, 9
Fraud
  accounting cycle, 151
  auditing information systems, 155
  cyber defense strategies, 153–154
  defending against, 150–155
  defined, 150
  financial meltdowns triggered by, 290
  general controls, 152–153
  internal controls, 153, 290–291
  occupational fraud, 151–152
  occurs, 289
  prevention and detection, 289–291
  risk factors, 289–290
  risk management, 289
  senior management financial reporting, 151
Free monitoring services
  Google alerts, 229
  Hootsuite, 229
  social mention, 228
  Twitter search, 229
Front-office operations, 315
Full-text similarity search, 187
Functional business systems (FBSs)
  business management systems (BMSs), 273
  vs. cross-functional business
      processes, 274–275
  management levels, 273–274
  transaction processing systems
      (TPSs), 275–276

G

GAAP (generally accepted accounting
    principles), 152
GAAP Financial Reporting Taxonomy, 287
Gantt chart, 403–404
Garbage in, garbage out (GIGO), 75–76
Generally accepted accounting principles
    (GAAP), 152, 286
General Motors (GM)
  Ally Bank, Overview of, 248
  geocoding, 350
  resolving channel conflict, 250
Geocoding, 350
Geographic information systems (GISs)
  in business, 351
  defined, 349
  geocoding, 350
  geospatial data, 349
  GIS-generated map, 350, 351
  infrastructure, 350
  location-tracking app, 350
  longitude and latitude, 349
Geospatial data, 332, 349
Ghost pages, 181
Ghost text, 181
Giant global graph, 211
GISs, *See* Geographic information
    systems (GISs)
Global e-Sustainability Initiative (GeSI), 434

Globalization, 8
Global mean temperature (GMT), 432–433
Global warming
  carbon cycle, 433–434
  climate change mitigation, 435–436
  Climate Group's SMART 2020 Report, 434–435
  GeSI, 434–435
  IT sector, 435
  mobile, cloud, and social carbon
      footprint, 436
  OCO-2, 435
  sustainability initiatives, 436
GMT (global mean temperature), 432–433
Goal seeking, 35
Go/no-go decision, 390
Google Glass, 418–419
Google's Street View, 421–422
Gray hat, 133
Groundswell, 209
Group dynamics
  defined, 120
  online brainstorming, in Cloud, 121
Group work, 120–121

H

Hackers
  classes of, 123
  defined, 127
Hacking
  defined, 132, 133
  industry operates, 133–134
Hacktivists, 133
Hadoop, 85–87
Hardware virtualization, 59
Hashtag(s), 223
Hashtag activism, 224
Health Insurance Portability and Accountability
    Act (HIPAA), 43
High fidelity, 219
Horizontal exchanges, 253
Hortonworks, 343
HTML (hypertext markup language), 204
Human resources (HR)
  benefits administration, 295–296
  compliance and ethics, 292–296
  defined, 399
  employee relationship management, 296
  ethical challenges and considerations, 296
  information systems, 292–295
  management and employee
      development, 295
  monitors compliance with antidiscrimination
      employment laws, 293
  performance evaluation, 295
  personnel planning and HR strategies, 295
  recruitment, 294–295
  SaaS, benefits of, 294
  training and development, 295
Hybrid recommendation engines, 191
Hybrid search engines, 168
Hypertext markup language (HTML), 204

I

IaaS (infrastructure as a service), 56, 57
IBM DB2, 73
ICT, *See* Information and communications
    technology (ICT)
Identity theft, cyberattack, 142
IDS (intrusion detection system), 137, 146, 148
Immediate consistency, 70
Inbound logistics, 278

Inbound marketing, 180
Incident response team (IRT), 158
Income statement, 286
Indexer module, 169
Indirect procurement, 252
Informal processes, 9
Information, 30
Informational search, 173
Information and communications
　　technology (ICT)
　　defined, 102
　　environment, 432
　　GMT, 432–433
　　IT and global warming, 433–436
　　people-first approach, 438
　　and sustainable development, 432–438
　　transform business and society
　　　technology, 436–437
Information architecture, 41
Information flows, 276
Information governance, *See* Data governance
Information management
　　business benefits of, 45–46
　　defined, 26, 42
　　information deficiencies, reasons for, 43–45
　　scattered data, 43
　　sharing and collaboration, 45
Information overload, 92
Information retrieval (IR)
　　services, 168
　　social media, 230–231
Information sharing, 120
Information silos, 43, 44, *See also* Data silos
Information systems (ISs)
　　characteristics of, 36
　　components of, 29–30
　　concepts and classification, 28–37
　　data, information, knowledge, and
　　　wisdom, 30–31
　　data properties in, 275
　　decision support system (DSS), 34–35
　　defined, 28
　　executive information system (EIS), 35–36
　　exist within corporate culture, 36–37
　　management information system
　　　(MIS), 33–34
　　security, 130
　　support enterprise applications, 270
　　transaction processing system (TPS), 32–33
　　types of, 31–32, 272
Informed user, 2, 21
Infrastructure as a service (IaaS), 56, 57
In-house development, 367–368
Insider fraud, 289
In-store tracking, 256
Integrated change control, 405–406
Integrated search vendors, 173
Intellectual property (IP)
　　defined, 141
　　finding, 176
　　theft of, 94
Internal control (IC), 153
Internal employment, 289
Internal threats, 137
Internal transactions, TPS, 32
Internet of Things (IoT)
　　advantages and disadvantages of, 123
　　defined, 16, 121
　　in developing nations, 436
　　group work and decision processes, 120–121

security and privacy in, 123
sensors, smart meters, and the smart
　　grid, 121–123
virtual collaboration, 120
Internet Protocol (IP), 109
Internet service providers (ISPs), 108
Intranet, 105, 230
Intrusion detection system (IDS), 137, 146, 148
Intrusion prevention system (IPS), 146
Inventory control systems
　　defined, 279
　　just-in-time inventory management
　　　systems, 279–280
　　lean manufacturing systems, 280
　　production/operations technologies, 280
　　quality control (QC) systems, 280
IoT, *See* Internet of Things (IoT)
IP (Internet Protocol), 109
IP address, 109
IPOS (input, process, output, and store), 28
IPS (intrusion prevention system), 146
IP Version 4 (IPv4), 109
IP Version 6 (IPv6)
　　defined, 102, 109
　　Sony builds, 102–103
Isolation, of data, 276
ISs, *See* Information systems (ISs)
IT career, 19–20
　　adds value to your performance, 19–21
IT consumerization, 11
IT ethics
　　competing responsibilities, 423
　　computer ethics, 441
　　ethical *vs.* unethical behavior, 420–423
　　in workplace, 440
IT governance, 156
　　frameworks, cyber defense, 155–157
IT infrastructure, 38, 48
IT innovation and disruption
　　social–mobile–analytics–cloud (SMAC)
　　　model, 13–14
　　technology mega trends, 14–16
　　using disruptive technologies, 16–17
IT management priorities, 7
IT project management mistakes, 410
IT security, 73
　　defense-in-depth model, 157–159
　　terminology, 148
IT strategic planning
　　and business disconnects, 359
　　business value drivers, 358
　　corporate and IT governance, 359
　　defined, 358
　　investments, 359
　　IT Steering Committee, 362
　　medium-term IT plan, 361
　　objectives of, 358
　　process, 361–362
　　SWOT analysis, 359, 360, 383
IT strategy
　　BIT (*See* Business–IT alignment (BITA))
　　BSC, 355, 377
　　defined, 354–355
　　in-house development, 367–368
　　Intel Reaps rewards, 355–357
　　sourcing (*See* Sourcing and Cloud services)

J

JavaScript, 204
Jive, 326

Job prospects, IT, 21
Joint Munitions Command (JMC), 314
Just-in-time (JIT)
　　defined, 279
　　inventory management systems, 279–280

K

Key performance indicators (KPIs), 40
　　BI strategy with business strategy, 92
　　BMSs, 273
　　data ownership and organizational
　　　politics, 76
　　data types and roles, 340
　　EIS, 39
　　project status report, 405
　　retailing technology, 243
Keyword(s), 169
Keyword conversion, 184
Keyword tricks, 181
Knowledge, 30
Knowledge sharing, 230–234

L

Lagging indicators, 374
LAN (local area network), 104, 116
Latency, 70
Latency-sensitive apps, 107
Leading indicators, 375
Lean manufacturing system, 280
Legal and organizational feasibility, 389
Lessons learned report, 408
Link spamming, 181
Local area network (LAN), 104, 116
Location-based advertising, 27, 28
Location-based marketing, 256
Logical design, 390
Long-term evolution (LTE), 110
Lost data, 44
LTE (long-term evolution), 110
LulzSec, 139

M

Machine-to-machine (M2M)
　　communications, 435
　　technology, 16
Maintenance, repair, and operations
　　(MRO), 253
Malicious (rogue) mobile applications, 138
Malware, 135
MAN (metropolitan area network), 104, 116
Management information systems (MIS), 33–34
Management levels, FBSs, 273–274
Manufacturing execution systems, 281
Manufacturing quality control (MQ)
　　systems, 280
MapReduce, 85–87
Marketing management
　　pricing of products/services, 285
　　profitability analysis, 285
　　salesperson productivity, 285
Mashup, 117, 226
Mashup social
　　RSS technology, 227
　　social monitoring services, 227–229
Master data
　　and data entities, 79
　　defined, 46
　　master reference file, 79
Master data management (MDM), 47, 78–79
Master file, 47
Master reference file, 79

M-commerce, 244
Media bandwidth, 106
MEDIATA, 27–28
Mega trends
  big data, 15
  connectivity, 14
  data analytics, 15
  defined, 14
  digitization, 15
  machine-to-machine technology, 15–16
Metadata, 185
Meta-search engines, 168
Metropolitan area network (MAN), 104, 116
Microblog, 223
Micropayments, 261
Microsoft Cloud, 324
Microsoft SQL server, 73
Milestones, 403
Millennials, 325
MIS (management information systems), 33–34
Miscellaneous errors, 132, 138
Mission, 273
Mobile app risky behaviors, 420–421
Mobile banking security risks, 263
Mobile bill payments, 261
Mobile biometrics, 148
Mobile browser, 256
Mobile check-in strategy, 241, 242
Mobile commerce
  competitive advantage, 255–258
  defined, 244
  hotel services and travel go wireless, 259
  mobile entertainment, 258–259
  mobile social networking, 259
Mobile communications, 4
Mobile display strategy, 241
Mobile entertainment, 258–259
Mobile infrastructure
  Wi-Fi and Bluetooth, 115
  Wi-Fi networking standards, 115–116
Mobile kill switch, 148
Mobile location-based marketing, 256, 259
Mobile marketing, 255
Mobile networks
  choosing solutions, 118–119
  circuit *vs.* packet switching, 111
  higher demand for high-capacity, 115
  increases in traffic and users, 114
  3G, 4G, 4G LTE, and 5G network
    standards, 110–111
  mobile infrastructure, 115–116
  wireless infrastructure, two components
    of, 116–117
Mobile payment, 242
Mobile phone card reader, 261
Mobile retailing, 255
Mobile search, 175, 256
Mobile SEO, 175
Mobile social networking, 259
Mobile transactions and financial services
  mobile banking, 262–263
  mobile payment systems, 260–262
  security issues, 263
  short codes, 263
Mobile visual search engine, 267
Mobility as a service, 58
Model, 26, *See also* specific models
Modem, 105
Modulation and coding, 105
Modulator, 105

Moral hazard, 290
MRO supplies, 253

N

National Highway Traffic Safety Administration
  (NHTSA), 422
Natural language processing, 185
Natural language search, 187
Navigational search, 173
Near-field communication (NFC), *See also*
    Mobile networks
  business use of, 117–118
  defined, 117
  mobile payment systems, 261
Negligent hiring, 427–428
Net neutrality, 108
Net semi-neutrality, 108
Network effect, 215
Network fundamentals
  functions supported by business
    networks, 106–107
  intranets, extranets, and virtual private
    networks, 105
  quality of service (QoS), 107–108
  terminology, 105–106
  types, 104
Network interface card (NIC), 59
Network servers, 48
Network virtualization, 59
Newsgroups, 210
NFC, *See* Near-field communication (NFC)
NIC (network interface card), 59
Nonlinear search and influence patterns, 244
Nonstandardized data formats, 44
NoSQL systems, 72

O

Objectives, 8
Object-oriented (O-O), 392
Occupational fraud
  access controls, 152
  administrative controls, 152
  business reporting and disclosure of
    violations, 152–153
  corporate governance, 151
  defined, 150, 289
  intelligent analysis and anomaly
    detections, 151–152
  physical controls, 152
  prevention and detection, 151–152
  Sarbanes–Oxley Act (SOX), 152–153
Office Graph, 326
Off-page SEO, 179–180
Offshoring, 370–371
OLAP (online analytical processing)
  systems, 72
OLTP (online transaction processing), 33, 71
Omni-channel retailing, 245
On-demand economy
  Airbnb Business Model, 3
  business models in, 3–4
  change in consumer behavior, 4
  defined, 4
  growth of, 5–6
  IT business objectives, 8
  IT's role in, 7
  low cost of entry, 6
  tech platforms enabled on-demand
    services, 3
  Uber Business Model, 3
On-demand services, 3

On-demand workers
  changes in work status, 18
  profile of U.S., 18
Online analytical processing (OLAP)
  systems, 72
Online banking, B2C, 246
Online communities, 210
Online transaction processing (OLTP), 33, 71
Online transaction processing systems
  (OTPS), 276
On-page SEO, 179–180
Onshore sourcing, 368
Ontology-based search, 187
Open graph, 215–216
Open Wi-Fi network, 421
Operating management corruption, 151
Operating systems, 111–112
Operations level, 274
Oracle 12c database, 72
Oracle's social network, 326
Orbiting Carbon Observatory-2 (OCO-2), 435
Order fulfillment process, 315–316
Organic search, 174, 178–181
Organic Valley, 306
OTPS (online transaction processing
  systems), 276
Outbound logistics, 278
Outsource relationship management (ORM)
  company, 372
Outsourcing
  challenges, 369
  five-phase outsourcing life cycle, 371, 372
  managing sourcing arrangements
    and SLA, 372
  risks and hidden costs, 370
OWL, *See* Web ontology language (OWL)

P

PaaS (platform as a service), 56, 57
Packet(s), 109
Packet switching, 111
PageRank, 180
Page repository, 169
Paid search
  advertising, metrics for, 184
  listings, 174
PAN (personal area network), 104
Patches, 144
Payload, 136
Payment Card Industry Data Security Standard
  (PCI DSS), 157
Pay-per-click (PPC)
  creating advertising campaign, 182–183
  defined, 174
PDoS (permanent denial-of-service), 137
People, 399
People-first approach, 437
Permanent denial-of-service (PDoS), 137
Personal area network (PAN), 104
Personal assistants and voice search, 175–176
Personal health information (PHI), 128
Personalized search, SEO, 180
Personally identifiable information (PII), 128
Petabyte, 66, 170
PHI (personal health information), 128
Phishing, 132, 134–135
Physical controls, 152
Physical design, 390
Physical theft/loss, cyberthreats, 138
Plaintext/clear text, 148

Platform as a service (PaaS), 56, 57
PMI® Project Management Body of Knowledge (PMBOK 5e), 398
Point of sale (POS), 37, 68
Portfolio management, 396
PostgreSQL, 73
Post mortem, 386
   activities, 407–408
   defined, 407
   lessons learned report, 408
PPM (project portfolio management), 396–397
Prioritize traffic, 107
Privacy
   addressing social media, 216
   civil rights, 424–429
   privacy paradox, 424–425
   recruiting, social media, 425–426
Private cloud, 52
Private social networks (SNSs), 219
Process improvement, 8
Procter & Gamble (P&G), 329
Procurement, 399
Product development, 8
Production and operations management systems
   CIM and MES, 281–282
   inventory control systems, 279–280
   logistics management, 278–279
   transportation management systems (TMSs), 278
Productivity, 7
Program management, 396
Project charter, 400, 401
Project Closing, See Post mortem
Project management
   benefit, 395
   business case, 396, 412–413
   characteristics of projects, 396
   defined, 395
   failure, 408–409
   IT jobs, 410
   IT project management mistakes, 410
   life cycle (See Project management life cycle)
   PMBOK, 398
   PPM, 396–397
   software, 413
   ten knowledge areas of, 398
   triple constraint, 397
Project management life cycle, 398
   execution, 403–404
   initiation, 400
   planning stage, 400–403
Project management office (PMO), 408
Project monitoring and controlling
   activities, 405
   baseline, 407
   critical path analysis, 406–407
   integrated change control, 405–406
   project status report, 405
   scope creep, 405
Project portfolio, 361
Project portfolio management (PPM), 396–397
Projects, 395
Promoted tweets, 224
Proof of concept (POC), 373
Protected classes, 426
Protocol, 109
Public cloud, 52

Q

Quality control (QC) systems
   inventory control systems, 280
Quality of service (QoS), 107–108
Quality score, 183
Query, 70
Query interface, 170
Query predictability, 70
Query processing capabilities, 70
Quick response (QR)
   codes, 241, 261
   time, 70

R

RAM (random access memory), 59
Ransomware, 135, 136–137
RAT (remote access trojan), 136
RDBMSs (relational management systems), 70
RDF (resource description framework), 185
Really simple syndication (RSS), 227
Real-time processing, 33
Real-time search, 177
Recommendation engines
   applications, 192
   collaborative filtering, 190–191
   content-based filtering, 189
   defined, 173
   filters, 189–192
   hybrid, 191–192
   limitations of, 191
Red flag, 290
Related searches/queries, 186
Relational database, 70
Relational management systems (RDBMSs), 70
Remote access trojan (RAT), 136
Remote wipe capability, 148
Reporting tools, 335
Responsibility matrix, 404
Responsiveness, 11, 364
Retailing technology
   consumer demands and behavior, 243–244
   omni-channel retailing concept, 244–245
Retrieval/ranking module, 169
Return on advertising spend (ROAS), 184
Retweet, 225
Reverse supply chain, 315
Rich snippets, 188
Risk, 146
Risk management, 289
Risk register, 404
ROAS (return on advertising spend), 184
Rogue app monitoring, 148
Rootkits, 135
Route data over third-party, 120
Routers, 106
RSS (really simple syndication), 227

S

SaaS (Software as a service), 54, 56–57
Safety stock, 279
Sales and marketing systems
   data-driven marketing, 284
   marketing management, 285
   sales and distribution channels, 284
   social media customer service, 284–285
SAN (server area network), 104
SAN (storage area network), 104
SAP Sybase ASE, 73
Sarbanes–Oxley Act (SOX), 43, 152–153, 155

SCADA (supervisory control and data acquisition) system, 141
Scalability, 72
SCM, See Supply chain management (SCM)
Scope creep, 405
Scrum, 394
SDDC (software-defined data center), 50–52
SDK (software development kits), 203
SDLC, See Systems development life cycle (SDLC)
Search engine(s), 168
Search engine marketing (SEM)
   defined, 172, 173
   growth of, 174
Search engine optimization (SEO)
   black hat vs. white hat, 181
   click-through rates (CTR), 179
   content and inbound marketing, 180–181
   defined, 166, 174
   functionality and programming, 179
   on-page and off-page, 179–180
   personalized search, 180
   relevance and credibility, 180
   strategies for, 178–180
   strategies of, 174
Search engine results page (SERP), 166
Search history, 176
Search on semantic/syntactic annotations, 187
Search technology
   for business success, 168–177
   search engines work, 168
   web directories, 168–169
   why search important for business, 172–177
Search tools button, 176
Semantic search engines, 168
Semantic web
   for business, 187–188
   defined, 185, 211
   search, 186–187
Senior management financial reporting fraud, 151
Sensors, 122
Sentiment analysis, 88
SEO, See Search engine optimization (SEO)
Server area network (SAN), 104
Server virtualization, 59
Service level agreement (SLA), 61
Service packs, 145
Service providers, 53
"Seven Deadly Sins of Project Management," 410
Shadow pages, 181
SharePoint, ESP
   collaboration and business intelligence, 324
   documents, 324
   intranet and extranet, 324
   Microsoft Cloud, 324
   Office Graph, 326
   Oslo App, 325–326
   Yammer, 324, 325
Sharing sites, 208
Short code, 263
Short message service (SMS), 241
Showrooming, 175, 241
Signal frequency spectrum, 106
Signatures, 136
Silo effect, 45
SLA (service level agreement), 61
Smart city, 122
Smart grid, 123

Smart meters, 121–123
SMS database strategy, 241
SNA (social network analysis), 211
SNS, *See* Social networking service (SNS)
SNSs (private social networks), 219
Social bookmarking, 177, 232
Social commerce, 244
Social engineering
  cyberthreats, 134–137
  defined, 133
Social graph, 211
Social logins, 216
Social media
  applications and services, 207–209
  attacks, 144
  bookmarking tools, 231–232
  defined, 202
  elements of, 208–209
  guidelines, financial institutions, 428–429
  information retrieval, tools for, 230–231
  more than Facebook, YouTube, and
    Twitter, 207–209
  optimization, 174
  privacy, 216
*Social Media: Consumer Compliance Risk
  Management Guidance,* 428
Social–mobile–analytics–cloud (SMAC), 13
Social monitoring services, 227
Social network analysis (SNA), 211
Social networking service (SNS)
  and communities, 210–220
  crowdfunding, 212–213
  defined, 207, 213–214
  discussion groups on, 231
  Facebook dominates, 214–216
  future of, 220
  Google takes on Facebook with G+, 216–217
  open graph initiative, 215–216
  power of crowd, 212
  private social networks, 219
  Second Life, 218–219
  with Snapchat, 217–218
  social logins, 216
Social network sprawl, 325
Social plug-ins, 205, 206
Social recruitment, 425
Social search, 175
Social stalkers, 426
Social VR, 219
Social web, 202
Software as a service (SaaS), 54, 56–57, 246
Software-defined data center (SDDC), 50–52
Software development kits (SDK), 203
SOPs (Standard operating procedures), 9
Sourcing and Cloud services
  cloud strategy challenges, 368–369
  managing IT vendor relationships, 373
  offshoring, 370–371
  on-premises systems, 368
  outsourcing, 369–372
  SLAs, 373–374
  tactical adoption *vs.* coordinated cloud
    strategy, 368
SOW (statement of work), 400
SOX (Sarbanes-Oxley Act), 43
Spam, 136
SPARQL protocol and RDF query language
  (SPARQL), 185
Spear phishing, 135
Specialized search vendors, 173

Spiders, 168
Sprints, 394
Spyware, 135
SQL (structured query language), 70
Stack, 56
Stakeholder(s), 399
Stakeholder integration, 8
Standard operating procedures (SOPs), 9, 275
Statement of work (SOW), 400
Stockouts, 279
Storage area network (SAN), 104
Storage virtualization, 59
Strategic planning, 273, 358
Strategic plans, 273
Strategic technology trends
  defined, 378
  description/examples, 378, 379
  ESSA Academy, 378, 379
  invest, 380
  scanning, 380
Structured data, 172
Structured decisions, 35
Structured query language (SQL), 70
Subscription monitoring services, 227–228
Sunk costs, 409
Supervisory control and data acquisition
  (SCADA) system, 141
Supply chain management (SCM)
  always-on supply chain, 316
  business goals, 314
  cloud computing and storage, 318
  defined, 301, 313, 314
  driverless vehicles and drones, 318
  flow of materials, data, and money, 315
  functions, 303, 304
  inventory and network optimization
    tools, 317
  logistics, 315
  Lowe's fresh approach, 328–329
  order fulfillment, 315–316
  predictive analytics, 317
  robotics and automation, 317
  sensors and automatic identification, 317
  3D printing, 318
  wearable and mobile technology, 318
Switches, 106
SWOT analysis, 19
Synchronous communication, 230
Systems development life cycle (SDLC)
  defined, 386
  implementation and testing, 390
  methodology (*See* Systems development
    methodology)
  support and maintenance, 391
  systems analysis, 390
  systems design, 390
  systems planning, 388–390
Systems development methodology
  agile methodology, 392–394
  DevOps, 394–395
  object-oriented analysis and design, 392
  Waterfall Model, 391–392

T
Tableau Desktop, 336
Tactical level, 274
Tactical plan, 361
Tangam's Yield Management Solution (TYM), 7
TCO, *See* Total cost of ownership (TCO)
TDoS, *See* Telephony denial-of-service (TDoS)

Technical feasibility, 389
Technology architecture, 41
Technology, entertainment, and design
  (TED), 353
Technology platform, 3
Technology stack, 3
Technology Vision report 2013, 6
TED, *See* Technology, entertainment, and
  design (TED)
Telephony denial-of-service (TDoS), 137
Templates, 400
Terms of service (TOS) agreement, 213, 216
Texting while driving, 422
Text mining, 88
Third-party *vs.* company-owned offshoring, 383
Threat
  actions, 138
  defined, 130
  intelligence, 89
3D bioprinting, 303, 423
3D printing, 318, 422–423
  additive manufacturing process, 301
  aerospace manufacturing, 303
  defense, 302
  defined, 301
  features and benefits of, 301, 302
  hardware stores, 302
  health care, 302–303
  industrial design, 303
  manufacturing on-demand, 303
  predictions, 301
  reproducing vintage car components, 303
  supply chain impact, 301–302
  worldwide revenue of, 301
Throttle traffic, 108
Time, 398
Time-to-exploitation, 145
Title VII of the Civil Rights Act of 1964, 293
TOS, *See* Terms of service (TOS) agreement
Total cost of ownership (TCO), 60
Total quality management (TQM), 280
TQM, *see* Total quality management (TQM)
Trade secrets, 141
Traditional BI market, 336
Traffic shaping, 108
Trail run, 373
Transactional search, 173
Transaction processing systems (TPS)
  batch *vs.* online real-time processing, 33
  defined, 32
  OTPS, 276
  processing impacts data quality, 33
  real time and batch processing, 276
Transmission control protocol/Internet
  protocols (TCP/IPs), 111
Transportation management systems
  (TMSs), 278
Triple constraint, 397
Trojan, 135
Trojan horse, 136
Tumblr blogs, 225
Tweet, 223
TweetDeck, 224
Twitterholic, 225
Twittersphere, 224
TYM (Tangam's Yield Management Solution), 7

U
UGC (user-generated content), 208
Uniform resource identifiers (URIs), 185

Unintentional threats
  computer systems failures, 133
  environmental hazards, 133
  human error, 132–133
  social engineering, 133
Unstructured data, 15, 172
Unstructured decisions, 35
URIs (Uniform resource identifiers), 185
USA PATRIOT Act, 43
Use-case
  description, 392
  diagram, 392
Usenet, 210
User-generated content (UGC), 208
Users categorization (tagging), 208

V
Valuation, 4
Value-added networks (VANs), 120
Value-added reseller (VAR), 305
Value chain model, 367–368
Value drivers, 358
Variance, 407
Vector, 136
Vendor management, 53–54
Vertical exchanges, 253
Vertical search engines, 177
Video blogs (vlogs), 206
Virtual communities, 210
Virtualization
  business continuity with, 60
  characteristics and benefits, 59–60
  defined, 59
  layer, 59
Virtual machines (VMs), 58–60
Virtual private networks (VPNs), 105

Virtual reality (VR), 59, 219
Virus, 135
VMs, *see* Virtual machines (VMs)
Voice biometrics, 148
Voice over IP (VoIP), 115
Vulnerability, 130

W
WAN, *see* Wide area network (WAN)
Wardriving, 421
Waterfall Model, 391–392
WBS, *see* Work breakdown structure (WBS)
Wearable technology, 12
Web 2.0
  AJAX Technologies for, 204
  constantly changing web, 201–202
  defined, 202
  markets, 209–210
  platform for services and social
    interaction, 202–203
  of social applications, networks, and
    services, 203–205
  social media applications and
    services, 207–209
  vs. Web 1.0, 203
  web technology, 205–206
Web 3.0 language(s), 185–186
Web directories, 168
Web ontology language (OWL), 185
Web search, for business, 176
Web technology, 205–206
What-if analysis, 35
White hat
  vs. black hat, 181
  defined, 133
Wide area network (WAN), 104, 116

Wi-Fi
  defined, 115
  networks, 421–422
  standards, 115–116
Wiki, 208
WiMAX, 110, 116
Wireless infrastructure
  GPS and Bluetooth, mashup of, 117
  WiMAX, 116
  WLANs, 116
Wireless local area network (WLAN), 104
Wireless marketing and advertising, 256
Wisdom, 31
WLAN, *see* Wireless local area network
    (WLAN)
Work breakdown structure (WBS), 402–403
World wide web (WWW)
  communicating on, 206
  defined, 202
  invention of, 202–203
Worm, 135

X
XaaS (anything as a service), 55–58
XBRL, *See* EXtensible Business Reporting
    Language (XBRL)
XML (extendable markup language), 204
XMLHttpRequest, 204

Y
Yammer, 324, 325

Z
Zero-day exploits, 136
Zettabyte, 114
Zombies, 136